COMPARATIVE POLITICS IN TRANSITION

FIFTH EDITION

New Horizons in Comparative Politics

Series Editor: Howard J. Wiarda

COMPARATIVE POLITICS IN TRANSITION

FIFTH EDITION

JOHN McCORMICK

Indiana University
Purdue University Indianapolis

THOMSON
™
WADSWORTH

Australia • Brazil • Canada • Mexico • Singapore • Spain
United Kingdom • United States

Comparative Politics in Transition, **Fifth Edition**
John McCormick

Executive Editor: David Tatom
Development Editor: Sarah Ebel
Assistant Editor: Rebecca Green
Editorial Assistant: Eva Dickerson
Technology Project Manager: Michelle Vardeman
Senior Marketing Manager: Janise Fry
Marketing Assistant: Teresa Jessen
Marketing Communications Manager: Nathaniel Michelson
Project Manager, Editorial Production: Paul Wells
Creative Director: Rob Hugel
Art Director: Maria Epes
Print Buyer: Barbara Britton
Permissions Editor: Joohee Lee

Production Service: Matrix Productions Inc.
Photo Researcher: Cheri Throop
Copy Editor: Sherri Dietrich
Cover Designer: Brian Salisbury
Cover Image: © Paul Almasy/CORBIS;
  © Alan Schein Photography/CORBIS;
  © Toshiyuki Aizawa/Reuters/CORBIS;
  © Press Information Department/Handout/Reuters/CORBIS;
  © Reza/Webistan/CORBIS
Cover Printer: Phoenix Color Corp
Compositor: International Typesetting and Composition
Printer: Courier Corporation/Westford

Library of Congress Control Number: 2005937014

ISBN-13: 978-0-495-00760-9
ISBN 0-495-00760-9

Thomson Higher Education
10 Davis Drive
Belmont, CA 94002-3098
USA

For more information about our products, contact us at:
Thomson Learning Academic Resource Center
1-800-423-0563

For permission to use material from this text or product, submit a request online at **http://www.thomsonrights.com** Any additional questions about permissions can be submitted by e-mail to **thomsonrights@thomson.com**

Foreword

by Howard J. Wiarda, Series Editor

With all the changes taking place in the world at the moment, fresh perspectives on government and politics are ever more important. Hence the development of Wadsworth's New Horizons in Comparative Politics series, which sets out to offer students and professors timely, readable, and current books in this exciting and booming field of political science.

The goal of the series is to provide books that are accessible while enhancing student understanding of the vital themes and approaches in comparative politics. At the same time, we hope that more senior students and scholars will find the conclusions and interpretations of their authors of value as well. Books in the series have been published on politics in Britain (Jorge Rasmussen), France (Ronald Tiersky), Russia (Steve Boilard), Mexico (George Grayson), China and Japan (Peter Moody), Latin America (Howard J. Wiarda), Africa (Carlene Edie), and Eastern Europe (Ivan Volgyes). Other books in the series include *An Introduction to Comparative Politics, European Politics in the Age of Globalization, Comparative Democracy and Democratization, and Non-Western Theories of Development*, as well as recently commissioned books on Germany, the Middle East, and other topics.

In offering this series, we have sought out authors who can balance scholarship with lively, readable writing. We have also made a conscious decision to move to a new generation of scholars who see things from a fresh perspective. Our objective has been to provide short, versatile volumes that can be used in myriad comparative politics courses, and we hope that some of the excitement and enthusiasm that our authors feel for their subject areas will rub off on students.

A lynchpin of this series for several years has been this major introductory comparative politics text by John McCormick, professor of political science at the Indianapolis campus of Indiana University.

It is rare these days for a single author to write a comparative politics text that covers all areas of the world. Most of us in this field are so specialized in our own countries, regions, or topics that we would not even attempt such a feat. Hence, most textbooks are written by teams of authors, each approaching the topic from their own individual perspectives. The multiauthor approach has its advantages, to be sure, but it can also result in anthologies and collections of uneven styles and points of view, with little connection to a common core, or even a sense of integration. McCormick's book avoids all these problems. It is an integrated introduction to the field, with a common set of themes that is woven throughout the manuscript like threads in a tapestry.

McCormick's prose flows nicely, and he includes the most important comparative politics concepts while using a provocative and innovative approach. He is also widely traveled and brings his own personal experiences into an approach that is new and fresh and that moves beyond older cold war thinking. He has updated and rewritten the entire text for this new edition to continue to provide a clear focus on political power and the way it is organized in developed and developing countries, Western and non-Western. His section on Islam has never been more important than it is today.

Moreover, McCormick has included a vast amount of useful information and interpretation. When I first read the manuscript, I was astounded not only at how well he writes but also at the huge storehouse of information he has developed, usefully and coherently organized around his integrating theses and outline. McCormick has true, in-depth expertise, not just in one or two countries but in all of the regions and countries covered in the book.

Adding to the value and utility of the book is the inclusion of suggested reading lists and study questions for each country, the listing of Web sites that will lead students to useful supporting information, the use of boxed features that highlight and draw out key issues and personalities, the inclusion of major country chronologies, and lists of key terms and names. The emphasis on true comparison is most obvious in the Comparative Exercise studies at the end of every case, which will help students look across the different cases and compare topics such as executives, legislatures, electoral systems, political parties, constitutions, and bureaucracies. In terms of readability and study aids, this fifth edition is better than ever before.

McCormick's book nicely complements the other books in our series and can be used either as a single text for a course in comparative politics, or as an integrating text that is supplemented by other books—hopefully from our series! *Comparative Politics in Transition*, fifth edition, is a significant accomplishment that continues to be a core part of this series.

Preface

If you are reading this book, then chances are that you have enrolled in—or are thinking about enrolling in—an introductory course on comparative politics or government. So what can you expect in this book and in the course?

The main goal of comparative politics is to study different political systems in order both to better understand the different ways in which people are governed, and to make comparisons that will give us the reference points that we need to help us understand what politics is about. As you study the chapters that follow, you will read about the structures of government, the different ways societies are governed, the channels through which people take part in the political process, and the ways political decisions are reached and implemented. You will read about presidents and prime ministers, parliaments and congresses, democracies and dictatorships, constitutions and coups, elections and assassinations, and heroes and villains. In short, you will be reading about all the elements that make up government in its many different and intriguing forms around the world.

At the heart of the book is the comparative method. In the ten case studies that make up the book, you will see how politics is approached in societies with values and priorities that are sometimes the same, but sometimes very different. The case studies represent a wide variety of political and economic systems, from the richest to the poorest, from the most stable to the most chaotic, and from the most successful to the least successful. You will see how some countries address similar problems, how other countries have different sets of priorities, how people relate to politics, and how comparison can help us draw up rules about politics and better understand our place in the global community.

These are the conventional goals of comparative politics, but this book has always taken an unconventional approach to achieving those goals:

- Unlike almost all other comparative politics textbooks, which still use the old cold war three-way division of countries (rich ones, red ones, and poor ones), this book is based around six arenas that offer a more realistic and balanced view of the way the world looks today.

- Unlike almost all those other textbooks, which focus heavily on rich industrialized countries and have a heavy bias toward Western Europe, this one has deliberately sacrificed two of the most popular case studies (Germany and France) and pays much more attention to the non-Western world, where most of the world's people live and whose importance is growing.

- Unlike almost all those other textbooks, which make few distinctions among the 135 countries of Africa, Asia, and Latin America, this one argues that we have to distinguish among countries that have developed new levels of wealth and stability (and are pulling away from the pack), countries that are best understood in light of the political influence of Islam, and countries whose progress has either stalled or has never really begun.

As you read this book, you will find that politics is constantly evolving and mutating and that you will be studying not just one moving target but several, and trying to come to grips with societies that are in a constant state of transition. If there is a single theme that ties the book together, it is the concept of change: its causes, its effects, and the impact it has on the structure and actions of government.

THE FIFTH EDITION

It has been encouraging to see how widely this book has been adopted for courses across the United States, in Canada, and in several other countries. Because the approach meets the needs of many instructors and students, this fifth edition uses the same basic structure and style, and most of the changes have come from updating developments in politics since the fourth edition went to press. Alterations have also been made in response to suggestions from students and instructors.

Case studies

The biggest change to the fifth edition is the addition of a new, tenth case study (Haiti), designed to provide an example of a marginal country. Otherwise, it keeps the same case studies as before, with the same basic structure as before: history, institutions, processes, and policies. All the cases have been thoroughly edited, the arguments have been tightened up, new and more recent examples have been inserted, more points of comparison have been injected, and all the key political, economic, and social data have been updated, including the results of the most recent elections.

The arenas

The historical sections in the part openers have been cut back to add more explanation of the features of each group of countries. A number of countries have also been moved from one arena to another in response to changes in those countries. For example, Estonia, Latvia, and Lithuania—since joining the European Union in May 2004—are now better approached as liberal democracies, and Zimbabwe has been demoted from a less developed country to a marginal country.

Boxes

About one third of these cover new topics. Every part opener now has a Checklist that briefly summarizes the key features of the countries in that group, and every case study includes boxes that focus on key personalities in history and/or politics, on key issues that influence government in the different case study countries, and on critical policy issues and political debates of the day. The material in the boxes continues to be overtly comparative, contrasting events, issues, and values across the ten cases.

Key Terms, Key People, and Study Questions

The lists of key terms and people at the end of every chapter have been expanded, with the terms highlighted in boldface where they appear in the text. New sets of study questions have been developed, designed to encourage students to think about similarities and differences among the case study countries, to guide their analysis as they read, and perhaps to give them ideas for term papers.

Comparative Exercises

These appear at the end of every case study and are designed to illustrate the similarities and differences among countries by looking in depth at specific institutions and processes, and to provide another source of ideas for term papers. They have all been updated for the fifth edition.

Internet sites

The lists of Web sites have been overhauled and updated. They are all on my home page at http://mypage.iu.edu/jmccormi/comp.html, and I will be adding new sites and updating URLs as necessary.

Further Reading

These lists have all been fully revised, with many new titles added. The focus continues to remain on the most recent work of the best-known scholars in each area, and a special effort has been made to go beyond the usual mainly American or European sources and to look at the work of local scholars and writers from each of the case study countries.

A NOTE ON SOURCES

In addition to the sources listed in the notes at the end of the book, I rely for news on a mixture of *The Economist*, CNN, MSNBC, National Public Radio, and BBC Online. For basic economic and social data in the book, I rely heavily on the United Nations, and particularly on the World Development Indicators database maintained by the World Bank, available on their Web site at www.worldbank.com.

ACKNOWLEDGMENTS

A book like this demands the help and support of a lot of people. Above all, I want to thank the nearly 1,500 students who have passed through my comparative politics classes at IUPUI since 1989. I wrote the first edition because of concerns that they and I had about the texts we were using, and their comments and questions have encouraged me to constantly refine and rethink my approach to this book. Wadsworth also solicited opinions from specialist outside reviewers, who both fortified my belief in the slightly unconventional approach of the book and made useful suggestions for changes and additions. For their help, input, and often detailed comments on the fourth and fifth editions, I would like to thank the following: Sean K. Anderson,

Idaho State University; Todd Bradley, Indiana University, Kokomo; Joy Chaudhuri, Arizona State University; Mark A. Cichock, University of Texas at Arlington; Scott Ditloff, University of the Incarnate Word; Jodi Finkel, Loyola Marymount University; Tricia Gray, University of Louisville; Samuel B. Hoff, Delaware State University; Neal Jesse, Bowling Green State University; Rebecca Kingston, University of Toronto; Becky Larsen, Brigham Young University; Ed Taylor, University of Oregon; and David Uranga, Pasadena City College. I would also to thank my colleagues Brian Vargus (for his comments on the U.S. chapter) and Scott Pegg (for his comments on the Marginal Countries part-opener), Michael Snodgrass of the IUPUI Department of History for his comments on the Mexico chapter, and Milind Thakar of the University of Indianapolis for his comments on the India chapter. My thanks also to the production team—particularly Sarah Ebel at Wadsworth and Aaron Downey at Matrix Productions—for their professionalism and patience. Finally, my love and thanks to my wife Leanne for her support and to my sons Ian and Stuart for their distractions and for their reminders of what is really important in life.

About the Author

John McCormick is professor and chair of political science at Indiana University–Purdue University Indianapolis (IUPUI). He has studied at Rhodes University (South Africa), the University of London, and Indiana University; and has been a visiting professor at Exeter University and the University of Sussex in Britain, and at the College of Europe in Bruges, Belgium. He has lived and worked in Britain, Kenya, Zimbabwe, South Africa, and the United States, and has traveled widely through North America, Europe, Southeast Africa, and Southeast Asia.

Before completing his Ph.D. in political science, he worked in the public sector for two environmental interest groups and was a consultant for a number of specialized agencies of the United Nations, including FAO and UNEP. His teaching and research interests lie in comparative politics and public policy, with particular interests in environmental policy, British politics, and the politics of the European Union.

His other publications include *Environmental Policy in the European Union* (London: Palgrave Macmillan, 2001), *The European Union: Politics and Policies* (Boulder, CO: Westview, 3rd Edition, 2004), and *Contemporary Britain* (London: Palgrave Macmillan, 2nd Edition, forthcoming).

Brief Contents

Contents

Tables and Figures

Boxed Items

INTRODUCTION

Without comparisons to make, the mind does not know how to proceed.

—Alexis de Tocqueville, French author, 1830s

To know ourselves we must know others and be able to see ourselves in relation to others.

—Thomas Symons, Commission on Canadian Studies, 1975

There is a famous Chinese curse: "May you live in interesting times." If living in interesting times is indeed a curse, then we are all in trouble. Life in the early years of the twenty-first century is changing so fast that it is often difficult to keep up. The forces driving these changes are many and complex, but at their core has been the rise of globalization. Whether we like it or not, we live in a global society in which politics and economics are inextricably linked. We import, we export, and decisions made in one country can have an impact in countries on the other side of the world.

The links are made more visible by the rise of new communications technology. Cell phones, email, and faxes offer us virtually instant contact with almost anyone in the world in a matter of seconds, at little cost, and—thanks to digital television and the Internet—we can find information on almost anything and update ourselves on news from around the world as it happens. When the United States was young, it could take weeks or months for political news to spread even from one state to another. Today, a bomb can go off in Baghdad, an election can be held in Brazil, the stock market can make gains in London, a politician can make a speech in South Africa, and we can hear about it within minutes and can often watch it live on television or the Web. Changes in local economies can have a worldwide impact, even the smallest regional conflicts can have international implications, and of course we are all affected by climate change, which is a truly global problem.

Links of this kind make it critically important for all of us to try to understand what is happening in politics, not just at the national level but at the global level. It can be difficult, to be sure, because of the speed of political change—and the disagreement on the causes of that change—but we must at least *try* to understand what is happening, and respond if necessary. One of the tools we have available to help us is comparative politics.

WHAT IS COMPARATIVE POLITICS?

politics The process by which people compete for power, influence, and resources.

Politics is the process by which two or more people make decisions on issues of mutual interest. Perhaps one of those people has control and the others do what he says, or perhaps they might decide to negotiate and reach a compromise. Either way, they

1

have a political relationship and they need to decide how best to relate to one another and how best to reach decisions. At the local level, politics is relatively simple, but as we move through communities, cities, states, countries, and into the international system, it involves more pressures and more decisions and becomes more complex and difficult to understand.

Political science has always used comparative tools, but comparison has become increasingly important in recent years because of the growing links across the international system. A political science professor may be a specialist in American politics, but the chances are that he or she will make comparisons between the United States and other countries to better understand and illustrate what is happening in the United States.

comparative politics
The systematic study of the differences and similarities among political systems.

Comparative politics involves studying the institutions, character, and performance of government and the political process in different countries to (1) better understand how politics works and (2) draw up rules about politics. Unlike physical scientists, social scientists do not have laboratories in which they can study political systems in their search for rules and laws. Instead, they use countries as laboratories and compare politics across those countries. This is the **comparative method**, which is one of the oldest tools of political science. It was used as early as the fourth century B.C. by the Greek philosopher Aristotle, who compared political systems to develop theories about which was best. We can (and do) study the politics of a single country, but to truly understand its features and characteristics, we need to compare that country with others.

Take the question of political parties. The United States is dominated by just two: the Democrats and the Republicans. Political scientists have developed plenty of explanations for that dominance: The two big parties are good at incorporating the policies of third parties, strongly ideological parties are not popular with American voters, the United States has a tradition of two-party politics, the two big parties control the electoral system to their advantage, and so on. But to fully understand why the Democrats and the Republicans are so strong, we need to study other democracies to see how their party systems have evolved. One explanation offered by comparison is that the United States lacks the kind of regional, religious, linguistic, or social divisions that have produced multiple political parties in many European countries. Another explanation is that the math of the American electoral system tends to produce a two-party arrangement, whereas many European countries use a system known as proportional representation, which makes it easier for small parties to win seats.

What are the benefits of studying politics using the comparative method?

- **Comparison can help us understand ourselves.** It has been argued that "knowledge of the self is gained through knowledge of others."[1] By studying the ways in which other societies govern themselves, we can better understand the character, origins, strengths, and weaknesses of our own system of government. Comparison can give us more insight into how power is distributed and limited, can give us a broader perspective of our place in the world, and can help us better understand our responses to different kinds of problems.

- **Comparison can broaden our options.** Studying other political systems can show us how similar problems are approached by different governments and perhaps offer us ideas that might help us improve the way we do things in our own country or avoid the mistakes made by others. How do other countries manage their education systems and distribute welfare? Which countries have the best record on controlling air and water pollution? Why do voter turnout figures vary so much from one country to another?

- **Comparison can broaden our horizons.** The novelist Mark Twain once remarked that travel was "fatal to prejudice, bigotry, and narrow-mindedness." Much the same can be said about the comparative study of different political systems. By studying the way other countries govern themselves and by trying to understand their problems and the way they see the world, we can build a more balanced view of the world, avoiding prejudice and **ethnocentrism** (seeing the world through our eyes rather than through the eyes of others), and better appreciating the variety and complexity of human society.

- **Comparison can help us draw up rules about politics.** Just as no credible zoologist would try to draw up rules about animal behavior without studying and comparing different species, no credible political scientist would try to draw up universal rules about political behavior without studying the structures and values of government in different countries. The study of different political systems can help us develop and test explanations of the trends and underlying principles of politics and help us better understand, explain, and predict political change.

- **Comparison can help us make sense of a confusing global system.** Keeping up with political changes in one country is difficult enough, but keeping up with political developments around the world creates multiple additional layers of complexity; we have to study multiple moving targets whose relationships with one another are always changing. Comparison can help us sort through the changes by helping us better understand the causes and effects of change, and better understand its impact on our lives.

ethnocentrism
A view of the world based on the superiority of a particular culture or race.

Comparison is not necessarily about deciding which political system is best or worst. Instead, it involves studying different systems with a view to (a) learning more about how and why they are different or the same and (b) understanding the effects of the differences and similarities. If a study of the French bureaucracy can help us understand why it is relatively efficient and professional and provide us with pointers to features that other countries might want to adopt, that is all well and good. But a comparison of the way the bureaucracies of France, Germany, Japan, and the United States are structured would provide us with more insight into the government of each country.

Although the benefits of comparative politics are many, political scientists have yet to agree on the best way of making the comparisons. It would be relatively easy if there were just a few countries to compare, but there are nearly 190, and although they are similar in some respects, they are different in others. Their political institutions come in varied forms, they organize power in different ways, their citizens use different channels to influence government, they have different economic philosophies, and they have remarkable social and cultural variety. One option is to compare principles, philosophies, institutions, or processes across countries. Thus we could take executives—presidents, prime ministers, monarchs, and military leaders—and try to draw conclusions about leadership as a philosophical or structural concept. This approach has its advantages, but it does not give us the opportunity to understand whole systems.

CLOSE-UP VIEW

WHAT ARE WE COMPARING?

The basic unit of comparison is the **state.** When you look at a map of the world, you will see it divided into 190 countries. But the term "country" is too imprecise for most political scientists, who instead prefer to talk about states. A state is a legal and physical entity that has four major features:

- It operates within a fixed **territory** marked by borders, and controls the movement of people, money, and goods across those borders.
- It has **sovereignty** over that territory and over its people and resources, and has the authority to impose laws and taxes within that territory.
- It is legally and politically **independent,** and operates the system of government that administers the territory.
- It has **legitimacy,** meaning that it is normally recognized both by its residents and by other states as having jurisdiction and authority within the territory.

The world has not always been divided into states, but certainly in the last 200 years or so the state system has become the standard by which we decide questions of jurisdiction and authority. Most of us think of ourselves as citizens of one state or another, and we are reminded of that when we have to produce a passport or even (depending on how long we plan to be abroad) a visa to travel from one state to another. To complicate the issue, states are often aligned with **nations,** or communities distinguished from each other by a common history, culture, and language. This alignment produces **nation-states.** But because the boundaries of nations and states rarely coincide, we are left with multinational states: territories inhabited by two or more national groups coming together under a common system of law and government. National divisions within states have been the root cause of many of the most troubling political problems, often leading to internal conflict, civil war, and even secession.

Critics of the state system argue that it is in decline, for a variety of reasons: states have been unable to guarantee peace for their citizens; globalization has created complex webs of political and economic ties that have weakened the independence of states; mass tourism and complex new patterns of migration have broken down the psychological borders among states; and internally divided states have become weaker as minorities have demanded greater self-determination and even independence. But, at least for now, the state remains our basic unit of comparison.

nation A group of people sharing a common culture, language, customs, and traditions.

Another option—used in this book—is to take the case study approach, which can be used both for developing explanations and for testing theories of political phenomena.[2] The method used in this book is to make some generalizations about country types—whether liberal democracies, Islamic countries, or marginal countries—and then to illustrate those types with one or two case studies.

To make this work, however, we need a system of **classification.** This way we can group countries with similar features and concentrate on how and why the groups—rather than individual countries—are different. The ideal system of classification is one that is simple, neat, consistent, and logical. Unfortunately, no one system has ever won universal approval, mainly because politics is a moving target and political systems are constantly evolving. The approaches taken by Aristotle (who distinguished between states ruled by one person, by a few people, and by many people) or the eighteenth century French philosopher Montesquieu (who distinguished between republics, monarchies, and despotic systems) would not tell us much about twenty-first century political realities because the world is a more complex and varied place than it was 2,300 years ago or even 250 years ago. More recent systems of classification include the following:

- The **structural-functional model,** which sees government as a system made up of structures (institutions) that perform certain functions, and compares how they perform.[3]
- The study of **sources of authority,** including traditional (or hereditary) authority, charismatic authority, and legal authority.[4]
- A system based around democratic/parliamentary systems (such as the United States or Britain), fascist/authoritarian systems (such as Nazi Germany), and communist systems (such as the old Soviet Union).[5]

These approaches may be simple and neat, but they fail to recognize the broader realities of national political systems or of the global environment of which they are a part, and they have never won general approval. A much broader approach was taken during the cold war (1945–1990), when we divided countries into **Three Worlds:**

- A First World of wealthy, democratic industrialized states, which included most of those countries in the Western alliance against communism.
- A Second World of communist regimes, which included most of those countries ranged against the Western alliance.
- A Third World of poorer, less democratic, and less developed countries, some of which took sides in the cold war, and some of which did not.

The system has a strange history. It came out of the *tiers monde*, the "third force" of French political parties in the 1940s that supported neither the government of the Fourth Republic nor the policies of Charles de Gaulle.[6] In 1952, the French demographer Alfred Sauvy borrowed the concept to describe a "third world" of countries that were choosing not to align themselves either with the West or with the Soviet bloc during the cold war.[7] The label stuck, and by the late 1960s the so-called developing countries of Africa, Asia, and Latin America were routinely being described as the Third World. Counting backwards, communist states were described as the Second World and industrialized democracies as the First World.

This system was simple and neat and provided evocative labels that could be slipped with ease into everyday conversation. The term *Third World* still elicits powerful images of poverty, inefficiency, underdevelopment, corruption, and political instability. But the system is misleading. The First World always had the most internal logic because its members had (and still have) the most in common. The Second World was always more of a problem because communism was interpreted differently by its members, and communism was never actually applied as anticipated by its most influential theorist, Karl Marx. As for the Third World, it never had much internal consistency because its 135 members had little in common: Some were rich, others were poor, some were democratic, others were dictatorships, some had civilian governments, others had military governments, some were industrialized, and others were agrarian.

A DIFFERENT WAY OF SEEING THE WORLD

The fatal blows to the Three Worlds system were struck by the end of the cold war, which not only saw many Second World countries adopting political systems and economic policies at odds with the principles of communism but also revealed many of the inconsistencies in the Third World. In particular, the emergence of a group of wealthy Asian and Latin American countries dispelled the popular image of the huddled masses of the Third World. Symbolically, U.S. President George H.W. Bush made a speech to Congress in March 1991 in which he spoke of the emergence of a **"new world order,"** and although neither he nor political science gave much definition to the concept, few doubted that he was right.

But the influence of the Three Worlds system lives on in political science, as a survey of other introductory comparative politics texts reveals. Some still overtly use the three-way classification, dividing the world into industrial democracies, communist and postcommunist systems, and Third World countries. Others use the system but have changed the labels, presumably to appear more modern. Yet others avoid using a system of classification altogether but still use a selection of country case studies that reflects the three-way division.

The Three Worlds also live on in the Western bias of many comparative political scientists. The First World has always attracted more study, partly because most political scientists come from the First World and partly because its features are more consistent, making it easier to study. This is why the authors of most comparative politics textbooks published in the United States typically devote as much as half their space to First World case studies, despite the fact that First World countries account for just 16 percent of the world's population, whereas Third World countries account for 55 percent of the population (or 76 percent if China is included).

So how is this book different? In short, it divides the world up into six arenas that are more representative of the variety of today's systems of government, and categorizes them using a combination of political, economic, and social variables.

Political Variables

Deciding how to distinguish among different political systems is difficult, because many different measures are available. We could categorize them on the basis of institutions (presidential versus parliamentary systems, for example), on the basis of philosophy (democratic versus authoritarian), or on the basis of levels of control (unitary versus federal). But this book opts for the broad view, arguing that the best way to understand different countries is to look at their records in meeting the basic needs of their people. It does this by examining several different performance indicators:

- The structures of their systems of government
- Their records on human rights and democracy

- The relationship between citizens and government
- Popular ideas about the role of the state
- Relative levels of political legitimacy

These concepts cannot be measured objectively, but one helpful indicator is the set of **Governance Indicators** developed by the World Bank. Based on data from 18 organizations, these develop six indicators of performance: voice and accountability, political stability, government effectiveness, regulatory quality, the rule of law, and the control of corruption. The Bank cautions that the margins of error make it impossible to produce precise rankings of countries, which is why the Bank's Web site makes it possible only to compare one country's ratings across all six indicators, or to compare multiple countries on one of the indicators. With these warnings in mind, the ratings for political stability and for the rule of law are shown in Table 1.

Another useful measure of democracy is the index developed by **Freedom House**, an international nonprofit organization (co-founded by Eleanor Roosevelt) that categorizes countries according to their records on political rights (the ability of people to participate in the political process) and civil liberties (including freedom of expression, the independence of the judiciary, personal autonomy, and economic rights). The rating system divides countries into three groups—Free, Partly Free, and Not Free—and gives them scores of 1 to 7 on the scales of political rights and civil liberties.

TABLE 1

World Bank Governance Indicators

Political stability (percentile)		Rule of law (percentile)	
Japan	90.3	Britain	94.3
Canada	87.0	Canada	93.8
Britain	73.5	United States	91.8
United States	56.2	Japan	88.7
China	51.4	Botswana	72.7
Mexico	50.8	Egypt	57.7
Egypt	34.1	India	57.2
Russia	33.0	Mexico	52.1
India	22.2	China	51.5
Haiti	14.6	Eritrea	36.1
Nigeria	10.3	Russia	25.3
Zimbabwe	8.6	Nigeria	5.2
Colombia	4.9	Haiti	1.0

Source: World Bank, World Development Indicators database, 2005, www.worldbank.org/wbi/governance.

TABLE 2

Freedom House Ratings

	Political rights	Civil liberties	Freedom rating
United States	1	1	Free
Britain	1	1	Free
Canada	1	1	Free
Japan	1	2	Free
Mexico	2	2	Free
India	2	3	Free
Nigeria	4	4	Partly Free
Russia	5	5	Partly Free
Egypt	6	6	Not Free
China	7	6	Not Free
Haiti	7	6	Not Free

Source: Freedom House, 2005, http://freedomhouse.org.

So whereas Canada and the United States do well (a rating of Free and a 1 on each scale), Russia does not do so well (Partly Free and a 5 on each scale) and Egypt does poorly (Not Free and a 6 on each scale) (see Table 2). We can quibble with some of the ratings, we can debate the meaning of "freedom," and the scale is by no means comprehensive or value-free, but it is a useful point of reference and discussion.

A third useful scale, which is more a measure of failure than of success, is the **Corruption Perception Index** developed by another nonprofit, Transparency International. This deals with only one part of the process of government and, as the title suggests, is as much about perception as about objective reality. Nonetheless it gives us a good idea of the relative levels of political effectiveness around the world—obviously, the more corrupt a society is the worse a job it is doing at governing itself. Not surprisingly, liberal democracies do well on this scale, and poorer countries much less well.

Economic Variables

gross domestic product
The value of the goods and services produced within the borders of a country.

gross national product
The value of the goods and services produced by a country, both internally and externally.

States are also classified in this book according to the size and structure of their economies. The standard measure of economic size is **gross domestic product (GDP),** which gives a dollar value to all the goods and services produced by a country in a year.* It is not a value of individual wealth, nor even of the wealth of a country, but a measure of productivity. Not everyone agrees that GDP is a helpful measure, in part because it is hard to be sure that everything is being counted (for example, we can do no more than guess at the size of the black market in some countries) and

*An alternative measure is **gross national product (GNP),** which adds to the total the value of all goods and services produced by a country's government and corporations overseas. It is less popular.

TABLE 3

Comparing Economies

	GDP (in billions of dollars)	Ranking		Per capita GDP (in dollars)	Ranking
United States	11,668*	1	Luxembourg	56,230	1
Japan	4,623	2	United States	41,400	5
Germany	2,714	3	Japan	37,180	9
Britain	2,141	4	Britain	33,940	13
China	1,649	7	Canada	28,390	21
Canada	980	9	Mexico	6,770	66
India	692	10	Russia	3,410	95
Mexico	676	12	Egypt	1,310	136
Russia	582	15	China	1,290	137
Egypt	75	48	India	620	168
Nigeria	72	50	Haiti	390	187
Haiti	4	133	Nigeria	390	187
Kiribati	0.06	184	Burundi	90	218
WORLD	40,888		WORLD	6,280	

* The 25 member states of the European Union together have a GDP that is greater than that of the United States.
Source: World Bank, World Development Indicators database, 2005, www.worldbank.org/data. Figures are for 2004.

in part because it is difficult to give a value to every economic activity; how do you measure the value of intellectual wealth, or of voluntary work, or the potential value of natural resources? GDP also does not take into account the real value of national currencies, some of which are overvalued relative to the U.S. dollar. To counteract this problem, some economists use **purchasing power parity,** which corrects for anomalies in the value of different currencies.

Despite its problems, GDP is the most common measure of economic wealth. It reveals that the United States is by far the wealthiest economy in the world, with a GDP of nearly $12 trillion. The Japanese, the Chinese, and the four big European countries follow, all with GDPs of between $1 trillion and $5 trillion. By contrast, the poorest countries in the world count their GDPs not in the trillions or the billions, but in the *millions* (see Table 3).

GDP provides a measure of the absolute size of national economies but does not take into account population size, so it is only of limited value to comparative politics. A more useful measure is GDP per person, which gives us a better idea of the relative economic wealth of different countries. If we divide GDP by population, we see that Luxembourg heads the table with a **per capita GDP** at more than $56,000, the United States is in the top five with $41,400, and countries such as Burundi, Ethiopia, and

purchasing power parity A method of calculating GDP or GNP of a country; the total is expressed according to the purchasing power of the national currency.

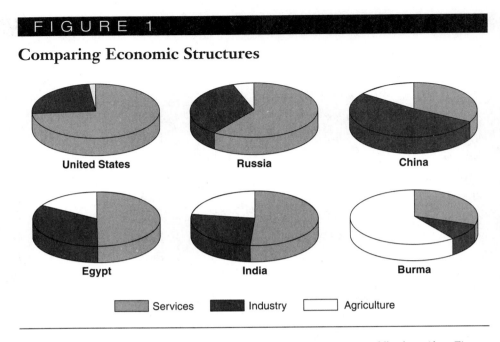

FIGURE 1

Comparing Economic Structures

United States   Russia   China

Egypt   India   Burma

Services   Industry   Agriculture

Source: World Bank, World Development Indicators database, 2005, www.worldbank.org/data. Figures are for 2002–2003 (except Burma, which are for 1999).

Malawi sit at the bottom of the league with a per capita GDP of less than $200. Put another way, it takes 460 Burundians to produce as much in a year as one American.

We can also tell much about the differences among countries by looking at **economic structure.** All economic activity falls into one of three categories: **industry** (which produces tangible, manufactured goods), **services** (which deal in intangibles, such as insurance, financial services, and retail), and agriculture. Generally speaking, the richer a country, the more it earns from services; the poorer a country, the more it earns from agriculture. Services are more profitable and are a sign of a sophisticated economy and an educated workforce. Agriculture is less profitable, relies on government subsidies in wealthy countries, and is often low-scale in poorer countries. So, in liberal democracies such as the United States or Canada, services account for as much as two-thirds of GDP and agriculture accounts for barely 2–3 per cent. By contrast, newly industrializing countries are still earning a lot from industry and less from services, whereas the poorest countries in the world have relatively little industry and many of their people still rely on agriculture for a living (see Figure 1).

Finally, we need to look at **economic policies,** because governments approach economic management in different ways. Free-market systems such as the United States, Britain, and Japan have less government control over the economy and less public ownership of industries and services, but centrally planned systems such as China have more government regulation and ownership. Meanwhile, emerging Asian and Latin American states have adopted increasingly free-market policies, and less developed countries have failed to develop economic stability and are handicapped by problems such as an overvalued national currency, high inflation, an inability to

industry An economic activity that transforms raw materials into tangible and usable products.

services Any economic activity that results in the provision of an intangible service.

TABLE 4

Economic Freedom Ratings

	Ranking	Score
Hong Kong	1	8.7
Singapore	2	8.6
New Zealand	3	8.2
Switzerland	3	8.2
United States	3	8.2
Britain	3	8.2
Canada	7	7.9
Japan	36	7.0
Mexico	58	6.5
India	68	6.3
Egypt	74	6.2
Haiti	78	6.0
China	90	5.7
Nigeria	90	5.7
Russia	114	5.0
Burma	123	2.5

Source: Fraser Institute, 2005, www.fraserinstitute.ca. Figures are for 2004.

raise taxes efficiently, corruption, inefficiency, and a large black market. Marginal countries have far less formal economic structure, and the question for them is less the role that government plays in the marketplace and more what they can do simply to impose some order on the economy.

One useful indicator of economic policies is the **Economic Freedom Index** developed by the Fraser Institute, a Canadian nonprofit that studies markets and the way they work. Arguing that the key ingredients of economic freedom are personal choice, voluntary exchange, freedom to compete, and protection of individuals and property, the Institute ranks 123 countries according to factors such as the size of government income and spending, how the law protects people and property, monetary policies, and trade policies. It then gives those countries a ranking on a scale of 10 to 1, with 10 being the freest. It gives Hong Kong and Singapore the highest ratings (8.8 and 8.6), places most liberal democracies in the range of 7.5 or better, and ranks Russia and China toward the bottom of the index, among a motley list of Asian and African states (see Table 4).*

---

* The Heritage Foundation, a U.S.-based think tank, has a similar Index of Economic Freedom which can be viewed on its Web site at www.heritage.org.

Social Variables

We can learn about different political systems by studying the structure of government institutions and the mechanics of political processes, but to better understand the *performance* of these systems, we need to look at the **quality of life** in different countries. In other words, what kind of job are they doing in terms of meeting the basic needs of their people? There are three standard measures of quality of life (see Figure 2):

- *Life expectancy,* or the age to which the average resident of a country can expect to live. This is used as an indicator of the quality of health care, but it can also say something about diet, environmental quality, and levels of public safety; life expectancy in countries torn by crime or civil war can be significantly reduced. The figures range from a high of about 75–82 years in the most successful countries, to about 55–65 in countries with medium levels of development, and a low of 38–50 in the most troubled countries.

- *Infant mortality,* or the number of newborn babies that die within 30 days of birth, expressed as a figure per 1,000 live births. This is another indicator of the quality of health care. Unfortunately, infant mortality is a fact of life, and even in the most medically advanced societies there will be some babies born with severe medical problems or dangerously premature, who will die. The figures range from a high of about 3–10 per 1,000 in the most successful countries to a low of as many as 130–150 per 1,000 in countries with the least advanced health care systems.

- *Adult literacy,* or the percentage of the population that can read and write. Unfortunately the definitions of literacy vary from one country to another, and even in countries that claim 100 percent literacy, there are many people who can do no more than read road signs and make only the simplest math calculations. Most industrialized countries claim literacy rates of 100 percent, whereas the rates in poorer countries can be as low as 40 percent.

One comparative measure of social conditions is offered by the **Human Development Index (HDI),** a ranking developed by the United Nations. Using a combination of life expectancy, adult literacy rates, educational enrollment, and per capita GDP, it rates human development for most of the countries in the world as high, medium, or low. On the 2004 index, Canada and the United States did well, ranking fourth and eighth respectively, whereas most other rich countries were in the top 30. By contrast, the poorest countries ranked at the bottom of the table, with Sierra Leone in last place at 177 (see Table 5).

THE SIX ARENAS

Using these three sets of variables (political, economic, and social) produces a system of classification based around six different arenas. The boundaries that separate the countries in each arena are debatable; some countries can be classified with more confidence than others, their features are often relative rather than absolute, and membership of the different arenas is transitory. Some countries firmly fit the characteristics of each

FIGURE 2

Comparing the Quality of Life

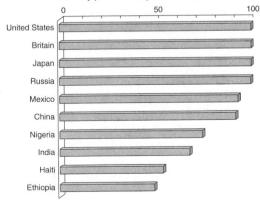

Source: World Bank, World Development Indicators database, 2005, www.worldbank.com. Figures are for 2002–2003. No figures available for adult literacy in Egypt.

TABLE 5

Human Development Ratings

	Ranking	Rating		Ranking	Rating
Norway	1	High	Mexico	53	Medium
Sweden	2	High	Russia	57	Medium
Australia	3	High	China	94	Medium
Canada	4	High	Egypt	120	Low
Netherlands	5	High	India	127	Low
United States	8	High	Nigeria	151	Low
Japan	9	High	Haiti	153	Low
Britain	12	High	Sierra Leone	177	Low

Source: United Nations Development Program, 2005, http://hdr.undp.org.

arena, and some are more peripheral (see Figure 3). Broadly speaking, though, the six arenas work out as follows.

Liberal Democracies

This arena contains 35 mainly European and North American countries with stable and legitimate systems of government; high Freedom House, Economic Freedom, and HDI ratings; wealthy free-market economies based mainly on services; and highly developed and generally efficient social services. If there were some kind of Darwinian scale of political evolution, it could be argued that liberal democracies have advanced further than any others. They are, however, not perfect. Capitalism is criticized for its focus on material wealth, and no one can claim to live in a society in which everyone has equal opportunity regardless of race, gender, religion, sexual preference, educational background, or economic circumstances. But liberal democracies have traveled a long way down the path to that ideal.

The **United States** is used as the first case study because it is obviously an important point of departure for Americans, but also because non-American students will find it important to understand how this powerful and influential system of government works. The American model has also been copied—in whole or in part—in many other countries, so we need to study the U.S. Constitution and American political institutions to understand why and how they have influenced and been adapted by those other countries.

Britain is used as the second case study because it is the home of the parliamentary system and of many of the ideas behind modern capitalism and democracy and because it provides some good contrasts with the United States. We could learn about parliamentary systems by studying Canada or Sweden, but we would always be referring to British precedent. The British political system is also interesting because

FIGURE 3

Overlapping Arenas

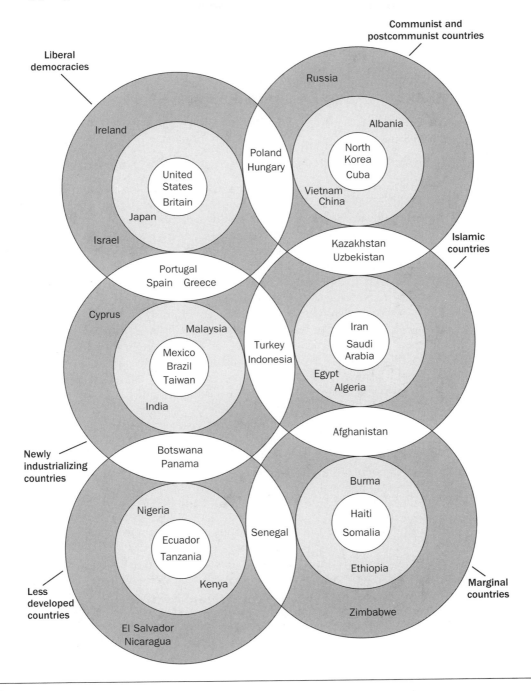

of the changes it has undergone since the end of World War II and continues to undergo as it develops a new role for itself as a mid-sized power and a member of the European Union.

Japan is included because of its economic importance in the world, because it shows how liberal democracy can take root outside the West, and because it is a parliamentary democracy with a distinctive political culture and some interesting variations on the parliamentary model. Japan's economic transformation since World War II has been remarkable, but it finds itself struggling to make reforms aimed at providing lasting political and economic stability. Its record may give us insight into the changes we can expect in Southeast Asian states that are experiencing rapid economic growth.

Communist and Postcommunist (CPC) Countries

This arena contains 26 mainly Eastern European and Asian countries whose modern histories have been dominated by one-party governments claiming to be communist and by economic policies driven by central planning and rapid industrialization. None of them are actually communist, nor have they ever been, and most have turned their backs on communism and headed off in several different directions. Some have moved into the liberal democratic orbit, some are moving into the Islamic orbit, and only five (China, Cuba, Laos, North Korea, and Vietnam) still officially subscribe to communism, but not always very convincingly. For now, though, they are still best understood in light of their "communist" past.

Russia is used as the first case study because of its importance to understanding the history of communism, because of its leading role in the former Soviet Union and in the demise of communism, and because of the problems of adjustment it shares with many of its Eastern European neighbors. As the erstwhile competitor to the Western alliance in the cold war, Russia also is a source of continuing fascination for North American and European students. Russia now faces the challenges of building a stable and democratic political system, restructuring its economy, and making related social adjustments.

China was chosen because it is an ancient culture, because it includes one-fifth of the world's population, and because of its rise to global economic power. It also helps bridge the gap between urban-based Soviet-style socialism and peasant-based socialism, showing how Marxism has been adapted to non-European and mainly agrarian societies. In some respects, it could also be approached as a newly industrializing country, but as long as the Chinese Communist Party holds on to its monopoly on power, China will remain best understood as a communist state.

Newly Industrializing Countries (NICs)

The label *newly industrializing* has been used by social scientists since the 1970s but has yet to make its way into the mainstream of comparative politics, despite its value to comparative analysis. It is applied in this text to 30 mainly Southeast and South Asian, Caribbean, and Latin American countries undergoing the kind of rapid political, economic, social, and technological change that occurred in Europe and

FIGURE 4

The Cases in this Book

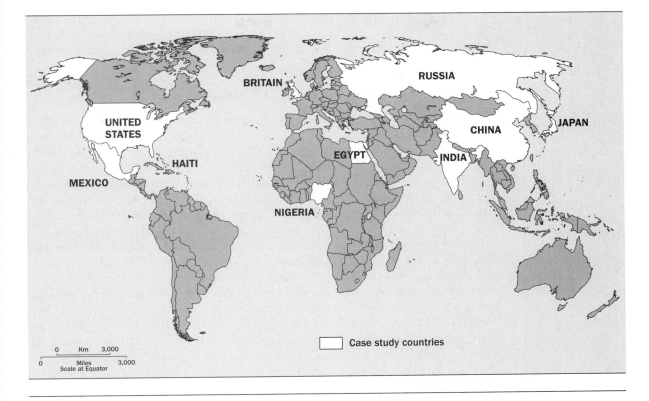

North America in the eighteenth and nineteenth centuries. These states are building stable systems of government; have high to medium Freedom House, Economic Freedom, and HDI ratings; enjoy a growing variety of channels of representation and participation; and are experiencing rapid industrialization and export-led economic growth.

   Mexico may have economic and debt problems, human rights abuses, and severe disparities in the distribution of wealth and political power, but its industrial base is rapidly expanding and it has seen political continuity since the 1930s. It also has obvious interest for the United States and Canada, given that all three countries are partners in the North American Free Trade Agreement (NAFTA). Mexico is a good point of comparison with the United States given that both countries began from a roughly equal political and economic base, yet evolved very differently. Political stability has helped promote economic growth in Mexico, which has in turn brought democratic reform.

   India is used as the second example of a newly industrializing country because it offers fascinating contrasts: It is a huge country with deep religious and ethnic divisions and great poverty and the vast majority of its people earn a living off the land, yet it has a vibrant and democratic political tradition and a record in industrial and technological development that has allowed it to launch its own space and nuclear weapons programs. Rapid population growth could soon make India the world's most populous country, but it needs to ensure that the quality of life for its people continues to improve quickly enough to prevent religious, class, and economic differences from boiling over and undermining the foundations of the Indian state.

Less Developed Countries (LDCs)

This arena consists of 35 mainly African, Central American, and Pacific Island states that have the potential to build political, economic, and social stability but face short-term handicaps. Some are building strong democratic records, some are politically stable but poor, others are overcoming major obstacles to rebuild their political and economic systems, and a few have great economic potential but many social handicaps. Most have elected civilian governments, although political stability is often compromised by corruption, social divisions, poor human rights records, and the intervention of the military. Most have a low per capita GDP, a limited economic base, and poorly developed social services, with medium to low Freedom House, Economic Freedom, and HDI ratings.

Nigeria is used as the case study because it is an ideal laboratory for the study of the problems of state-building in the postcolonial era. It has experimented with different forms of civilian government in an attempt to build stability, but it has suffered from many years of military government. Nigeria also provides insight into the problems of sub-Saharan Africa, an area about which most North Americans know much too little. Its ethnic and religious divisions exemplify problems elsewhere in the continent; they led to civil war in the late 1960s and have undermined Nigeria's experiments with civilian government. The challenges facing Nigeria include building a common national identity and a stable system of government and reducing the role of the military in politics.

Islamic Countries

Where this book breaks most obviously with convention is in approaching Islamic countries as a separate arena. It does this because Islam is the only major monotheistic religion in the world that offers its adherents an entire way of life, including a political system and a body of law. It also does this because Islam is the key political and social force in most of the countries with Muslim majorities. The failure of the West to understand the political nature of Islam is unfortunate, but the growing conflict between Islamic extremists and the West has encouraged us to pay more attention to the nature of Islam, and more political scientists now appreciate its ideological significance. The ongoing tensions between Islam and the West also underline the importance of better understanding these countries.

The arena includes 26 mainly North African and Middle Eastern states where Islam is the religion of the majority and where it plays a significant actual or potential role in politics and government. Although Islamic countries have very different levels of political, economic, and social development, their adherence to Islam is ultimately the most important factor in understanding how they work. However, several countries are excluded because they are better understood (at least for now) in other contexts: The Islamic republics of the former USSR are still influenced by their communist past, Indonesia and Turkey are secular states best approached as NICs, and most sub-Saharan African states with large Islamic populations are better understood as LDCs.

Egypt was chosen as the case study because of its key role in the Islamic world, the Middle East, and the Arab world; because of its strategic importance; because of what its history and political development say about the changing relationship between Islam and the West; and because of the tension in Egypt between religious revivalism and secular modernism, which is common to many Islamic states. Egypt is struggling to build its economy; to stay on good terms with Israel, its Arab neighbors, and the West; and to prevent the activities of Islamic opposition groups from spilling over into revolution. Given Western concern for stability in the oil-rich Persian Gulf, Egypt's welfare is at the forefront of North American and European foreign policy interests.

Marginal Countries

This arena coincides with the UN definition of the poorest countries in the world, which it describes as "least developed countries." However, whereas the UN uses only per capita GDP, economic structure, and adult literacy to make its calculations, marginal countries are defined here according to a broader set of political, economic, and social criteria. These are the most troubled countries in the world, with problems that range from persistent political instability to deep social divisions, few independent or competing sources of political power, a limited economic base and widespread poverty, few natural resources or exports, sometimes serious public health problems, and—in some cases—deliberate isolation from the international community and disputed legal status. There are 36 altogether, and they are found mainly in Africa.

Haiti is used as the case study because of the contrasts it offers to its neighbors (it is the poorest country in the Americas, with the highest rates of poverty and infant mortality, the lowest rates of literacy and primary education, and the lowest life expectancy), because of the challenge of understanding why a country that has been independent almost as along as the United States should be in such trouble, and because it is physically close to the United States. There are many analysts who now argue that the problems of failing or failed states like Haiti pose critical challenges to liberal democracies; with a troubled country such as Haiti on our doorstep, it is important that we try to understand the source of its problems and the potential solutions to those problems.

THE CASE STUDIES

Every case study used in the book is structured around the same four questions: Who governs? How do they govern? How do people take part in politics? With what results? To do this, and to help the process of comparison, each case study is divided into the same four sections:

- **Political development and political culture.** History tells us how political systems have evolved, which is essential to understanding them today. For example, it would be difficult to understand Russian politics without knowing about the influence of Stalin or to understand Indian or Nigerian politics without appreciating the impact of colonialism. Each case study begins with an overview of how government and the state have evolved in that country and then looks at the key features of political culture or the prevailing political values and attitudes of its citizens.

- **The political system.** Understanding how political institutions work is essential for comparison. We need to know how they function, how they relate to each other, from where they derive their authority, the limits that are placed on their powers, and the impact that citizens have on their work. To these ends, this section describes the institutional "rules" of the political system and analyzes and explains the relationships among its elements.

- **Elections and parties.** Government consists of a network of systems and processes, with leaders and citizens relating to each other in a large and complex series of games. This section focuses on the inputs into those systems, or the ways in which people take part (or are prevented from taking part) in politics. They may do this through voting, lobbying, demonstrating, or supporting political parties and interest groups, but they may also do it through bribery, intimidation, violence, and murder.

- **Public policies.** Just as we need to understand institutions and inputs, so we need to understand the outputs of politics: what governments actually do or do not do to meet the needs of their citizens. Although most governments routinely deal with dozens of policy issues, this section in each case covers two of the most important: economic policy and foreign policy. The goal is to use these examples to compare the policy priorities of each country, to understand how agendas evolve, and to see how policies are made and implemented.

The case studies are carefully structured so that the same material is covered in each, allowing comparisons to be made across all ten countries.

KEY TERMS

classification
comparative method
Corruption Perception
 Index
Economic Freedom
Index
economic policies
economic structure
ethnocentrism
Freedom House Index
Governance Indicators

gross domestic product
 (GDP)
gross national product
 (GNP)
Human Development
 Index (HDI)
independent
legitimacy
nation
nation-state
new world order

per capita GDP
political culture
purchasing power parity
quality of life
sources of authority
sovereignty
state
structural–functional
 model
territory
Three Worlds system

COMPARATIVE POLITICS ONLINE

Every chapter of this book has a list of recommended Web sites relating to politics in the different countries covered. There are also a growing number of Web sites that offer general information on multiple countries. Among the best are the following:

Political Resources on the Net: www.politicalresources.net
Offers a wealth of information on every country in the world, including elections, parties, government institutions, and the media.

Elections around the World: www.electionworld.org
Related to the above site, with all the latest news on elections.

Inter-Parliamentary Union: www.ipu.org
A site containing useful information and statistics on legislatures around the world.

Library of Congress: http://lcweb2.loc.gov/frd/cs
Contains brief studies of countries all over the world, including the ten in this book.

United Nations: www.un.org
Official Web site of the UN, with links to all its specialized agencies.

BBC News: http://news.bbc.co.uk
Probably the best source of truly international news on the Web.

CIA World Factbook: www.cia.gov/cia/publications/factbook
Contains basic political, economic, geographical, and demographic information on every country in the world. Updated annually.

Amnesty International Online: www.amnesty.org
Home page of the respected human rights organization, which includes reports on the human rights situation in nearly 150 countries.

Part I

LIBERAL DEMOCRACIES

Democracy is the worst form of government except all those other forms that have been tried from time to time.

The best argument against democracy is a five minute conversation with the average voter.

—Winston Churchill, British statesman

Liberal democracies are the most successful societies in the world. They are the freest and most stable, the wealthiest and most productive, and they have the strongest records on human rights and on providing their citizens with basic social services. They are not perfect by any means and are still troubled by a host of problems, including racism, sexism, elitism, exploitation, political corruption, poverty, corporate greed, and threats to the environment. But by most objective measures, they have more fully met the needs of more of their citizens than any other type of political system.

It should be relatively easy to describe and understand the major features of liberal democracies, because we all think we know how to define democracy—free elections, freedom of speech, the rule of law, civil rights, and government by "the people." But the reality is not so simple. Liberal democracy is a complex idea surrounded by a fog of semantic confusion. The word "*liberal*" is widely misunderstood by Americans, and no political concept has been studied in as much detail as "*democracy*"; yet it has been so loosely applied that it sometimes seems that almost any society can be described as democratic if the definition is stretched far enough.

Broadly speaking, liberal democracies have six major features in common.

Liberalism

liberalism A political ideology that supports limited government, individual freedom, social toleration, and the redistribution of resources.

One of the most universal of all political concepts, **liberalism** is at the heart of what we understand by modern politics and economics. But we first have to appreciate that it has at least three different meanings. For most Americans, it is an ideological concept, in the sense that a liberal is someone who believes in greater government involvement in people's lives as a way of redistributing wealth, equalizing opportunity, and correcting social wrongs. In this sense, liberalism means support for a managed economy, social welfare, higher taxes, and affirmative action, or, in the views of its critics, "big government." It was used pejoratively during the 2004 U.S. presidential election; President George W. Bush often dismissed the policies of his challenger Senator John Kerry as "liberal," but Kerry was unwilling to fully associate himself with the label.

For our purposes, liberal has two quite different applications, both of them associated with restrictions on the power of government:

limited government A form of government in which sovereign power is limited by law.

- **Classical liberalism** is an arrangement designed to achieve **limited government,** usually through a **social contract,** which is an agreement between government and citizens regarding their obligations to one another. The broad idea is that government will work in the interests of the people while citizens will respect the law. The embodiment of a social contract is a constitution, a document designed to outline the powers of government, the limits on the powers of government, and the rights of citizens. The ideal is to provide majority rule with minority rights.

capitalism An economic system driven by profit, private ownership, and supply and demand.

- **Economic liberalism** (otherwise known as **capitalism**) is an approach to the marketplace based on a belief in private property, a limited government role in the economy, and the promotion of a free market driven by supply and demand. As with most concepts in the social sciences, capitalism is not absolute, because no market is completely free: Governments influence production and choice through taxes, regulations, and welfare and often own and operate key public services, such as schools and universities, postal services, and transport systems. But economic liberalism is based on the idea of limiting the role of government in the economy.

If we combine the classical and economic notions of liberalism, then almost all North Americans and Europeans are liberals, because they believe in limited government and a free market. But these beliefs are no more than ideals, because even in the most democratic societies governments are often accused of accumulating too much power.

Democracy

In its most basic sense, democracy means government or rule by the people, and comes from the Greek words *demos*(people) and *kratos* (strength). In its purest form, a **direct democracy** would be one in which everyone who lived under the jurisdiction of a government was asked his or her opinion every time the government made a decision. Because most societies are too big to be run this way, they opt instead for a **representative democracy,** or a system in which citizens elect others to represent their views and interests when decisions are made on law and public policy.

democracy A political system in which government is based on a mandate from the people.

Because elections and elected officials are subject to many different pressures and influences, the views of voters are not equally reflected in the democratic process. This has prompted the development of different theories about how democracy works in practice. For example:

- **Elite theory** argues that most democracies are controlled by a ruling class. The Greek philosopher Plato (c. 428–348 B.C.) was the first to suggest that in every society a minority makes most of the decisions.[1] Many theorists since then have

CHECKLIST

LIBERAL DEMOCRACIES
What Are Their Features?

- Representative systems of government based on regular, fair, secret and competitive elections
- Well-defined, consistent, and predictable political institutions and processes
- A high degree of public loyalty to the state
- A variety of institutionalized forms of political participation and representation, including multiple political parties with a variety of platforms
- Protection of individual rights under the law
- A belief in human equality
- An active, effective, and protected opposition and respect for freedom of speech

- Postindustrial, wealthy and free-market economic systems based mainly on services and industry, driving the world's biggest multinational corporations
- High levels of urbanization, with advanced infrastructure
- Advanced technology
- A relatively high quality of life when measured by the provision of education, health care, and other basic services
- High ratings on the Freedom House, Economic Freedom, and Human Development indexes
- Significant regional and global influence

Where Are They?

There are 35, and they are found mainly in North America, Europe, and East Asia/Australasia:

Australia	Hungary	Norway
Austria	Iceland	Poland
Belgium	Ireland	Portugal
Canada	Israel	Slovakia
Cyprus	Italy	Slovenia
Czech Republic	Japan	South Korea
Denmark	Luxembourg	Spain
Estonia	Latvia	Sweden
Finland	Lithuania	Switzerland
France	Malta	United Kingdom
Germany	Netherlands	United States
Greece	New Zealand	

argued that although elected officials rely on individual votes to win office, once in office they often make decisions as a result of the pressures put on them by their networks of supporters.

- **Group theory,** or **pluralism,** argues that democracy should be seen not so much in individual terms as in group terms. It has been suggested that instead of the term *democracy* we should use the term **polyarchy** (rule by many).[2] A pluralist society is one in which politics is driven by competition among different groups, with the

pluralism The distribution of power among several institutions, allowing government to be influenced by competing groups, values, and demands.

TABLE 1.1

Different Forms of Government

In addition to *democracy*, Greek has given us the roots for many of the terms used to describe different forms of government. Here are some examples:

Anarchy	Absence of government (from *anarchia*, or non-rule)
Aristocracy	Rule by a hereditary class (literally, rule by the best)
Autarchy	Self-rule
Autarky	Self-sufficiency (from *autarkeia*)
Autocracy	Rule by one person
Autonomy	Self-government
Bureaucracy*	Rule by government officials
Gerontocracy	Rule by the elderly (from *geron*, an old man)
Hierarchy	Rule by different levels/degrees (it originally meant sacred rule)
Kleptocracy	Rule by criminals (literally, thieves)
Meritocracy	Rule by achievement and ability
Monarchy	Rule by one (typically hereditary)
Oligarchy	Rule by a few or a group
Plutocracy	Rule by the wealthy
Polyarchy	Rule by many
Theocracy	Rule by religious leaders (literally, rule by God)
Timocracy	Rule of honor, arising out of aristocracy
Tyranny	Absolute rule (from *turannos*)

* A hybrid French–Greek word.

government supposedly acting as an honest broker. Power is not equally distributed but is manipulated by the groups with the most influence, which may be based on wealth or numbers. These groups may be corporations, special interest groups, labor unions, or regional interests, or they might be based around gender, race, age, religion, or social class.

Whichever theory we apply, the typical features of a democracy include the following: government by elected officials, regular elections at which all eligible voters can make their choices, few (if any) restrictions on the rights of all adults to vote, competing political parties offering a variety of ideological platforms, multiple channels through which citizens can express their views and influence government (such as interest groups and a free press), freedom of speech, an independent court system, and a constitution. Perhaps most important, democracies believe in the **rule of law,** meaning that all citizens are equally subject to the same body of laws, which limit the powers of elected officials and protect the rights of citizens. In practice, though,

rule of law The process by which power is determined and limited according to a body of laws to which everyone is equally subject.

there are many ways people can get around the law, find loopholes, or use their wealth or position to escape prosecution. Equal application of the law is an ideal rather than a reality.

Stable State Systems

One of the advantages enjoyed by liberal democracies is that they all have relatively stable state systems. The evidence of that stability can be found in the following: strong and generally well-respected political institutions and legal systems, political processes that are mainly consistent and predictable, relatively efficient and professional bureaucracies, and the absence of serious challenges to territorial integrity. Of course, there are exceptions to every rule: all liberal democracies have economic and social divisions, not all of their citizens are always entirely happy with the way they are governed, and several have nationalist or separatist movements (such as the Scots in Britain, the Quebecois in Canada, and the Catalans in Spain), but few of these problems threaten the fabric of the state. The story is different in less developed countries and marginal countries (see Parts IV and VI). In the worst cases, there is little sense of national unity or identity, national government may be out of touch with the people, and the internal divisions of states can lead to social conflict, civil war, genocide, and even the breakup of states.

Postindustrialism

Liberal democracies have undergone economic and political change that has taken them from feudalism (see later discussion) through an industrial revolution to a postindustrial, service-based economy. Most wealth in liberal democracies is generated by **industry** and **services;** as noted in the Introduction, the former produces tangible goods such as cars, furniture, electrical appliances, and other consumer products, and the latter are intangibles, such as retailing, entertainment, tourism, banking, and insurance. Whereas services account for about two-thirds of national wealth in liberal democracies, agriculture and industry tend to dominate in poorer countries, which usually have a smaller service sector.

Because they are **postindustrial,** liberal democracies are also highly urbanized, with anything from 75 to 95 percent of their people living in towns and cities. This means that power tends to be focused in cities, and politics tends to be dominated by urban interests. As a general rule, the wealthier a country, the smaller its rural population and the fewer the people earning a living directly off the land. Agriculture in most liberal democracies is mechanized, intensive, and productive. Liberal democratic economies also produce a wide variety of goods and services and are built on a well-developed and diverse infrastructure with efficient and sophisticated transportation and communication systems.

postindustrial society A society in which most wealth and economic activity is based on the provision of services.

High Quality of Life

Most people in most liberal democracies have a high standard of living when measured by the availability of jobs, education, health care, consumer choice, and basic services. They have effective health care, education, and welfare systems, and they can expect to live relatively long and healthy lives. Educational levels are high, population growth rates are low, and calorie consumption is at or above minimum needs. Although liberal democracies still have problems such as illiteracy, poverty, discrimination, crime, pollution, and homelessness, these are normally much worse in poorer countries.

Global Influence

Liberal democracies have converted their wealth and stability into political, economic, and military power. Their wealth has given them the means to exert influence over trade, currency exchange rates, and the prices paid for goods and services. North American, European, and Japanese banks and corporations have become the world's major sources of investment funds, the poorest countries often rely on aid from liberal democracies, and liberal democracies are the biggest influence on the policies of international lending agencies such as the World Bank. The bigger liberal democracies have converted their economic wealth and technological prowess into military power, making countries such as the United States, Britain, and France among the most powerful in the world.

THE EVOLUTION OF LIBERAL DEMOCRACY

Although the origins of democracy can be traced back to the early city-states of Greece and Rome and to early Chinese and Indian cultures, all of which developed ideas emphasizing the role of the people in government, modern liberal democracy is mainly a product of changes that came to European society between the thirteenth and nineteenth centuries. At the heart of those changes was a shift in power away from landowning monarchs and aristocrats to a broader demographic base.

The End of Feudalism (13th to 14th Centuries)

feudalism A hierarchical system in which most people own little and are subservient to an aristocracy that controls most of the land and political power.

The most common political system in Europe until the Middle Ages was **feudalism,** a rigidly hierarchical class system that allowed little, if any, social or economic mobility. At its base were the peasants, who made up the vast majority of the population, owned nothing, and had little control over their lives. They lived, worked, and died on estates operated by aristocrats, who controlled their movements and settled all legal questions. The aristocracy in turn answered to the monarch, who sat alone at the apex of the system, owned most or all of the land, and granted the aristocrats rights to the estates in return for services (usually military) on the basis of an oath of loyalty. Monarchs could be removed by murder or by defeat in war, but otherwise they ruled by **divine right,** meaning that they claimed to answer to no one but God, and certainly not to the peasants or the aristocrats.

divine right The belief in medieval Europe that monarchs or sovereigns ruled by the consent of God.

European feudalism began its long decline in 1215, when King John of England, at the insistence of his barons, signed the Magna Carta. This agreement for the first time placed limits on the power of the monarch, a process that was taken a stage further in 1265 with the creation of the first British parliament. Only aristocrats could be members, and they were not elected, but it was the first alternative form of government to a monarchy. The key to subsequent democratic change in Europe was the emergence of a balance between the crown and the nobility, allowing the nobility their independence while preventing royal absolutism. In countries where royal absolutism persisted (as in Russia), democracy did not emerge.[3]

The Reformation and the Enlightenment (16th to 18th Centuries)

Feudalism was underpinned by the Catholic Church, which acted as an international authority exercising most of the real political power in Europe in the Middle Ages and whose authority only finally began to be questioned with the Reformation. The way was led by the German monk Martin Luther (1483–1546), who criticized papal corruption and luxury and argued that individuals should be allowed to worship God directly, rather than through the intermediary of the church. In effect, he was arguing in favor of individual rights and against the powers of the church and the state.

In 1651, as England recovered from one of its civil wars (which led to the brief removal of the monarchy), a book titled *The Leviathan* was published, written by Thomas Hobbes (1588–1679). In arguing for the restoration of the monarchy, Hobbes suggested that people were selfish and that life without government would be "solitary, poor, nasty, brutish and short." He said that if people were to protect themselves from the unrestrained state of nature and the evil of others, they had to submit themselves to government with absolute power, or a "leviathan" that dominated society. No one had the right to resist or revolt against that power, unless the ruler tried to take the life of a citizen, in which case the contract between ruler and citizen was broken.[4]

One of Hobbes's younger contemporaries was John Locke (1632–1704), who took the opposite view by arguing that humans were rational and self-interested (rather than selfish). He argued that people had "natural rights" to life, liberty, and property and that they entered into a social contract with government to protect these rights. Locke wrote that the only true basis for the power of government was the consent of the governed and that it was the duty of government to protect the rights of citizens. He disputed the divine right of monarchs and argued that men were born equal with rights that no monarch could take away. The transfer of powers from the monarch and the church to the people in England was confirmed in Locke's lifetime with the Bill of Rights, drawn up in 1689 following the restoration of the monarchy to confirm the supremacy of parliament over the monarch.

The spread of liberalism was confirmed in 1776 with the American Declaration of Independence, a radical statement of principles that were taken a stage further in 1787 with the publication of the U.S. Constitution. This was the first written constitution in the world and the kind of social contract proposed by Locke and the French philosopher Jean-Jacques Rousseau (1712–1778) (author of *The Social Contract* and a man often credited with inspiring the French Revolution of 1789). The U.S. Constitution was also based on the principles of limited and representative government outlined by Locke. With the separation of powers (three branches of government and a division of powers between the federal government and the states), it set out to ensure that no one arm of government could accumulate too much power.

THE MOST EXCLUSIVE CLUB IN THE WORLD

The strength of liberal democratic ideas has been helped by the strong patterns of political and economic cooperation that have emerged among liberal democracies, particularly since World War II. Even before the war had ended, representatives of 44 countries met at **Bretton Woods,** New Hampshire, to discuss their plans for the postwar world and agreed to promote global free trade. Out of Bretton Woods came the World Bank, the International Monetary Fund (IMF), and the General Agreement on Tariffs and Trade (GATT, which was replaced by the World Trade Organization, or WTO, in 1995). The World Bank and the IMF have provided financing to encourage economic development and international trade, and the reduction of barriers to global free trade is negotiated under the auspices of the WTO.

Three other organizations have helped liberal democracies to work together:

- **North Atlantic Treaty Organization (NATO).** Although peace was achieved in Europe in 1945, the Soviet Union seemed to pose a threat to the new order, as a result of which Western Europe and North America created NATO in 1949 to guard against Soviet attack. NATO succeeded in its aim of protecting the Western alliances, and also

helped underpin democracy and capitalism. Its success was vividly illustrated in 2004 when seven Eastern European countries—including Bulgaria, Romania, Slovakia, and Slovenia—all joined NATO. But since the diplomatic fallout in 2002–2003 between the United States and some of its key European allies over the invasion of Iraq, a question mark has hung over the future of the organization.

- **Organization for Economic Cooperation and Development (OECD).** Founded in 1961, and sometimes nicknamed the "Rich Man's Club" because its members include the world's major economic powers, the OECD coordinates and promotes the economic policies of member states, helps expand ties between them and poorer countries, and promotes world trade. In recent years its founding members have been joined by Hungary, Poland, Mexico, and South Korea.

- **G-8 Group.** Beginning in 1975, the leaders of the seven wealthiest members of the OECD (Britain, Canada, France, Germany, Italy, Japan, and the United States) began holding annual summits as the G-7 Group. They initially discussed global economic issues, but with time the agenda broadened to include political issues. Russia has since joined, pushing membership to eight.

The Rise of the Nation-State (17th to 19th Centuries)

During the European feudal era, political allegiance was based on the relationship between monarchs and their vassals. Military control over land, personal agreements, and the exchange of favors and obligations were key components of the system. The relationship between the ruler and the ruled in Europe was gradually formalized and institutionalized, particularly when monarchs began raising money (or imposing taxes) to meet the costs of waging war. This led to the development of more structured and intensified systems of control and the emergence of what eventually became the international state system in which we live today.

A group photo of the most exclusive club in the world: the leaders of the Group of Eight wealthy industrialized countries. Front row: George W. Bush (United States), Jacques Chirac (France), Tony Blair (United Kingdom), Vladimir Putin (Russia), and Gerhard Schroeder (Germany). Back row: Paul Martin (Canada), Junichiro Koizumi (Japan), Silvio Berlusconi (Italy), and José Manuel Barroso (President of the European Commission).

Something like the modern frontiers of European states began to emerge in the fourteenth century, but it was not until the sixteenth and seventeenth centuries that the earliest European states really began to take shape, beginning with England and France. Until the nineteenth century, borders in Europe were still loose and people could cross them freely, but the nineteenth century saw the growth of **nationalism,** as the citizens of different nation-states placed their own interests and values above those of their neighbors or competitors. Borders began to be more jealously protected, the limits of state sovereignty began to be marked out, and the foundations of the modern state system began to take shape.

The Industrial Revolution (18th to 19th Centuries)

Until the Middle Ages, European economies were based on agriculture. Most people worked on large estates operated by aristocrats and had neither wealth nor power. The balance began to change as agriculture became more productive, more land was tilled, and more efficient methods were developed for growing and harvesting crops and breeding livestock. Farmers became richer, society became more varied and complex, freedom of choice expanded, and a new class of merchants and entrepreneurs emerged. As this class won more political power, the influence of monarchs, aristocrats, and the church was eroded still further.

The agricultural revolution was followed by an **industrial revolution:** Human energy was replaced by mechanical energy, cheaper and more efficient methods of smelting iron and producing steel were discovered, and technological breakthroughs led to the invention of cotton-spinning machines and the steam engine. Britain was the first country to witness these changes, mainly because its monarch had less control over the economy, the population was growing rapidly (creating a large new market), there was less domestic political discontent than elsewhere in Europe, and feudalism had weakened (creating a less rigid class structure).[5]

Adding momentum to these developments was the work of the Scottish philosopher Adam Smith (1723–1790). In *The Wealth of Nations*, published in 1776, he outlined most of the basic concepts of what we now call capitalism.[6] He criticized the traditional belief that a state's power was based on its wealth and that a state should keep as much wealth as possible within its borders by encouraging exports and limiting imports. He argued instead that supply and demand was the most efficient way of meeting society's needs. He wrote of the power of the "invisible hand" of the marketplace and argued that economies should be supported by a limited form of government that would maintain law and order and guarantee contracts and a stable currency, but little more. In other words, he was supporting a hands-off, free-market approach to economic management.

Early industrialization was made possible by changes in the distribution of political power, and politics was itself changed by industrialization. The number of people working on the land fell as the urban working class grew. With the rise of a new entrepreneurial capitalist class, aristocrats no longer had a monopoly on economic wealth, and the commercial and industrial classes were much less willing than before to tolerate limits on their freedom of choice.[7] The new urban middle and working classes demanded greater input into the political system, trade unions formed to represent the workers, the vote was extended, towns and cities grew, and the new capitalists used their power to bring about changes in representation. In 1854, the English philosopher John Stuart Mill published his classic *On Liberty*, which argued in favor of civil liberties and minority rights (but against free-market economics, which he believed would bring about exploitation and the virtual enslavement of workers).[8]

Despite all of these new democratic tendencies, the political changes of the post feudal era were not aimed at giving rights to all citizens but rather only to a privileged few. The American Declaration of Independence says that "all men are created equal," but it might as well have been worded "all white male property and slave owners are created equal." Adam Smith may have praised the free market, but he had little respect for the working class, believing that the modern industrial worker who spent his whole life performing simple operations "generally becomes as stupid and ignorant as it is possible for a human to become."[9] Even Karl Marx, the alleged champion of the working class, had little respect for workers as a group.

The Spread of Liberal Democracy
(17th to 19th Centuries)

With a finite population and domestic market, there was a limit to how far European industry could be supported by the home market. As the need for new markets, new sources of raw materials, and cheap labor became more obvious, Spain, Portugal, Britain, France, the Netherlands, and other European countries set off overseas to explore and conquer. The Spanish were the most active in the sixteenth and seventeenth centuries, followed by the French. By the nineteenth century, Britain had become the dominant imperial power, establishing a presence on every inhabited continent. Some of its colonies (such as Canada and Australia) were created for settlement, whereas others (such as India and most of Britain's African colonies) were created for economic exploitation, particularly of raw materials and labor.[10]

To protect themselves and their trade interests, the Europeans expanded their military power. When Britain won the edge over its French and Dutch rivals, the world entered the **Pax Britannica,** or the peace policed by Britain. One of the results was that many British political values were exported or copied elsewhere, providing a foundation for the spread of liberal democracy. This developed strong roots in countries that were settled by British immigrants (such as the United States, Canada, Australia, and New Zealand) but not in those taken over by force and for economic exploitation.

LIBERAL DEMOCRACY TODAY

The principles of liberal democracy today form the basis of politics and government throughout North America, Europe, Japan, and Australasia, although some converts have been relatively recent. Germany and Japan did not begin to emerge as nation-states until the 1860s, and both underwent devastating experiences with failed democracy and dictatorship before finally settling with liberal democracy after World War II. Norway has governed itself only since 1905, Finland was part of the Russian Empire until 1917, and Ireland was under British administration until 1922. Until the mid-1970s, Spain and Portugal were dictatorships, Greece was under a military government from 1967 to 1974, and the Czech Republic, Estonia, Hungary, Latvia, Lithuania, Poland, Slovakia, and Slovenia were part of the Soviet bloc until 1991; all are now members of the European Union, an organization that has had a profound impact on the spread of democracy throughout Europe (see Close-Up View, page 118).

Although we call these countries liberal democracies, they are neither purely liberal nor perfectly democratic. Not only is the free market limited by government regulation and public ownership, but civil liberties and rights are often compromised, as they have been in Northern Ireland, prompting extremist groups in some cases to respond with violence. In Japan, political power is concentrated in the hands of bureaucrats and party leaders. In the United States, several groups (including ethnic minorities, and homosexuals) still do not have equal opportunities, and questions hover over the nature of electoral politics. In all liberal democracies, women have less political power and opportunity than men, do not earn as much as men for equal work, and are still prevented from rising to positions of corporate and political power as easily as men. Despite these problems, liberal democracy has been stable and lasting, and no country with a sustained history of liberal democracy has ever freely or deliberately opted for an alternative form of government.

Liberal democracy has many attractions, and many of its ideas have taken root in other countries, with varied results. Since the end of the cold war in 1989–1990, for example, Eastern Europeans have turned increasingly to liberal democratic ideas, and countries such as Hungary, Poland, and the Czech Republic have joined the ranks of liberal democracies. Countries in other parts of the world are also developing democratic traditions (for example, India, Mexico, and Costa Rica), and even some sub-Saharan African states (notably Botswana) have recently started moving away from personal and one-party rule toward multiparty democracy. Some analysts have suggested that such trends represent an expansion of liberal democracy, but it is too early to be sure.

KEY TERMS

Bretton Woods	feudalism	polyarchy
capitalism	group theory	postindustrialism
classical liberalism	industrial revolution	representative democracy
democracy	industry	rule of law
direct democracy	liberalism	services
divine right	limited government	social contract
economic liberalism	nationalism	
elite theory	Pax Britannica	

KEY PEOPLE

Thomas Hobbes	Jean-Jacques Rousseau	John Stuart Mill
John Locke	Adam Smith	Plato
Martin Luther		

STUDY QUESTIONS

1. What are the responsibilities of government?
2. Are individual rights absolute? If not, what limits are acceptable?
3. Which is the most compelling theory of democracy: elitism, pluralism, or a combination of the two?
4. What does *majority rule* mean, and how are minority rights protected?

LIBERAL DEMOCRACIES ONLINE

There are no Web sites for liberal democracies as such, but the sites of the following key international organizations provide useful insight into liberal democratic goals and values:

European Union: http://europa.eu.int
North Atlantic Treaty Organization: www.nato.int
Organization for Economic Cooperation and Development: www.oecd.org
World Trade Organization: www.wto.org

FURTHER READING

Almond, Gabriel, and Sidney Verba, *The Civic Culture: Political Attitudes and Democracy in Five Nations* (Princeton, NJ: Princeton University Press, 1963), and *The Civic Culture Revisited* (Newbury Park, CA: Sage Publications, 1989). Classic studies of political ideas in selected liberal democracies.

Dahl, Robert Alan, *On Democracy* (New Haven, CT: Yale University Press, 2000). An accessible introduction to democracy, providing a history of the concept and a discussion of its qualities.

Mandelbaum, Michael, *The Ideas That Conquered the World: Peace, Democracy, and Free Markets in the Twenty-First Century* (New York: Public Affairs, 2002). An analysis of the role of these three concepts in shaping the world.

Parenti, Michael, *Democracy for the Few*, 7th Ed. (Belmont, CA: Wadsworth, 2001). A short and pithy critique of American democracy that raises some challenging and controversial questions about many treasured assumptions.

Tilly, Charles (Ed.), *The Formation of National States in Western Europe* (Princeton, NJ: Princeton University Press, 1975). A good survey of the rise of the nation-state.

CHAPTER 1

UNITED STATES

UNITED STATES: QUICK FACTS

Official name: United States of America

Capital: Washington, D.C.

Area: 3.56 million square miles (9.22 million sq. km)

Languages: Overwhelmingly English, with some minority languages (notably Spanish)

Population: 291 million

Population density: 82 per square mile (32 per sq. km.)

Population growth rate: 1.1 percent

POLITICAL INDICATORS

Freedom House rating: Free

Date of state formation: 1776

System type: Republic

Constitution: Written; published 1787

Administration: Federal; 50 states

Executive: President elected for maximum of two four-year terms

Legislature: Bicameral Congress; Senate (100 members, two from each state, serving six-year renewable terms), and House of Representatives (435 members, serving two-year renewable terms)

Party structure: Multiparty, but two dominant parties (Democrats and Republicans)

Judiciary: Separate Supreme Court (nine members appointed for life by president and confirmed by Senate)

Head of state: George W. Bush (2001–)

Head of government: George W. Bush (2001–)

ECONOMIC INDICATORS

GDP (2004): $11,668 billion

Per capita GDP: $41,400

Distribution of GDP: Services 74 percent, industry 25 percent, agriculture 2 percent

Urban population: 77 percent

SOCIAL INDICATORS

HDI ranking: 8

Infant mortality rate: 7 per 1,000 live births

Life expectancy: 77.4 years

Illiteracy: 0 percent of people aged 15 and older

Religions: Predominantly Christian, with many denominations

INTRODUCTION

As the world's biggest military power and one of its two biggest economic powers (the other being the European Union), the United States has been deeply affected by the changes that have come to the world in the last few decades. During the cold war it led the Western alliance against the threats posed by the Soviets and their clients. Today the United States faces a new set of challenges, few of which have straightforward military or political solutions. Not only is it caught up in a struggle against global terrorism, but it also faces economic competition on an unprecedented level, against a background of spiraling budget deficits, a growing trade gap, and an addiction to oil that seems unwilling to go away.

Meanwhile, the United States is so deeply split within itself that it is sometimes called the "50:50 nation." Although divisions are nothing new to Americans, their sources and effects pose more challenges to policymakers today than they have for many years. Not only are there broad philosophical differences between conservatives, liberals, and moderates, but there are also ongoing racial divisions, growing economic divisions between the rich and the poor and between different parts of the country, and strong differences of opinion on a wide range of political and social issues, from abortion to gun control, religion, capital punishment, gay marriage, immigration, and the appropriate role of government in the lives of citizens.

In economic terms, the United States is still the dominating global actor: It has the world's biggest economy in absolute terms, with a GDP of nearly $12 trillion, and one of it's biggest in per capita terms, at nearly $41,500. It is a large country— the fourth biggest by land area after Russia, Canada, and China—and the third biggest by population after China and India. It has a wealth of natural resources, from land and minerals to fuels, forests, and cropland. The U.S. dollar is the world's strongest and most respected currency, and the United States is a major trading power, the world's biggest producer of natural gas and nuclear electric power, and the second biggest producer of crude oil and coal. U.S. corporations feature heavily on the *Fortune* Global 500 list of the world's largest industrial corporations, which is topped by Citigroup and General Electric. Within their respective fields, Wal-Mart, Chevron Texaco, Walt Disney, Boeing, Microsoft, and others are major players.

In social terms, three important changes are taking place that are redefining the balance of power in the United States. First, the population is becoming more racially diverse. The proportion of white Americans has fallen since 1970 from 87.5 percent of the total to about 68 percent today. Blacks long made up the biggest minority (about 12.8 percent of the population) but have recently been overtaken by Latinos (13.7 percent of the population),[1] and the proportion of Asian Americans is also growing rapidly (nearly 4 percent of the population). Second, there has been a shift in the balance of population away from the older industrialized states of the Midwest and the Northeast and toward southern and western states such as Florida, Texas, and California, whose role in national politics has grown in tandem. Finally, Americans are growing older as birth and fertility rates have declined and people live longer: the median age is up from 29.4 years in 1960 to 35.7 years today,[2] and the proportion of the population aged 65 years or older is up from 9.7 percent to 12.4 percent.

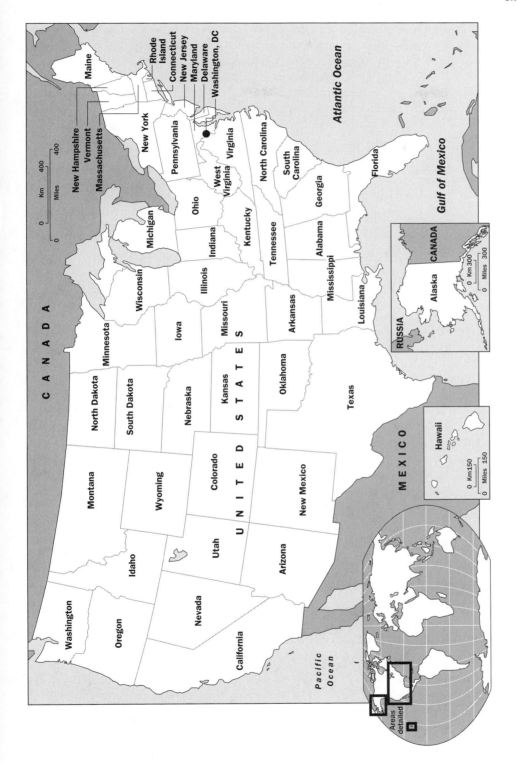

This has not only put more pressure on the health care system but has also meant a greater burden on social security, and has created an increasingly powerful interest group in the form of retirees.

In political terms, the United States is unique among liberal democracies in the structure of its government: it is based on three separate branches whose powers are shared, checked, and balanced with one another. This structure has been copied or adapted in several Latin American and African countries, but every other liberal democracy has opted instead for variations on the theme of the British parliamentary system (see Chapter 2). The United States is also unusual in the extent to which power is decentralized by the federal system, with states and local governments being responsible for much of the day-to-day administration of their communities and a political culture that shies away from **"big government"** (regulation and large government programs). Finally, it is alone among liberal democracies in the monopoly on power held by two political parties and in the relatively weak role these parties play in government.

big government
The concept of an active government that involves itself in people's lives through regulation and expansive programs.

POLITICAL DEVELOPMENT

The United States is an old country, but most Americans have very little sense of their own history beyond a sometimes selective and even idealized version of America's relationship with democratic values. Unlike Europeans, for whom history is important for an understanding of themselves and of their relations with each other, Americans live more in the present and the future and tend to think more in terms of what might be, rather than what once was. Europeans originally emigrated to North America to find new beginnings, and even today Americans like to reinvent themselves, changing homes and jobs more often than almost anyone else, particularly the relatively immobile Japanese.

The peculiar circumstances of the United States in the late eighteenth century drove it to develop what were then unique ideas about government, including a written constitution and a political system in which powers were divided horizontally among the institutions of government and vertically between national government and the states. Since then, politics has been driven by debates over the appropriate role of government and the best balance between the institutions of government. There have been problems and failures along the way, and the American model of democracy is far from perfect (see Critical Issues, p. 68), but the long-term result has been the creation of a successful and dynamic society whose influence is felt all over the world.

The Colonial Era (1607–1776)

Although the Americas were inhabited by native peoples when Columbus made his first voyage of discovery in 1492, the modern political values of the United States are ultimately the product of European philosophy. The United States was settled by Europeans, Europeans continued to arrive in large numbers in the nineteenth and early twentieth centuries, and although immigrants from Latin America and Southeast Asia have changed the social and cultural balance of the United States in the last generation, it is still ultimately a product of the European political and cultural tradition.

The British were the first to settle and develop North America in any great numbers, with the first arrivals coming in the early 1600s and settlement accelerating with the Puritan migrations of the 1630s. By the early 1700s, Britain had colonized the entire eastern seaboard, setting up colonies that were governed by appointed governors with substantial powers and by elected bicameral legislatures. British monarchs tightened their control over the colonies, but not so much that the colonists were encouraged to think about independence. The mood began to change in the 1760s, when new taxes and duties were imposed on the colonies and criticism of British interference in American domestic affairs began to grow. Revolution broke out in April 1775, the colonies declared independence in July 1776, and the creation of the new state was confirmed with the surrender of British forces at Yorktown in October 1781.

State-Building (1776–1865)

For its first few years, the United States was a loose association governed by the **Articles of Confederation,** under which Congress had the power to make war and peace, conduct foreign affairs, and borrow and print money, but could collect taxes or enforce laws only through the states. A combination of problems—the financial difficulties of fighting the war with the British, the barriers to trade among the states, and the handicap posed by the lack of a single currency—led to a Constitutional Convention in 1787 designed to address the defects of the Articles of Confederation. The result was a new federal system in which power was divided, checked, and balanced among the states and three major branches of national government: the president, a bicameral Congress representing the states and the people, and a judiciary. The Constitution came into force in June 1788, and in 1789 George Washington became the first president.

The years following independence saw the United States steadily expanding westward from the original 13 colonies, and by 1787 the western frontier of the United States had reached the Mississippi. With the Louisiana Purchase from France in 1803, the United States doubled in size. Texas was annexed in 1845, the Pacific Northwest was absorbed in 1846, and the Southwest was ceded by Mexico in 1848. Meanwhile, a revolution in transport connected much of the eastern half of the country with roads, canals, and railroads. The national economy began to diversify, the most notable changes being the emergence of the cotton- and slave-based economy of the southern states, and—in the north—the development of cities and industry and the steady growth of immigration from Europe; between 1790 and 1860 the population of the United States grew from 4 million to 31 million.

The economic and social divisions between the North and the South spilled over in 1860 with the election as president of Abraham Lincoln, a member of the northern-based, antislavery Republican Party. Secessionist views picked up steam in the South, leading to the declaration in February 1861 of the Confederacy (eventually joined by 11 states) and the outbreak in April of the **Civil War.** The war lasted four years, cost half a million lives, brought an end to slavery, and obliged Americans to make important new choices about their future political, economic, and social development.

Reconstruction and Growth (1865–1945)

Following the Civil War, the United States was transformed from a society in which half of all workers had been employed in agriculture to one in which industry played the dominating economic role. It was the age of the railroad and the entrepreneur, of technological change, of the growth of monopolies and cities, and of expansion to the West. The influence of political parties began to decline as that of interest groups—representing the new sectors that emerged out of these economic changes—began to rise.

After spending much of its first century focused on internal matters, the United States become more active in world affairs in the later decades of the nineteenth century, its main focus being on commerce with eastern Asia and on watching political developments in the Caribbean and Central America. Its new role as an emerging global actor was emphasized by its brief war with Spain in 1898, the decision to enter World War I in April 1917, and its involvement in the peace conference at Versailles in early 1919 and in the creation of the League of Nations.

The years of prosperity that followed the war ended with the Wall Street crash of October 1929, which ushered in the **Great Depression.** Unemployment soared to 25 percent, prompting the federal government to take a radically different approach to economic and social issues. President Franklin D. Roosevelt took office in 1933 and announced his **New Deal** program aimed at economic recovery, help for the victims of the depression, and new approaches to financial regulation. Notable among the changes of the 1930s were the introduction of social security and the creation of public works programs.

While these developments were taking place at home, problems that had been unresolved—and even created—by the Versailles conference were feeding into the growth of Nazism in Germany, and Hitler's expansionism in Europe sparked the outbreak of World War II in September 1939. The United States initially chose to remain neutral, but the Roosevelt administration gave economic and military assistance to Britain and then entered the war following the Japanese attack on Pearl Harbor in December 1941. It quickly took over the leading role in planning and fighting the war, in both the European and Pacific theaters.

Pax Americana (1945–)

cold war A war of words and ideas between the Western and Soviet blocs between 1945 and 1990.

With the end of the war in 1945, the old regime under which world affairs had been dominated by European powers was replaced by a new one in which there were two military superpowers: the United States and the Soviet Union. The two now engaged in a new kind of global hostility in which conventional military conflict was replaced by a **cold war** of words and ideas between the Americans, the Soviets, and their respective allies. The conflict occasionally broke out into fighting wars between clients of the two sides, as in Korea in 1950–1953, Vietnam in the 1960s and early 1970s, and Afghanistan in 1979–1989. The United States became actively involved in promoting its objectives on several different fronts and continents.

At home, the economy began a period of sustained expansion, with mass production and consumerism feeding off each other and growing numbers beginning to enjoy the benefits of an improved quality of life. Behind the façade, however, there was

TABLE 1.1

Key Dates in U.S. History

1492	Christopher Columbus unwittingly reaches the West Indies
1585	First English colony established at Virginia
1607	First permanent English settlement at Jamestown, Virginia
1620	Arrival of pilgrims aboard the *Mayflower*
1775	Outbreak of the American Revolution
1776	Declaration of Independence
1781	War of Independence ends, Articles of Confederation take effect
1787	Writing of the Constitution (came into effect 1788)
1803	Louisiana Purchase doubles size of United States
1845	Annexation of Texas
1848	Southwest ceded to United States by Mexico
1849	California gold rush
1861–1865	Civil War
1870	Black men given the right to vote
1917	United States enters World War I
1920	Women given the right to vote
1920–1933	Prohibition
1929	(October) Wall Street crash ushers in Great Depression
1941	(December) Japanese attack on Pearl Harbor brings United States into World War II
1945	(May) End of European war; (August) End of Far Eastern war
1950–1953	Korean War
1954	*Brown* v. *Board of Education* decision ends segregation
1962	(October) Cuban missile crisis
1965–1973	Height of the Vietnam War
1971	Voting age reduced from 21 to 18
1972–1974	Watergate scandal; President Richard Nixon resigns August 1974
1990–1991	United States leads coalition to respond to Iraqi invasion of Kuwait
1994	(January) Free trade agreement among United States, Canada, and Mexico comes into force; (November) Republicans take control of both houses of Congress for first time in 40 years
1995	(April) Oklahoma City bombing kills 169 people
1998	(December) Impeachment proceedings begin against President Bill Clinton
1999	(February) Senate votes not to convict Clinton; (April) United States leads NATO attack on Yugoslavia
2000	(December) George W. Bush declared winner by U.S. Supreme Court in contentious presidential election
2001	(September) Terrorist attacks on World Trade Center and Pentagon kill 3,100 people; Bush administration response includes invasion of Afghanistan
2003	(March–April) Controversial U.S.-led invasion of Iraq
2004	(November) President Bush wins a second term
2005	(August) Hurricane Katrina kills more than 1,000 people and causes widespread devastation in Alabama, Mississippi and Louisiana

simmering social discontent. Many Americans were denied opportunity or were dissatisfied with their situations, and the tensions boiled over into a period of political and social turbulence. Cold war neuroses brought a Red Scare that reached a trough of absurdity with the anti-Communist witch-hunt organized by Senator Joseph McCarthy in 1950–1954. The civil rights movement used the court system successfully to challenge **segregation,** the continuing problem of racism becoming a key policy concern throughout the late 1950s and early 1960s. At the same time, women began to be more assertive in their demands for political, economic, and social equality.

The assassinations of John F. Kennedy in 1963 and of Martin Luther King, Jr. and Robert F. Kennedy in 1968 forced many Americans to think about the violence that ran through their culture. The **Great Society** programs of the Johnson administration—aimed at combating poverty and discrimination—expanded the activities of the federal government in social policy but also emphasized the gaps between aspirations and realities. Americans were deeply split in the late 1960s and early 1970s over the war in Vietnam, and faith in government leaders sustained a heavy blow with the Watergate scandal. These events, combined with the energy crises and economic problems of the 1970s, brought doubts and disillusionment to replace the optimism of the 1950s.

In 1980 Ronald Reagan was elected president, pulling vital support from a religious right that was in favor of a redefinition of moral values. He moved the United States into conservative positions on economic and social issues, and worked to revive the American spirit, proclaiming that it was "morning in America." **Reaganomics** was based on addressing double-digit inflation, high interest rates, and unemployment by cutting back on the role of the government in the economy and reducing taxes. At the same time, Reagan moved to restore the U.S. presence in global affairs by rebuilding the military. While the United States came out of recession, and both inflation and unemployment fell, the combination of reduced taxes and increased military spending contributed to a dramatic increase in the federal budget deficit and the national debt, which—during the Reagan years alone—grew from $1 trillion to $3 trillion. (By 2005, bolstered by the tax cuts and increased defense spending of the Bush administration, it stood at a record $8 trillion.)

By the 1990s, there was a growing division within American society about the appropriate role of government and about the direction that the United States should be taking on social, economic, and foreign policies. On the political right, conservatives argued that the government was too involved in making choices for citizens, the economy was stifled by too much regulation, and most of the country's social problems could be addressed by a return to "traditional" family values. On the political left, liberals argued that there were still too many people who were denied their share of the rights and opportunities afforded by the American model of democracy, that social discrimination remained a critical problem, and that government should be more assertive in promoting equality.

Despite strong economic growth during the 1990s, including low unemployment and inflation and high productivity and consumer confidence, there were concerns that Americans had become polarized, that politics in the United States was driven less by voting and parties than it was by special interests, and that elected officials in Washington, D.C. had forgotten the needs and priorities of

Reaganomics
An economic philosophy based on reducing taxes and the government regulatory burden on the economy.

their constituents. Polls regularly found low levels of faith and trust in government and elected officials, a view that was not helped by sex scandals and charges of perjury surrounding President Clinton, leading to his attempted impeachment in 1998 by a Congress dominated by Republicans (more than a few of whom had skeletons in their own closets). Paradoxes also continued to color the relationship between government and the people. How could the wealthiest country in the world still have 15 percent of its population living in poverty? How could the country with the best medical technology in the world have infant mortality rates that were higher and a life expectancy that was lower than those in several other liberal democracies? How could a country built on the sanctity of equality and individual rights still witness as much discrimination as it did against women, ethnic minorities, and gays?

The United States Today

In December 2000, after a hotly contested and controversial election, George W. Bush was confirmed as 43rd president of the United States. He had run on a platform driven heavily by domestic issues, and—as with many of his predecessors, including Bill Clinton—had little real understanding of the problems and challenges of the international system. But following the terrorist attacks of September 2001, he found himself pulled into a new kind of problem in foreign policy: the international struggle against terrorism. Winning plaudits for his quick decision to invade Afghanistan, he engaged in a much more divisive issue when he turned his attention to Iraq, which he accused of developing weapons of mass destruction and of being part of an "axis of evil" that included Iran and North Korea.

When it came in March 2003, the US-led invasion of Iraq—although supported by a small number of other governments—was widely criticized by majority public opinion in most parts of the world, and by a significant minority of Americans. Questions were raised about the legality of the war, about the wisdom of ending decades of U.S. policy by launching a preemptive attack on another country, and about the holding in Guantanamo Bay of terrorist suspects. Questions were also raised when the Bush administration oversaw the biggest reorganization of U.S. government in 50 years as many different agencies were brought together under a new Department of Homeland Security. More questions were raised with the passage of the USA Patriot Act, which gave the federal government unprecedented powers to look into the personal affairs of Americans.

When no weapons of mass destruction were found in Iraq, opposition to the war grew, and although Bush was reelected with a majority in November 2004, it was difficult to ignore the fact that anti-Americanism in many parts of the world had reached an all-time high, and that the United States was itself deeply divided over the war and over the policies of the Bush administration. Bush had run for office in 2000 claiming to be a uniter and not a divider, and yet his policies had been implicated in bringing out many of the underlying divisions in American society. Encouraged by the philosophy of **neoconservatism,** he believed in using American force in the international system to its full capacity, and in acting unilaterally if necessary. At home, he seemed to run counter to the traditional

IS AMERICA EXCEPTIONAL?

One of the ongoing themes in American studies over the years has been **exceptionalism:** the idea that the United States is a unique society, that its people inhabit a unique place in the world, and that its values—political, economic, and social—offer both hope and unusual opportunities for the rest of humanity.[3] The notion dates back to the first settlers, and to the suggestion by John Winthrop, Governor of the Massachusetts Bay Colony, that the Puritans should create "a city upon a hill" that would mark a clear break from the corrupt society they had left behind. The term "exceptional" was first used by Alexis de Tocqueville in the 1830s in his study *Democracy in America*.

Many Americans have since seen themselves and their country as special, as charged with saving the world from itself, and as being responsible for sustaining a high level of spiritual, political, and moral commitment to this destiny. One historian suggests that exceptionalism "permeates every period of American history and is the single most powerful agent in a series of arguments that have been fought down the centuries concerning the identity of America and Americans."[4] There is a deeply religious element to the notion, which is reflected in the views of some Americans that their country is "blessed" and in the way American presidents will habitually end their speeches with the phrase "God bless America." George W. Bush has been one of the most active

champions of the idea, with his repeated claims that the United States is "the brightest beacon for freedom and opportunity in the world." In his speech to the Republican National Convention in September 2004, he even argued that "like generations before us, we have a calling from beyond the stars to stand for freedom."

The idea of American exceptionalism is controversial, in part because almost every country can claim to be exceptional in its own way, and in part because the claims of uniqueness raise troubling questions about the way American leaders think and act. Putting it bluntly, it has been suggested that many Americans think of themselves as better than anyone else, and that the term exceptionalism "encompasses obnoxious superiority, irritating paternalism, ugly undertones of racism and imperialism, and has been linked to the excessive nationalism of a chosen people."[5] In a similar vein, it has been suggested that "Americans generally tend to strike the world as pushy, preachy, insensitive, self-righteous, and usually, anti-French."[6] The philosophy has fed in to a kind of American triumphalism, with many academics and political leaders claiming that the United States is the world's last remaining superpower and that it is unchallenged by anyone; this in turn may encourage unilateralism, isolationism, and a general feeling of moral and cultural superiority that is unlikely to win the United States many friends overseas.

exceptionalism The belief that the U.S. is somehow a unique and exceptional society with a mission to change the world in its image.

understanding of political conservatism by expanding rather than contracting the powers of government.

Are the policies of the Bush administration part of a sea-change in political culture in the United States, and of a successful program to complete the shift of the country to the political right (as many scholars and many leaders of the Republican Party have claimed)? Or are they just the transient policies of a single administration? Is the United States out of touch with thinking in other parts of the world, or is it providing the kind of leadership the world should expect from a military super-power? Only time will tell.

POLITICAL CULTURE

Champions of the American system of government routinely emphasize the importance of individual liberty in American political culture and values such as a belief in political equality, equality of opportunity, equal sharing of the material rewards of democracy, and equal access to the political process. They almost seem to suggest that these are somehow uniquely American values, or at least that they are much more centrally a part of the American political system than is the case in other liberal democracies (see Political Debates, page 46). However, there are at least two problems with this notion. First, these are all characteristics that are common to all liberal democracies. Second, the gap between aspiration and achievement is as significant in the United States as in other liberal democracies. To appreciate the features that truly distinguish political culture in the United States, we need to look beyond the ideals and focus our attention elsewhere.

Patriotism and Optimism

The United States is without question the most patriotic of liberal democracies. We can see this in the respect shown to the flag, the national anthem, and the military. In no other country has there been the same level of debate as in the United States about flag burning as a form of political expression, and in no other country are military veterans shown so much respect as public servants. Opinion polls confirm the levels of patriotism: 80 percent of Americans routinely describe themselves as being "proud" or "very proud" of being American. The figures for most European countries are in the range of 40 to 60 percent and for Germany are as low as 20 percent.[7]

Most Americans are also relatively optimistic about the opportunities and choices they face and about the quality of life they enjoy or expect their children to enjoy. Europeans since World War II have seen their lives changed dramatically, and many as a result are doubtful about what the future holds (even though the quality of life is far better than it was even a generation ago). Americans, on the other hand, generally have a positive attitude about the condition of their country. Even in the face of persistent problems such as poverty, racism, drugs, and violence, they have a high level of faith in political institutions and the process of government. Even knowing that domestic conditions are not always perfect and that the motives behind U.S. foreign policy have not always been noble, most still believe that the United States is better, stronger, and freer than any other country. This optimism has taken a knock in recent years with the rise of anti-American feeling in many parts of the world, but the belief by Americans in the rightness of the American way continues to survive.

Individualism and Self-Determination

To a much greater extent than is true of any other liberal democracy, most Americans believe that government should play a limited role in their lives. It should provide selected public services, uphold the rule of law, and help individuals to achieve their goals, but it should not make too many decisions on behalf of individuals. This is why socialism is so unpopular (or, actually, misunderstood) in the United States, why it is the only liberal democracy without a national health care system (which many Americans—tellingly—like to call "socialized medicine"), and why large government programs are so often criticized, even by the people who benefit from those programs. There has always been a frontier mentality in American society and a feeling that distance from government is good. This is partly why many immigrants came to the United States from Europe, why the opening up of the western United States in the nineteenth century was so significant, and why civil liberties—such as freedom of speech—are so much a part of political discourse among Americans.

Aspirational Politics

Most Europeans approach politics from the perspective of the "here and now" and within the limits of what they believe is possible. By contrast, political debate in the United States is peppered with words such as *dream* and *vision*. The creation of the ideal society is a work in progress, but the ultimate goal is achievement of the **American Dream.** This is rarely defined but is generally associated with ideas of the United States as a land of opportunity where initiative and hard work can bring success, which is usually measured by material wealth and private property. The dream is there, but many Americans are still denied equality of opportunity, and the divisions in American society suggest that the sentiment in the second paragraph of the Declaration of Independence—that all men are born equal—is still more an aspiration rather than a reality. The consequences of Hurricane Katrina in August 2005 emphasized many of the structural problems of American society. For many, they showed that racism and economic divisions were both still factors in politics, questions were asked about the priorities of government, and the inability of federal and state agencies to respond quickly and effectively to emergencies—and to work together—was tragically underlined.

A Shift to the Right

Although most Americans hold moderate or centrist positions on most issues, there has been a debate in the United States about the signs that the country is becoming more conservative, particularly on social issues.[8] This has been reflected not just in growing support for the Republican Party, but also in the way that moral issues have been climbing up the political agenda, and in the questions raised about the size of the gap between church and state. Whether it is a question about posting the Ten Commandments on public buildings, about displaying "In God We Trust" on bank notes and coins, or about the wisdom of stem cell research or ending the lives of patients in a persistent vegetative state, religious values overlap with public policy on many issues. A key example has been the abortion debate. Abortion has been legally available in most liberal democracies for decades and is rarely discussed anymore in Europe. But in the United States the debate has been kept alive by an active disagreement between pro-life and pro-choice campaigners. The former hope to see a conservative future Supreme Court overturn the 1973 *Roe* v. *Wade* decision that established a woman's right of access to abortion, and the latter work to protect that decision.

POLITICAL SYSTEM

In addition to the typical features of a democracy (including representative government and support for the rule of law), four key principles give American government its distinctive personality:

- It is a **republic,** or a political system in which all members of government are either elected or appointed by elected officials. (Britain, Canada, and Japan are not republics, because they all have monarchs, who are not elected.)
- It is a **federation,** or an administrative system in which national and local levels of government have separate and independent powers and responsibilities.
- There is a **separation of powers** among a legislature responsible for making laws, an executive responsible for overseeing the application of those laws, and a judiciary responsible for checking the constitutionality of the laws and actions of government.
- A system of **checks and balances** divides powers and responsibilities and obliges the key institutions—and the different levels of government—to work together to make and implement policy.

This combination makes the United States unusual among liberal democracies. Of the 35 liberal democracies in the world, only 23 are republics, only 6 are federations (the rest are unitary systems in which most political power is vested in national government), and almost all have fused executives and legislatures: Their heads of government are prime ministers who depend for their power on having the support of a majority of members of the national legislature.

republic A political system in which all members of the government are elected.

THE CONSTITUTION

The Constitution of the United States was the first document of its kind in the world and has been the model for most of the **constitutions** that have since been developed by other countries. It is the centerpiece of the American political system, the blueprint by which the United States is governed, and the subject of much debate and analysis among lawyers and scholars. It does four things:

- It outlines the structure of government, which is based around three branches of government within a federal system.
- It distributes powers among the different elements of government, giving Congress the power to coin, raise, and spend money; to regulate commerce with other countries;

constitution A set of rules outlining the structure, responsibilities, and powers of a government.

and to declare war. It also gives the president command of the armed forces, wide authority over foreign policy, the power to make selected appointments, and the power to veto legislative proposals from Congress.

- It distributes powers between the federal government and the states; for example, the states cannot sign treaties with other countries or have their own currencies.

- It describes limits on the powers of government. Many of these were outlined in the first ten amendments to the Constitution, passed in 1791 as the Bill of Rights. These were designed to preserve certain individual rights, such as freedom of religion, speech, and the press, and the right to a speedy public trial.

The Constitution can be amended, in a two-stage process, to meet changed circumstances. First, amendments must be proposed, either by two-thirds of both houses of Congress or by two-thirds of state legislatures. Then the amendments must be ratified by three-fourths of state legislatures, usually within 7 to 10 years. Thousands of amendments have been proposed, but only 33 have won enough support in Congress to be considered and only 27 amendments have been ratified. The most recent was in 1992; it forbids members of Congress from giving themselves a midterm pay raise. The low number of amendments can be interpreted in one of two ways: it is either a sign that the original Constitution was so well written that it has not needed much change, or it is a sign that political disagreements have made it difficult to make any changes.

There are three other ways in which the Constitution can be affected, without a formal amendment. First, the Supreme Court can issue decisions on whether or not laws and the actions of government are constitutional. Second, many of the details of the structure of government have been changed by laws passed by Congress. For example, laws have established the size of the House of Representatives and the Supreme Court and have created all federal courts below the level of the Supreme Court. Finally, the Constitution is affected by custom and tradition, out of which have developed political parties, party leadership, and party conventions.

THE EXECUTIVE: PRESIDENT

executive The part of government responsible for implementing policy and executing laws.

The presidency of the United States is often described as one of the strongest government offices in the world. In terms of the resources presidents have at their disposal, this is true: The president is commander-in-chief of the world's most powerful military force and makes decisions affecting one of the world's two biggest economies. However, compared directly with the powers of the leaders of other democracies, presidents are often hamstrung: They are limited by the terms of the Constitution, their policy options are limited by Congress, and many of the most important decisions about government and policy are made outside the White House. In reality, the power of the president boils down to two important factors: the incumbents' ability to persuade, and their ability to build coalitions of support inside and outside Congress.

The framers of the Constitution feared anarchy and tyranny in about equal measure and wanted to make sure that the powers of the executive and the legislature checked each other. Throughout the nineteenth century, Congress dominated the

TABLE 1.2

Modern Presidents of the United States

Term	Name	Party
1933–1945	Franklin D. Roosevelt	Democrat
1945–1953	Harry S. Truman	Democrat
1953–1961	Dwight Eisenhower	Republican
1961–1963	John F. Kennedy	Democrat
1963–1969	Lyndon B. Johnson	Democrat
1969–1974	Richard M. Nixon	Republican
1974–1977	Gerald Ford	Republican
1977–1981	Jimmy Carter	Democrat
1981–1989	Ronald Reagan	Republican
1989–1993	George H.W. Bush	Republican
1993–2001	Bill Clinton	Democrat
2001–	George W. Bush	Republican

government and few presidents were able to exert substantial leadership; this is partly why so few early presidents—the exceptions including Washington, Jackson, and Lincoln—made much of a mark. How many Americans really know very much about Martin van Buren, John Tyler, Franklin Pierce, or Chester Arthur? The situation changed with Franklin Delano Roosevelt (1933–1945), the first president to fully exert the powers of the office rather than simply respond to Congress. Since then, the power and influence of the presidency has changed beyond all recognition,[9] for five main reasons.

First, as the population of the United States has grown, so have people's needs. Responding to them has demanded a more systematic way of evaluating priorities, so presidents have won more powers to set the policy agenda, which in turn has motivated them to work harder at winning congressional support. Second, the president is better placed to respond quickly to policy needs than Congress, which is big, cumbersome, and divided along party lines. Third, the emergence of the United States as a superpower has given more influence to the president, who has had a large amount of freedom to set foreign policy. Fourth, presidents are more newsworthy than Congress and have exploited this to manipulate the media and public opinion to their advantage. Finally, the presidency itself has grown, making it easier for presidents to respond to a broader set of policy issues. George Washington had just 1 staff member, Lincoln had 4, and Roosevelt had 50; by contrast, George W. Bush has more than 2,000 people working directly for him.

In terms of the qualifications for the office, the Constitution says that anyone who is a natural-born citizen, is older than 35 years, and has been a U.S. resident for at least 14 years can be president. In practice, however, every president so far has been a white male, and most have had English, German, or Scandinavian heritage and have come from states with large populations. In terms of experience, elected political background is important, preferably as a state governor or a U.S. senator. Governors used to be prime contenders for the presidency, but this changed in the 1960s and 1970s, when a rash of former senators ran, including the Kennedy brothers, Barry Goldwater, Richard Nixon, and George McGovern. Then came Watergate, and the reaction against Washington "insiders" and big government gave the advantage to state governors: Jimmy Carter from Georgia, Ronald Reagan from California, Bill Clinton from Arkansas, and George W. Bush from Texas.

The "enumerated" constitutional powers of the president are modest: They include being commander-in-chief (although what this means is not specified) and having the powers to grant pardons, to make treaties (with Senate approval), to nominate ambassadors and Supreme Court judges, and to veto congressional bills. More generally, the powers of the presidency have expanded into at least ten different spheres:

head of state The person who symbolically represents a state and all the citizens of that state.

- **Head of state.** The president is the symbolic leader of the United States, supposedly representing the entire country rather than just the people who elected him into office. In this sense, he carries out many of the duties reserved in other countries to the monarch or to non executive presidents; these include receiving ambassadors and foreign political leaders, making goodwill tours, providing a unifying influence, and acting as a national father figure at times of crisis. This can be time-consuming but can also be politically useful—the more that a president can associate himself with popular feelings of patriotism and national unity, the more persuasive he can be at winning support for his policies. George W. Bush showed this clearly with the fallout from the attacks of September 11, 2001, when most of the country rallied around him in his calls for a war on terrorism.

head of government The person who runs the government of a country and in whom executive power is normally vested.

- **Head of government.** The president is also a politician, a representative of his party, and the champion of his particular set of policy objectives. In this role, he needs to keep the support of the voters who elected him into office, the members of Congress on whom he depends to vote his programs into law, the Washington establishment, and the national media. Unlike his father, George W. Bush has been effective at keeping and expanding the core base of his support; however, he has also alienated those Americans who do not support his policies.

- **Commander-in-chief.** The president is in charge of U.S. armed forces and of making decisions on their involvement in military operations. His powers declined as a reaction to the role of the presidency in taking the United States into Vietnam and making most of the key decisions on the war. The 1974 **War Powers Act** made it illegal for presidents to commit U.S. troops overseas for more than 60 days without congressional approval. But George W. Bush reasserted his military powers when he was able to convince Congress in 2002 to give him sweeping authority in preparation for the 2003 invasion of Iraq.

- **Chief executive.** The president is head of the federal cabinet and of the federal bureaucracy. He uses this power to make sure that Congressional laws are executed.

GEORGE W. BUSH

© AFP/CORBIS

Born in Connecticut in 1946 but raised in Texas, President George W. Bush was educated at Yale and Harvard, leaving the latter with a business degree. (This set him apart from most other contemporary American politicians, who are products of American law schools.) He joined the National Guard as a pilot before following his father into the oil business. He lost a run for the U.S. Congress in 1978 and underwent a personal crisis before changing his life around at the age of 40. He made several successful business deals, including becoming part owner of the Texas Rangers baseball team, and then in 1994 he followed his father and grandfather into politics by being elected governor of Texas. He was returned for a second term in 1998. Meanwhile, his brother Jeb had been elected governor of Florida.

His presidential campaign of 1999–2000 was notable for raising record amounts of financial support. He positioned himself on the moderate right of the Republican party, describing himself as a "compassionate conservative" and campaigning on issues such as poverty, education, and minority concerns. After a close-run race against Democratic challenger Al Gore, in which many voters complained

that there was little to differentiate the two, the result was so close that Gore initially conceded defeat on election night. But he then withdrew his concession when it became clear that there had been problems with some of the voting machines, notably those in Florida. After four weeks of legal debate, the case went to the U.S. Supreme Court, which split along party lines in declaring Bush the winner.

Bush has been a controversial politician, deeply admired by his core base of supporters but more aggressively disliked by his critics than many modern presidents. Few have questioned his personal charm and integrity, but some have questioned his intellectual abilities and the long-term implications of his policies. He initially won high public approval ratings, but he attracted criticism from overseas for his unilateralist positions on a number of issues, ranging from climate change to the International Criminal Court, antiballistic missile treaties, and free trade. His decision to invade Iraq, with or without the support of the United Nations or other national governments, was without doubt the most controversial decision of his presidency. But he has also made controversial choices on domestic matters, for example instituting tax cuts and increasing military spending, taking the federal budget deficit and the national debt to record levels. He has also unsuccessfully tried to reform the social security system, even in the face of majority public opposition. He won reelection to a second term in November 2004, but by the smallest percentage margin for a sitting president in U.S. history. Within a few months, his political troubles had caused his public opinion ratings to fall to the lowest levels of his presidency.

- **Agenda setter.** Using his "bully pulpit," a term used by Theodore Roosevelt, the president has considerable influence over setting the national political agenda. He does this in part through the annual State of the Union address, which is an opportunity to outline the issues and problems he considers important. Every president has a well-developed strategy for the media, which tend to regard almost anything the president does—whether making an important policy speech to buying a new family dog—as newsworthy.

- **Foreign policymaker.** Presidential candidates usually emphasize domestic issues in their campaigns for office, but when it comes to the realities of governing they have much more freedom to maneuver over foreign policy. As well as having sole power to negotiate treaties with other countries, and to extend diplomatic recognition to foreign governments, they also tend to lead Congress in deciding the priorities of foreign policy.

- **Economic leader.** Congress alone has powers over fiscal policy (taxing and spending), but the White House must develop the federal budget and presidents can influence the direction taken by economic policy. Indeed, the political fortunes of presidents often rise and fall with the state of the economy, and the president is usually closely identified in the public mind with economic issues, such as the rate of economic growth and inflation. As Bill Clinton's advisor James Carville once famously quipped, "It's the economy, stupid."

- **Moral leader.** Unlike the citizens of any other liberal democracy, most Americans look to the president to set the moral tone for the country. A president is expected to be a good family man and a churchgoer, and is expected to be something close to a model citizen: honest, compassionate, open minded, good humored, and competent. Europeans expect the same values of their leaders, but are much less ready to look to them for moral leadership, and more willing to forgive lapses in their private lives. Imagine the U.S. president admitting to an affair while in office (as did British prime minister John Major) or to having an illegitimate child (as did French president François Mitterrand).

- **Crisis manager.** Life is often unpredictable, and crises break to which government must respond, such as war and conflict, natural disasters such as hurricanes and floods, the taking of hostages, and acts of terrorism. As one person, the president is in a better position to respond quickly than is Congress, and so is expected to provide leadership in such instances.[10]

- **Party leader.** Although American political parties have their own governing committees and chairs, the president becomes de facto leader of his party while in office, and the goals of the party are heavily influenced by his programs.

Against the background of all these roles—and the constitutional powers of the president—the job performance of individual presidents is ultimately tied to other, more informal and often less quantifiable factors. These include the president's ability to communicate his program and message, his capabilities as an organizer and the builder of a governing team, his political skills (how well or how badly he is able to work with others to build support for his program), his sense of direction (or what president George H.W. Bush once famously described as "the vision thing"), and his emotional intelligence: how well he manages anger and stress, how secure he feels in himself, his sense of moral character, and so on.[11]

To do their jobs, presidents have become dependent on an expanding body of people and institutions that collectively come to represent "the presidency." Most notable among these are the staff within the White House itself, including the chief of staff, the press secretary, congressional liaison staff, and a string of advisors on a whole host of policy issues. These are all appointed by the president and help keep him informed, but they also become associated in the public mind with the administration.

The president also governs with the help of the cabinet, which consists of the heads of 15 key government departments, including defense, justice, the treasury, and homeland security. The president nominates cabinet heads, who must then be confirmed by the Senate. They come from a variety of backgrounds—some are business people, others have experience in state or federal government, and some are friends or associates of the president. Cabinets in parliamentary systems are like governing committees, are deeply involved in making political decisions, and meet as often as once per week; by contrast, the U.S. cabinet is more of an advisory body which rarely meets as a group.[12]

The president is also helped by a vice president, whose job is traditionally considered one of the least important in government. Vice presidents may be "a heartbeat away from the presidency," but most have spent their time in relative obscurity, their role dependent almost entirely on the president. The significance of the office may be changing, though: Several modern vice presidents have used the office as a launch pad for a bid for the presidency, and it has been clear that George W. Bush's vice president—Dick Cheney—has played a central role in both making the policies of the administration and in conveying them to the media and the public.

THE LEGISLATURE: CONGRESS

Despite being the political institution that is closest to the people, Congress is the least popular of the three branches of government.[13] There are several reasons for this: Its work is more visible, it does not have the same aura as the other institutions, and it is most closely involved in the process of lawmaking and so is more deeply involved in the struggles of politics. When Americans complain about big government, they are usually talking about Congress, which is ironic given the number of supporters of small government among its members. Americans admire and respect the presidency, but opinion polls find that being a member of Congress is one of the least admired of all professions.

The Constitution gives Congress several powers, including the authority to levy taxes, borrow money, coin money, declare war, raise armies, determine the nature of the federal judiciary, and regulate commerce with foreign governments and among states. In practice, however, the powers of Congress rest mainly in four areas:

- **Law-making.** Congress is where federal laws are introduced, discussed, and either accepted or rejected.
- **Oversight.** Congress checks on the work of the federal bureaucracy, making sure that it carries out the intent of Congress.

©John McCormick

The Capitol Building, home of the United States Congress in Washington, DC. Congress was designed to represent the interests of the people and to be the most powerful branch of government, but it has lost both popularity and its power to the presidency, particularly since the mid-twentieth century.

- **Budgetary matters.** Congress has the final say over the federal budget, which is developed by the White House Office of Management and Budget but must be approved by Congress.

- **Confirming appointments.** The Senate has the power to check and confirm all key presidential appointees except those who work directly for the president in the White House.

Congress was designed by the framers of the Constitution to be the most powerful branch of government, and so it was for about 150 years; few presidents were able to challenge congressional power, and most of the key political struggles took place within Congress rather than between Congress and the president. During the twentieth century, however, presidential powers grew and decision making within Congress was decentralized. The result has been more of a balance between the two branches, which need each other to govern effectively.

Legislation can be introduced in either of the chambers of Congress (with the exception of revenue bills, which can be introduced only in the House). All bills are immediately sent to the relevant committee, are then sent for debate by the chamber as a whole before being voted on, and are then sent to the other chamber where they go through the same stages. If a bill passes both chambers, it is then sent to the president, who can either sign it into law or exercise presidential veto power. A presidential veto can be overridden in Congress by a vote of more than two-thirds of the members of both chambers. Those chambers are the Senate and the House of Representatives.

Senate

The Senate is designed to represent the states in the sense that equal representation is given to them all, regardless of size. Each of the 50 states elects two senators, for a total of 100. They serve six-year renewable terms, and elections are staggered so that one-third of the members stand for reelection every two years. This system ensures that smaller states are relatively overrepresented and larger states are relatively underrepresented; this is why the 500,000 residents of Wyoming have the same level of representation as the 35 million residents of California.

Sessions of the Senate are overseen by a president, who is—ex officio—the vice president of the United States. This is a largely symbolic position, and the president of the Senate can cast a vote only in the case of a tie; most of the time, the president is represented by a junior senator acting as president pro tempore. Much more significant is the post of **Senate majority leader,** held by a member of the majority party in the Senate. The majority leader schedules debates, assigns bills to committees, coordinates party policy, appoints members of special committees, and generally oversees the functioning of the Senate to suit the purposes of the majority party.

In terms of its powers over introducing, discussing, and voting on legislation, the Senate has equal powers with the House of Representatives. However, it has the unique power of approval over presidential nominations for appointments to the cabinet, the Supreme Court, lower federal courts, key government agencies such as the Federal Reserve Board, and ambassadorial posts.

House of Representatives

The House of Representatives is the lower chamber, which is designed to represent the people in the sense that every member is elected from a district of roughly equal size. The House has 435 members elected for renewable two-year terms, all of whom come up for reelection every two years. According to the Constitution, all congressional districts must be reapportioned every 10 years to reflect changes in the population. Because of these changes, southern and western states such as Florida and California have picked up new seats in recent years at the expense mainly of older industrial states such as New York and Pennsylvania.

The leader is the **Speaker of the House,** who comes from the majority party. In contrast to the Speaker in parliamentary systems, whose main job is to keep order during debates and who is expected to be nonpartisan (see Chapter 2), the Speaker of the House is a partisan leader with considerable powers: The Speaker presides over debates, recognizes members who wish to speak, votes in cases of a tie, interprets questions of procedure, and influences the committee system by assigning bills to committees and deciding who sits on special and select committees.

THE JUDICIARY: SUPREME COURT

The Supreme Court has nine members, nominated by the president and confirmed by the Senate for lifetime terms, with one of their number appointed as Chief Justice. The Court is responsible for ensuring that the laws and actions of government fit with the letter or the spirit of the Constitution. This is a power known as **judicial review,** which was not described in the Constitution but which the Supreme Court won for itself in the *Marbury* v. *Madison* decision of 1803. There is nothing in the Constitution, either, about lower federal courts, but a complex system of district courts and courts of appeal has been built over time, and now hears about ten million cases per year.

Plaintiffs who lose their cases in lower courts can appeal to have them heard by the Supreme Court, which receives about 6,000 to 7,000 petitions every year but usually agrees to review only about 90 to 120 cases that it believes have important constitutional implications. Since World War II, the Court has paid particular attention to cases relating to civil liberties, civil rights, and social equality. Among the most famous of its decisions were *Brown* v. *Board of Education* in 1954, which ended racial segregation in schools; *Miranda* v. *Arizona* in 1966, relating to the rights of criminal defendants; and *Roe* v. *Wade* in 1973, which prohibited states from outlawing abortion.

There are about 750 federal court judges in all, who must be nominated by the president and approved by the Senate. Court appointments have become increasingly politically charged as the role of the courts in the political system has changed. Theoretically, judges are supposed to execute and clarify the meaning of the law, and not actually make law, but this is no more than an ideal, because court decisions can often have important policy implications. For that reason, the ideological biases of judges have become a critical issue in debates over appointments, with both parties in Congress working to block the confirmation of judges whom they consider to be too partisan. This is particularly true of the Supreme Court, whose judges can be removed from office only for serious dereliction of duty.

SUBNATIONAL GOVERNMENT

federalism An administrative system in which local units of government have powers independent of those of the national government.

The United States is a federation, in which powers are divided between the national government in Washington, D.C., and the governments of the 50 states, each of which has its own constitution, elected governor and state legislature, and constitutional court. Within states, power is further subdivided, with separately elected bodies for city and county government. Although the federal government is responsible for most aspects of economic, foreign, and defense policy, state and local governments are responsible for managing most of the welfare system, maintaining state highways, managing land use, executing many federal laws and regulations, and overseeing education and policing.

The United States is far too big and heterogeneous to be governed under the kind of unitary systems of administration used in Britain and Japan, which would also fly in the face of American political culture and its emphasis on keeping government as close as possible to the people. Although federalism helps deal with the size and diversity of the country, allows different states to adopt different positions on key issues that are more in tune with local opinion, and offers citizens more opportunities for participation in government, it also creates problems. It slows the process of decision making (which can be a good thing or a bad thing, depending on circumstances), it can make people too focused on narrow goals and values rather than looking at the broader national interest, and it can hamstring the ability of national government to even out economic and social differences within a country.

ELECTIONS AND PARTIES

The American electoral and party system is rife with ironies. First, voters are faced with more elected offices and elections than in any other liberal democracy, yet turnout rates are among the lowest in the world. Second, American political culture places great emphasis on democracy and civic duty, yet as the number of eligible voters has increased, the proportion who actually vote has fallen. Finally, the United States has some of the oldest political parties in the world, yet Americans are offered fewer choices in the way of parties with a realistic chance of winning office than any other liberal democracy, and those parties play a relatively weak role in politics.

All three of these phenomena are related and are a reflection of declining party identification among American voters. They are also indicative of a number of features of the political system that discourage voters from taking an active role in politics:

- **The parties are too similar.** Compared with parties in other liberal democracies, the differences between the mainstream of the two major U.S. parties—the Democrats and the Republicans—are not very great. If they were more clearly polarized, more voters might be motivated to go to the polls.

- **Voter mobilization is ineffective.** Whereas they once had grassroots organizations with which people identified and which were good at engaging voters and supporters, state party organizations have become more independent. The Republicans showed signs in the 2004 election that they were addressing the problem, particularly by mobilizing conservative Christian voters, but whether this was part of permanent change or not remains to be seen.

- **There are too many elections, and they last too long.** This has become a particular problem with presidential elections, for which early candidates may begin campaigning as much as two years before the event itself. In the year leading up to the election, media coverage is so intensive that it runs the risk of boring many voters.

Because ordinary Americans do not engage in politics as much as they might, this leaves more opportunities for motivated minorities to have more influence over the

LOW VOTER TURNOUT

One of the most distinctive features of U.S. elections is the low voter turnout. European elections usually attract about 65 to 90 percent of eligible voters, and about 55 to 60 percent of voters turned out at the most recent elections in Canada, Japan and Russia (See Figure 1.1 opposite). But presidential elections in the United States now attract only about 50 to 55 percent of eligible voters (down from 60 to 65 percent in the 1960s), and turnout at midterm congressional elections is as low as 35 percent (down from 45 to 50 percent in the 1960s). As the number of people who are eligible to vote has increased, the percentage turnout has fallen. The United States now ranks 139th out of 172 countries in the world in voter turnout.

The low voter turnout has been explained by a variety of factors: Some voters are deeply dissatisfied with the electoral process and with government, and feel that turning out will make no difference to their lives; other voters are satisfied with their lives and the state of the country, and also feel that voting will make no difference. Others claim that the procedure for registering and voting is too time-consuming, but this is probably a reflection of their lack of interest in politics, because voting is usually a quick and simple procedure.

Whatever the causes of low voter turnout, though, it has several worrying effects. First, government tends to respond to those who make the loudest demands (the squeaky wheel gets the grease), so those who don't vote will not have their voices heard by government. And when we realize that certain groups of people—notably ethnic minorities and the young—vote less than the national average, it should be no surprise that elected leaders will not listen so readily to their concerns. Second, elected officials tend to look like—and reflect the views of—the people who vote. Concerns have been raised about the lack of diversity in Congress, where professional, white, middle-aged men outnumber all other demographic groups—but part of the reason for this is that voter turnout among professionals, whites, the middle-aged and men is higher than the national average. Finally, low turnout reduces the level of legitimacy conferred on government and reduces the accountability of elected officials. Despite these concerns, and even though attempts have been made to improve turnout by running registration drives and making registration easier, the absence of so many voters at the polls is not something that seems to worry most Americans very much.

political process. Nowhere is this more problematic than in the relationship between money and politics. Jesse Unruh, Speaker of the California state legislature in the 1960s, once quipped that "Money is the mother's milk of politics." This has always been an issue, notably in the nineteenth century, when political favors were openly bought by many of the owners of the new corporations then being born in the United States, but it has become a particular bone of contention since changes made in the 1970s to campaign finance laws.

The main problem is the high cost of elections, which is a result mainly of the need for first-time candidates—many of whom may be unknown to voters—to reach a large constituency. In the record-breaking 2000 congressional elections,

FIGURE 1.1

Comparing Voter Turnout

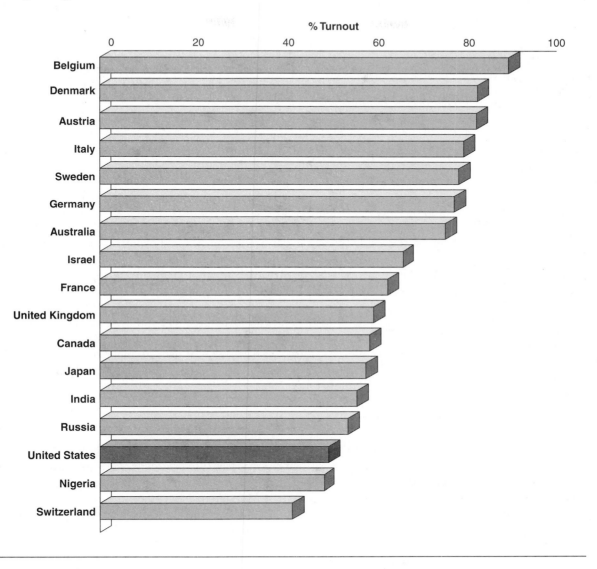

Source: Electionworld, 2005, www.electionworld.org. Figures are for eligible voters, and for the most recent legislative elections in each country. U.S. figure is for the 2000 presidential election.

the average candidate spent nearly $420,000, with House candidates spending an average of $275,000 and Senate candidates—because they had to cover more ground—spending an average of more than $1.3 million. Total spending on congressional elections in 2000 reached a record of just over $1 billion, up from about $200 to $300 million per season in the early 1970s. Presidential campaigns are the most expensive of all: In 2004, about $1 billion was spent by presidential candidates and national conventions. George W. Bush raised nearly $270 million, or three times as much as he raised in 2000, and Democratic challenger John Kerry raised nearly $235 million, or six times as much as had ever been raised by a Democratic nominee.[14]

Although American political culture places a premium on equality and access to government, the costs of running for office have become so high that only those with access to large sums of money can now realistically hope to win. Furthermore, changes to the law in 1974 forced candidates to be less reliant on a few large sources of funding and to raise money from a broader constituency. At the same time, a loophole was created by which donors who wanted to give more than they were allowed by federal law could make donations to the national party committees, which could channel the money to state parties faced with less demanding state regulations. This **"soft money"** loophole has become increasingly controversial in recent years, adding to demands for reforms to campaign finance laws.

Another controversial feature of campaign financing is the **political action committee (PAC).** PACs are set up by interest groups to channel money to candidates running for office. A complex body of laws places limits on how much money any one PAC can give to any one candidate directly, but they are also allowed to give money to parties and to spend money promoting particular issues that may help their favored candidates. PACs are controversial because they are a form of institutionalized bribery; they will expect "their" candidates to support bills in which their members have an interest.

THE ELECTORAL SYSTEM

winner-take-all An electoral system in which the candidate winning the most votes wins office.

Most elected officials in the United States serve an unlimited number of fixed-year terms, the only exceptions being executives (the president, state governors, and city mayors), most of whom serve limited terms. Congressional elections are always held on the first Tuesday after the first Monday in November in even-numbered years, and presidential elections take place on the same day every four years. The system is based on the **winner-take-all rule,** meaning that the winning candidate does not have to win a majority (more than half the votes cast) but simply a **plurality** (the largest number of votes).

plurality The outcome of an election in which the candidate with the most votes wins, without having a majority.

Elections in the United States are longer, more numerous, and more expensive than in any other liberal democracy. To give citizens the opportunity to have as much say as possible in government, elections are held for offices ranging from the president of the United States down through multiple and often obscure offices in state and local government. The weakness of political parties has combined with the need for candidates to make themselves known to the electorate to produce a system in which a long process of familiarization is required, resulting in election campaigns that can last several months and—as noted earlier—can be expensive.

A notable feature of American elections is the system of **primaries** that are held for most key offices. Rather than parties choosing who will run for office in their name, as is the case in parliamentary systems, the choices are made in the United States by voters casting ballots in primaries. Voters choose from among competing potential candidates, and the winner is then adopted by the party to run in the general election. Primaries are democratic in the sense that they leave it up to voters to choose party candidates, but they also add time and expense to the electoral process, weaken political parties, and give a few—sometimes unrepresentative—voters considerable impact on the outcome of the nomination process.

The Presidential Election

Without question the dominating event in the American electoral calendar is the race for the presidency, which is the focus of intense national and international media scrutiny and has become a long, drawn-out process. There are four key stages in the process.

The first stage is the informal "preprimary" season, when the media begin talking about possible candidates and some of the candidates begin forming exploratory committees to look into the possibility of running. The season usually begins about two years before the actual election (although speculation can begin much earlier), and the likely front-runners are often decided by the amount of attention paid to them in the media. As long as 18 months before the election, the main contenders will start to campaign in key states, and some may already have picked up enough sense about the balance of public opinion to have withdrawn. This still often leaves as many as a dozen contenders for the major parties who may start appearing in television debates as much as a year before the election.

The second stage is the formal primary season itself, which begins in the February before the election with votes in New Hampshire and Iowa. It runs until June, peaking on "Super Tuesday" in March, when several states hold their primaries on the same day. The front-runners for the major parties may be decided early in the process, or the contest may take longer to decide. Either way, the primary season ends in late summer with the holding of national party conventions. At one time, it was left to the conventions to confirm the choice of candidate for the major parties, but in recent elections that choice has already been made and the conventions are little more than self-indulgent media events designed to crown the candidates.

The third stage is the final campaign between the candidates, which traditionally runs from Labor Day in September until election day in November. All campaign spending by the major candidates ends, and their costs are met out of public funds. Media coverage of the candidates intensifies, and it has become usual for the Republican and the Democrat to hold televised debates (although these are not so much one-on-one debates as carefully managed opportunities for the candidates to outline their programs). Sadly, there is none of the face-to-face debate with opponents or with the public that occurs in most European countries, and American presidential candidates rarely expose themselves to challenging public or media events, or to potentially hostile audiences.

The final stage is the election itself. Even though the candidates for the Republican and Democratic parties are the only ones with a realistic chance of winning, as many

FIGURE 1.2

Presidential Electoral Trends in the United States

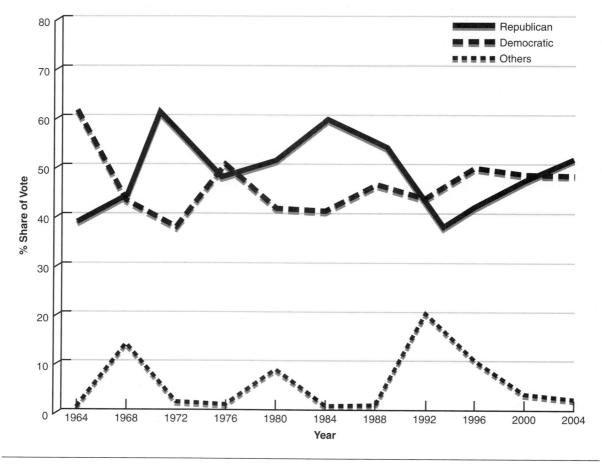

as a dozen candidates have run in recent elections, and the 1990s saw the emergence of significant third-party challenges for the first time in decades (see Figure 1.2). Voters do not vote directly for the competing candidates, who are instead chosen indirectly through an **electoral college.** Devised at the time of the writing of the Constitution, this was a compromise between those who wanted Congress to select the president and those who wanted the people to elect the president. One of the effects of the college is that candidates are encouraged to focus all their efforts and attention on the larger states; they often bypass smaller states or states they are sure to win or lose. Given that there are 538 electoral votes and that the winner needs only a plurality of those votes to win, a president could theoretically be elected by winning pluralities in just the dozen largest states.

Legislative Elections

Every two years, all 435 members of the House of Representatives and one-third of the members of the U.S. Senate run for reelection. As with the presidential race, candidates must all be selected in primaries, but incumbents are rarely seriously challenged and reelection is usually assured.

Legislative primaries attract much less media and public interest than their presidential equivalents, but this does not mean that candidates do not spend a proportionate amount of effort and money in running for office. This is particularly true of Senate campaigns, where competition is more intense and in which there is greater public interest.

Local Elections

Americans can vote in a wide range of elections at the local level, from those for state governors and legislators to those for mayors, city councilors, chiefs of police, district attorneys, state auditors, library trustees, coroners, town clerks, and local school boards. The races for governors and mayors are usually the most hotly contested and draw the most voter interest, with those for local positions being less interesting, if only because most voters know little about the competing candidates.

POLITICAL PARTIES

Almost every introductory textbook on American politics includes a chapter on parties. But instead of discussing what the different parties stand for, those chapters are mainly about the history of parties, about party organization, and about party conventions and the prospects for third parties. Look at textbooks on politics in other liberal democracies, by contrast, and you will find much less history, and much more about the role of parties in politics today. The difference is a reflection of the relatively weak role that parties play in American politics.

Only 13 percent of Americans describe themselves as strong Republicans and 19 percent as strong Democrats, while the number of independents has risen from 23 percent in the 1950s to about 34 percent today.[15] This suggests that American voters have become disillusioned with the major parties, leading to much discussion in recent years about a realignment of party politics and the declining partisanship of the electorate. American voters often make their choices at elections on the basis of personalities rather than parties, even to the point of voting for candidates from another party: About 9 to 13 percent of Republicans have routinely voted for Democrats running for the presidency in recent years, and as many as 26 percent of Democrats voted for Republican Ronald Reagan when he ran in 1980 and 1984.

Although there are many political parties in the United States representing a variety of ideological and regional interests, the party system has been "duopolized" since the nineteenth century by the Republicans and the Democrats. They have won every presidential election in modern history, and between them they have long held almost all the seats in the U.S. Congress (see Figure 1.3). The stranglehold of the

FIGURE 1.3

Legislative Electoral Trends in the United States

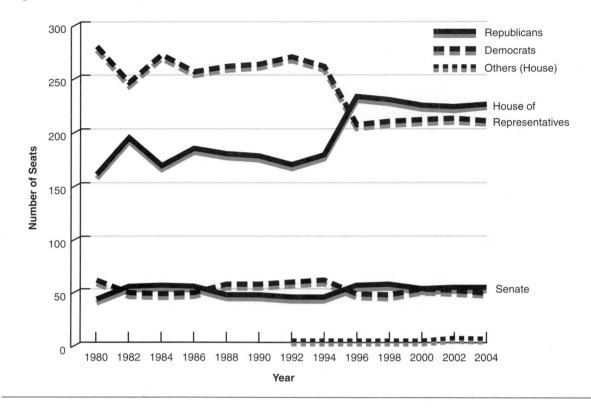

two parties is based on a variety of factors: They have been able to alter their electoral strategies to ensure that breakaway parties or minor parties fail to develop much influence or win seats; they are automatically included on general election ballots, whereas third parties must meet the requirements (such as filing petitions) set by different states; they dominate the middle ground of American politics, which is where most American voters place themselves; and the unpopularity of parties or candidates with strong left-wing or right-wing ideological positions has ensured that the two major parties remain little different from each other.

Republicans

Otherwise known as the GOP (Grand Old Party), the Republican Party traces its roots back to the Civil War, when Democrats opposed to slavery broke away to form the new party. The Republicans went on to win almost every presidential election for the next 50 years, and then alternated with the Democrats in the White House after World War II, under the presidencies of Eisenhower, Nixon, Reagan, and the two Bushes. After 40 years in opposition in Congress, the Republicans won back a majority in 1994. Most members are moderate conservatives, but the party contains many shades of opinion. Most Republicans today are either traditional conservatives, keen on minimizing the role of government in the economy, or neo-conservatives, driven by a desire to institutionalize their religious and moral values by limiting access to legal abortion, promoting prayer in schools, and controlling pornography.[16] The Republicans tend to have the advantage among voters with higher incomes and better education, among social conservatives, among suburban voters, and in the South, where there has been a shift from solid Democratic support to solid Republican.

Democrats

The Democratic Party traces its roots back to the 1820s and long had its most important base of support in the South. After decades spent mainly in political opposition, the party was swept into office in 1932 on the back of demands that government take a more hands-on approach in dealing with economic and social problems in the wake of the Great Depression. After World War II, it held the White House during the Truman, Kennedy, Johnson, Carter, and Clinton administrations and held a 40-year majority in both houses of Congress before losing it to the Republican takeover of 1994. The Democratic Party has traditionally been the party of the disadvantaged and continues to be a moderate left-wing party, favoring social welfare, regulation of big business, and environmental management. It has the advantage in New England and in older industrial states, among poorer Americans, religious minorities, and the less educated, and it has a very clear advantage among blacks and among voters in inner city areas.

Minor Parties

The United States has a long history of minor parties, but the control exerted by the two major parties over the electoral process has combined with the math of the winner-take-all system to prevent any of them from becoming nationally prominent. A recent example is the Reform Party, a moderately conservative party which was formed around the presidential bid of Texas billionaire H. Ross Perot in 1992; Perot was widely suspected of taking away enough votes from Republican George Bush to help Bill Clinton win the presidency that year. It went on to run candidates in several state elections, notably former professional wrestler Jesse Ventura, who served as governor of Minnesota in 1998–2002. Another national party is the pro-environmental Green Party, which ran Ralph Nader as its presidential candidate in 2000 and took enough votes away from the Democrats to help George W. Bush win. Finally, the Libertarian Party holds a number of conservative positions but has not yet had an impact on the presidential election. None of these parties has yet won seats in Congress, even though they won more than 15 million votes—or 5.3 percent of the total cast—in the 2000 elections.[17]

HOW HEALTHY IS AMERICAN DEMOCRACY?

Americans and their political leaders often portray the United States as the pinnacle of democracy, yet the U.S. model of democracy is full of contradictions.[18] Consider the November 2000 presidential election. Not only were there voting irregularities and technical problems that left many votes uncounted, but the winner of the popular vote—Democrat Al Gore, who won 50,999,897 votes, or 543,895 more than his Republican opponent George W. Bush[19]—did not win the election. Why not? Because presidents are elected through the Electoral College, where George W. Bush won 271 votes to Gore's 266. Meanwhile, Green Party candidate Ralph Nader won nearly three million votes (almost 3 percent of the total) but won no Electoral College votes.

Democracy includes the ideas that (1) every voter should be allowed to cast just one vote, (2) every vote should have equal weight, and (3) the candidate with the most votes wins. The U.S. model of democracy failed on all three counts in 2000. Consider some additional problems:

- The borders of voting districts are decided in most states not by independent commissions but by the majority political party in each state, which will routinely draw those districts in such a way as to maximize the chances of its members winning congressional seats.

- There is relatively little public funding of elections in the United States, which means that candidates must raise money from private sources. Among these are groups representing a variety of special interests, most notably corporate interests and single-issue interest groups, whose views strongly influence the behavior of elected officials, occasionally running counter to majority public opinion.

- Presidents and presidential candidates are so shielded now from the public that real political debate involving leaders has all but died. During the 2004 presidential campaign, for example, George W. Bush gave public speeches only before carefully handpicked crowds of supporters, and kept himself out of the reach and the earshot of his critics.

- On the international scene, the United States has been accused of double standards, holding other countries to high expectations on human rights, and to treating itself differently from other countries by refusing to sign international agreements on issues as varied as land mines, nuclear testing, climate change, and the rights of children.[20]

Under the circumstances, how can we be sure that the interests of all Americans are being effectively represented in government? Just how healthy is the American model of democracy?

POLICIES AND POLICYMAKING

Public policy in the United States is driven by a combination of constraints and opportunities that is unique to the American political system. As with all liberal democracies, it has a political system in which many different actors give input to the process, from elected officials to voters, parties, interest groups, the media, and private corporations. At the same time, expectations regarding the role of government are relatively modest. Whereas most Europeans are used to—and prefer—large government programs and a relatively high degree of state intervention in social affairs, Americans give more weight (in theory at least) to the idea of self-determination. Government is expected to do less than is the case in most other liberal democracies, although in fact it is significantly involved—through regulation, the provision of welfare, subsidies to states, and contracts to private business. The role of government is also influenced by at least five other factors.

First, government must respond to the needs of a society that is more diverse than that of any other liberal democracy. As noted earlier, race is a key factor, partly because ethnic minorities make up about 32 percent of the population and partly because racism is still a problem in the United States. In almost every respect—educational opportunities, housing, life expectancy, and so on—there are significant differences between whites, blacks, and Latinos, and Americans are regularly reminded of the implications of these differences. Age is also a factor: As Americans live longer and the population becomes older, the social security and health care systems come under more pressure.

Second, the freedom of action that the president, Congress, or the courts have on policy is limited by checks and balances and by the absence of party unity in Congress. Neither the president nor Congress can act alone in making policy or responding to needs and crises. They must constantly reach compromises to ensure that their programs are put into effect, laws are passed, and money is spent. Not only is power divided horizontally, but there is also a vertical division between the federal government in Washington, D.C., and the governments of the states. The states have a high degree of freedom over policy in a variety of areas—notably education, policing, and criminal justice—and federal law and policy usually depend on the cooperation of the states for successful implementation.

Third, the abilities of the federal government to get anything done are severely constrained by the realities of the budget. The size of the U.S. federal budget has grown to match the expansion of federal government activities: It was $60 billion in 1962, $500 billion in 1982, $1.9 trillion in 2000, and $2.6 trillion in 2005. However, most spending is made in a limited number of areas. About half goes to payments to individuals in the form of social security, health care, and other benefits; 15 percent goes to grants to state and local governments; 14 percent is spent on defense; 11 percent goes to pay interest on the national debt; and everything else must be covered by the remaining 5 percent. Furthermore, the federal government does not have much room to maneuver, because about two-thirds of all spending is mandatory, or committed, and cannot be redirected at will. Finally, the United States has dug itself into a large budgetary hole by building up a large national debt: Thanks mainly to the tax refunds and increased defense spending of the Bush administration, the budget deficit reached a record $700 billion in 2005, and the national debt a record $8 billion.

Fourth, the options facing the federal government are influenced by the fact that the United States is the world's last remaining military superpower and has obligations as a global leader. Isolationists within the United States argue that it should pull back from these obligations, whereas neoconservatives argue that, should the United States remain active in world affairs, it should do so on its own terms rather than working through the United Nations or in concert with allies. But these are minority views, and successive administrations continue to argue that the United States must protect its economic and strategic interests as part of a global community. This has become particularly critical since the launch of the war on terrorism, which has resulted in more money than ever being spent on the military.

Finally, the United States is a free-market economic system with some of the largest corporations in the world, so the private sector has much influence over the directions taken by policy. It accounts for nearly two-thirds of GDP and 85 percent of employment, and corporations inevitably have a key role to play in labor relations, setting pay scales, the opening of new factories and the closing of old ones, the revitalization of decaying urban and rural areas, and the development of new technology.

The effect of all these pressures is that although policies are driven by the president and Congress, they are only two among a variety of actors in the American policy system. The decisions made by national government in the United States are affected by a complex interplay involving the private sector, government agencies, state legislatures and city councils, governors and mayors, the media, interest groups, the courts, public opinion, foreign governments, and international organizations.[21]

ECONOMIC POLICY

The U.S. economy is one of the two biggest in the world in absolute terms. With a GDP of nearly $12 trillion, it is slightly smaller than the European Union, and although it has less than five percent of the world's population, it accounts for nearly 25 percent of global economic output. Economists have not always agreed on the explanations for the growth and success of the U.S. economy, but it has involved an element of trial and error.

Until the Great Depression of the early 1930s, the United States supported classical economic theories of the kind associated with the writings of Adam Smith, who argued that the market economy was a self-adjusting mechanism that worked best if left alone. Recession would stay away, inflation and unemployment would stay low, and productivity would stay high if the economy was left to the forces of the marketplace. The Great Depression shattered this view: Unemployment jumped to 25 percent and was still at 18 percent in 1936, seven years after the Wall Street crash of 1929. With questions being asked about the ability of the market to stabilize itself, the theories of British economist John Maynard Keynes began to win support.

Keynes argued that the government should involve itself in economic policy by manipulating demand through the budget. His ideas were reflected in the 1946 Employment Act, which committed the federal government to taxing and spending policies aimed at promoting maximum employment. This worked well during the 1950s and 1960s, but the popularity of Keynesian theory was undermined in the 1970s when the United States experienced stagflation (concurrent inflation and economic stagnation). President Reagan described Keynesian economics as "the failed policies of the past," and opted instead for **supply-side economics** (or neoclassical economics). The argument here was that taxes penalize hard work, creativity, investments, and savings, so they should be cut, government spending should be held in check, regulations should be minimized, and government should work to stimulate supply rather than demand.

The floor of the New York Stock Exchange on Wall Street in New York City. For many, Wall Street represents the heart of global capitalism. The remarkable growth of the U.S. economy in the 1990s was reflected in record trading activity on the floor of the exchange, but not everyone has benefited from America's new wealth, and there is a large gap between the rich and the poor.

Under Reagan, taxes were lowered, especially for the wealthy. The 1981 Economic Recovery Tax Act cut the top income tax rate from 50 percent to 29 percent, and the average income tax rate fell to 23 percent. The assumption was that this would free up money for investment, encourage people to work, and redistribute wealth and opportunity through a "trickle-down" effect. Unfortunately, Reaganomics also reduced federal government income at a time when the Reagan administration was increasing spending on the military from 4.5 percent of GNP to 6.5 percent. Although inflation fell and productivity grew during the Reagan years and unemployment fell from more than 10 percent to 5 percent, the national debt nearly tripled.

By 1991, the United States was in a **recession** (meaning two consecutive quarters of economic decline), a problem that contributed to the defeat of George Bush in the 1992 election. The economy then rallied and by the end of the decade GDP and industrial production was growing at 3 to 4 percent annually, unemployment was at 4 percent, several regions of the country had labor shortages, and consumer price inflation was running at 2 to 3 percent. The market was so buoyant that President Clinton's popularity rating was at 60 percent or higher even while Congress was holding impeachment hearings against him in early 1999. The United States was meanwhile supporting free trade, pressuring countries that protected their markets (notably China), and signing the North American Free Trade Agreement (NAFTA) with Canada and Mexico in 1993. The national debt continued to grow during the Clinton administration, but agreement was reached between the White House and Congress on the budget, and 1999 saw a budget surplus for the first time since the Nixon administration in the late 1960s.

Not all the news is good, however. After making astonishing profits for entrepreneurs and shareholders, the bottom fell out of the new technology market in 2001–2002, greatly reducing personal savings and pension plans for many. A string of accounting scandals during the same period led to the collapse of major corporations such as Enron and WorldCom, and undermined public faith in corporate America. The U.S. **trade deficit** continued to grow, reaching more than $600 billion in 2004. This is a problem because foreign investors must fund the difference by lending the United States money, and they are becoming worried by the size of the deficit and are withdrawing funds, lowering the value of the U.S. dollar. The United States also continues to lack a comprehensive energy policy and relies heavily on imported oil, raising the prospect of an energy-price shock to the economy. There has been a steady loss of manufacturing jobs to countries where workers are paid less, and although the shortfall has been met by more jobs in the service sector, many of these are poorly paid. The gap between the rich and the poor has grown to the point where the poorest 40 percent of Americans now make 15 percent of the national income, while the richest 40 percent make 67 percent of the national income. Americans save little as a percentage of their income, so there is less money available for investment. At the same time, they borrow a lot, and personal bankruptcies have reached an all-time high.

The U.S. economy may be the biggest national economy in the world, but several trends suggest that the United States is facing new threats and levels of competition that it has not seen since before World War II; most of these come from Europe and China. In his first term in office, George W. Bush became focused on the war on terrorism, and although this initially won him high public approval ratings, his critics charged that he was not spending enough time addressing the underlying threats to long-term economic growth and success: the budget deficit, the national debt, the trade deficit, the persistence of poverty, and the American addiction to oil. Hurricane Katrina offered Americans a shocking lesson in the extent to which the country is still handicapped by gaps between the rich and the poor, and by a lack of adequate investment in infrastructure.

FOREIGN POLICY

As the world's only remaining military superpower and—with the European Union— one of its two economic superpowers, the United States is a dominant force in international relations. It does not have the world's biggest military—China's is bigger—but it spends more on defense than the next ten countries combined, and it has the world's biggest military arsenal, the most technologically advanced weapons systems, and the ability to launch quick and devastating attacks almost anywhere in the world with minimal loss of personnel. But there is much debate among Americans about just what kind of role the United States should be playing in the world and about how U.S. foreign policy interests should be defined. During the cold war, the overriding objectives were to contain the Soviet Union and to limit the spread of communist influence. With the end of the cold war, however, the world has become a less predictable place. U.S. foreign policy interests were beginning to shift away from defensive and strategic issues toward economic and trade issues, but then came the September 2001 attacks and a new set of issues moved to the top of the agenda.

The worldview held by policymakers in the United States has combined with shifts in public opinion to move U.S. foreign policy in different directions. For the first century and a half after independence, **isolationism** was the norm—the general feeling was that the U.S. should not become involved in developments outside the Americas. The **Monroe Doctrine** of 1823 (named after President James Monroe) declared that the western hemisphere would be off-limits to colonization or intervention by European states, but the doctrine was little more than symbolic because the United States lacked the military power to back it up. Furthermore, the United States did not cut itself off from international affairs: There were conflicts and war with Mexico, commercial ties with Japan and Korea in the late nineteenth century, involvement in the internal affairs of several Latin American and Caribbean states, and a war with Spain in 1898 over Cuba. On the global stage, however, the Europeans —notably Britain, France, and Germany—held the balance of power, and the United States restricted its foreign policy interests to the western hemisphere.

This began to change with the two world wars of the twentieth century, which pulled the United States into a more active global role. The turning point was World War II (1939–1945), which had two effects on U.S. foreign policy. First, European powers emerged from the war economically and militarily drained, and Britain and France were under pressure to dismantle their empires. As Europe's relative influence declined, the influence of the United States and the USSR grew. Second, this new arrangement made it difficult for the United States to revert to isolationism, because it found itself pursuing strategic and ideological interests in many parts of the world. At the heart of those interests was the cold war, during which the United States was active in protecting Western Europe from the threat of communism (through the North Atlantic Treaty Organization (NATO)), and in containing and deterring the spread of communist influence in many other parts of the world. It fought a war in Korea in 1950–1953, and then, driven by the **domino theory** (allowing one state to fall to communism would lead to similar outcomes for neighboring states), became involved in propping up the government of South Vietnam against communist incursions from the north. The war dragged on until the fall of Saigon in April 1975, cost 56,000 American lives, became increasingly unpopular, and raised many questions about the broader motives behind U.S. foreign policy.

The United States also entered a nuclear arms race with the Soviet Union, prompted in part by the 1958 launch by the Soviets of Sputnik (the first global satellite) and in part by the failed Soviet attempt in 1962 to site nuclear warheads in Cuba. President Nixon hoped that confrontation with the Soviets could be replaced with negotiation, to which end the United States and the USSR pursued a policy of **détente** aimed at reducing tensions between the two superpowers. During the 1970s and 1980s, the concerns of the United States were focused on several critical regional issues, including the Arab-Israeli conflict, the Iranian revolution in 1979, the

Iran-Iraq war of 1980–1988, and disputes in the Caribbean and Central America (Nicaragua, Panama, and Grenada, among others). At the same time, the Reagan administration put more pressure on the "evil empire" of the Soviets, increasing spending on the military by more than $100 billion annually and launching research on a Strategic Defense Initiative intended to defend the United States against incoming Soviet missiles.

The end of the cold war is usually dated from the reunification of Germany in October 1990. In 1991, President George H.W. Bush made a speech in which he spoke of a **"new world order,"** giving some identity to the nature of the post–cold war world, but never fully explaining what he meant. The term implied that rather than the balance of power being driven by competition between the United States and its allies on one side and the Soviets and their allies on the other, there were now multiple centers of power in the world and a variety of new issues. In fact the phrase "new world disorder" might have been more apt. Nowhere have the doubts about the new challenges facing the international system been more clear than in the war on terrorism that has moved into high gear since September 2001. Unlike states, which usually launch sustained attacks with troops and military hardware, terrorists strike against different targets at different times, using different methods. And whereas conventional war involves military forces fighting against each other for dominance—civilians mainly being hurt in the crossfire—terrorism by definition involves attacks on both military and civilian targets with a view to literally terrorizing governments into changing policy.

The response of the George W. Bush administration to the threat of terrorism has been controversial. On the one hand, American neoconservatives believe that the United States should use its power in its own interests, and should not necessarily work with the international community to deal with problems that are seen as a threat to U.S. interests. But whereas the 2001 U.S.-led invasion of Afghanistan was generally welcomed and supported both inside and outside the United States, the 2003 invasion of Iraq was much more questionable, because it was promoted less by Iraq's links with terrorism than by allegations—never proven—that it was producing weapons of mass destruction. It was also criticized because it was a preemptive strike, a tactic that the United States had never used before on such a scale. Finally, it was criticized by those who argue that the Bush administration has largely ignored the causes of terrorism, including widespread criticism of U.S. policy on Israel/Palestine and the presence of the U.S. military in Saudi Arabia, the holy land of Islam. Rather than making the world a safer place, they charge, Bush's policy has made it more dangerous.

The United States may still be the world's biggest military power, but it is far from omnipotent. This was shown clearly in Vietnam, and has been shown again more recently with the inability of the U.S. military to stem an insurgency in Iraq that has cost hundreds of American lives, and has brought death and destruction to Iraqis and their property. Public and political opinion within the United States is divided on the future of foreign policy; some Americans prefer to maintain the multilateralist policies of the cold war era, when the United States worked in conjunction with its allies through international organizations, while others take a more unilateralist line, believing that the United States should use its power to preserve U.S. interests, with or without the support of its traditional allies.

U.S. POLITICS IN TRANSITION

The twentieth century was often described as the American century, a reflection of the extent to which the newfound military and economic power of the United States made it a global leader, notably after World War II. Its population grew and became more affluent, its corporations became world leaders, its economy became the engine of worldwide economic growth, and it led the Western alliance in its opposition to the Soviet bloc during the cold war.

At the same time, the United States went through important internal political and social change. Women and ethnic minorities became more integrated into the political system, and demographic changes led to a redefinition of the balance of power—the population became older and more ethnically diverse, suburbs expanded at the expense of downtown areas, and southern and western states grew relative to the old industrial northern states. Cynicism about politics fueled a reaction against politics-as-usual and contributed to declining support for political parties and falling turnout at elections.

The United States today faces new debates about the nature of politics (notably the influence of interest groups and structural problems with campaign funding). It also faces many pressing domestic social needs (notably the persistence of poverty and racism) and must redefine its place in a world in which the sources and the nature of international threats has changed. The next few years promise to be an interesting time in American politics as politicians and voters rethink their priorities.

KEY TERMS

American Dream
Articles of Confederation
big government
checks and balances
Civil War
cold war
Democrats
détente
domino theory
electoral college
exceptionalism
federation
Great Depression

Great Society
isolationism
judicial review
Monroe Doctrine
neoconservativism
New Deal
new world order
plurality
political action
    committee (PAC)
primaries
Reaganomics
recession

republic
Republicans
segregation
Senate majority leader
separation of powers
soft money
Speaker of the House
supply-side economics
trade deficit
War Powers Act
winner-take-all

KEY PEOPLE

George H.W. Bush
George W. Bush
Bill Clinton

John F. Kennedy
Richard Nixon
Ronald Reagan

Franklin D. Roosevelt
George Washington

STUDY QUESTIONS

1. What kind of challenges does the United States face, domestically and internationally, and how should it respond?
2. Is the United States an exceptional society, and—if so—how?
3. Is the United States becoming more conservative, and—if so—what are the indications?
4. Have the principles of the U.S. Constitution kept up with the needs of the American people?
5. Is the presidency accumulating too much power?
6. Does the Electoral College any longer serve a useful purpose?
7. Is low voter turnout something Americans should worry about?
8. Are there too few political parties in the United States?
9. How healthy is American democracy?
10. What are the features of the new world order, and should the United States be taking a unilateral or a multilateral approach to addressing global problems?

THE UNITED STATES ONLINE

There are hundreds of Web sites dealing with U.S. politics and government. The following list is just a small selection of mainly official sites.

White House: www.whitehouse.gov
U.S. Senate: www.senate.gov
U.S. House of Representatives: www.house.gov
Supreme Court: www.supremecourtus.gov
Democratic Party: www.democrats.org
Republican Party: www.rnc.org
Thomas: http://thomas.loc.gov
Contains a wealth of information on the workings and activities of Congress.
CNN/AllPolitics: www.cnn.com/ALLPOLITICS
A useful site containing the latest political news from CNN.

FURTHER READING

Barbour, Christine, and Gerald Wright, *Keeping the Republic: Power and Citizenship in American Politics* (Boston: Houghton Mifflin, 2001), and Susan Welch, John Gruhl, John Comer, and Susan M. Rigdon, *Understanding American Government*, 9th Ed. (Belmont, CA: Wadsworth, 2003). Two of the dozens of introductory U.S. politics texts on the market.

Barone, Michael, et al., *The Almanac of American Politics* (Washington, DC: National Journal, biannual since 1980). A handbook of information on Congress, with descriptions of members, their districts, and their voting records.

Lieven, Anatol, *America Right or Wrong: An Anatomy of American Nationalism* (New York: Oxford University Press, 2004). A critical and controversial study of the U.S. role in the world, which charges that American global leadership and the war on terrorism could be undermined by American nationalism.

Peters, B. Guy, *American Public Policy: Promise and Performance*, 6th Ed. (Washington DC: CQ Press, 2003). An introduction to public policy in the United States, with chapters on the policy process and on seven key policy areas.

EXECUTIVES

Americans have lived for nearly 220 years with the idea that the functions of government should be divided: The legislature makes laws, the executive oversees the application of those laws, and the judiciary ensures that the laws and actions of government fit with the terms of the Constitution. This principle of the separation of powers is usually attributed to the eighteenth-century French philosopher and political theorist Baron de Montesquieu (1689–1755), even though it was implicit in the writings of Aristotle and also addressed by John Locke. Montesquieu believed that the most obvious sign of despotism was when a single leader combined all three powers and that the best way to limit the powers of government was to make sure that the three roles were separated from each other as clearly as possible and balanced against each other.

Although virtually every political system in the world has equivalents of each of these three "branches" of government, power is divided among them very differently, and the role of the executive varies substantially.

- **The parliamentary executive.** This is the most common form of executive, found in Britain and in all those countries that have adopted the British parliamentary system, including almost all European states, Canada, Australia, New Zealand, India, Israel, and most Caribbean states. The executive consists of a prime minister and a cabinet, is drawn from the legislature, depends on party numbers in the legislature for its power, and coexists with a symbolic head of state. Prime ministers are typically leaders of the party with the majority of seats in the legislature or—if there is no majority party—leaders of the biggest party, or of the multiparty coalition that has come together to form the government. Prime ministers govern with the help of a cabinet of ministers drawn from the majority party or coalition. There is no constitutional

limit to how long prime ministers stay in office, provided they call elections as required, their party wins enough seats, and they keep the support of enough members of the legislature.

Under this arrangement, the executive and the legislature are fused, because prime ministers are always members of the legislature and so are most (or all) of the members of the cabinet. They usually all stand for election at the same time as all the other members of the legislature. If members of the prime minister's party vote against the government or drop out of the governing coalition, the prime minister's position is weakened and the executive could even fall if there is a rebellion among members of the governing party or coalition or if the prime minister loses a vote of confidence.

- **The limited presidential executive.** This is the second most common form of executive, found in the United States and in all those countries that have adopted the American model; they include most Latin American states and several African and Asian states. The executive consists of a president elected separately from the legislature for a limited number of fixed-length terms and who has most of the powers that are divided in the parliamentary system between the head of state and the head of government. Presidents govern with the help of a cabinet of ministers, who are usually nominated by the president and confirmed by one of the chambers of the legislature. Presidents are not formally leaders of their parties, and their position does not depend on them having the support of a majority of members of the legislature; while in office, they can usually only be removed by death or impeachment.

Under this arrangement, the executive and the legislature are separate, because neither the president nor the members of the cabinet can be members of the legislature, and there is a system of checks and balances between the two. Presidents have limits placed on their powers, but they also have independent responsibilities (particularly over foreign policy); it helps if they have a sympathetic legislature, but they can outwit the legislature if they are able strategists, and they usually have the power to veto proposals from the legislature. In contrast to the parliamentary executive, they do not lose office if there is a rebellion among members of their party in the legislature, and they do not face votes of confidence.

- **The dual executive.** This is a more unusual arrangement, found in Austria, Cyprus, Egypt, Finland, France, Portugal, Russia, and a few Eastern European states. It involves a mixture of the parliamentary and presidential systems, dividing executive powers between an elected executive president serving fixed (but not always limited) terms and a prime minister and cabinet who head the largest party or coalition in the legislature. The president is head of state but also has considerable powers over policymaking, sharing these with the prime minister in his or her role as head of government. The president and the prime minister do not need to come from the same party; if they do, the prime minister tends to be a functionary of the president, but if they do not, the prime minister can develop more independence.

  Under this arrangement, the executive and the legislature are separate, but the president depends on having the cooperation of the prime minister—and preferably the support of a majority of members of the legislature—to govern effectively. There is no clear separation of powers, and clever (or devious) presidents can take the credit for successful policies while blaming their prime ministers for failed policies. Presidents do not lose office if there is a rebellion among members of their party in the legislature, and they do not face votes of confidence. But if voters return the opposition to power in a legislative election, these presidents can find their hands tied. However, if no one party has a majority—as has been the case recently in Russia—clever presidents can also exploit divisions in the legislature to make policy.

- **The unlimited presidential executive.** This is the kind of system commonly found in African states without military governments. The president coexists with a legislature, but the president's party is usually the dominant party and the president has so many powers that the legislature is little more than a rubber-stamp institution. There may be limits on the length of presidential terms, but there are no limits on the number of terms, and the president is usually assured of reelection. The balance of power lies squarely with the executive, opening the door to authoritarian leadership.

As these examples show, the role of an executive is heavily dependent upon both the powers of the office, and the relationship with the legislature. The American model may seem the weakest of the four—at least in terms of the powers given by the Constitution to the president—but this depends on a complex combination of the leadership qualities of the president, his standing in public opinion, and his relationship with Congress. Although the parliamentary executive and the dual executive seem to put too much power into the hands of one person, it is not unqualified power; leaders in these systems rely heavily on the base of their support in the legislature. Without a strong following, a British prime minister can be removed from power, and a Russian or French president can be a lame duck.

BRITAIN

BRITAIN: QUICK FACTS

Official name: United Kingdom of Great Britain and Northern Ireland

Capital: London

Area: 94,249 square miles (244,103 sq. km, about the size of Oregon)

Languages: Overwhelmingly English, with some regional languages (Welsh, Gaelic)

Population: 59 million

Population density: 628 per square mile (242 per sq. km.)

Population growth rate: 0.2 percent

POLITICAL INDICATORS

Freedom House rating: Free

Date of state formation: Debatable; arguably 1066

System type: Parliamentary democracy with a constitutional monarchy

Constitution: Unwritten

Administration: Unitary

Executive: Prime minister and cabinet

Legislature: Bicameral Houses of Parliament; House of Lords (currently undergoing structural reformation) and House of Commons (659 members). Lords are appointed; MPs are elected to renewable five-year terms

Party structure: Multiparty, with two dominant parties (Labour and Conservative) and several smaller parties

Judiciary: No separate judiciary; House of Lords is highest court of appeal

Head of state: Queen Elizabeth II (1952–)

Head of government: Tony Blair (1997–)

ECONOMIC INDICATORS

GDP (2004): $2,141 billion

Per capita GDP: $33,940

Distribution of GNP: Services 72 percent, industry 27 percent, agriculture 1 percent

Urban population: 89 percent

SOCIAL INDICATORS

HDI ranking: 12

Infant mortality rate: 5.3 per 1,000 live births

Life expectancy: 77.6 years

Illiteracy: 0 percent of people aged 15 and older

Religions: Predominantly Anglican, with Catholic and Presbyterian minorities

INTRODUCTION

Britain is one of the standard case studies in comparative politics, and with good reason. As well as being the birthplace of the parliamentary system, elements of which are found in every liberal democracy, it is also the birthplace of the industrial revolution and the modern notion of capitalism, and as such has long had an important influence on economic developments in the rest of the world. It is also a leading member of all the key international organizations, notably the North Atlantic Treaty Organization (NATO), the UN Security Council (on which it has veto power), the European Union (EU), and the G-8 group of major economic powers. Finally, it is the birthplace of the English language, which has become the global language of business, communications, diplomacy, trade and—increasingly—everyday conversation.

Once one of the world's great powers, Britain since 1945 has had to adjust to a change in its global position and in the view that Britons hold of themselves. The transition has not always been easy, but Britain today has forged a new identity for itself as a medium power built on hundreds of years of evolutionary political development, and boasting one of the most successful and dynamic economies in Europe. Economic growth—combined with a downturn in the fortunes of Germany and France—has helped make Britain the fourth biggest economy in the world with a GDP of $2.1 trillion.

In economic terms, Britain has all the typical features of a postindustrial free-market society. It is one of the world's biggest producers of natural gas and coal. It exports a variety of manufactured goods and has plenty of prime agricultural land, but it has relatively few other natural resources and must import raw materials such as cotton, wool, rubber, and tin. Like all its European neighbors, Britain is a small, crowded, and highly urbanized country. With a population of nearly 60 million, it has a population density of nearly 630 people per square mile (compared to about 80 people per square mile in the United States and about 8 per square mile in Canada).

In social terms, it has several important divisions:

- **Regional identity** is strong, with cultural and political differences among the English, the Scots, the Welsh, and the Northern Irish (see Political Debates, p. 88).

- **Social class** was long a defining characteristic of British society, with a hierarchy in place by which most Britons placed themselves—or were placed—in the upper, middle, or working class. The class system still exists, but the expansion of the middle class has made the system both less obvious and more complex.

- **Race** has become a more important issue since the 1950s with the immigration of increased numbers of nonwhites from the Caribbean and the Indian subcontinent. Today about 7 percent of the population is nonwhite, and although ethnic minorities have become more successfully integrated in recent years, racism remains a problem in some of the larger urban areas, notably London.

In political terms, Britain is distinct from most other countries in its record of evolutionary development, driven by what has been described as a "genius for

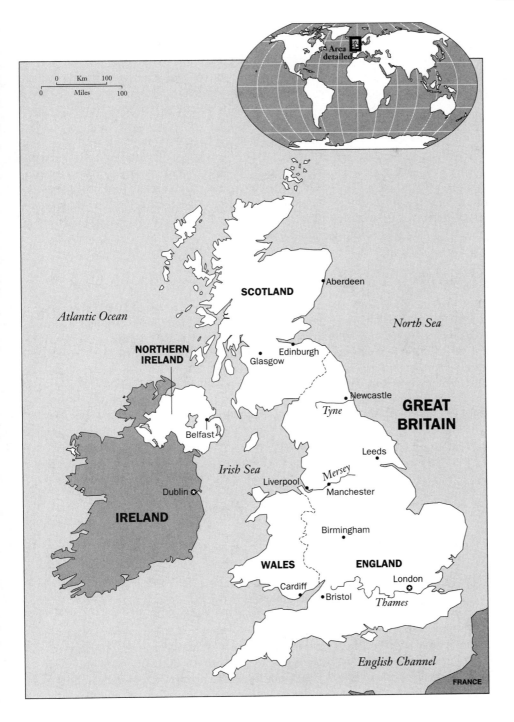

0 Km 100
0 Miles 100

Area detailed

Atlantic Ocean

SCOTLAND

Aberdeen

North Sea

NORTHERN
IRELAND

Edinburgh
Glasgow

Newcastle

GREAT
BRITAIN

Tyne

Belfast

Leeds

Irish Sea

Mersey

Liverpool

Manchester

Dublin

IRELAND

Birmingham

WALES

ENGLAND

London

Cardiff

Bristol

Thames

English Channel

FRANCE

nonviolent progress."[1] There has been violence, it is true, and Britain's democratic record is far from spotless: Questions are regularly raised about government secrecy, social inequalities, and an electoral system that handicaps smaller political parties, and British governments until recently were often criticized for allowing human rights abuses in Northern Ireland. But concessions and change have usually come quickly enough to avoid the kinds of political problems often experienced by other European states.

The evolutionary process continues today. The government of Tony Blair—in power since 1997—has made changes to the constitution of a kind that would be difficult to engineer in the United States. Political powers have been devolved to the regions, reforms have been made in the electoral system, for the first time in history there is an elected mayor of London, changes have been made to the upper chamber of the British Parliament (the House of Lords), and laws have been changed to ensure greater protection for individual rights.

POLITICAL DEVELOPMENT

Most liberal democracies have at some point experienced a war or a revolution leading to the introduction of a new or substantially altered system of government: Germany had a new system imposed on it after World War II, France adopted a new constitution in 1958, and Spain began a transition to democracy following the end of the Franco dictatorship in 1975. By contrast, Britain has never permanently replaced one system of government with another, but has instead made changes that have built on the foundations of existing arrangements. For that reason, understanding the British political system means reviewing more than 2,000 years of history.

Early Invasions from the Continent (55 B.C.–A.D. 1066)

Britain's early history was dominated by repeated invasions by its continental neighbors. The native people of the British Isles were the Celts, who arrived between 800 and 200 B.C.; they are the ancestors of the Irish, Scots, and Welsh of today. When the Romans invaded in 55 B.C. and occupied what is now England and Wales, the Celts were pushed west and north and England developed a social, economic and political system very different from that of the rest of the British Isles. When the Romans left at the beginning of the fifth century, they created a political vacuum into which moved several waves of invaders, notably Germanic tribes such as the Angles and the Saxons (from which come the names *England* and *Anglo-Saxon*).

A mission in 597 from the Pope in Rome brought Christianity to Britain, preceding a wave of Viking invasions in the eighth and ninth centuries. These were followed in 1066 by the last successful invasion of Britain, by William, Duke of Normandy. This brought political stability and centralization to England, but the English and the Celts remained divided ethnically, culturally, and linguistically. Religious differences were added in 1534, when King Henry VIII dissolved England's ties with the Roman Catholic Church and created the Church of England. The Scots today are mainly Catholic and Presbyterian, while the English are mainly Protestant.

The End of Feudalism and the Expansion of the State (1215–1707)

Until about 800 years ago, Britain—like all of Europe—was a feudal society. Sovereign power lay in the hands of monarchs, who ruled by divine right and governed the peasant majority through a land-owning aristocracy. The powers of monarchs and aristocrats began their long and sometimes violent decline in 1215 when King John signed the **Magna Carta,** a document that obliged him to consult with his aristocrats before levying taxes and prevented him from arbitrarily arresting or seizing property from his subjects. It did little more than confirm the privileges of the aristocrats, but it was an important first step in the transfer of power.

A second step was taken in 1265 with the convening of the first British **Parliament.** It was unelected, met only sporadically, and was dominated by the aristocracy, but monarchs came to rely on it for political support. Tensions between crown and Parliament remained, however, finally boiling over in 1642 with the outbreak of a civil war between monarchists and parliamentarians. This led to the declaration of a brief republic (1649–1660) under the military dictatorship of Oliver Cromwell. When King James II (1685–1688) tried to win back the divine right of monarchs, a Bill of Rights was drawn up which confirmed the supremacy of Parliament over the monarch.

Parliament The legislative body in the Westminster system of government.

Meanwhile, war and attrition led to the dominance of England over its Celtic neighbors; a union with Wales was formalized in 1536–1542 and with Scotland in 1707. For its part, Ireland was steadily subjugated and by the late eighteenth century had to all intents and purposes become part of the British state.

Economic and Political Change (17th–19th Centuries)

Beginning in the late 1600s, Britain underwent wide-ranging economic change, which led in turn to political and social change. New and more efficient processes for smelting iron and making steel were developed, the steam engine was invented, industry was mechanized, and large-scale business enterprises emerged. This in turn brought about improvements in transport, which led to the growth of commerce and markets. As the birthplace of the **Industrial Revolution,** Britain was forged into the world's first and most powerful industrial state and by the mid-nineteenth century was producing two-thirds of the world's coal, half its steel, half its cotton goods, and virtually all its machine tools.

Parliament was still dominated by aristocrats representing mainly rural areas, many of which had only a handful of voters and in some of which a seat in Parliament could be bought. The new middle class of industrialists and entrepreneurs found this unacceptable, and pressure for change led to reforms in the nineteenth and early twentieth centuries that eliminated corrupt electoral districts; extended the vote to the wealthy, the upper middle class, and women; introduced secret voting; sparked the growth of mass-membership political parties; created single-member parliamentary districts with roughly equal populations; and took most remaining significant political powers away from the aristocratic House of Lords.

The Imperial Era (18th Century to Early 1960s)

With its industry growing, Britain's priority was to find new markets and sources of raw materials and to build on its competitive advantage over its European rivals, particularly France. Thus began an expansive program of colonization. After losing its 13 American colonies in 1781, Britain colonized Australia, Canada, New Zealand, parts of West Africa, most of southern and eastern Africa, many Caribbean and Pacific islands, the Asian subcontinent, and parts of Southeast Asia. At its height during the late Victorian era, the **British Empire** included about a quarter of the world's population.

The beginning of the end of the imperial era came with World War I, when the cream of a generation of young British men died in one of the most brutal and mismanaged conflicts in the history of warfare. The United States and the Soviet Union began to emerge as economic and military powers, a transition that was finally confirmed by World War II. Britain entered the war in 1939 as the world's biggest creditor nation, and although it played a key role in fighting and winning the war, it emerged six years later as one of the world's biggest debtor nations. It suffered widespread physical damage, its economy was devastated, its political influence diminished, its export earnings were halved, and most of its colonies were agitating for independence.

Postwar Adjustment and the Welfare State (1945–1975)

Although its economy prospered in the 1950s and 1960s, Britain saw its influence relative to other countries—notably the United States, Japan, and Germany—beginning to decline. The most obvious explanation for this was the dismantling of its empire—India and Pakistan became independent in 1947, and over the next 20 years there was a steady program of decolonization. The decline could also be blamed, however, on the cost of the war, handicaps posed to industrial relations by class divisions, an education system that was prejudiced against business as a career, low levels of mobility within the labor force, inadequate investments in industry and in research and development, and high levels of government involvement in production and employment.[2]

The postwar period saw the completion of a welfare state and the shift to a managed economy. Pensions had been introduced in 1908 and national health and unemployment insurance in 1911,[3] but the welfare system was completed only after 1945, when voters wanting a new start swept a socialist Labour government into power. A National Health Service was created that provided free care for almost everyone; there was an expansion of welfare for the unemployed, the ill, and families with children; and basic services such as railroads and the steel industry were nationalized.

Succeeding Conservative governments agreed to follow roughly the same policies, and—whether the Conservatives or Labour were in power—British politics became driven by a **consensus** on the maintenance of welfare and of managing economic demand so as to sustain full employment. Nonetheless, the British economy, plagued by growing industrial unrest, continued its relative decline through the 1960s and 1970s. In 1976, the Labour government of Harold Wilson had to ask the International Monetary Fund for a loan to help offset a run on the pound and to help Britain service its debts. A new low was reached during the "winter of discontent" in

consensus The point at which all opinions converge to a conclusion with which everyone can agree.

TABLE 2.1

Key Dates in British History

1066	Norman invasion
1215	Magna Carta signed
1265	Parliament founded
1536–1542	Union with Wales
1642–1649	Civil war leads to the deposition of the monarchy
1649–1660	Cromwell's republic ends with restoration of the monarchy
1707	Union with Scotland
1914–1918	World War I
1918	Women older than age 30 given the right to vote
1922	Irish independence
1928	All women given the right to vote
1939–1945	World War II
1945	First Labour government elected
1947	Independence of India and Pakistan
1957–1968	Independence of most of Britain's African colonies
1969	Civil unrest breaks out in Northern Ireland
1973	Britain joins the European Economic Community
1979	(May) Margaret Thatcher wins first of three elections
1982	War with Argentina over the Falklands/Malvinas
1990	(November) Thatcher resigns as leader of Conservative party and prime minister; replaced by John Major
1991	(January) British forces take part in U.S.-led Gulf War
1992	(April) Conservatives win fourth successive election victory
1994	Opening of English Channel tunnel connecting Britain and France
1996	Controversy breaks out over mad cow disease and sales of British beef in the rest of the European Union
1997	(May) Election of Tony Blair as prime minister ends nearly 18 years of Conservative government; (August) death of Diana, Princess of Wales
1998	(April) Peace agreement signed in Northern Ireland
1999	(March–April) Britain joins NATO in air attacks on Serbia/Kosovo; (May) first elections to Scottish and Welsh assemblies; (October) hereditary peers sit in the House of Lords for the last time; (November) Northern Ireland regional government meets for the first time
2000	(May) Elections held for first-ever elected mayor of London
2001	(June) Tony Blair elected to a second term; (September) 250 Britons killed in terrorist attacks on New York and Washington, D.C.
2002	(January–February) Britain chooses not to join 12 European neighbors in adopting the new European currency, the euro
2003	(March) Britain joins the U.S.-led invasion of Iraq
2005	(May) Tony Blair elected to a third term as prime minister; (July) 52 people killed in London in suicide bombings linked to Muslim extremism

WHAT'S IN A NAME?

Despite Britain's prominence in the world, many non-Britons are still confused by its name. The United Kingdom of Great Britain and Northern Ireland (its official title) is actually four countries in one: Great Britain—made up of England, Scotland, and Wales—and Northern Ireland. England predominates because it conquered and assimilated the others; because it is home to more than four out of five Britons; and because London is the wealthiest part of the country and is the political, financial, cultural, and communications capital of Britain. However, Scotland, Wales, and Northern Ireland are also part of the United Kingdom (UK), so it is wrong to call the whole country "England"; it is usually known either as Britain or the United Kingdom.

The relationship among the four countries has not always been an easy one, with concerns about the cultural, economic, and political dominance of England, and movements to protect and rebuild minority cultural identity. There are many reminders of the differences among the four: Each has its own flag, culture, "national" sports teams, writers, and artists; Scotland, Wales, and Northern Ireland have their own regional political parties; Scotland and Northern Ireland have legal and educational systems that are separate from those used in England and Wales; and the Church of Scotland is separate from the Church of England.

Despite the existence of a "United" Kingdom, regionalism is a factor in national politics,[4] and some in Scotland and Wales even support the idea of complete independence. Pressure since the 1960s for **devolution** (the transfer of powers from the national government in London to regional governments) led the Blair government to agree to the creation of **regional assemblies** for Scotland, Wales, and Northern Ireland in 1998–1999. Supporters of devolution hoped that this would reduce demands for independence, particularly in Scotland. However, opinion polls are inconclusive on how far the Scottish independence movement has grown, with recent surveys finding between one third and one-half in favor.

Regionalism is not simply about national divisions but also about divisions within the four countries. The Scots have different religions, and there are cultural rivalries between highlanders and lowlanders. The Welsh are divided economically between the old industrial centers of the south and the agricultural regions of the north and between those who speak Welsh and those who do not. Northern Ireland suffers a variety of religious, economic, and cultural divisions and is split between those who support continued union with Britain and those who do not. Finally, England has many distinctive regional identities, so the values, attitudes, and priorities of people who live in the economic powerhouse of London and its suburbs are different from those of people who live in the rural and small-town communities near London, in the farmlands and the tourist centers of the southwest, in the old industrial areas of the midlands and the north, and in the dales of Yorkshire and the mountains and lakes of Cumbria.

1978–1979 when public-sector workers went on strike across Britain, almost shutting the country down.

A landmark event took place in 1973, when Britain joined the European Economic Community (EEC). A free-trade agreement among selected Western European states, the Community—created in 1958—was aimed at bringing down the barriers to trade and movement of people, with the goal of creating a unified European market. Dreamers even talked about the possibility of the eventual creation of a United States of Europe. Britain was slow to warm to the Community, arguing that its main interests lay outside Europe, but it quickly changed its mind and joined.

The Thatcher Revolution

Reflecting growing public concern about the state of the economy and about growing international competition, a Conservative government under Margaret Thatcher was elected in 1979 and launched a program of wide-ranging change. She claimed to reject the wisdom of consensus politics, arguing that government was too big, there were too many government-owned businesses and services, and that special interests (especially labor unions) had too much influence on government. Employing her own distinctive brand of "conviction politics," Thatcher launched an assault on socialism and labor unions and worked to create a new "enterprise culture" aimed at making British industry more competitive. **Thatcherism** became the watchword in politics and economics, its most enduring element being **privatization,** or the sale of state-owned services and industries to the private sector, a policy that has since been copied in many other countries.

privatization The selling of government-owned businesses, industries, and services to private owners.

The impact of Thatcherism on Britain is debatable. Her supporters argue that she spurred the changes needed to reverse Britain's economic decline by freeing up the marketplace, cutting the power of unions, reducing dependence on welfare, and promoting a **stakeholder culture** in which more Britons became involved in creating their own wealth and opportunities. But according to her critics, she failed to meet the needs of the underclass, allowed too many people to slip through the safety net of welfare, and widened the gap between the "haves" and the "have nots"; the number of millionaires grew sharply as a result of her tenure, but so did poverty and homelessness, and many believed that Britain became a less caring society. Britain today has a poverty rate of 18 percent, the worst in Western Europe.

Britain Today

Membership in the European Union has combined with the effects of Thatcherism to bring great change to Britain. It is visible in the renewal of cities, in the rise of a new entrepreneurial spirit that has transformed the attitudes of business and industry, and in the growth of the middle class and the consumer society. The average Briton is healthier, better educated, and better off than before, and there is a new spirit of liveliness and optimism, at least among the younger generations. Not only has its economy rediscovered the competitive culture that made it so strong in the nineteenth century, but many aspects of politics (notably election campaigns) have taken on a more vibrant character.

The legacy of Thatcherism has been reflected in the policies pursued since May 1997 by the Labour government of Tony Blair. Astonishing political analysts with the scale of its victory, the rejuvenated Labour Party swept the internally divided Conservative Party out of office after 18 years in power, winning a large majority. Under Tony Blair, "New" Labour abandoned many of its traditionally socialist ideas and adopted key elements of the Thatcher program. Blair has underlined the importance of the free market but has also emphasized the need to improve education, rebuild the national health care system, and take a tough stance on crime. But Blair will probably be best remembered for two things: the dramatic changes he has made to the structure of government (including setting up regional assemblies for Scotland and Wales, and reforming the upper chamber of Parliament, the House of Lords), and his decision to support the U.S.-led invasion of Iraq in 2003, which was deeply unpopular and lost him considerable political support.

There is little question at the beginning of the new millennium that Britain is once again undergoing significant political change. The Blair government wants to see it compete more effectively on the global stage, to have a more constructive relationship with its partners in the EU, to invest more heavily in its human capital, and to build a society that is less dependent on government. Blair has also been outspoken in his opinion that Britain should be "repackaged" as a society that has deep roots in history and culture, but which is forward-looking and economically dynamic. But public opinion is divided on just how far he has been able to follow through on these goals.

POLITICAL CULTURE

Tying down the political values of a society is always difficult, especially one with as long a history as Britain. Generally, though, most political scientists agree that the British are pragmatic, have faith in their political system (but not necessarily politicians), and are politically moderate, but that government is not sufficiently transparent, in the sense that people do not have as much access as they should to the workings of government.

Pragmatism

The British tend to keep their feet on the ground when it comes to their expectations of government and their aspirations for their own lives. They take an empirical approach to problem solving, shying away from theory and looking instead at the practical reality of policies. In the United States, argues Vivien Hart, "the emphasis has been on what democracy is and should be, while Britain has been characterized by a more pragmatic and less urgent emphasis on what democracy is and can be."[5] The two approaches bring out one of the key differences between Americans and Britons: Americans tend to have an optimistic (some would say naive) view of the possibilities for democracy—American political leaders will often sprinkle their speeches with words such as *dream* and *vision*—but Britons tend to place more faith in what has been tried and tested. This is not to suggest that the British do not dream or that they are opposed to innovation (quite the contrary), but rather that they are less apt to overreach than are Americans.

Among older Britons, realism has spilled over into pessimism, making many gloomy about the changes they have seen. The media tend to perpetuate the problem through their fascination with everything from lowered educational performance to the poor record of the national soccer team in international tournaments. While older Americans often talk about making life better for their children, many older Britons grumble that life was better and safer when they were younger. But most of the basic indicators—such as health care, education, economic wealth, individual freedoms, crime rates, and the state of the environment—suggest that life for most Britons has improved significantly in the last 30 years.

Faith in the Political System

Writing about the orientation of individuals toward political systems, Robert Dahl argues that favorable feelings indicate an "allegiant" orientation, neutral feelings reflect apathy and detachment, and unfavorable feelings reflect alienation.[6] Political alienation is often obvious in Italy and France and among disadvantaged Americans who feel cut off from government. Britain, by contrast, is marked by strong feelings of allegiance, reflected in the fact that most people still feel they can influence government.[7] These feelings are tied closely to the long history of political stability and evolutionary change in Britain, which contrasts with the often revolutionary and violent change that has come to political systems in other European states.

Most Britons have a high degree of faith in their political system and are more patriotic and trusting of their fellow citizens than are most of their European neighbors. However, the sense of allegiance is on the decline due to a combination of changes in the class system, a growing respect for succeeding through effort and hard work rather than through privilege, a reduction in individual dependence on the state, a concern that the political system is not as responsive as it should be, and a declining respect for politicians in the wake of a number of headline-making financial and political scandals in the late 1980s and early 1990s, and deeply held doubts about Tony Blair's motives in supporting the U.S.-led invasion of Iraq in 2003. Recent studies suggest that the British are more willing to use unconventional forms of political participation than the citizens of any other democracy, such as signing petitions, attending lawful demonstrations, joining a boycott or wildcat strike, and even—for 13 percent of Britons—refusing to pay taxes.[8]

Social Liberalism

In contrast to many Americans, most Britons take liberal positions on social and moral issues, and this has an impact on public policy and expectations of government. For example, capital punishment was outlawed in 1965, homosexuality and abortion have been legal since 1967, and British television has nothing like the degree of censorship found in the United States. Perhaps most astonishing to Americans, all handguns were banned in Britain in 1998. The spark for this was a mass killing at a school in 1996, of the kind that is tragically all too common in the United States. The response to such outrages in the United States tends to be hand-wringing about social problems and personal responsibility; the response in Britain was to place the blame squarely on the availability of guns and to tighten the already substantial controls. Part of the difference between British and American attitudes toward social issues may be rooted in the relative role of religion in the two societies. About two-thirds of Britons still claim to believe in God, but, except in Northern Ireland, church attendance has been steadily declining, and only about 13 percent of the population now actively participates in religious activities,[9] compared with about 43 percent in the United States.

A Closed Society

The British tend to be a private people, hence the often-quoted phrase that an Englishman's home is his castle. Perhaps because Britain is such a crowded country where a premium is placed on personal space, the British can often seem a little standoffish to visitors. This sense of privacy is reflected in the secrecy that often surrounds the functioning of government. Issues of national security are subject to secrecy in every democracy, but government critics charge that state secrets are too narrowly defined in Britain. Those critics say that this has helped increase the power and reduce the accountability of the police, weakened the power of Parliament at the expense of central government, promoted the use of surveillance, reduced the right to personal privacy, and allowed the government to interfere with media freedom.

Such secrecy has become increasingly unacceptable and there has been a movement in recent years for greater freedom of information. Successive governments have promised more open administration, and information has become more freely available, but the most significant changes have come during the Blair administration, which has opened up the bureaucracy and made government departments subject to performance reviews based on their services to the public.

POLITICAL SYSTEM

There are six key principles that give the British system of government its personality:

- It is a **constitutional monarchy** in which the monarch has symbolic power, and all government is carried out in the name of the monarch, but the prime minister is the true political leader.
- It is a **unitary state,** meaning that unlike the division of powers in the American federal system, most significant political powers are concentrated in national government, and local government is relatively weak. But this has changed recently with the creation of the Scottish, Welsh and Northern Irish regional assemblies.
- There is a **fusion of the executive and the legislature,** rather than the separation found in the American system. In Britain, the members of the executive (the prime minister and senior government ministers) are almost all serving members of Parliament.
- **Parliament is sovereign,** meaning that it has the ultimate power and right to make or abolish any law it wishes. But this is also changing, thanks to the increasing body of law made at the level of the European Union, which supercedes national law.
- There is a belief in **responsible government,** meaning that government ministers are responsible to Parliament for the management of their departments.
- Britain is a **member of the European Union,** and as such is subject to the common laws and policies of the EU.

In contrast to the atypical features of the U.S. system of government, most of the principles of British government are typical of the parliamentary system of government, and are found in different forms in virtually every liberal democracy except the United States.

THE CONSTITUTION

Most democracies—like the United States—have written constitutions in which the powers of government and the rights of the governed are outlined. However, constitutions do not necessarily have to take the form of a single written (or "codified") document; they can be more abstract, consisting of laws and customs that have the same function as a single written document. Britain has taken the latter course in that it lacks a codified document and is governed instead on the basis of constitutional principles. These principles come from five major sources:[10]

- **Common law,** or judgments handed down over time by British courts. Among the more significant are those dealing with freedom of expression and the sovereignty of Parliament.
- **Statute law,** or Acts of Parliament that override common law and have the effect of constitutional law. They include laws that outline the relative powers of the two houses of Parliament.
- **European law,** since Britain is subject to laws adopted by the EU, which override British laws where the two conflict, in those policy areas where the EU has primary authority. These include trade, agriculture, social issues, and the environment.
- **Traditions and conventions** that do not have the force of law but have been followed for so long that they are regarded as binding. For example, there are no laws stating that the prime minister and cabinet should come out of the majority party in Parliament; this is simply a tradition.
- **Commentaries** written by constitutional experts such as Walter Bagehot and Albert Venn Dicey (author in 1885 of *The Law of the Constitution*).

Where the U.S. Constitution spells out how government works and the U.S. Supreme Court has the power to interpret and build upon those rules, the rules of government in Britain are determined "on the basis of what has proved to work rather than on abstract first principles."[11] Supporters of this approach argue that the absence of a codified constitution allows for greater flexibility, but critics argue that there is too much potential for the abuse of powers by a strong prime minister. The result has been growing support for a written constitution, which is now favored by about 80 percent of Britons.

THE MONARCHY

Except for a brief spell between 1649 and 1660, when a republic was proclaimed, Britain since the tenth century has been a **monarchy**. This literally means "rule by one," but more specifically it means a system governed by someone who typically comes to that position by birth or heredity. British kings and queens once had a virtual

monarchy A political institution characterized by nobility, aristocracy, and heredity.

monopoly on political power but began giving it up with the Magna Carta, and the monarch is now little more than a ceremonial head of state, expected to be a neutral symbol of history, stability, tradition, and national identity. It is often said that the monarch reigns but does not rule. The present monarch—Queen Elizabeth II— is limited to the following so-called **reserve powers:**

- **Calling new elections.** She has the right to dissolve Parliament and call new elections, although in practice she does this only at the request of the prime minister.
- **The power of veto.** Just as presidents of the United States must sign all new congressional bills before they become law, the Queen gives the Royal Assent to every piece of new legislation. Theoretically, this gives her the same right of veto as an American president, but it is no more than a symbolic power; the last time a monarch vetoed a law was in 1707.[12]
- **Conferring with the prime minister.** She meets with the prime minister at confidential weekly meetings, during which she has the right "to be consulted, the right to encourage, and the right to warn."[13] She also has access to secret government documents.
- **Forming a government.** After an election is over, the prime minister must formally meet with the Queen to request her permission to form a government. If he has a solid majority, this is a formality. But if no one party has an absolute majority, the Queen steps in as an arbitrator, and—on the advice of the prime minister—can name the person she thinks is in the best position to be able to form a government. Queen Elizabeth has had to do this three times since she came to the throne in 1952.
- **Address to Parliament.** At the annual State Opening of Parliament (usually held in November), she gives an address in which she outlines the government's program (much like the State of the Union in the United States). However, the address is written by the government, and the Queen simply reads it aloud.
- **Symbol of the state.** Above all, the Queen is "a visible symbol of unity"[14] and the symbol of supreme executive authority. She is commander-in-chief, many public duties are carried out in her name, and British postage stamps, coins, and banknotes bear the Queen's image instead of the name of the country. As head of the Commonwealth (see section on Foreign Policy), the Queen also symbolizes Britain's relationship with its former colonies.

For centuries, the monarchy was imbued with an aura of mystery, and little was publicly known about its inner workings; in the words of the nineteenth-century constitutional authority Walter Bagehot, it was important not to "let in daylight upon magic." This has all changed in the last generation as the private lives of Prince Charles (heir to the throne), Prince Andrew, and their ex-wives and girlfriends have become the focus of intense media coverage. Prince Charles has also caused controversy by being more willing than previous heirs to comment on public issues such as the state of British architecture, education, and the environment.

As an individual, Queen Elizabeth is popular, but opinion polls show that public support for the monarchy has slipped since the mid-1980s from 85 to 90 percent to about 70 to 75 percent. The death of Princess Diana, former wife of Prince Charles, in August 1997, sparked a reappraisal aimed at making the monarchy more relevant to public life in Britain. The once unthinkable—that a divorced heir to the throne could become king—has been accepted; Prince Charles married his long-time friend Camilla Parker-Bowles (herself divorced) in April 2005, although the British public has been divided over whether or not they want to see Prince Charles succeed to the throne. One of the great strengths of the British monarchy—and the major reason it has lasted so long—is that it has been more adaptable than many of its continental European counterparts. The changes it now faces are just the latest in a long series of adjustments it has had to make to keep up with the times.

THE EXECUTIVE: PRIME MINISTER AND CABINET

The monarch may be Britain's head of state, but the head of government is the prime minister, who provides policy leadership and oversees the implementation of the law through a cabinet of senior ministers. By definition, the prime minister is the leader of the political party or coalition with the most seats in the lower chamber of parliament, the House of Commons. As long as they can keep the support of their party in Parliament, prime ministers have much power over deciding which laws will be passed and which policies adopted. In fact, within the scope of their jobs, they have more power than presidents of the United States, whose decisions are constantly checked and balanced.

As head of government, the prime minister sets the national political agenda, oversees the military, appoints ambassadors, manages crises, leads his or her party, and represents Britain overseas.[15] There are two foundations to the prime minister's authority:

- **The power to call elections to the House of Commons.** These must be held at least once every five years, and prime ministers will usually call them when the polls indicate that their party has the best chance of winning. More rarely, they may have to call an election because they have lost a parliamentary vote or the support of their party.

- **The power of appointment.** As well as being party leader, the prime minister decides on the size of the cabinet, calls and chairs cabinet meetings, appoints and removes members of the cabinet and other senior government officials (about 100 people in all), regularly reshuffles the cabinet (bringing in new members and either removing existing members or moving them to new posts), and can even reorganize government departments. By contrast, U.S. presidents need Senate approval for cabinet appointments and the reorganization of departments.

British prime ministers are normally seasoned national politicians who have worked their way up through the ranks of their party and Parliament. They must be members of the House of Commons and usually serve a long apprenticeship before winning the leadership of their parties; John Major and Tony Blair rose to the top relatively quickly, serving as members for 11 years and 14 years, respectively, before becoming prime ministers.

TABLE 2.2

Postwar Prime Ministers of Britain

Date	Prime minister	Governing party
July 1945	Clement Attlee	Labour
February 1950	Clement Attlee	Labour
October 1951	Winston Churchill	Conservative
May 1955	Anthony Eden	Conservative
January 1957*	Harold Macmillan	Conservative
October 1959	Harold Macmillan	Conservative
October 1963*	Alec Douglas-Home	Conservative
October 1964	Harold Wilson	Labour
March 1966	Harold Wilson	Labour
June 1970	Edward Heath	Conservative
February 1974	Harold Wilson	Labour
October 1974	Harold Wilson	Labour
April 1976*	James Callaghan	Labour
May 1979	Margaret Thatcher	Conservative
June 1983	Margaret Thatcher	Conservative
June 1987	Margaret Thatcher	Conservative
November 1990*	John Major	Conservative
April 1992	John Major	Conservative
May 1997	Tony Blair	Labour
June 2001	Tony Blair	Labour
May 2005	Tony Blair	Labour

*In these years, leadership of the governing party changed—through health, resignation, or loss of political support—without a general election being held.

cabinet A group of heads of government departments and senior administrators.

Prime ministers govern with the help of a **cabinet,** which, as in the United States, consists of all the heads of senior government departments (such as the foreign secretary and the defense secretary), numbering about 20 to 24 in all. In the United States, cabinet members cannot be members of Congress and cabinet experience is rarely a launch pad for a presidential bid. In Britain, by contrast, the cabinet is always appointed from within Parliament and is an essential testing ground for anyone with aspirations to becoming prime minister. Senior cabinet members become national figures, and reputations can be made and broken according to their performance in the cabinet.

While U.S. presidents rarely meet with their cabinets, the British cabinet meets frequently and is an important part of the policymaking structure of government: Between

PEOPLE IN POLITICS

TONY BLAIR

In almost every sense, Tony Blair has proved an unusual prime minister and an unusual leader of the Labour party. Born in Scotland in May 1953 of Scottish and Irish parents, he was raised in middle-class comfort in England, attending private schools and studying law at Oxford (where he had his own rock group—called Ugly Rumours—and apparently did a passable impression of Mick Jagger). He practiced as an attorney from 1976 to 1983, specializing in employment and industrial law. In 1980 he married another attorney, Cherie Booth.

Blair was elected to Parliament in 1983 as representative for Sedgefield in northern England, and was appointed to the shadow cabinet in 1988, holding first the energy portfolio and then the job of shadow home secretary (dealing with issues such as policing). In 1994—at the age of just 40—he was elected leader of the Labour Party and moved quickly to abandon some of its more left-wing policies and to bring it closer to the center of the political spectrum. In May 1997, he became the third-youngest prime minister in British history, the first prime minister born after World War II, and the first truly postimperial prime minister.

Exemplifying the potential powers of a strong prime minister, Blair used his 178-seat majority in the House of Commons to bring significant changes to the structure and character of British government. These included the creation of regional assemblies in Northern Ireland, Scotland, and Wales; proposals to change the electoral system; changes to the structure of the House of Lords; and discussions about a Bill of Rights that could not be overridden by Parliament. At the same time, he made greater use of the referendum as a means of putting major issues to a public vote.

Blair easily won reelection in June 2001, his majority reduced by just 12 seats. But there were signs of flagging enthusiasm for his leadership: voter turnout at the 2001 election was down from 71 percent to 59 percent, he drew criticism for continued problems with Britain's public services (notably health care, education, and transport), and he controversially supported President Bush's invasion of Iraq in 2003, flying in the face of majority opinion both among the British public and within his own party. But the Conservatives—who also supported the invasion—were unable to mount an effective opposition, and Blair won a third term in May 2005, although his majority was greatly reduced, and public enthusiasm for his leadership had tailed off. He said it would be his last election. Gordon Brown, Britain's finance minister (on the left in the picture), is widely expected to succeed Blair as Labour leader (and as prime minister).

© 2005 Getty Images

them, the prime minister and cabinet constitute **Her Majesty's Government.** Although prime ministers meeting in the cabinet are technically no more than "first among equals" (*primus inter pares*), their powers of appointment and agenda setting mean that loyalty to the leader is an essential prerequisite for cabinet members. The cabinet functions on the basis of **collective responsibility,** meaning that once it has made a policy decision, all members are expected to support that decision in public regardless of their personal feelings and to take responsibility for its success or failure. If the government loses an important vote in Parliament, or a vote of confidence, the whole cabinet is expected to resign.[16]

collective responsibility An understanding that all decisions made by a group are taken collectively.

The manner in which prime ministers govern depends on their different management styles.[17] Margaret Thatcher led from the front and was infamous for her forcefulness and for stretching the powers of her office almost to their limit. She appointed several weak ministers to the cabinet who could be easily controlled, she reduced the number of cabinet meetings, and she fired 12 ministers in 11 years. By contrast, John Major made more use of his cabinet, allowed a greater variety of opinion, emphasized collegiality and consensus, and intervened less in the affairs of departments.

Tony Blair has developed a reputation for imposing strong discipline on his party and his cabinet, driven by his agenda of changing its ideological tilt. He has delegated discretion to strong ministers prepared to follow the government line, emphasized collegiality in the cabinet, and worked to identify himself in the public mind with populist images, including his personal role in planning Britain's millennium celebrations and his invitations to 10 Downing Street—the London home of the prime minister—of celebrities involved in the arts. His desire to manage—and even to micromanage—has led to charges by his critics that he tries to control too much and that the office of prime minister has become more presidential.[18] How much of this is a function of his leadership style, and how much a function of his unpopularity in the wake of the invasion of Iraq, is debatable.

THE LEGISLATURE: PARLIAMENT

The British parliamentary model is one of Britain's most successful exports; in whole or in part it has been copied by every other liberal democracy, including the United States. Also known as the **Westminster model**—because the Houses of Parliament are situated in the district of Westminster in central London—it dates back more than 700 years. Parliament has three main functions: it is where laws are introduced, discussed, and either rejected or accepted; it is where existing laws are amended or abolished; and it is responsible for checking on government policy and debating major issues. It may seem powerful, but because a prime minister with a good majority can usually rely on the loyalty of party members, Parliament usually spends most of its time debating or confirming the program of the government and has much less power in relative terms than the U.S. Congress.

Westminster model The system of government associated with the British parliamentary model.

Parliament has two chambers with different structures and powers.

House of Lords

The so-called upper house, the Lords recalls the days when Britain was ruled by aristocrats. Members must be **peers,** which meant—until 1999—that they were either

© Jeremy Horner/CORBIS

The British Houses of Parliament, on the banks of the River Thames in London. After centuries of struggle with the monarchy, Parliament won supremacy following the English civil war. The British parliamentary model—in which executive and legislature are fused—has since been the basis of systems of government in many other countries.

hereditary or were appointed to the House for a life term as a reward for public service or political loyalty. Nearly 1,200 peers had the right to sit in the Lords, although only about 800 ever actually attended, and only about 300 were regular participants—members who attended received no salary, only expenses.

The pre-1999 Lords was not elected, so it was both unrepresentative and undemocratic, but it had little power. It could introduce its own legislation, and all bills going through Parliament had to be approved by the Lords, but its decisions could be overruled by the Commons and bills on taxation or spending did not need the approval of the Lords. However, it had more time to debate issues than the Commons, it often debated controversial issues, it could force concessions from the Commons, and it was a useful point of access for lobbyists.

While in opposition, the Labour Party had long threatened to abolish the House altogether once it came to power, but the Blair government took a more moderate position. After removing the rights of hereditary peers to sit in the House in 1999, Blair appointed a commission to decide what form the new chamber should take.

Proposals ranged from an all-appointed chamber to a fully elected chamber, but there was no political agreement on how to proceed, as a result of which the House of Lords today is in a state of limbo, with an unclear future. For now, at least, it has four kinds of members:

- **Hereditary peers.** A group of 92 has been allowed to stay on pending the next stage in the process of reform.
- **Religious leaders.** These consist of the two archbishops and 24 bishops of the Church of England. (This is an interesting concept for Americans raised on the idea of a separation of church and state.)
- **The law lords.** These are 12 nominated judges who function as the supreme court of appeal for civil and criminal cases (except in Scotland, which has its own legal system). They are headed by a Lord Chancellor and hold their positions until the age of 75.
- **Life peers.** Numbering about 600, these are mainly people who have been in public service and are rewarded with a life peerage by the Queen on the recommendation of the prime minister. All former prime ministers are usually offered a peerage, as are other people prominent in public life, such as actors, musicians, and entrepreneurs. Many life peerages are political rewards, where favors are returned, or where peerages are given to build party numbers in the Lords. (Knights—such as Sir Elton John and Sir Paul McCartney—are not members of the House of Lords.)

Except for the bishops, most members of the House of Lords belong to one of the major political parties (in 2005, there were 203 Conservative peers and 202 Labour peers), but a significant number will typically declare themselves as independents—they are known as "crossbenchers."

House of Commons

The House of Commons is the more powerful chamber of Parliament, and has five major roles: to represent, to make laws, to keep the prime minister accountable, to be a forum for national debate, and to act as a recruitment pool for members of government.[19] It consists of 646 **Members of Parliament** (MPs) elected by direct universal vote from single-member districts. Debates are presided over by a Speaker, who is elected by the House from among its members and usually comes from the majority party. Unlike Speakers in the U.S. House of Representatives, who act as the partisan leaders of their party, the British Speaker is more of an arbiter who keeps order and maintains the flow of business in the House.

To encourage debate, the chamber of the House has been kept small, with benches rather than seats (see Figure 2.1). The governing party sits on one side, with the prime minister and senior ministers on the front bench. MPs without government office, or with only junior office, sit behind the front bench and are known collectively as **backbenchers.** The next biggest party in Parliament sits across from the governing party and acts as the official opposition. Its leader sits directly opposite the prime minister, beside a shadow cabinet of opposition MPs responsible for keeping

Floor Plan of the House of Commons

1. Speaker
2. Clerks
3. Prime minister
4. Cabinet
5. Government party
   backbenchers

6. Leader of opposition
7. Shadow cabinet
8. Main opposition party backbenchers
9. MPs of other opposition parties

up with—and challenging—their counterparts on the government front bench. The **leader of the opposition** and the **shadow cabinet** are formally recognized and salaried positions. If the opposition wins a majority in an election and becomes the government, the leader of the opposition would normally become prime minister and many members of the shadow cabinet would become the real cabinet. In other words, the shadow cabinet is a government in waiting.

Anyone who has seen the Commons in action will wonder how it ever achieves anything. As the news weekly *The Economist* once put it, MPs "snigger and smirk. They sneer and jeer. They murmur and yawn. They gossip salaciously in the bars. They honk and cackle when the Prime Minister or his opposite number is trying to talk. They are like unruly schoolchildren, egged on by the frisson of a chance of being spanked by [the] Speaker but knowing they will usually get away with naughtiness." In fact, like the U.S. Congress, most of the real work of Parliament is done in committees, where specialists go over the details of bills and invite outside experts to give testimony. The chamber of the Commons is normally quiet, except during controversial debates or **Prime Minister's Question Time,** a half-hour session that is held every Wednesday afternoon during which MPs can ask the prime minister for information on government policy.

Party discipline is much tighter in the British system than in the U.S. Congress, because MPs are expected to vote with their parties. But rumbles of discontent are normal and party revolts have led to 7 of the 11 Conservative leaders since 1900 being unseated by a vote within their own party. This last happened in November 1990, when Margaret Thatcher lost the leadership of her party. Many in her party thought she could not win another election, so a challenge was mounted during the normally routine annual leadership election. She won, but not by a big enough margin to retain her credibility, so she resigned and was replaced as leader—and prime minister—by John Major. A breakdown of party cohesion—usually dubbed a "back-bench rebellion" if it is big enough—is normally interpreted as a sign of weakness and can lead to the fall of a government, the resignation of a prime minister, or even the calling of a new general election. Tony Blair lost his first ever parliamentary vote in November 2005, when many members of his own party voted against his proposal to allow the police to detain suspects in terrorist cases for up to 90 days without charge. Although Blair survived, his grip on power was clearly damaged.

THE JUDICIARY

It is ironic that Britain—home to John Locke (1632–1704), the political theorist whose ideas about a social contract and the separation of powers are at the core of the U.S. Constitution—has neither a written constitution nor a constitutional court. The U.S. Supreme Court has the power to interpret the U.S. Constitution (the power of judicial review), but Britain has no direct equivalent. Instead, judicial review is carried out in a complex system of courts topped by a Court of Appeal and the House of Lords, where law lords will hear final appeals in five-person benches. Appointments to the higher courts are made either by the Lord Chancellor (who is a member of the cabinet) or by the prime minister after consultation with the Lord Chancellor. Unlike the U.S. Supreme Court, whose work often grabs the headlines, and where appointments are politically charged, the work of the law lords very rarely makes the headlines in Britain.

One of the constitutional changes proposed by the Blair government was to create an independent British Supreme Court, which would become the highest court of appeal in the country, and would also rule on disputes about the authority of the British Parliament and the Scottish and Welsh regional assemblies. Appointments to the court were to have been made by the Secretary of State for Constitutional Affairs, from a short list drawn up by an independent commission. But the House of Lords blocked the proposal in March 2005.

The role of judicial review in the British system is changing with the growing powers of the **European Court of Justice.** One of the key institutions of the EU, the Luxembourg-based Court does not yet have a European constitution to interpret (a draft of one was agreed on in 2004, but was put on ice in 2005 after national votes in France and the Netherlands went against ratification), but it does have a series of treaties and a growing body of European law, whose primacy over national law is established. The European Court is slowly developing the same kind of relationship with the British government as the U.S. Supreme Court has with state governments, and it acts as the final court of appeal on matters of European law.

SUBNATIONAL GOVERNMENT

Federations like the United States and Canada have national and local levels of government with independent powers and distinct rights and responsibilities. Britain, by contrast, is a **unitary state,** where local government units have so little independent power that they can be reformed, restructured, or even abolished by the national government. However, changes made by the Blair administration are altering the balance of power between national and local government.

Scotland and Wales were given their own elected regional assemblies in 1998; the first elections for these were held in May 1999. Members of both are elected for fixed four-year terms and have a variety of powers over local issues such as education, health services, housing, transport, and policing. The 129-member Scottish Parliament also has limited tax-raising powers, but the 60-member National Assembly for Wales does not. The 108-member Northern Ireland Assembly has powers over local issues and also has two councils that address joint policymaking with Ireland and with the British Parliament. The creation of these regional assemblies has eaten into the idea of a unitary state, replacing it with something like a quasi-federal system.

England has no regional assembly but instead has a complex patchwork of unitary and two-tier local authorities, responsible for issues such as education, transport, housing, highways, local services, refuse disposal, and the police. Interestingly, London—which, with its surrounding suburbs, is home to about one-third of the British population—had no elected city government from 1986 to 2000. It had been governed by a Greater London Council, whose leader was the Labour politician Ken Livingstone, dubbed "Red Ken" by the tabloid media. He became a thorn in the flesh of the Thatcher government, so—illustrating the powers of national government over local bodies—she abolished the council in 1986. The Blair administration decided that a city the size of London needed its own government, so he created an elected 25-member Greater London Assembly, and—much to the chagrin of the Blair administration, which promoted its own "official" Labour candidate—Livingstone in May 2000 became London's first-ever directly elected mayor.

unitary state A state in which all significant power rests with the national government, and in which local units of government have little or no independent power.

 ELECTIONS AND PARTIES

As with all liberal democracies, Britain has many channels through which its citizens can take part in politics, express their opinions, and have their views reflected in government policy. These include regular elections, political parties representing multiple sets of positions across much of the ideological spectrum, a broad and active interest group community, and one of the most diverse and well-respected media establishments in the world. The options have increased in recent years as the number of elections and parties has grown, the electoral system has diversified, and the number of sources of political news has increased. Only about one in ten Britons has a sustained interest in politics, but most take some periodic, intensive interest in politics (usually in the lead-up to elections), and most are well informed about national and international politics.

THE ELECTORAL SYSTEM

As noted in Chapter 1, the United States is a large country with several levels of government, each with its own elections, each with its own system of primaries, and each with multiple elective offices. These factors combined mean that the United States has more, longer, and more expensive elections than any other liberal democracy. By contrast, Britain is a small country, has a unitary system of administration, offers its voters no primaries, and has relatively few elective offices. Hence the election process is simpler, cheaper, and quicker. Parties choose who will run in their name, elections for the executive and the legislature are combined, and no party has more than one leader. And because these leaders are normally established public figures, they do not need the expensive and lengthy process of public familiarization demanded of candidates in U.S. elections.

While Americans elect 500,000 officeholders at many different levels, British voters are faced with just three sets of elections.

The General Election

Members of the lower chamber of Parliament—the House of Commons—are chosen in the general election, which is run on roughly the same lines as elections to the U.S. House of Representatives. The UK is divided into 646 constituencies (electoral districts) of roughly equal population size, each represented in the House of Commons by a single Member of Parliament. At least once every five years, all 646 seats must be contested in a general election, on a date chosen by the prime minister. The prime minister must give at least 18 days' notice of the election (excluding weekends and public holidays). Almost everyone older than age 18 can vote, and turnout is normally about 70 to 75 percent, which is about average for Western Europe but considerably higher than the figures in the United States (50 to 55 percent in presidential election years and about 35 percent in midterm elections).

Election campaigns in the United States can last several months (even several years), but British general election campaigns normally last just three to four weeks, and voters make a straight choice among the candidates from the different parties standing in their district. The choices are made easier by the fact that parties have strong ideological consistency and there is stronger party identification among voters, who tend to vote more for parties than for individuals. The differences in emphasis are visible on campaign posters and bumper stickers—in Britain, the name of the party dominates, whereas in the United States, the name of the candidate dominates.

As with the U.S. House of Representatives, the British general election uses the winner-take-all system (sometimes also known as first-past-the-post), under which the winning candidates do not need a majority, but can win with a plurality—in other words, they simply need to win more votes than any other candidate. This system has been increasingly criticized in recent years because although it may be quick, cheap, and simple, it is not always fair. It tends to favor parties that have large blocks of concentrated support around the country but works against the interests of parties whose support is more thinly spread; the former tend to win seats, while the latter more often come in second or third. The effects of this were clear in the 2005 general election, when Labour won 35 percent of the vote but 55 percent of seats in the House of Commons. Meanwhile, the Conservatives won 32 percent of votes and 30 percent of seats (a slightly more equitable result), and the third-placed Liberal Democrats won 22 percent of the vote but just 10 percent of seats.

The Blair administration has talked about replacing the winner-take-all method with a form of **proportional representation (PR)** under which parties contesting elections would receive a number of seats in Parliament in proportion to their share of the vote. This system is commonly used elsewhere in Europe and is also used in combination with winner-take-all in Japan and Russia (see Chapters 3 and 4). British voters had their first taste of the system in 1998–1999 with elections to their new regional assemblies and to the European Parliament. The short-term prospects of it being adopted for the general election are slight, though, because of opposition from both the major political parties and a lack of public support.[20]

proportional representation An electoral system in which political parties win seats in proportion to their share of the vote.

European Elections

As a member of the EU, Britain has the right every five years to elect 78 representatives to the 732-member **European Parliament (EP)** in Strasbourg, France. Direct elections to the EP have been held only since 1979, and many British voters have mixed opinions about the EU, so turnout at European elections in Britain is among the lowest in the EU: After running at about 36 percent (far below even the modest EU average of about 55 percent), it fell to an all-time low of 23 percent in 1999, before climbing back up to 39 percent in 2004. These figures are also a reflection of the limited powers of the EP, which can neither introduce nor make the final decision on adopting new laws. Its powers are growing, however, and as they do, more voters may be encouraged to turn out.

Candidates are fielded by the same parties that contest general elections at home. At the 1994 elections, Labour won 63 of the British seats and the more Euroskeptical Conservatives won just 19. By contrast, the 1999 elections were a major blow for Labour, whose share of seats fell to 30; the Conservatives won 39 seats, and the balance was won by smaller parties, including the Greens. This turnaround was seen as a reflection of a shift throughout Europe to right-wing parties calling for a slowdown in European integration and as a critical comment by British voters on the EU. However, it was also affected by Britain's decision to adopt for the first time the same system of proportional representation used for EP elections in the other 14 EU member states. Instead of having 78 single-member districts and declaring the candidate in each district with the most votes the winner, Britain was divided into several much larger multimember districts, competing parties put forward lists of candidates, and the seats were divided up among the parties according to the proportion of the vote each received. At the 2004 elections, both Labour and the Conservatives lost seats, and fringe anti-EU parties made gains.

Local Government Elections

Because Britain is a unitary state and local authorities have limited power, most voters do not take part in local elections. Members are elected to district, county, city, and town councils on a fixed four-year cycle, but voters usually make their choices on the basis of national issues and the performance of the national government, they vote along party lines, and turnout is rarely better than 40 percent. However, the situation may change as the new regional assemblies get off the ground. Because the assemblies have power over a variety of local government issues, the stakes in the elections have been raised. Turnout at the first elections in 1998–1999 was not inspiring—58 percent in Scotland and 46 percent in Wales—but this may improve with time. Scottish and Welsh assembly elections are based on a combination of winner-take-all and PR, while regional and European elections in Northern Ireland use a variation of PR known as the single transferable vote (STV) (see Comparative Exercise, p. 223).

POLITICAL PARTIES

Britain has a wide range of political parties, covering many ideological positions. Most have strong internal organization, and voters tend to be loyal to parties, using them to provide the reference points for their political opinions and for the choices they make at elections. But although several dozen parties contested the 2005 general election and 9 won seats in Parliament, Britain since World War II has been a two-party system dominated by Labour and the Conservatives. Between them, these two parties usually take about 70 to 75 percent of the vote and about 85 to 90 percent of the seats in Parliament (see Figure 2.2). However, this may change as the use of proportional representation in local and European elections allows smaller parties to win seats, build experience, and establish a stronger national reputation.

FIGURE 2.2

Legislative Electoral Trends in Britain

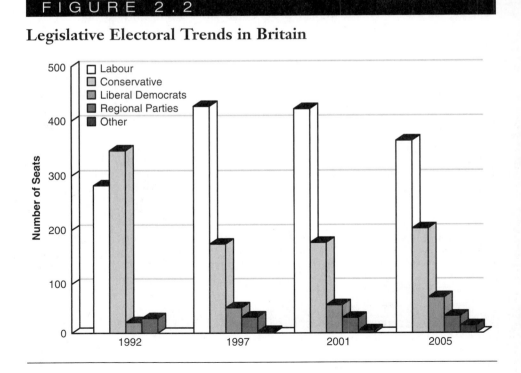

Labour

The **Labour Party** was founded in 1900 and first came to prominence in the 1920s but only won outright power for the first time in 1945. It immediately set about building a welfare state and a managed economy, nationalizing key industries, and creating the National Health Service, a social security system, and a subsidized education system. It lost power in 1951 but returned in 1964 and again in 1974 under the leadership of Harold Wilson. Labour went into opposition in 1979, losing four straight general elections and undergoing a crisis of confidence before finally regaining power in 1997 under the leadership of Tony Blair.

The Labour Party's failures in the 1980s were blamed on a combination of the political shrewdness of Conservative prime minister Margaret Thatcher, a string of "unelectable" party leaders, and the growing unpopularity of many of its more traditional socialist policies, including state ownership of key industries, support of labor unions, and redistributing wealth through taxation. The extent of its internal problems was emphasized in 1981 when a group of moderate Labourites broke away to form the Social Democratic Party (SDP). This merged with the Liberal Party in 1988 after helping to encourage Labour to rethink and moderate its policies. The shift in Labour's philosophy was symbolized by its decision to replace its red flag symbol with a red rose, which sent a much less militant and threatening message to voters.

Tony Blair was elected party leader in May 1994 and made it clear that he opposed business as usual. He moved quickly to "modernize" the party and to distance it from its more radical ideas by adopting what he called a new "left-of-center agenda." One of his first priorities was to abandon the controversial Clause Four of the Labour Party constitution, which pledged "common ownership of the means of production, distribution and exchange"; in other words, Labour gave up its promise to undo privatization, one of the most successful of Margaret Thatcher's policies. Clause Four was abandoned in 1996, and since then Labour has stood for more overtly free-market economic policies of the kind associated with the **third way** in politics. A concept that has never been clearly defined, it is usually described as a philosophy that lies somewhere between the kind of right-wing conservatism and capitalism associated with the Reagan and Thatcher governments and the left-wing liberalism and economic management associated with socialist parties in Western Europe. It has also been described as "capitalism with a conscience" or "market socialism."[21]

The Labour victory in May 1997 was astonishing in almost every sense. Labour was swept back into office with a 179-seat majority, while Conservative representation in the Commons was halved, the party lost all its seats in Scotland and Wales, and even senior members of the cabinet (including several future contenders for the leadership of the party) lost their seats. Debates have since raged about the reasons behind the Labour victory and the Conservative defeat.[22] Britain at the time had rates of unemployment and inflation that were among the lowest in Europe (6 percent and 3 percent, respectively). The Conservatives were also the party of Margaret Thatcher, whose policies of privatization and undermining the powers of labor unions had been popular and effective. However, the turnaround symbolized a yearning among Britons for change and a concern that Conservatives had paid too little attention to social problems. There was also clearly some tactical voting in the election, with

Labour and Liberal Democratic supporters voting for the other party in districts where one of them was in a strong position to challenge the incumbent Conservative.[23] Finally, a new generation of young people who had known nothing but Conservative government was voting for the first time; 52 percent of under-25-year-olds voted Labour, up from 35 percent in 1992. Many analysts also argued that the vote was ultimately less for Labour than against the Conservatives.

Voters were not quite so complimentary to Labour in the 2001 election. Blair was given a second term in office with his majority barely changed, but voter turnout was just 59 percent, one of the lowest levels ever. This was interpreted as criticism of the Blair administration for the continuing problems in Britain's public services and as a lack of enthusiasm for the opposition Conservative Party, which was deeply divided on key issues. Blair was returned to a third term in office in 2005, his majority down to just 62 seats. This was still a significant margin of victory, and it marked the first time in its history that Labour had won a third successive election. But his margin of victory was the lowest for a party in the modern era, and enthusiasm for Tony Blair had clearly lost its luster, thanks in large part to his decision to support the 2003 invasion of Iraq. Blair entered his third term somewhat humbled, and aware that he would not be able to complete his program of change without working more closely with others.

The Conservatives

The origins of the **Conservative Party** (also known as the Tories) date back to the late seventeenth century. They have held power for 36 of the 58 years since the end of World War II but, despite the number of their postwar election victories, have never won more than 42 to 44 percent of the national vote and fell to a new low of 30 to 32 percent in the 1997, 2001, and 2005 elections.

Much like U.S. Republicans, the Conservatives are a probusiness, antiregulation political party, with many shades of opinion: Right-wingers in the party emphasize social discipline, authority, continuity, and morals, while moderates emphasize the creation of wealth and efficient economic organization. Until 1975, when Margaret Thatcher became party leader, Conservative policies changed little, irrespective of the leader. Thatcher broke with tradition, and for more than a decade the party developed policies that reflected her values. She supported monetarist economic ideas of the kind favored by Ronald Reagan, such as controls on government spending, reducing the role of government in the marketplace, low taxation, and a free market. She also promoted private enterprise and private ownership, believed in a strong global role for Britain and close Anglo-American relations, and was hostile to many aspects of European integration.

Although the Conservatives fought the 1997 election against the background of a strong economy, they faced an electorate that was tired of internal party squabbles; the party had become particularly divided over the issue of Europe, with some of its members arguing in favor of greater support for European integration and some arguing that the process of integration had already gone too far. The Conservatives had also been hurt by a number of financial scandals involving prominent backbenchers (which became known as the "sleaze" factor). John Major was unable to pull the party together, it went into the election 20 percentage points behind Labour in opinion polls, and it sustained its worst election defeat in more than 160 years.

Following his defeat, John Major gracefully resigned the party leadership (although he stayed on as an MP) and was replaced by William Hague, who faced the difficult task of uniting the Conservatives and making them a true party of opposition. The task proved a hard one, however, given the popularity of Tony Blair and the Labour government. By 1999, the Conservatives were in a state of crisis, and Hague was unable to unite the party, or to capitalize on public concerns about the state of health care and education. The net number of Conservative seats increased by just one at the 2001 election, encouraging Hague to step down as party leader. Instead of picking a moderate who might have been able to unite the party, the Conservatives chose the right-wing and almost unknown Iain Duncan Smith, who was able to do little to improve party fortunes. He quickly fell by the wayside, being replaced in 2003 by Michael Howard. In the wake of the 2005 election defeat, Howard stepped down and was replaced by the young and untested David Cameron. Whether he is able to turn the party around and to pull it out of the rut into which it has fallen remains to be seen.

Liberal Democrats

A small, moderate center party, the Liberal Democratic Party was created in 1988 when members of a Labour splinter group (the Social Democratic Party, or SDP) joined forces with the Liberal Party, one of the oldest parties in Britain and for many years the major opposition to the Conservatives. The last Liberal prime minister (David Lloyd George) left office in 1922, and Liberal support declined dramatically. For a while in the 1980s, however, an SDP-Liberal Alliance seemed poised to take over from Labour as the major opposition party. The renamed Liberal Democrats contested their first general election in April 1992, winning nearly 18 percent of the vote but only 20 seats. In the 1997 election they more than doubled their representation in Parliament, winning 46 seats, the best result for a third party since the 1920s. They added six more seats in 2001, and ten more in 2005. Although still very small, new attention has been paid to them by political analysts. They have been led since 1999 by Charles Kennedy (b. 1959).

Other Parties

There are many other small parties in Britain, most of which represent regional interests. The Scottish National Party campaigns for devolution for Scotland and has undergone a revival in recent years, winning 27 percent of the seats in the Scottish Parliament in 1999. Its then-leader, Alex Salmond, went so far in September 1999 as to predict that Scotland would be completely independent before 2007, the 300th anniversary of the union of England and Scotland. Meanwhile, its Welsh counterpart, Plaid Cymru, won 28 percent of the seats in the Welsh assembly. Both also have a few seats in the House of Commons. There are also nearly a dozen parties that are active only in Northern Ireland; the biggest are the Ulster Unionists, who represent continued union for Northern Ireland with Britain, while the smaller Sinn Fein has campaigned in the past for the reunification of Ireland.

While candidates for the larger parties must go through a rigorous selection procedure, British law allows almost anyone to stand for Parliament under almost any guise, even from prison. The only formal requirement is the payment of a deposit of £500 (about $900), which is returned if the candidate wins more than 5 percent of the vote. Candidates who fail to cross the 5 percent barrier are described as having lost their deposit, the most galling possible result in an election.

POLICIES AND POLICYMAKING

As in most liberal democracies, public policies in Britain are made, implemented, and evaluated through a complex process involving many different actors: The public arena, Parliament, parties, the cabinet, the bureaucracy, the media, and interest groups. While postwar governments had a tendency to bargain, compromise, and build consensus—resulting in incremental rather than radical change—the changes introduced by the Thatcher and Blair governments have taken policy in Britain in some surprising and notably different new directions.

Britain is technically a constitutional monarchy, but because monarchs have lost all but their symbolic power, control over decision making rests with the government (the prime minister and the cabinet). The government works closely with senior bureaucrats and is accountable to Parliament, which alone has the power to make, amend, and abolish laws, at least in areas where authority has not been transferred to the EU and regional assemblies. Because a solid government majority means that Parliament usually does little more than confirm most government decisions, Parliament's main value is that it provides a point of access for citizens and interest groups, and parliamentary debates and questions help keep the government accountable.

Bureaucrats play an important and often unseen role in government, helped as they are by several advantages over government: They hold long-term appointments, compared with the high turnover among ministers; they have access to the papers of previous ministers, which new ministers do not; and they are powerful traffic police, overseeing the flow of information from ministers to departments and vice versa. Bureaucrats are also closely involved in the development of proposals for new laws, and in negotiations over new policies and regulations.

Outside government, the most important influence on policymaking in Britain is the interplay between public opinion, the media, and interest groups. Prime ministers constantly look at their standing in the polls, calculating the popularity of their decisions and the chances for their parties in the next election. U.S. presidents can shield themselves to some extent from public criticism by exploiting the aura surrounding their office and using checks and balances to spread the blame for failed policies and claim credit for successful policies. By contrast, the unitary structure of Britain means that the prime minister and cabinet are held more directly accountable, so much of what they can and cannot do is tied to their standing in the polls and to their relationship with their party. This was never more clear than when Tony Blair campaigned for reelection in early 2005 against a background of criticism for his support of the war in Iraq.

ECONOMIC POLICY

There have been dramatic changes in the direction of British economic policy since World War II, as the country first had to adjust to its reduced position in the global system, and then had to adjust to the impact of a massive program of postwar government planning. Under the postwar consensus, the Conservatives and Labour agreed that—whichever was in power—they would work to maintain welfare, full employment, a mix of private and public ownership, and the traditional features of the constitution and would agree on policies through compromise involving discussions between government and interest groups, particularly labor unions. Although this approach brought prosperity to Britain in the 1950s, the economy by the 1960s was not growing as quickly as those of Germany, Japan, or the United States. Conservatives pointed the finger of blame at "creeping socialism," leading to a **British disease** consisting of three main features:

- **The growing costs of welfare,** which demanded higher taxes and reduced the incentives for entrepreneurs to invest or for workers to improve their productivity. At one time, the wealthiest Britons were subject to a so-called supertax of 95 percent of their earnings, and many became tax exiles as a result.
- **The power of labor unions,** which intimidated the government by calling frequent strikes and demanding higher wages for reduced working hours. By the 1970s, some of the best-known figures in national politics were union leaders.
- **A large public sector.** The postwar Labour program of nationalization had resulted in the government taking over large sectors of the economy, including airlines; railroads; and the coal, natural gas, iron, steel, and electricity supply industries. Critics argued that public ownership created inefficient monopolies, leading to reduced quality, inadequate investment, and stagnation.

Liberals questioned the role of creeping socialism. If welfare was to blame, they asked, why did other countries with extensive welfare and high tax rates (such as France and Sweden) not have similar problems? Their explanations for Britain's problems focused less on workers and more on management, which they blamed for failing to compete in the new global market and for failing to invest in new machinery and technology. Allied to this, the class system ensured that entrepreneurial activity and the creation of "new" money were sniffed at by many of those with "old" money, and managers failed to communicate with their workers. Confrontation became more common than cooperation in relations between managers and workers, leading to bitterness, low productivity, and a sense of "us versus them."

Whatever the causes, Britain had seen 10 to 15 years of relative economic decline by 1975. In that year, Margaret Thatcher became leader of the Conservative Party. Accepting most of the standard conservative explanations of the British disease, she argued that major changes were needed if Britain's problems were to be effectively addressed. After winning office in 1979, she pursued several key economic policies.

The rapidly changing skyline of London's financial area, showing a mix of the old and the new. London plays a role in the national and international economy unmatched by the capital city of any other country. Some are concerned that the importance of London as a global financial center may be compromised if Britain continues to stay out of the euro zone.

First, she set about reducing the power of labor unions, refusing to stand down in the face of strikes and union demands. The confrontation peaked in 1984–1985, when the National Union of Mineworkers (NUM) threatened to bring down the Thatcher government by stopping the supply of coal and the generation of electricity. Thatcher had anticipated the confrontation and had given the National Coal Board incentives to produce more coal, thereby building coal stocks. During the strike itself, a breakaway union kept producing coal, so Thatcher was in a position to ignore the demands of the NUM (which she described as "the enemy within"[24]). The strike collapsed, helping bring an end to the era of strong labor unions.

Second, the Thatcher administration lowered taxes. The top rate of income tax was reduced from 83 percent to 40 percent, and the basic rate fixed at 35 percent, the goal being to encourage small entrepreneurs and more private investment. Many new businesses were started, and although many failed, there was an average net increase of new firms, the number of self-employed people grew from 7 percent of the labor force to 11 percent, there was a rise in British overseas investment, and the number of private shareholders tripled between 1979 and 1989.[25]

CRITICAL ISSUES

IMPROVING THE QUALITY OF LIFE

Like all liberal democracies, Britain is a **welfare state,** or one in which government makes provision under the law for those in need, particularly the elderly, sick, poor, disabled, and indigent. Elements of a welfare system have been in place since the sixteenth century, but the foundations of the current system were laid in 1906 with the creation of state schools and the provision of state pensions, free school meals for children, and unemployment benefits. After World War II, a social security system was created to help the unemployed, widows, and the retired, and a National Health Service was founded that provides mainly free medical services to anyone not already covered by other programs.

The social security system is now the biggest item on the national government budget, accounting for about 28 percent of government spending. The second biggest item (15 percent of spending) is the National Health Service (NHS), which—with a total workforce of about one million people—is the single biggest employer in Western Europe. Public opinion on the NHS is divided. Few question the principle of universal free medical care and there is much pride in the concept of the NHS, but there have been complaints about poor standards, low pay and long hours for doctors and nurses, the amount of time it sometimes takes for a patient to see a doctor, and the waiting time in accident and emergency departments in hospitals.

Most critics have argued that the best response is to spend more money, and the Blair administration has responded accordingly: Spending on the NHS increased at an annual rate of 6.4 percent in 1999–2004. Other critics argue that the shortfall of staff is the real problem. Some of the methods used to address this issue—such as launching overseas recruitment drives for doctors and nurses or sending patients to other European countries for treatment—have created their own controversies.

Despite its problems, the effects of health care have improved life significantly in Britain: Life expectancy is now 75 years for men and nearly 80 years for women, putting Britain above countries that spend more on health care, such as Germany and the United States. Meanwhile, death rates from cancer and coronary heart disease have fallen, and the number of people smoking has been nearly halved since the mid-1970s. Unfortunately, the trends in two other areas are negative: Britain has the worst drug problem in Western Europe, with nearly five deaths per 100,000 people in 1999, compared with about two in Italy and Germany, and less than one in France; and Britain is seeing rising numbers of people who are overweight or obese. In 1980, just 7 percent of Britons were classified as obese, but today the number is more than 20 percent.

Third, Thatcher sold off publicly owned companies—so successfully that this policy of privatization was copied in many other countries. Between 1979 and 1989, 40 percent of previously state-owned industries were sold to the private sector, including British Aerospace, Jaguar, British Airways, and Rolls Royce. Profits and productivity in many of these companies improved, but whether as a result of privatization or of a general improvement in the management methods of British industry is unclear.[26] Among the most notable of the privatizations was the sale to their occupants of public housing, greatly expanding private home ownership and improving the quality of housing stock.

welfare state A state that provides through law for people in need, such as the poor, the elderly, and the handicapped.

Finally, Thatcher encouraged competition. By reducing government subsidies, her administration tried to make basic services more competitive, efficient, and self-supporting. It tried, for example, to encourage universities to rely less on subsidies and to raise funds for themselves. Thatcher also tried to encourage the growth of the private health industry to help make public health care more efficient.

Did Thatcherism address Britain's economic problems? The answer depends on whom you ask. Her supporters argued that she freed Britain from big government and powerful unions and restored an entrepreneurial spirit. However, her critics noted that the poor remained relatively poor, the economic rift between the Britain's prosperous south and the industrial north persisted, and the number of homeless people increased. Cuts in public spending led to a decrease in the quality of many public services, including education and health care. The high school dropout rate grew, the quality of secondary education declined, and the reduction of university subsidies led to fewer places for students and faculty.

Overall, though, there is little doubt that there has been an aggregate improvement both in British economic health and in the attitudes of business toward customers. The relative decline has been halted, and since the mid-1990s Britain has had one of the fastest-growing economies in the EU; it overtook both Italy and France, and today stands as the fourth biggest economy in the world after the United States, Japan, and Germany. Building and road construction have expanded, there are more private homeowners and shareholders, and the number of luxury cars on the roads has increased. Class distinctions have declined as the middle class has grown, and competition has helped improve the choices available to consumers and the quality of service provided by retailers. By 2005, the unemployment rate was one of the lowest in Europe (4.7 percent), the inflation rate was a healthy 1.9 percent, and GDP was growing faster than that of France, Germany, or Japan. As one observer put it in late 2002, "For more than a decade now there has been something seriously right with the British economy."[27]

The free-market philosophy has been so enthusiastically rediscovered that when Tony Blair became leader of the Labour Party in 1994 he set about "modernizing" the party and committing it to the maintenance of some of the more popular aspects of Thatcherism, most notably privatization. Indeed, many of the elements of the Labour manifesto as it went into the 1997 election sounded more conservative than socialist. They included a balanced budget, independence for the Bank of England, efforts to reduce welfare dependency, promotion of the work ethic, close ties to business, and a rejection of special deals for labor unions. At the same time, however, the Blair government emphasized the need to deal with the problems of the underclass and to pay greater attention to improving education and health care.

Although substantial changes have come to the priorities of domestic economic policy in the last 20 years, the biggest overall influence on that policy today is the EU. Britain now does about 55 percent of its trade with its EU partners, compared with about 15 percent with the United States and 3 percent with Japan. There has also been a substantial flow of foreign investment into Britain, most coming from other EU states, but much also coming from the United States and Southeast Asian corporations that see Britain as a useful base from which to make inroads into the European market.

One of the most troubling issues facing the Blair government today is whether Britain should take part in the single European currency, the **euro.** Thanks in part to the rising U.S. budget and trade deficits, confidence in the U.S. dollar has fallen in recent years, and the euro seems to be on its way to fulfilling the hopes of many Europeans that it will compete with the U.S. dollar as the most influential unit of international exchange. But the idea of a single currency has been controversial in Britain, which was not among the 12 countries that adopted the euro in 2002. The Blair government launched a program in 1999 aimed at promoting greater awareness of the benefits of joining and promised to put the idea to a national referendum following the 2001 general election, but public opinion against the euro hardened in 2002–2003, encouraged by the growing strength of the pound and economic problems in continental Europe. There was still no sign of a referendum on the horizon as this book went to press.

FOREIGN POLICY

As the world's policeman and major imperial power during the eighteenth, nineteenth, and early twentieth centuries, Britain once traded with almost every part of the world, had its troops stationed on every continent, and had a navy that controlled the world's oceans. It is now only a middle-ranking economic and military power, but it is still a significant actor in world affairs: It is one of the five countries with veto powers on the UN Security Council, it is a member of the G-8 group of industrialized countries, it is a nuclear power, and it still has a significant (and efficient) military. However, Britain's aspirations are more modest than they once were, and it has narrowed its foreign policy interests to focus today on three main arenas: the EU, its relationship with NATO and the United States, and its role in the Commonwealth.

Britain and the European Union

When Europeans began building ties of economic cooperation among themselves in the 1950s and 1960s, they concentrated on reducing the barriers to trade and on building a common European market, with free movement of money, goods, services, and people. European integration has since broadened and deepened significantly. There are now very few remaining barriers to internal trade, and EU residents can live and work in any of the 25 member states (citizens can even vote in local elections in some of them). Intra-European investment and corporate mergers have grown, and internal transport networks are expanding. The European flag—a circle of twelve gold stars on a blue background—is an increasingly common sight throughout the EU; the member states have brought domestic laws into line with European law; and the EU has a growing network of administrative and lawmaking bodies, headquartered mainly in Brussels and Luxembourg.

The British have always been reluctant Europeans, but since joining the European Economic Community—precursor to the EU—in 1973 they have had to rethink their attitudes toward their neighbors. British economic dependence on the EU was forcefully illustrated in 1996 by a crisis surrounding suspicions that a disease afflicting British cattle (bovine spongiform encephalopathy, or mad cow disease) could be spread to humans. Britain's EU partners boycotted British meat and insisted on drastic remedial action, leading to a political standoff that took several years to resolve.

Some Britons remain hostile to what they see as the federalist tendencies of the EU, but increasing numbers (particularly professionals and those in their 20s and 30s) are now arguing the benefits of membership. Ironically, Britain has one of the best records in the Union on changing its national law to fit with EU law on issues as diverse as trade, agriculture, the environment, public health, transportation, and employment. Perhaps nothing better symbolized Britain's new ties to its neighbors than the completion in 1994—after many false starts—of a rail tunnel under the Channel between England and France. Despite its financial troubles, the tunnel is a key element in the high-speed rail network that is slowly linking all the major cities and regions of the EU.

One area in which the EU has made only mixed progress has been the development of a common foreign and security policy. Backed by the vast size of the European market—which now accounts for 28 percent of global GNP—the 25 member states have largely worked as one on global trade issues, and have agreed on a large number of common positions on foreign policy. But they lack the political unity to work together on security and defense issues. Several member states (such as Finland and Ireland) are neutral, Germany is not allowed by international law to commit its troops outside the NATO area, and the two major military powers—Britain and France—often have different policy priorities. Britain is a supporter of the NATO alliance and U.S. leadership, but Germany and France tend toward a more independent European position on security issues. The divisions became particularly clear in 2002–2003, when the governments of Britain, Spain, and Italy supported plans by the Bush administration to attack Iraq while France and Germany were both actively opposed.

Many hurdles still must be crossed before the EU has a common foreign policy, but widespread public hostility to the policies of the Bush administration has helped; public opinion polls have recently found large majorities of Europeans in favor of Europe building policies that are independent of those of the United States, and there are growing signs that Europe is flexing its economic muscle to exert political power on the world stage (see Close-Up View, page 118).

The Atlantic Alliance

Along with Canada, the United States, and most other Western European countries, Britain has been committed since 1949 to the common defense policies of the North Atlantic Treaty Organization (NATO). NATO was founded to counterbalance the threats posed by the Soviet Union, and Britain subsequently relied heavily on U.S. missiles and personnel to back up its own defenses. Britain has been an active participant in NATO activities; for example, it took a leading role in Operation Allied Force, the NATO attack on Serbia in March–April 1999 that came in response to the ethnic cleansing visited on the predominantly Albanian province of Kosovo. Tony Blair became one of the most vocal spokesmen in favor of the attack, and Britain committed air, sea, and ground forces to the operation. With the end of hostilities, the British military played a dominating role in reconstruction, making up one-third of the peacekeeping force sent in to Kosovo. With the cold war long over, however, questions are now being asked about NATO's role in the world, about the U.S. role in European defense, and about Britain's own defense priorities.

Britain and the United States have long had a **special relationship,** which the United States has often used as a conduit for its relations with the rest of Western Europe. The relationship was closest during the Roosevelt-Churchill years and again during the Reagan-Thatcher years, cooled during the first Clinton administration, but then warmed with the election of Tony Blair. Although Britain joined most (but certainly not all) of its EU partners in the U.S.-led coalition against Iraq following its invasion of Kuwait in 1990, it was alone in providing political and military support for U.S. efforts to pressure Iraq into removing obstacles to UN arms inspectors in 1998. Britain also split with its EU partners in 2002–2003 when it backed the United States in building up pressure on Iraq to come clean on its stocks of weapons of mass destruction. In March–April 2003, nearly one-quarter of all Britain's military personnel fought alongside U.S. troops in the attack on Iraq. While the French in particular are wary of U.S. influence in European foreign and security policy, Britain has long been a supporter of **Atlanticism,** promoting the idea of working with the United States and encouraging the United States to maintain a military presence in Europe.

Britain and the Commonwealth

The third—and least politically important—of the arenas of British foreign policy is the **Commonwealth.** An outgrowth of the British Empire, and known until 1949 as the British Commonwealth, this is an organization that consists of 54 countries, most of which were once British colonies and dominions. Members include Australia, Canada, New Zealand, many Caribbean states, India, Nigeria, and most eastern and southern African countries (such as Kenya, South Africa, and Zambia). Based originally around white dominions such as Australia and Canada, the Commonwealth grew and became increasingly multiracial in the 1950s and 1960s as Britain's former colonies won their independence. It now includes 27 percent of the world's population and has even brought in countries that were not British colonies: Namibia joined in 1990 and Mozambique in 1995.

Less a political alliance than an economic and cultural alliance, the Commonwealth remains a significant commitment for Britain, not least because the Queen is head of the Commonwealth and *de jure* head of state in 14 Commonwealth countries (including Australia, Canada, and several Caribbean states such as Grenada and Jamaica, where the Queen is represented by a governor-general). The wealthier Commonwealth countries have provided economic assistance to poorer members, and the ties offered by the Commonwealth have proved useful as a means of promoting diplomatic relations among the members. The Commonwealth has also occasionally taken on a more overtly political role, as when South Africa was expelled in 1961 because of its policies of apartheid (it rejoined in 1994), and when Nigeria was suspended in 1994 and Zimbabwe in 2002 because of the authoritarian policies of their governments.

The Commonwealth today has a mainly cultural role, thanks in part to its use of English as the sole official language. Among its political and economic objectives are the promotion of democracy, good government, human rights, the rule of law, and sustainable economic development and the development of regional investment funds to promote trade across and within the Commonwealth.

CLOSE-UP VIEW

EUROPE: THE NEW SUPERPOWER

Britain is a member of the European Union (EU), an organization that began life in the 1950s as an attempt to develop a common European market and promote economic cooperation among Western European states. It has since taken on many of the features of a new level of government, moving toward the development of a federal Europe. Britain refused to join at the outset, convinced that its future lay outside Europe, but quickly began to realize that there were strong reasons for participating. It eventually joined in 1973, and since then EU membership has redefined Britain's relationship with the rest of Europe and redefined Britain's place in the world.

Several European institutions have been created, including a European Commission responsible for proposing and implementing European laws, a directly elected European Parliament, and a European Court of Justice. A major development took place in early 2002, when 12 member states (excluding Britain) gave up their national currencies and replaced them with a new European currency, the euro. In May 2004, ten new mainly Eastern European members joined, moving the EU into the territory of the former Soviet Union, expanding membership to 25 countries, and bringing the total population to 453 million. The effect of this has been to create a new economic superpower that poses strong competition to the United States. The economy of the EU is bigger than that of the United States, and the EU accounts for more than one-third of global merchandise trade (three times as much as the United States). It has also become the biggest mergers and acquisitions market in the world, helping European corporations move up the list of the world's biggest.[28]

Although the EU has no plans to compete with the military power of the United States, its evolution has raised questions in the minds of many about claims that the United States is the world's lone remaining superpower. That may be true if power is measured only in military terms, but if the idea of power is expanded to include economic and political influence, then the European Union has joined the superpower club. This is not just a factor of the size and reach of Europe, but also of the growing unpopularity of U.S. policy around the world. The 2003 invasion of Iraq, for example, may have been supported by the governments of Britain, Italy, Spain, Poland, and other European countries, but opinion polls found between 70 and 90 percent of Europeans opposed the war. No longer so obviously needing the U.S. security shield that was so important during the cold war, and gaining new confidence as its economy grows, Europe is becoming more assertive in its opposition to U.S. policy. As both a member of the European Union and a close ally of the United States, Britain today finds itself in a difficult situation.[29]

BRITISH POLITICS IN TRANSITION

Britain is distinguished from almost every other country in the world by its long and evolutionary history of political development. Relative peace and prosperity allowed it to build enduring political institutions and to be home to many influential political and economic thinkers. Stability also provided the foundations for an industrial revolution and for the creation of a huge empire.

However, the contribution of two world wars; the end of empire; and the rise of the United States, Japan, and Germany as economic powers forced Britain to

undergo a process of political and economic change that has not yet ended. It began
by restructuring its economy, building a welfare system, and rethinking both its military role in the world and its attitude toward its European neighbors. Changes of
this magnitude inevitably lead to introspection, but after a long period of pessimism
there are signs that Britain's political and economic readjustment has begun to develop some long-term stability.

In economic terms, the most significant change has come out of a redefinition of
public and political attitudes toward the role of the state. Institutionalized dependency has been replaced by the idea that individuals must take more responsibility for

their own opportunities. Membership in the EU has brought many changes, but the most significant changes that have come recently have been constitutional. The monarchy is reforming itself in light of demands that it become more relevant, power is being devolved to the regions in response to demands for greater self-determination, and a reappraisal of the structure of government is underway as the Blair administration considers reform of the electoral system and of the House of Lords.

KEY TERMS

Atlanticism
backbenchers
British disease
British Empire
cabinet
collective responsibility
Commonwealth
consensus
Conservative Party
devolution
euro
European Court of
  Justice
European Parliament
(EP)
European Union
general election

head of government
head of state
Her Majesty's
  Government
Industrial Revolution
Labour Party
law lords
leader of the opposition
Magna Carta
Member of Parliament
  (MP)
monarchy
Parliament
peers
prime minister
Prime Minister's
  Question Time

privatization
proportional
  representation (PR)
regional assemblies
reserve powers
shadow cabinet
special relationship
stakeholder culture
Thatcherism
third way
unitary state
welfare state
Westminster model

KEY PEOPLE

Tony Blair
Winston Churchill

Margaret Thatcher
Queen Elizabeth II

David Cameron

STUDY QUESTIONS

1. How have the different historical experiences of the United States and Britain impacted their respective political systems?

2. What are the main differences between the American presidential model and the British parliamentary model of government?

3. Who has the more realistic expectations of government: Americans or Britons?

4. Is a written constitution necessary?

5. What are the advantages and disadvantages of having a monarchy?

6. Would a President's Question Time be a useful addition to the way the United States is governed? What difference might it make?

7. With the creation of regional assemblies in Britain, is there a case for replacing the House of Lords with a chamber more like the U.S. Senate?

8. What are the advantages and disadvantages of the flexible election calendar of Britain and the fixed-term system used in the United States?

9. What are the costs and benefits of having an identifiable opposition party and leader?

10. What are the implications of a united Europe for the global role of the United States?

BRITAIN ONLINE

10 Downing Street: www.pm.gov.uk
Houses of Parliament: www.parliament.uk
Official home pages for the office of the prime minister, the House of Commons, and the House of Lords, with links to other useful sources of information.
British Monarchy: www.royal.gov.uk
Web site for the monarchy, with news and information on activities of the Royal Family.
BBC News: http://news.bbc.co.uk
Electronic Telegraph: www.telegraph.co.uk
Times (of London): www.timesonline.co.uk
Some of the best Web sites for news on politics in Britain. The BBC is also an excellent source of international news.
Europa: http://europa.eu.int
Official Web site of the European Union.

FURTHER READING

Clarke, Peter, *Hope and Glory: Britain 1900–1990* (London: Penguin, 1996). A good general history of Britain during the twentieth century.

Coxall, Bill, Lynton Robins, and Robert Leach, *Contemporary British Politics*, 4th Ed. (Basingstoke: Palgrave Macmillan, 2003); Dunleavy, Patrick, Andrew Gamble, and Richard Heffernan Peele (Eds.), *Developments in British Politics* 7 (Basingstoke: Palgrave Macmillan, 2003); Budge, Ian, Ivor Crewe, David McKay, and Ken Newton, *The New British Politics*, 3rd Ed. (Harlow: Pearson Educational Limited, 2004); Jones, Bill, and Dennis Kavanagh, *British Politics Today*, 7th Ed. (Manchester: Manchester University Press, 2004). Four examples of the many surveys of British politics that are available.

Hennessy, Peter, *The Prime Minister: The Office and its Holders Since 1945* (Basingstoke: Palgrave, 2000). A detailed study of the nature of the office and the characters of the officeholders, from Attlee to Blair.

McCormick, John, *Contemporary Britain* (Basingstoke: Palgrave Macmillan, 2003). Designed as a general introduction to the history, politics, society, and economy of Britain.

Stothard, Peter, *Thirty Days: Tony Blair and the Test of History* (New York: HarperCollins, 2003); Naughtie, James, *The Accidental American: Tony Blair and the Presidency* (London: PublicAffairs, 2004). Two interesting assessments of Tony Blair's role as prime minister, with an emphasis on his part in the 2003 invasion of Iraq.

COMPARATIVE EXERCISE

HEADS OF STATE

In the Comparative Exercise for the United States, we looked at executives, or the people responsible for overseeing the execution of policy and law. If that was all they did, they would be nothing more than glorified bureaucrats—what makes them different is that they also provide leadership, doing what they can to encourage others in government to adopt their policies and their views about society's needs, and setting the national agenda. Leadership is a difficult term to define, but when it comes to managing countries, leaders are expected not just to be administrators but to inspire as well. In other words, we are looking for people not only to run the government but also to represent the interests of the state. What is the difference between the two roles?

A **head of government** is usually an elected leader with a particular set of values and goals that appeals to the people who voted him or her into office. Heads of government have specific agendas driven by particular biases, which may be ideological, economic, religious, regional, or nationalistic. They report to their parties and the supporters of their parties, and they tend to be concerned mainly with the immediate interests of their government and with the views of the people who paid their campaign expenses or voted them into office. They will try to encourage members and supporters of opposition parties and groups to support their policies, but will generally pay less attention to the interests and wishes of the opposition. Once in office, they appoint all or most of the other senior members of government, who then become part of their administration.

A **head of state** is someone who may or may not be elected but who uses his or her office to represent the interests, goals, and values of the entire population. The head of state is expected to be politically neutral, to rise above partisan politics, to look beyond the immediate interests of the incumbent government, to be a symbol of the country and its people, and to be the primary nonpolitical representative of the country in dealings with other countries. Heads of state will usually have a few political powers, but only enough to support their roles as arbiters (for example, stepping in to nominate a head of government in the event that no one party or coalition wins a majority of seats in the legislature). They will have few, if any, powers of appointment to political office.

In terms of how they go about allocating the responsibilities of the head of state, most countries have opted for one of two models:

- **Nonexecutive Heads of State.** A number of countries have chosen to separate the functions of head of state and head of government, placing them in the hands of two different people. Several countries have monarchs as heads of state. In the case of liberal democracies, kings and queens (or emperors in Japan) have lost all their significant and direct political powers, play only a marginal role in government, and have been reduced to being symbolic heads of state; technically, they are known as constitutional monarchs, because their powers are limited by a constitution. Monarchs attain their positions by birth or heredity, being the eldest sons or daughters of the previous monarch, usually keeping the job for life and—upon their death or abdication—passing the title on to their eldest son or daughter, or closest living heir. Despite the argument by their critics that they are elitist and undemocratic, monarchies are still surprisingly common: They can be found in several Western European states (including Britain, Spain, Belgium, Denmark, and Norway), several Arab states (including Jordan, Morocco, and Saudi Arabia), several Asian states (including Bhutan, Brunei, and Nepal), and several countries that were once

British colonies still recognize the British monarch as their head of state (including Australia, the Bahamas, Canada, Jamaica, and New Zealand).

Several countries—including a few that once had monarchies—have opted for nonexecutive presidents as their heads of state, giving most of the duties of monarchs to people elected as president for fixed terms of office. Presidents may be former politicians, but once they have become president they are expected to be neutral and symbolic figureheads and to show no political or ideological biases in their dealings with the government, their citizens, or other countries.

How they come to office and how long they serve varies from one country to another. Some presidents are elected directly by the people (for example, Austria, Iceland, and Ireland), while others are elected by members of the national or local legislatures or a combination of both (for example, Germany, Greece, India, Italy, and Turkey). Terms in office vary between four and seven years.

- **Executive Heads of State.** Other countries have opted to give their heads of state executive powers, blurring the line between the roles of head of state and head of government.

In Finland, France, Portugal, and Russia—among others—the president is an elected politician, usually with a party identification and an ideological bias, and is expected to be head of state while sharing executive responsibilities with an elected head of government. In the French case, the president is elected for renewable seven-year terms, and once in office makes all the key appointments to government. However, the prime minister and council of ministers must have the support of the legislature. If the legislature is dominated by the president's party, then the prime minister will tend to be a functionary of the president, who will dominate the political system. But if the prime minister comes from a different party, he or she will have much more independence and the president will be more a head of state than a head of government.

In the United States, most Latin American countries, and several Middle Eastern and African states, the president is the chief executive and has the combined roles of head of state and head of government. In other words, one person is expected to be both the neutral figurehead of the country and the political leader of government. The line separating the two roles almost disappears, which can work to the advantage of the president; a president who runs into political trouble can try to rise above politics by taking on the persona of a statesperson, leaving it to the legislature to become mired in the day-to-day politics of administration. On the other hand, presidents also have to do a convincing job of making the people believe that they have not become too partisan and too focused on the interests of their voters and party.

The ways different countries divide the responsibilities of head of state and head of government can have a significant impact on the way government functions, and on the way citizens relate to government. For many, it is important to have a psychological link with government or the state, and that link may be broken unless they have a nonpolitical leader who represents the interests of the entire country, rather than just one political party. At the same time, monarchies in particular have been criticized for promoting elitism and social class, a problem that creates its own kinds of divisions.

3

*J*APAN

JAPAN: QUICK FACTS

Official name: Japan (Nippon)

Capital: Tokyo

Area: 144,807 square miles
(375,050 sq. km, slightly smaller than California)

Languages: Japanese

Population: 127.6 million

Population density: 886 per square mile (340 per sq. km.)

Population growth rate: 0.1 percent

POLITICAL INDICATORS

Freedom House rating: Free

Date of state formation: Fifth century (approximately)

System type: Parliamentary democracy with a constitutional monarchy

Constitution: Published 1947

Administration: Unitary

Executive: Prime minister and cabinet

Legislature: Bicameral Diet; House of Councillors (247 members), and House of

Representatives (480 members). Councillors are elected for renewable six-year terms, representatives for renewable four-year terms

Party structure: Multiparty, undergoing substantial change

Judiciary: Independent 15-member Supreme Court modeled on U.S. Supreme Court

Head of state: Emperor Akihito (1989–)

Head of government: Junichiro Koizumi (2001–)

ECONOMIC INDICATORS

GDP (2004): $4,623 billion

Per capita GDP: $37,180

Distribution of GDP: Services 68 percent, industry 30 percent, agriculture 1 percent

Urban population: 79 percent

SOCIAL INDICATORS

HDI ranking: 9

Infant mortality rate: 3 per 1,000 live births

Life expectancy: 81.7 years

Illiteracy: 0 percent of people aged 15 and older

Religions: 85 percent Shinto and Buddhist

INTRODUCTION

Of the world's 35 liberal democracies, 33 are either European or come out of the European tradition. The two exceptions are Japan and South Korea, where Western ideas of liberal democracy have been grafted onto societies that remain distinctly non-Western. It is often argued that Japan is modern but not Western and that its experience proves that it is possible for a society to advance economically and technologically without losing sight of its cultural and social identity. The most obvious signs of its modernity can be found in its economic and technological development, which has become the stuff of legend. Meanwhile, the traditional values are most obvious in the unique features of its political system, where Western ideas about democracy have intermingled with Japanese ideas about faction, obligation, and group identity.

In absolute terms, Japan has the world's second biggest economy after the United States, with a GDP of more than $4.6 trillion. In per capita terms, it ranks in the top ten at just over $37,000 (compared with nearly $41,500 in the United States and $34,000 in Britain). It has few natural resources, few minerals, and limited farmland and must import most of its iron and energy needs and nearly one-third of its food needs. However, it has turned adversity into opportunity by protecting its domestic market with formal and informal barriers, and by developing a manufacturing sector that leads the world in engineering, machinery, road vehicles, and electronic products. This helped make Japan rich during the 1960s, 1970s, and 1980s, but a combination of problems—including a troubled banking system, corporate difficulties, bad investment choices, a too-powerful bureaucracy, and a political system that seems to be immune to reform—brought an economic downturn in the 1990s. Japan's economy contracted, with GDP falling by nearly one-fifth between 1995 and 2001.

Like Britain, Japan is a small, crowded country, with a population density nearly 12 times greater than that of the United States. About 27 million people (more than 20 percent of Japan's population) live in and around Tokyo, the world's largest and most expensive city. History and geography have combined to create a society that puts a premium on consensus, conformity, and compromise and in which people allow the state to intervene in their lives to a greater degree than in the United States. Its physical and historical isolation have also ensured that Japan is relatively homogeneous: There are no major national minorities or regional languages, most of its people are Shinto or Buddhist, and Japan's strong social hierarchy is rarely seriously questioned. Minorities make up just 2 percent of the population and include about two million *burakumin* (or "village people," whose position is much like that of India's untouchables) and about 700,000 descendants of Koreans brought to Japan as forced labor before and during World War II.

In political terms, Japan is a relative newcomer to liberal democracy. It was a feudal society until 1868, when it embarked on a short-lived experiment in parliamentary democracy, followed by a brief imperialist era when Japan conquered large parts of the neighboring east Asian mainland and went to war with the United States and

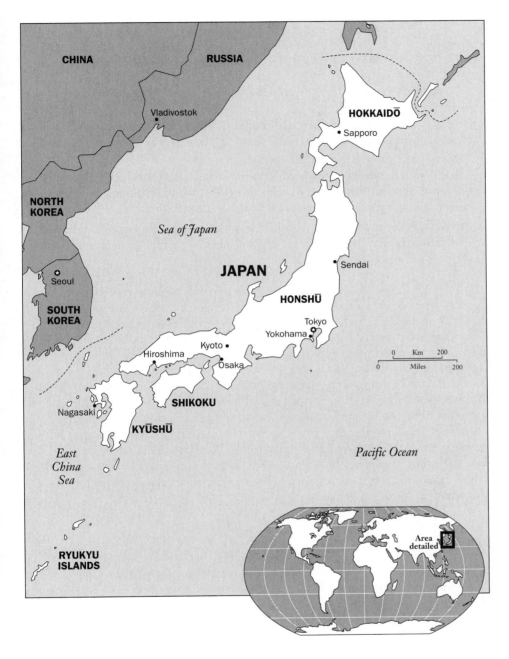

CHINA

RUSSIA

Vladivostok

HOKKAIDŌ

• Sapporo

NORTH
KOREA

Sea of Japan

JAPAN

Sendai

Seoul

HONSHŪ

SOUTH
KOREA

Tokyo
Yokohama

Kyoto •
Hiroshima
Osaka

SHIKOKU

Nagasaki

KYŪSHŪ

*East
China
Sea*

Pacific Ocean

0　　　Km　　200

0　　　Miles　　200

RYUKYU
ISLANDS

Area
detailed

its allies. Parliamentary democracy was forced on Japan during the U.S. occupation after World War II and has generally worked well, although there are several important differences between the Japanese and British parliamentary models:

- Britain is more pluralistic, while Japan tends to be paternalistic, elitist, and factional.

- British prime ministers lead and become dominating figures in politics, while Japanese prime ministers tend to be party functionaries and do not stay in office long.

- Britain is dominated by two political parties, but one party had a monopoly on the office of prime minister in Japan from 1955 to 1993, although there has been recent talk of the emergence of a two-party system.

- Britain is governed by a prime minister and cabinet, while Japan is governed by an **"iron triangle"** consisting of big business, senior bureaucrats, and senior members of the governing party.

iron triangle The close relationship that exists in Japan (and the United States) between the government, the bureaucracy, and big business.

For a modern society and an economic superpower, Japan has seen a surprisingly high incidence of political corruption. Much is the result of an electoral system that long encouraged factionalism and forced members of the same party to run against each other. Matters are made worse by a bureaucracy that is powerful and elitist, and has too close a relationship with big business. Recent prime ministers have tried to reform the system so that government becomes more accountable and politics moves away from deal making among politicians and bureaucrats out into the public arena. After many failed attempts, changes were finally approved to the electoral system in 1994, setting off a confusing game of musical chairs among Japan's political parties. The stability that was supposed to emerge from these changes has not yet taken root, and the web of obligations in which political leaders and civil servants are often caught has undermined attempts to stop Japan's economic decline. Critics argue that reform is impossible because the problems are built in to the entire structure of government.[1]

POLITICAL DEVELOPMENT

Britain's physical separation from the European continent long helped isolate it from the political and social upheavals that affected its mainland neighbors. The same has been true of Japan, whose physical isolation from the Asian mainland has helped create a strong sense of identity that has allowed the Japanese to adhere to their own political and social values while copying the best that others have to offer.

The Early Japanese State

The ancestors of the Japanese came from the mainland, most likely by way of Korea. Society was originally based around clans using a system of heredity, and the practice of adopting foreign models began in the sixth century, when Buddhism, Confucianism, and Chinese script were introduced from China. Traditional beliefs in nature worship were nonetheless preserved and distinguished from Buddhism by the name **Shinto** (or "way of the gods"), which remains the major religion of Japan.

Also on the Chinese model, a permanent imperial capital was founded in the eighth century near Kyoto and a centralized administrative structure created. Emperors ruled Japan, but their power declined as they rewarded members of their families with grants of land, thereby reducing their revenues and influence. The power shift was confirmed in 1192, when following a series of brutal civil wars, Japan was united under a military dictatorship. Yoritomo Minamoto was appointed by the emperor as **shogun** (or general) and had enough independent power to found a separate capital at Kamakura. The title of shogun became hereditary, and for nearly 700 years the shoguns were the major force in Japanese government.

The Shoguns (1192–1868)

While Japanese emperors were kept powerless and often in poverty at the imperial capital in Kyoto and peasants and merchants were kept at the lower end of the political structure, the shoguns ruled through a complex hierarchy of territorial lords (*daimyo*) and warriors (*samurai*). The *samurai* lived by the *bushido*, a code of conduct based on loyalty, obligation, and self-discipline.

By the beginning of the seventeenth century, power had shifted to the Tokugawa shogunate, which ruled Japan from its new capital at Edo, dividing the rest of Japan into semiautonomous feudal domains ruled by *daimyo* and their subordinate *samurai*. In the 1630s, the Tokugawas closed Japan off from the outside world, creating *sakoku*, or "the **closed country**." Christianity was forbidden; no one was allowed to leave; and the Dutch were the only Westerners allowed to trade with Japan, but only from a strictly controlled island enclave in Nagasaki harbor.

Japan now entered a period of 250 years of peace and isolation, during which Edo became the largest city in the world. The country came under centralized and authoritarian bureaucratic rule, with a well-established system of law and order and flourishing free enterprise. Although the shoguns were supposedly in charge, real power was wielded by a council of four or five advisors, establishing a tradition of collective leadership that still persists today. By the nineteenth century, however, it had become clear that the system was unable to keep pace with the social changes brought by economic development or to resist the demands of Western countries impatient to trade with Japan. The U.S. was casting particularly hungry eyes at Japan and China, with American businessmen keen to capitalize on the development of the U.S. west coast by trading with Asia, and missionaries keen to spread "civilization" and Christianity.[2]

The end of Japanese isolationism came in July 1853, when commodore Matthew Perry of the U.S. Navy sailed into Tokyo Bay with a demand from President Millard Fillmore that Japan open its doors to trade. The Tokugawas no longer had the power to resist, and a treaty was signed with the United States in 1854, granting limited trading concessions. Agreements with European powers followed. Ironically, this fulfilled the worst fears of Japanese rulers about destabilizing foreign influences. The shogunate lost prestige, the last Tokugawa shogun abdicated in 1867, and the Emperor Meiji was restored to power in 1868. Japan now entered a period of radical change.

Limited Democracy and Imperialism (1868–1945)

The **Meiji restoration** of 1868 marked the watershed between the old regime and the new era of modernization. The new emperor symbolically moved to Edo, which was renamed Tokyo (or Eastern Capital), and after much debate it was decided in 1871 to abolish the feudal system and to create a new system of government that could lead Japan into the Western-dominated state system. Realizing that it would be impossible to expel the "barbarian," Japan's leaders decided instead to copy foreign models. An imperial declaration in 1868 included the ruling that "knowledge shall be sought throughout the world in order to strengthen the foundations of the Imperial rule."[3]

Shopping around for what they defined as the best of everything, Japanese leaders copied the British parliamentary system (although they included a powerful executive along Prussian lines), French local government, the Prussian (German) civil service, the American system of currency, the Belgian banking system, and the Prussian and French military. They also systematically studied European constitutions before drawing up and adopting the 1889 Meiji Constitution, based mainly on the Prussian model.

Eagerness to learn from other countries, coupled with Japanese self-discipline, led to rapid industrialization, the building of a powerful new military, a new sense of national consciousness, and a doubling of the population between 1867 and 1913. The changes helped Japan win two wars against major enemies: China (1894–1895) and Russia (1904–1905). Taiwan (then Formosa) was ceded to Japan after the Sino-Japanese war, Korea and much of Manchuria (in what is now northern China) were occupied after the Russo-Japanese war, and an Anglo-Japanese alliance was formed in 1902 in the face of concerns about Russia. Japan was now a regional power.

Although it had based its new political system on the parliamentary model, Japan practiced only a limited form of democracy. The 1889 constitution created a cabinet and a bicameral **Diet** (parliament), but the emperor still ruled by divine right and appointed the prime minister and cabinet. Competing political parties nevertheless emerged, and in 1918 a commoner became prime minister for the first time. The powers of the emperor were preserved, but the Diet won more power and there was a shift toward multiparty parliamentary democracy.

Japan's leaders hoped that democracy and economic progress could be underwritten by peaceful trade with the rest of the world, but several obstacles prevented this from happening: a tendency toward factionalism, secret deal making, corruption (which undermined the credibility of the political system), and the Great Depression in the 1930s. The depression not only hurt the economy, leading to reduced export earnings and unemployment, but also worsened rural poverty, and—because many members of the military came from rural areas—fed into the dissatisfaction of the military with the civilian government.

Among junior army officers and right-wing intellectuals at the time of the depression there was a feeling that Japan's economic ills could be blamed on politicians and capitalism. There were calls for a restoration of imperial rule, a new social order, and a policy of imperialist expansion, generating several attempted coups and the assassinations of ministers, industrialists, military leaders, and in 1932, the prime minister. With the civilian central government losing control to the military, Japan

T A B L E 3 . 1

Japan: A Timeline

1192	Beginning of the shogun era
1274, 1281	Attempted Mongol invasions of Japan
1500–1600	Civil war
1603	Beginning of the Tokugawa shogunate
1639	Japan cuts its links with the Western world
1853	Commodore Perry sails into Tokyo Bay
1868	Meiji restoration
1889	New constitution established, followed by legislative elections in 1890
1894–1895	War with China, occupation of Formosa (now Taiwan)
1904–1905	War with Russia, occupation of Korea
1923	Earthquake in Tokyo region kills more than 100,000 people
1929–1931	Great Depression
1932	Japanese establish state of Manchukuo in Manchuria
1937	War breaks out between China and Japan
1941	Japan attacks Pearl Harbor; declaration of war by the United States
1945	Atom bombs dropped on Hiroshima (August 6) and Nagasaki (August 9); USSR declares war on Japan (August 8); Japan surrenders (August 15)
1945–1952	U.S. military occupation
1947	New constitution comes into force; Japan renounces war
1951	Peace Treaty and Mutual Security Treaty signed with United States
1955	Liberal Democratic Party takes power for the first time
1956	Japan joins United Nations
1960	Renegotiation of the Mutual Security Treaty with the United States
1973	Global oil crisis inflicts economic shock on Japan
1988	News breaks of the Recruit scandal
1993	Elections result in the end of a 38-year monopoly on power by the Liberal Democrats
1994	New electoral laws bring major changes in the makeup of the Japanese party system; (June) Tomiichi Murayama becomes the first socialist prime minister since 1948
1995	(January) Earthquake in Kobe leaves 6,000 dead; (March) nerve gas attack on Tokyo subway leaves 12 dead and thousands hurt
1996	The Liberal Democrats return to power in a minority government
1997	Asian financial crisis affects Japanese economy
2001	(April) Junichiro Koizumi becomes prime minister
2002	(September) Koizumi visits North Korea
2005	(September) Koizumi wins reelection in a landslide

Note: The Japanese normally give the family name first, followed by the given name (hence Koizumi Junichiro rather than Junichiro Koizumi). This textbook goes with the normal Western practice of placing the given name first.

in 1932 formalized its occupation of Manchuria by establishing the puppet state of Manchukuo under the heir to the Chinese throne. Its actions broke international law, and Japan withdrew from the League of Nations. In 1937, Japan invaded China, capturing the Chinese capital of Nanjing and slaughtering tens of thousands of civilians. Japan then allied itself with Germany and Italy in 1940, signed a nonaggression pact with the Soviet Union in 1941, and invaded Indo-China.

On December 7, 1941, Japan attacked Pearl Harbor in Hawaii, bringing a declaration of war by the United States and Britain. The Japanese attacked the British and the Dutch in Southeast Asia; seized Burma, Malaya, the Philippines, and Singapore in 1942; and seemed poised to attack Australia and India. An Allied counterattack halted the Japanese advance between May and August 1942 in the Coral Sea and at the islands of Midway and Guadalcanal. American forces then island-hopped across the western Pacific while Chinese, British, and Australian forces attacked from the south and west. American forces landed in Japan at Iwo Jima in February 1945, and the United States delivered the final blow in August with the dropping of atomic bombs on Hiroshima and Nagasaki. Shortly after a declaration of war by the Soviet Union, Japan surrendered.

Germany and Italy had identifiable leaders during the war, but the Japanese tradition of collectivism had persisted, frustrating Western attempts to apportion blame after the war. The prime minister in 1941–1944 had been Hideki Tojo, but he was little more than the representative of the army. Emperor Hirohito ultimately accepted responsibility, but because of debates about the exact powers of the emperor, he was never seen in quite the same light as Hitler or Mussolini and remained on the throne until his death in 1989. Tojo and other military officers, on the other hand, were tried and executed as war criminals.

The Occupation (1945–1952)

Japan emerged from World War II with its economy in ruins, with its social and political systems fragile and confused, and under foreign occupation for the first time in its history. U.S. General Douglas MacArthur was appointed the **Supreme Commander for the Allied Powers (SCAP)** and was charged with disarming, democratizing, and permanently demilitarizing Japan.[4] He oversaw the creation of a political and social system that combined elements of the prewar system with elements of Western-style democracy and also arranged for the writing of a new constitution, which was approved by the Japanese legislature and went into force in May 1947.

Once agreement had been reached on the constitution, there was little reason for the occupying forces to remain, except that some formula was needed to deal with the emerging postwar Soviet threat. Under the new constitution, Japan renounced war as a sovereign right, so an arrangement was made by which the occupation would end in April 1952 and Japan would have its sovereignty restored, but it would also "invite" the United States to station forces in Japan. The Soviets opposed this plan, as did Japanese pacifists, but attention was diverted in 1950 by the outbreak of the Korean War and the plan went ahead. The Japanese Peace Treaty was formally signed in September 1951, becoming effective in April 1952 and returning Japan to its pre-1854 borders. Japan and the United States also signed the **Mutual Security**

Treaty, under which U.S. forces continued to be stationed in Japan, bringing it firmly into the Western sphere of influence.

The Rise of the New Japan

When the U.S. occupation ended, Japan began applying its new political system. The 1946 elections had been contested by no fewer than 267 "parties," although most of these were either local parties or the personal organizations of individual politicians.[5] Over the next ten years, coalitions and attrition reduced the number, and by the late 1950s the Liberal Democratic Party had emerged as the dominating force in politics. A pattern of consensus government was also reestablished, in which power was exercised by the bureaucracy with the support, encouragement, and sometimes influence of the Liberal Democrats.

Building on a base of political stability, Japan since 1947 has developed strong trading ties all over the world and has invested heavily in other countries. Within barely a generation, isolationism and feudalism had given way to a new system of democratic government that helped Japan become one of the world's major economic powers and made household names of corporations such as Canon, Fujitsu, Honda, Mitsubishi, Sony, Toshiba, and Toyota. Japan became the world's biggest creditor nation, its stock market one of the most influential, its currency (the yen) one of the strongest, and its banks among the world's largest. Japan established its place as a world leader in the development of new technology and the application of that technology to efficient and dependable manufactured goods.

Underneath the impressive figures, though, there have long been concerns that Japan's political modernization has not kept pace with its economic growth, leading some to question whether the political system has measured up to the needs of an economic superpower. Public faith in government was particularly shaken by a string of political and financial scandals. News of one of the biggest broke in 1988, when it was revealed that political donations had been given in 1985–1986 to leading politicians and senior government officials in the form of shares in the Recruit Corporation, an information and property conglomerate. When Recruit shares were offered publicly in late 1986, the new shareholders reaped instant and large profits. News of the scandal led to the resignation of 42 politicians and bureaucrats, including finance minister Kiichi Miyazawa and—eventually—prime minister Noboru Takeshita. He was replaced by Sosuke Uno, but he resigned within weeks after news broke that he had once kept a mistress. (After 13 years of hearings and court cases, the chairman of Recruit was finally given a suspended jail term in March 2003.)

Subsequent scandals revealed bureaucratic corruption in the ministry of health that allowed 2,000 hemophiliacs to contract AIDS through transfusions of tainted blood, incompetence in a government response to a devastating 1995 earthquake in the southern city of Kobe that left more than 6,000 people dead, and questions about public safety following a 1995 nerve gas attack on a Tokyo subway by a religious cult called Aum Shinrikyo that left 12 people dead and more than 5,500 hurt.

Critics of the status quo began calling in the early 1990s for a "third opening," which, like the trade openings of 1853–1854 and the SCAP occupation of 1945–1952, would bring the kinds of changes to government, education, and economic and foreign policy Japan needed to become a true superpower. But the first two openings took place under authoritarian governments, and in the 1990s Japan lacked either the political leaders who could build a consensus on the need for reform, or who could build the authority to impose it.[6] The monopoly of the Liberal Democratic Party was finally broken in 1993–1994, but this proved to be only a temporary break, because the party came back in a minority government in 1996 and has been a member of the coalitions that have since ruled Japan.

Japan Today

In the 1980s, the name *Japan* was a watchword for economic power. Today, it is in danger of becoming a watchword for the inability of a political and economic system to keep up with new opportunities and pressures for change. Although the increasing number of Japanese cars and electronic goods in the United States was once seen as symbolic of the economic threats posed by Japan, it has slowly come to matter less. Japan is still an economic powerhouse, but it entered its longest postwar recession in the mid-1990s, and its GDP fell by 17 percent between 1995 and 2001 (U.S. GDP grew over the same period by 47 percent). While industrial production continued to grow, and unemployment in 2005 was running at 4.4 percent (compared to 5.1 percent in the United States), retail sales and consumer confidence fell, the Tokyo stock market was down a remarkable 77 percent from its highest level, and Japan was the only major liberal democracy to experience deflation.

Politically, Japan remains a difficult country both to understand (at least for outsiders) and to reform. It needs leadership, but the idea of leadership—or at least of individuals rising above the pack—runs counter to political culture (see later discussion). So instead of transparency (an open political system) and accountability, there is obfuscation and a tendency to hide behind the protective barrier of the group. Prime ministers who are appointed to office on a promise of reform typically end up being cautious and/or conservative, and business continues as usual. Change is occurring, though, regardless of the policies pursued by Japanese leaders: The electoral system has been reformed, government ministries have been reorganized, younger Japanese are rebelling against formality and conformity, and the number of independents elected to the Diet has grown.[7] The problem lies in the relatively slow pace of change and the political and economic effects this could have on Japan in light of the much greater pace of change witnessed by other liberal democracies.

POLITICAL CULTURE

Japan may be a liberal democracy, but the changes it has seen in the last century have come so rapidly that many traditional aspects of Japanese political culture remain intact, or—at least—play an important residual role in understanding Japanese political culture. The emphases of the culture are typically placed on group orientation, hierarchy, mutual obligation, and consensus. Several of these have come under increasing criticism for acting as a brake on Japan's political modernization and for contributing to instability in the leadership of the world's second biggest economy. But at least one expert on Japan asks whether they are any longer accurate or adequate descriptions of how Japanese behave in social situations.[8]

Social Conformity and Group Identity

Although almost every community has some kind of social hierarchy, it is particularly obvious in Japan, where people are divided into groups that are not only ranked in relation to each other but also internally. Where politics in most liberal democracies is driven by majoritarian democracy and by winners and losers, decisions in Japan tend to be made by consensus, there is little room for individualism, and emphasis is placed on the group. This is visible, for example, in the emphasis on teamwork in Japanese corporations.

Japanese politicians occupy their posts not necessarily because they are good leaders but because of their seniority, their acceptability to the group, their paternalistic concerns for the people, and their ability to build consensus rather than impose their preferences on others. The emphasis on group leadership is one reason few outsiders can name Japanese politicians—few rise above the pack, rock the boat, or threaten the political status quo. Conformity is visible in the way so many Japanese dress alike, and group solidarity is reflected in the way many of the most successful politicians come from families with a tradition in politics. For example, Prime Minister Junichiro Koizumi's father and grandfather were both members of the Japanese legislature.

The collective society is also behind a Japanese version of the exceptionalism that is part of American society; many Japanese think of their country as unique,[9] assume that their culture cannot be adopted by foreigners, and have a poor record of assimilating non-Japanese. For example, the descendants of the Koreans who were brought to Japan as laborers during World War II are still denied jobs in the bureaucracy, cannot vote, and are generally treated as second-class citizens. Similarly, Japanese-owned companies outside Japan rarely involve non-Japanese managers in high-level decision making.

Loyalty and Obligation

Group identity is also reflected in Japanese ideas about loyalty and obligation, which tend to be based on emotion rather than formal legal contracts.[10] Political power is based on a web of social and financial ties that bind a small political elite and promote nepotism and factionalism. These values help explain the Japanese support for militarism and imperialism in the 1930s, promoted by military leaders under the guise of loyalty to the emperor. Loyalty is reflected today in the way workers tend to stay with one company all their lives, and obligation is reflected in the frequency of influence peddling in politics. Allied to the notion of group identity and loyalty is the achievement ethic. As the performance of Japanese business and industry shows, the Japanese are goal-oriented, but their goals are driven less by personal ambition than by collective achievement.

A Male-Dominated Society

Europe and Japan both have a feudal past, but most European countries have left that past behind. In Japan, however, paternalism is still a feature of social and political relations, and in no other liberal democracy is the gender gap so obvious or the

CRITICAL ISSUES

WOMEN IN POLITICS

The role of women in politics has improved in most liberal democracies in recent years, but their access to elected office and to the highest levels of government varies from one country to another. The roll call of female prime ministers has grown—including Margaret Thatcher in Britain, Angela Merkel in Germany, Edith Cresson in France, Kim Campbell in Canada, Jenny Shipley and Helen Clark in New Zealand, and Gro Harlem Brundtland in Norway—but a more telling measure of their changing status in government is reflected in the numbers of women being elected to legislative office (see Figure 3.1).

- The record in Japan, with its traditional paternalism, is relatively poor: Less than 5 percent of members of the House of Representatives were women in 1999, a decrease from 1946, when the figure was 8.4 percent. By 2005 the figure was up slightly to 8.9 percent, but this was still far less than the average for Europe (18.5%) or for Asia (15.1%).

- The U.S. Congress has seen growing numbers of women members but still does not have a strong record. Only 15 percent of members of the House of Representatives were women in 2004 and only 14 percent of senators, yet women make up just over half the population of the United States. Proportionately, ethnic minorities are better represented.

- The 1997 election in Britain saw the proportion of women elected to Parliament double, from 9 percent to more than 18 percent. A total of 120 women were elected, all but nine of whom represented the Labour Party, which had made a particular effort to field women candidates. In 2005 the figures were almost unchanged.

- Britain and the United States compare well to Italy and France (both about 11 to 12 percent), but every country pales by comparison to the Scandinavians and the Dutch, all of whom are in the range of 36 to 45 percent.

Although there is nothing to suggest that different sexes, races, or religions are necessarily better represented by their own members, the diversity of the membership of legislatures is a strong indicator of how far a society has gone in removing discrimination and barriers to professional achievement. The data suggest that—for women at least—Japan still lags far behind most other countries.

feminist movement so weak. Women earn just over half as much as men, and while most other liberal democracies have seen the number of women in politics grow, the number of women in Japanese politics has actually fallen since World War II (see Critical Issues), and they have also made only limited inroads into the higher levels of corporate Japan.[11] The underlying reason (or excuse) for this paternalism is tradition and the social order. Despite this, Japanese women have a close sense of group identity, in contrast to women in other liberal democracies, and their social position has improved since the prewar era, when they were regarded by men as little more than chattels. Women were given the vote in 1945 (mainly because General

FIGURE 3.1

Women in Legislatures

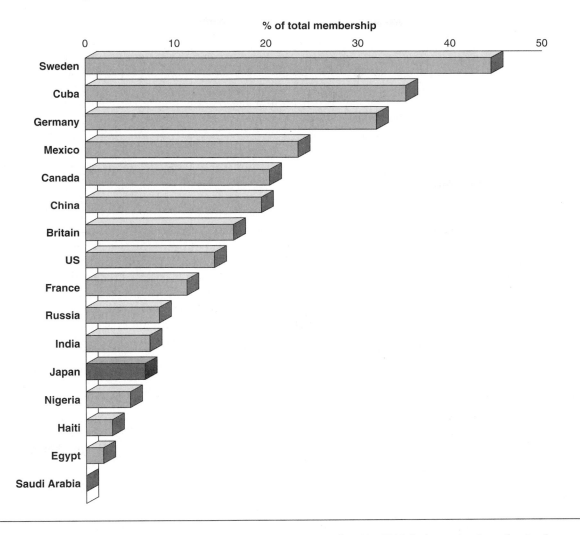

% of total membership

Source: Inter-Parliamentary Union Web site, 2005, www.ipu.org. Figures are for 2001–2005, for lower chambers of national legislatures.

MacArthur insisted) and the 1947 constitution gave them equal legal status with men for the first time. The divorce rate has increased at least partly because more women demand more from life than being housewives and mothers, and the number of women college graduates has grown. However, opportunities for women in business, politics, and the professions are still limited.

POLITICAL SYSTEM

Japan is a liberal democracy, with many of the same political institutions, values, and processes as the United States, Britain, or Canada. In all these countries, democracy is influenced by the activities of groups representing economic, social, and special interests, and policy decisions are often reached through a process in which these groups bargain with elected officials. But where Japan parts company with the others is in the extent to which it has institutionalized group politics, and in the emphasis placed on achieving a consensus. The methods used to build that consensus include personalism, factionalism, the exchange of political favors, and an almost constant process of bargaining within and among big business, political parties, and the senior levels of the bureaucracy. For these reasons, Japan is often called a **patron-client democracy**.

The pressure and desire to break with this tradition has grown in recent years, driven by increased cynicism toward government among voters and by political scandal, which has been a problem for decades but seems to have become worse. Changes were made to the structure of the political system in 1994–1996; most important, the old electoral system—in which members of the same party were obliged to run against each other and which resulted in many small parties winning seats—was replaced by a mixed system of winner-take-all and proportional representation (PR). This helped make the party system more stable, but not enough for critics of group politics—calls are still being made today for additional reforms, including a reduction in the number of members of the legislature elected by PR.

THE CONSTITUTION

Like Britain, Japan was governed for most of its history without a written constitution, relying instead on custom and tradition. But while Britain still has no written constitution (in the sense of there being a single, codified document), Japan has had two in modern times.

The first of these was the Meiji Constitution, adopted in 1889, partly to convince Western countries that Japan should be taken seriously and treated equally and partly to lay down rules on the distribution of power, promoting social discipline and national unity so that Japan could deal with the economic and security challenges posed by the West.[12] The Meiji Constitution was authoritarian and was based on the ideas that government was omnipotent and benevolent and gave rights and liberties to citizens as gifts. The constitution itself was portrayed as a gift to the people from the emperor, who alone had the right to amend it (although he never did). Despite its limitations, the constitution provided a bridge for Japan's transition from a feudal to a modern society. It also gave rise to a tradition of party politics and electoral competition, resulting in power being devolved to a new generation of leaders.

The Meiji constitution was replaced by the **1947 constitution,** the one in force today. Symbolizing the extent to which World War II was a watershed in Japanese history, the new document did not come out of Japanese political tradition, nor was it even written by the Japanese themselves. Seeing the disagreement among Japanese leaders about the future course of their country, General MacArthur instructed his Government Section to write the constitution, which it did in just six days in 1946. Had the Japanese themselves done the job, it might have been less liberal and more paternalistic. The fact that it was written by foreigners—in less than a week—is remarkable. That it was generally accepted by the Japanese, even though it includes many principles alien to Japanese political culture, is even more remarkable. That it is still working nearly 60 years later—so far completely unrevised—is most remarkable of all.

The new constitution created a parliamentary system similar to the one that had existed until the late 1920s and replaced the emperor-based state with the doctrine of popular sovereignty. It guaranteed basic human rights, renounced war and the maintenance of military forces, abolished the aristocracy, severely limited the powers of the emperor (who had to renounce his divinity), and created a new supreme court. In short, it replaced the prewar system, in which civilian and military groups had been allowed to exercise the powers of the emperor, with a new system in which authority was clearly centered in the new legislature (the Diet), which was controlled by a popular vote. Where the prewar distribution of power and responsibility had been unclear, the new constitution clearly defined the lines of responsibility. Although conservatives disliked the limits placed on the military and the emperor and wanted him instead to be declared head of state, the constitution has remained in effect, essentially unchanged, to this day.

THE EMPEROR

Both Britain and Japan are constitutional monarchies, meaning that their governments are headed by hereditary leaders who have almost no real political power but whose job is to act as the symbolic leader of the country. One technical difference between the two jobs is that the British monarch is head of state, but the Japanese emperor—according to the constitution—is only the "symbol of the state." The distinction stands as a reminder of the modern role of the emperor, who was an important element in the political system until much more recently than the British monarch.

The job has been held since 1989 by Emperor Akihito, the 125th descendant of the first emperor of Japan and the son of Emperor Hirohito (1902–1989), who holds a controversial place in Japanese history because of questions about his part in Japan's role in World War II. Much like the British king or queen, Akihito (b. 1933) presides over openings of the Diet, his seal is needed for important state documents, and he confirms the person chosen to be prime minister by the Diet. He is also a living embodiment of the history and culture of Japan, even more so than most other monarchs: although Japan has used the Gregorian calendar since 1873, the numbering of years in Japan is still based on the reign of the emperor. So 2005 was Heisei 16, or the 16th year of the reign of the Heisei emperor Akihito. He will be succeeded in due course by Crown Prince Naruhito and his wife Masako. So far, none of Akihito's sons have themselves had sons, raising the prospect that Japan will have to change its laws to allow a woman to succeed to the title.

Despite being members of the oldest dynasty in the world, with a continuous line said to go back 2,600 years, Japanese emperors have rarely personally ruled the country. From 1192 until 1868, they were kept in isolation at Kyoto while the shoguns ruled Japan from Kamakura and then Edo. When the rule of the shoguns ended in 1868, real power fell into the hands of coalitions of elites surrounding the throne. Until World War II, emperors were surrounded by an aura of near-divinity that contrasted sharply with the way most European monarchs were seen by their subjects. Hirohito was treated with such reverence that in his early years his court tailors were not allowed to measure him for his clothes, because this would have meant touching him. His status misled many people into thinking that he had more power than he actually had, but because the power structure in prewar Japan was unclear, it was difficult for the Allies to decide what role Hirohito had played in World War II. But Japan's defeat in the war made the emperor seem less god-like, and the 1947 constitution finally stripped the emperor and surrounding institutions of all direct political power. The altered role of the emperor was symbolized in 1958, when Crown Prince Akihito was allowed to marry a commoner, Michiko Shoda.

THE EXECUTIVE: PRIME MINISTER AND CABINET

In the British system, the parliamentary agenda is driven by the prime minister, who governs with the help of the cabinet, but cabinet members play only a supporting role. By contrast, Japanese prime ministers have few opportunities to show or exert much leadership and are among the weakest heads of government of any liberal democracy.[13] The Japanese prime minister is more like the keeper of the helm than the captain of the ship, and few leave a lasting personal stamp on government. Turnover in recent years has been so rapid that Japan is sometimes jokingly called a *karaoke* democracy: While the United States had two presidents and Britain had two prime ministers between 1992 and 2005, Japan had eight prime ministers, serving average terms of 18 months each.

Limits are placed on prime ministerial power by the bureaucracy, factions within political parties, party leaders, and the consensus style of Japanese politics. Their standing in the polls is only marginally important to their power base, some may not even have policies of their own, and few succeed in making substantial changes in government policy. But this does not mean that they are completely powerless: They can hire and fire members of the cabinet, and they do not face the same checks and balances as U.S. presidents. Even so, prime ministers are usually less important than the policies of the governments they lead.

Technically, the Diet chooses the prime minister from among its members. Because the lower House of Representatives has more power than the upper House of Councillors and because political parties tend to vote together, what in effect happens is that the prime minister comes out of the majority party (or coalition) in the House of Representatives. But unlike in Britain, where the leader of the biggest party or coalition becomes prime minister, in Japan it is the person who wins the most political support who takes over the top job.

From 1955 to 1993, Japan was ruled by a single party, the **Liberal Democratic Party (LDP).** Although supposedly a united political party, the LDP is actually made up of several factions, each with a different leader (see Close-Up View, p. 154). During this period, the prime minister was not necessarily the leader of the LDP, nor even the leader of the biggest faction, nor even the leader of *any* faction, but rather the person who won enough support among the competing factions to form a government. LDP prime ministers were rarely changed at elections, nor did their positions depend on how popular they were with voters; they were usually changed in midstream as a result of several weeks (sometimes even months) of negotiation within the party. There is a dictum that power and popularity are not synonymous in Japanese politics, well illustrated by the recent history of the office of prime minister.

- August 1993 saw the first non-LDP government in 38 years taking power. It was a seven-party coalition headed by **Morihiro Hosokawa,** and it had political reform and economic deregulation at the top of its agenda. Although popular, Hosokawa's grip on power was weakened by stories about skeletons in his political closet, including financial indiscretions, and by disruptive infighting within the coalition. It finally collapsed in April 1994, when Hosokawa resigned and a key coalition partner—the Social Democrats (SDPJ)—pulled out.

- A new coalition led by **Tsutomu Hata** was formed but lasted just two months before the SDPJ once again pulled out, this time concerned that there was a conspiracy to marginalize them. To almost universal astonishment, the SDPJ then struck a deal to form a coalition with their old enemies the LDP, and in June 1994 SDPJ chairman **Tomiichi Murayama** became the first socialist in 46 years to hold the office of prime minister. Murayama was leader of the far left of the SDPJ and a well-known parliamentarian, beloved of cartoonists for his distinctive long gray eyebrows. Under his leadership, the SDPJ abandoned its opposition to the existence of a Japanese military and came out in favor of including Japanese troops in UN peacekeeping operations and of the security alliance with the United States. But Murayama proved an unimaginative leader and was widely held responsible for the slow government response to the 1995 Kobe earthquake and the nerve gas attack on the Tokyo subway. He resigned in January 1996, leading to rumors that he had done so in return for a promise from the LDP that it would help the SDPJ boost its declining support among voters before the next election.

- Murayama was replaced by LDP president **Ryutaro Hashimoto.** Arrogant, quick-tempered, and colorful, Hashimoto made it clear that he wanted to give the office of prime minister a more assertive role in government. He called early elections in October 1996, the first in many years to be contested by two major party groups led by two distinctive candidates: Hashimoto himself and Ichiro Ozawa of the New Frontier Party. The LDP failed to win a majority, but won enough seats to form a minority government headed by Hashimoto. But he resigned in July 1998 following LDP losses in elections to the upper chamber of the Diet—the House of Councillors—for which he accepted responsibility.

- Former foreign minister **Keizo Obuchi** was appointed to see out the remainder of Hashimoto's term. Thought of as a caretaker and nicknamed "Mr. Ordinary,"

TABLE 3.2

Postwar Prime Ministers of Japan

Date	Prime minister	Party
April 1945	Kantaro Suzuki	
August 1945	Naruhiko Higashikuni	
October 1945	Kijuro Shidehara	Progressive
May 1946	Shigeru Yoshida	Liberal
May 1947	Tetsu Katayama	Socialist
March 1948	Hitoshi Ashida	Democrat
October 1948	Shigeru Yoshida	Democratic Liberal
October 1952	Shigeru Yoshida	Liberal
December 1954	Ichiro Hatoyama	Democrat
November 1955	Ichiro Hatoyama	Liberal Democrat
December 1956	Tanzan Ishibashi	Liberal Democrat
February 1957	Nobusuke Kishi	Liberal Democrat
July 1960	Hayato Ikeda	Liberal Democrat
November 1964	Eisaku Sato	Liberal Democrat
July 1972	Kakuei Tanaka	Liberal Democrat
December 1974	Takeo Miki	Liberal Democrat
December 1976	Takeo Fukuda	Liberal Democrat
December 1978	Masayoshi Ohira	Liberal Democrat
July 1980	Zenko Suzuki	Liberal Democrat
November 1982	Yasuhiro Nakasone	Liberal Democrat
November 1987	Noboru Takeshita	Liberal Democrat
June 1989	Sousuke Uno	Liberal Democrat
August 1989	Toshiki Kaifu	Liberal Democrat
November 1991	Kiichi Miyazawa	Liberal Democrat
August 1993	Morihiro Hosokawa	Coalition
April 1994	Tsutomu Hata	LDP coalition
June 1994	Tomiichi Murayama	LDP coalition
January 1996	Ryutaro Hashimoto	LDP coalition
July 1998	Keizo Obuchi	LDP coalition
March 2000	Yoshiro Mori	LDP coalition
April 2001	Junichiro Koizumi	LDP coalition
November 2003	Junichiro Koizumi	LDP coalition
September 2005	Junichiro Koizumi	LDP coalition

Obuchi surprised everyone by taking control of the office and winning strong public approval ratings. But he failed to carry out more electoral reforms, drawing criticism from his coalition partners. In July 1999, a newly formed left-wing party—New Komeito—joined the coalition, giving it a majority in the House of Councillors for the first time. This was intended to strengthen Obuchi's hand but was seen by voters as a cynical bid to strengthen the LDP by making a deal with its political enemies. Public support for Obuchi was beginning to slip when—in March 2000—he suffered a stroke and died.

- The prime ministership was now taken over by **Yoshiro Mori,** a politician who had been tainted by scandal and who was unpopular from the outset of his term in office. Nevertheless, he led the LDP into the June 2000 general election, and although turnout was low (just 62 percent) and the LDP lost 10 percent of its seats in the Diet, Mori was able to form a new government. By early 2001 was so reviled that some polls had his approval rating as low as 9 percent, making him one of the most unpopular prime ministers in Japan's postwar history.

- In April 2001, **Junichiro Koizumi** became Japan's 29th postwar prime minister, at the head of an LDP-led coalition. LDP leaders had wanted to return Ryutaro Hashimoto to office, but the party membership demanded a vote, and gave overwhelming support to Koizumi; he won just 51 percent of the vote among the LDP's members in the Diet, but 87 percent of local political leaders voted for him. The results were interpreted as a clear message that voters were tired of mainstream politics. But Koizumi was unable to deliver on many of the changes that were expected, and quickly lost public support (see People in Politics).

Although prime ministerial politics in Japan and Britain are very different, the two jobs have similar powers, and the relationship between executive and legislature in both countries is similar. The Japanese prime minister has the same basic powers over policy, the power to call elections, and the power of appointment. One key difference lies in the role of the cabinet, which by law can have no more than 20 members. While the British cabinet is an important power base for the prime minister and a core part of the government of Britain, the Japanese cabinet is little more than an executive committee of the Diet. British ministers make policy and take collective responsibility for their decisions, but Japanese ministers look out for their departmental interests first and place the interests of the government second. Ministers are usually given their posts as political favors, and cabinet turnover is normally high.

THE LEGISLATURE: THE DIET

The name of the Japanese legislature is usually translated into English with the anachronistic term Diet, even though the most accurate translation of the Japanese name (*Kokkai*) is National Assembly. It has all the typical lawmaking powers of a legislature, and—like the British Parliament—it has powers over the budget, can unseat

JUNICHIRO KOIZUMI

Taking over the helm of Japanese politics in April 2001, Junichiro Koizumi—like several of his predecessors—was hailed as someone who could bring change to Japanese politics and economic policy. He came from a political family, both his father and grandfather having served as representatives and as cabinet ministers, and Koizumi himself had spent 28 years in the House, part of it as a minister. He was a critic of the Japanese faction system and came over well in the media, helped by his distinctive wavy grey-black hair, his willingness to break with tradition, and his fondness for both opera and heavy metal rock music. One of his ministers once described him as "weird."

He started out with a public approval rating in the range of 80 to 90 percent, led the LDP to impressive gains in elections to the House of Councillors in July 2001, appointed cabinet ministers on the basis of merit rather than their membership in factions, and 5 of his 17 ministers were women. He then announced an ambitious reform program, including the privatization of government-owned businesses, a new tax system, an overhaul of the banking system, and spending cuts aimed at reducing the budget deficit. He even came close to achieving pop celebrity, running his own email magazine in which he proclaimed, "I am Koizumi the lionheart."

However, doubts quickly arose about how far he was prepared to go with reform, particularly when he intervened to save several large and inefficient businesses from bankruptcy. He then fired his popular foreign minister, Makiko Tanaka, who had developed a reputation as someone prepared to stand up to the bureaucrats in her department. In a controversial move, he visited Yasukuni, a shrine in Tokyo to Japan's 2.5 million war dead, which includes a small number of war criminals. Despite the outcry from his first visit in August 2001 and criticism from China, South Korea, and other Asian countries, he made a second visit in 2002. Then senior members of his party became involved in corruption scandals, and his party did poorly in local elections. And

like many other national leaders, his support of the U.S.-led invasion of Iraq—and his decision to commit Japanese troops in support of the invasion—also cost him politically.

Koizumi had been elected prime minister by a vote involving the entire membership of the LDP, rather than just party leaders, who had wanted to appoint one of their own. In Japanese terms, his victory was revolutionary, and—to use that tired phrase—a mandate for change. But Koizumi showed that he was willing to use factionalism to get his own way, a philosophy that combined with his cautious approach to Japan's economic problems and his slowness to institute political reforms to reduce his base of support. He was able to pull the LDP through the November 2003 elections, but by July 2004 his approval ratings had fallen below 40 percent. When his plans to privatize Japan's postal system were defeated in the House of Councillors, Koizumi called a snap general election in September 2005. His coalition was returned in a landslide, and Koizumi promised to press ahead with the reforms. But he was also expected to step down when his term as leader of the LDP ended in September 2006.

the prime minister and cabinet through a vote of no confidence, holds a question time for members of the cabinet, and has a range of specialist committees. There is one key difference, though: While the British Parliament defers to the power of the prime minister and cabinet, the Japanese Diet defers to the power of the governing party or coalition and to the bureaucracy.

Like most liberal democratic legislatures, the Diet has two chambers.

House of Councillors (*Sangi-in*)

The House of Councillors is the upper house, consisting of 247 members. Of these, 149 are elected from 47 local government units known as **prefectures,** and the remaining 98 are elected using proportional representation; hence they represent the whole country, not individual districts. Councillors serve fixed six-year terms, with half coming up for reelection every three years. The House is presided over by a president chosen from among its members.

The House of Councillors replaced the prewar House of Peers, an almost direct copy of the old British House of Lords. Members of the House of Peers included the imperial family, hereditary aristocrats, army representatives, and government appointees. The U.S. occupation authorities after World War II argued that Japan did not need an upper house because it was a unitary state and did not have local government units that needed separate representation at the national level. The Japanese, on the other hand, argued that a second chamber was needed to check the popularly elected lower chamber. In any event, an upper house was created, but with no clear idea about what it should do, beyond giving the prefectures some representation. It can reject bills from the lower house, but treaties and budgetary matters do not need its agreement. Its most important role in recent years has been in allowing voters to comment on the record of the government between elections to the House of Representatives.

House of Representatives (*Shugi-in*)

The House of Representatives is the lower—and more powerful—of the two houses of the Diet. Until 1994, it had 511 members elected using a complex system based on multimember districts, but electoral reforms replaced this with the present system, which has 480 members elected using a combination of 300 single-member districts and 180 seats filled by proportional representation. Elections must be held within four years of each other, but as with the British House of Commons, the House of Representatives rarely sees out a full term. The lower house chooses the prime minister, passes laws, passes the budget, makes treaties, and can override an upper house veto with a two-thirds majority. It is presided over by a speaker, along British and American lines.

The weakness of the Diet relative to the bureaucracy is symbolized by the fact that the Diet meets for only five months per year, two months of which are usually tied up over the annual budget debate. By contrast, the British Parliament meets for seven months, and the U.S. Congress for eight months. Further weaknesses are

The National Diet building in Tokyo. It was opened for use in 1936, replacing temporary wooden structures that had been burned down twice. The completion of the new permanent building confirmed Japan's transition from an imperial to a parliamentary system of government.

added by the large number of political parties represented in the House (typically six to seven in recent years), the divisions within the major parties created by factions, and the tradition of consensus politics that makes most members disinclined to disagree with the executive.

THE JUDICIARY: SUPREME COURT

One of the legacies of the U.S. role in designing the postwar Japanese political system is the existence of a separate Supreme Court with the power of judicial review. Separation of the judiciary from the executive was motivated by American plans to decentralize Japanese government. The allied occupation force under SCAP transferred authority over the courts from the Ministry of Justice to a new Supreme Court, giving it powers as the guardian of civil rights and liberties written into the new constitution. Although similar in their general goals, the U.S. and Japanese courts are different in their details:

- While the U.S. Supreme Court has 9 justices appointed by the president and confirmed by the Senate, the Japanese court has 15 judges, 14 of whom are chosen by the cabinet from lists submitted by the court itself. The chief justice is appointed by the emperor on the recommendation of the cabinet.

- While U.S. Supreme Court justices have jobs for life, new members of the Japanese court must be confirmed by a popular vote at the next general election and again at the next general election following ten years of service. Partly because of their lack of activism, Japanese Supreme Court justices remain little-known public figures and are regularly reconfirmed.

- Much of the justification for setting up the U.S. Supreme Court came from the need to have an authority that would rule in disputes between the states and the federal government. As a unitary state, Japan does not have such disputes, so the Japanese court has less to do.

- While the United States is one of the most litigious societies in the world, in which people often go to court as a first resort rather than a last resort, the Japanese preference for consensus encourages them to attach less importance to formal rules and regulations than they do to custom. Most Japanese assume that disputes can be worked out through informal discussion and compromise, and falling back on laws and rules is often seen as an admission of failure. One consequence of this is that Supreme Court decisions in Japan impact a narrower range of policy issues than is the case with the U.S. Supreme Court.

Probably the most important difference between the U.S. and Japanese courts is their relative roles in politics. The U.S. Supreme Court is supposed to be a neutral arbiter that simply rules on the constitutionality of government laws and actions. However, it has often been activist and thus has had a key role in influencing public policy. For example, it addressed the core issue of racial segregation in its 1954 decision *Brown* v. *Board of Education*, and it addressed abortion in its 1973 decision *Roe* v. *Wade*. By contrast, the Japanese Supreme Court tends to avoid using its powers of judicial review and becoming involved in controversial public issues. It is also inclined to support the government, rather than acting as a check on the powers of the executive or the legislature. Reflecting its limited role in politics, it is barely ever discussed in texts on Japanese politics.

SUBNATIONAL GOVERNMENT

With its small size, heavy population density, social homogeneity, and consensual political culture, Japan is a ready candidate for a centralized system of government. No surprise, then, that it is a unitary state. During the American occupation, SCAP policy was to make sure that a clearly identifiable source of political authority was created, while also recognizing that elected local government was a vital element in grassroots democracy.[14] General MacArthur was particularly keen to encourage small independent farmers, and SCAP also gave powers over education and the police to local government. It has been argued that SCAP was motivated by the American experience of the "frontier" and independent-minded citizens, an approach that was inappropriate in a Japan that had long been used to centralization. One result was that decentralizing reforms instituted by SCAP were reversed by the Japanese once the occupation had ended.[15]

Japan today is highly centralized, and local government is correspondingly less important. There are two main levels of local government: the 47 prefectures, which in turn coordinate the activities of the municipalities, which may be cities, towns, or villages, depending on the distribution of population. Just as in Britain, but unlike the United States or Canada, local units of government have no independent powers; they can be created, abolished, or reorganized by central government. But while Britain has seen regular disputes between central and local government, Japanese local government generally operates as a willing and efficient channel for the implementation of central government policies. Local governments are allowed to collect only 30 percent of their own revenue needs, depending for the rest on grants from central government.

Given its size, Tokyo—home to one in five Japanese—plays a substantial role in national politics. It is the political, economic, social, and communications hub of Japan, and it wields major influence over the entire country. The April 1999 election for governor of Tokyo was particularly important because the incumbent—a former television comedian named Yukio Aoshima—had decided not to run again, having been overwhelmed by the city's economic, social, and environmental problems. The race was won by Shintaro Ishihara, an outspoken former LDP politician who ran as an independent. Ishihara had come to national prominence in the late 1980s by coauthoring a best-selling book titled *A Japan That Can Say No*; in the book he argued that Japan should stop falling in with U.S. demands on foreign policy and should revise the constitutional principle renouncing war, an idea for which there is growing support in Japan.[16]

 # ELECTIONS AND PARTIES

Japan has most of the typical structural features of a liberal democracy except for a truly competitive party system. The dominance of the Liberal Democrats in 1955–1993 reduced other parties to a token opposition, and voters had a bigger impact on internal party politics than they did on competition among parties.[17] The influence of voters was further reduced by the secrecy surrounding government, which prevented voters from feeling involved in national issues. Most important, though, power in government has always depended more on the support of the bureaucracy than on that of voters.

It became clear in the late 1980s and early 1990s that voters—especially younger ones—were becoming tired of political corruption, of the factions that divided the parties, and of the role of special interests. Changes were made to the election laws in 1994, but opinion polls in 1996 revealed that about half of all voters still did not identify with any of the parties on offer. They made their point by voting with their feet: Turnout at elections fell from 70 percent during the 1980s to 67 percent in 1993 and in recent elections has hovered at about 60 percent. The 1994 election laws were aimed at making elections less expensive and thus less prone to bribery and corruption. Combined with recent changes in the lineup of political parties, however, all they did was make the party system more fluid and make clear the need for further reforms.

The frustrations continue today, with the gap between the priorities of leaders and voters symbolized by the rebellion that took place within the LDP in 2001—the party rank-and-file elected Junichiro Koizumi as prime minister in place of Ryutaro Hashimoto, the preferred candidate of the party leadership. If voters were tired of corruption and mainstream politics in the 1990s, they are even more tired of it today. The problem, though, is that the political leaders who must make the needed changes benefit too much from the current system, and they face a powerful bureaucracy that is deeply hostile to change.

THE ELECTORAL SYSTEM

There are no primaries in Japan, and official election campaigns are restricted by law to a maximum of 30 days. The result is that Japanese elections are as short as those in Britain, but they are not always as cheap or as simple.

Legislative Elections

Japan uses a combination voting system for elections to the Diet. Of the 247 members of the House of Councillors, 149 are elected using the single-member system and 98 are elected by the country as a whole using multimember districts and proportional representation. Members of the House serve fixed six-year renewable terms and elections are staggered, with half the members coming up for reelection every three years. At the election, each party publishes a list of at least ten candidates, ranked in order of priority. Voters choose one of the competing lists, and when the votes are totaled, the seats are divided in proportion to the votes cast.

In the House of Representatives until 1994, there were 511 members, all elected using the single nontransferable vote (SNTV) system (see Comparative Exercise, p. 222. There were 129 districts, each represented by between two and six members. Every voter in each district voted for one candidate only, and when the votes were totaled, the two to six candidates with the most votes were declared elected, even if they all came from the same party. Although this system provided a fairer reflection of voter preferences than a single-member system, it also created a number of problems:

- It led to a large number of parties winning seats in the Diet.
- It weakened interparty competition and strengthened intraparty competition by forcing candidates from the same party to run against one another. Because they had no substantial policy differences, they had to use other methods to win, including personal appeal, networks of supporters, and the purchase of political

support. The system also encouraged the formation of factions within parties as candidates sought whatever advantages they could over their competitors.[18]

■ Although electoral districts were supposed to be regularly reapportioned to take account of demographic changes, this did not happen often enough to keep pace with the shift of the population from rural to urban districts. The result was that some members of the Diet represented as many as six times more voters than other members. The LDP was unwilling to change the system for fear that it would lose seats, but a reapportionment was forced on them in 1986 by the Supreme Court, and the LDP ended up losing fewer seats than it had anticipated.

Revisions to the Public Offices Election Law passed since 1994 have given the House of Representatives the same system used in the House of Councillors: It now has 480 seats, of which 180 are elected by PR and 300 by the single-member system, for renewable terms of a maximum of four years. Voters cast two ballots: one for a candidate and one for a party. There are 11 PR districts, which overlap the single-member districts, and candidates can run in both. Thus, if they lose in a single-member district, they might still win enough votes to be elected under PR. Ironically, this system favors the LDP and works against smaller parties, which became clear when it was tried for the first time in 1996 and several smaller parties lost many of their seats.

Electioneering in Japan is controlled by the strongest restrictions found in any liberal democracy. This is a legacy of campaign rules passed in 1924, when the government assumed that voters were not sophisticated enough to understand the differences among parties and so might be an easy target for the growing socialist movement. Even today, door-to-door canvassing, signature drives, mass meetings, polling, unscheduled speeches, parades, and literature produced by candidates are either illegal or strictly regulated. Candidates are instead limited to a small number of government-sanctioned mailings, newspaper advertisements, and radio and TV announcements.

Local Government Elections

In addition to the Diet elections, Japanese voters take part in a variety of local elections. Mayors and members of the assemblies of villages, towns, and cities are elected, as are governors and assembly members of Japan's 47 prefectures. As in all unitary systems, however, the significance of local government elections is relatively minor, except as a potential (but not always reliable) indicator of support for political parties.

POLITICAL PARTIES

Japan does not have a long history of party politics. Several parties were formed after the Meiji restoration, but they were not constitutionally recognized, and any potential for the development of a multiparty system was halted in the 1930s with the Great Depression and the rise of Japanese militarism. The party system was reborn after 1945 and has since gone through considerable and often confusing change.

From 1955 to 1993, every government was formed and led by the LDP, which dominated both houses of parliament until 1989, when the party lost its majority in the House of Councillors for the first time. Changes in the party system took another dramatic turn in the 1993 elections to the House of Representatives, when defections from the LDP resulted in big losses and the emergence of three new parties. A new multiparty coalition government was formed under Prime Minister Morihiro Hosokawa, and the LDP went into opposition for the first time since 1955. Hosokawa was to remain in office for barely eight months, however, and realignments in the late 1990s brought rapid turnover in the office of the prime minister. There were predictions that a two-party system might emerge, with the LDP on the right and the New Frontier Party (NFP) on the left, but this idea died in late 1997 with the collapse of the NFP. The closest that Japan now has to an opposition party is the centrist Democratic Party.

Running from left to right on the political spectrum, the five main parties active in politics today are as follows.

The Japan Communist Party (JCP) (*Nihon Kyosanto*)

Founded in 1922 with Soviet support, the Japan Communist Party was not legalized until 1945. It won 10 percent of the vote in 1946, but it became increasingly militant and was torn by an internal battle between pro-Soviet and pro-Chinese factions. It purged these factions in the 1960s and softened its stance. As it became wealthier and more respectable, radicals charged that it had become too close to the establishment, and many switched their allegiance to the Socialists. With the collapse of Soviet-style communism, the party lost 10 of its 26 seats in the House of Representatives, but it regained them all in 1996 as left-wing voters abandoned the discredited Socialist Party and disenchanted LDP supporters cast protest votes for the JCP. The 2003–2005 elections saw its representation in both chambers of the Diet cut to single figures.

Social Democratic Party (SDP) (*Shakai Minshuto*)

The Japan Socialist Party (JSP) was long Japan's main opposition party. It was part of a short-lived coalition government with the Democratic Party in 1947, and its support grew quickly enough to alarm Japanese conservatives into forming the LDP, which took power in 1955. The Socialists won 33 percent of the vote in 1958 but subsequently lost support because of their more militant policies: arguing that the maintenance of a military was unconstitutional (which was true), supporting unilateral conventional disarmament and "unarmed neutrality," criticizing the U.S.-Japanese relationship, and opposing nuclear power.

In 1986, leadership of the party fell to Takako Doi, a former law professor notable for being Japan's first female party leader. She rapidly established herself as a popular and outspoken figure, began moderating the policies of the party, and exploited the scandals then rife in the LDP to help the JSP win a large block of seats in the upper house in 1989 (although this was as much a protest against the LDP as a sign of growing support for the JSP). It also changed its name to the Social Democratic Party (SDP). In the interests of forming a coalition with the LDP in 1994, it abandoned almost all its traditional policy positions, disgusting many of its supporters. Despite reappointing Takako Doi leader, the party became a shadow of its former self, and in 2005 won just seven seats in the House of Representatives.

FIGURE 3.2

Legislative Electoral Trends in Japan

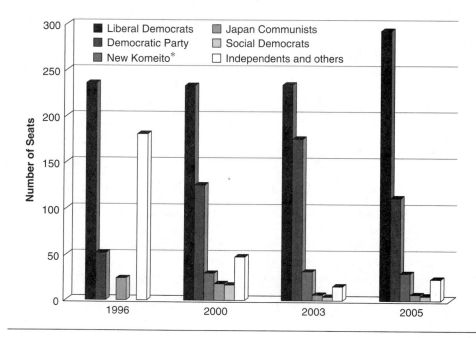

Figures are for House of Representatives only.
* Ran in 1996 as part of the New Frontier Party.

Clean Government Party (CGP) (*Komeito*)

New Komeito is the political wing of Japan's largest lay Buddhist organization. It was created in 1998 on the center-left of the political spectrum as a result of a string of changes in the party system dating back to the early 1990s, when the cumulative effect of scandals, political arrogance, unfulfilled promises of political reform, and a growing feeling of voter powerlessness was beginning to prove too much for the LDP. Groups of disaffected LDP members of parliament broke away during 1992–1993 to form three new parties: the Japan New Party, the Japan Renewal Party, and the New Harbinger Party. These then joined forces with four other small parties—including Komeito (founded in 1964) and the Social Democrats—to form the multiparty coalition that finally broke the LDP's 38-year grip on power in 1993.

In December 1994 the New Frontier Party (NFP) united no fewer than nine opposition groups under the leadership of Ichiro Ozawa, an aggressive and ambitious opposition politician who was behind the rebellion among LDP members that led to the loss of its majority in 1993. The NFP proved to be a formidable force, winning more votes than the LDP in elections to the House of Councillors in July 1995 and winning 31 percent of the seats in the House of Representatives in October 1996. However, its failure to win a majority caused grumbles of dissent within the party. To remove some of his critics, Ozawa disbanded the NFP in December 1997, and most of its members agreed to create New Komeito. This then entered into a coalition with the LDP.

Democratic Party of Japan (DPJ) (*Minshuto*)

Among the parties that broke away from the Liberal Democrats in 1992–1993 was the small, moderately left-wing New Harbinger Party (*Shinto Sakigake*). Although it had as many as 23 seats in the House of Representatives, it was not as actively pro-reform as it claimed and quickly lost support. In August 1996 it finally broke apart, with defectors forming the centrist Democratic Party under the joint leadership of a popular former health minister, Naoto Kan, and Yukio Hatoyama, a member of a wealthy family often compared to the Kennedys because of its long lineage in politics. More defections pushed DPJ numbers in the House up to 52, and the emergence of the Democratic Party as the major opposition to the LDP-Liberal government was confirmed at the June 2000 elections when it won 127 seats. Its share of seats rose to 177 in 2003, making it the de facto opposition to the LDP, and it made further gains in the July 2004 elections in the House of Councillors, mainly at the expense of smaller parties. Two months later it elected Katsuya Okada as its new leader. Relatively young (b. 1953), telegenic, and an opponent of factions, he was widely seen as the first serious non-LDP contender for the prime ministership in many years. But following the DPJ's poor showing in the 2005 elections, when it lost about one-third of its seats, Okada resigned and was replaced by the even younger Seiji Maehara (b. 1962).

Liberal Democratic Party (LDP) (*Jiyuminshuto*)

The LDP can trace its roots back to the 1870s, but it was reformed in 1955 when the two main conservative parties (the Liberals and the Democrats) joined forces to prevent the Socialists from winning power. It then became the dominating influence in Japanese politics, regularly winning more than 50 percent of the vote. However, a string of scandals and mounting criticism of the electoral system steadily drove away its supporters, and it suffered its heaviest blow in 1993 when many of its members defected. After winning only 44 percent of the vote in the general election, it went into opposition. It regained some of its lost ground in 1994, forming a minority government with the support of the Socialists and the New Harbinger Party. It has been in government ever since, but always in coalition with other parties.

The LDP is a classic example of Japanese consensus politics. It is a mainstream, pro-business party, but it is less a party than a coalition of factions; hence the common jibe that the LDP is neither liberal, nor democratic, nor even a party. Each faction is headed by a senior party figure, every LDP member of parliament is associated with one of these factions—of which there are usually five to seven but as many as ten—and party leadership is decided by interfactional bargaining. So strong was the LDP in 1955–1993, and so important was the role of faction, that the real

FACTIONALISM IN JAPANESE POLITICS

Understanding all the changes that have come to the Japanese party system in the last few years is challenging enough by itself, but the existence within many of these parties of factions tied to competing political leaders adds an additional layer of complexity. The word *faction* is the nearest English translation of the Japanese word *habatsu*. Unlike the common Western notion of factions as ephemeral and self-seeking, Japanese factions are usually permanent and well organized, and only the communists and New Komeito have been able to achieve the kind of discipline needed to prevent the emergence of *habatsu*.[19]

Factionalism was encouraged by the pre-1994 electoral system, which obliged candidates from the same party to compete against each other in multimember districts. The LDP has been particularly famous for its factions, which have their own leaders, policies, and political funds and run their own campaigns. Although they were officially disbanded several years ago, they are still part of LDP politics. There are factions too in opposition parties (such as the Social Democrats), in government ministries, businesses, higher education, and even schools of sumo wrestling. Wherever they are found, they serve the same basic purposes of providing group identity and personal connections, and encouraging individual and group advancement.

Factions may help prevent too much centralization of power and allow different policies to be discussed within one party, but the problems they cause are legion. They weaken the power and authority of party leaders, encourage elitism and nepotism, and contribute to the prominent role of money in Japanese politics; the factions provide the money and contacts to help with election campaigns, and the bigger factions regularly raise more money for their candidates than the parties raise as a whole.

struggles for political power in Japan took place within the LDP rather than among the different parties.

There were several explanations for the longtime dominance of the LDP:

- It presided over the economic boom that began in the 1950s, so it was able to argue that it was the party of experience and could meet popular expectations for stability and economic prosperity.

- The factions do not provide real policy alternatives so much as they promote their leaders to positions of power. Party leaders find it more important to win the support of other members of the party than to win the support of voters. Factionalism in the LDP prevented the party from responding to the changing place of Japan in the world while it was in power, and it threatens to leave Japan in a position of stalemate when its major trading partners demand less protectionism and a greater Japanese contribution to global security issues.

- Opposition parties were unable to cooperate long enough to form a government, and the major opposition party—the Socialists—differed significantly with the LDP only on foreign policy issues, thus failing to offer a distinct ideological alternative.

- The LDP has an impressive network of grassroots supporter groups (***koenkai***), consisting of friends and supporters with personal (rather than political) ties to Diet members; the *koenkai* are less concerned about party policies than about ensuring the reelection of their representatives.[20]

- Japanese voters tended to be conservative, preferring continuity and consensus. They regularly showed signs that they might be about to drop the LDP, periodically voting against the government in by-elections and local elections and giving the Socialists a majority in the House of Councillors in 1989. At general elections, however, they always went back to the LDP. Even at the height of the Recruit scandal in 1990, when the popularity of the Takeshita government fell to a dismal 3.9 percent, the LDP won more than 50 percent of the vote at national elections.

- The LDP is a chameleon party, adapting its policies to meet the changing tastes and needs of voters. Ostensibly conservative, it has members whose positions cover points from the left to the right of the political spectrum, leading critics to charge that it has no ideology at all.

- With its extensive contacts in business and the bureaucracy, the party has long been able to raise more money than its opponents and has also had much more power of patronage at its disposal. Although usually an advantage, this also paved the way for repeated cases of bribery and political scandal.

Although it lost its majority in the House of Representatives in 1993, and currently governs in a coalition with New Komeito, the LDP has remained the biggest party in the Diet by far. It came back into government as part of a coalition in 1994 and has retained its preeminence in recent general elections. After several months of declining popularity, Prime Minister Junichiro Koizumi called a snap election in September 2005, the centerpiece being his program of overhauling the Japanese banking and business world. Voters responded by increasing LDP representation, giving the LDP-New Komeito coalition 326 of the 480 seats in the House of Representatives. But it was unclear how Koizumi would use his new mandate, and how much he would be able to achieve if he followed through on his promise to step down as prime minister in September 2006.

POLICIES AND POLICYMAKING

Elected officials in most liberal democracies feel at least a little responsible to the voters and keep a wary eye on opinion polls, but elected officials in Japan are less concerned about public opinion than about personal ties to voters in their districts and their relationship with party leaders, faction leaders, and senior bureaucrats. As the central actor in politics and policymaking, the LDP has been able to rely on the Japanese preference for pragmatism and consensus. The result is that policy initiatives in the party arena have been driven mainly by developments within the LDP and driven more by internal competition than by the competition offered by other parties.

Policymaking in Japan is also heavily influenced by the special place of the **bureaucracy** in the power structure. Bureaucrats, by definition, are supposed to implement

bureaucracy The government institutions charged with the daily administration of a society.

rather than make policy, but Japanese bureaucrats have several features that distinguish them from their counterparts in most other liberal democracies:

- The bureaucracy is efficient and, as such, has contributed to Japan's postwar economic and political success. Japan is one of the few countries (France being another) where being a bureaucrat is a high-status occupation, subject to demanding entrance exams. The higher levels are dominated by the top graduates of the best law schools, notably those at the universities of Tokyo and Kyoto.

- Bureaucrats are government leaders. Japan is governed by a class of administrators who first run government ministries, then retire to become corporate executives or to sit in the Diet.[21] This "revolving door" is common in the United States as well, and is criticized in both countries. In Japan it is described as *amakudari*, or "descent from heaven."

- More than in any other liberal democracy, policy decisions are made out of public view and mostly within government ministries. This process has reached the point where there is a standing joke that the Diet passes a law, and the bureaucrats then write it. Put another way, "the politicians reign and the bureaucrats rule."[22]

In short, public policy in Japan is made not so much as a result of all the activities we normally associate with pluralism, such as electoral competition, interest-group pressure, public debate, and political parties reflecting the views of voters, but rather as a result of what has unhappily come to be called **Japan Inc.**: bargaining within an iron triangle involving the higher levels of the governing political party (or coalition), the bureaucracy, and big business.[23]

ECONOMIC POLICY

It is rare these days to read or hear any reports about the Japanese economy without coming across the word *crisis*. After its remarkable growth during the 1970s and 1980s, when Japan was routinely described as an emerging economic superpower, there has been little but bad news over the past decade: falling GDP, record unemployment, declining share prices, a falling trade surplus, record numbers of bankruptcies, a growing national debt, and a banking system in trouble. These and many other problems are indicative of a system in trouble, leaving analysts undecided as to where the blame lies, or whether Japan can recover. One administration after another has tried to address the problem, but so far without much success.

Japan's economic record after World War II was remarkable. Barely two generations ago, Japan was a militaristic and predominantly agrarian society. As recently as the mid-1960s, more Japanese worked on farms than in factories, and the label *Made in Japan* was synonymous with inferior and rapidly disposable products. But the Japanese economy grew at an average annual rate of 10 percent (three times the U.S. rate), laying the foundations for Japan's emergence in the 1970s and 1980s as an economic powerhouse.

The country's economic success was based on importing raw materials (it has little coal, oil, or steel of its own) and turning them into superbly designed consumer and industrial products that are still synonymous with quality, reliability, and durability; Japanese road vehicles, machinery, and consumer goods swept both the home and the export markets, and almost every North American and European owns at least one Japanese consumer product. Japan became by far the world's largest source of surplus wealth for international investment, and parallels were drawn between Japan's record and those of other Southeast Asian states, with the implication that countries such as South Korea, Taiwan, Malaysia, and Indonesia could be the Japans of the future. (See Part III.)

At the same time, Japan was economically vulnerable because of its need to import so much. This encouraged it to protect its industry from foreign competition by imposing formal and informal barriers on imported manufactured and consumer goods, making them expensive to Japanese consumers and making it difficult for Europeans and North Americans to break into the Japanese market. In 1982, manufactured goods accounted for just 25 percent of Japan's import bill. That figure is now nearly 60 percent, but even that is still short of comparable figures for Germany, Britain, or the United States, where manufactured goods account for 70 to 80 percent of the import bill. Protectionism has also helped Japan build a large trade imbalance with most of its trading partners: In 2003, its imports totaled nearly $385 billion in value, but its exports were worth nearly $472 billion, leaving it with a healthy $87 billion trade surplus. By contrast, the United States was importing goods with a value of $1.3 trillion, but exporting goods with a value of just $725 billion, leaving it with a trade deficit of about $580 billion (up from $245 billion in 1998). (See Figure 3.3)

Explanations for Japan's remarkable economic record included the national character of the Japanese, the effort invested by Japanese industry in product design and development, and the unfair trade practices employed by Japan. Initially, Japan was helped by a global economic system that encouraged exports by keeping the yen cheap against other currencies. It also invested heavily in new plants and equipment during the 1950s, laying the foundation for later economic growth. The energy crisis of the early 1970s slowed that growth, but it encouraged Japan to conserve energy and develop new fuel- and labor-efficient technology, which in turn lowered the break-even points of Japanese industry.

Other key factors in Japan's economic success included the following:

- A close relationship between government and business, which allowed Japanese companies to borrow much more than their American counterparts and protected established industry from competition while encouraging the growth of new industries.

- A close relationship between government, business, and labor unions, which has meant that the number of days lost through strikes is among the lowest in the liberal democratic world, and workers are not only highly productive, but they tend to put the good of the company before their own personal welfare

- Major investments in new technology and research and development, where the emphasis has been on greater automation

- High levels of household savings. While most Americans (like their political leaders) like to spend money and live on credit and fail to achieve even the modest suggested goal of saving 10 percent of their income, the Japanese save a remarkable 23 percent of their income, much of which is invested, thus helping economic development.

FIGURE 3.3

Comparing Trade Balances

Suplus or deficit as a percentage of
total trade, measured in U.S. dollars

Source: Based on figures in World Trade Organization Web site, 2005, www.wto.org. Figures are for 2003.

Along with the economic successes, the value accorded to discipline, conformity, and group behavior has created a prosperous and successful society. The streets are clean, there are few drug problems, there is an efficient transport system, the crime rate is one of the lowest in the world, the primary and secondary education system is one of the best in the world (Japanese pupils spend longer at school than American pupils, devote more time to homework, follow a compulsory national curriculum, and are subject to stricter discipline), and the Japanese live longer than almost anyone else, including nearly four years longer than Americans.

Unfortunately, economic growth has come at the expense of quality of life. Remarkably little has been invested in environmental protection, welfare, and basic services, and the Japanese work long hours, driven partly by the high cost of living but mainly by notions of loyalty and obligation toward their employers. This has led to *karoshi* (death from overwork) and to the filing of court cases against companies by the families of workers who have died relatively young from heart attacks or strokes;

CAN JAPAN CHANGE ITS WAYS?

Japan is a society full of interesting contradictions. On one hand, opinion polls suggest that the Japanese are happier than the citizens of most liberal democracies, and the data reveal a society that is more socially and economically equal, with a bigger middle class and smaller income disparities than in the United States or almost any Western European country. On the other hand, there are elements of the Japanese way that are causing social and economic difficulties:[24]

- It is an unusually homogeneous society, but it is also one in which anything foreign is kept at a distance. For a city of its size, Tokyo is notable for its lack of racial diversity, and unlike many other economically successful countries, Japan has kept out immigrants who might have helped fuel economic growth. It has also kept out ideas and practices that might help it solve its economic problems. The record of liberal democracies suggests that one of the keys to political and economic success is openness and transparency, commodities that are undersupplied in Japan.

- As the Japanese live longer, the population is growing older. At the same time, younger Japanese are marrying later—or not at all—and having fewer children. These trends are typical of liberal democracies, but there are some interesting differences in the Japanese case. Where more Europeans and Americans are having children outside marriage (62 percent of all births in Iceland, 40 percent in Britain, and 33 percent in the United States[25]), this is still frowned upon in Japan, where just 1 percent of children are born outside marriage. Also, there is a tradition in Japan that the wife of an eldest son will take care of her parents-in-law when they grow older. With more Japanese women pursuing careers, this is an increasingly unwelcome prospect, so more are delaying marriage.

- The number of Japanese in their 20s is falling, which is already having an impact on the labor market; it is placing a greater burden on the young to look after the elderly and to meet the bill for social security and health care, and it places greater pressure on older Japanese to work longer. Furthermore, an older society tends to be more conservative and more resistant to change.

There is little question that although Japan still reflects many traditional social values, it is also undergoing fundamental change. But it is debatable whether these changes can help it address the core contradictions in its political and economic systems: a belief in democracy and capitalism, yet an inability to make either of them work in the same way as most other liberal democracies.

labor laws have recently been changed to limit companies with more than 30 employees to a 40-hour working week. Despite their work ethic, the Japanese have less purchasing power than Europeans or North Americans. Not only are consumer goods relatively expensive, but land and real estate prices are among the highest in the world. Cities are crowded, housing is in short supply, homes are small, and commuters often have to travel up to two hours a day each way between home and work. Finally, there is a growing sense of disillusionment and alienation among Japanese, as well as a

Rapid economic growth has brought new wealth and affluence to Japan since the 1960s, but it has also compromised the quality of life for many Japanese. Tokyo is crowded and polluted and has the highest cost of living of any city in the world.

gradual breakdown of old systems of discipline, amounting to something like a national identity crisis.[26]

To these problems has now been added the specter of an economy in decline. Just what has happened is a puzzle, mainly because of the difficulty of differentiating business and politics.[27] The problem of Japan Inc.—and the heavy dependence of the government, the bureaucracy, and big business on one another—has made it difficult for each to make independent judgments. One result is that the government subsidizes inefficient businesses to keep unemployment low or builds public works projects (such as airports and bridges) that no one needs simply to keep their networks of supporters happy. In return, many of the companies pay off the politicians or bureaucrats, and voters routinely make sure their representatives are returned to office. The most infamous relationship between the bureaucracy and business is *amakudari*. More generally, there is so much secrecy within the political system, and so little accountability, that it is difficult to apportion blame, and the people who should be responsible for making the changes have no motivation to take action. Under the circumstances, it is difficult to see how Japan can reform itself.

FOREIGN POLICY

Japanese foreign policy since World War II has been influenced by three short sentences contained in Chapter II, Article 9, of the 1947 constitution:

> Aspiring sincerely to an international peace based on justice and order, the Japanese people renounce war as a sovereign right of the nation and the threat to use force as a means of settling international disputes.
>
> In order to accomplish the aim of the preceding paragraph, land, sea and air forces, as well as other war potential, will never be maintained. The right of belligerency of the state will not be recognized.

Just as the Allied powers restricted the rearming of Germany after World War II, so this clause was included in the Japanese constitution to prevent the reemergence of Japanese militarism. Although it may have kept the Allies happy, it has provoked much controversy within Japan, has not been strictly followed, and has complicated Japan's relations with the United States and with its immediate neighbors.

Japan and the United States

The rise of economic powers such as Britain and France was accompanied by a parallel growth in their military power. By contrast, Japan and postwar Germany were prevented from using their economic power to become threats to regional security. Japan was restricted to being little more than a regional representative of U.S. foreign policy, a role underpinned by the U.S.-Japanese Mutual Security Treaty of 1954, by which it agreed to the stationing of U.S. troops on its soil. Japan has also maintained the **Self-Defense Force (SDF),** whose job during the cold war was to provide the United States with intelligence, serve the interests of the Western alliance in the western Pacific, prepare to repel invaders, and keep open the sea lanes supplying Japan. To underpin this policy, the United States stations about 45,000 military personnel and 190 aircraft in Japan at an annual cost of $6 billion, half of which is paid by Japan.

Although this arrangement has generally worked well, it has occasionally shown signs of strain. U.S. and Japanese economic and defense interests are linked together closely, but the two countries are economic rivals. There has been particular concern in the United States (less so today than in the 1990s) about the inroads made into the U.S. automobile and appliance markets by Japanese products and about Japanese investment. When Japanese companies purchased Rockefeller Center in New York and Columbia Pictures in 1989, news headlines decried the sale of U.S. "landmarks" to Japan. (Interestingly, the sale of such "landmarks" as Pillsbury, Burger King, and Holiday Inn to British companies elicited almost no response at all.) The concern was as much as anything driven by the trade imbalance at the time between the U.S. and Japan.

Meanwhile, dissident voices in Japan argue that Americans have lost the ability to compete, that Japanese dependence on the U.S. military is wrong, and that Japan's economic power gives it the right to a stronger voice in world affairs and that it should not necessarily defer to the United States. The 1990–1991 Gulf War heightened tensions. Because Japan imports about 70 percent of its oil from the Middle

East, many in the United States felt that it was obliged to help in the war effort. Japanese public opinion was opposed to the war but in favor of helping the allies, if only to avoid U.S. criticism. Japan eventually agreed to pay $13 billion toward the cost of the war effort, but not without controversy that ultimately threatened the tenure of Prime Minister Toshiki Kaifu. Japan remained remarkably quiet as tensions in the Gulf built again prior to the second Iraqi war in 2003, but since the end of the cold war there has been a growth of Japanese military activities abroad: The SDF has been involved in UN peacekeeping operations in Cambodia, Mozambique, and East Timor, and in 2004 the Koizumi government surprised many by sending more than 500 Japanese troops to Iraq to help with rebuilding; this was Japan's first deployment in a combat zone since World War II.

Japanese-U.S. relations were strained in 1995 when three U.S. servicemen abducted and raped a 12-year-old girl on the island of Okinawa. One of a chain of islands south of the Japanese mainland, Okinawa is home to about 29,000 U.S. military personnel. Against a background of growing doubts about the U.S. presence, the incident set off mass protests and led to a September 1996 referendum in which 90 percent of Okinawans supported a cutback in U.S. presence. The Japanese government essentially ignored the result, raising questions about the gaps between public policy and public opinion.

The visits made by prime minister Junichiro Koizumi to the Yasukuni shrine for Japan's war dead were interpreted by some as symbolic of his desire—shared by an increasing number of Japanese—to see Japan play a more assertive role in world affairs, to cease hiding the Japanese military behind the label "Self-Defense Force," to develop a more active role for Japan's military in alliance with the United States, and to at least reinterpret—if not revise altogether—Article 9.[28] Achieving the change will be difficult though, because of opposition within Japan to anything that even hints at militarism, and concerns from Japan's neighbors, particularly China and South Korea, who still remember with disquiet their unhappy experiences at the hands of the Japanese.

Japan and Its Neighbors

Japan officially spends only 1 percent of its GNP on defense, not as much as most European nations (2 to 3 percent) or the United States (about 5 percent). In fact, creative accounting hides the fact that it probably spends closer to 2 percent of GNP. This means that it has the third largest military budget in the world, amounting to almost as much as Britain and France combined. Even this is too small to provide Japan with more than a token defense capability, however.

Despite its vulnerability, Japan has tried to limit its global activities and has kept a low profile in international disputes. Its main priority has been to stay friendly with everyone and to build trade, but this has brought criticism that it is taking a free ride at the expense of the United States and not giving the United States a fair deal on trade in return. Japan is now torn between continuing to be a regional arm of U.S. foreign policy and building closer relations with Russia, China, and other Asian nations.

The debate over Japanese policy on the two Iraqi crises seemed to reflect the lack of direction in Japanese foreign policy, but it is not only the Japanese who are confused. For all the criticism that was leveled at Japan by the United States and others at the time of the 1990–1991 Gulf War, it is unlikely that anyone (even the Japanese themselves) would look favorably on an expansion of the Japanese military. Japan now finds itself torn between military self-sufficiency, meeting the responsibilities and expectations that come with economic wealth, and meeting the goal of nonbelligerence required by its U.S.-written constitution.

In recent years, Japan has become interested in spreading its influence to poorer countries. For example, it has the biggest national foreign aid budget in the world (nearly $8 billion in 2003–2004, compared to the $7 billion given by the United States), has cut tariffs on the import of tropical products from poorer countries, has taken steps to help reduce the debt burden of these countries, and has increased its investments in Southeast Asian countries. Given its dependence on imported raw materials and trade, Japanese planners want to encourage economic development in countries such as India and China, with their potentially huge consumer markets, and in newly industrializing countries such as Indonesia and Malaysia.

JAPANESE POLITICS IN TRANSITION

Japan has seen a dramatic transformation in the last 60 years. Defeated in war and economically devastated, it was faced in 1945 with the challenge of adopting a new political system imposed on it by the terms of the peace settlement, becoming more fully a part of the international community, and building economic independence against a background of limited natural resources.

There are no questions about its economic success. In 1946, it had a GDP of just $1.3 billion, and more than half its workforce was employed in agriculture. Its GDP today is nearly 3,300 times bigger, its industries and services have grown by leaps and bounds, and barely one in ten Japanese now works in agriculture. Japanese products, sold all over the world, have become synonymous with quality and durability.

However, although Japan has become wealthy, many argue that its political system has not modernized as quickly or as effectively as its economy. Vested interests, factionalism, and deal making have dominated the policymaking process, self-interest on the part of party leaders has helped perpetuate a corrupt electoral system, and Japan has been left with a strangely archaic way of governing itself. It now faces the challenges of opening its markets to its trading partners, finding a new role for itself at the heart of an Asia filled with rapidly growing economies, and reforming its political system in a way that takes government out of smoke-filled rooms and moves it more fully into the public arena.

KEY TERMS

amakudari
closed country
Diet
emperor
factionalism
Japan Inc.
koenkai

Liberal Democratic
   Party
Meiji restoration
Mutual Security Treaty
patron-client
   democracy
prefectures

Self-Defense Force (SDF)
Shinto
shogun
Supreme Commander
   for the Allied Powers
   (SCAP)
1947 constitution

KEY PEOPLE

Emperor Akihito   Douglas MacArthur   Ichiro Ozawa
Junichiro Koizumi   Katsuya Okada

STUDY QUESTIONS

1. What is the difference (if any) between modernization and Westernization?
2. What evidence is there of social hierarchies in the United States and Britain, and how do their political consequences compare with those of Japanese social hierarchy?
3. It is often said that Japanese prime ministers are caretakers or functionaries, rather than leaders. To what extent could the same be said of U.S. presidents and British prime ministers?
4. Which is best for government and the people: regular or slow turnover in the office of the executive?
5. To what extent is factionalism a part of politics in other liberal democracies? Is it something peculiarly Japanese?
6. Compare and contrast the power and role of political parties in Japan and the United States.
7. What are the costs and benefits of a single-party-dominant system like that of Japan?
8. Is Japan an economic superpower?
9. Should Japan be allowed to take care of its own defense?
10. What reforms are needed to bring stability to the Japanese political system?

JAPAN ONLINE

The Japanese Government: www.mofa.go.jp/j_info/japan/government
Web site maintained by the Japanese Ministry of Foreign Affairs, with links to a variety of government departments.
Kantei Home Page: www.kantei.go.jp/foreign/index-e.html
Home page of the office of the prime minister, which includes links to other government institutions.
House of Representatives: www.shugin.go.jp/index.nsf/html/index_e.htm
Home page of the Japanese House of Representatives.
Liberal Democratic Party: www.jimin.jp/jimin/english/index.html and **Democratic Party of Japan:** www.dpj.or.jp/english/index.html
Home sites for Japan's two major political parties.
Asahi Shimbun: www.asahi.com/english/english.html
Japan Times: www.japantimes.co.jp
News in English from two of Japan's major daily newspapers.

FURTHER READING

Curtis, Gerald L., *The Logic of Japanese Politics: Leaders, Institutions and the Limits of Change* (New York: Columbia University Press, 1999). A survey of the state of Japanese politics, with predictions on how matters are likely to evolve.

Kerbo, Harold R., and John A. McKinstry, *Who Rules Japan? The Inner Circles of Economic and Political Power* (Boulder, CO: Prager, 1995). A study of the elites who rule Japan, their methods and motives, and their role in Japan's postwar economic growth.

Nathan, John, *Japan Unbound: A Volatile Nation's Quest for Pride and Purpose* (New York: Houghton Mifflin, 2004). A study of Japan's recent social and economic changes, which argues that the country is going through a national identity crisis.

Schlesinger, Jacob M., *Shadow Shoguns: The Rise and Fall of Japan's Postwar Political Machine* (Stanford, CA: Stanford University Press, 1999). An assessment of the link between economic wealth and political corruption in Japan, by a former member of the Tokyo bureau of the *Wall Street Journal*.

Stockwin, J. A. A., *Governing Japan: Divided Politics in a Major Economy*, 3rd Ed. (Oxford: Blackwell, 1999) and Ian Neary, *The State and Politics in Japan* (London: Blackwell, 2002). Introductions to Japanese political institutions, processes, and culture.

LEGISLATURES

Legislatures are the institutions within political systems that are responsible for making laws. The legislative process normally involves the introduction of proposals (or bills), discussion and amendment, and the acceptance or rejection of those proposals. The effect of these duties is to give legislatures at least four major roles in the political system: They legitimize government policies, represent the views of the people, act as a national debating chamber in which views are exchanged about government policies, and oversee and supervise the work of the executive and the bureaucracy.

Legislatures come in a variety of forms. The key differences among them are based on their relationship with the executive, the nature of the representation they provide, the terms of office of their members, and their organizational structure.

- **Relationship with the executive.** The vast majority of the world's legislatures are deliberative bodies that tend to follow the lead of the executive rather than having any real independence or the ability to set the policy agenda. Particularly in parliamentary systems such as those in Britain, Japan, and Canada, where the prime minister and most members of the cabinet are also members of the legislature and where their ability to lead depends on tight party discipline within the legislature, the powers of legislatures relative to the executive have tended to decline. Hence they have become more a source of votes and support for the goals of the executive than a source of key policy initiatives or places where important decisions are made. This is particularly true in more authoritarian systems, such as Egypt, where the legislature is little more than a rubber stamp for the policies of the leadership, which uses it as a means to legitimize power.

The only exceptions to these supportive legislatures can be found in the United States and in political systems that have adopted the U.S. model. Where there is a true separation of powers and a system of checks and balances, legislatures become important sources of policy initiatives, and executives must often work hard to win the support of legislators to see their pet programs voted into law. A failure to win an important vote in a parliamentary system could result in the fall of the government and the resignation of the prime minister, but it is not unusual for a vote in the U.S. Congress to go against the plans of the president.

- **The nature of representation.** Legislatures are the embodiment of the idea of representative democracy, meaning that voters elect into office legislators who are then supposed to represent their views when policies are debated and bills are voted on. In authoritarian systems, where elections are manipulated and executives wield most of the power, this process is usually a sham. Nowhere is this more obvious, for example, than in China, where only the Chinese Communist Party is allowed to field candidates at elections, where the National People's Congress meets once annually for sessions of two or three weeks, and where "representatives" do little more than discuss and endorse decisions already made by the party.

Even in liberal democracies, there are questions about how far legislators really represent the views of voters. They may be influenced by much narrower agendas, for several reasons. First, because they are members of parties with different ideologies and have been elected by voters who support those parties, legislators may have an ideological bias that means they represent only the opinions and values of that particular group of voters. Second, some may decide to be delegates, in the sense that they are driven by majority opinion among their constituents, regardless of their party affiliation. Third, some may see themselves as trustees, being driven by what they feel is in the best interests of their constituents. Finally, some will be influenced by special interests that have bought their support by being key sources of campaign funding.

In parliamentary systems, where party discipline is tight and members of the same party are expected to vote as a group, legislators will be led from above rather than from below. This means that they will tend to vote as their party leaders instruct rather than being influenced by the views of their constituents or of special interests. Japanese legislators have the added complication of being responsible to their different factions and may make their decisions out of a sense of obligation to faction leaders rather than being influenced by the party leadership or their constituents.

- **Terms of office.** Legislators in democratic systems are usually elected directly by voters and most commonly for terms of between four and five years. This is enough time to allow them to make their mark on government and to allow voters to assess their impact, but it is also a short enough time to allow voters to review their performance at elections. The United States has gone to two extremes, using a fixed two-year election cycle for members of the House of Representatives, which forces members into almost constant campaigning and fund-raising, and a fixed six-year cycle for the Senate, which produces relatively little turnover. The United States has opted for fixed terms for its legislators, but

parliamentary systems usually have maximum terms, allowing their executives to call new elections at any time within those terms. The method used can have a significant impact on the nature of politics: With fixed terms, legislators are assured of a particular period of time in which to reach their goals and can time their actions accordingly; with maximum terms, legislators can never be sure when the next election will come and are much more subject to manipulation by the executive as a result.

- **Internal structure.** Legislatures are structured in many different ways, depending on how they are elected and what kind of representation they are expected to provide. The United States, Canada, Britain, and Japan all have bicameral legislatures, but these are relatively rare—about two-thirds of the world's national legislatures are unicameral, meaning that they have just a single chamber. Two chambers are normally found only in large or diverse countries and are designed to give two different kinds of representation. In federal systems such as the United States, Germany, and Australia, the upper chambers normally provide equal representation for states, regardless of how big or small they are, while lower chambers give equal representation to the people. Legislation may have to go through the same stages in both chambers—as is the case in the U.S. Congress—but upper chambers will often be weaker than lower chambers and may only have the power of delay.

For their part, lower chambers tend to be designed to represent the people in the sense that members come from districts of equal size. In most parliamentary systems, the executive—the prime minister and cabinet—comes from the lower chamber, giving it more political significance.

Part II

COMMUNIST AND POSTCOMMUNIST COUNTRIES

The theory of communism may be summed up in one sentence: Abolish all private property.

—Karl Marx

Communism doesn't work because people like to own stuff.

—Frank Zappa, American musician

One of the defining global ideologies of the twentieth century was communism, which provided the foundation for politics, economics, and society in about two dozen countries, and spawned political parties in many more. But with the collapse of the Soviet Union in 1990, communism also seemed to collapse. Only five countries still officially claim to be communist (China, Cuba, Laos, North Korea, and Vietnam), but the claims are much stronger than the hard evidence; China and Vietnam, for example, have made so many free-market reforms that they are now seen as part of the capitalist economic revolution that is transforming Asia. The only country that still comes close to old-style communism is North Korea, where Kim Jong Il runs the only remaining Stalinist dictatorship in the world.

Elsewhere in the former communist world, change is the prevailing order. The USSR itself broke up into 15 independent countries, some of which (notably Russia and the Ukraine) have moved unsteadily toward a democratic and free market future, while others (including Belarus and Turkmenistan) still hang on to the repressive policies of the Soviet years. Meanwhile, most Eastern European countries have moved quickly to shake off the heritage of communism and to transform themselves into liberal democracies. Estonia, Latvia and Lithuania—three former Soviet republics—are now members of both NATO and the European Union, and several of the newly independent states that came out of the breakup of Yugoslavia (such as Croatia and Macedonia) are also now looking to EU membership.

So why continue approaching the communist world as a distinctive group of countries? The simple answer is that the driving force in most of them, that best explains their current political situation, is their attempt to adjust to the collapse of the ideas that for so long underpinned the structure of their governments and economies. Just as the philosophies of John Locke and Adam Smith have long been at the heart of life in liberal democracies, so the writings of Karl Marx, Vladimir Lenin, and Mao Zedong continue to drive decisions in nearly 30 countries, whether in a positive sense (as something to be achieved) or in a negative sense (as something to be avoided).

Before looking at the features of communist and postcommunist (CPC) countries, it is important to be clear about the differences among three fundamental concepts:

- **Socialism.** This philosophy is based on the argument that the best way to remove social inequalities is through government ownership of key industries and services and through the redistribution of wealth and resources by taxing the wealthy and providing extensive welfare. Elements of socialism can be found in most liberal democracies—even the United States—in the form of progressive income taxes (the more you earn, the more you pay), social security, public health care, subsidized education, and the regulation of economic activity.

- **State socialism.** This takes socialist ideas much further and is based on large-scale state intervention in the economy, the centralization of political authority, government by a single political party supported by a large bureaucracy, state ownership of property, and the virtual elimination of the free market. The most extreme form of state socialism was the **totalitarianism** associated with Joseph Stalin in the Soviet Union between 1928 and 1953: complete government control of the political system, the economy, and the private lives of citizens.

- **Communism.** This is an end state, which has been described in theory but has never been achieved in practice on a large scale. Theoretically, communism would involve the elimination of the state system and private property and the creation of a classless, nonexploitive, and self-governing society in which there would be no political institutions, wages, or prices. The USSR came nowhere close to achieving these goals and actually eradicated many of the essential prerequisites for real communism, such as a strong **civil society**: a community of individuals and groups capable of acting separately from the state on the basis of pluralism, tolerance, civility, and mutually acceptable rules.

No country has ever been truly communist, and to describe the USSR or China as such was never correct. For most socialist thinkers, communism has always been an ideal that would follow the creation of a socialist state. This, at least, was the official claim of the USSR (the Union of Soviet *Socialist* Republics), whose 1977 constitution argued that a developed socialist society was "a necessary stage on the road to communism" and that the goal of the Soviet state was to lay the foundations of "a classless communist society in which there will be public, communist self government."[1] In fact, the USSR by the 1980s was far from achieving that goal. For their part, Chinese leaders still claimed in 1989 that their country was headed toward the achievement of "genuine" socialism at some distant and unknown time. By 1995,

totalitarianism A political system subject to total state control, where no individual rights or privileges are recognized.

communism A social, economic, and political system in which power and property are held in common.

CHECKLIST

COMMUNIST AND POSTCOMMUNIST COUNTRIES
What Are Their Features?

- Representative systems of government with regular elections, but with mixed results and a mixed application of democracy. Authoritarianism in some, the lingering effects of a heritage of authoritarianism in others.

- Political institutions and processes that are still undergoing redefinition, and where links between the government, the bureaucracy, and opposition groups are still often unclear.

- Mixed public feelings about the role of the state.

- A growing variety of forms of political participation and representation in most, all channels controlled by the governing party in a few.

- A mixed record on protection of individual rights under the law.

- Official claims of a deep respect for human equality, but a record on human rights ranging from indifferent to poor.

- The development of an active opposition and increased respect for freedom of speech in some, little or no opposition tolerated in others.

- Increasingly free-market policies in most, but heavy state control in some, and economic difficulties in almost all, including inefficiency, incompetence, and corruption, mainly arising out of the heritage of central control.

- High levels of urbanization in most, but with varied quality infrastructure.

- Improving technology.

- A mixed record on the provision of basic services, ranging from excellent in some to poor in others.

- Mixed ratings on the Freedom House, Economic Freedom, and Human Development Index rankings.

Where Are They?

There are 26, and they are mainly in Eastern Europe and Asia:

Albania	Cuba	Romania
Armenia	Georgia	Russia
Azerbaijan	Kazakhstan	Serbia and Montenegro
Belarus	Kyrgyzstan	Tajikistan
Bosnia and Herzegovina	Laos	Turkmenistan
Bulgaria	Macedonia	Ukraine
Cambodia	Moldova	Uzbekistan
China	Mongolia	Vietnam
Croatia	North Korea	

public enthusiasm for socialism and political appeals to socialist goals were hard to find.[2] Today, it is understood that China is moving quickly toward becoming a free-market system, and that democracy must follow in short order.

So none of the CPC countries are truly communist, but instead they have practiced variations on the themes of socialism and state socialism. Most are now moving away from state control and are undergoing three levels of transformation: political, economic, and social.

Political Transition

In theory, communism is the most purely democratic of all political systems because it is based on a governing structure in which everyone plays a part and has an equal role. The late Chinese leader Deng Xiaoping once claimed that Chinese democracy was "the broadest democracy that has ever existed in history" and was superior to Western-style "bourgeois democracy."

In practice, the principles of communism were so distorted and abused by leaders with their own narrow agendas that most communist states became the antithesis of individual and social freedom, denying their citizens most of the political rights and liberties associated with liberal democracy. Communism included severe abuses of human rights, systematic repression, the elimination of opposition, controls on freedom of speech and movement, and the construction of a **police state:** one in which power is distributed and stability maintained by force and intimidation and in which civil liberties are routinely abused. The critics of communism would argue that these problems were inevitable; supporters would counter that the ideals of Marx and Lenin were never properly applied and that Soviet-style communism was an aberration.

> **police state** A state in which power is distributed and stability maintained by force.

Most communist states developed a centralized system of government, where power was in the hands of a small elite and was supposedly directed at mobilizing the masses in the interests of building socialism. This usually produced four kinds of political institutions:

- **A single political party,** which went well beyond political parties in liberal democracies in its attempts to make and implement policy and to control and direct government, the bureaucracy, and even the private lives of citizens.

- **A hierarchical government structure** that was supposedly separate from the party but was actually heavily controlled by the party.

- **A large and usually inefficient bureaucracy,** which was subordinated to the party and used to implement the party's political, economic, and social goals.

- **A complex network of "social organizations."** Many of these looked like liberal democratic interest groups and even (in some cases) alternative parties but were actually used by the party to gather information and impose additional social control, usually by mobilizing and socializing workers on behalf of the party.

While China, Cuba, and North Korea still hold on to these institutions, most other postcommunist states have switched instead to the institutions and systems we associate with liberal democracy. These new institutions are often still weak, the boundaries between the responsibilities of the state and the individual are not yet clear, and some governments—most notably the Niyazov regime in Turkmenistan—still pursue old-style authoritarianism. But competitive multiparty systems are generally on the rise, the structures of government and the bureaucracy have been reorganized, and citizens have many more channels for the expression of their views. Communist and socialist parties are still active and prominent in a few CPC countries, but their influence has declined.

A public performance in the Kim Il Sung Stadium in Pyongyang, capital of North Korea, in 2002. Such organized displays of support for the regime were once a common feature of communist systems; North Korea is now one of the last countries remaining that still goes through the motions of old-style mass events designed to showcase the symbols of state socialism.

Meanwhile, the record on human rights in most CPC countries has improved. This has been particularly true in Eastern Europe, where most governments have abandoned the vestiges of the old totalitarian methods of conducting political business. It is less true in some of the former Soviet republics and in China and Cuba, both of which still have a poor record on human rights. It is least true in North Korea, which grimly hangs on to its old Stalinist ways, including systematic human rights abuses (there are an estimated 200,000 political prisoners in North Korean jails), a complete absence of media freedom, a single political party, and a complex cult of personality surrounding Kim Jong II.

Economic Transition

Because communism emerged mainly in economically underdeveloped countries, its leaders emphasized modernization and industrialization, moving beyond economic growth to include wider social change.[3] Communist governments became heavily involved in running industry and in regulating the economy. In most cases, this meant the virtual elimination of the free market and competition. It also meant the creation of state-owned monopolies and a centrally planned **command economy** in which huge government departments used quotas, price controls, subsidies, and five-year plans to decide what would be produced, where and when it would be produced, how it would be distributed, and at what prices it would be sold.

command economy
Economic system in which all decisions about production, supply and costs are made by government planners.

Virtually all CPC states are now cutting back on the role of government in the economy and are switching to free-market methods. Most have sold off state-owned monopolies to private owners and shareholders; have allowed the development of competition; and are letting the marketplace determine supply, demand, and prices. Russia and the other former Soviet republics are finding this a painful process, but China and Vietnam are making a more orderly transition, slowly allowing the private sector to expand and compete with state-owned industries and services.

Social Transition

Centralized political and economic control in the old communist regimes meant that individual citizens came to rely heavily on the state: It was the only significant employer, it ran all the basic services (such as transport, health care, and education), and it made all the decisions about the supply and the cost of goods and services. Centralized control also meant restrictions on the movement of people; international travel was allowed only for a privileged few (almost always ranking party members), and even domestic travel was often controlled through internal passports. At the same time, communist economies were often geared more toward the development of a strong military or toward the rapid development of industry, and governments were proportionately less interested in the welfare of individuals and the needs of consumers.

In the postcommunist era, the citizens of most CPC states are learning to look after themselves and to make more of their own decisions about their lives and about the choices they make. They are allowed virtually free movement, although many cannot afford to exploit the new opportunities available to them. Governments have switched their economic focus away from the military and toward the provision of basic services, but in terms of access to education and health care, postcommunist states lag far behind liberal democracies. Most CPC countries have only a Medium ranking on the Human Development Index, infant mortality is about two to three times the rate in liberal democracies, and their citizens have a life expectancy that is typically 5 to 10 years shorter.

THE PRINCIPLES OF SOCIALISM AND COMMUNISM

Socialism and communism—much like democracy and capitalism—have undergone a convoluted evolutionary process that has resulted in the development of many variations on several central themes, most of them based on the ideas of Karl Marx. However, if he had been able to see how his ideas were adapted to the different situations in Russia, China, and Latin America, he probably would have been shocked.

Marx and Marxism

Modern socialism was a response to the rise of European industry in the early nineteenth century. Industrialization produced a class system in which wealth was unequally distributed, voting rights were limited, and unemployment, poverty, child labor, and malnutrition were rife. The **utopian socialists**—such as Claude Henri Comte de Saint-Simon and Pierre Joseph Proudhon—believed that change was best achieved through a patient reform of existing institutions. One person who tried to put such reforms into practice was Robert Owen (1771–1858), who rose from being a child laborer to becoming part owner of the largest steel mills in Scotland. In 1824 he came to the United States and created a communal society at New Harmony, Indiana. When his experiment failed, Owen returned to Britain to continue his reforming efforts and later became one of the founders of British socialism.

Karl Marx was much less patient. He built on the emerging ideas of socialism and ultimately provided the foundation for all modern communist and socialist thinking. Marx argued that all history was a tale of class antagonism and that this was particularly clear in the social divisions and exploitation emerging out of the industrial way of life in Western Europe. He identified two classes—the **proletariat** (the workers) and the **bourgeoisie** (the middle- and upper-class employers and owners of production)—and argued that the state represented the interests only of the bourgeoisie. Because workers were paid so poorly, their purchasing power was kept at a minimum, causing overproduction and underconsumption and leading to periodic economic crises.

Marx warned that it was only a matter of time before workers organized themselves and overthrew the ruling class. But, he said, the historical conditions would have to be right before this happened. Revolutions were most likely to come to advanced industrial societies with a large proletariat, such as the United States, Britain, Germany, or France, where capital was concentrated in the hands of a few. The transition was likely to come peacefully in the United States and Britain, but he believed that it would be more violent in more authoritarian states such as Germany and France.

For Marx, who lived in poverty most of his life, private property was at the root of all key social problems; he criticized it for creating social divisions and antagonism and for alienating humans from one another, and he argued that people would have their dignity and freedom restored only when it was abolished. He predicted that revolution would bring about a **dictatorship of the proletariat.** This would lead to the end of the class system, the withering away of the state, and the creation of a classless, nonexploitive communist society in which everyone would have equal opportunities, would work for the common good, and would take back from society what they needed: "From each according to his abilities, to each according to his needs," as he put it.

For a while in 1848 it seemed as though Marx's predictions might come true because there was a surge of revolutionary activity in several continental European countries, during which Marx himself was forced to escape to Britain. The surge died down, however, and Europe never again came so close to revolution, partly because workers and labor unions won concessions on working conditions and voting rights. Marx died long before any of his ideas were applied, but after his death, Marxist parties sprang up across Europe and even in the United States. The American Socialist Party was founded in 1901, won nearly 1,200 local offices in its heyday, and ran Eugene V. Debs

Marxism Marx's belief that the structure of industrialized societies could be explained by the tensions arising out of class struggle.

proletariat The workers in a capitalist industrial society who have little or nothing to sell other than their labor.

bourgeoisie The middle or upper-middle class property owners created by capitalism.

MARX AND LENIN

They never met each other, but Karl Marx (1818–1883) and Vladimir Lenin (1870–1924) will probably always be spoken of in the same breath as the most influential thinkers in the evolution of socialist ideas. Marx was mainly a theorist. Lenin was both a thinker and an organizer; he took Marxist ideas and applied them to the particular circumstances of Russia at the beginning of the twentieth century.

Marx was born in Trier, Prussia (in what is now Germany). After studying at the Universities of Berlin, Bonn, and Jena, he began a lifelong collaboration with Friedrich Engels (1820–1895), and between them they developed much of the theoretical foundation of socialism and communism. Marx's writings on economic and social issues made him so unpopular with the authorities that he moved to Paris, then to Brussels, and in 1849 to London, where he spent the rest of his life, living mainly on financial support from Engels and from relatives. Among his many writings, *The Communist Manifesto* and *Das Kapital* stand out as the most influential. He died in 1883, having outlived his wife Jenny and five of their seven children. At his funeral, Engels described Marx as "the best hated and most calumniated man of his time."

Lenin was born Vladimir Ilyich Ulyanov in Simbirsk, Russia. His opposition to the tsarist regime was sparked by the execution in 1887 of his brother Alexander, implicated in an attempt to assassinate Tsar Alexander III. After finishing his law studies, Ulyanov traveled abroad, where he came into contact with many leading exiled socialists. Returning to Russia, he was arrested in 1895 and banished to Siberia from 1897 to 1900. Upon release, and to make it more difficult for the Russian police to keep track of his movements, he renamed himself Lenin, after the River Lena in Siberia.

During the 1890s he studied the prospects for revolution in Russia from a Marxist perspective and concluded that Russian workers would not develop a revolutionary consciousness spontaneously. He argued instead that the key to success was a small party of dedicated professional revolutionaries, who could force the revolution without losing sight of Marx's basic ideas and theories. Following the failure of the 1905 revolution, Lenin went back into exile in Europe, helping to set up the newspaper *Pravda* in 1912. He returned to Russia after the March 1917 overthrow of the tsar and led the coup of November 1917. Lenin survived an assassination attempt in 1918 and the civil war of 1918–1922, but in May 1922 he suffered a stroke from which he never fully recovered. After two more strokes, he died in January 1924 at age 53. His body was embalmed and subsequently lay in state in a mausoleum built in Red Square next to the Kremlin walls.

Leninism Lenin's revolutionary principles, including a vanguard party, democratic centralism, and worldwide revolutionary activity.

as its presidential candidate. Debs won nearly 6 percent of the vote in the 1912 election, one of the best results ever for a minor party in the United States.

Lenin and Leninism

Among those influenced by Marxist philosophy was the Russian Vladimir Ilyich Ulyanov, otherwise known as Lenin. He argued that the chances of a revolution in Europe were diminishing with the emergence of a small class of relatively wealthy workers and that Marxism had to be adapted to fit new circumstances. Marx had argued that revolutionary socialism would come to industrialized countries through the efforts of the workers; Lenin believed it could also come to less industrialized countries such as Russia if the peasants, ethnic minorities, and other aggrieved groups were mobilized. His adaptation of Marx added several original ideas to socialism:

- **The vanguard party.** Lenin argued that a dedicated and professional vanguard would have to foment and guide the revolution on behalf of the proletariat, promoting revolutionary consciousness among the workers using agitation and propaganda (or *agitprop*).[4] Other European Marxists believed that Russia had to advance much further industrially before it would be ready for revolution and criticized Lenin for trying to force the process. They also argued that his vanguard would simply replace the old elite with a new elite and that this would undermine the possibility of a socialist workers' revolution. They were proved right when the vanguard party become a permanent and elitist feature of the Soviet system.

- **Democratic centralism.** For the vanguard party to succeed, Lenin argued, it had to be carefully organized around the idea of democratic centralism: free political discussion and free elections within one hierarchical party. Every level of the party would elect the next highest, and decisions would be passed down through the ranks. The party would in turn control every other organization and social unit, from the family to the school to the factory. This principle is often blamed for paving the way for the totalitarian rule of Stalin.

- **Imperialism as the highest stage of capitalism.** Lenin talked of the need for a worldwide struggle against capitalism and tried to explain why revolution had not occurred in Western countries, as Marx had predicted. He argued that the profits of colonialism allowed capitalists to pacify their workers by paying them better, thereby postponing the revolution.[5] At the same time, imperialism was making class exploitation and polarization a global phenomenon. Lenin predicted that the colonies would accept only so much exploitation before eventually fighting for their independence. The struggle against capitalism would then spread back to Europe when workers lost the concessions bought from the profits of colonialism.

- **Comintern.** In 1919, two years after the Russian revolution, Lenin formed the Third Communist International (or Comintern), a network of 35 national communist parties. Until it was disbanded in 1943, Comintern coordinated the activities of those parties, giving them advice and helping them build a local following in their own countries. Probably the most successful product of Comintern was the Chinese Communist party.

Unlike Marx, Lenin was able to apply his revolutionary ideas, and he and Leon Trotsky (1879–1940) became the driving forces behind the Russian revolution of November 1917. But his sudden death in 1924 set off several years of infighting within the Soviet communist party, the leadership ultimately going to Joseph Stalin. Lenin's legacy was summed up in the term **Marxism-Leninism,** coined in the USSR after his death to describe a combination of Marx's theoretical analysis of capitalism and Lenin's doctrine of revolutionary action.

democratic centralism The process by which a single, hierarchical party governs a society.

Marxism-Leninism A combination of Marx's economic theories and Lenin's revolutionary methods.

Mao and Maoism

Maoism Mao's application of communism to rural societies such as China, rejecting elitism, and emphasizing communalism and social experimentation.

Marx had focused on a worker revolution and argued that peasants had no role to play. Lenin cultivated the peasants, but support for the Russian revolution came mainly from urban workers. By contrast, the Chinese revolution (when it came) was spearheaded by a peasant army raised and trained by Mao Zedong (1893–1976). Few countries were as far from Marx's idea of an industrial-capitalist society as China, but Mao nonetheless helped spark a revolution affecting one-fifth of humanity.

Mao's major contribution to socialist theory was to rethink Marxism-Leninism to suit rural and agricultural societies and to develop a populist and anti-elitist form of Marxism with some uniquely Chinese influences. For example, China had long regarded foreigners as barbarians, an idea that Mao perpetuated by encouraging resentment against imperialism and anyone who had profited from dealing with foreigners. He argued that authority should be questioned and criticized by the people, and he worked to make communism less reliant on the kind of bureaucratic elite that was emerging in the USSR under Stalin. He stressed communalism, small-scale social and economic units, and a rejection of elitism.[6] Mao also emphasized thought reform and indoctrination, building on Chinese ideas of the state as the supreme educator. To discourage elitism, for example, he ordered that students, professionals, and other urban residents be sent off occasionally to work on farms and in factories.

Maoism was more radical than Marxism and, because it applied Marxism to rural societies, was also attractive to nationalist movements in less industrialized Asian, Latin American, and sub-Saharan African states. Mao had argued in the 1920s that "political power grows out of the barrel of a gun," and he used a peasant army and revolutionary guerrilla warfare to take power in China. His methods inspired nationalist movements such as those led by Fidel Castro in Cuba and Ernesto "Che" Guevara in Bolivia. This led some U.S. foreign policymakers to simplistically equate nationalism with communism, leading them to withdraw support from nationalists and to instead support oppressive right-wing regimes because they were anticommunist. The best known example of this came in Vietnam; the United States and its allies refused to help the newly independent North Vietnam in 1954, mainly because its leader, Ho Chi Minh, was a communist. The United States went further by supporting the government of South Vietnam, becoming involved in one of the most tragic and costly wars in U.S. history.

COMMUNISM TODAY

Communism is dead in most countries and is very unwell in a few others, although some of the more optimistic Marxists insist that it has simply reached the end of its first epoch. Its critics argue that it was always structurally flawed, strongest in its critique of capitalism and weakest in its provision of blueprints for change. Its supporters argue that it was never applied in the way Marx predicted; was abused by Lenin, Stalin, and Mao; and has been unfairly discredited. Wherever the truth lies, most former strongholds of communism have abandoned the Soviet model of government—and perhaps even communism as an ideology—altogether.

The changes arguably began in China in the 1980s with the reformist policies of Deng Xiaoping, who combined limited free-market policies with Chinese socialism.

The watershed in the collapse of communism, however, came during the administration of Mikhail Gorbachev in the USSR (1985–1991). Gorbachev came to office determined to undo the abuses of Stalinism and the lethargy of the Brezhnev years and to make the Soviet model of socialism more efficient and more democratic. He had no intention of presiding over the end of communism, but the changes he launched took on a life of their own. After giving up Soviet control over Eastern Europe, he lost power, the Soviet Union broke up in 1991, and the former Soviet republics abandoned state socialism.

The long-term prognosis remains mixed. In Russia, the government has struggled to liberalize the economy and to democratize the political system, using legal and illegal means. Pro-reformists won their rearguard action against communist and nationalist hard-liners opposed to reform, but have struggled to keep the lid on simmering separatist problems on Russia's southern border. The 1993 constitution created a new and more democratic political system, but democratic ideals have not yet taken firm root in Russian society and economic conditions have been less than perfect. Much depends on how much longer it will take for the benefits of democracy and capitalism to be broadly felt, and on how far Putin-style authoritarianism will be allowed to evolve.

In other former Soviet republics, developments have been varied. Georgia, Kyrgyzstan, and Ukraine have all seen popular movements for reform, bringing pro-Western governments to power and holding out the possibilities of democracy and increased stability. But Kazakhstan, Tajikistan, and Uzbekistan have all seen their leaders extend their terms in office against a worrying background of authoritarianism, flawed elections, and economic problems. Meanwhile, Armenia and Azerbaijan have seen ongoing civil unrest, Saparmyrat Niyazov in Turkmenistan has been made ruler for life and has built himself a cult of personality, and in Belarus the government of Aleksandr Lukashenko continues to rule with an iron fist.

The future for the Eastern European states that were once under Soviet control is much more certain, because most have moved quickly into the liberal democratic camp. NATO has been joined by ten of its former "enemies": Bulgaria, the Czech Republic, Estonia, Hungary, Latvia, Lithuania, Poland, Romania, Slovakia, and Slovenia. All these countries have also now joined the European Union, or (in the case of Bulgaria and Romania) will be joining soon, and three of them (the Czech Republic, Hungary, and Poland) have joined that bastion of capitalism, the Organization for Economic Cooperation and Development (OECD). The EU has meanwhile sent investment and development aid to Eastern Europe, helping underpin the switch to free-market economic policies and the building of democratic, multiparty political systems.

KEY TERMS

bourgeoisie	dictatorship of the	proletariat
civil society	proletariat	socialism
Comintern	Leninism	state socialism
command economy	Maoism	totalitarianism
communism	Marxism	utopian socialists
democratic	Marxism-Leninism	vanguard party
centralism	police state	

KEY PEOPLE

Fidel Castro	Vladimir Lenin	Leon Trotsky
Friedrich Engels	Karl Marx	Deng Xiaoping
Mikhail Gorbachev	Ho Chi Minh	Mao Zedong
Kim Jong Il	Saparmyrat Niyazov	

STUDY QUESTIONS

1. Is communism still a useful analytical tool for comparative politics?
2. How well do the values of communism fit with human nature?
3. Is the Marxist analysis still relevant to an understanding of modern society?
4. Where would you look to find socialism or social democracy practiced in liberal democracies today?

COMMUNISM AND SOCIALISM ONLINE

Marxists Internet Archive: www.marxists.org/txtindex.htm
Provides information on the works of Karl Marx and key Marxists.
Marxism Page: www.anu.edu.au/polsci/marx/marx.html
A site maintained by the Australian National University, which includes introductory material on Marxism and the text of *The Communist Manifesto*.
Socialist International: www.socialistinternational.org
The home page of the London-based Socialist International, with links to many socialist parties.

FURTHER READING

Drakulic, Slavenka, *How We Survived Communism and Even Laughed* (New York: Harper Perennial, 1993) and *Café Europa: Life After Communism* (New York: Penguin USA, 1999). Two books written by a Croatian journalist, reflecting on life under communism and how Eastern Europe has changed.

Muravchik, Joshua, *Heaven on Earth: The Rise and Fall of Socialism* (San Francisco: Encounter Books, 2002). The fortunes of socialism, told through the lives of its major thinkers and practitioners.

Schram, Stuart, *The Thought of Mao TseTung* (Cambridge, MA: Cambridge University Press, 1989). A commentary on the principles of Maoism.

Tucker, Robert C. (Ed.), *The Marx–Engels Reader* (New York: W. W. Norton, 1978). A comprehensive introduction to the lives and works of Marx and Engels.

Wolff, Jonathan, *Why Read Marx Today?* (New York: Oxford University Press, 2002). An analysis of the continuing relevance of Marxism to an understanding of modern society.

RUSSIA

RUSSIA: QUICK FACTS

Name: Russian Federation

Capital: Moscow

Area: 6,592,800 square miles (17,075,400 sq. km)

Languages: 82 percent of the population speaks Russian

Population: 143.4 million

Population density: 22 per square mile (8 per sq. km.)

Population growth rate: –0.4 percent

POLITICAL INDICATORS

Freedom House rating: Partly Free

Date of state formation: June 12, 1991

System type: Federal republic with dual executive

Constitution: 1993

Administration: Federal

Executive: Executive president elected by direct popular vote for maximum of two 4-year terms

Legislature: Bicameral Federal Assembly, with upper Federation Council (178 members appointed by the president) and lower State Duma (450 elected members)

Party structure: More than 30 parties are currently active, of which five have developed a broad following, but a stable multiparty system has not yet emerged

Judiciary: Constitutional Court (19 members appointed for 12-year terms by the president and confirmed by the Federation Council)

Head of state: Vladimir Putin (1999–)

Head of government: Mikhail Fradkov (2004–)

ECONOMIC INDICATORS

GDP (2004): $582 billion

Per capita GDP: $3,410

Distribution of GDP: Services 61 percent, industry 34 percent, agriculture 7 percent

Urban population: 73 percent

SOCIAL INDICATORS

HDI ranking: 57

Infant mortality rate: 16 per 1,000 live births

Life expectancy: 65.7 years

Literacy: 99% of people aged 15 and older

Religions: Predominantly Russian Orthodox, with significant Muslim, Buddhist, and Jewish minorities

INTRODUCTION

Russia has undergone such dramatic changes since 1985 that we have all had to rethink our perceptions of the country, its government, and its national identity. For nearly 70 years, Russia dominated the Union of Soviet Socialist Republics (USSR), a country that most Westerners feared or distrusted and largely misunderstood. The USSR was a communist country, governed by a single political party, whose leaders controlled the state, the economy, and society, sometimes lapsing into totalitarianism. The Soviet Union broke up in 1991, and Russia became an independent country that has moved toward democracy and free-market economics, but with mixed results. Is it on its way to a stable and successful liberal democratic future, or is it having trouble leaving behind its authoritarian past and surviving its social divisions? The jury is still out.

At nearly 6.6 million square miles, Russia is the largest country in the world; it stretches across 11 time zones and is nearly twice the size of the United States. Using a straight conversion against the U.S. dollar, Russia is a poor country: It has a GDP of about $582 billion, which works out to $3,410 per capita, or about one-twentieth the figure for the United States. But using purchasing power parity, Russian GDP rises to more than $1.3 trillion, or nearly $9,000 per capita, suggesting that the Russian economy is more substantial than it at first appears. But Russia is still far from a postindustrial, service-based economy.

Russia's main economic challenge is making the transition from an economy that was centrally planned and geared toward the military to a free-market system geared toward the consumer. It has a wealth of natural resources, including land, minerals, oil, natural gas, timber, gold, coal, and iron, but it lacks the capital and technical expertise to fully exploit these resources, most of which are in **Siberia,** the huge and sparsely populated eastern expanse of the country. It also has the potential to build successful corporations, but few are yet in the position to take on foreign competition. When the western United States was being opened up in the nineteenth century, it was helped by capital investment from Europe; Russia's best hope may also lie in foreign investment, but first it must achieve greater economic and fiscal stability, more efficient government, and more open markets.

Economic reforms have so far proved difficult to apply, leading to hardships for many Russians. They could once rely on the state to provide jobs and to subsidize food and basic services, but they now face shortages, lost jobs, falling wages, rising prices, and a shift to a free-market system with which they have little familiarity. Industrial output, agricultural output, and GDP have all grown, but they have not met their potential. Meanwhile, inflation has fluctuated wildly from a high of 350 percent to a low of 15 percent, and attempts to build economic stability have been undermined by organized crime and the black market. Although these problems are serious, Russians have long been fatalistic, all too familiar with hard times and sacrifice. There have been regular predictions of social unrest, rebellion, and violence, but most Russians continue to survive, as they have done many times before.

In social terms, Russia still reflects its imperial past; the Russian empire that emerged between the mid-fifteenth century and the nineteenth century incorporated many different ethnic groups, and even in today's new Russia there are still 60 to 90 national

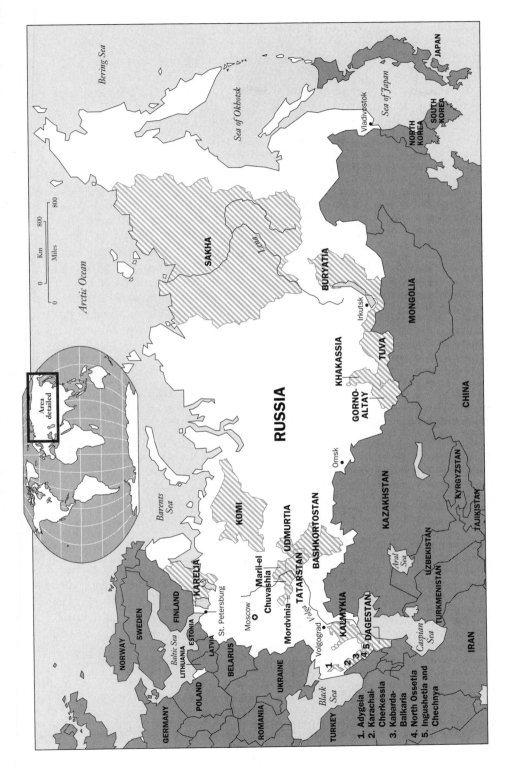

minorities, including Tatars, Ukrainians, Bashkirs, and even 840,000 Germans—together they account for nearly 20 percent of the population. Several of these groups, especially in the volatile Caucasus region, resent being under the control of Moscow and are agitating for independence. To further complicate matters, up to 25 million Russians still live in neighboring former republics of the USSR, posing a problem for relations between Russia and those republics.

In political terms, the key challenge facing Russia is that of building a multiparty democracy in a country that has known only monarchy, one-party rule, totalitarianism, or oligarchy. The Communist Party of the Soviet Union (CPSU) had a monopoly on power from 1917 to 1991, and although the changes that have taken place since then have made Russia more democratic, its new leaders have never lost sight of the Soviet tradition of strong and centralized executive authority and they still find it hard to tolerate criticism and opposition; president Vladimir Putin in particular has caused concern with his strong-arm tactics. On paper, the Russian political system looks much like that of France, with an executive president, a separately elected legislature, and a prime minister nominated by the president and confirmed by the legislature. In practice, Russia faces a divisive struggle for control between an executive armed with considerable powers, a legislature in which no one party has yet been able to win a majority, and a cluster of often-rowdy regional politicians. Against this background, Russian politics remains volatile and the prognosis for the future uncertain.

POLITICAL DEVELOPMENT

For hundreds of years, Russia was a feudal empire, with most of its citizens bypassed by political and economic developments in nearby Europe. In the last 90 years, however, Russians have seen dramatic change. The revolutions of 1917 removed a centuries-old and autocratic monarchy that made way for several decades of brutal repression under the Stalin administration. Then came the tensions of the cold war and the Gorbachev "revolution" of the late 1980s, which ended decades of central planning and one-party government. Finally, the breakup of the Soviet Union created an independent Russia, which has once again had to redefine itself and its place in the world.

The Russian Empire (15th Century to 1917)

For most of its history, Russia was more an imperial power than a nation-state. From humble beginnings in the ninth century, it was liberated in the fifteenth century from more than 200 years of Mongol control by Ivan the Great (1440–1505), who set up his capital at Moscow. Under Ivan the Terrible (1533–1584), Russia expanded into Kazan, Astrakhan, and Siberia. Peter the Great (1682–1725) laid the basis for the country's military and industrial growth; Russia became a European power, the nobility adopted European culture and values, the army and bureaucracy were based on European models, and the new capital—St. Petersburg—was overtly a European city. Through all these changes, however, Russia remained a feudal system, in which the vast majority of Russians remained powerless peasants (or serfs), a small aristocracy controlled virtually all national wealth, there were no free elections or free speech, most people lived in crushing poverty, land was often arbitrarily seized and redistributed, and the tsars violently suppressed opposition. Despite efforts at reform during the nineteenth century and the emancipation of the serfs in 1861, Russia remained rigidly divided into classes, with the tsar and the nobility jealously guarding their rights.

Unlike other more pragmatic European monarchs, the last tsar, Nicholas II (1894–1917), failed to respond to the pressures for change. Popular opposition was led by the Social Revolutionary Party and the smaller Russian Social Democratic Labor Party (RSDLP), a Marxist party founded in 1898. At its Second Congress in London in 1903, the RSDLP split into two factions: the Mensheviks (or "minority"), who advocated a mass membership party, and the more elitist **Bolsheviks** (or "majority"). Led by Lenin, the Bolsheviks subscribed to his idea of a vanguard party and developed a tight and disciplined structure with Lenin's authority at the core. Russia came close to revolution in 1905, when it was defeated in a war with Japan, but the tsar survived with the help of the military. A new parliamentary assembly (the Duma) was convened in 1906, but Nicholas II was never able to fully accept the idea of limits on his power.

Lenin and the 1917 Revolutions

In 1917, Russia underwent two revolutions, which grew out of three interconnected factors: the huge losses suffered by Russia in World War I; the theories of Karl Marx and the related ideas of Russian thinkers; and the leadership skills of Lenin and Trotsky, who were able to identify themselves with the popular issues of peace and the redistribution of land. Feeding off Russian losses in the war, worker demonstrations and food riots in March 1917 turned into a revolution against Tsar Nicholas, who abdicated and was replaced by a provisional government, which made the fatal error of continuing the war.

In April, Lenin returned from exile in Europe and began campaigning for an end to the war and the creation of a socialist state. In November, he and his followers staged a second "revolution" (actually a coup rather than a popular uprising),[1] took over the government, and established a one-party socialist state. He changed the name of his party to the Communist Party, abolished the class system, and created the Red Army. In March 1918 Lenin negotiated a peace treaty with Germany at Brest-Litovsk, which he was able to repudiate when Germany was defeated. In July 1918, the tsar and his family were shot to death on the orders of the Bolsheviks.

Lenin's new state was almost immediately split by a civil war between Lenin's Red Army and White Armies led by former tsarist generals intent on overthrowing the Bolsheviks. The Whites were defeated in 1922, but Soviet Russia found itself the only socialist revolutionary state in the world, cut off by a Western economic blockade. Faced with a war-ravaged economy, falling industrial and agricultural output, and public discontent, Lenin decided in 1921 to compromise on his principles by launching a **New Economic Policy,** based partly on free enterprise policies designed to encourage peasants and small businessmen. Before he could press these reforms, however, he died.

A succession struggle followed, with the most obvious successor—Leon Trotsky—being pushed aside by a trio of party leaders, including Joseph Stalin. Stalin organized and manipulated the party bureaucracy to establish personal control over the party and to confirm the party's control over the country.[2] After a brief collective leadership, Stalin had by 1928–1929 made his office of first secretary of the CPSU the most important in the party hierarchy, and he won uncontested control over both the party and the country. Over the next 25 years, Stalin stamped his personal mark on the USSR, creating the system that was to persist until the late 1980s.

TABLE 4.1

Key Dates in Soviet/Russian History

1147	Founding of Moscow
1812	Napoleon invades Russia, advancing as far as Moscow
1861	Emancipation of the serfs
1914	Outbreak of World War I
1917	(March) Revolution ousts Tsar Nicholas II; (November) a coup brings Bolsheviks to power under Lenin
1918–1922	Russian civil war; establishment of USSR (December 1922)
1924	Lenin dies
1929–1933	Collectivization of agriculture leads to famine
1941	Hitler attacks the USSR
1945	The USSR emerges from the war with control over much of Eastern Europe
1953	Stalin dies
1957	*Sputnik* becomes first satellite in space
1961	Yuri Gagarin first human in space
1962	Cuban missile crisis
1979	Soviet invasion of Afghanistan
1985	Gorbachev becomes general secretary of the CPSU
1991	(June) Boris Yeltsin elected president of Russia; (August) failed coup attempt by communist hardliners; (December) Gorbachev resigns, USSR ceases to exist
1992	Price controls are lifted; Russia takes over the UN Security Council seat formerly occupied by the USSR and joins the International Monetary Fund
1993	(September–October) Hard-line deputies occupy Congress in attempt to set off an uprising against Yeltsin; (December) new Russian constitution approved, new legislature elected
1994	(December) Yeltsin sends troops into Chechnya to quell uprising
1995–1996	Elections indicate a resurgence of support for the communists
1996	(July) Yeltsin reelected president; (August) ceasefire declared in Chechnya; (November) Yeltsin undergoes major heart surgery
1998	Yeltsin causes alarm by hiring and firing three prime ministers
1999	(August) Hostilities break out again in Chechnya; (August–September) bombs explode in Moscow, killing more than 300 people; (December) pro-reform parties make gains in State Duma elections; Boris Yeltsin suddenly resigns as president
2000	(March) New presidential elections result in victory for Vladimir Putin; (August) nuclear submarine *Kursk* sinks with loss of 118 lives
2002	(June) The EU and the United States announce that they consider Russia a market economy; (October) Chechen hostage incident at Moscow theater leaves more than 120 dead
2003	Putin administration deeply critical of U.S.-led invasion of Iraq
2004	(March) Putin elected to a second term; several East European countries—including former Soviet republics Estonia, Latvia, and Lithuania—join NATO and the European Union; (September) School siege in Beslan leaves 350 dead, many of them children

The Stalin Era (1928–1953)

Under Stalin, the USSR moved further away from Marxist principles and toward a totalitarian style of government that was distinctive enough to earn its own label in the dictionary of political science. **Stalinism** is an absolutist, inflexible, and highly undemocratic version of communism that demands unquestioning support for the state and a belief in the unchallenged authority of the party and its leaders. (This is much the kind of system that still exists today in North Korea.) Abandoning Lenin's idea of promoting global revolution, Stalin's priority was to build "socialism in one country" and make the Soviet Union a political, industrial, agricultural, and military model for others. Stalin also created a society based on the systematic use of terror, the elimination of human rights, and a cult of personality (providing the inspiration for Big Brother in George Orwell's novel *1984*).

Stalin also established a **command economy** in which all decisions that are driven by the free market in a liberal democracy were made by state planners: they decided what should be produced, when it should be produced, where it should be delivered, and at what prices it should be sold. A series of **five-year plans** set production figures with the goal of increasing industrial production by 100 percent, and meanwhile the Soviet bureaucracy became bigger and more inefficient. Stalin forced millions of farmers into huge new collective farms, eliminating an entire social class (the *kulaks*, or wealthy peasants) and causing a famine that claimed several million lives. He also closed down all small shops, arranged for the state to take over all services, and promoted one-party rule. The CPSU infiltrated every part of Soviet life, creating a new class of privileged political leaders and dashing any real hope of achieving Marx's goal of a classless society. Finally, Stalin ruled through the use of terror, making sure that his opponents were silenced, killed, or sent off to labor camps in Siberia.

Stalinism Stalin's political, economic, and social values, including centralized economic planning, a cult of personality, a police state, and mass terror.

The Cold War (1945–1990)

Stalin was succeeded as Soviet leader by Nikita Khrushchev, whose priority was to end the years of terror. In February 1956 he electrified the Twentieth Party Congress of the CPSU with a "secret speech" denouncing the excesses of Stalin and extolling the virtues of collective leadership. The speech was not made public in the USSR until 1989, but it set the tone for Khrushchev's policies of reform, which influenced a new generation of party members, including Mikhail Gorbachev and Boris Yeltsin, both then in their mid-20s.

Khrushchev continued the attempts to build industry and agriculture, with limited success. To prove Soviet technological prowess, he launched a space program that sent the first satellite (*Sputnik*) into space in 1957 and the first human (Yuri Gagarin) in 1961. The Khrushchev years also saw the perpetuation (in fits and starts) of the cold war. Tensions between the two superpowers peaked in 1962 with the Cuban missile crisis, when U.S. President John F. Kennedy had a battle of wills with Khrushchev over the stationing of Soviet nuclear warheads in Cuba. The warheads were withdrawn, but for a few weeks in late 1962 the world stood on the brink of nuclear war.

With his popularity falling in the wake of repeated policy failures and concerns about his erratic style of leadership, Khrushchev was ousted by the CPSU in 1964 and replaced by the more conservative Leonid Brezhnev. The bold reforms ended, and Soviet leaders became older, less imaginative, and more concerned with the

PEOPLE IN HISTORY

JOSEPH STALIN

The man ultimately responsible for shaping Soviet government and bureaucracy was Joseph Stalin (1879–1953), whose power and influence was so great that by 1985 the USSR was more Stalinist than Marxist-Leninist. Born Joseph Vissarionovich Dzhugashvili in Georgia, Stalin trained for the priesthood before being expelled from his seminary and joining the political underground in 1900. He took part in bank robberies aimed at raising funds for the Bolsheviks and in 1912 changed his name to Stalin ("man of steel"). Arrested several times, he was exiled to Siberia in 1913 but returned to Petrograd (formerly St. Petersburg) in 1917. In 1922 he became first secretary of the Communist Party, a position he held until his death.

Stalin outmaneuvered his rivals following Lenin's death so that by 1928–1929 he had become the undisputed ruler of the USSR. His main rival, Leon Trotsky, was exiled in 1929 and murdered by Stalin's secret police in Mexico in 1940. Other rivals—such as Georgy Zinoviev, Lev Kamenev, and Nikolai Bukharin—were murdered, executed, or exiled. Pursuing mass control through mass terror,[3] Stalin launched a program aimed at making the USSR a world power, using systematic oppression to enforce his reforms. In the process, perhaps as many as 20 million people died from famine, execution, or war. Many millions more were purged, or exiled to concentration camps (or gulags) in Siberia. To support his policies, he even began a project in the late 1930s to rewrite Soviet history.

In June 1941, Hitler invaded the USSR, setting off what the Soviets called the Great Patriotic War. Following the siege of Leningrad, the Soviet army advanced deep into Eastern Europe, allowing Stalin to expand Soviet control over neighboring countries to the west. Europe was divided into eastern and western blocs, laying the basis for the cold war.

Stalin died from a brain hemorrhage in March 1953. His cult of personality had been so effective that prisoners in Siberian *gulags* (labor camps) wept at the news and more than 400 people died in the crush to see his embalmed body lying in state beside that of Lenin in Moscow's Red Square. As part of Khrushchev's campaign of de-Stalinization, Stalin's body was removed in 1961 and buried in a modest grave between the Lenin Mausoleum and the Kremlin walls.

maintenance of the status quo. There was a major military buildup that led to near parity with the United States, and the Soviet Union helped several nationalist movements in Africa and Asia. The Brezhnev era culminated in the ultimately disastrous decision by the Soviets in 1979 to invade Afghanistan, which led to a costly and unpopular war. When Brezhnev died in November 1982, he was followed by two transitional leaders, the reformist Yuri Andropov (1982–1984) and the conservative Konstantin Chernenko (1984–1985). Both were elderly and in poor health, and both died in office. The way was then cleared for the rise of Mikhail Gorbachev, the man who, in his words, now set about launching the second Russian revolution.

Gorbachev and Yeltsin (1985–1999)

Gorbachev denounced the stagnation of the Brezhnev era and set out to make many of the reforms envisioned by Khrushchev and Andropov. There were two core planks to his program: ***perestroika***, or the "restructuring" of the Soviet economic and political system, and ***glasnost***, or "openness," meaning a willingness to encourage more public discussion of key issues and a greater frankness in admitting mistakes. A third plank—*demokratizatsiia*, or democratization—had been added by 1988. Gorbachev's goal was not to dismantle the state socialist system but to make it more efficient and more democratic and to reduce the role of central planning. But his position was undermined by several problems:

- He lacked legitimacy. He preached democratic accountability, but was never popularly elected to office and insisted on maintaining the CPSU monopoly long after other groups had demanded equal rights.

- He found himself caught between liberals who thought his reforms were too timid and conservatives who thought they had gone too far. Partly because of the entrenched power of the Soviet bureaucracy to sabotage and delay his changes and partly because of his own caution, Gorbachev lost control.

- His reforms brought into the open the underlying tensions among the Soviet republics, sparking nationalism and secessionism. As these grew, it became doubtful that anyone could have kept the USSR together.

In August 1991, on the eve of the signing of a new union treaty that would have redefined the relationship among the Soviet republics, a group of communists staged an attempted coup in Moscow. Although it quickly failed, Gorbachev's credibility was fatally undermined, and he quickly lost control. He resigned as president of the USSR on December 25, 1991, and the following day the Soviet Union ceased to exist. Where there had once been a superpower, there were now 15 independent countries. The biggest and most influential was Russia, which just six months before had elected Boris Yeltsin as its president.

Yeltsin found himself plagued by the same problems that had faced Gorbachev: balancing the demands of reformers and hard-liners, trying to promote greater political and economic liberalism, and trying to negotiate a new federal treaty that would keep Russia from civil war. The changes were given urgency by attempts made during 1993 to unseat Yeltsin, peaking in September when he dissolved the Russian legislature, the Congress of People's Deputies. A small group of conservatives barricaded themselves inside the Congress building and gave the acting presidency to Yeltsin's biggest critic—his own vice president, Alexander Rutskoi. Yeltsin lined tanks up outside the Congress building and ordered them to fire, the attempted coup failed, and Rutskoi and many of his supporters were briefly jailed.

Throughout 1992 and 1993, Russian politics was diverted by a conflict between conservatives and reformers anxious to stake their claims before the new political system was committed to paper with a new constitution. The constitution was "approved" in a hurried public referendum in December 1993, and a new legislature was elected. But questions remained about Russia's stability. Despite threats from communists on the left and nationalists on the right, a civil war in the southern republic of **Chechnya** (see Critical Issues, p. 216), and his own health problems, Yeltsin managed to be elected to a second term as president in July 1996. But trust in government fell to an all-time low, the legislature failed to be an effective source of

perestroika Mikhail Gorbachev's policy of restructuring the Soviet Union's political and economic system to reduce the control of central government and promote efficiency.

glasnost A policy in Gorbachev's USSR of encouraging more open debate about the problems facing the country.

policy ideas or of opposition to the president, nationalist problems in the south boiled over into renewed war and urban terrorism, wealth and power continued to accumulate in the hands of a new elite, the value of the ruble fell as inflation grew, confidence in the banking system declined, and unemployment grew. In December 1999, Yeltsin suddenly resigned. He was replaced as acting president by his prime minister, Vladimir Putin, who was elected president in his own right in March 2000.

Russia Today

Russia has undergone considerable change since 1991, and the general trends have been toward greater democracy, a freer market place, and a more cooperative stand on issues of foreign policy. But many questions remain. Will the democratic changes be lasting, and how quickly can they be consolidated in a society that has known nothing but authoritarian rule? Can Russians learn how the free market works? Can Russia define a new place for itself in the world that keeps citizens and outsiders happy? Superficially, the signs seem positive, but significant problems still need to be overcome.[4] The economy is growing, but there is too little foreign investment. There is still considerable resistance to change, both among Russians and among old-style bureaucrats. Infrastructure is in an advanced state of decay. The quality of life for most Russians is poor: The population is unhealthy, relatively poorly educated, aging quickly, and shrinking in size. And Russia is still struggling to come to terms with its new status as a former superpower.

On the political front, the structure of government is still "top down" rather than "bottom up," and government is still in the mode of providing leadership rather than listening to what the people want. This has worsened under Vladimir Putin, who is clearly more an autocrat than a democrat. His rise to power as prime minister was based on overseeing a bloody government response to the uprising in Chechnya, an event that did not augur well for those concerned about the tradition of authoritarianism in Russian politics. He has since continued to show a worryingly heavy hand in his management of Russia, whether through his intolerance of criticism in the media, through the increased powers he has given to the security services, or through the way he has expanded his powers over regional governments. In September 2004, about 350 people—many of them children—were killed in a hostage crisis in a school in the town of Beslan in the southern Russian province of North Ossetia, after demands had been made for the release of Chechen rebels. Putin used the incident as the excuse to further expand his control, claiming the need to deal with terrorism and stop the disintegration of Russia. Is he simply a strong leader who believes in strong responses to problems, or is he using Russia's difficulties to strengthen both his own power and the power of the presidency? Only time will tell.

POLITICAL CULTURE

One of the effects of the collapse of communism and the breakup of the USSR has been to allow political scientists to open the hood, examine the engine of traditional Russian political culture, and study the effects of communism. Recent events suggest a strong continuity between public attitudes toward politics and government from the pre-Soviet era through to the present, with authoritarian tendencies and a preference for strong leadership. But there are also signs of discontinuities, with increasing openness, tolerance, and support for individual rights. Overall, it is often argued that Russia's failure to come to terms with its past is the biggest obstacle it faces in its attempts to build a stable and open liberal democracy.[5]

An Authoritarian Tradition

Russians have known little but authoritarian government. The tsars clung to autocracy long after most other European monarchs had given up their powers to popularly elected assemblies, and government during the tsarist era was centralized, bureaucratic, authoritarian, and intrusive.[6] The Soviet experience after 1917 was little different because tsarist autocracy was replaced by Leninist elitism, which was followed by Stalinist totalitarianism. Russia since 1991 has seen more democracy than the country has ever had, but democracy is having trouble taking root, in large part because Russians have had to learn how it works, in part because of the unwillingness of presidents Yeltsin and Putin to entirely abandon authoritarian methods, and in part because many Russians look back nostalgically on the authority and unity of the past.

Strong Leadership

Russians tend to like strong leaders, and public opinion surveys shortly after the breakup of the USSR found that people were more concerned with the state providing order than they were with it ensuring their civil liberties.[7] Many older Russians in particular (for whom life in the new Russia has only become worse) still admire Stalin as someone who provided a stable and tightly regulated social order and whose use of force is often excused as being "necessary for the time." Views such as these have been both a cause and an effect of a tradition of Russian political **patrimonialism:** a sense of leaders as father figures. Boris Yeltsin's attempts in 1992 to circumvent the legislature and use his powers of decree to bring about his own ideas of change were consistent with this tradition, although his actions were sharply criticized by some. The tradition also helps explain the emergence of something close to a cult of personality surrounding Vladimir Putin. Although strong leadership has its place, no political system that relies on the fortunes and methods of one person can hope to develop long-term stability.

patrimonialism A political system based on a leader as a father figure who has limited accountability to his people but who claims to understand their interests and needs.

Closed Politics

Liberal democracies have a tradition of relatively open politics, where most political decisions are publicly discussed and citizens can express their opinions. In Russia, by contrast, most decisions traditionally have been made behind the scenes with little (if any) public discussion. Closed politics was described as "the basic identifying characteristic" of the Soviet political system in the 1970s. It left most Soviet citizens feeling that there was little they could do to influence government, and many were disinclined to express their political opinions or bring their influence to bear on the decisions of government.[8]

The relative openness of the post-Soviet era has given Russians an unaccustomed level of freedom to express their opinions, although polling in Russia is still in its infancy and many Russians are still uncomfortable about sharing their views. The vestiges of secrecy remain; it was often difficult to be sure, for example, about the seriousness of Boris Yeltsin's heart problems during 1996, when his handlers at first said he was suffering from fatigue, a cold, or laryngitis, and he all but disappeared from public view for weeks. A liberal democratic leader in similar circumstances would have found it nearly impossible to keep such illness a secret.

The Collective Society

While liberal democracies place great value on individualism and self-determination, Russian society tends to much more group-oriented. Even after the emancipation of the serfs in 1861, they owned land not individually but collectively. Opinion polls during the Soviet era showed a high level of support for state planning and ownership of the economy, for state ownership of transport and communications, for collectivist public welfare in the fields of education and health care, and for living in a welfare state. There was also wide support for the idea that the state should not only look after the material welfare of its citizens but their spiritual welfare as well. The Soviet era is gone, but big government is still widely supported. It has been argued that the key to understanding Russian political culture is sobornost, meaning an attachment to collectivism and an opposition to individualism.[9]

Fear of Chaos

nationalism The promotion of national values and interests above those of the wider community.

Liking order and fearing chaos, Russians historically have leaned toward conservatism.[10] They have been preoccupied with national security and fear of foreign invasion, particularly from the west, where the land is flat and difficult to defend. Russian **nationalism** is partly a reaction to these fears, and many Russians place a heavy reliance on the state to maintain order and security. Given the extent of the changes the Russian people have experienced in the last few years, many believe that their country is headed toward "the abyss." These traditions make it difficult to build democracy, given that democracy by definition involves a high degree of uncertainty.

POLITICAL SYSTEM

"The most dangerous time," wrote the French historian Alexis de Tocqueville, "is when a bad government begins to reform itself." Seldom has this been more true than in Russia since the breakup of the Soviet Union. Nearly 145 million people have had to rethink their old assumptions as a society once founded on one-party rule and central economic planning has struggled to adopt an open, competitive political and economic system. The transition has not been easy, torn as Russia has been between those who want the status quo and those who want change. Even among those in favor of change, there are doubts about exactly how to achieve that change.

The Soviets claimed that their political system was democratic, but all real power was focused in the Communist Party of the Soviet Union (CPSU), which was run by an elite that made all policy, which was implemented in turn by a bureaucracy directed by the party. Mikhail Gorbachev tried to make the system more democratic and efficient, but had barely warmed to the task before he lost control. He left his successors with the challenge of building a new system while having to be careful about how quickly they abandoned the old system, for fear of leaving Russia without direction or generating a backlash among disgruntled Russians.

Under its new constitution, Russia has a political system much like that of France or Egypt: In what is known as a **dual executive,** it has both a directly elected president and a prime minister who is appointed by the president and confirmed by the legislature. But Russia's legislature has been split among a confusing array of new political parties, none of which has yet won enough support to form a majority. This has played into the hands of an already powerful presidency, and Vladimir Putin has been able to exploit the growth of a pro-Kremlin cluster of parties to extend his control over Russia. Supported by the preference that most ordinary Russians have for strong leadership, he has taken the kinds of actions that would be impossible in a liberal democracy.

dual executive A political system in which executive power is shared between an elected president and an appointed prime minister.

THE CONSTITUTION

When the Soviet Union collapsed, Russia inherited the 1978 constitution of the Russian republic, which was amended so many times during 1990–1991 that work was begun on drafting an entirely new document. The job was complicated by the fact that no previous Soviet or Russian constitution had clearly spelled out the relative powers of executive and legislature. Concern grew within the legislature (the Congress of People's Deputies) that Boris Yeltsin was using the hiatus to consolidate presidential power before the relationship between executive and legislature was committed to paper.[11] Their concerns sparked the attempted coup of September–October 1993.

In December 1993, elections were held to the reformed Russian legislature (by then renamed the Federal Assembly), and the new constitution was put to a public referendum. Voter turnout was just under 55 percent, and just 58 percent of those who voted (32 percent of all eligible voters) expressed their approval. In other words, 68 percent of eligible voters either voted against the constitution or did not vote at all. This was hardly a popular mandate, but the constitution went immediately into force. It created a federal republic in which power is shared between an elected and powerful executive president, the Russian government (consisting of a prime minister and federal ministers), a bicameral Federal Assembly, a complex high court system, and 89 local government units. The legacy of the Soviet era encouraged the framers to open the constitution with a lengthy bill of rights (Articles 17–64) that not only established the personal freedoms normally associated with a democracy but went into more detail, including the right to a private life, nationality, artistic expression, ideological diversity, and even protection from being subjected to medical experiments without consent.

Amendments can be proposed by the president, either chamber of the Federal Assembly, and even by a group of at least 20 percent of the deputies of either chamber of the Assembly. Most amendments must be approved by a three-quarters majority in the Federation Council (the upper chamber of the Federal Assembly), a two-thirds majority in the State Duma (the lower chamber of the Federal Assembly), and a straight majority in two-thirds of local legislatures.

THE EXECUTIVE: PRESIDENT AND PRIME MINISTER

Executive power in the old Soviet system was theoretically vested in a prime minister and Council of Ministers; in reality, all real power lay with the CPSU, and the *de facto* leader of the Soviet Union was the general secretary of the CPSU, the post to which Mikhail Gorbachev was elected in 1985. In March 1990, Gorbachev was hastily elected by the reformed Soviet legislature to a new post of executive president, in an attempt to shift authority from the party to the government and to make the executive more accountable to the people. But it was too little too late, and the office was eliminated with the collapse of the USSR in 1991. Boris Yeltsin—who had been elected president of Russia just six months before—now became leader of an independent Russia. He struggled to establish the new office between 1991 and 1993, finally winning a legal base with the passage of the 1993 constitution. He was reelected in 1996 and resigned on December 31, 1999. As required by the constitution, his prime minister Vladimir Putin stepped in as acting president and was confirmed in the post at the March 2000 presidential elections.

With his headquarters in the Kremlin in central Moscow, the president is elected for a maximum of two four-year terms; serves as head of state, commander-in-chief, and overseer of foreign policy; and has considerable tools of power at his disposal:

- **The power to issue edicts.** So long as they do not contravene the constitution or federal law, the president can issue edicts that have the force of law unless and until the legislature passes laws that supersede them. Yeltsin used this power extensively, for example when he privatized state-owned industries, reformed the banking system, and took on organized crime. Among the edicts issued by Putin: reestablishing mandatory training for military reservists, censoring news from Chechnya, and allowing the 15-year old Mir space station to be destroyed by crashing back to earth in 2001. The president can also introduce draft laws to the State Duma and even bypass it altogether with a referendum.

- **The power of appointment.** The president can appoint and dismiss the prime minister and federal ministers, move ministers from one job to another, and even influence the appointment of senior ministerial staff. The president can also appoint the heads of all major government agencies, such as the Russian Central Bank, nominates justices to the Constitutional Court (who must win approval by the Federation Council), and can appoint and dismiss military commanders and ambassadors. The State Duma must approve all key appointments, but if it turns down the president's nominee for prime minister three times in a row, then new elections are called for the Duma. Because most members of the Duma want to see out their full term, they are unlikely to push a president that far; they would be more likely instead to pass a vote of no confidence in the government. In the event of such a vote, the president can either dismiss the prime minister or ignore the vote, but—if it was passed again within three months—the president would either have to replace the prime minister or dissolve the Duma and call a new election.

- **The power to call elections.** The president can dissolve the State Duma and call new elections at any time. But to prevent presidents from arbitrarily dissolving the Duma and holding repeated elections until they get a result they like, presidents

```
TABLE 4.2
```

Postwar Leaders of Russia

CPSU party leaders	Prime ministers
(1922) Joseph Stalin	(1941) Joseph Stalin
1953 Georgy Malenkov	1953 Georgy Malenkov
1953 Nikita Khrushchev	
	1955 Nikolai Bulganin
	1958 Nikita Khrushchev
1964 Leonid Brezhnev	1964 Alexei Kosygin
	1980 Nikolai Tikhonov
1982 Yuri Andropov	
1984 Konstantin Chernenko	
1985 Mikhail Gorbachev	1985 Nikolai Ryzhkov (Acting)
	1990 Ivan Silayev
	1991 Valentin Pavlov

Presidents

1991 Boris Yeltsin	1991 Boris Yeltsin
	1992 Yegor Gaidar (Acting)
	1992 Viktor Chernomyrdin
	1998 (April) Sergei Kiriyenko
	(Aug) Viktor Chernomyrdin (Acting)
	(Sept) Yevgeny Primakov
	1999 (May) Sergei Stepashin
	(Aug) Vladimir Putin
1999 Vladimir Putin (Acting)	
2000 Vladimir Putin	2000 (May) Mikhail Kasyanov
	2004 (March) Mikhail Fradkov

cannot dissolve the house if it is considering impeaching them, during a state of national emergency or martial law, or within a year of a vote of no confidence.

- **The power of veto.** Like their American counterparts, Russian presidents must sign all bills before they can become law, and they have the power of veto, although the Duma can overturn the veto with a two-thirds majority.

- **Martial law and a state of emergency.** If presidents believe there is a threat of aggression against Russia, they can introduce martial law (under which they can use the military to control and govern using direct force) or declare a state of emergency (under which normal legislative and judicial powers are suspended). They must have the approval of the Federation Council to do either.

Although some of these powers border on dictatorial, they are not unlimited. The president has to take public opinion into account, and can also be impeached by the Federation Council for treason or a serious crime. But much like the "high crimes and misdemeanors" clause in the U.S. Constitution, this is an ambiguous idea that is open to wide interpretation, and impeachment is difficult to actually achieve: It must be brought by one-third of the members of the Duma, its grounds must be confirmed by the Constitutional Court and the Supreme Court, and it must then be confirmed by a two-thirds majority in both chambers of the Federal Assembly.

As in the United States, the presidency in Russia is much more than the individual who holds the office. Both presidents have a supporting network of offices and institutions that play a key role in determining the character of an administration; for the Russian president these include the State Council (a consultative forum created by Putin in 2000 and made up of Russia's 89 regional leaders),[12] the Executive Office (with representatives from nearly 40 government agencies), and the Security Council (which gives advice on national security). So impressive are the powers of the office that it has been called a **superpresidency,** and has even been compared with the old tsarist imperial court.

The president governs with the help of the Government of the Russian Federation: the prime minister, several deputy prime ministers, and about two dozen federal ministers, the most influential of which are the four "power ministers": foreign, interior, intelligence, and defense. The main jobs of the government are to draft the federal budget, oversee economic policy, and oversee the implementation of law and policy by the bureaucracy. Neither the prime minister nor the ministers need come from the largest party or coalition in the Federal Assembly; they simply need to win the approval of the State Duma. If and when one party wins a majority in the Duma, however, these posts will almost certainly be filled by members of that party.

The prime minister has a thankless task, caught between executive and legislature. The president sets the broad direction of government policy, but the prime minister—who is a member of the State Duma—has to take care of the details and work to get the president's program through the Duma. The prime minister helps select ministers, advises the president on policy, and—because there is no vice presidency—is next in line to become president if the incumbent dies, resigns, or becomes permanently incapable of governing. The prime minister takes power as acting president, but new presidential elections must be held within three months. When Yeltsin resigned in December 1999, he was replaced by Vladimir Putin and new elections were held in March 2000.

Russian prime ministers to date have been largely unknown at the time of their appointment, and have been expected to be loyal and unthreatening. Yeltsin's prime minister from 1992 to 1998 was Viktor Chernomyrdin, a moderate liberal on economic issues and the former chairman of Russia's state-owned natural gas monopoly, Gazprom. He made so much money out of its privatization that when he became leader of a new party called Our Home Is Russia in 1995 wits quickly dubbed it Our Home is Gazprom. Chernomyrdin was both loyal and a good manager, with a style that was so understated as to be dull. After several years of stability in the office of prime minister, Yeltsin caused much head-scratching during his second term by suddenly appointing and dismissing a string of five prime ministers in less than 18 months (1998–1999). Some saw this as a sign that he wanted to prevent any one prime minister from becoming too powerful or popular[13] while others saw it as a sign

VLADIMIR PUTIN

© AFP/CORBIS

After several years of uncertainty under the unpredictable leadership of Boris Yeltsin, the helm was passed to a new generation of leaders in December 1999 when Yeltsin resigned and was replaced as acting president by his prime minister, the relatively unknown Vladimir Putin. Putin's tenure was confirmed in March 2000, when he convincingly won Russia's second presidential election. His age, vigorous good health (he is a judo expert), and decisive leadership stood in stark contrast to that of the ailing Yeltsin.

Vladimir Vladimirovich Putin was born in 1952, and after graduating from Leningrad State University in 1975, he joined the KGB, the Soviet intelligence organization. Exactly what he did there has never been clear, but he is not thought to have had a stellar career and spent ten years working in what

was then East Germany, where his two daughters were born. In 1989 he returned to Leningrad State University as an administrator, later working for reformist St. Petersburg mayor Anatoly Sobchak. He was then brought to Moscow to work for deputy prime minister Anatoly Chubais, and was named prime minister by Boris Yeltsin in August 1999.

As prime minister, Putin won support within Russia—but criticism from abroad—by pursuing an aggressive response to the rebellion in Chechnya. His rhetoric about the restoration of Russia's status as a great power led to concerns both at home and abroad that he might prove to be an autocrat, but he won the March 2000 presidential election convincingly, winning more than 52 percent of the vote, pushing the communist Gennady Zyuganov into a distant second place, and avoiding a second-round runoff. He comfortably won election to a second term in 2004.

As president, Putin has focused on the economic reconstruction of Russia, has shown less opposition to the expansion of NATO than was once feared, has built strong relations with the Bush administration (although he was critical of the 2003 U.S.-led invasion of Iraq), and has built closer ties with the European Union. Opinions about him are still divided, however. Supporters see him as a decisive modernizer, a democrat, and a supporter of free-market policies, but his critics point to his occasionally authoritarian methods and the emergence of a cult of personality, and wonder whether he has a hidden agenda. Many of those who remember the cold war still find it hard to trust Russia or Putin. While he once said that "anyone who doesn't regret the passing of the Soviet Union has no heart, but anyone who wants it restored has no brains", he also commented during his April 2005 state of the nation address that the collapse of the Soviet Union was "the greatest geopolitical catastrophe of the 20th century." His term of office is scheduled to end in March 2008.

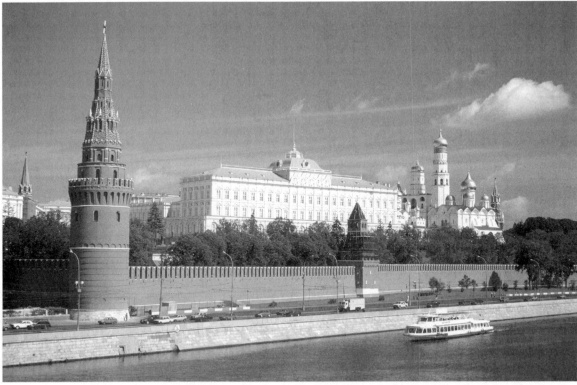

The Kremlin in central Moscow, home of the office of the president of Russia. The Kremlin was a well-known symbol of Soviet power during the cold war and remains a potent symbol today of the authority of the presidency in the new Russian political system.

that he was out of control. Yet others suggested that he may have made the changes to create contenders for the presidential election in 2000. Strategically, nothing could have made it more difficult for the communists to win the election.

Putin has had two prime ministers. His first was Mikhail Kasyanov (b. 1957), a technocrat and free-market economist with an eight-year career in the Ministry of Finance, mainly as Russia's chief debt negotiator but including several months as Russia's finance minister. Kasyanov confounded those who predicted that he would not last long and quickly became a close Putin confidante. But then just two weeks before the March 2004 presidential election, Putin replaced his entire government, and appointed as prime minister Mikhail Fradkov (b. 1951), a former Russian trade minister and ambassador to the European Union.

Just as the real power of the president of the United States took decades to evolve, so it will take time for the balance of power in the Russian system to be settled.[14] In much the same way as the outlines of the U.S. presidency were set by the personality of George Washington, so Boris Yeltsin stamped his own mark on the office in the way he used his actual or implied powers. For now, the evolution of the presidency lies in the hands of Vladimir Putin and how he uses the office to deal with the other arms of government and with Russia's political, economic, and social problems. His power is nearly absolute, thanks to his constitutional powers, his control of both chambers of the Russian legislature, and his new abilities to control regional governments (see the following section). It is difficult to see real opposition to Putin or his successors emerging any time soon.

THE LEGISLATURE: FEDERAL ASSEMBLY

During Soviet days, the national legislature was the 1,500-member Supreme Soviet, its lower chamber elected from local districts and its upper chamber from the 15 republics. Meeting only twice each year for sessions of three to five days each, it did little more than rubber-stamp party decisions, the real power being held at other times by a 39-member Presidium, whose members were appointed by the party leadership and which could take any action that was constitutional, provided that it was ratified by the Supreme Soviet. In his attempts to turn the Soviet Union from a "party-governed" state into a "law-governed" state, Gorbachev created a tricameral Congress of People's Deputies and a smaller and more powerful Supreme Soviet, which sat for two sessions of four months each year. (Compare these with China's legislative bodies—see pp. 243–246.)

When the USSR broke up, Russia's own republican parliament became the supreme legislative body. This was virtually a mirror image of the Gorbachev model, with a Congress of People's Deputies elected for five-year terms, a smaller and more powerful bicameral Supreme Soviet, and a prime minister and Council of Ministers. Elements of this system worked their way into the 1993 constitution, but the powers of the executive and legislature were more clearly defined and the old system was replaced with a Federal Assembly consisting of two chambers.[15]

The Federation Council

Much like the U.S. Senate, the Federation Council is designed to represent the regions. But unlike the Senate, it is relatively weak, and—thanks to the lack of any explanation in the Russian constitution about how it should be "formed"—has been manipulated by Vladimir Putin for his own ends. It initially consisted of two representatives from each of the 89 "subjects" of Russia (regions and republics), for a total membership of 178. They were replaced in 1995 by the chief executives and the chairs of local legislatures in each of the subjects; in other words, its members became members by virtue of holding office in local government. But questions were raised about how these officials could be regional and national politicians at the same time. Another change came in 2000, when—in an attempt to limit the powers of the regional leaders, who he felt had accumulated too much influence over national politics—Vladimir Putin steered a new law through the State Duma that stripped the local leaders of their rights to sit in the Council, replacing them with 178 full-time representatives appointed by local legislatures and their executives.

The Council has jurisdiction over relations between the federal government and the regions and republics and can discuss all laws passed by the Duma, but its approval is needed only for laws involving economic or defense issues (although the State Duma can override a Council veto with a two-thirds majority). It confirms presidential nominations to the Constitutional Court and Supreme Court, must approve changes to the internal borders of Russian subjects, must approve decisions by the president to declare martial law or a state of emergency, schedules presidential elections, and has the sole power to initiate impeachment proceedings against the president.

The State Duma

The State Duma is Russia's major lawmaking body and the focus of real political power in the Federal Assembly. It has 450 members elected for maximum four-year terms, half by proportional representation and half on a winner-take-all basis. None of the elections held since 1993 has given any one party a majority in the Duma, but pro-Kremlin parties won a stranglehold after the December 2003 elections, giving Putin a strong foundation on which to pursue his legislative program.[16] The Duma is overseen by a chairman (equivalent to a Speaker) who would normally be appointed from the majority party, but because no one party has had a majority, chairs so far have been compromise appointees with relatively little political influence.

As well as its key role in the lawmaking process, the State Duma must confirm the president's choice for prime minister and must approve all government ministers except defense, foreign affairs, and internal affairs. It can also introduce motions of no confidence in the government. If these are passed by a majority, the president can either ignore them or dismiss the prime minister, but if they are repeated within three months, the prime minister must be dismissed and replaced. Given the current balance among the parties in the Duma, there is no prospect of a vote of no confidence succeeding without multiparty support. An example came in March 2001 when the communists—accusing Putin of "suicidal" policies and talking of a decade wasted on so-called "democratic reforms"—called for a vote. They were initially supported by the Unity Party, which backed the proposal because it hoped it could win more seats in the subsequent election. But when Unity withdrew, the motion was soundly defeated.

The Russian lawmaking process has two notable differences from that of the U.S. Congress:

- The Federal Assembly can discuss and adopt both federal laws and constitutional laws (which change or clarify the constitution).
- Proposals for new laws can be submitted by the president, the government, either house of the Federal Assembly, legislatures of local units of government, or even the Constitutional Court and Supreme Court. Of the more than 3,300 bills that went through the Duma in 1996–1999, nearly half came from the Duma itself, but 20 percent came from the government, 16 percent from regional assemblies, 9 percent from the Federation Council, and 5 percent from the president.[17]

Once passed by the State Duma, federal laws must go within five days to the Federation Council, which has just two weeks to vote in favor or against. A rejection can be overruled by a two-thirds majority in the Duma, or else the law is sent to a conciliation committee to settle the differences. Once a law has been adopted by the Assembly, it must be submitted to the president within five days and the president has two weeks to sign it or reject it. A presidential veto can be overruled by a two-thirds majority of both houses of the Assembly.

The Assembly is relatively weak in relation to the president, handicapped as it is by the absence of a majority party or a strong opposition (which would give it more power to contest presidential policy), by the president's powers to issue edicts and decrees, and by ongoing uncertainty about the balance of power between the executive and the legislature. Putin has taken advantage of the situation by manipulating the Assembly to his own ends.

THE JUDICIARY: CONSTITUTIONAL COURT

Russia has a Constitutional Court, which—like most such courts—has the task of protecting and interpreting the constitution. It does this by resolving disputes over political jurisdiction (including disputes between federal government departments) and making sure that the legislative and executive branches abide by the constitution. It has 19 members nominated for 12-year terms by the president and confirmed by the Federation Council.

In its early days the Court had no constitution to defend or interpret (other than the discredited 1977 version), so its members were unable to define a place for themselves in the new Russian system[18] or to act as neutral arbiters as Yeltsin and the legislature bickered. The passage of the 1993 constitution provided the legal foundation for the Court's powers, but its structure was only finally settled with the passage of a 1994 law. The Court has since faced four major challenges: building legitimacy for the constitution, giving more definition to the principles and objectives of the constitution, establishing a tradition of judicial review, and promoting public respect for the rule of law in a society in which both the law and the constitution were discredited by being manipulated to suit the ends of the CPSU.

Russia also has a Supreme Court, which is the highest court of appeal for civil, criminal, and administrative cases and has the power of oversight over the activities of lower courts. Meanwhile, a Supreme Arbitration Court deals with economic and business matters, and the constitution also provides for a single, centralized system of prosecution, headed by a prosecutor-general.

SUBNATIONAL GOVERNMENT

The USSR was legally a federation, but in practice it was governed more like a unitary state. It consisted of 15 republics, which varied in size and power from the vast and sprawling Russian Soviet Federated Socialist Republic (RSFSR), which covered 76 percent of the land area of the USSR, to the three Baltic republics (Estonia, Latvia, and Lithuania), which made up less than 1 percent of the land area of the USSR. Elections provided the same illusion of democracy as those at the federal level, but the heads of local government bodies were appointed by the general secretary of the CPSU and were accountable to no one but the higher levels of the party.

Throughout the Soviet period, ethnic and cultural differences were swept under the rug because Marxism-Leninism stipulated that such differences would disappear under communism. Official policy was to promote Russian language and culture and even to encourage non-Russians to identify themselves as Russian. Few realized just how much resentment this caused until Gorbachev came to power and his reforms released pent-up demand for change. Every Soviet republic declared sovereignty during 1990–1991, Russia included. In an attempt to save the union, Gorbachev announced plans to draw up a union treaty that would give the republics greater powers, but he was too late. The proposed signing of the treaty on August 20, 1991, sparked the attempted coup of August 19 by hard-liners opposed to its more liberal terms. Ironically, this ended any real possibility of the Soviet Union surviving, and it was formally dissolved four months later.

Under the 1993 constitution, Russia now has 89 equal "subjects," or components: 21 republics, 6 krays (territories), 49 oblasts (provinces), 2 "cities of federal significance" (Moscow and St. Petersburg), and 11 autonomous okrugs, all of which have their own government institutions and their own systems of law. Until recently, republics had their own elected presidents and krays and oblasts had elected governors. But several of the regional leaders developed strong independence and became a thorn in the flesh to the Putin administration—hence the change of law in 2000 by which they were replaced in the Federation Council with appointed representatives, and the controversial change of law in 2005 that now allows the president to appoint regional governors (see the following section, "Local Elections").

 ELECTIONS AND PARTIES

One of the biggest challenges faced by the new Russia has been to break with the legacy of a system in which political power was centralized and representation was token and to build in its place a system that allows citizens to take part in democratic decision making and encourages government to actually respond to their opinions and concerns. Russians have had little experience with democracy, so the transition has not been easy.

During the Soviet era, all significant policy decisions were made by the **Communist Party of the Soviet Union (CPSU).** Voters were offered no choice at the polls, all interest groups were overseen by the party, and the media were controlled and censored. Gorbachev began developing a more open society, but he neither lifted all controls on the media nor allowed the free expression of opposition sentiment, inside or outside government. In 1993 Russian voters—for the first time—were offered real choices at the polls, and they have since cast their votes in three presidential elections, four sets of legislative elections, and multiple local elections. They are becoming used to the idea of choice, but the evolution of a stable democratic system is still undermined by the strength of the presidency, the weakness of the legislature, and the instability of the party system.

THE ELECTORAL SYSTEM

The USSR was governed on the Leninist principle of democratic centralism, meaning that limited democracy existed within a single legal party, the CPSU. In theory, every level in the party delegated its authority to the next highest level through the electoral process. All decisions passed down by the higher levels were to be followed by the lower levels, but the higher levels were also supposedly accountable to the lower levels. In reality, rank-and-file party members had little impact on party policy, all electoral nominations were controlled by the CPSU, and because the CPSU claimed to represent the public interest, only one CPSU-approved candidate was slated for each seat. The CPSU decided the dates of elections, made all the arrangements, counted the ballots, and even organized light entertainment to keep voters amused. According to official statistics, turnout was never less than an unbelievable 99 percent.

The March 1989 elections to the Soviet Congress of People's Deputies were quite different. The CPSU was still the only legal party and the elections were still organized by the party, but anyone could be nominated to run for office and nearly 75 percent of districts were contested. The result was that several high-ranking party officials were defeated, and a number of reformers and government critics won office. Among these was Boris Yeltsin, who survived an attempt by the CPSU to discredit him and won 89 percent of the vote in his Moscow district, defeating the official CPSU candidate.

In March 1990, new elections were held for the Russian Congress of People's Deputies, still under the control of the CPSU. When the USSR ceased to exist in 1991, Congress became the supreme legislative body of Russia and its hard-line communist deputies tried to block Yeltsin's reforms. He finally suspended the legislature in September 1993 and called new elections. This sparked the September occupation of the Congress building and the attempt to overthrow Yeltsin. With the end of the siege in October, the way was cleared for new elections in December 1993, the first under the new constitution and the first contested by multiple parties.

There are two interesting options for Russian voters that are not available to most American voters. First, on both the presidential and legislative ballots, they have the option of voting "Against All Candidates." At the 2003 State Duma elections, nearly 5 percent of voters took this option, so that "Against All Candidates" won more votes than many smaller parties, and even well-established parties such as Yabloko. Second, reflecting the changeability of Russian party politics, a significant number of candidates are elected as independents. The number is usually high immediately after an election, but then falls as most of them attach themselves to a political party. But if Vladimir Putin has his way (see below), independents will be a thing of the past.

The Presidential Election

Russian presidential elections are much shorter and cheaper than their U.S. counterparts, mainly because they do not include primaries. Anyone can run, provided that they register and collect one million signatures to qualify for inclusion on the ballot. Voter turnout has been healthy and consistent, running at about 64 to 70 percent. Once the votes are counted, a candidate who wins more than 50 percent of the vote is declared elected. If no one crosses the 50 percent barrier, the top two finishers must run off against each other in a second round held within 15 days. In 1996 Boris Yeltsin barely won the biggest share of the vote in the first round with 35.3 percent of the total, followed by the Communist candidate, Gennady Zyuganov, with 32 percent. In the runoff between these two, Yeltsin was elected with nearly 54 percent of the vote. Significantly, nearly four million voters—about 5 percent of those who turned out—made a political statement in the second round by voting for "none of the above" (see Table 4.3).

The March 2000 election was different both in its character and its outcome. A change of leadership was inevitable (because Yeltsin could not run again), and 11 candidates contested the election. The clear front-runner was former prime minister and

TABLE 4.3

Results of Presidential Elections in Russia

	Candidate	% share		Ideology/party
1991*	Boris Yeltsin	57.3		None
	Nikolai Ryzhkov	16.9		Communist
	Vladimir Zhirinovsky	7.8		Liberal Democrat
	Others	10.9		
	Turnout: 69.2%			
		First round	**Second round**	
1996	Boris Yeltsin	35.3	53.8	None
	Gennady Zyuganov	32.0	40.3	Communist
	Alexander Lebed	14.5	—	Russian Communities
	Grigory Yavlinsky	7.3	—	Yabloko
	Vladimir Zhirinovsky	5.7	—	Liberal Democrat
	Others	2.2	—	
	None of the above	3.0	4.8	
	Invalid ballots	1.4	1.0	
	Turnout: 69.8% in first round; 68.9% in second round			
2000†	Vladimir Putin	52.5		None
	Gennady Zyuganov	29.4		Communist
	Grigory Yavlinksy	5.9		Yabloko
	Vladimir Zhirinovsky	2.7		Liberal Democrat
	Others	9.4		
	None of the above	1.9		
	Turnout: 68.8%			
2004†	Vladimir Putin	71.2		None
	Nikolai Kharitonov	13.7		Communist
	Others	10.8		
	None of the above	3.5		
	Turnout: 64.3%			

*Russia in June 1991 was still a Soviet republic, so this was a regional rather than a national election.
†No second round was needed because Putin won more than 50% of the vote in the first round.

incumbent acting president Vladimir Putin, whose lead in opinion polls was never seriously challenged. Putin won the first round with more than 52 percent of the vote, ensuring that a runoff was unnecessary. Gennady Zyuganov came in second with a slightly smaller share of the vote (down from 32 percent in the first round in 1996 to just under 30 percent), and all the remaining candidates were in the single-figure range. The March 2004 election produced few surprises. Gennady Zyuganov stepped aside to make way for a new candidate for the troubled Communist Party, and no other candidates were able to mount a strong challenge. They included Irina Khakamada (daughter of a Japanese communist who claimed that she was "not afraid of the terrorists in power") and Oleg Malyshkin of the Liberal Democratic Party (standing in for party leader Vladimir Zhirinovsky). Putin was again elected in the first round, with a handy 71 percent of the vote, while the Communist share of the vote was more than halved.

Legislative Elections

The most important legislative elections are those to the State Duma. Following the lead of several European states, Russia adopted a mixed voting system for the lower house, in which voters cast two votes. Half the 450 members are elected using the same winner-take-all, single-member district system used in the U.S. House of Representatives or the British House of Commons, with the candidate who wins the most votes in each of the 225 districts winning the seat, irrespective of whether that candidate has a majority. The remaining 225 seats are filled using proportional representation (PR) based on party lists. Voters cast a second vote, but this time for a party rather than an individual. The seats are then filled by parties in proportion to the number of votes they receive, provided only that they win at least 5 percent of the national vote. Only the biggest parties with the broadest base of support win seats under the PR element. (As this book went to press, legislation was under consideration that would abolish the winner-take-all element, converting the Duma to purely PR elections. This would have the effect of eliminating independents.)

The first three sets of elections in the 1990s were all regarded as relatively free and fair, and as a big improvement on the way elections were run during the Soviet era. But by 2003 there were concerns about manipulation. Observers from the Organization for Security and Cooperation in Europe (OSCE) charged that the elections were distorted by government bias, including the use of taxpayer money and state television to promote parties that supported the Putin administration, and described them as a "regression in the democratization of Russia." But Putin unsurprisingly hailed them as "another step" in the democratization of Russia, and despite Western concerns about his strong-arm tactics, the results seemed to show that he was well regarded by a majority of Russians.

Local Elections

Russians also go to the polls to elect officials to local government, but so far these elections have not been held at the same time as the presidential elections, as many of them are in the United States. A series of gubernatorial elections held in the last four months of 1996 allowed voters to confirm or reject leaders previously appointed

FIGURE 4.1

Legislative Electoral Trends in Russia

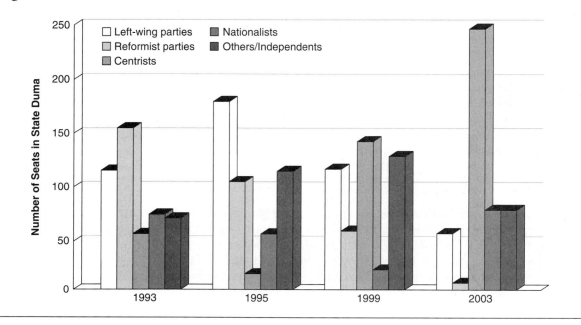

by Yeltsin, thereby extending democracy to local government. But with Putin's efforts to rein in unruly and sometimes corrupt provincial leaders, local elections have lost much of their significance. A major change came in early 2005, when—claiming the need to strengthen Russia's defenses against terrorism in the wake of the Beslan incident—Putin was able to push a law through the Duma giving him the power to appoint top regional leaders, such as governors, who would then be confirmed locally. The move was widely criticized outside Russia—and by Putin's critics at home—for giving him too much power.

POLITICAL PARTIES

One of the most important transitions that Russians have had to make has been from Soviet-style party politics (only one legal political party, which was indistinguishable from government) to modern multiparty politics, with a multitude of parties to choose from, all of them independent from the state.

The old CPSU—set up as a temporary vanguard by Lenin—was converted by Stalin into a permanent and all-pervasive part of the Soviet political system. Membership—open only to the privileged few—was a basic condition of promotion to any position of leadership, whether this was managing a factory, a college, or a trade union. Party organization was hierarchical, beginning at the grassroots with more than 440,000 primary party organizations, to which every party member belonged, and moving up through local, provincial, and republican levels to the national level, where the CPSU was dominated by a Party Congress (which met only once every four or five years) and a Central Committee (which ran the party between meetings of the Congress). At the top of the pyramid was a governing **Politburo,** the heart of real power in the USSR, which included among its members the president, the prime minister, the foreign and defense ministers, the head of the KGB security agency, and senior military officers. Its senior member was the general secretary of the CPSU, who was the de facto leader of the USSR. This was the job held by Stalin, Khrushchev, Brezhnev, Gorbachev, and other Soviet leaders.

The party system today is quite different: Russians are faced with a wide range of competing political parties that offer different views about Russia's problems and priorities and different ideas about how the country should be governed. So many parties have come and gone, and their membership has been so unstable and changeable, that they were once jokingly called "taxicab" parties because they seemed to go around in circles, stopping occasionally to let old members jump out and new members climb aboard. The prospects for a more orderly system were improved in 2001 when the State Duma passed a law limiting the number of small political parties that could take part in elections; no party can now compete unless it has at least 50,000 members and branches in at least half of Russia's 89 provinces. But the system is still in a state of flux, and there are still many different parties representing the entire political spectrum; they include several communist parties (including a Bolshevik party), a feminist party called Women of Russia, a party for retirees (the Russian Pensioners Party), and even parties supporting a return of the monarchy.

Mainstream Russian parties now fall into four major groups.[19]

Left-Wing Parties

The dominant party on the left of Russian politics is the reformed **Communist Party** of the Russian Federation (KPRF), which—not surprisingly—has been the most actively anti-reformist. The Communists are all that remains of the old CPSU, and although they have tried to reassure foreign investors and Russian entrepreneurs that a communist government would not restore state ownership and a planned economy, few have been convinced. Their former presidential candidate Gennady Zyuganov was an apologist for Stalin (blaming his worst excesses on Stalin's acolytes), spoke of his hopes for a voluntary future reunification of the former Soviet republics, wrote of his concerns about Jewish influence in the world, often criticized capitalism, and blamed the West for the fall of the USSR.

The Communists won only 14 percent of State Duma seats in 1993, but then surprised many by winning nearly a quarter of the vote in 1995 and the biggest block of seats in the Duma (up from 65 to 157). Zyuganov used this as a launchpad for his bid for the presidency in 1996, promising to restore order to Russia and briefly being described as a possible winner—until Yeltsin was able to snatch victory from the jaws of defeat. The fact that Zyuganov attracted 40 percent of the vote in the second round of the presidential election was a reflection of the extent to which communism still appealed to many Russian voters. The party was attracting voters who felt worse off because of economic reforms, notably blue-collar workers and retirees. The Communist share of seats fell to 113 in the December 1999 State Duma elections, but the party has since fallen on hard times: It won just 53 seats in the December 2003 State Duma elections, and its candidate Nikolai Kharitonov picked up less than 14 percent of the vote in the 2004 presidential election. The party attracts little support among younger Russians, there have been struggles over ideology within the party, and more militant communists have moved to more radical parties on the left.

Reformist Parties

This has been the most changeable part of the Russian party spectrum, with parties coming and going and changing their names, making it difficult to keep up. At the 1993 State Duma elections, the main party in this group was Russia's Choice, which was led by first deputy prime minister Yegor Gaidar and strongly supported Yeltsin's economic policies. It won the biggest block of seats in the Duma (96), but the party suffered from residual ill feelings among voters about the economic "shock therapy" program promoted by Gaidar. The reformist banner was taken up in 1995 by Our Home Is Russia, a coalition of parties led by Viktor Chernomyrdin, describing itself as the "party of the establishment" and supporting the current market reforms. It won the second biggest block of seats in the Duma (55) and—although Boris Yeltsin as president was not allowed to ally himself with any one party—tended to be most closely in tune with his policies.

Also on the moderate left has been Yabloko, whose name is an acronym derived from the names of its founders: Grigory Yavlinsky, Yuri Boldyrev, and Vladimir Lukin (a former ambassador to the United States). Founded in 1993, the party won the fourth biggest block of seats in the 1995 Duma elections (a modest 45), and Yavlinsky emerged as one of the contenders for the 1996 and 2000 presidential elections. Relatively young and liberal, he is a Harvard-trained economist and former advisor to presidents Gorbachev and Yeltsin, favors a gentler transition to a market economy, and warns of the dangers of public monopolies being replaced with private ones. Yabloko won just 22 seats in the 1999 elections, and just four seats in 2003.

Centrist Parties

This segment of the party spectrum has seen great growth in recent years. Starting out modestly with two major parties—the Party of Russian Unity and Women of Russia—it grew during 1999 with the rise of Unity, created just three months before the December 1999 State Duma elections and designed to be a platform for then–prime minister Vladimir Putin, to be a counterweight to another centrist party, **Fatherland-All Russia,** a coalition set up by Moscow mayor Yuri Luzhkov, former Russian prime minister Yevgeny Primakov, and several regional governors. Both groups of parties supported the view that Russia should become a market economy but that there should be a high degree of state intervention and regulation, and in 1999 won 139 seats between them.

The two parties formed the **United Russia** coalition in preparation for the 2003 elections, and won 222 seats, the biggest block of seats yet won by any one party or party group in postcommunist Russia. Putin—like Yeltsin before him—has tried to stay out of party politics, claims to be nonideological, and to look for solutions to problems from across the political spectrum.[20] However, he made clear in the lead-up to the 2003 election his support for United Russia, and there were fears that the party might win the two-thirds majority needed to change the constitution and perhaps give

Putin a third term in office, but this did not happen. Nonetheless, the pro-Kremlin parties after the 2003 election—including United Russia, the People's Party, Motherland (set up just a few months before the election), and the Liberal Democrats—among them had 316 seats, enough to give Vladimir Putin an overwhelming legislative force to help him achieve his policy goals.

Nationalist Parties

Once a potentially important part of the party spectrum, the nationalists—united mainly by their concerns about Russia's place in the world—have become much less influential than they once might have been. In 1995 they included the Congress of Russian Communities (KRO), founded to promote the interests of the 25 million ethnic Russians living in neighboring former republics of the USSR. One of the leaders of KRO was Alexander Lebed, an Afghan war veteran who became a well-trusted figure in Russian political life and came third in the first round of the 1996 presidential election. Within days he had been appointed national security advisor by Boris Yeltsin, ensuring that many of his supporters would vote for Yeltsin in the second round (which they did). After brokering a ceasefire in Chechnya in August 1996, he was fired by Yeltsin in October, probably because his usefulness to the president had expired. He was subsequently elected governor of Krasnoyarsk, a key industrial region in Siberia, before dying in a helicopter crash in 2002.

The most notorious of the nationalist parties is the Liberal Democratic Party (LDPR). Despite its name, this is a neofascist party that surprised many in the West by winning 70 seats in the 1993 State Duma elections. Many LDPR supporters resented Russia's loss of empire and the influence of the West, and believed that an alternative to capitalism could be developed. Its leading figure is Vladimir Zhirinovsky, whose popularity once attracted comparisons with the rise of Hitler in Germany in 1933. Zhirinovsky threatened to launch nuclear attacks on Japan and Germany, spoke of taking Alaska back from the United States, and promised to respond to Russian feminism by finding husbands for all unmarried women. His poor showing in the 1996 presidential election (he won just under 6 percent) started a decline that was confirmed in the 1999 State Duma elections, when the party won just 17 seats. It more than doubled its representation in 2003, by which time they had joined the pro-Kremlin block of parties in the Duma.

POLICIES AND POLICYMAKING

Establishing who was in charge during the Soviet era was relatively simple; policy was made by the leadership of the CPSU and implemented by the state bureaucracy under party supervision, while the average citizen was barely consulted. In the new Russia, policy is no longer made by a single dominant party—beyond that, all we can say with certainty is that the hierarchy of power has become fluid and changeable. The early struggle for power between the executive and legislature was won by the executive, but whether Putin plans to use that power to help him make essential changes or to solidify the dominance of the executive is still not entirely clear. The uncertainties are compounded by ongoing struggles over authority, by party divisions within the State

SHOULD BUSINESS AND POLITICS MIX?

In the United States, business and politics have always had a close relationship. Business has been a major source of funding for candidates for public office, and government has been supportive of the goals of the private sector, within reason. Russia, as a new addition to the ranks of capitalist systems, has not yet worked out how to deal with the relationship, a problem that has been compounded by the emergence of the **oligarchs:** entrepreneurs who exploited privatization and changes in economic policy in the 1990s to build massive business empires, particularly in energy and banking, and used their new power during the Yeltsin administration to influence government. Several of the most prominent played important roles in helping Yeltsin win reelection in 1996 and then committed enormous financial resources to helping Yeltsin stay in power. In the run-up to the 2000 election, they used their media influence to attack two of the contenders for the presidency, Moscow mayor Yuri Luzhkov and former prime minister Yevgeny Primakov.[21]

Vladimir Putin hinted when he became president that he expected the oligarchs to keep out of politics, in return for which he would not investigate too closely the legality of the methods used by the oligarchs to accumulate their wealth. But when he hounded into exile two of the best known

of the oligarchs—Boris Berezovsky (who had widespread interests in the oil business and the media) and Vladimir Gusinsky (head of the Media-Most conglomerate, which owned NTV, the second largest Russian television station)—it became clear that he was moving against potential sources of opposition in the corporate sector.[22]

No conflict between Putin and corporate Russia has attracted more attention than his campaign against Mikhail Khordokovsky, a billionaire several times over and chief executive of Yukos, Russia's largest oil company. In the lead up to the 2003 State Duma elections, Khordokovsky financed two opposition political parties (Yabloko and the Union of Right Forces), and openly criticized Putin's performance as president. In October, after several months of investigations into Yukos, the oil magnate was arrested when armed and masked members of the FSB, the Russian security police, boarded his corporate aircraft in Siberia. He was tried on charges of fraud, tax evasion, embezzlement and running a criminal organization, and in May 2005 was found guilty and sentenced to nine years in jail. This was widely interpreted as a political decision, designed to warn off any other oligarchs who planned to support the opposition to President Putin.

Duma, by the definition of "Russia," and by a debate over the direction of economic and foreign policy. In both spheres, the priorities of nearly 145 million people have had to be redefined: Russians have had to give up the (false) security of an economic system in which all key decisions were made for them and the supply of basic needs was guaranteed, and they have had to rethink their relationship with a world in which they once had major influence. The transition has not been easy.

ECONOMIC POLICY

In liberal democracies, production and consumption are driven mainly by supply and demand, with the role of government limited to regulation, taxes, welfare, and subsidies. By contrast, the USSR maintained a command economy in which government decided supply, distribution, and prices. No private enterprise was allowed, so everyone with a job worked for the state, all property was owned by the state, and all key services were provided by the state. At the core of the system was **Gosplan,** the State Planning Committee, which drew up five-year plans listing targets for economic production, coordinating the operations of more than 60 economic ministries and more than 130 million employees.

Central planning brought rapid industrialization and impressive economic growth, helping the Soviet Union build a powerful military machine and become a nuclear superpower. Beneath the veneer of achievement, however, the system was inefficient and irrational, and although the standard of living improved, it could not keep up with the West and probably lingered well below its true potential. The emphasis on military spending drew investment away from the civilian sector, and there was too little investment in infrastructure or in the rural economy.

Mikhail Gorbachev was not the first to attempt to reform the system (Nikita Khrushchev had tried and failed before him), and he offered neither a new diagnosis of Soviet economic problems nor even a new set of prescriptions. Where he differed was in his willingness to actually make changes. He began cautiously, easing restrictions on farms and factories, promoting small private businesses, allowing farmers to lease land and workers to lease businesses from the state, and allowing the managers of state enterprises to make more of their own decisions and sell some of their produce directly to consumers. Then in September 1990 Gorbachev launched a 500-day program aimed at turning the Soviet Union into a free-market system. He accepted the principle of private property, gave ownership of industrial assets to the republics, decentralized the tax system, and outlined a timetable for privatization, cutting the federal budget deficit, and ending subsidies to state enterprises. But it was all too late; he failed to alter the structure and attitude of the CPSU, and his policies meant few positive changes for Soviet citizens, who saw only a visible decline in the short-term quality of their lives.

Boris Yeltsin built on the changes begun by Gorbachev, but he faced the same obstacles. He opted for **"shock therapy,"** taking his first revolutionary step in January 1992 when he lifted price controls on selected consumer goods, services, machinery, and equipment. He also agreed to a stringent budget aimed at reducing Russia's deficit and cutting military spending. Finally, he built on Gorbachev's plans for privatization, while also making it clear that he wanted to keep state ownership of strategic resources such as water and forests and to carefully control the sale of property and businesses to foreign investors. His changes were bolstered by loans from foreign banks and governments, and from the International Monetary Fund (IMF), which Russia joined in March 1992. But real wages fell, inflation worsened, exports declined, and imports grew. Even though the European Union and the United States both declared that they considered Russia a market economy in 2002, Putin inherited a long list of problems from his predecessor:

- **Controlling inflation.** From its peak of 350 percent in 1992, inflation fell but was still running at about 13 percent in early 2005. The ruble had lost much of its value, falling from 30 rubles to the dollar in 1991 to an astonishing 5,800 rubles by mid-1997. A new ruble was introduced in mid-1997, with a rate of five to the U.S. dollar, but by early 2003 this too had fallen, to 32 to the dollar. One of the consequences of inflation has been a worrying flight of capital as assets are moved abroad rather than being invested locally.

© Heidi Bradner/Panos Pictures

A local resident trudges the snowy streets of Norilsk, the northernmost city in Siberia, and the world's second largest city lying north of the Arctic Circle. Sitting on top of some of the largest nickel deposits in the world, Norilsk was declared a closed city for foreigners in 2001, and even Russians cannot visit without a travel permit.

- **Improving industrial output.** After falling by nearly 10 percent in 1997–1998, output grew by 12 percent in 1998–1999, but it had fallen back to 5 percent in 2005. To make matters worse, the quality of production remains variable, thanks mainly to the obsolescence or decay of much of the physical plant in Russian factories. So poor has been the quality of Russian aircraft manufacture, for example, that staff members of the Russian civil aviation authority refuse to fly anywhere— even within Russia—on Russian-made planes.

- **Making Russia more self-sufficient and competitive in the global market.** After falling for several years, GDP has been growing since 1999 at rates of between 4 and 9 percent annually. But some of the growth has been due to increases in the international price of oil (Russia is a major producer), and the Russian consumer goods industry has so far failed to rise to the challenge posed by imports of superior Western products. Also, Russia needs to export more and to reduce its heavy reliance on exports of raw materials.

- **Making the benefits of economic growth more widely felt.** According to official estimates, more than one-third of Russians were living below the subsistence level of $520 per year in 2003. (Contrast this with the government definition of poverty in the United States: $19,350 for a family of four.) So big is the wealth gap between the cities and the rural areas that in 1997 Moscow alone was generating nearly half the entire Russian federal budget.[23]

- **Dealing with decaying infrastructure.** So much of the USSR's limited economic wealth was invested in the military that other sectors often suffered. Buildings, roads, and bridges were badly designed and constructed, and industrial machinery and equipment were inadequately maintained. Even today, much of Russia's infrastructure is outdated and in a poor state of repair. There have been improvements in industry because of increasing private ownership and investment, but public services have declined.[24] Most Russians make do, but the absence of infrastructure handicaps attempts to rebuild the economy.

- **Reducing unemployment and closing the income gap.** Liberal democracies are founded on a substantial and secure middle class. There is an emerging middle class in Russia, but unemployment is high (believed to be in the range of 7 to 10 percent, although official figures are not available). New wealth has come to a few Russian entrepreneurs, and it is becoming increasingly common to hear *biznesmeni* discussing corporate *imidzh* over a meal in Moscow restaurants, but most Russians have not yet benefited from economic change, and homelessness is widespread.

- **Generating investment.** Much is already coming from outside Russia, but this tends to fan the flames of nationalism and does not help Russians themselves learn the pitfalls and possibilities of capitalism. To make matters worse, Russia needs investment and loans from abroad to help fuel its economic recovery, but its national debt in 2001 stood at nearly $155 billion, and it has several times defaulted on its debts, making lenders disinclined either to lend it more or to cancel its debts.

- **Addressing the crisis in the banking system.** Russian banks have faced financial problems, the government has not been able to bail them out, and several have gone bankrupt. Ordinary Russians have so little faith in private banks that they make few long-term deposits. Embarrassment has been added by the involvement (usually unwitting) of local and foreign banks in money laundering—by which money acquired criminally in Russia is made "respectable"—and in capital flight as Russians with money move it overseas to keep it safe. A large part of the problem has stemmed from the persistence of Soviet-era attitudes, notably in the person of the president of the central bank, Viktor Gerashchenko. Once described as "the worst central banker in history,"[25] he maintained time-consuming red tape, employed too many staff, and refused to make public key pieces of information, such as the size of the bank's reserves. He resigned in March 2002.

THE CHECHNYAN PROBLEM

There are about 60 to 90 national minorities in Russia,[27] many of whom live on the margins of the country and several of whom want greater self-determination and even full independence. The most serious nationalist problem has come in the semi-independent republic of Chechnya, where resentment about Russian power has led to civil war and has spilled over into terrorist incidents that have rocked Russian society.

Many Chechens—who have lived as a Muslim minority within Russia since being conquered in 1858—saw the breakup of the USSR as an opportunity to win independence. When a September 1991 coup brought former Soviet air force general Dzhokhar Dudayev to power, tensions mounted, leading to a Russian attack in December 1994. Vicious fighting over the next 20 months claimed the lives of several thousand Russian troops and as many as 100,000 Chechens— about one-tenth of the population. Dudayev himself died in an April 1996 missile attack, and in May a ceasefire was negotiated that left Russia without any authority in the republic. In early 1999 the Chechen government announced plans to phase in Islamic *sharia* law, and in August Chechen-led Islamic rebels began to invade from neighboring Dagestan as part of a campaign to set up an independent Islamic republic in the north Caucasus.

The Russian government claimed that Chechens were behind bomb attacks in Moscow in August 1999 that left more than 300 people dead, and the new Putin government responded with force but, instead of relying on recruits and conscripts as in 1994–1996, used professional soldiers and worked to win public support both inside and outside Russia. Facing international criticism but backed by domestic public opinion, Russia launched an air and land attack on Chechnya, razing the capital of Grozny and generating a flood of refugees to neighboring republics. Direct control from Moscow was instituted in May 2000.

During 2001, human rights groups expressed concern about violations in Chechnya, citing allegations of torture, widespread detentions, and mass killings. In October 2002, Chechen rebels took 800 people hostage in a Moscow theater. Most of the rebels and 120 hostages were killed when Russian troops stormed the building. More violence followed: A December 2002 suicide bomb attack in Grozny killed more than 50 people, a December 2003 bomb on a train in southern Russia killed 40, a suspected suicide attack in a Moscow subway in February 2004 killed 40, and in August 2004 two passenger planes crashed shortly after takeoff from Moscow, killing 89 and raising suspicions of another terrorist bombing. Chechen rebels have described the conflict as a war of liberation, but Vladimir Putin calls it an anti-terrorist operation. The problem continues to test the multinational identity of Russia and the administrative abilities of its government, while acting as another flashpoint on the borders of the deeply troubled Middle East.

■ **Dealing with crime.** Russia still has a large black market. Although bartering is the purest form of capitalism and helps people learn the value of goods and services, it reduces the ability of a government to raise taxes and plays into the hands of organized crime. Crime bosses may control as many as four out of every ten businesses in Russia. They have also been involved in the murders of businesspeople, journalists, and politicians, such as the shooting death in November 1998 of Galina Starovoitova, a leading reformist politician. Such incidents are symptomatic of a broader problem within the justice system, which is notoriously incompetent and whose failings have allowed crime to grow: Russia now has the second highest per capita homicide rate in the world after South Africa.

- **Curbing corruption.** Putin has reduced the influence on politics of the oligarchs (rich businessmen) who were prominent during the Yeltsin years, the amount of bureaucratic paperwork demanded of businesses has fallen, and a government Audit Chamber has been investigating the financial practices of state-run agencies. But the links between government, the bureaucracy, and business are still close, and Transparency International ranked Russia 90th out of 145 countries on its 2004 Corruption Perceptions Index.[26]

Russia has considerable human capital and a wealth of natural resources, but it is still a long way from being able to exploit its potential to its fullest. The Putin administration has shown that it is impatient for change, and claims to be committed to the development of a competitive market economy,[28] but faces the challenge of capitalizing on that potential before economic and social decay go too far. One of the administration's priorities is to see Russia given membership in the World Trade Organization (WTO). Under the WTO's rules, applicants must convince all existing members of their genuine commitment to a market economy. With China's accession at the end of 2001, Russia now believes that it too should be allowed to join but faces opposition from its largest trading partner, the European Union (EU). The EU wants to be sure that Russia has made the changes needed to provide its trading partners and investors with access to all key sectors of the Russian economy and that it is dealing effectively with corruption. A number of Russian executives are also opposed, but for different reasons: they worry that joining the WTO would mean direct competition from efficient Western multinational corporations.

FOREIGN POLICY

Throughout the cold war, Soviet foreign policy was driven by strategic competition with the United States and its allies. For Americans, it often seemed that the enormous Soviet military machine posed a constant threat to peace and security, that the USSR took an aggressive posture, and that the West should respond in kind. Yet Soviet foreign policy during the cold war was based on a long tradition of insecurity stemming from the difficulties of defending the largest country in the world: "Russia is always stronger, and weaker, than it looks," went the adage.

Its insecurities were behind the creation of an East European buffer zone after World War II, in which economic ties were formalized in 1949 with the creation of the Council of Mutual Economic Assistance (Comecon) and military ties in 1955 with the Eastern European Mutual Assistance Treaty (the **Warsaw Pact**), the Soviet counter to the North Atlantic Treaty Organization (NATO). Subsequent events in Eastern Europe reflected the extent to which Soviet policy was aimed at ensuring the "cooperation" of its satellite states: the suppression of reform movements in Hungary in 1956 and Czechoslovakia in 1968, the building of the Berlin Wall in 1961, and the crackdown on the Solidarity labor union in Poland in the early 1980s. Meanwhile, the USSR gave support to Cuba and to nationalist movements in Angola, Ethiopia, and Somalia, counterbalancing the aid given by the United States and its allies to their client states in Africa and Asia.

Not all was hostility. The nuclear Non-Proliferation Treaty was signed in 1968 with the U.S. and Britain, the Strategic Arms Limitation Treaty (SALT I) was signed in 1972, in 1975 the 35-nation European Security Conference was convened, and discussions on SALT II might have resulted in a second arms reduction treaty but for the 1979 Soviet invasion of Afghanistan. The Brezhnev administration sent troops in to prop up a pro-Soviet government and quickly found itself bogged down in a military quagmire, fighting Afghan guerrillas supported by the West. By the time Soviet forces were withdrawn by the Gorbachev administration in February 1989, the war had cost more than 15,000 Russian lives. In terms of damage to national pride, it had been the Soviet Vietnam.

Gorbachev introduced a philosophy of "New Thinking" based on the argument that Soviet security depended on a political, rather than a military, relationship with the West. He entered into talks with the United States aimed at making cutbacks in nuclear and conventional weapons, paving the way for reductions in the Soviet military presence in Europe. In Eastern Europe, he refused to intervene militarily as communism began to collapse and the Soviet hegemony dissolved. The symbolic end to that hegemony came with the dismantling of the Berlin Wall in 1989 and the reunification of Germany in October 1990.

Russia during the Yeltsin years was more introverted, its leaders too focused on domestic problems to take an active role in foreign affairs and disappointed by the lukewarm response of the West to its economic and social needs. Russia inherited the Soviet seat on the UN Security Council but pursued a **"Russia First"** policy driven by its traditional mistrust of the West.[29] Yeltsin and U.S. President Bill Clinton developed a warm personal relationship, and they met more times than all their postwar predecessors combined, but Yeltsin's few overseas visits were aimed mainly at attracting economic support and at building ties with Russia's neighbors. The only major international disputes in which Russia's name was raised were the crises in the former Yugoslavia, where Western countries were slow to deal with the Serbs because of their traditional links with Russia.

A key item on the military policy agenda is Russia's relationship with NATO, the "winner" of the cold war. In 1994 NATO introduced a Partnership for Peace program aimed at promoting military cooperation and strengthening ties between NATO members and Eastern Europe. Signatories had to declare their commitment to democracy and the principles of international law. Russia joined in May 1994 and, by the end of 1996, 26 countries had joined, including all 15 former Soviet republics except Tajikistan. However, NATO remained unpopular in Russia, as shown by the public and political outcry against the NATO-led attack on Yugoslavia in 1999.

More recently, the controversial issue has been the expansion of full NATO membership to Eastern Europe. It has not been welcomed by Russia, but plans have proceeded regardless: the Czech Republic, Hungary, and Poland joined in 1999, and were followed in 2004 by Bulgaria, Romania, Slovakia, Slovenia, and—more significantly—the former Soviet republics of Estonia, Latvia, and Lithuania. The Putin administration continues to oppose expansion but realizes that there is little it can do to stop it, and there is even a minority within Russia that sees eventual Russian membership as inevitable. Meanwhile, there has been a reappraisal of NATO's role, which is increasingly focused on building political links among its members and their allies, providing political support for security operations, and redefining "the enemy," with much talk of the need for a common approach to terrorism.

Following the attacks of September 11, 2001, there were signs of warming relations between the West and Russia, with the Putin administration supporting the U.S. war in Afghanistan and even backing down on its initial opposition to plans by the Bush administration to develop a ballistic missile defense system and to withdraw from the 1972 Anti-Ballistic Missile treaty. Putin made a number of successful visits to Western Europe and made it clear that he wanted to better understand the goals of the European Union, membership of which expanded in 2004 to the Czech Republic, Estonia, Hungary, Latvia, Lithuania, Poland, Slovakia, and Slovenia. He also stressed that Russia's earlier implied criticism of American global leadership and its talk of the importance of strong relations with China and North Korea were in the past. Putin may have been motivated by two key philosophies: his own war against Islamic insurgency in Chechnya and his belief that building a strong and modern Russia needs investment and encouragement from the West.[30]

Meanwhile, the state of the Russian military remains a cause for concern. Once a formidable fighting force, which protected the USSR against the Nazi invasion in 1941 and then pushed Hitler's war machine back into the heart of Germany, the Russian military today is a shadow of its former self. It is still large (although no one knows exactly how large because many commanders exaggerate numbers to collect more pay, rations, and equipment), and it still has nuclear missiles and other advanced weapons. But it is top-heavy and badly paid; morale is low following failures in Chechnya; its equipment is old; and alcoholism, drug addiction, and suicide are common among its youngest conscripts. Putin has plans to reduce troop numbers and build a smaller and more professional military by 2007, but he faces many bureaucratic hurdles.[31]

The future for Russian foreign policy depends in large part on how economic reforms go at home. Many older Russians still hark back to the "good old days" when the USSR was a superpower, and they are wary of any attempts to compromise Russian economic independence or to encircle Russia. This is partly why nationalist political parties have struck a chord with many Russians. The challenge for Russia, for Eastern Europe, and for the Western liberal democracies is to ensure that Russia is able to redefine its position in the world without feeling that its interests are compromised. It will be no easy task.

RUSSIAN POLITICS IN TRANSITION

"I cannot forecast to you the action of Russia," once quipped Winston Churchill. "It is a riddle wrapped in a mystery inside an enigma." He was speaking in 1939 about Russia's potential war aims, but the sentiment still applies today; Russia is not easy to understand. Since the breakup of the Soviet Union, Russia has undergone a transition on at least three fronts: from empire to nation-state, from one-party state socialism to liberal democracy, and from a command economy to a free-market system. The magnitude of these changes—and their impact both on Russia and on the rest of the world—is enormous. Without help, the right political and economic choices, and plain good luck, Russia will not become the liberal democracy that the West would like to see.

Russians themselves have shown only mixed levels of support for the values and beliefs that support such a system. At the very least, they must organize and participate and must learn an entirely new set of rules about their place in the system relative to one another and to their government. Equally important, economic decline must be reversed and social discontent must be addressed. Russian nationalism is partly a reflection of widespread dissatisfaction with the old system, the change brought about by the new system, and the uncertainty inherent in transition. Russia's challenges in the 1990s were complicated by the lack of a stable government or opposition within the State Duma. Since then, the office of president has won more definition, the party system is settling down, and the Duma is slowly becoming a more effective policymaking body. Worrisome elements of the tradition of Russian authoritarianism remain, however, and Russia still has some way to go before it meets the definition of working free-market democracy.

KEY TERMS

Bolsheviks
Chechnya
closed politics
command economy
Communist Party
Communist Party of the
   Soviet Union (CPSU)
Constitutional Court
dual executive
edicts

Fatherland-All Russia
Federation Council
five-year plans
glasnost
Gosplan
nationalism
New Economic Policy
oligarchs
patrimonialism
perestroika

Politburo
Russia First
Siberia
shock therapy
Stalinism
State Duma
superpresidency
United Russia
Warsaw Pact

KEY PEOPLE

Mikhail Fradkov
Mikhail Gorbachev
Nikita Khrushchev

Vladimir Putin
Joseph Stalin

Leon Trotsky
Boris Yeltsin

STUDY QUESTIONS

1. By the time Gorbachev took power in 1985, was the USSR predominantly a Marxist, a Leninist, or a Stalinist state?

2. Is Russia under Putin headed toward becoming a liberal democracy?

3. Does the dual executive help or hinder the prospects for political change in Russia?

4. How does the structure of federalism in the United States and Russia compare?

5. What signs are there—if any—that the authoritarian tradition is still a factor in Russia today?

6. Has Russia become the "party-governed" state for which Mikhail Gorbachev hoped?

7. If adopted in the United States, would a two-round presidential election improve or detract from the quality of American democracy?

8. What impact has the mixed winner-take-all/proportional representation electoral system had on the way Russia is governed?

9. What is the significance of the Chechnyan problem for Russia's stability?

10. What problems do the tradition of Soviet central planning pose for economic reform in Russia?

RUSSIA ONLINE

There are Web sites for the **Russian government** (www.gov.ru), the **presidency** (http://president.kremlin.ru/eng), and the **State Duma** (www.duma.ru), but they are mainly in Russian. Among the most useful English-language sites are the following:

Russia on the Net: www.ru/eng/index.html

Russia on the Web: http://members.valley.net/transnat

Two megasites that provide links to a variety of other sites on news, politics, and business.

Russia Today: www.einnews.com/russia

Radio Free Europe/Radio Liberty: www.rferl.org

Pravda: http://english.pravda.ru

The Russia Journal: www.russiajournal.com

A variety of sources of news on Russia, *Pravda* ("Truth") being the former CPSU party paper and *The Russia Journal* being a Moscow-based weekly.

FURTHER READING

Herspring, Dale R. (Ed), *Putin's Russia: Past Imperfect, Future Uncertain*, 2nd Ed. (Lanham, MD: Rowman and Littlefield, 2004). An edited collection of studies of the impact of Vladimir Putin, with chapters on state and society, the economy, the military, and foreign policy.

Hosking, Geoffrey, *Russia and the Russians* (Cambridge, MA: Harvard University Press, 2001). A general history of Russia that raises important questions about the viability and purpose of the Russian state.

Kelley, Donald R., *Politics in Russia and the Successor States* (Fort Worth, TX: Harcourt, 1999). An introductory survey, with chapters on the constitution, political culture, institutions, parties, and policies.

Sakwa, Richard, *Russian Politics and Society*, 3rd Ed. (London and New York: Routledge, 2002), and Remington, Thomas F., *Politics in Russia*, 3rd Ed. (New York: Longman, 2003). Two general surveys of Russian politics, covering political culture, institutions, process, and policies.

White, Stephen, Alex Pravda, and Zvi Gitelman (Eds.), *Developments in Russian Politics 5* (Durham, NC: Duke University Press, 2001). The Russian volume in the excellent Palgrave/Duke series, with chapters on the presidency, parties, policies, and the non-Russian former Soviet republics.

ELECTORAL SYSTEMS

One of the hallmarks of a democracy is an electoral system in which every citizen can take part in regular, free, and fair elections. However, elections are truly fair only if every vote cast has equal weight and if seats are divided among candidates competing for office in a way that reflects the balance of opinion in the electorate. Ideally, electoral systems should also produce stable governments, where a single party is in charge or a workable coalition of two or more parties can be agreed. Unfortunately, these ideals are difficult to achieve, because the math of most electoral systems means that some votes count more than others. For example, it can take more votes to help one party win seats in a legislature than another party. In an effort to achieve balanced elections, several different electoral systems have been developed, which fall into one of four categories: plurality, majority, proportional representation, and combination systems.

- **The plurality system.** Otherwise known as winner-take-all or first-past-the-post, this is used for elections to the lower chamber in most English-speaking democracies, including the United States, Canada, and Britain. The country is divided into districts with roughly equal population size, and each district is contested by candidates representing different parties. Every voter casts a single vote, and the candidate who wins the most votes (a plurality) wins the district.

  The system is simple, usually inexpensive (except in the United States), does not require much thought from voters, and gives each district a single representative. However, because it works in favor of parties that have solid blocks of support around the country (they win seats) and against parties whose support is more widely and thinly spread (they more often come second or third), it often leads to victorious parties winning a much bigger percentage of seats than votes. It also provides no representation for voters who vote against the winner.

- **The majority system.** This is used in countries such as Australia and France and is set up in such a way as to require the successful candidate to win a majority of the votes. Like the plurality system, it is based on single-member districts, but the similarities end there. Australia uses a system known as alternative vote, which requires that voters—instead of voting for a single candidate—must rank all the candidates running in their district. The candidate with the highest average score wins. The system is not as simple as the plurality system because it demands more thought by voters, who have to develop an opinion about every candidate. It can also lead to even more disproportionate results than the plurality system.

  One variant is the dual ballot, used for presidential elections in Austria, Finland, France, Portugal, and Russia, and for legislative elections in France. Under this system, multiple candidates compete against one another in the first ballot, and a winner is declared if he or she wins more than half the vote. If no one wins more than half the vote, a second ballot is held that usually involves just the two highest-placed candidates in the first round. The second round is usually preceded by bargaining among parties as the two final candidates try to encourage voters from other parties to support them.

- **Proportional representation (PR).** This is widely used in continental European liberal democracies but has so far been adopted by neither the United States nor Canada. Political parties win seats in proportion to the number of votes they receive, but PR comes in many different forms, none of which produces an exact reflection of the popular vote.

The most basic form is the party list system. This divides a country into districts with roughly equal population size that are much bigger than the districts used in the plurality system and that are represented not by a single member but by multiple members. Each of the contesting parties publishes a list of candidates, ranked in order of preference. Voters then choose among the parties, and the seats are divided up among the parties in proportion to the vote they receive. So, in a ten-member district, if Party A wins 50 percent of the vote, the first five people on its list are elected. If Party B wins 30 percent of the vote, the first three people on its list are elected, and so on. A threshold is also usually used so that no party wins any seats unless it wins at least 5 percent of the vote.

A more complex version of PR is the single transferable vote (STV). Voters must choose at least one candidate and must rank all the candidates they like, writing 1 next to the name of their favorite, 2 next to their second choice, and so on. To be elected, a candidate must win a minimum number of votes (or a quota), which is worked out by dividing the number of valid voting papers cast by the number of seats to be filled plus one. So if the number of votes cast in a district is 500,000, and there are five seats to fill, the quota would be $500{,}000 \div 5 + 1 = 83{,}000$. First preference votes are then counted, and any candidate winning more than 83,000 votes is elected. All the surplus votes for winning candidates are then transferred to other candidates. So if Joe Smith wins 100,000 first preference votes, his surplus is 17,000. All 100,000 of his first-preference votes are examined again to establish the distribution of second-preference votes among the other candidates. If Ann Jones receives 80,000 of the second-preference votes cast by Joe Smith supporters, then in addition to the 70,000 first preference votes she has received (not enough to get her elected), she receives $17{,}000 \div 100{,}000 = 0.17$ of an additional vote for each second preference, or $80{,}000 \times 0.17 = 13{,}600$ votes. This puts her above the 83,000 minimum, and she is elected.

Although this is an achingly complex system as far as the electoral officials are concerned, it gives voters much more control over how their votes are used than is the case with the party list system. It also ensures that no votes are wasted, because voters know that all their preferences will be taken into account. It was used in the United Kingdom for the first time in the Northern Ireland assembly elections in 1998.

- **Combination systems.** These use plurality and PR together, with some seats being decided with one system and others with the second system. The main advantage is that voters end up being tied to individual representatives and smaller parties are able to win seats. Combinations are used for legislative elections in Japan and Russia and have also been used for elections to the Scottish and Welsh regional assemblies in Britain. For example, Scotland has 129 seats in its assembly, 73 of which are decided by the plurality system, and the remaining 56 of which are divided among eight parliamentary regions, each represented by seven members. Voters cast two ballots: one for their constituency member and one for a party. Constituency winners are determined by a plurality, and the regional seats are divided among the parties according to the proportion of the seats they win. The plurality system usually works in favor of bigger parties, whereas the regional system works in favor of smaller parties, which tend to win no seats under the plurality system.

Looking at these options, it is clear that the plurality system is the simplest and quickest, but it is also potentially the least fair. The other options may take more thought and effort, but they have the benefit of more accurately reflecting voter preferences.

CHAPTER 5

CHINA

CHINA: QUICK FACTS

Official name: People's Republic of China (Zhonghua Renmin Gonghe Guo)

Capital: Beijing

Area: 3,695,000 square miles (9,571,300 sq. km) (slightly larger than the United States)

Languages: Predominantly standard or Mandarin Chinese, with many dialects and several minority languages

Population: 1,272 million

Population density: 351 per square mile (14 per sq. km.)

Population growth rate: 0.6 percent

POLITICAL INDICATORS

Freedom House rating: Not Free

Date of state formation: 1949

System type: Socialist republic

Constitution: Published 1982

Administration: Unitary

Executive: Premier and State Council

Legislature: Unicameral National People's Congress of nearly 3,000 members, with Standing Committee of 20 members; members of Congress serve 5-year terms

Party structure: Dominated by the Chinese Communist Party (CCP)

Judiciary: No separate judiciary

Head of state: President Hu Jintao (2003–)

Head of government: Premier Wen Jiabao (2003–)

ECONOMIC INDICATORS

GDP (2004): $1,649 billion

Per capita GDP: $1,290

Distribution of GDP: Services 33 percent, industry 52 percent, agriculture 15 percent

Urban population: 32 percent

SOCIAL INDICATORS

HDI ranking: 94

Infant mortality rate: 30 per 1,000 live births

Life expectancy: 70.8 years

Literacy: 92 percent of people aged 15 and older

Religions: None officially sanctioned, but Confucianism, Taoism, and Buddhism were traditionally prevalent

A note on spelling: There are two systems for the Romanized spelling of Chinese words and names: the 19th-century Wade-Giles system and the Hanyu Pinyin system preferred by China today. This text uses Hanyu Pinyin, but gives Wade-Giles equivalents where they are more familiar.

INTRODUCTION

Of all the countries in this book, probably none is undergoing such fundamental transition as China. Once one of the backbones of the communist world, China today is steadily moving toward capitalism, and the result is that we are having to rethink the way we look it. Recent recalculations of data suggest that China has one of the world's biggest economies , a discovery that has led to a spate of predictions over the last decade that it could become the world's next economic superpower.[1] This depends, though, on three major factors: Will the free-market tendencies that China has seen in the last decade persist? Will political liberalization keep pace? And will Chinese leaders be able to control the speed of change and avoid the shock therapy that Russians have had to endure?

Although China's economic potential has been clear to China watchers for a long time, it became headline news in 1994 when the World Bank—using questionable official statistics and the purchasing power parity (PPP) method—announced that the Chinese economy was much bigger than previously thought. The news encouraged the major liberal democracies to take a new interest in the Chinese market. The figures have since grown further, and in 2004 China had a GDP of $1.65 trillion, or—in PPP terms—$7.1 trillion, which placed it second only to the United States. But the figure should be treated with caution, because in relative terms China is still a poor country, with a per capita GDP of just $1,290 (or $5,530 using PPP calculations).

The most notable feature of the People's Republic of China (PRC) is its sheer size. It has about the same land area as the United States, but it has nearly five times the population—with nearly 1.3 billion people, it is by far the most populous country in the world, with nearly 4.5 times as many people as the United States. That population is relatively young and, because most of China is uncultivable mountain or desert, is concentrated along the east coast, where 90 percent of the population lives on 17 percent of the land. No surprise, then, that some of the biggest and most crowded cities in the world are in China, including Shanghai (13.5 million) and the capital, Beijing (11.3 million).

Despite the positive economic growth figures, an estimated one-third of all Chinese live in poverty, and two-thirds live in the rural areas and make a living off the land. More than half of China's wealth is generated by industry, with services making a relatively modest contribution of 33 percent of GDP. China is the world's biggest coal producer and has rich deposits of iron ore, but it lacks mining and distribution capacity. Self-sufficient in oil until the mid-1990s, it now has to import more of its energy needs. All of China's postrevolutionary leaders have agreed on the need for industrialization and modernization, but they have disagreed on the means of achieving those ends. In the 1950s and 1960s, Mao Zedong occasionally used draconian measures to build the national economy through mass mobilization and Stalinist five-year plans. In the 1980s, his successors began liberalizing the economy, encouraging a limited free market, consumerism, and an open-door policy toward the West that continues today.

In social terms, China is relatively homogeneous. The vast majority of its people are ethnic Han Chinese, and only about 7 percent belong to an ethnic minority

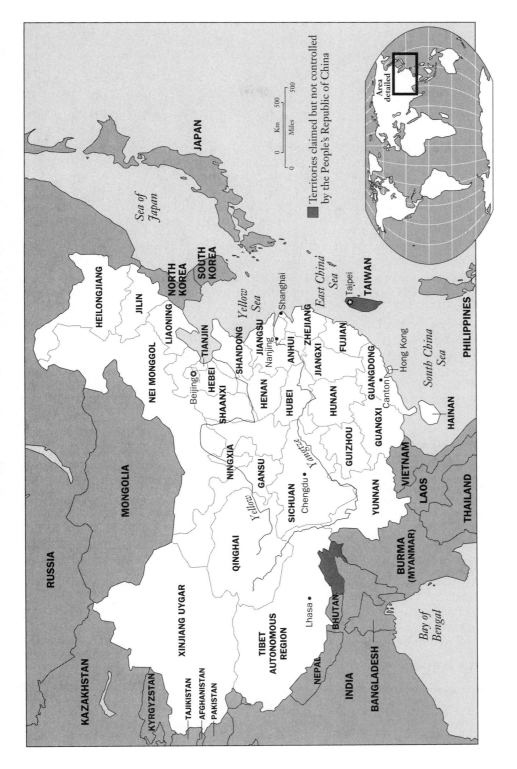

Territories claimed but not controlled by the People's Republic of China (of which there are about 55 to 60). But given the sheer size of China, some of those minorities are big enough to make up the population of a medium-sized country: There are about 17 million Thais, 6 million Mongols, and 5 million Tibetans. Many of these groups live in areas thought to have rich mineral resources, and others live on the borders of China, close enough to related groups in other countries to pose a potential threat to China's territorial integrity. To complicate matters, the Han Chinese tend to see aliens as culturally inferior and have had a poor record of assimilating minorities.

In political terms, China underwent dramatic and often confusing changes during the twentieth century that pulled it in several different directions. For centuries it sat in splendid isolation, but the arrival of European traders in the nineteenth century paved the way for changes in the first half of the twentieth century that left China struggling to build a new identity and a viable system of government. These changes included a nationalist revolution in 1911 that ended several thousand years of imperial rule, a second revolution in 1927–1928 that brought a decade of quasi-fascist nationalism, and a civil war that launched China in 1949 on a course of socialism that was confused by the often idiosyncratic ideas of Mao Zedong.

Chinese politics since the revolution has been commonly described with words such as *corporatism, obedience*, and *bureaucracy*, rather than *individualism* or *democracy*,[2] and policy has been heavily influenced by the personalities of leaders such as Mao and his most prominent successor, Deng Xiaoping. China today is more stable and peaceful than it has been for decades, and a new generation of pragmatic and technocratic leaders has brought economic liberalization. However, it still has a poor record on human rights, the Chinese Communist Party still has a monopoly on government, and power is determined by struggles within the ruling elite rather than by the wishes of the citizens.

POLITICAL DEVELOPMENT

China has the longest recorded history of any country in the world, dating back more than 3,600 years. For most of that time, the Chinese lived under an imperial system of government, relatively untouched by the outside world. China called itself Zhongguo (Middle Kingdom), thought of itself almost literally as the center of the world, and regarded all other cultures as peripheral. Chinese culture was rich and sophisticated, making great strides in the arts and the sciences and developing an intricate political system and social structure. However, the old imperial China is not the modern socialist China, which is mainly a product of events that have taken place in the last 90 years, including three revolutions (1911, 1927–1928, and 1949), periods of near anarchy, and lengthy debates about the goals of political, economic, and social development.

The Imperial Era (1766 B.C.–A.D. 1911)

Prerevolutionary China was based on an agrarian economy and governed by the ideas of Confucius (551–479 B.C.), a philosopher who lived during the late Zhou dynasty. **Confucianism** was a secular and ethical system of moral rules and principles, but although it was akin to a religion, it had no institutionalized church and was more tolerant toward other systems of thought than Christianity. Officially denounced in the 1970s as the root of all China's evils, it is now being taken more seriously again.

Confucian theory taught the importance of obeying the authority of the emperor, but it also promoted "government by goodness," arguing that the emperor (the Son of Heaven) had the right to govern (the Mandate of Heaven) only so long as he ruled with honor and virtue. If rulers set a good example, they would not have to use coercion to rule; if they did not, the right to rule could be withdrawn. The government of goodness also depended on all citizens knowing their roles, so Confucianism provided a social code governing interpersonal relationships, emphasizing (like Japan) conformity and self-discipline and discouraging individualism. Emperors ruled through senior government officials, or mandarins, who won appointment through an examination system that was theoretically open to anyone but that was based largely on a test of their "morality" and knowledge of Confucian ethics. The mandarins formed a small but powerful ruling elite, running a sprawling and hierarchical bureaucracy.

The decline and fall of the last of China's 24 imperial dynasties—the Qing Manchus (1644–1911)—began in the early nineteenth century when the dynasty was unable to respond to the needs of a growing population for land and food. Imperial credibility was further weakened by the opium war with Britain in 1839–1842, which resulted in China being forced to open its doors to traders and missionaries from the outside world and to cede harbors (such as Hong Kong and Shanghai) to European powers. Growing resentment sparked the **Taiping Rebellion** of 1850–1864, led by the failed Confucian scholar Hong Xiuquan, who believed he was Jesus Christ's younger brother and responsible for bringing Christian morality to China. The rebellion cost an estimated 20 to 40 million lives before being put down with Western help. Financially and politically drained, the Manchus suffered a final blow when China was ignominiously defeated by Japan in the war of 1894–1895.

Nationalism and Chaos (1911–1949)

With pressures for revolutionary change mounting, Sun Yat-sen (1866–1925), an expatriate Chinese physician, founded a secret society among Chinese living abroad in 1894. From headquarters in Tokyo and Hanoi, Sun's followers launched a number of attacks on the Manchu regime, finally succeeding (on their 11th attempt) in October 1911. However, Sun's government relied on the military for its authority, was undermined by continuing Western inroads into China, understood little about how Western democracy worked, and was unable to win the allegiance of the people; it soon lost control and China fell into chaos.

Between 1916 and 1926, China was torn apart by warlords fighting among themselves for power. Sun was nominally leader, but he had no real power or credibility. In 1922, having failed to win help from the West, Sun signed an agreement with the Soviet Comintern through which he received help to transform his Nationalist Party (the **Guomindang**) and to provide arms and training for the Chinese army. In the interests of national reunification, he also entered a brief and acrimonious coalition with the new Chinese Communist Party (CCP), which had been founded in 1921.

When Sun died in 1925, he was replaced by his senior military commander, Chiang Kai-shek (1886–1975), who abhorred communism and set about defeating the warlords and uniting China. In an attempt to unify the Nationalists, Chiang launched a lightning strike against the CCP in June 1927 (the "Shanghai Massacre") and expelled Soviet advisors. He then set up his own right-wing nationalist government in Nanjing, which was widely recognized in the West as the legitimate government of China. Although he improved the administrative and educational systems and built a modern German-trained army, Chiang made the fatal mistake of doing nothing about land reform, leaving the peasants poor and unhappy.

Some Chinese now began seeing the solution to their problems in the CCP. Outlawed by Chiang in 1927, it was forced to survive as underground groups in cities and as small experimental councils in the rural areas. It came under the influence of Mao Zedong, who built a base of support in Jiangxi province, to which the party headquarters was moved in 1931. Three years later, a Guomindang campaign forced Mao to uproot his 150,000 followers and move them west and then north on the 6,000-mile **Long March.** The migration lasted a year, and the party lost almost 90 percent of its number to disease, starvation, and nationalist attacks, but Mao was now beyond the reach of the nationalists and he was able to strengthen his control over the CCP.

In 1936 Chiang was obliged to agree to a second alliance with the CCP to stave off the Japanese, who had invaded Manchuria in 1931 and begun moving southward. Mao's Red Army suffered repeated military defeats but nevertheless expanded its membership; by 1945, when Japan surrendered and civil war broke out in China between the Guomindang and the Red Army, Mao was in a strong position. Attempts by the United States to mediate failed, and in 1949 Chiang fled with his followers to **Taiwan,** an island off the coast of mainland China. On October 1, 1949, the People's Republic of China was proclaimed in Beijing.

The Communist Era (1949–)

China under communism has been relatively united and relatively immune from outside interference. Within its borders, however, there has been enormous social upheaval, considerable violence, disruptive political change, and a vocal debate about how best to achieve the goals of socialism. The **shifting lines** of the debate saw radicals wanting to force the process by pursuing an ideological commitment to Marxism-Leninism-Maoism and pragmatists arguing that change needed more than an ideological commitment.

Mao clearly played a central role in the creation of the PRC and the restoration of China's independence, but his leadership was flawed, especially after 1957; his goals of combating bureaucracy, improving health care and education, and encouraging popular participation and self-reliance were laudable, but the methods he used were often self-defeating.[3] He saw his first priority as the redistribution of land, which was still in the hands of a privileged few; the majority of Chinese were tenant farmers. In 1950, 300 million landless peasants were given their own plots, but it soon became obvious that many of these plots were too small to support a family, so the government set up new and bigger cooperatives, on the lines of Stalinist collectivization.

T A B L E   5 . 1

China: A Timeline

1815	First British envoys arrive in China
1839–1842	Opium wars with Britain; Britain gains Hong Kong
1850–1864	Taiping rebellion
1894–1895	Sino-Japanese war
1911	Nationalist revolution
1916–1926	Era of the warlords
1921	Founding of the Chinese Communist Party
1925	Death of Sun Yat-sen
1927	Shanghai massacre
1927–1937	China under Guomindang rule
1934–1935	Long March
1937–1945	Sino-Japanese war
1945–1949	Chinese civil war
1949	Proclamation of People's Republic of China and of the Republic of China (Taiwan)
1949–1953	Land redistribution program and execution of 2 to 4 million owners of large estates
1951	China invades Tibet
1950–1953	Korean War
1953	First five-year plan
1954	First constitution of China published
1958–1960	Great Leap Forward
1964	China detonates its first atom bomb
1966–1969	Great Proletarian Cultural Revolution
1971	China admitted to UN; Taiwan expelled
1972	Meeting of Mao Zedong and Richard Nixon
1976	(January) Death of Zhou Enlai and (September) Mao Zedong
1979	(February–March) Chinese invasion of Vietnam
1982	New constitution brings an end to Maoism
1989	(June 4) Tiananmen Square massacre; Dalai Lama wins Nobel Prize for peace
1992	CCP declares establishment of a market economy an official goal
1993	Jiang Zemin becomes president
1995	(February) China's population reaches 1.2 billion
1997	(February) death of Deng Xiaoping; (July) Hong Kong returned to China after 155 years of British rule
1999	(May) NATO bombing of Chinese Embassy in Belgrade; (December) Macau returned to China after 442 years of Portuguese rule
2001	(April) midair collision between U.S. spy plane and Chinese fighter jet; (December) China joins the World Trade Organization
2002	(November) Jiang Zemin retires as CCP general secretary; Hu Jintao takes over
2003	(March) Hu Jintao becomes president; (October) launch of China's first manned spacecraft
2005	(April) First meeting for 49 years between leaders of Chinese communist and nationalist parties

Mao's second priority was to build industry. He initially followed the Stalinist model of long-term centralized planning based on five-year plans. These produced impressive growth rates, but they relied too heavily on professionals and bureaucrats, ignoring millions of peasants. To promote debate on how the party should relate to the people, to reduce the urban-rural divide, and to diffuse the growing criticism of his policies, Mao in 1957 allowed public discussion of China's problems, declaring that he would "let one hundred flowers bloom, let one hundred schools of thought contend." Alarmed at the extent to which his critics took up his invitation, he then decided to decentralize industry and agriculture and—by substituting capital (of which China had little) with manpower—encourage the Chinese to use their own resources to launch the **Great Leap Forward** (1958–1960).

Great Leap Forward An aggressive attempt by Mao to accelerate Chinese economic change.

Vowing that China would progress "20 years in a day," Mao mobilized the peasant masses, put the unemployed to work, forced the employed to work harder under almost military discipline, and launched a systematic program of indoctrination to create a new breed of "complete communists" and a classless society. The Great Leap Forward ended in failure, in part because peasants received little reward for their labor. Matters were made worse by a falling out between China and the USSR, the withdrawal of Soviet technical aid, and floods and famines in 1959–1961 that led to an estimated 15 to 20 million deaths. Agriculture was set back by nearly a decade, and Mao, heavily criticized for being arrogant and impatient, came close to losing power. The new president of China, Liu Shaoqi, effectively became the leader of the country and quickly moved to reintroduce private farming plots and markets.

In an attempt to regain his lost influence, Mao turned his attention to ideological reform and in 1966 launched a program of mass criticism known as the **Great Proletarian Cultural Revolution.** Supposedly a debate on the nature of the revolution, it was actually a scheme to neutralize Mao's opponents by attacking bureaucrats, "intellectuals," Confucianism, and those accused of wanting to follow the "capitalist road," such as Liu Shaoqi and Deng Xiaoping (then CCP general secretary). Radical students known as Red Guards ran criticism sessions, and tens of millions of leaders and "intellectuals" (anyone with a high school education) were sent to the rural areas to work on the land and to discuss Maoist thought, as contained in the famous *Little Red Book* (see People in History, p. 233). Public education and government came to a virtual standstill, Deng Xiaoping was disgraced, and Liu Shaoqi was dismissed in 1968. (He died in prison in 1969 but was later hailed as a hero.)

Cultural Revolution Mao's program of ideological reform aimed at strengthening his control over China.

The period 1966–1976 is now described as the Ten Catastrophic Years. The early 1970s saw an aging Mao withdraw from public life, and China increasingly came under the steadying influence of premier Zhou Enlai, one of the most widely respected of all China's modern leaders. Zhou began rebuilding the economy and the bureaucracy and established a collective leadership for the party. The deaths of both Zhou and Mao in 1976 intensified a power struggle that had been brewing since 1973 between radicals and pragmatists. Mao's widow, Jiang Qing, and three other radicals formed a "Gang of Four," which worked to continue Maoist ideas. They were quickly arrested by Mao's designated successor, Hua Guofeng; put on trial; and later jailed for life.

Hua was never able to build a solid base of support, and through most of the 1980s, China was under a collective leadership: The party was run by general secretary Hu Yaobang and the government by premier Zhao Ziyang, while Deng Xiaoping

P E O P L E   I N   H I S T O R Y

MAO ZEDONG

The towering influence in the history of China during the twentieth century was Mao Zedong (1893–1976), instigator of the 1949 communist revolution; leader of China for 27 years; and a man of exceptional personal power, prestige, and ruthlessness.

Mao was born in rural Hunan province in south-central China. In 1918 he was hired as an assistant at Beijing National University by Li Dazhao, a professor of history, economics, and political science. Influenced by Li and by the writings of Marx and Lenin, Mao joined the CCP and in 1928 organized a series of uprisings in Hunan; when these failed he was dismissed from his posts in the CCP. The party split and Mao left for the mountains of Jiangxi province, where he established the Chinese Soviet Republic and became leader of the CCP. In 1931 Chiang Kai-shek launched a series of campaigns against Jiangxi aimed at eliminating the communists, finally forcing Mao to leave with his followers on the Long March. Thousands died on the march (including Mao's first wife), but it established him as a legendary figure and convinced millions that he offered China the best hope for peace.

From a new base in Shaanxi, Mao rebuilt the Red Army, and while China was at war with Japan (1937–1945), he extended his control. The civil war of 1945–1949 ended in victory for the Communists, and Mao became first chairman of the People's Republic of China. His tenure saw the introduction of policies aimed at establishing and cementing a distinctly Chinese revolutionary ideal (the "Chinese Road to Socialism"), which brought many social improvements, but which also brought famine, civil disorder, and economic ruin; Maoism was ultimately responsible for the loss of millions of lives. Despite his failures, he became the focus of a cult of personality and was acclaimed the Great Helmsman (although his second wife, Jiang Qing, became increasingly powerful as Mao grew older and more unsteady). He died in September 1976, at age 82.

The Maoist cult was sustained by the publication of the *Little Red Book* of quotations from Mao.[4] Although many dealt with themes such as public service, personal responsibility, and moral virtue, the more militant have been longer remembered:

- Political power grows out of the barrel of a gun.
- Politics is war without bloodshed, while war is politics with bloodshed.
- All reactionaries are paper tigers.
- People of the world, unite and defeat the U.S. aggressors and all their running dogs!

(who had been rehabilitated in 1974) functioned as the power behind the throne. Deng implemented a policy of Four Modernizations: industry, agriculture, national defense, and science and technology. Where Mao had looked for a Chinese road to socialism, Deng spoke of "socialism with Chinese characteristics." He also oversaw the drafting in 1978 of a new constitution that established liberalizing tendencies, leading some to call democracy the **Fifth Modernization.**

Deng's economic reforms went well beyond anything envisaged in the USSR by Mikhail Gorbachev. Mao had argued that elements of capitalism could be used as a means to the end of achieving true socialism; Deng developed this idea by running the economy on a mixture of capitalism and socialism, allowing factories and farms to produce for market demand as long as they filled their basic state quotas and to buy raw materials through the market rather than depending on central allocation; he also allowed more prices to be set by supply and demand. Whether China has adopted capitalism or has merely changed the way it plans and manages socialism is a topic of debate inside China and abroad. Deng himself said in the early 1960s that he supported private farming, arguing: "It doesn't matter if the cat is black or white as long as it catches mice." Whatever the truth is, economic liberalization has led to rapid growth and a consumer boom that at times has threatened to run out of control.

Although Deng Xiaoping was able during the early 1980s to replace conservatives at the head of the party and the government, he was unable to take complete control. The party elected the conservative Li Peng to the post of premier in 1987, dismaying members of the growing Chinese pro-democracy movement. In the autumn of 1988, Li launched an austerity program in an attempt to control inflation. In April 1989 the death of the reformist general secretary of the CCP, Hu Yaobang, encouraged students to put up posters and hold meetings, ostensibly as a memorial to Hu, but actually to draw wider attention to their demands for democracy and freedom. By late April, peaceful pro-democracy demonstrations had begun to grow in several major towns and cities. More than a million students occupied **Tiananmen Square** in Beijing, demanding greater democracy and an end to corruption[5] and planning to occupy the square until the June 20 meeting of the Chinese legislature, the National People's Congress.

When a number of party leaders (most notably Zhao Ziyang, the new CCP general secretary) appeared willing to talk to the students and to support political reform, the way was cleared for the opening of the most serious battle within the CCP since the Cultural Revolution. Conservatives such as Premier Li Peng and President Yang Shangkun were pitted against reformers such as Zhao, presenting the party with a crisis of credibility.

Fears that the demonstrations would spread led to a clampdown on June 3–4, when the army was sent in to break them up, a move endorsed by Deng Xiaoping. No one knows how many died in and around the square; the government claimed about 200 (most of whom were soldiers), but Western media estimates went as high as 7,000. The most generally accepted figures are now in the range of 1,000 to 1,500, a toll that included soldiers from the Beijing garrison, which apparently rebelled and took the side of the students. The massacre proved a victory for the conservatives, who strengthened their position when Zhao was removed from all his party posts at the end of June and replaced as general secretary by Jiang Zemin. The West, which had begun to warm to China during the 1980s, was suddenly reminded once again of the repressive nature of Chinese government. At the same time, it also became clear that a generation gap was emerging and that many younger Chinese no longer shared the political views of their elders.

China Today

China since Mao has been described as a "consultative authoritarian" regime, meaning that the Communist Party has increasingly recognized the need to gauge public opinion and win public support but still suppresses dissent and retains ultimate political power.[6] Deng began working in the mid-1980s to raise a "third generation" of leaders who would continue building on his economic and political reforms, but he became increasingly frail and reclusive and it was clear that his reforms were still not complete when he died in February 1997. An intensified struggle for power followed and was resolved in September when Jiang Zemin, Deng's hand-picked successor, was reelected as general secretary of the CCP. Questions surfaced about his hold on power, and there were concerns abroad that he may have had plans for a newly assertive foreign policy, but—except for an aggressive posture toward Taiwan—China under Jiang was relatively quiet and continued to build links with its Asian neighbors and its major trading partners.

In 2001 China's place in the global economic system underwent a fundamental change when it joined the World Trade Organization (WTO). Membership means that China must open up its markets to foreign investors and importers, and it also means that there is more pressure for China's economic policies to be coordinated with those of other WTO members. The economy is growing rapidly, and Chinese products are working their way into consumer markets all over the world; it is virtually impossible, for example, to buy children's toys in the United States that are not made in China, and the same can be said increasingly for electronic appliances. But China also faces important economic concerns, such as underdeveloped industrial infrastructure, growing unemployment, and pressure for the government to create as many as nine million jobs annually just to keep up.

Meanwhile, political change continues. In 2002–2003, China underwent its most substantial change of leadership since the 1970s, bringing in a so-called **"fourth generation."** It began in November 2002 when Jiang Zemin was replaced as party leader by Hu Jintao. (See People in Politics, p. 242) Formerly vice president of China, Hu had been identified ten years before as Jiang's successor by Deng Xiaoping.[7] Hu's hold on the leadership was strengthened in March 2003 when he also became China's president. Although this is a job with more symbolic power than real power, it nonetheless ended Jiang's formal leadership role. Meanwhile, Wen Jiabao replaced Zhu Rongji as premier of China in March 2003, and Wu Bangguo replaced Li Peng as chairman of the Standing Committee of the National People's Congress. In short, in the space of just four months, the entire leadership of China had been replaced. The change was emblematic of the transformation in the way China sees itself, and is seen by the rest of the world. Under the old leadership it was introverted, and was never seen by the West during the cold war in the same light as the former Soviet Union. But today it is increasingly extroverted, a rapidly growing actor in international economic relations, and a country that is attracting increased attention from outside.

POLITICAL CULTURE

Several thousand years of political continuity gave imperial China a political culture that was both stable and sophisticated. The imperial system was bound together by Confucian ideals that emphasized morality and authoritarianism and by social and political systems that were both elitist and hierarchical. The 1949 revolution had a disruptive effect on political values and norms, but it did not completely clean the slate; many elements of traditional political culture remain intact, although many new values and norms have emerged.

Kinship and Communalism

Like Japan, China has traditionally been a collective society marked by group orientation. Individual well-being, economic security, and the definition of political functions were traditionally based around kinship and the family unit, outside of which few social organizations existed. The head of the family was held responsible for the behavior of members of the group, who could bring collective honor or shame to the family. Recourse to the law or to the intervention of government officials was rare, because most disputes were settled locally and family heads were responsible for punishing wrongdoers. In short, everyone became his brother's keeper.[8] A good example of the emphasis on the group is the strategy known as "creating your own society," under which a group takes care of itself. For example, if a construction unit is employed on a major new project, it will provide its own housing, education, and health facilities rather than relying on government agencies.[9]

The Importance of Consensus

consensus The point at which all opinions converge to a conclusion with which everyone can agree.

It may sometimes seem as though China since 1949 has lurched back and forth between rule by conservatives and rule by reformers. In fact, radical change has consistently been rejected, delayed, or watered down in the interest of reaching a **consensus**.[10] Allied to this has been a traditional preference for gradual and cautious change. A good example was the issue of restoring ranks to the Chinese military; the idea was first proposed in 1980, and the army received new uniforms in 1984, but because of disagreements between retired and active officers over whether the retired officers should receive formal ranks, the ranks were not actually restored until October 1988.[11] The emphasis on consensus and gradualism may also explain why China has achieved many of the same reforms as those once proposed by Mikhail Gorbachev for the USSR, but over a longer period of time and without the same explosive consequences.

The Dominance of the State

Although the legal system may impinge little upon the life of the average Chinese citizen, politics impinges upon their lives almost daily. Even the most minimal political activity means regular exposure to propaganda, attendance at meetings, and the regular expression of support for government policy. China since 1949 has witnessed massive and pervasive political education and indoctrination and a system of government whose policy decisions have reached into the home, the school, the workplace, and every other sphere of human existence to a greater extent than in almost any other society (including Stalinist Russia). This has created a society that emphasizes the state, the party, and the idea of mass cooperation at the expense of individualism and competition. At the same time, though, Chinese political culture is not opposed to political liberalization, and one of the challenges that continues to face the CCP is correctly gauging the pressures for democratic change. Its grip on society has loosened in recent years and with it the dominance of the state.

A Poor Record on Human Rights

The argument that China could become the next global superpower tends to focus on two measures: its growing economy, and the sheer size of its population. But being a superpower is not just about size—it also involves wielding political influence, and that tends to require credibility. For example, while not everyone in the world agrees with U.S. foreign policy, the pronouncements of American presidents matter because the United States is a democracy, and it has both the economic power and the military power to back up its words, and deep invested interests in political events around the world. The same cannot be said for China, whose biggest handicap—in terms of global influence—is its poor record on **human rights.** It is widely criticized for executing hundreds of dissidents every year, for using torture to achieve political ends, for stamping out dissent among ethnic minorities, for continuing to threaten neighboring Taiwan with violence, and for continuing its illegal occupation of Tibet, more than half a century after it invaded the country. And it should not be forgotten that the CCP has a monopoly on political power, and Chinese voters are offered no choices at elections.

human rights Rights that belong to all humans, including freedom from hunger, want, and persecution.

POLITICAL SYSTEM

There are many political scientists who question whether it is worth studying formal political institutions, on the grounds that they do not tell the real story about how government and politics work. About few societies is this question more often asked than China. Its institutions are a façade for a complex and changeable political process where everything is not as it seems, and understanding how decisions are made in China involves reading between the lines. The gap between formal structures and informal realities can be summarized in four key principles:

- China is a **unitary state** in which all significant power is centralized in the national government. Although it officially subscribes to Leninist democratic centralism, local government has little independence. The sheer size of China suggests that a federal system might be more suitable, and although there has been a continuing debate about how much power should be delegated to local government, this enormous country is still governed by a small group of people based at the apex of government in the capital city of Beijing.

- All real power lies with the **Chinese Communist Party.** As in the former USSR, China has an intricate governmental structure, with a cabinet, a legislature, and a network of supporting agencies and so-called mass organizations. But they do little more than legitimize the decisions already made by the party leadership and subscribe to the authority of that leadership.[12] The relationship between party and government has been described as one between a principal and an agent: The party has formal political authority (based mainly on its power to appoint and promote government officials), while the government does the actual work of running the country.[13]

- Deciding who actually runs China can be difficult because **titles are not always what they seem** and there is a mismatch between power and rank.[14] China has had periods of collective leadership; holding formal office is not a requirement for leadership; and identifying the source of real power is less a question of understanding the political hierarchy and the powers of officeholders than of understanding links across institutions, personal networks, and the standing of key figures in the system. For example, Deng Xiaoping, "paramount leader" of China from 1978, never held any of the highest offices in government and formally retired in 1987, yet he remained de facto leader of China by virtue of his personal power and influence until his death in 1997. Even though Jiang Zemin left most of his offices in 2002–2003, he too seemed to want to pull strings behind the scenes.

- There has long been **an important supporting role for the military in politics.** During the Cultural Revolution, when government broke down, the military became the dominant political institution. In recent years, as power has shifted from a generation of leaders who were veterans of the Long March and the sustained guerrilla war of the 1930s and 1940s, the power and influence of the military has declined. However, it was still strong enough to cause sleepless nights for China's leaders during the Tiananmen Square demonstrations in 1989, when some units of the People's Liberation Army (PLA) took the side of the demonstrators.

THE CONSTITUTION

In liberal democracies, constitutions usually focus on the structure of government and the rights of individuals, and political parties play an independent and separate role in government. By contrast, the Chinese constitution not only describes the system of government but it also spells out the programs and policies of the CCP. The goals of the party are further elaborated in the constitution of the CCP itself, which in many ways is more politically significant than the state constitution, is more regularly revised, and offers important indicators of new policy directions being taken by China's government.

There have been four state constitutions since 1949. The first, published in 1954 after several years of debate, was replaced by new versions in 1975, 1978, and 1982. Together with their various amendments, each provides a good indication of the changed thinking of new leaders. For example, the 1954 constitution reflected Mao's ideas on government and society, and although these themes can be traced through the 1975 and 1978 versions, the 1982 constitution finally deleted lavish praise for Mao. Each of the revisions also steadily shifted powers from the state to the party, and recent amendments have shown growing acceptance of the role of the nonstate sector of the economy, which has moved from being "a complement to the socialist public economy" to being "an important component of the socialist market economy."[15]

The 1982 state constitution took two years to draft and was reportedly read and debated at several million meetings held across the country before being adopted by the National People's Congress in December 1982. With 138 articles, it is one of the longest constitutions in the world. It describes China as "a socialist state under the people's democratic dictatorship led by the working class and based on the alliance of workers and peasants." It emphasizes the importance of continuing "socialist modernization" and argues that it is China's fundamental goal to follow the socialist road and "step by step to turn China into a socialist country." Although it vests all power in the people, it also emphasizes that China is led by the CCP, functioning as the vanguard of the people under the guidance of Marxism-Leninism-Mao Zedong Thought.

Articles 33–65 contain an impressive list of the rights and duties of citizens, including freedom of speech, the press, assembly, association, demonstration, and religion and the right to criticize any state organ or functionary. However, Article 51 says that the exercise of personal rights may not infringe upon the interests of the state or society, or upon the freedoms and rights of other citizens, and Article 54 prohibits acts "detrimental to the security, honor and interests" of China. These clauses clearly allow the party or the government to neutralize any dissent regarded as being against the national interest and to limit the civil rights and liberties listed in the constitution.

POLITICAL LEADERSHIP

The government of communist countries such as China and the former Soviet Union can seem enormously complex, especially when all is not as it seems, when labels and titles do not always accurately identify the people and institutions with the real power, and when the formal flowcharts do not really capture the essence of the decision-making system.[16] Studies of Chinese leadership are peppered with words such as *fluid, ambiguous, shadowy,* and *flexible.* The key feature of that leadership has been the dominant role of a single individual: first Mao, then Deng, then Jiang, and now Hu Jintao. Mao and Deng owed their power and influence mainly to their political abilities and charisma, while Jiang owed his mainly to his positions as party leader, president, and commander in chief. Try as he might, Jiang never had the status or authority of Mao or Deng. Indeed, given the increasingly technocratic nature of Chinese government, the unwillingness of the Chinese people to be manipulated as blatantly as they were by Mao, and China's increasing integration into the global system, it is unlikely that old-style paramount leaders will ever be seen again in China. But much depends on how Hu Jintao uses his steadily accumulating power.

Normally, the de facto leader of China is the general secretary of the CCP, but even this is not a fixed rule. After 1978, Deng Xiaoping was effectively the "paramount leader" of China, but the most senior posts he ever held were party vice chairman and chairman of the party's Military Commission (a post from which he retired in 1989). By 1993, the only position of any kind that Deng held was the presidency of China's bridge association. Technically, General Secretary Jiang Zemin was the leader of the party, and thus of China, but it was always clear that Deng was in charge. Much the same was expected of Jiang Zemin following his 2002 retirement; for two years, Jiang retained the important position of chairman of the Military Commission, and many of the members of the Politburo were his acolytes.

The key to making sense of all this is to appreciate three key points:

- Personal relationships (or *guanxi*) are a more important indicator of who has power in China than formal titles.
- Leadership and the distribution of power depend on political maneuvers among a small group of people at the apex of the party (mainly the Standing Committee of the Politburo).

TABLE 5.2

Postrevolutionary Leaders of China

Party Leader*	Premier	Chairman of Standing Committee of NPC	President of Republic People's of China†
1949 Mao Zedong	1949 Zhou Enlai	1949 Mao Zedong	1949 Mao Zedong
		1959 Liu Shaoqi	1959 Liu Shaoqi
			1966–1982 vacant
		1966 Dong Biwu (acting)	
		1975 Zhu De	
1976 Hua Guofeng	1976 Hua Guofeng	1976–1978 Sung Qingling (acting)	
		1978 Ye Jianying	
	1980 Zhao Ziyang		
1981 Hu Yaobang			1982 Li Xiannian
		1983 Peng Zhen	
1987 Zhao Ziyang	1987 Li Peng		
		1988 Wan Li	1988 Yang Shangkun
1989 Jiang Zemin			
		1992 Qiao Shi	
			1993 Jiang Zemin
	1998 Zhu Rongji	1998 Li Peng	
2002 Hu Jintao	2003 Wen Jiabao	2003 Wu Bangguo	2003 Hu Jintao

* Chairman, 1949–1982, then general secretary.
† Chairman of Chinese People's Political Consultative Conference (1949–1954), Chairman of the PRC (1954–1966), and president of China from 1982.

Note: In 1978–1997, the "paramount leader" of China was Deng Xiaoping, who held none of the positions listed above.

- The driving force behind Chinese politics in recent decades has been the struggle between reformists and conservatives. (There are close parallels on all these points between China and the former USSR, and more than a fleeting similarity with elements of politics in Mexico and Egypt.)

Much like in Japan, power in China is based around factions, which are based less on ideological differences than on personal relationships. Power is also based on the particular leadership skills of perhaps no more than two or three people and on the abilities of these leaders to keep control, a process that involves regular purges of rivals and opponents. For example, Mao held on to power for decades, but only because he regularly dismissed or shuffled his lieutenants. Around him he built what has been described as a "first generation" (or echelon) of supporters, most of whom were veterans of the Long March.[17] Among those shuffled during these changes was Deng Xiaoping, who was purged from the highest levels of the party no fewer than three times.

With Mao's death in 1976 and the arrest of the Gang of Four, at least two major factions emerged within the party leadership: the "Whatever" group of Mao loyalists led by premier Hua Guofeng and including veteran economists and technocrats, and a group of reformists led by Deng Xiaoping and including veteran party and military leaders.[18] Beginning in 1978, Deng and his reform-minded supporters wrested power for themselves, forming a second generation of leaders. Deng used many of the same methods as Mao to retain power, carrying out purges of his own and using a mix of "cajolery, compromise, and threat" to keep his faction together.[20] He arranged in 1981 for the reformist Hu Yaobang to replace Hua Guofeng as CCP general secretary, but Deng had to remove him in 1987, apparently to placate conservatives within his faction. His successor, Zhao Ziyang, was in turn removed from power in 1989 for being too unwilling to crack down on the Tiananmen Square demonstrations.

Realizing that many of the members of the second echelon were old and ailing, Deng developed a third generation of leaders who would build on the economic reforms he had begun. This group, which steadily rose to a new prominence in the Politburo, was both younger and more technocratic than its predecessors. By the early 1990s, the most prominent of the reformists was Jiang Zemin. Conservatives were represented by premier Li Peng (often described after Tiananmen Square as "the most hated man in China"). Li forged his own alliance with President Yang Shangkun (whose power base rested with the military) and Chen Yun, another member of the Standing Committee of the Politburo and an advocate of central planning.[21] With the retirement of Yang in 1993 and the death of Chen in 1995, Li's star appeared to be on the wane and Jiang's position strengthened. Jiang's hold on power was confirmed in September 1997 when the Central Committee reelected him to a new term as general secretary. Li, meanwhile, had to be content with the relatively weak post of chairmanship of the National People's Congress.

In 2002–2003, the leadership of China passed to a new **fourth generation** of leaders, headed by Hu Jintao. The China they inherited was quite different from that ruled by the first generation, and significantly different even from the China of the third generation. Hu was in charge of an economy from which the state was steadily retreating, a political system in which the future of the CCP was in question, and a society that was beginning to show the first cracks resulting from policies that were not keeping up with needs.

THE EXECUTIVE: STATE COUNCIL

The highest executive office in the Chinese state system is the State Council, the nearest functional equivalent to a cabinet. Normally meeting once per month, the Council is elected by the National People's Congress and consists of the **premier** of China, as many as a dozen vice premiers, and the heads (and their deputies) of ministries and government departments. Membership of the Council has occasionally been as low as 30 but currently runs at about 60 to 70.

Until the late 1980s, when it began to develop some independence, the Council was little more than the executive arm of the party, responsible for making sure party policies were implemented by government ministers. Membership of the Council overlapped with that of the Central Committee and Politburo of the party, where

PEOPLE IN POLITICS

HU JINTAO

© 2005 AFP/Getty Images

In November 2002 the world's biggest country had a change of leadership. Yet the event barely made a dent in international news headlines, and the incoming leader was wrapped in a veil of anonymity—even the Chinese people knew very little about him. His name was Hu Jintao, and his accession to the leadership of China was the result not of a popular vote, nor a party vote, nor even of the wishes of his predecessor Jiang Zemin, but had been arranged years before by Deng Xiaoping, who did not live to see his protégé take office. Under the circumstances, questions were immediately asked about just how much power Hu really had. Even today, he is still a little mysterious, and much less is publicly known about him than about either of his predecessors.

Born in 1942 in Anhui province, Hu is the first communist Chinese leader whose career began after the 1949 revolution. He trained as a hydro-electric engineer, joining the CCP in 1964 at the height of the Cultural Revolution. In 1988 he became CCP leader in Guizhou province, and from 1988 to 1992 he was CCP leader in Tibet, where he developed notoriety for his crackdown on antigovernment protesters. He was promoted to the Politburo in 1992, a sign that he had been informally chosen by Deng Xiaoping as eventual successor to Jiang. He was introduced to the outside world in late 2001 when he undertook a tour of Russia and Europe (but not the United States). He became vice president of China in 1998, CCP general secretary in November 2002, and president of China in March 2003.

Hu has had the same challenge as Jiang Zemin before him: making the leadership his own. The challenge was complicated by the fact that Jiang had not nominated Hu as his successor and by the fact that Jiang remained active in the background, refusing to give up the chairmanship of the Central Military Commission, thus remaining commander-in-chief of China's vast armed forces. When Jiang finally resigned the position in September 2004 and it went to Hu, the move was seen as representative of the fact that a new generation of leaders had finally taken charge of China. Hu is now in charge of the party, the state, and the Chinese military, and it has only been recently that he has begun to give a hint of what he stands for. Observers note with concern his determination, his fundamentalism, his desire for control, and his willingness to both clamp down on criticism and dissent, and to take a tough line on dealings with Taiwan.[19]

most policy decisions were made, leaving the Council with little more than executive responsibilities. The Council has begun to reassert itself in recent years, though, particularly as the former military heads of ministries have been replaced by a new generation of civilian technocrats.

Because meetings of the full Council are too large to function efficiently, the key decisions are made by a small inner cabinet consisting of a premier and a group of vice premiers (about 15 people in all). The premier, the nearest equivalent to a prime minister in a parliamentary system, is arguably the second most powerful person in China after the leader of the party. The dominating personality in the history of Chinese executive politics was Zhou Enlai, premier from 1949 until his death in 1976. Thanks to Zhou's close relationship with Mao, membership of the Council remained stable during the Cultural Revolution and the Council was a pool of relative calm during the upheaval of the revolution.[22] Zhou, a moderate, had groomed Deng Xiaoping to be his successor as premier, but Deng was purged in January 1976 following Zhou's death. Zhou was followed by Hua Guofeng and the pragmatist Zhao Ziyang, a linchpin of the collective leadership that governed China through the mid-1980s. In 1982 a decision was made to limit premiers to two consecutive five-year terms. In 1987 the office went to Li Peng, foster son of Zhou Enlai and one of the key figures in the suppression of the 1989 democracy movement. Despite his public unpopularity and regular predictions in the early 1990s that his downfall was imminent, he began a second term as premier in 1992. He was succeeded in 1998 by Zhu Rongji, architect of China's recent economic reforms.

Zhu retired in 2003 after just one term and was replaced by Wen Jiabao. Trained as a geologist and with a good reputation as a communicator, Wen was one of the most popular members of the party leadership, serving as vice premier before being promoted to the top job in government. As premier, he is charged with overseeing China's economic policy.

THE LEGISLATURE: NATIONAL PEOPLE'S CONGRESS

Theoretically the "highest organ of state power," the unicameral National People's Congress (NPC) is the nearest equivalent China has to a legislature. Its members are elected for five-year terms, although these can be shortened or lengthened. The Congress normally meets once per year, but during the Cultural Revolution it met only once in ten years. On paper, it represents the people of China and has the power to make and enforce laws, to amend the constitution, to designate and remove the premier and the State Council, and to elect the president of the Supreme People's Court. In reality, its powers are limited in several ways:

- It is huge and unwieldy. Its membership began at 1,226 members in 1954, peaked at a staggering 3,459 members in 1978, and was down to just under 3,000 in the Tenth NPC (2003–2008).

- Although the NPC has the power to discuss, pass, and oversee the execution of laws, it is allowed to do little more than discuss and endorse decisions already made by the party.

T A B L E   5 . 3

Political Institutions in China

Party	Government	Bureaucracy
	President Hu Jintao, 2003–	
General Secretary Hu Jintao, 2002–	**Chairman** Wu Bangguo, 2003–	**Premier** Wen Jiabao, 2003–
Standing Committee 6–8 members. Apex of the Chinese political system. Meets regularly.	**Standing Committee** About 135 members. Meets bimonthly.	**Standing Committee** About 15 members: premier, vice premiers, senior counselors. Meets twice weekly.
Politburo 18–28 members elected by Central Committee. Meets monthly.		
Central Committee About 200 senior party members. Meets annually for varying periods.		**State Council** About 60–70 members: premier, vice premiers, heads of ministries and commissions. Meets monthly.
National Party Congress About 2,000 delegates; meets once every 5 years for 1–2 weeks to confirm party policy.	**National People's Congress** Unicameral, with 2,970 members elected by provincial congresses. Meets once per year for 2–3 weeks.	
Local party groups Provincial, county, and primary party organizations.	**Local, county, and provincial congresses**	**Government ministries**

- Delegates are only indirectly elected by the people. Voters elect local congresses, which elect county congresses, which elect provincial congresses, which finally elect the NPC. Membership is structured so that workers, peasants, intellectuals, and soldiers have occupational representation, and delegates tend to be appointed as a reward for exemplary work and public service rather than because they have particular administrative abilities. This has raised questions about the quality of delegates and their ability to understand the issues discussed by the Congress.

- Congresses meet only briefly, for one session of two to three weeks every year (usually in March or April). Even then they rarely meet in full plenary session, spending most of the time in group sessions. During meetings, delegates can question senior government ministers, submit motions, make suggestions, and raise questions about government policy, but there is obviously a limit to what can be achieved.

The National People's Congress in session in the Great Hall of the People, Beijing. The sheer size of China's legislature—coupled with its short meetings—means that it is able to achieve little beyond confirming policy decisions that have already been reached by the Chinese Communist Party.

■ Unlike liberal democratic legislatures, where most of the real work is done in specialist committees, the NPC has no committees. This denies delegates the opportunity to become specialists or to spend time working through the details of legislative proposals and party policy.

Its huge size, short sessions, and lack of real power suggest that the NPC is simply a rubber stamp for the party, but it has not always accepted the party line; it has been known occasionally to criticize the party leadership and, particularly since the mid-1980s, has not always been unanimous on votes. The NPC certainly has more real powers than the old Supreme Soviet of the USSR.

Standing Committee of the NPC

When the NPC is in recess, its work is carried out by a Standing Committee, which is roughly equivalent to the Presidium of the Supreme Soviet in the former USSR. Elected by the NPC, the Committee meets twice per month and consists of a chairman, several vice chairs, and senior members of Congress. Although membership has run as high as 175, it has settled down in recent years to about 135. The powers of the Committee have changed over time, but they now include the right to declare and enforce martial law, oversee NPC elections, supervise the work of the State Council and Supreme People's Court, appoint and remove members of the State Council on the recommendation of the premier when the NPC is not in session, and serve as the interim NPC when Congress is not in session. It also runs a series of specialist committees dealing with issues such as foreign affairs, finance, and education.

The Chinese Head of State

China has a presidency (and a vice presidency), but the significance of the post has waxed and waned depending on the other positions held by the incumbent. The presidency was usually held by a semiretired former leader of China, but in the 1990s Jiang Zemin held both the presidency and the job of general secretary of the communist party, as does Hu Jintao today. This combination has made both men more like the president of the United States in the sense that they have both carried out political and nonpolitical jobs at the same time.

The office of president traces its roots back to the 1954 constitution, which provided for the election by the NPC of a chairman and vice chairman of the People's Republic. The chairman effectively became the head of state, with all the ceremonial duties this entailed, but he also had significant political powers: For example, he could hire and fire the premier, vice premiers, and other members of the State Council. Mao was elected first chairman in 1954 but did not stand for reelection in 1959 and so was replaced by Liu Shaoqi. Mao, however, remained chairman of the CCP Central Committee, so Liu was unable to use his position to challenge Mao's leadership and fell from grace in 1966. After several years in abeyance, the powers of chairman and vice chairman were revived by the 1982 constitution when new posts of president and vice president of China were created. Both positions are filled for a maximum of two five-year terms by a vote of the Standing Committee of the NPC.

The Cadres

Although not exclusively a part of the legislative system, nor of the party system, cadres are a defining part of the Chinese system of government. China has the world's biggest bureaucracy and a long history of bureaucratic government. Chinese leaders since 1949 have expanded the bureaucracy, while trying to limit its powers by keeping its structure simple and efficient and making sure that it remains responsive to party pressure. Central to this policy has been the role of the cadre, usually defined simply as a party worker but actually a figure of authority within the party or state bureaucracy, who may or may not be a party member. Cadres include the leaders of production units, officials in public institutions (such as schools or hospitals), members of the PLA, or anyone in a position of leadership.[23]

Mao saw the cadres as revolutionaries who were essential to the promotion of the party line and to the achievement of the goals of the revolution. They are chosen less as a result of educational achievement than because of their ideological correctness, loyalty, hard work, and administrative ability. At the lower levels, they are the primary link between the people and the party and government, and the success or failure of government policies has often depended on the competence and abilities of cadres. For example, they became the focus of both public and party criticism during the Cultural Revolution.

THE JUDICIARY: SUPREME PEOPLE'S COURT

China does not have an independent constitutional court like the United States, Japan, or Russia. Instead, it has a dual judicial system consisting of local people's courts answering to a Supreme People's Court and to a Supreme People's Procuratorate.

The judiciary and law enforcement agencies exist less to protect individual rights than to enforce party and state policies and regulations.[24] Justice is administered through a system of more than 3,000 people's courts at the district, county, municipal, and provincial levels. All these answer to the Supreme People's Court, which is accountable in turn to the NPC. The president of the Supreme Court is elected by the NPC, and its other members are appointed by the NPC Standing Committee. Members of lower-level courts are elected or appointed by the corresponding state organ at each level. For its part, the Procuratorate traces its roots to Chinese imperial days and to the Napoleonic civil code, which also influenced the Soviet legal system. A procurator is a monitor who reviews the work of government bodies, making sure they observe the constitution and deciding whether cases should be brought to trial.

Chinese courts developed a reputation for independence during the 1950s, a reputation that came under attack during the Cultural Revolution, when the formal court system was regularly bypassed. The 1982 constitution restored their independence, although questions remain about the extent to which this is respected in practice. Law enforcement in China relies less on a formal legal system than on ideological control. Whereas the rule of law dominates liberal democracies, the party dominates in China. Class enemies (however that concept is defined) were long treated as different from—and unequal to—class allies, especially during the Cultural Revolution, when the administration of law was taken out of the hands of the formal legal system and placed in the hands of mass groups, notably the Red Guards.

SUBNATIONAL GOVERNMENT

Because it is a unitary state, all effective political power in China rests with the national government and the leadership of the party. Although China subscribes in theory to the principle of democratic centralism, local government has little if any real power or independence.

The most important local government units are the provinces, or *sheng* (22 in all), four major municipalities (Beijing, Chongqing, Shanghai, and Tianjin), two Special Administrative Regions (Hong Kong and Macao), and five "autonomous" regions for ethnic minorities. Provincial government in China is roughly equivalent to state government in the United States, except that all provincial leaders are appointed by central government. Another feature unique to Chinese local government is the military regions, of which there are 11. The significance of these regions is heightened by the political role of the military, which—as noted later—has been particularly important during times of civil unrest.

Below the provinces are 210 prefectures (*diqu*), 2,080 rural counties (*xian*), and nearly 290 municipal districts and townships (*shi*). The lowest level of government was once the commune, introduced in 1958 and consisting typically of about 10,000 people. The original intention was that communes would become the focus for almost all political, social, and economic activity and that the government could use them as the front line for the modernization of China. However, most were either too small or too large for the job, and they were finally wound up during the early 1980s. The township has since largely replaced the commune, with powers over the administration of law, education, public health, and family planning. In the rural areas, local administration is overseen by nearly 1 million village committees.

China is a multinational state, although ethnic minorities make up only about 7 percent of the population. Among the minority groups are the Zhuangs, Tibetans, Mongols, and Koreans. Although small in number, they are spread out so thinly in the more hostile regions of China that they inhabit nearly 60 percent of Chinese territory. More important, most of this territory is on China's borders, raising the constant danger of minority grievances spilling over into border disputes involving related ethnic groups in neighboring countries. The most serious of these problems, and the one that has attracted the most world attention, concerns the autonomous region of **Tibet.** Annexed by China in 1951, Chinese troops were sent into Tibet in 1959 to put down a rebellion, and the Dalai Lama, spiritual and political leader of the Tibetan theocracy, went into exile. He has since been joined by more than 10,000 Tibetan refugees and has posed a constant embarrassment to the Chinese government, drawing attention to Chinese repression, agitating for the creation of an autonomous Tibet, and winning the 1989 Nobel Prize for peace for his efforts.

THE PEOPLE'S LIBERATION ARMY

Most brief surveys of the politics of different countries pay little attention to the military, except when the military plays an active role in politics (see Chapters 8 and 10). One of the exceptions to the rule is China, where the People's Liberation Army (PLA) has regularly played a critical political role. Established in 1927–1928 as the Red Army, its first political officer was Mao Zedong, and its members were at the core of the Long March. During World War II the army perfected its guerrilla warfare techniques, motivated by the strategic ideas that people were more important than weapons and that winning the hearts and minds of the people could overcome even the most sophisticated military hardware (a principle convincingly illustrated in Vietnam in the 1960s and 1970s, and raised more recently in connection with events in Iraq). The PLA has been involved in few foreign military excursions, being used instead as a means of extending and consolidating internal political control. In many ways, it has been the third major arm of the political structure, working as an extension of the party and the government.

The PLA is not only an army, air force, and navy in the conventional sense, but it also recruits for the party, educates and informs people, and was used by Mao to act as an example to the people. Members of the PLA were encouraged to work on farms and in factories, and the PLA even went so far as to abolish ranks in 1965 in order to stand as an example of egalitarianism. (The ranks were reestablished in the mid-1980s.) During the Cultural Revolution—when regular government effectively broke down and many government posts went unfilled—the PLA took over administrative duties, kept the Chinese economy functioning, and essentially held the country together. In any other country, it might have used the opportunity to stage a coup; instead, it helped neutralize the Red Guards and restore the party to power.[25]

The PLA came directly under Mao's command and played a vital role in helping Deng Xiaoping win power upon Mao's death in 1976. Since then, the party leadership has tried to reduce the influence of the army by delegating powers of internal security to other agencies, reducing the number of military men in the Politburo, cutting the size of the PLA, and playing down the army's role as the guardian of socialist ideological purity. The tension between the party and the military remains, however. It became particularly obvious during the Tiananmen Square demonstrations just how much the party still relied on the PLA to control dissent and how nervous the party leadership had become about the possibility of an army revolt. That the army would back Deng was not certain; several military regions made it clear they had divided loyalties, and many soldiers were reportedly killed in fighting between rival units. Ultimately, the massacre was spearheaded by the 27th PLA, which helped restore the political power of conservatives within the CCP.

China's armed forces today (at just under three million members) are the world's largest. Chinese arms sales are also growing, and China is now the world's fourth largest arms exporter after the United States, Russia, and Germany.

ELECTIONS AND PARTIES

Voting is a small and relatively insignificant part of political participation in China. Voters elect only the members of their local people's congresses, the schedule of elections is regularly changed, and the party system is dominated by the CCP. How this has affected turnout is difficult to say; official figures have not been released since the 1956 elections, when 86 percent of voters turned out. Because elections are so marginal to an understanding of the Chinese political process, most studies of Chinese politics refer to them only in passing,[26] and more emphasis is placed on other channels through which citizens can take part in the political process, most of which have a more direct effect on party policies.

THE ELECTORAL SYSTEM

Chinese voters (the legal voting age is 18) take part directly in only one election, that of delegates to county and district congresses. Every other election above the local level is indirect; members of county or district congresses elect delegates to provincial congresses for five-year terms. These delegates in turn elect delegates to the NPC for five-year terms. Although the 1982 constitution fixed the terms of local congressional delegates at three years, elections in postrevolutionary China have been sporadic, with as few as two years and as many as 13 years between them. The 1982 constitution even stipulates that the term of the NPC can be extended if necessary.

The entire electoral process is overseen by the CCP, which controls the election committees that draw up the approved slates of candidates for every elective office. Until 1980, only one candidate was put forward for each office, so the party effectively determined the outcome of every election. In this sense, elections were little more than exercises in building consensus, with agreement on candidates being decided in advance by the party and the election itself functioning simply as a rubber stamp. Public and media debate in 1978–1979 about the fairness of this system led to changes in electoral laws after 1980; these changes allowed multiple candidates in elections, a more open nomination process, and the use of secret ballots. Little is known in detail about how subsequent local elections have fared; although the party has been known to interfere in the outcome of elections by actively supporting its preferred candidates, unpopular local party officials have occasionally lost reelection.

POLITICAL PARTIES

Political parties in liberal democracies exist to put forward different sets of policy options and leaders, allowing voters to choose the direction in which they want their country to move. Parties are subservient to the state and can be removed or kept in office by voters casting ballots at regular elections. (For more on this, see Comparative Exercise, pp. 264–265.)

In China, there is only one significant political party—the Chinese Communist Party—and it is the source of all political power, controls all other political organizations, plays a key role in deciding the outcome of elections, and dominates both state and government. Policy changes come not through a change of party at an election or a meaningful public debate, but rather through changes in the balance of power within the leadership of the party. The dominant role of the party is symbolized by the Chinese flag, which consists of one large gold star and four small stars on a red background; the four smaller stars represent the four major classes (peasants, workers, petty bourgeoisie, and owners of enterprises), and the large star represents the party.

(Strictly speaking, China is a multiparty system because there are eight other sanctioned "democratic parties and groups" with alternative policy platforms, including the Democratic League and the National Construction Association. However, they have very few members—numbered in the tens of thousands—and are really little more than professional associations, although they could one day become the nuclei of alternative parties. One of the few direct challenges to CCP rule came in 1998 with the launch of the China Democracy Party, which was quickly closed down by the government and its members arrested or harassed.[27])

The CCP in 2003 had a membership of 64 million, making it bigger than many large countries and the largest party political organization in history. Despite this, it remains elitist, since only about 7 percent of the adult population are members. As with the old Communist Party of the Soviet Union (CPSU), membership provides status, career opportunities, and personal influence. Application is a convoluted process, requiring careful screening. Once admitted, a member is expected to perform tasks set by the party; study the works of Marx, Lenin, and Mao; reject factionalism or personal gain; be loyal; undertake self-criticism; and generally set a good example. The Gang of Four apparently launched a "crash admittance" program aimed at boosting party numbers in the mid-1970s; attempts have since been made to weed out "unfit or unqualified" members, with the goal of improving the professionalism and competence of party members in support of China's modernization plans.[28]

Although party membership is growing, the balance of that membership is changing. The drop in the number of urban Chinese employed by state-owned businesses has also meant a fall in the number of party branches that were once so much a part of their lives, and—at least in towns and cities—the party is increasingly associated with government departments and institutions, rather than the economic sector.[29] And where the Chinese once accepted and followed the dictates of the party (at least in public), it is now coming under increased criticism for China's fast-growing crime problems, the steady emergence of an economic class system that has led to the growth of an underclass, and economic changes that are causing social unrest and unemployment.

Party strategy and policies constitute the **"party line,"** a concept that is often difficult to pin down but is nevertheless regularly quoted as the principal guide to the direction of Chinese politics. Despite the official criticism of faction, party politics is ultimately driven by factionalism, clientelism, and the establishment of personal ties and networks.[30] Leaders rise and fall according to their abilities to make (and keep) friends and allies in the right places and to identify and control, sideline, or eliminate their opponents. In that sense, the CCP is not so different from a conventional liberal democratic political party.

The structure and role of the CCP follows almost exactly the hierarchical model of the old CPSU. At the lowest level are about 3.5 million **primary party organizations (PPOs),** formed wherever there is a minimum of three full party members. They can be formed in the workplace or local neighborhoods or within units of the People's Liberation Army, and each has a committee elected for three-year terms. Primary party organizations, the major point of contact between the party and the masses, are overseen in turn by provincial and county-level party organizations. These have committees elected for five-year terms, have considerable power over economic activities, and have responsibility for convening provincial and county party congresses. Despite this show of concern for the input of the people, however, real power is focused at the national level, and the party is ultimately a closed institution on which outsiders have no significant influence.

Organizationally, the national party has five major bodies.

National Party Congress

In theory at least, the National Party Congress (not to be confused with the National People's Congress) is the highest organ in the party hierarchy. It meets once every five years, although it did not meet at all between 1945 and 1956, nor between 1958 and 1969, thanks in part to the upheavals created by Mao's policies. The 1982 party constitution still allows meetings to be convened early or postponed "under extraordinary circumstances." Congresses are usually convened in Beijing, are attended by more than 2,000 delegates, and meet for no more than two weeks (although the

Ninth Congress in April 1969 met for 24 days, presumably to clear up some of the backlog of work that had accumulated since 1956). Given their size and the rarity of their meetings, they have time to do little more than rubber-stamp party policies and decisions. The most recent Congress met in 2002.

In theory, delegates are selected at lower party levels; in practice, allocations are engineered by the party leadership to ensure representation of the military and the central party, often at the cost of seats for representatives from the provinces. Normally, the National Party Congress does little more than hear a report by the chairman of the party, hear another report on changes to the constitution, and—more significantly—"elect" members to the Central Committee, although all it really does is confirm a list already drawn up by the party leaders. Nonetheless, balloting and politicking have occasionally produced changes in the list and there are now more candidates than there are posts for party positions, so even influential figures have been known to fail to be voted into the Central Committee. Generally, however, the Congress has little significant power.

Central Committee

As in the former Soviet system, the Central Committee is the major governing body of the party. Although it rarely initiates or introduces policies, it must approve the policies of the leadership. As with most Chinese political institutions, size is again a determining factor in the powers of the Committee; as membership of the CCP grew, and as appointment to the Central Committee was used increasingly as a means of rewarding service to the party, so Committee membership grew from just over 40 members in the mid-1950s to almost 350 members in 1982, settling down to about 200 today. The Committee usually meets annually for varying periods, during which time it elects members of the Politburo and of the Standing Committee of the Politburo.

Central Secretariat

Working as an adjunct to the Politburo, the Secretariat has up to a dozen members; meets twice weekly; provides administrative backup; plays a key role in developing policies; and evaluates the choices for appointments to senior party, state, and military positions. It is appointed by the Standing Committee of the Politburo.

Political Bureau (Politburo)

Ultimate party power in China (and therefore ultimate political power) lies in the Politburo of the CCP and most notably in the Standing Committee of the Politburo. The Politburo, which meets about once a month to initiate and discuss party policy, takes collective responsibility for its decisions. It is within this small group of about 18 to 28 people that power—and the leadership of China—is negotiated, given, and taken away.

Although the Central Committee technically elects the members of the Politburo, this has not always been the case. Until 1975, membership was determined entirely by Mao and merely confirmed by the Central Committee. Mao's choices were determined

CLOSE-UP VIEW

THE FALUN GONG: A THREAT TO THE PARTY?

The Chinese Communist Party has always been good at identifying potential sources of competition for power and has usually moved quickly to ensure that they have never developed into a significant threat. One such potential threat on which attention began to focus in 1999 was the Falun Gong, a movement variously described as a sect, cult, or religion. Its members practice a combination of breathing exercises (*qigong*), Buddhism, Taoism, martial arts, and faith healing.

Although it claims to have its origins in prehistoric culture, Falun Gong has only begun to attract wider interest since 1992, when its self-proclaimed leader Li Hongzhi set up a study center in Beijing. It now claims to have a following of more than 100 million worldwide, of which 70 million live in China. If that claim is true, then the group has a larger number of members than the CCP, a statistic that is enough to give party leaders pause for thought. It also claims to be apolitical and argues that it is neither a religion nor a cult. However, between 10,000 and 20,000 adherents staged a demonstration in April 1999

outside the compound in Beijing where China's senior leaders live. This not only frightened the leadership and caused it much embarrassment but also indicated that the movement was well organized.

Reflecting the extent to which the CCP regarded the Falun Gong as a threat, Jiang Zemin used the June 1999 anniversary of the founding of the CCP to make a speech denouncing "feudal, superstitious, or other negative practices." His comment came in the midst of his attempts to restore the moral authority of the party in light of a growing number of instances of corruption and against a background of growing debates about a spiritual vacuum that many felt was aflicting China. Critics of the CCP argued that although it had provided political and economic direction, it did not meet all the needs of the Chinese people. Not only had religion been dismissed by Marxists as the "opium of the people," but—more immediately—party leaders believed that a movement such as Falun Gong could quickly compete with the party for the attentions of the people.

by seniority, loyalty, and usefulness to Mao and by contributions made to his rise to power.[31] The result was that there was relatively little change in membership, most Politburo members came from the military, and the average age of members climbed to well over 70, leading some to describe China as a gerontocracy. Deaths and replacements brought the average age by the mid-1980s down to just over 60, and the military members had been replaced by younger and more professional members. The membership stays relatively young today under the leadership of Hu Jintao.

Standing Committee of the Politburo

When the Politburo is not in session, the party is run by a Standing Committee of six or seven members. This meets about twice per week and constitutes the most powerful and senior group of individuals in the entire Chinese political system. At the head of this group sits the general secretary of the party (or chairman until 1982).

After the changes of 2002–2003, this group included Hu Jintao (general secretary), Wen Jiabao (premier), and Wu Bangguo (chairman of the NPC Standing Committee).

 POLICIES AND POLICYMAKING

Pinning down the processes, individuals, and principles involved in policymaking in China is difficult, and foreign political scientists have developed different models over the last 30 years in attempts to better understand the system. Some have focused on particular policy areas (such as education and agriculture) and some on the struggles within the top levels of Chinese leadership. One study of Chinese policymaking[32] argues that three key principles are involved:

- There is a fragmented bureaucratic structure of authority, involving 25 to 35 top leaders, senior bureaucrats, and government ministries.
- Consensus building is central to the process, mainly because of the cooperation needed from the lower levels of government.
- Decision making is a lengthy, disjointed, and incremental process.

Another study concludes that because Mao fashioned the political institutions of China on those of Stalinist central planning, he brought to China some of the flaws of the Stalinist system. These included the creation of a heavily centralized and chronically overloaded decision-making system. The system compelled policymakers in China to maintain dysfunctional policies for long periods and to rely on simplistic performance indicators. It also discouraged party subordinates from drawing attention to policy problems, preferring to wait until the failure was acknowledged by the party itself.[33]

The Chinese leadership claims to believe in the value of ensuring that public policy is openly debated within the party system and down through the many levels of government. There is an element of truth in this claim, as reflected in the way that policies have occasionally been changed or abandoned as a result of public debate, officially permitted or not. China is not a democracy in the Western sense, but the views of the Chinese public, and the outbreak of occasional civil disorder, have not always passed unnoticed by the leadership. Public opinion also plays a role in influencing the balance of power at the apex of the party; for example, Premier Li Peng may have kept his post following Tiananmen Square, but his policies were unpopular, and he apparently softened his hard-line position. Recent changes in the direction of Chinese economic and foreign policies also suggest a softening of the official party line and reduced state and party control over people's lives.

ECONOMIC POLICY

Until Mao's death, China was a poor country that subscribed to central economic management, relying on a series of five-year plans to map out its development goals.

Skyscrapers in the Pudong financial district of Shanghai, silhouetted against the sun. The pace of new construction in Shanghai has been emblematic of the pace of China's economic development. But it has been cut back recently after evidence revealing that the city is sinking at a rate of nearly half an inch each year.

It initially enjoyed rapid agricultural and industrial growth, but this was followed by several years of stagnation during the Great Leap Forward and the Cultural Revolution, when there was little order and not enough investment in the agricultural sector, which survived nonetheless, growing almost every year and being hurt as much by weather as by politics.

Over the last decade, the West has had to reassess its image of China as new economic figures have revealed a dynamic society that, despite widespread poverty and high unemployment, has the makings of an economic giant. The first step in its transformation was the proclamation in 1978 of an open-door policy aimed at expanding trade, opening up production to factors of supply and demand, reducing the role of central planning, and introducing what some have described as **"Market-Leninism."** Incentives for workers and peasant farmers that had been removed during the Cultural Revolution—including promotions, bonuses, and wage increases—were reintroduced. Greater emphasis was placed on light industry over heavy industry and on the expansion of production in consumer goods. Finally, greater support was given to domestic research and development, and China proved more open to the idea of importing foreign technology. This in turn meant that it needed more foreign exchange, which led to a decision to boost the tourist industry, to expand exports, and to encourage foreign companies to invest in China.

During the 1980s, further changes were made, including a decision to introduce "household contracts" for farmers. Under this system, a household was allocated a piece of land (for use but not for sale) and was required to meet state quotas, but it was allowed to sell whatever it produced over the quotas and keep the profit. Collective agriculture ceased to exist, and rural residents saw increases in both income and consumption. In urban areas, the state gave up its monopoly on services and—largely to deal with high unemployment—allowed the creation of small businesses and collectives.[34]

The middle class grew, overall unemployment fell, public ownership of land declined, the Chinese economy grew at more than 9 percent annually, and exports grew at 15 percent annually. However, planners wrestled with trying to combine the new market economy with the vestiges of the old centrally planned system, and foreign investor confidence stumbled following Tiananmen Square, which was itself brought on at least in part by growing public complaints about a fall in the standard of living.

During the 1980s, China set up a number of special economic zones aimed at attracting foreign investment, a program that was given new significance in 1997 when Hong Kong reverted to China after 155 years of British rule. The enclave had already been used as a conduit for Chinese trade and investment connections with the rest of the world and as a source of foreign exchange, investment, trade, and expertise. Now a Special Administrative Region, it continues in the same role and is helping bring significant changes throughout the Chinese economy.

Chinese industrial production has grown rapidly in recent years and China is relying less on state production and more on the private and collective sectors. Trade between China and the rest of the world is also growing, foreign investors are finding China more attractive than Russia (investing $45 billion in China in 1998 alone), and capitalism is no longer officially condemned in China (not even by the party newspaper the *People's Daily*, which has run editorials in favor of more open markets). Perhaps nothing symbolized the new era as much as the opening in 1993 of a Ferrari dealership in China.

Problems remain, however, not least of them being pollution, worsening crime rates, and corruption among party and government officials, who have been implicated in everything from running smuggling rings to extorting illegal taxes from peasants. Another problem is population growth. Improvements in health care have helped more babies to survive and more people to live longer, so China now has nearly 1.3 billion people, most of whom are concentrated in arable coastal areas and several huge cities. Population growth fell from 1.5 percent in 1990 to 0.9 percent in 2000, and was down to 0.6 percent in 2003, but even this means that there are more than 16 million more Chinese every year, straining and even defeating attempts by economic planners to keep up with demand. Deciding that drastic measures were needed, the government introduced a **one-child policy** in 1979, limiting every family to no more than one child. Not only did this lead to widespread resentment, but because boys were more useful in economic and labor terms to poor families, it also promoted infanticide, with firstborn girls often being murdered.

A related problem is the lag between supply and demand in education. One of the reasons several Southeast Asian countries have seen rapid economic growth in recent years is that they have improved their schools; adult male literacy in many of these countries runs at 90 percent or more, and there have been notable increases in the provision of secondary education. In China, 16 percent of adults are still illiterate, and postsecondary education is the privilege of a small minority (less than 2 percent, compared with about 30 percent in the United States). To make matters worse, there is the "lost generation": As many as 30 million Chinese were forced to drop out of school during the Cultural Revolution and had no formal education at all. Many are now in their 40s and 50s, and instead of playing a central role in society, they are on the periphery. Students today who see little future in China—among them the best and brightest of the new generation—try to go abroad for their university education, and very few return.

An important economic breakthrough came in December 2001, when—after 15 years of diplomatic pressure and negotiation—China joined the World Trade Organization. Membership obliges China to open its markets to other countries (notably its banking, insurance, telecommunications, and agricultural sectors), increases pressure on China to make capitalist reforms, and over the long term may encourage greater openness and accountability in government. On the other hand, it could open China to a level of economic competition that it may not be prepared to face, which could worsen unemployment and promote financial instability.[35] Like the United States, China also has a worryingly high level of reliance on imported oil, which will increasingly hold its economy ransom to changes in the world oil price.

China is not yet a market economy, and it has structural weaknesses that could complicate, or even undermine, the reforms it has made and continues to make: In particular, industry suffers from poor quality output, low productivity, and a shortage of skilled workers. Economic problems have led to growing dissatisfaction, as has the corruption that continues within the CCP and the continued existence of an elitist party system. The structural problems of the Chinese system were emphasized in March–April 2003 by the slowness of the government response to the outbreak of severe acute respiratory syndrome (SARS). It showed that the Chinese government was poorly equipped to handle crises, even those that threatened to undermine China's economic progress. But whatever happens, changes in the nature of the global marketplace are combining with a shift of power to a new technocracy to make it difficult for the CCP to resist demands for democratization.

FOREIGN POLICY

The United States and China in the nineteenth century both preferred not to be involved in world affairs, but the twentieth century saw both being much influenced by their place in the world, with very different results. While the United States abandoned isolationism and actively tried to determine the outcome of external events, China spent more time reacting to those events and trying to understand its place in the global system. From the isolation of the imperial era, China switched to the unwilling dependence of the nationalist era, went through the shifting coalitions of the communist era (being initially pro-Soviet and then falling out with the USSR), and finished the century with attitudes that indicated growing accommodation with the rest of the world, although neither side really knew what to think of the other.

Throughout the imperial era, China had little to do with the outside world and considered all other cultures inferior. Outsiders were known as *yang guizi* ("foreign devils"), anything from abroad (goods, people, or ideas) was described as *yang* (foreign), and anti-Western feelings ran so high that wild rumors spread among the more superstitious peasants, including one that Westerners ate their children.[36] Then China was violently and unwillingly drawn into closer relations with the outside world, a process that contributed to the collapse of the imperial order. Britain began the process by forcing concessions in the 1830s on trade in opium and winning a foothold in Hong Kong. France, Portugal, the United States, Japan, and other countries subsequently wrested similar agreements out of the Chinese, so by the turn of the century China had given up much of its economic and political independence. The arrival of Western ideas, and the inability of China to oppose them, encouraged many Chinese to rethink the nature of Chinese society, led many to resent the influence of the West, and sowed the seeds of nationalism.

Chinese resentment toward the West deepened after World War II, when Mao—who had led China's fight against the Japanese—was not invited to the conferences convened to plan the postwar world. When the West then supported Taiwan and refused to recognize the PRC, Mao—driven by his overarching interest in rebuilding China—decided to "lean to one side" in foreign policy. He portrayed the United States as the archenemy of the Chinese people, formed an ideological alliance with the USSR in the struggle against capitalism, and for much of the 1950s followed the Soviet model of economic development. He also promoted China as a champion of decolonization, sending Zhou Enlai to the founding conference of the Nonaligned Movement in 1955 (see the Introduction to Part III), and winning new friends in Southeast Asia and sub-Saharan Africa. To limit Western influence in Southeast Asia, China helped North Korea and North Vietnam, and worked to isolate Taiwan (see Political Debates, p. 260).

By the late 1950s, ideological differences had emerged between China and the USSR, not least over the role of the peasants (whom Mao respected but the Soviets did not) and attempts by Soviet leader Nikita Khrushchev to improve relations with the United States. Unprepared to accept any cooperation with the West, Mao cut ties with the USSR in 1960–1961, and the Sino-Soviet split developed into a bitter war of words and ideology, along with active disputes over their joint border. By the late 1960s, China was beginning to see the United States as less of a threat than the USSR. Following the 1968 Soviet invasion of Czechoslovakia and Sino-Soviet border clashes in 1969, Sino-U.S. relations took a new turn in 1971 as secret talks began between Zhou Enlai and Henry Kissinger, the national security advisor to

U.S. President Richard Nixon. China was admitted to the United Nations in October 1971 at the expense of Taiwan, and the new friendship was confirmed in February 1972 with Nixon's remarkable visit to China and meeting with Mao, encouraged by the desire of both nations to form a strategic partnership against the USSR.[37] In 1978, the United States agreed to recognize the People's Republic of China as the sole legitimate government of China, and in 1979 Deng made the first visit by a Chinese leader to the United States. Trade and cooperation between China and the United States, and between China and Japan, has since grown steadily.

China's relations with its near neighbors have not always been close, leading many to question the sincerity of the claim in the preamble to the 1982 constitution that China supports "mutual respect for sovereignty and territorial integrity...noninterference in each other's internal affairs...and peaceful coexistence." China was strongly critical of the Soviet invasion of Afghanistan in 1979 and of aggressive Soviet posturing on the Chinese border, but it has occupied Tibet since 1951 and shows no inclination to withdraw. China was also worried about the close ties that had developed between the USSR and Vietnam in the 1970s and about the Vietnamese invasion of Cambodia in 1978. Vowing to teach Vietnam a lesson, China launched a limited and inconclusive invasion in February–March 1979; instead of humiliating Vietnam, the PLA lost more than 30,000 men. Under Deng Xiaoping, China became more extroverted, opening itself to investment from—and trade with—the outside world, abandoning the Stalinist and Maoist models of economic development, and making itself almost overnight into a newly industrializing country in the character of Taiwan and South Korea.[38] At the same time, it followed "an independent foreign policy," a phrase thought to mean that it would not align itself with either superpower or that it may simply have been trying to work out some consistency in its relations with its Asian neighbors.[39]

The Tiananmen Square massacre brought widespread revulsion, provided a reminder of the authoritarian nature of Chinese government, and caused a shift in Chinese relations with the rest of the world. Since 1989, China has restored its tarnished image to some extent through its constructive role in encouraging peace in Cambodia and through supporting—or at least not opposing—allied action against Iraq in the aftermath of the August 1990 invasion of Kuwait.[40] As a potential economic superpower, however, China needs (and probably wants) to be taken more seriously and is taking an increasingly assertive role on the world stage. It has had several disagreements with the United States over trade (the Clinton administration briefly tried to make an issue of Chinese commercial piracy in 1994–1995), has renewed its aggressive posture toward Taiwan, and has taken a more assertive stance on ownership of the Paracel and Spratly Islands in the South China Sea; the seabed around them is thought to contain oil, natural gas, and other valuable mineral resources.

China has the world's biggest military, but it poses only a limited threat to any but its nearest neighbors. This may be changing, however. It is a nuclear power and has been building up and modernizing both its short-range ballistic missiles and its long-range strategic missiles. It is also expanding its navy, although it is still very small. China poses nothing like the threat once posed by the Soviet Union, but its growing economic power may give it the wealth over the longer term to back up its political values with hard military capacity.

POLITICAL DEBATES

ONE CHINA OR TWO?

Ever since its creation in 1949, China has been variously dogged, embarrassed, irritated, and annoyed by the status of the other China that was created that same year: the Republic of China, otherwise known as **Taiwan.** Taiwan has been an international outcast since the 1970s, but its economic success and military power have ensured that it cannot be ignored, and tensions between the two Chinas have grown in recent years as Taiwan has decided to become more assertive of its rights.

A Japanese colony from 1895 until 1945, Taiwan was returned to Chinese sovereignty just in time to be taken over by the Nationalists, under the leadership of Chiang Kai-shek, as they retreated from Mao's Red Army. Violently suppressing his opponents and winning the support of a U.S. government alarmed at the spread of communism, Chiang claimed that his government was the legitimate government of all China and made the recovery of the mainland one of his primary goals.

While Mao's China experienced political and economic turbulence during the 1950s and 1960s, Taiwan developed its agricultural and industrial base with the help of foreign investment and by the early 1970s had all the hallmarks of a newly industrializing country. However, as part of the strengthening of relations between the United States and China, China's seat in the United Nations was taken away from Taiwan in 1971 and given to the PRC, beginning a process by which Taiwan was steadily pushed out of the international community. Chiang died in 1975, and in 1979 the United States withdrew its diplomatic recognition of Taiwan. A political outcast it may be, but Taiwan's economy has flourished and its political system has liberalized. It held its first competitive presidential elections in 1996 and today has a per capita GDP about six times that of mainland China and a substantially better record on almost every social indicator, from infant mortality to education. Opinion has been divided in recent years about whether Taiwan should continue to seek reunification with China or should declare itself an independent state.

Tensions between the two Chinas began to heat up again in 1995 following attempts by Taiwan to strengthen its international status by, among other things, being readmitted to the United Nations. The PRC responded by holding military "exercises" in the straits of Taiwan. The restoration of Hong Kong and Macao to China, in 1997 and 1999, respectively, was accompanied by talk of a **"one country, two systems"** policy that may one day encourage reunification. But in 1999, Taiwan insisted on opening talks with the PRC on a "state-to-state" basis, further angering the Chinese government. While the United States has continued to refuse to recognize Taiwan, there is considerable support for it within the U.S. Congress, Taiwan remains an important market for U.S. arms sales, and the Bush administration has upset China with its pro-Taiwan position.

An uneasy peace currently prevails in China's foreign relations. In recent years it has moved to strengthen ties with its Asian neighbors, continues to ensure the isolation of Taiwan, and has joined the WTO. Relations with the United States have generally been warm, although Taiwan remains a potential point of dispute. China has also continued to talk about the dangers of a U.S. "hegemony," has systematically stolen nuclear secrets from the United States for more than 20 years, and saw an out-pouring of nationalist rage following the NATO bombing of the Chinese Embassy in Belgrade in May 1999 during the Kosovo military action. There is a growing consensus that China has an important role to play as a regional power in Southeast Asia, but questions remain about the implications of changes in economic policy for China's status as one of the last officially "communist" nations in the world.

CHINESE POLITICS IN TRANSITION

China is undergoing economic changes of a kind that promise to make it one of the major powers of the twenty-first century. However, its search for a political form and for answers to its economic needs since 1948 has brought social upheaval, economic experimentation, and human tragedy on a huge scale. The question now is whether it can continue to make the changes at a pace needed to keep up with the demands of its huge and growing population. A strong China could present opportunities for trade and the promotion of democratic values to one-fifth of the human population, but that strength could also pose a threat if the nationalism that often colors the words of Chinese leaders and the actions of the Chinese people is channeled in the wrong direction. At the same time, the world faces the real danger of a weak China with internal divisions, social problems, rising crime, and unemployment, where leaders might try to divert attention away from internal problems by being more aggressive on foreign policy, notably toward Taiwan and other near neighbors.

The economic and political changes begun by Deng and developed by Jiang remain incomplete, and it will be some time before we can really see the extent to which reform has taken root in Chinese society. The steady rise of the Chinese consumer and entrepreneur will continue to place growing pressure on the leadership for democratic change. In 2002–2003 China underwent its most substantial change in leadership for a generation. We will have to wait and watch to see what impact that change will have on China, and on its place in the world.

KEY TERMS

cadres
Chinese Communist
   Party
Confucianism
Falun Gong
Fifth Modernization
fourth generation
Great Leap Forward
Great Proletarian
   Cultural Revolution

Guomindang
Long March
Market-Leninism
National People's
   Congress
one-child policy
one country, two systems
party line
People's Liberation Army
Politburo

premier
primary party
   organizations
shifting lines
standing committees
Taiping Rebellion
Taiwan
Tiananmen Square
Tibet

KEY PEOPLE

Deng Xiaoping   Mao Zedong   Wu Bangguo
Hu Jintao   Wen Jiabao   Zhou Enlai
Jiang Zemin

STUDY QUESTIONS

1. What changes did Mao make to Marxism and Leninism to make them more appropriate to the Chinese setting?
2. Does China have a Marxist-Leninist system?
3. Is it still appropriate to think of China as a "communist" country?
4. Is China a newly industrializing country?
5. The relationship between party and government in China has been described as one between a principal and an agent. To what extent can the same be said of the relationship between parties and government in liberal democracies?
6. Who governs China?
7. How does leadership change in China, and how does the process compare with changes of leadership in liberal democracies?
8. What will China look like in 20 years?
9. What differences are there between the methods used by Chinese leaders to win control and the methods used by politicians in liberal democracies?
10. Is China a superpower?

CHINA ONLINE

ChinaSite: http://chinasite.com
China Today: www.chinatoday.com
Megasites with links to sites on Chinese news, government, politics, the economy and social issues.
South China Morning Post: www.scmp.com
China Daily: www.chinadaily.com.cn
Good sources of news on Chinese and Asian affairs; the first is a Hong Kong–based daily newspaper, and the second is the online version of the major English-language Chinese daily newspaper.

FURTHER READING

Benewick, Robert, and Paul Wingrove (Eds.), *China in the 1990s* (Basingstoke, UK: Macmillan, 1999). An edited collection of chapters on Chinese politics, economics, social issues, and public policies.

Dreyer, June Teufel, *China's Political System: Modernization and Tradition*, 3rd. Ed. (New York: Longman, 2000). An introduction to the Chinese political system, with chapters on history, the economy, education, and foreign policy.

Nolan, Peter, *China at the Crossroads* (Cambridge: Polity Press, 2005). An assessment of the changes that China has been undergoing, which argues that it faces complex problems arising out of its rapid growth.

Saich, Tony, *Governance and Politics of China*, 2nd Ed. (New York: Palgrave, 2004). Another good survey of Chinese politics, including chapters on economic, social, and foreign policy.

Wang, James C. E., *Contemporary Chinese Politics: An Introduction*, 7th Ed. (Upper Saddle River, NJ: Prentice Hall, 2001). One of the standard introductions to Chinese politics, society, and culture.

COMPARATIVE EXERCISE

POLITICAL PARTIES

A political party is an organization that brings together people with similar views about how to govern societies and tries to pursue its goals by getting its members elected into political office. Parties normally have six major functions: (1) developing a series of goals behind which voters can unite to influence policy, (2) recruiting members and supporters to help promote the party platform, (3) mobilizing voters and raising funds to promote the campaigns of their candidates, (4) providing the reference points that help voters make sense of the policy options before them, (5) giving candidates and elected officials a label by which voters can tell them apart from opponents, and (6) encouraging elected officials to work together to support or oppose bills working their way through legislatures.

Parties usually organize around ideological differences, but they can also be based around social class, economic status, religion, or regional differences. They use varied methods, they often relate in different ways to voters and to the institutions of government, and although some are the servants of the political system, others sit at the very core of that system. Their impact depends in large part on how much competition they have.

- **One-party systems.** These are found mainly in dictatorships or communist systems. As was the case in the USSR—and as is the case in China today—monopoly parties do not offer voters choices but instead work to extend the reach of government and to ensure uniformity of purpose among voters. They often try to give the impression of democracy without actually giving voters the opportunity to have much impact on policy, which is made by the party leadership, using elections as a means of giving its decisions an aura of legitimacy.

- **One-party-dominant systems.** These are fairly rare and are usually found in authoritarian regimes, such as Mexico (until recently, anyway), Egypt, and several African states. One political party not only holds the executive and a majority of seats in the legislature but also controls the electoral commission and so is able to determine the outcome of elections. In Mexico, the Institutional Revolutionary Party (PRI) was able to dominate politics between 1929 and 2000 by reaching out to all the elites and interest groups it needed to win power, by bargaining with the groups it needed and pursuing policies that those groups favored, and by manipulating the electoral system. As Mexicans became better educated and more affluent, however, they became less easy to manipulate.

  Single parties can also dominate in democracies. In India until the 1990s, the Congress Party was consistently either the governing party or the biggest party, its power underpinned by a combination of the charisma of the Nehru-Gandhi dynasty and a divided opposition. Similarly, Japan was dominated until 1993 by the Liberal Democratic Party, which was flexible and clever enough to outwit the opposition and ultimately became associated in the minds of voters with Japan's postwar economic success.

- **Two-party-dominant systems.** These are fairly common and are mainly the product of the winner-take-all electoral system, which helps parties with large blocks of support to turn votes into seats; smaller parties with more thinly spread support more often come in second or third. It is not unusual for one or the other of the two parties to lose support and be supplanted by another party, but the two-party dominance is maintained by the electoral system. Britain is an example, having been dominated by the Liberals and the Conservatives, now by Labour and the Conservatives. The United States is another example, where there is little likelihood of a third party being able to compete effectively with the Republicans or the Democrats. They are both moderate parties that contain many shades of opinion, party discipline tends to be loose (members of Congress from one party often cross over to vote with the other), they run elections in most states and can manipulate electoral districts to increase their chances of winning seats, and while voters tend to vote for candidates rather than for parties, the majority also look for candidates who are associated with either the Republicans or the Democrats.

- **Multiple-party systems.** In several European countries (notably Germany, France, and Italy), there are so many political parties that few ever win a majority, governments are routinely formed by coalitions of two or more parties, the coalition partners usually have to make more effort to reach compromises, and governments can be fragile. This has not affected political stability in Germany, but Italian coalitions can often depend on parties with fewer than a dozen members who can hold all the others to ransom and exert an influence out of all proportion to their size and following. Coalitions collapse so often that in the period 1945–2005, Italy had more than 55 governments.

Electoral systems that are based on proportional representation contribute to multiple-party systems by making it easier for small parties to win seats and harder for large parties to win clear majorities. A government based around multiple parties will be obliged to take note of a much broader selection of political values and policy ideas, but it will also be less able to provide leadership and consistent policies.

Interest groups are related to political parties, the main difference being that they do not nominate members to run for office under the name of the group, working instead to influence government from outside. They can do this by raising funds and channeling them to parties or candidates, giving candidates or elected officials seals of approval or disapproval or encouraging their members to vote for particular parties or candidates. Whereas parties try to build mass followings and win as many votes as possible from members and nonmembers alike, interest groups are usually more focused in terms of their goals, values, and policies. Whereas parties mainly look for the support of their members and supporters only at election time, interest groups may attract more sustained involvement from most of their members. So while there may be a few dozen serious political parties at most in any one country, there may be tens of thousands of interest groups, varying greatly in their size, goals, methods, and relationship to the political system.

Part III

NEWLY INDUSTRIALIZING COUNTRIES

We face neither East nor West; we face Forward.

—Kwame Nkrumah, prime minister and president of Ghana

There was a time in the 1950s and 1960s when the label *Third World* almost made sense. Most of the countries of Asia, Latin America, and non-Soviet Asia had been colonized at one time or another, had comparable records of development, and saw themselves affected by cold war tensions that were mainly beyond their control. They were far from identical in terms of their political features, economic values, and social aspirations, but enough connections could be made among them to give the idea of the Third World some semblance of consistency.

This is no longer true. Since the end of the cold war, it has become clear that the differences among the countries of the Third World far outweigh the similarities. Their political systems come in different forms, they have different levels of economic development, they play different roles in the global economic system, and they have had different experiences with social development. The most notable development has been the emergence of a group of newly dynamic countries with improving democratic records, increasingly productive economies, and social conditions that are improving to keep pace. These newly industrializing countries (NICs, pronounced "nicks") have long been recognized as a subgroup on the margins of comparative politics, but at no time have their distinctive features been more clear than in the age of globalization. Their emergence not only has implications for their citizens, but also for the global economy and for the economies of their major trading partners.

NICs are usually described according to their economic features, distinguished by measures such as per capita income, manufacturing rates, gross domestic product (GDP), and the contribution of manufacturing to GDP.[1] This is why they are sometimes known as "emerging economies" or (in the case of Southeast Asian countries) "tiger economies." But those economic changes have important political and social

267

NEWLY INDUSTRIALIZING COUNTRIES
What Are Their Features?

- Generally improving records of representative government and regular, fair, secret, and competitive elections

- Increasingly well-defined, consistent, and predictable political institutions and processes

- Improving levels of public loyalty to the state

- A variety of institutionalized forms of political participation and representation

- Improving records on the protection of individual rights under the law

- A belief in human equality, if sometimes imperfectly implemented

- An active, effective, and protected opposition, and respect for freedom of speech

- Postindustrial and free-market economic systems based mainly on services and industry, and driven by a vigorous export market

- Rapid urbanization and improvements in the quality of infrastructure

- Advanced technology

- A relatively high quality of life when measured by the provision of education, health care, and other basic services

- High to medium ratings on the Freedom House, Economic Freedom, and Human Development indexes

- Increasing regional and global influence

Where Are They?

There are 30 NICs, and they are mainly in Latin America, Southeast Asia, and the Caribbean:

Antigua and Barbuda	India	St. Lucia
Argentina	Indonesia	St. Vincent and the Grenadines
Bahamas	Jamaica	South Africa
Barbados	Malaysia	Sri Lanka
Brazil	Mauritius	Taiwan
Chile	Mexico	Thailand
Costa Rica	Panama	Trinidad and Tobago
Dominica	Philippines	Turkey
El Salvador	Singapore	Uruguay
Grenada	St. Kitts and Nevis	Venezuala

implications, making it essential that we recognize them for their broader distinctiveness, and that we try to better understand why they have progressed while so many of their poorer neighbors have not.

Broadly speaking, NICs have seven major features in common.

Emerging Democracy

NICs have improving democratic records, revolving around increasingly fair and competitive elections that offer the real prospect of changes of leadership. Their citizens have a choice of political parties with ideological variety, an increasingly free press, a variety of channels for political representation and participation, and legal systems that better protect their civil rights and civil liberties. They have moved away from the kinds of erratic, corrupt, and personalized systems of government that were once the hallmarks of the Third World and have developed more structured, legalized, and predictable systems of decision making.

Democracy is qualified in some NICs (such as Indonesia and Malaysia), political violence is still a problem in others (notably India and Sri Lanka), and the leaders of NICs such as Singapore and Turkey still use occasionally authoritarian methods to exert control, but the underlying trend in NICs is toward greater public account-ability, greater respect for the rule of law, and greater political choice. Some NICs also suffer internal divisions, but these divisions do not threaten their underlying sta-bility. A good contrast is offered by India (a NIC) and Nigeria (a less developed country, or LDC). Both have almost every kind of religious, ethnic, regional, and economic division known to humanity; but, while Indian democracy weathers the storms they generate and is bolstered by a growing sense of an Indian national iden-tity, Nigerian government is undermined by corruption and by ethnic and religious divisions, which have often degenerated to the point where the military has stepped in to keep order.

Export-Led Growth

A stroll around the average North American home will reveal one of the clues to the success of NICs. The clothes many of us own may bear Western corporate trademarks, but they are probably made in countries such as Costa Rica, India, Indonesia, and Thailand. The same is true of the televisions, VCRs, DVD players, phones, comput-ers, refrigerators, and ovens we own; unless they are Japanese, they are probably made (for Western corporations) in a NIC; for example, I am writing this book on an Amer-ican PC that is made in Thailand and I have an American phone on my desk that is made in Malaysia. (Increasingly, though, the electronic appliances in our homes are made in China, which itself has many of the characteristic features of a NIC.)

The explanation lies in the export policies of NICs. Instead of exporting low-profit primary products that can be converted into high-profit manufactured goods in the rich industrialized countries, NICs make these goods themselves. They once protected domestic economies from imports and subsidized local producers, but they have increasingly opened up their markets and taken part in international ne-gotiations on free trade. As well as giving tax breaks to exporters and setting export targets, they have also developed the urban labor pools needed to attract foreign investment. Japan and South Korea were once the source of cheap and expendable consumer goods, but they combined quality with quantity to overcome the disad-vantages of being resource-poor and became export-led economic powers. The same is happening now in Chile, Indonesia, Singapore, and the other NICs, some of which may be the Japans or the South Koreas of the future.

The growth of their manufacturing sectors has helped NICs to return some of the fastest economic growth rates in the world, with annual increases in GDP and in-dustrial production that often outpace those in liberal democracies (see Figure III.1). They have adopted liberal trade policies, they are building diverse economies and

FIGURE III.1

Comparing Levels of Economic Growth

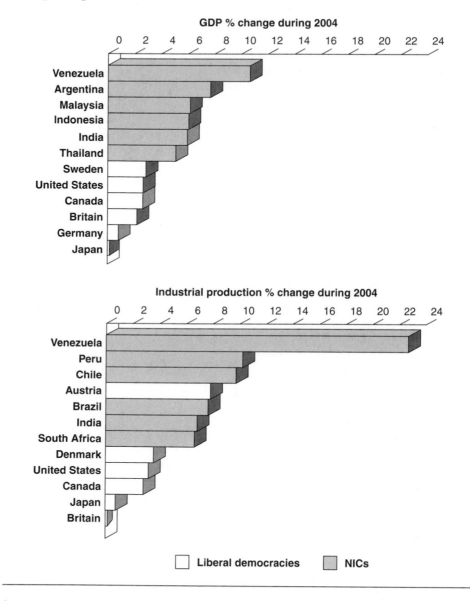

GDP % change during 2004

Industrial production % change during 2004

Liberal democracies   NICs

Source: *The Economist*, various issues, early 2005.

producing a variety of goods and services, they are replacing low-profit agricultural exports with high-profit manufactured exports, and their governments have had good records in controlling inflation. Industry and services are making a growing contribution to their national wealth: Services usually account for 45 to 65 percent of GDP, industry 25 to 40 percent, and agriculture less than 15 percent. Most NICs now have a per capita GDP in the range of $2,000 to $9,000, which is low compared to liberal democracies ($20,000 to $35,000) but high compared to LDCs and marginal countries ($1,000 or less).

Urbanization

Not only are NICs becoming wealthier, but the shift of the workforce from agriculture to industry has brought in its wake a movement of people from the rural areas to the cities. So big have some cities become that many have been elevated to the status of **megacities** (cities with more than five million people). In 1950 there were just eight megacities (six of them—including New York—in wealthy industrialized countries). Today there are 41, and most of them are in Asia and Latin America; they include Mexico City, Mumbai (formerly Bombay) and Sao Paulo (18 million people each), Calcutta and Buenos Aires (13 million), and Jakarta (10 million). It is estimated that by 2030, two-thirds of the world's population will live in cities—most of them in the NICs of today.

The growth of the urban population of NICs has contributed to an expansion of the middle class and the development of large new consumer markets, which has in turn helped the economic growth of NICs. Urbanization has also changed the balance of political power: City dwellers tend to be better educated, more likely to organize for political change and more inclined to make demands for democratic change. At the same time, though, the growth of urban populations has often outpaced the availability of jobs, and city governments have been unable to keep up with the demand for services. This has meant more urban slums, inadequate public transport, traffic congestion, worsening crime, problems with water and energy supply, and often severe air and water pollution. Nothing so clearly illustrates the gap between the urban rich and the poor as conditions in Brazil's big cities, where the wealthy elite ape the lifestyle and manners of Beverly Hills, and yet one third of the population lives in sprawling *favelas*, or slums.

New Levels of Foreign Investment

Just as the United States economy grew with the help of large infusions of foreign investment during the nineteenth century, so the growth of NICs has been underpinned by foreign investment aimed at building export capacity. Keen to exploit cheap labor and the growing consumer markets of NICs, Western corporations have invested heavily in Southeast Asia and Latin America. This has brought new wealth and opportunities to NICs and has made the products we buy in our stores much cheaper. Unfortunately, it has also meant job losses in manufacturing in liberal democracies, and for NICs it has meant the exploitation of workers, common instances of child labor, and the operation of **sweatshops** where men, women, and

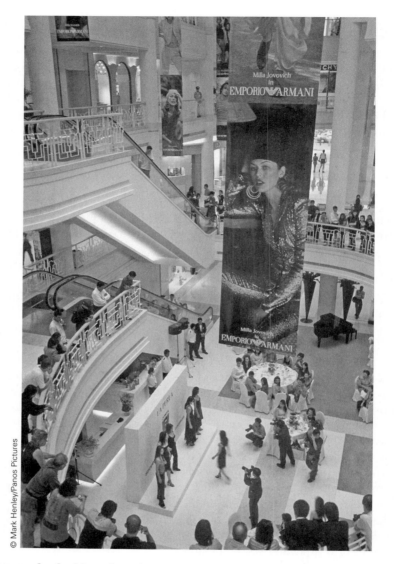

This scene of a fashion show in progress might be in Paris, London or New York. In fact it is inside a luxury shopping mall in Bangkok, the capital of Thailand. Not all Thais have access to such opulence, of course, but images such as this fly in the face of stereotypical views of a Third World burdened with poverty.

outsourcing The process by which jobs are moved from richer countries to those where labor is cheaper.

children work long hours for little pay. In many ways, NICs are experiencing the same labor conditions as today's liberal democracies saw when they were undergoing their industrial development in the nineteenth and twentieth centuries.

Cheap labor in NICs has also led to a phenomenon with which we are becoming increasingly familiar: **outsourcing.** In their attempts to cut costs or increase profits,

CRITICAL ISSUES

MEASURING NATIONAL WEALTH

The standard measure of national wealth is gross domestic product (GDP), defined as the total value of all goods and services produced by a country within its territory in a year. It tells us the absolute size of economies, but to make it useful for comparison, we need to divide it by population to give us a per capita figure. This reveals that Luxembourg and Switzerland are the most productive countries in the world, with a per capita GDP, respectively, of nearly $46,000 and $42,000; the United States ranks fourth with nearly $38,000; and Ethiopia is the least productive, at just $90 per person per year. The world average is about $5,500.

GDP is a useful means of measurement, but it presents several problems. First, production may not always be the best measure of human welfare, and material wealth is not the only indicator of the relative ability of societies to meet the basic needs of their members. Second, it is often mistakenly interpreted as a measure of income or personal wealth, but all it measures is the value of production. The per capita GDP of the United States is $38,000, but the average American has a personal income of just $30,000. Third, it may not give an accurate picture of the relative wealth of different societies. Poorer societies may have considerable wealth in the form of minerals, land, water, forests, or ecological variety, which has not yet been exploited but which signifies that they are resource-rich and therefore wealthy, at least potentially.

Finally, there is a problem with the way that GDP is calculated. It is usually expressed on the basis of a straight conversion from local currencies into U.S. dollars at the official exchange rate. But currencies in poorer countries may have an inflated value, and costs of living vary from one country to another. To give us a more accurate idea of the relative wealth of countries, some economists prefer using a calculation known as **purchasing power parity (PPP),** which is based on comparing the value of goods using the purchasing power of each national currency. The result has been a dramatic recalculation of the relative size of national economies. For example, China's economy leaps from $1.4 trillion to nearly $6.5 trillion, and India's from $600 billion to more than $3 trillion. These recalculations have given comparativists food for thought as they consider how to measure economic wealth, and have further emphasized the significance of NICs in the global economy.

corporations in liberal democracies are increasingly cutting jobs at home and—with the help of new technology—employing workers in NICs to do the same jobs. So when American consumers phone a company to make a purchase, increasingly the chances are that they will be speaking to a sales representative in India or the Philippines. Outsourcing is nothing new, but little attention was paid to it during the 1990s because the number of jobs outsourced from the United States was less than the number created. The kinds of jobs being outsourced also did not arouse much comment because they were typically unskilled technical jobs. But when white collar jobs began moving overseas, and the volume of outsourcing began to grow, the issue moved up the political radar, becoming an issue in a U.S. presidential election for the first time in 2004.[2]

purchasing power parity A method of calculating GDP or GNP of a country; the total is expressed according to the purchasing power of the national currency.

An Efficient Bureaucracy

A key factor in the success of liberal democracies has been the development of efficient, responsive, and professional bureaucracies. Governments can pass all the laws and regulations they want, but they mean nothing unless they are implemented. Effective implementation depends on having bureaucrats who are motivated, educated, well paid, and well trained and whose career advancement is based more on merit than on nepotism. So while LDCs such as Venezuela and marginal countries such as Zimbabwe are handicapped by bureaucratic corruption and incompetence, NICs such as Chile and Indonesia have become more like liberal democracies in the sense that government departments and agencies have a stronger record on overseeing the implementation of laws and regulations.

Social Development

Many NICs have religious, ethnic, and regional problems; many of their citizens lack steady jobs and access to basic public services; and poverty is still a critical problem. However, they are investing much more capital in their people than are neighboring LDCs and are building better hospitals, schools, and roads. The overall quality of life is also improving, as reflected in the statistics: While the citizens of most African LDCs can expect to live an average of 54 years, those of NICs can expect to live an average of 66 to 69 years. Similarly, while infant mortality rates in African LDCs are as high as 80 to 90 per 1,000 live births, the rates in NICs are about 40 to 60 per 1,000 live births. On the Human Development Index, most NICs sit just below liberal democracies with a ranking of High or Medium.

NICs also differ from their poorer neighbors in the extent to which they have invested in infrastructure: they have built strong transportation systems, provided commercial energy and other utilities to a growing number of their people, and developed modern communication systems. Taking advantage of improvements in technology, some NICs have actually leapfrogged over liberal democracies, building new transport and telecommunications systems that are technologically superior to the often much older systems in Europe or North America. Improvements in infrastructure have underpinned economic growth, provided social stability, and reinforced political stability.

New Regional and Global Influence

The new economic wealth and political stability of NICs has given them stronger voices regionally and globally. The Southeast Asian "tiger" economies are becoming magnets for workers from poorer neighboring states and are being taken more seriously as trading partners by North Americans and Europeans. Many NICs are also strengthening their regional influence through cooperative groups such as the ten-member Association of South East Asian Nations (ASEAN) and Mercosur, which has four South American members.

The power of NICs is reflected in their increasingly important role in international trade negotiations, underpinned by the growing percentage of global imports and exports for which they account. This has made them more aggressive negotiators, as reported by Jeffrey Garten, an undersecretary for commerce in the Clinton administration. During global trade negotiations in Geneva in 1994, he recalls that the Europeans wielded considerable power, as expected, but that what surprised him was the skill and energy of negotiators from Asia and Latin America: "These men and women had a superb grip on the trading rules and how to negotiate them. They also had a strategic concept of how they wanted to shape the new World Trade Organization … and what they wanted the new body to accomplish."[3] The significance of NICs lies mainly in their new role in global manufacturing and in the extent to which the rich industrialized countries now rely on them as a source of cheap manufactured goods.

THE EMERGENCE OF NICs

Why has a select group of NICs left the Third World behind? How have they built democratic traditions and expanded their economies when many other countries with very similar backgrounds have not? To find the answer to these questions, we first need to look at the legacy of **colonialism** (the one experience that almost all Third World states had in common) and at the postcolonial experience of these countries. We will then look at some of the explanations for the emergence of NICs and—in Parts IV and VI—look at why other countries have remained poorer and less stable.

colonialism The process by which citizens of one territory live in and control another territory.

The Colonial Era (1450–1970)

A colony is a settlement established in a territory by citizens of a foreign state. The settlement may be small and temporary or large and permanent; either way, its inhabitants answer wholly or partly to the authority of the mother state, with their social and economic life sustained in the colony. By this definition, almost every country in the world has been colonized at one time or another. However, the most significant and sustained program of colonization in world history was launched by the Europeans in the fifteenth century and affected every region of the world, directly or indirectly. Their motives varied by time and place:

- **Settlement.** In some cases (such as the Americas, Australia, New Zealand, and southern Africa), people left the mother country with the idea of permanent settlement, displacing or subjugating native populations.

- **Extraction.** In some cases, imperial powers (or private companies from those powers) were looking to exploit raw materials, and discouraged settlement. The Dutch, for example, established trading posts in the East Indies (now Indonesia) in the seventeenth and eighteenth centuries but prohibited permanent settlement. They more or less succeeded there, but failed in South Africa, where the descendants of the earliest Dutch settlers, the Afrikaners, still live today.

- **Strategic advantage.** Competition was behind almost all colonization, but some colonies were created primarily for strategic reasons. For example, Gibraltar was ceded to Britain by Spain in 1713 and maintained as a garrison defending the western entrance to the Mediterranean; Hong Kong was ceded to Britain by China in 1842 and acted as the gateway for trade between China and the world.

The first phase of colonialism began in the mid-fifteenth century with the Portuguese and the Spanish, who colonized most of what is now Latin America, developing an economy based on plantations and mining, and eventually destroying native civilizations and replacing them with a *mestizo* (mixed-race) society. The second phase came in the seventeenth century with Dutch interest in the eastern spice trade and the first British and French settlements in North America. Britain and France began a bitter colonial rivalry, competing in the Caribbean, southern Asia, and North America. By the mid-eighteenth century, Britain had won the upper hand, colonizing most of Canada, the American colonies, Australasia (where the main motive was settlement), and India (where the main motive was first trade, then strategic advantage over the French and the Dutch).

With the independence of the United States in 1776 and of most of South America in 1810–1830, a third phase of colonialism began in the nineteenth century when Europeans trained their sights on trade with Africa, their interests clearly reflected in the names they gave to stretches of the West African coast: the Slave Coast (now Nigeria), Grain Coast (Liberia), Ivory Coast, and Gold Coast (Ghana). As trade grew, Europeans created permanent settlements, protected their interests, competed for strategic gain, and moved inland. The competition accelerated with the "Scramble for Africa," when Britain, France, Portugal, Belgium, Germany, Italy, and Spain raced to stake their claims to Africa. The division of the spoils was confirmed at the Berlin Conference in 1884–1885, which left almost no part of Africa untouched.

The final phase of colonialism began in the early twentieth century when Europeans turned their attention to the Middle East. Here the main competitors were again Britain and France, and the main motive was strategic advantage. The Suez Canal, for example, was built to promote trade with India, but it later took on strategic value (see Chapter 9).

By the beginning of the twentieth century, there were about two dozen independent nation-states in Europe and the Americas and several dozen colonies in Africa and Asia. Most of South America was independent, as was China and Japan, but global political and economic power lay firmly in the hands of the Europeans and North Americans.

decolonization The process by which major imperial powers began to withdraw from their colonies in the mid-twentieth century.

Despite this, the first signs of a desire for self-determination and independence began to emerge in the colonies. Pressure for **decolonization** began to grow in the Middle East, where Egypt was given sovereignty in 1922, and Iraq and Lebanon in 1932 and 1944, respectively. The pressures intensified after World War II, from which the European colonial powers emerged on the brink of economic collapse. Unable any longer to justify or support colonialism, they began to withdraw from Asia and Africa.

The independence of India and Pakistan in 1947 marked the beginning of the most intensive period of new state formation in history, with independence given to 95 countries in just 40 years, more than doubling the number of sovereign states in the world. In 1957, Ghana became the first African state to win independence. France withdrew virtually overnight from 14 of its colonies in 1960, Britain had granted independence to most of its colonies by 1968, and Portuguese dictators grimly put down guerrilla wars in its colonies until being overthrown by a military coup in 1974.

Developing an Identity (1955–)

Prospects for the newly independent countries of Asia and Africa were not good. Because most had been used as sources of cheap raw materials and labor, little investment had been made in them or their people. Since their frontiers had been set not by competition among the inhabitants of those regions (as was the case in Europe) but by colonial powers competing with one another, many were also artificial creations with almost every social division known to humanity. Recognizing their weaknesses, the more ambitious Third World leaders began investigating ways of developing a common front, promoting economic and political solidarity, and building common foreign policies.

The first such attempt came with the creation of the Nonaligned Movement in 1955, when 29 countries met to establish positions that would allow them to avoid taking sides in the cold war. The United Nations at that time had only 59 member states, so the creation of a bloc of 29 nonaligned countries seemed to augur well for the future influence of the Third World. **Nonalignment** was based on a set of principles, including the importance of national sovereignty, the equality of nations, and noninterference in the internal affairs of other states. Members agreed not to join military pacts dominated by the superpowers, but this goal was undermined from the start when some aligned themselves with the communist bloc (for example, North Vietnam and Cuba), and others with the Western alliance (for example, Pakistan and the Philippines).[4]

nonalignment The belief by the leaders of newly independent African and Asian countries in the 1950s that they should not take sides in the cold war.

The Nonaligned Movement today has 114 members, representing about half the world's population. But although it has been a symbolic rallying point for Asian and African diplomacy, it has amounted to little more than a gesture, undermined by political and economic divisions among its members. Since the end of the cold war, the concept of nonalignment has been weakened and the movement has switched its focus to issues such as reform of the United Nations, a new system of international relations, solidarity among its members, and an end to nuclear proliferation.

More important as a forum for the expression of the views of African, Asian, and Latin American states has been the United Nations, where the governments of these countries make up two-thirds of UN membership. But none of them has the power of veto in the Security Council enjoyed by the United States, Britain, France, Russia, and China, and the bargaining power of poorer states has been undermined by the dependence of many of them on UN assistance and by the declining credibility of the United Nations. Even so, African, Asian, and Latin American delegates have used their numbers to place their concerns on the UN agenda. They have also tried to renegotiate the terms of the global economic system, first through the **United Nations Conference on Trade and Development (UNCTAD)** (created in 1964), which works to maximize trade, investment, and development opportunities for poorer countries, and then through the **Group of 77 (G-77)**, which originally consisted of the 77 countries that took part in the first UNCTAD conference, but which now (confusingly) has 133 members.

G-77 used its voting powers in the UN General Assembly to campaign for the creation of the **New International Economic Order (NIEO)**. A response to the liberal economic order dominated by rich industrialized countries and geared toward the promotion of free trade, the idea of the NIEO was launched in 1974. The goal was to reform the global trading and financial system so that it was not weighted against poorer countries, mainly by negotiating new trade agreements that would allow these countries to make greater profits out of their exports of raw materials. But the supporters of the NIEO lacked the political power to achieve their goals, and in the end it was little more than a rallying point for the Third World.

In 1989, G-77 shifted the focus back to itself, and after asking what its members could do to help themselves, agreed on a Global System of Trade Preferences (GSTP). Much like the General Agreement on Tariffs and Trade, this was designed to promote and sustain trade and economic cooperation among its members by reducing barriers to trade. The problem, though, is that most G-77 countries export more in the way of low-profit raw material and agricultural products than in high-profit manufactured goods, and even where they export the latter, it is often only wealthy liberal democracies that can afford to import them in significant quantities.

Despite all these attempts by poorer countries to renegotiate the terms of the global economic system, NICs have emerged from the pack by simply taking on the rich industrialized countries at their own game. They have exploited their two greatest resources—plentiful cheap labor and often substantial natural resources—to undercut labor markets in the liberal democracies and attract new investment. This has been used to invest in infrastructure and to shift their economies away from a reliance on agriculture to a much heavier reliance instead on industry and services.

NEWLY INDUSTRIALIZING COUNTRIES TODAY

It is often said that the nineteenth century was the British century and that the twentieth century was the American century. All the key indicators suggest that the twenty-first century could belong to Asia or Latin America. These are the two regions of the world where we will have to look for the next great economic powers—and with economic power comes political influence. Already, four of the world's biggest economies are NICs (India, Brazil, Mexico, and Indonesia), and—although it is not classified as a NIC in this text because of its poor record on democratization—it is only a matter of time before China, already the biggest emerging economy in the world, joins the ranks of the NICs.

Just as the new focus of economic development has switched to NICs, so has the focus of democratization. These countries are not just earning new wealth and global economic influence, but they are achieving new levels of political stability. As their citizens have become healthier, wealthier, and better educated, they have demanded political change. Indeed, democratization has been a critical element in the process by which economic development has proceeded. The West could not avoid noticing changes in Argentina, Brazil, India, Malaysia, the Philippines and South Africa, but these countries long played only a marginal role in international affairs. Today, they are among the most important engines of economic growth and democratic change in the world.

Argentina, Brazil, and Uruguay have seen an unfortunate cycle of economic booms and busts in recent years, but the underlying trends are positive. Argentina and Chile are both learning to deal with the legacy of unpleasant military dictatorships, while the

2002 election in Brazil of Luiz Inacio Lula da Silva (known as Lula) showed that even a former shoeshine boy and sheet metal worker could make it to the top of Brazilian politics. Meanwhile, several Caribbean NICs have diversified beyond tourism into banking and financial services, which in the case of the Bahamas has made it a magnet for illegal immigration from Haiti. Nearby Jamaica may suffer widespread crime and poverty, but it has stable political institutions, free and fair elections, and a free press.

Meanwhile the "tiger" economies of South and Southeast Asia have also seen growing political stability and social development. The small city-state of Singapore may be infamous for the role that the government plays in trying to control the lives of its citizens, whether encouraging them to have more children or to be more polite to each other, but it is also one of the most prosperous countries in the world, with a high standard of living and the kind of wealth that attracts both foreign investment and immigrant workers. The government of India is backing away from state intervention in the economy, allowing more Indians to prosper, and providing economic freedoms to match India's much-vaunted democratic freedoms. Nearby, Indonesia, Malaysia, the Philippines, Taiwan, and Thailand are all lead players in the rise of new economic powers.

KEY TERMS

colonialism
decolonization
export-led growth
Group of 77
megacities

New International
   Economic Order
nonalignment
outsourcing
purchasing power parity

sweatshops
United Nations
   Conference on Trade
   and Development
   (UNCTAD)

STUDY QUESTIONS

1. Is there anything that the experience of liberal democracies in the nineteenth century can tell us about the political and economic changes being witnessed by NICs today?

2. Is there anything in the Japanese experience to suggest that some NICs may be the Japans of the future?

3. Is political stability possible without economic growth? Is economic growth possible without political stability?

4. There is an old saying that if you cannot bite, you should not show your teeth. What would it take to give NICs the ability to "bite" in their relationship with rich industrialized countries?

NICs ONLINE

Group of 77: www.g77.org
Web site of the Group of 77, with information on its goals and programs.
UNCTAD: www.unctad.org
Web site of the UN body that has played a key role in the economic development of
   poorer countries.

Nonaligned Movement: www.nam.gov.za
Web site of the nonaligned movement, containing information on its meetings and
objectives.
South Movement: http://southmovement.alphalink.com.au
An unofficial guide to the Nonaligned Movement, from Australia.

FURTHER READING

Garten, Jeffrey, *The Big Ten: The Big Emerging Markets and How They Will Change Our Lives*
(New York: Basic Books, 1997). A study of the political and economic potential of ten
Third World states, including India, Mexico, Brazil and Argentina.

Harris, Nigel, *The End of the Third World* (London: Penguin, 1990). Although now dated, still
an interesting study of the reasons NICs emerged and why the concept of the Third World
is misleading.

Marber, Peter, *From Third World to World Class: The Future of Emerging Markets in the Global
Economy* (Cambridge, MA: Perseus Publishing, 1999). A New York investment manager argues that free trade is good for the United States and for emerging economies.

Weatherby, Joseph N., et al., *The Other World: Issues and Politics of the Developing World*, 4th
Ed. (New York: Longman, 2000). A general introduction to the politics, policies, and problems of the non-Western world.

MEXICO

QUICK FACTS

Official name: United Mexican States

Capital: Mexico City

Area: 737,000 square miles (1,908,000 sq. km) (almost three times the size of Texas)

Languages: Predominantly Spanish, with several indigenous languages

Population: 102 million

Population density: 133 per square mile (51 per sq. km.)

Population growth rate: 1.4 percent

POLITICAL INDICATORS

Freedom House rating: Free

Date of state formation: 1821

System type: Presidential republic

Constitution: Published 1917

Administration: Federal, with 31 states and the Federal District of Mexico City

Executive: President, elected for a single 6-year term

Legislature: Bicameral National Congress: Senate (128 members elected for six-year terms) and Chamber of Deputies (500 members elected for three-year terms). Members may not serve consecutive terms

Party structure: Multiparty

Judiciary: Supreme Court (11 members appointed for life and confirmed by Senate)

Head of state: Vicente Fox Quesada (2000–06)

Head of government: Vicente Fox Quesada (2000–06)

ECONOMIC INDICATORS

GDP (2004): $676 billion

Per capita GDP: $6,770

Distribution of GDP: Services 70 percent, industry 26 percent, agriculture 4 percent

Urban population: 74 percent

SOCIAL INDICATORS

HDI ranking: 53

Infant mortality rate: 23 per 1,000 live births

Life expectancy: 74 years

Literacy: 90% of people aged 15 and older

Religions: Predominantly Catholic

INTRODUCTION

Mexico is not a country that often appears in international news headlines, yet the changes that have taken place there since the late 1970s have been revolutionary and have affected all of the Americas, including the United States. A program of democratization has been so successful that the Institutional Revolutionary Party—in power without a break since 1929—lost its majority in the Mexican Congress in 1997 and lost the presidency in 2000, elections are now much more competitive, and Freedom House has changed Mexico's ranking from Partly Free to Free. Almost equally significant has been Mexico's program of economic reform, which has brought greater freedom to a market with 102 million consumers and has broadened the base of the world's ninth biggest economy, its eighth biggest producer of oil, and its biggest Spanish-speaking country.

All of this has been happening right on the doorstep of the United States, yet although the two countries share a 2,000-mile border and a nearly 500-year history, most Americans know or care remarkably little about Mexico. Most of those who travel there head for border towns like Tijuana or resorts like Cancun and do not much try to experience or understand Mexico on its own terms. But change is in the air. Latinos are now the biggest ethnic minority in the United States (nearly 14 percent of the population), and Mexican Americans make up about 60 percent of those Latinos; in parts of southern Texas and California, Latinos are in a majority (see Close-Up View, p. 291). The United States, Canada, and Mexico have also been partners since 1994 in the **North American Free Trade Agreement (NAFTA)**, which has meant an increased overlap of U.S. and Mexican interests on issues as varied as immigration, trade, tourism, labor, water supply, drugs, and the environment. Mexico's stability and welfare is of direct interest to the United States, a reality that was graphically emphasized in late 1994 by the collapse of the peso and the speed with which the Clinton administration led a multinational rescue mission.

In economic terms, Mexico is still large and poor, with a per capita GDP of just over $6,700, but it has many of the classic features of a newly industrializing country, including export-led growth, a service-based economy, a rapidly developing industrial base, and often startling economic and social paradoxes. It is common to hear talk of two Mexicos: one wealthy, urban, and modern and the other poor, rural, and traditional. One in ten Mexicans is illiterate, yet one in six goes on to higher education (a figure comparable to that of many European countries). Mexico City is a nightmare of congestion, yet it has an extensive subway that carries more passengers every day than the New York City subway. Within sight of urban slums with open sewers you might see smartly dressed investment brokers driving to work in air-conditioned luxury cars, using cell phones to close a deal or make a restaurant reservation.

In social terms, Mexico has few serious religious problems. More than 90 percent of Mexicans are Catholic and *mestizo* (of mixed Spanish and Native American blood). About 5 percent of the population is pure Native American, descendants of the Mayas, Zapotecs, Tarascans, and Aztecs. They may be few, but they have had a greater impact on Mexican society and politics than their northern cousins have had

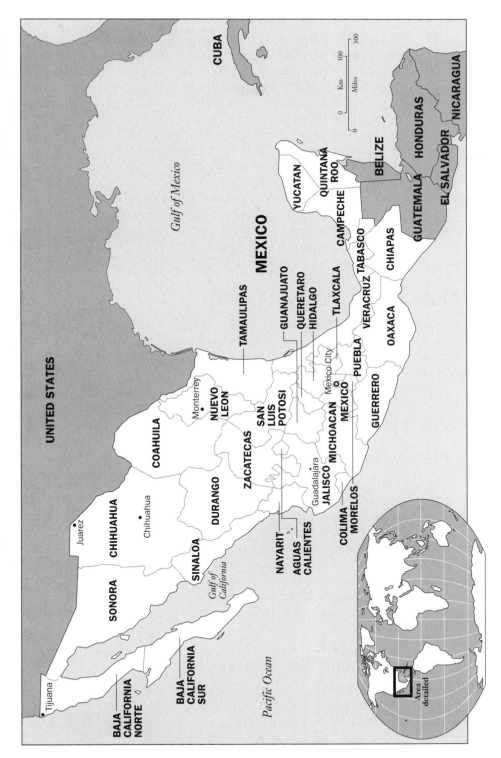

on U.S. society. Because the term *Indian* has cultural rather than racial connotations, it is possible to move across cultures,[1] but this does not mean that there is any less ethnic discrimination than is found in the United States. Like their American cousins, native Mexicans are poorer and more politically marginalized than *mestizos*. Their problems have been exemplified by problems in several poor southern states, which have occasionally spilled over into violence and have also emphasized the economic gaps between rich and poor in Mexico.

The Mexican political system has some similarities to the U.S. system: It is a federal republic with a separately elected president and legislature. In practice, though, there are important differences. Mexican presidents have much more power than their U.S. counterparts, and despite the existence of a federal structure, the political system is heavily centralized. This has left political scientists undecided about how to describe Mexico. Some call it authoritarian; others use words such as *bureaucratic*, *elitist*, and *patrimonial* when trying to describe it. But reforms to the electoral system have made Mexico more democratic, and the old assumptions about the nature of the political system no longer hold true.

POLITICAL DEVELOPMENT

Unlike either the United States or Canada—which come mainly out of the European tradition and where the early colonists did not try to integrate with natives but destroyed them or pushed them aside and seized their land—Mexico is a product both of its European and its Native American heritage. It is, as the Mexican Nobel laureate Octavio Paz once put it, a "land of superimposed pasts"[2] and continues today to be a melding of European and Native American ideas about law, government, and society.

The Precolonial Era

Until the fifteenth century, native peoples such as the Mayas and the Aztecs inhabited most of what is now Mexico. The Aztecs arrived in central Mexico from the arid north in the twelfth century, building their capital at Tenochtitlán (now Mexico City). Subduing their enemies, they built an empire with its own local governments, a centralized tax and court system, and ruling castes of religious and military leaders. In many ways, modern Mexican politics reflects the centralized and hierarchical Aztec system, but despite the sophistication and reach of native society and despite the remaining Native American cultural influence in Mexico, modern Mexican politics is mainly a product of changes that have taken place since the arrival of the Europeans.

Spanish Occupation (16th Century to 1821)

The Spanish arrived in 1519 under the command of Hernán Cortés, subjugating the Aztecs relatively easily. Not only did the Spaniards have better weapons but they also had horses (which the Aztecs had never seen before), and they were helped by the resentment of tribes under Aztec rule who took the opportunity to rebel. By the middle of the sixteenth century, the whole of what is now Mexico (along with large parts of what is now the southwestern United States and Central America) had been conquered and occupied. Unlike North America, where British settlers rarely intermarried with Native Americans, the mixing of Spaniards and Native Americans was encouraged, creating a new *mestizo* culture that gradually moved up the social ladder. In addition, the Spanish left Mexico with a significant religious heritage in the form of Catholicism, which went beyond being a religion and became embedded in political culture.[3] The Spanish also brought diseases to which the natives had no immunity, such as measles and smallpox. In the more than 300 years of Spanish occupation, the native population fell from 17 million to 6 million; nearly three million natives died in epidemics of one unidentified disease in the mid-sixteenth century alone.

Partly inspired by the American Revolution, Mexican revolutionaries began agitating for independence in the early nineteenth century. The struggle became one between Spanish administrators (the *peninsulares*) on the one hand and Mexicans of Spanish descent (*criollos*) and *mestizos* on the other. Many of Mexico's revolutionaries were more radical in their thinking than their U.S. counterparts, inspired as they were by the French Revolution. There was strong support, for example, for racial equality.

Independence and War (1821–1848)

After a long struggle (1810–1821), Mexico finally won its independence in 1821 and then tried to build its own empire in central America. However, its economy was weak; it lacked the stability needed to attract foreign investment; and doubts about the kind of society Mexicans wanted to build led to a power struggle between liberals calling for a democratic, federal system of government and conservatives favoring a more centralized system.[4] Politics broke down in revolution, rigged elections, and rapid changes in leadership; in the first 50 years of independence alone, there were 30 presidents.

Mexico's development was also affected by conflicts with the United States. In 1825 Mexico invited Americans to settle in and develop Texas, which was then part of Mexico. By 1830, about 20,000 settlers had arrived, alarming Mexico into banning further immigration and trying to tighten its control over the new immigrants in 1835. The immigrants responded in 1836 by declaring their independence and requesting U.S. annexation. Although General Antonio López de Santa Anna defeated the defenders of the Alamo mission in San Antonio, he was defeated at the battle of San Jacinto and forced to agree to Texan independence. In 1845 the United States annexed Texas over Mexican protests, and fears of U.S. expansionism precipitated the war of 1846–1848, which ended with Mexico ceding half its land area (including what are now California, New Mexico, Arizona, and part of Texas) to the United States.

Mexico saw further threats to its independence when France, Britain, and Spain demanded reparations for losses suffered during the war. Napoleon III of France took advantage of Mexico's internal weaknesses in 1864 by declaring a French-dependent Mexican empire with Archduke Maximilian of Austria as emperor. A resistance movement overthrew and executed Maximilian in 1867, and Benito Juárez became president. This introduced many political changes, including stronger civil liberties, regular elections, reductions in the powers of the church, and expanded public education. These changes did not amount to a new liberal order, however, and in 1877 the military government of José de la Cruz Porfirio Díaz came to power.

The *Porfiriato* (1877–1910)

Díaz dominated Mexican politics for 35 years, serving as president for all but one four-year term (1880–1884). During the era that came to be known as the *porfiriato*, Mexico enjoyed political stability and economic expansion. National income, foreign investment, and trade all grew; the railroads were expanded; and vast new tracts of land were opened to settlers. However, economic gains came at the cost of political freedom. Díaz ended free elections, curtailed freedom of speech and the press, put down dissent in the rural areas, ignored the separation of powers and states' rights, and tried to suppress Native American culture. Elections were held, but the results were rigged. Large landholders became wealthy, but peasants lost their land and were forced to become laborers, and the majority of Mexicans remained illiterate. The middle classes were unhappy about being excluded from power and demanded greater democracy. When Díaz announced that he would step down in 1910 and then changed his mind, a rebellion broke out. His forces quickly defeated, Díaz resigned and went into exile in 1911.

Revolution and Civil War (1910–1917)

Much like the 1917 Russian Revolution, the **Mexican Revolution** came mainly out of the middle and upper classes. But while their Russian counterparts claimed that they wanted to end the inequalities of the tsarist regime and to spread political and social justice, Mexican revolutionaries were mainly interested in opening up opportunities for themselves and in reducing the power and influence of foreign capitalists. The first revolutionary leader of Mexico was Francisco Madero, a member of a wealthy landowning family. Although he restored freedom of the press and individual property rights, he let too many officials from the Díaz era stay in office and failed to make the kind of reforms that would have won him the support of the peasants. In 1913 he was murdered in a U.S.-sponsored coup led by the brutal and corrupt Victoriano Huerta. A brief and violent civil war broke out, with three competing groups ranged against Huerta: a peasant army led by Emiliano Zapata, an army of workers and cattlemen led by Francisco "Pancho" Villa, and a group of ranchers and businessmen led by Venustiano Carranza. More than a million people died in the war, Carranza was in control by 1915, and Villa and Zapata were both later assassinated.

In 1917 a new constitution was drawn up that has been the basis of Mexican government ever since. Radical and progressive, it included many of the same basic ideas as the U.S. Constitution (including separation of powers, federalism, and a Bill of Rights), but differed in giving the state control over all natural resources, the federal government the right to redistribute land, and workers greater rights than they had in the United States.

The Mexican Revolution is often described as one of the first great social revolutions of the twentieth century, predating both the Russian and Chinese revolutions. Revolutions supposedly involve major political and social change, but although Mexico may

T A B L E   6 . 1

Key Dates in Mexican History

1519	Spanish occupation begins
1810–1821	War of independence
1821	Independence of Mexico
1836	Independence of Texas
1846–1848	War with the United States
1848	Loss of New Mexico and California territories to the United States
1864–1867	Rule of Archduke Maximilian of Austria
1877–1911	*Porfiriato*
1910	Outbreak of the Revolution
1913–1917	Civil war
1917	Publication of the Mexican constitution
1929	Creation of National Revolutionary Party, precursor to PRI
1938	Creation of Pemex
1953	Women given the right to vote
1968	Mexico City Olympic games; massacre of student demonstrators
1977	Electoral law changed to add 100 seats elected by proportional representation to the Chamber of Deputies
1982	Debt crisis
1985	Mexico City earthquakes kill 20,000
1986	Mexico joins the General Agreement on Tariffs and Trade (GATT) and signs a loan agreement with the International Monetary Fund (IMF); number of seats in Chamber of Deputies elected by proportional representation increased to 200
1992	Mexico signs the North American Free Trade Agreement
1994	(January) Mexico joins NAFTA, and insurrection breaks out in southern state of Chiapas; Mexico joins the OECD; (December) Ernesto Zedillo takes office, promising to govern with respect for the rule of law; loss of foreign investor confidence leads to devaluation of peso
1994	(March) assassination of PRI presidential candidate Luis Donaldo Colosio; (September) assassination of PRI secretary-general José Francisco Ruiz Massieu
1995	(January) President Clinton bypasses Congress to authorize economic rescue package for Mexico
1996	(August) Political reform package unanimously passed by both houses of Mexican Congress
1997	(June) PRI loses its majority in the Chamber of Deputies for the first time; Mayor of Mexico City elected for the first time
1999	(November) First ever primary to choose PRI presidential candidate
2000	(July) National elections; PRI loses the presidency for the first time in 71 years, and loses its majority in the Senate; (December) Vicente Fox takes office as president
2001	(February) George W. Bush chooses Mexico for the first foreign trip of his presidency
2003	(July) PRI regains its plurality in mid-term Congressional elections

have enjoyed more freedom of expression, more tolerance of opposition, and more open criticism of government after the revolution, its political system was still authoritarian. Even today, one in four Mexicans lives in poverty, women are politically and economically marginalized, land is unequally distributed, and concerns about Mexican economic independence remain an important public issue. This is why many Mexicans argue that the goals of the revolution have not yet been met and that the revolution is continuing.

Stabilizing the Revolution (1924–1940)

Of the early postrevolutionary presidents, two in particular made key contributions to Mexico's political development. The first was Plutarco Elías Calles (1924–1928), who in 1929 created the National Revolutionary Party as a way of perpetuating his political influence.[5] Its name was changed in 1945 to the **Institutional Revolutionary Party,** or PRI (pronounced "pree"), and it went on to govern Mexico for the rest of the century. Even more influential was Lázaro Cárdenas (1934–1940), the most left-wing of Mexico's presidents. He redistributed more land than his seven predecessors combined, supported labor unions, and—most important—launched a program of nationalization. Concerned at the extent to which Mexican companies were controlled by foreigners, particularly Americans, he brought several industries under state control and in 1938 created the state oil corporation, today called Petróleos Mexicanos **(Pemex).** This so upset the United States and other countries that they began a boycott of Mexican oil. For all these changes—aimed at economic and political equality and stability, and at asserting Mexican independence—Cárdenas remains the most revered of Mexico's twentieth-century presidents.

Portillo and the Oil Crisis (1976–1982)

After Cárdenas, Mexico's economic and political development paved the way for steady economic growth in the 1960s and 1970s, but signs of underlying structural problems began to emerge. Falling agricultural exports indicated a loss of competitiveness, leading in turn to middle-class discontent. This was reflected in the events of the summer of 1968, when students used the media spotlight provided by the Mexico City Olympics to demand political liberalization. A government crackdown resulted in as many as 500 students being killed by the army, leading in turn to a crisis of political legitimacy. To make matters worse, Mexico's economy was in trouble.

Taking advantage of new profits from oil price increases in the 1970s, the government of Luis Echeverría (1970–1976) launched an expensive oil exploration program that found vast new oil resources. This encouraged his successor José López Portillo (1976–1982) to follow a more liberal line in domestic politics and economic policy, making him popular with investors and the upper and middle classes and moving toward greater independence from the United States in foreign policy. Heavy investments were made in transport, industry, communications, health care, and education, and hundreds of thousands of jobs were created. But the high spending brought inflation and encouraged more imports and fewer exports. When the price of oil began to fall, Mexico borrowed to cover its spending, building a large national debt. In 1982 Mexico came close to defaulting on its debt, prompting talk of a "Third World

THE MEXICAN DIASPORA

The term *diaspora* refers to the broad community of a group of people, transcending national borders. In the case of Mexicans, it refers to everyone of Mexican origin living both inside and outside the country. The latter group has been growing: According to U.S. Census data for 2000, there are now 18 to 21 million people of Mexican origin living in the United States. The majority are U.S. citizens, but about 9 million are Mexican-born and mainly still citizens of Mexico, and about 3 to 4 million are illegal residents. Another 300,000 arrive each year illegally in the United States, and an estimated 1 to 3 million arrive every year to work in seasonal agriculture.

The expansion of the diaspora has implications for both Mexico and the United States. It is significant for Mexico because so many of its skilled and unskilled workers have left for better paying jobs in the United States, taking away an important part of Mexico's labor pool but also providing an important source of foreign income; it has been estimated that Mexicans living in the United States send as much as $13–14 billion annually back to their families at home. It is also significant because of the large numbers of Mexican voters who now live in the United States; so many, in fact, that during the 2000 Mexican presidential election, the major candidates visited the United States to campaign among expatriate Mexicans. The constitution has allowed them to

vote since 1996, but a law actually making this possible was only passed by the Chamber of Deputies in March 2005, and its fate in the Senate was still uncertain as this book went to press.

The expansion of the diaspora is significant for the United States for several reasons. Most obviously, Mexican workers—both legal and illegal—play an increasingly important role in the American economy, providing a growing proportion of the unskilled labor force, for example, especially in agriculture. There are concerns about the quality of life for many of these workers, who are exploited in a way that would not be tolerated if American workers were involved. There are also concerns about the impact of illegal immigration from Mexico on national security and the war on terrorism because of the increased demand for false identity documents. Finally, immigration is changing the social, cultural, and political makeup of the United States. This is particularly true in border states such as Texas, New Mexico, Arizona, and California, where the population of Mexican origin makes up 20 to 25 percent of the total. In several American border towns, such as San Antonio, Calexico, Nogales, Douglas, El Paso, Laredo, and Brownsville, there are Latino majorities in the range of 75 to 95 percent. Most Mexican immigrants once settled on the border, but migration in recent years has expanded throughout the United States.

debt crisis." Chastened, the Mexican government began a shift away from centralized economic management to a more open and competitive free-market system.

In 1986 Mexico joined the General Agreement on Tariffs and Trade (GATT), in 1994 it became a member both of NAFTA and of the Organization for Economic Cooperation and Development (OECD), and recent governments have pursued a policy of privatization—all signs of a more liberal line on the economy. However, the fragility of Mexico's economic development was emphasized by the collapse of the peso in late 1994, to which the Clinton administration responded with a $50 billion international rescue package of loan guarantees to again help Mexico avoid defaulting on its debt. Drug trafficking has also grown alarmingly and has been made more difficult to control because of widespread police and political corruption, harming U.S.-Mexican relations.

At the same time, the fragility of Mexico's political development was emphasized by unrest in the poor southern states of **Chiapas,**[6] Oaxaca, and Guerrero. Complaining about being cheated out of their land and being denied basic services, and feeling the effects of falling coffee prices, peasants in Chiapas rebelled in January 1994. Led by the charismatic Subcomandante Marcos, their masked and pipe-smoking leader, several hundred members of the Zapatista National Liberation Army (named after Emiliano Zapata) seized several towns and denounced NAFTA as a "death sentence" on Mexico's natives. Thousands of troops were sent in to put down the rebellion, resulting in more than 150 deaths. The Zapatistas stopped fighting almost immediately, and a peace agreement was eventually signed, but troops stayed on in Chiapas.

Meanwhile, a series of electoral reforms encouraged the rise of opposition parties and gave them more seats in the national Congress. The share of the PRI vote fell steadily as the governing party lost the support of unions and of a middle class hurt by Mexico's worsening economic problems. In 1997 PRI lost its majority in the Chamber of Deputies for the first time, and in 2000 lost its majority in the Senate and—most remarkable of all—lost the presidency of Mexico. The new president, Vicente Fox, came from the opposition National Action Party (PAN), and promised fiscal reform, sustainable economic growth, more social spending, political decentralization, and a more assertive foreign policy.

Mexico Today

Just in the last decade, Mexico has undergone a major political transformation. Most important is that it has begun to evolve into a healthy multiparty democracy, and the Fox administration was unable to manipulate government like its predecessors; in fact, the balance between executive and legislature has changed to the point where there is often gridlock, and much needed tax, energy and labor reforms have fallen prey to partisan bickering.[7]

On the economic front, the state has retreated from the marketplace in the wake of an extensive program of privatization, under which inefficient state-owned monopolies have been replaced by more competitive privately owned businesses better placed to take on international competition. Mexico now has a bigger GDP than that of Spain, India, South Korea, or Russia, and its new economic status was confirmed in 1994 when it joined OECD. Until then, OECD had been a club for the world's liberal democracies; Mexico's accession was confirmation that it could finally sit alongside the world's richest and most democratic countries.

Despite these changes, Mexico is not yet a liberal democracy. Its political institutions have not developed the necessary consistency and predictability, there is still much to be done to improve the quality of life for its people (especially those living in rural areas), corruption is still a major problem in government and public services, unemployment is still high, manufacturing is suffering (especially from competition from Asia), the middle class faces many problems, public safety leaves much to be desired, and Mexico's record on human rights still needs improvement. Questions also remain about the extent to which Mexico has actually reformed itself, or whether the old bad habits of PRI may return to influence the direction of politics. But in almost every other respect, the trends are positive.

POLITICAL CULTURE

There is a tension in Mexican society between democracy and authoritarianism. It has been said that while North American political culture is driven by the values of John Locke and liberalism, Latin American political culture is "elitist, hierarchical, authoritarian, corporatist, and patrimonialist."[8] Economic pressures and calculated changes to the system of government have begun to challenge these traditions in Mexico, promising to fundamentally rearrange the relationship between government and people. Put another way, economic modernization has increased the demand for political modernization.[9] For now at least, Mexican political culture has six main features.

The Continuing Revolution

While Americans tend to focus on the future, even to the point of sometimes failing to learn the lessons of history, Mexicans hark back to the past, to missed opportunities and unfulfilled dreams. Most have faith and pride in the 1917 constitution, agree with the goals of the Revolution, and support their political institutions. Revolutionary principles and national aspirations are perpetuated by the myths built around heroes as varied as Cuauhtémoc (the last Aztec emperor and leader of the opposition to the Spanish conquistadors), Pancho Villa, Benito Juarez, and Emiliano Zapata. At the same time, Mexicans recognize that the constitution is a work in progress and that it contains many goals that have not yet been met. Its supporters argue that Mexico is democratizing but that there are still many handicaps to the final achievement of democracy. For example, a strong presidency was seen as essential to helping Mexico restore order and build strong political institutions after the Revolution, but first there had to be economic growth. Now that Mexico is richer and has a growing middle class, there are greater opportunities for political modernization.

Nationalism

For many Mexicans, the history of their country has followed a pattern in which they have repeatedly had to defend themselves against more powerful foreigners. In some cases, the threats have taken the form of direct military confrontation, such as those between Mexico and Spain in the early nineteenth century, between the United States and Mexico in 1846–1848, and between Mexico and France in the 1860s. In other cases, the threats have been economic, such as the foreign investment that took place during the *porfiriato*. Debates over NAFTA and the 1995 bailout of the peso once again raised the issue of economic dominance by the United States. It is not uncommon to hear Mexicans refer wistfully—and in all sincerity—to their country as a colony of the United States.

Hierarchy and Elitism

Like many of its Latin American neighbors, Mexico has many of the hierarchical features of the Catholic Church. Spanish Catholicism was based on the idea that political authority emanated from God, and all lower levels of society had progressively less power and status. Mexican society is still class-based, with people and groups ranked within the political system and real power held by an elite whose attitudes are both paternalistic and authoritarian. The elite was once made up almost exclusively of the military; today it consists mainly of technocrats (technical experts) and of the entrepreneurs who have benefited most from privatization.

The Corporatist State

corporatism An arrangement by which groups in society are incorporated into the system of government.

Mexico offers a good example of a phenomenon most often found in Latin American societies: **corporatism.** A corporatist state is one in which groups representing the major social and economic interests are incorporated by government. The groups are given privileged official positions, access to government, and permission to bargain with the government on public policies, in return for which their members must respect and support the policies agreed on. This tends to create a system that is top-down and elitist, is based heavily on patronage, and works against political or economic liberalism. In the Mexican case, the most important groups are workers, peasants, and the "popular" sector (mainly the middle classes, small businesspeople, government employees, and the professions).

The signs of corporatism in Mexico are becoming harder to find. Democratic changes have coupled with improved education to make workers and peasants more difficult to manipulate and have also taken power away from the governing elite and distributed it to a broader, popular base. Meanwhile, economic changes have opened up the Mexican marketplace. The result has been a move away from the corporatist traditions of the last 70 years and toward the pluralist ideas associated with liberal democracy.[10]

Centralism and Corruption

camarilla A network of people with common political interests, tied to a particular political leader.

Mexico may be a federal republic, but power traditionally has been centralized in the ruling political party, and political power often revolves around *camarillas*: groups of people who have political interests in common and rely on one another for political advancement. Each has a single leader or mentor at its core.[11] In such systems, personalities become more important than ideology or policies in determining political behavior, and power revolves around patron-client relationships, with followers providing support in return for political favors. Political careers often depend heavily on "old-boy networks," which contribute to the corruption that is a common feature of Mexican politics.

Machismo

Although many of the ideas in the Mexican constitution reflect those in liberal democratic constitutions, not all have been put into practice, in part because *machismo* (assertive masculinity) is still a central characteristic of Mexican political culture. *Machismo* expresses itself in the political marginalization of women, who won the right to vote only in 1953 and still rarely move into positions of authority within government. It can also be seen in political violence, such as demonstrations, riots, kidnappings, political assassinations, and even guerrilla warfare. Government occasionally responds with its own kind of violence, which may take the form of direct repression or human rights abuses. Recourse to violence may also be a symptom of the feeling among more frustrated Mexicans that nonviolent participation is futile.

POLITICAL SYSTEM

Superficially, the Mexican political system looks much like the U.S. system: Both countries are federal republics with executive presidents, a bicameral legislature, an independent judiciary, a system of checks and balances, and competing political parties. In both countries, the president appoints cabinet members and ambassadors, with Senate approval. And both have written constitutions that can be amended by a proposal put forward by two-thirds of Congress and approved by state legislatures (a majority in Mexico, three-quarters in the United States).

Appearances deceive, however, because there are at least two critical differences between the United States and Mexico:

- Despite the separation of powers and the system of checks and balances, the Mexican presidency is a powerful office, with Congress and the judiciary playing mainly supporting roles. The president has wide-ranging control over appointments to key positions in government, can issue decrees and declare states of emergency (like his Russian counterpart), and has substantial powers of patronage at his disposal.

- Despite the fact that Mexico is a federation, the federal government has many more powers relative to the states than is true of the United States. This is partly due to the constitution, which gives the federal government opportunities to intervene in the affairs of Mexico's 31 states, and partly due to economic and political realities: Mexico City is so big and so dominant (about one in five Mexicans live in and around the city) that its power and influence over national affairs far outstrips that of any urban area in the United States or Canada. It is so influential, in fact, that the second most important and powerful job in Mexican politics is the mayor of Mexico City.

Two developments in the last few years have made a difference. First, the powers of the president have declined—for example, he can no longer appoint his successor as he once could. Second, the end of PRI's monopoly has meant that it can no longer control politics through patronage and through managing the electoral process as it once could, and there is real multiparty competition in Mexico for the first time in its history. Elections are more honest and competitive, the checks and balances between president and legislature now finally mean something, and power is being redistributed to a broader, popular base.

THE CONSTITUTION

Adopted in 1917, the Mexican constitution is one of the oldest in Latin America, the major legacy of the Revolution, and the blueprint by which progress in meeting the goals of the Revolution is measured. Nineteenth-century Mexican constitutions drew heavily on the U.S. Constitution and were seen less as blueprints for government than as outlines of goals to which Mexico aspired. The 1917 constitution was different in that it was grounded more firmly in the realities of Mexico, and as such had characteristics that made it different from its U.S. counterpart.

One of its core principles is **economic nationalism.** As Mexican revolutionaries wrote the constitution, they cast worried glances over their shoulders at the looming economic power of the United States. To protect Mexican interests, they included limits on foreign investment and foreign ownership of land and other natural resources, denied anyone but Mexicans the right to own land or water resources, and—in the controversial Article 27—vested ownership of all minerals and other underground resources in the state. Ideas like these have become increasingly difficult to defend as Mexico has had to open up its market under the pressures of globalization and under the terms of NAFTA and the other free trade agreements of which it is a part.

A second core principle is the gap between church and state. In the United States, that gap is sometimes ambiguous and often hotly contested, but in Mexico—at least until recently—there have been few such ambiguities. Until reforms to the constitution in 1992, the church had no legal standing, which meant that priests could not vote (although many did), and it was barred from owning property or taking part in politics. This did not stop church leaders from campaigning for social justice, however; priests have been active in defending the rights of native Mexicans, in criticizing electoral fraud, and in speaking out about the problems of poverty. During the PRI era, Mexicans frustrated with the weakness of opposition parties often turned to the church as a vehicle to express their political demands.[12] Among his other moldbreaking characteristics, Vicente Fox became the first openly practicing Catholic president since the Revolution, and he promised to allow the church a greater role in public and political life.

A third core principle is slightly more ironic. While Mexico for decades was ruled by a strong presidency and a single political party, the constitution was actually designed to prevent anyone from accumulating too much power. It does this mainly by placing limits on the number of terms that can be served by elected officials: the president is limited to a single six-year term, and no members of Congress or of state and local governments can be elected to the same public office for consecutive terms.

In the United States, amending the constitution is both controversial and time-consuming, needing the support of a complex mixture of national politicians and the states—this is partly why there have only been 27 amendments in more than 215 years. American politicians rely instead on changes in the law to bring about changes in the structure of government. By contrast, the Mexican constitution is relatively easy to change: amendments need the support of only two-thirds of members of Congress. The result is that Mexican leaders often propose constitutional amendments even for trivial matters. For example, while he was still a local politician in 1994, Vicente Fox successfully petitioned for an amendment that would allow him—the son of a Spanish mother—to run for the presidency. More broadly, presidents have often used the constitution to legitimize controversial policy issues. The result is that the Mexican constitution has been amended nearly 350 times in nearly 90 years. A package of electoral reforms in August 1996 alone involved 18 amendments, and President Fox was quick to propose more amendments when he came to office. All these changes have led its critics to ask whether the constitution still reflects the goals and principles of the Revolution.

THE EXECUTIVE: PRESIDENT

Presidents dominate the Mexican political system: All real political power flows from—and revolves around—the president, who decides the policies and character of Mexican government. This was particularly true between 1929 and 2000, when PRI had a monopoly on the presidency, but it would probably have been true whichever party was in government, simply because of the powers that come with the job. So powerful is the office that the term *presidencialismo,* or **presidentialism,** has been coined to describe the phenomenon; it means that most power lies in the hands of the president and that all policy, whether good or bad, stems personally from the president.[13] (Consider how this compares with the superpresidency in Russia—see Chapter 4.) The Mexican presidency is (or was) so powerful that during the 71 years that PRI controlled the office, not a single president ever had his legislation turned down by Congress.

Like his U.S. counterpart, the Mexican president has both formal (explicit) and informal (implicit) powers. The formal powers include the power of appointment, which goes well beyond the equivalent powers of the U.S. president:

- Mexican presidents can appoint and dismiss cabinet members, control party nominations for Congress and state governors, appoint the leadership of Congress, and appoint the heads of state-owned banks and industrial enterprises.

- Through the power of decree (the *reglamento*), the president can decide how a law passed by Congress is enforced.

- He has the power to use the armed forces for external and internal security, to declare a "state of siege," and to assume emergency powers.

- He also has a host of other powers, from the substantial (the power to control and regulate foreign investment in Mexico), to the potentially substantial (the power to give concessions for radio and TV channels), to the relatively trivial (the power to oversee the writing and updating of primary school textbooks).

Informally, the power of appointment allows presidents to build a system of patron-client relationships, dispensing power and influence in return for loyalty. Mexican cabinets have 18 to 22 members and routinely include the heads of government departments but also include the director of Pemex (the state oil company), the director of the Central Bank, and the mayor of Mexico City.

TABLE 6.2

Postrevolutionary Presidents of Mexico

Date	President	Party
1917–1920	Venustiano Carranza	PNR
1920	Adolfo de la Huerta	PNR
1920–1924	Alvaro Obregón	PNR
1924–1928	Plutarco Elías Calles	PNR
1928–1930	Emilio Portes Gil	PNR
1930–1932	Pascual Ortiz Rubio	PNR
1932–1934	Abelardo Rodríguez	PNR
1934–1940	Lázaro Cárdenas	PNR
1940–1946	Manuel Avila Camacho	PRM
1946–1952	Miguel Alemán Valdés	PRI*
1952–1958	Adolfo Ruiz Cortines	PRI
1958–1964	Adolfo López Mateos	PRI
1964–1970	Gustavo Díaz Ordaz	PRI
1970–1976	Luis Echeverría Alvarez	PRI
1976–1982	José López Portillo y Pacheco	PRI
1982–1988	Miguel de la Madrid Hurtado	PRI
1988–1994	Carlos Salinas de Gortari	PRI
1994–2000	Ernesto Zedillo Ponce de León	PRI
2000–	Vicente Fox Quesada	PAN

* PRI began life as the National Revolutionary Party (PNR). It was reorganized in 1938 by President Cárdenas and renamed the Mexican Revolutionary Party (PRM), and in 1945 was renamed the Institutional Revolutionary Party (PRI).

Mexican presidents can also exploit the aura of their office for political ends. As heads of state, U.S. and Mexican presidents often attract the kind of respect reserved in parliamentary systems for monarchs or nonexecutive presidents. This was long carried to the extreme in Mexico, where care was taken to immunize the president from criticism and to hold cabinet ministers or others in government responsible for policy failures.[14] But now that the one-party monopoly is over, presidents are much more open to criticism and the challenges from the opposition.

Mexican presidents serve a single six-year term, or *sexenio*. In theory, they are directly elected by the people. In practice, the popular vote was all but meaningless until 2000, because the PRI candidate always won, and he was chosen as candidate through a secret selection process within PRI known as ***dedazo***, or pointing the finger. This usually consisted of the following steps:[15]

- By about four years into his term, the president would have finalized the membership of his cabinet, and it was understood that his successor would come from that cabinet lineup.
- At the end of his fifth year, the president might replace the party chair with someone sure to be sympathetic to his choice of successor. After talking with former presidents, party leaders, and leaders of the military, the labor movement, and the business community, he would give the party chair a list of "precandidates" from which his successor would be chosen. The list was then made public, supposedly to gauge public opinion and encourage public debate. At this point, the successor was popularly known as *el tapado* (the "hidden one" or the "hooded one").
- After about two months of "debate," the name of the successor was made public, and a party convention ratified the choice. The successor then launched a national campaign to build public recognition and held meetings with local party leaders.
- The election was held the following July, the winner would then begin assembling his new cabinet team, and he would be inaugurated in December.

How incumbents chose their successors was thought to depend on the kind of person the outgoing president thought Mexico needed in the following *sexenio*, how the potential successor performed under the outgoing administration, how well he was regarded by key political and economic interest groups in the country, and the kind of personal and political relationships the outgoing president had developed. Personal links were also important, because they increased the likelihood of ex-presidents being able to influence their successors.

An attempt was made in 1988 to make the nomination process more democratic, with a dissident group within PRI demanding greater openness in selecting a successor for Miguel de la Madrid. When it failed, one of its leaders—Cuauhtémoc Cárdenas—broke away from PRI and ran against Salinas, the anointed PRI candidate. Heading a coalition of parties on the left, Cárdenas officially won 31 percent of the vote, while the right-wing National Action Party (PAN) candidate (Manuel Clouthier) won nearly 17 percent. Although most independent estimates suggest that Cárdenas probably won, Salinas was declared the winner, but with the slimmest margin of any PRI candidate for president (50.7 percent) and only after a lengthy delay in announcing the results, blamed on a "breakdown" in the computers counting the votes.[17]

The most revolutionary change to the selection process came in 1999, when the *dedazo* system was replaced by an open primary. Fulfilling a promise made soon after coming to office, President Ernesto Zedillo had ordered a review of the selection process, the results of which were published in May 1999. They showed that 70 percent of PRI party members were in favor of a primary, in which all registered voters would be allowed to take part. The result was that for the 2000 election, for the first time, all three major parties chose their candidates for the presidency through primaries.

PEOPLE IN POLITICS

VICENTE FOX

© 2005 AFP/Getty Images

The 2000 presidential election was a landmark event in Mexican political history. For the first time in 71 years, the candidate of the Institutional Revolutionary party lost and Mexico saw a change at the helm with the victory of Vicente Fox, the candidate of the National Action Party, the main right-wing opposition party. The incumbent governor of the rural central Mexican state of Guanajuato at the time, Fox's arrival meant not only a change of party, but a new governing style and a change of direction for Mexico.

Born in Mexico City in 1942, Fox was raised in Guanajuato. He studied business at the Ibero-American University in Mexico City and earned a diploma from the Harvard School of Business. He joined Coca-Cola in Mexico in 1964 as a supervisor, and by 1979 had become president of the company's operations in Mexico and Central America. He was elected to the Mexican Congress in 1988 and lost the fraudulent race for the governorship of Guanajuato in 1991 before winning at his second attempt in 1995. Along the way Fox was married, and he and his wife adopted four children, but by the time he ran for the presidency he was divorced.

His record as governor was good, with unemployment in Guanajuato down, exports growing, increased federal funds for schools and farmers, and a balanced budget. On the campaign trail Fox became known for his cowboy image and brash style; he rarely wore suits, instead dressing his six-foot five-inch frame in open-necked shirts or T-shirts and often wearing a belt with a large buckle bearing his name. Running on a moderately conservative platform, his policy priorities included championing the rights of Mexico's indigenous population, resolving the conflict in Chiapas, reforming the bureaucracy, and making changes to the constitution (including a requirement that cabinet appointments be approved by Congress and that Mexicans overseas be allowed to vote in elections).

Fox initially won high approval ratings and unanimous support for his first budget, but his tax reform proposals were unpopular, and critics charged him with being too cautious in pursuing his promises for change. His popularity was also affected by the economic downturn that affected both the United States and Mexico in 2002–2003, and by the success of a reenergized PRI to block his promise to "transform" Mexico—this was given a boost when PAN lost nearly one-third of its seats at the 2003 Congressional elections. Fox was also hurt by rumors that his wife Marta Sahagún planned to run for the presidency in 2006. So weak was he by 2004 that debate had already begun about the front-runners to replace him in the July 2006 election.[16]

All Mexican presidents so far have been men, they have come mainly from politically prominent, urban, upper-middle-class families, and—particularly in recent years— they have served apprenticeships not as **políticos** (elected officials) but as **técnicos** (government bureaucrats). Until Fox they had all been graduates of the National Autonomous University (UNAM) in Mexico City, and several (including de la Madrid, Salinas, Zedillo, and Fox himself) attended graduate school in the United States. Fox has broken the mold in several ways, having been raised in a rural part of Mexico and having been elected as a state governor before running for the presidency.

THE LEGISLATURE: CONGRESS

Mexico's national legislature looks much like its U.S. counterpart in the way it is structured and managed, but it has traditionally had much less power, prestige, or influence over the president and, until recently, did little more than legitimize the actions of the president and rubber-stamp the policies of PRI. Its real significance lay in its informal functions: PRI used it as a safety valve for opposition parties, and seats in Congress were used as rewards for party workers or as a means of recognizing second-level leaders within PRI.

This all began to change in the late 1970s as PRI changed the electoral system to give opposition parties more seats in Congress. As opposition numbers grew, and as PRI's share of the vote fell, Congress became more openly critical of the president and won more real power. It became a major political actor as a result of the 1997 elections, when PRI lost its majority in the lower Chamber of Deputies for the first time. Although opposition parties were divided among themselves, PRI could no longer rely on deputies to support the program of the president, whose grip on power began to loosen. With Vicente Fox's victory in 2000, the role of Congress changed completely. Instead of rubber-stamping the president's policies, it became the chief source of opposition. This was especially true after the 2003 elections, when PRI won back its plurality in the Chamber of Deputies.

The Mexican Congress has two chambers.

Senate

Like its U.S. counterpart, the Senate represents the states. It has 128 members, with four coming from each of the 31 states and four from the Federal District of Mexico City. Senators serve six-year terms, and all run for reelection at the same time as the president (a system of staggered elections was introduced in 1991 but suspended in 1993). PRI had a monopoly of Senate seats until 1976, when the Popular Socialist Party was given a seat in return for keeping quiet about fraud in a state election in another part of the country. In 1988 the opposition Cárdenas Front won four Senate seats, and in 1993, electoral reforms not only increased the number of seats in the Senate from 64 to 128 but also changed the electoral process so that the biggest party in every state won three seats, and the second biggest won the fourth. As a result, the 1994 elections saw 32 opposition senators elected, the 1997 elections saw 51 elected, and the 2000 elections saw 68 elected and PRI losing its majority for the first time.

The Mexican Chamber of Deputies in session. Long exploited by the governing Institutional Revolutionary Party to prove its "democratic" credentials, the Chamber has recently won more powers relative to the presidency and is increasingly becoming a meaningful source of policy ideas and political opposition.

Chamber of Deputies

Like the U.S. House of Representatives, the Chamber of Deputies represents the people rather than the states. Its 500 members are elected for three-year terms through a direct universal vote. As with the Senate, PRI once had a lock on the chamber, which until 1977 had 320 members—300 elected from single-member districts that PRI was virtually guaranteed to win and 20 elected from party lists by proportional representation, giving opposition parties a few seats in Congress. To give those parties greater representation, PRI increased the number of party list seats to 100 in 1977 and then to 200 in 1988, where it now stands. In the 1988 elections, opposition parties won few of the single-member seats, but won almost all the party list seats. This gave them 48 percent of the seats in the Chamber, enough to at least temporarily meet their demands for government influence and to deny PRI the two-thirds majority needed to amend the constitution. Their share of seats fell in 1991, but they won majorities in 1997, 2000, and 2003, obliging PRI to reach more accommodations with the opposition parties to move business along.

There are several important differences in the structures of the U.S. and Mexican Congresses:

- Since a Mexican constitutional amendment in 1928, consecutive terms in either chamber have been forbidden, so senators and deputies must skip a term before being eligible for reelection. Members of Congress who cannot get enough of politics have been known to move alternately from one chamber to the other, and even to have spells in state or local government.

- While the U.S. Congress—particularly the Senate—is often used as a platform for a bid for the presidency, the preference among presidents from PRI for appointing technocrats as their successors minimized the importance of experience in Congress. President Fox broke the mold with his background as an elected state governor, and PRI has changed its own party rules to require that anyone seeking nomination as its presidential candidate should have experience in elective office.

- The U.S. Congress has powerful committees and an extensive body of staff that can generate information, but Mexican members of Congress have only a few staff each and must still rely heavily on the executive branch for information and policy ideas.[18] This obviously places them at a disadvantage.

The new independence and importance of Congress was underlined in late 2001 by a fight over a tax reform program submitted by President Fox. To increase tax revenues and reduce government dependence on fluctuating oil income, Fox proposed a number of changes, including raising taxes on food and medicine. Critics charged that the plan would place an excessive burden on the poor, and after nine months of haggling, even the president's own party dropped its support. Congress proposed an alternative plan that would shift the burden more to business and the wealthy, mainly by taxing a selection of luxury items, including cell phones and computers. The debate gave Congress a new sense of purpose and—after more than 70 years as a supporting actor in government—emphasized its newly assertive role in politics. It also showed that the president could no longer make any assumptions about the support he would receive from Congress but instead had to negotiate and appeal to public opinion.[19] In this sense he was becoming much more like his American counterpart.

THE JUDICIARY: SUPREME COURT

Although theoretically equivalent to the U.S. judicial system (and similar in structure), the Mexican judiciary has traditionally played only a supporting role in government and has been more apolitical than its U.S. counterpart. It has occasionally—and usually reluctantly—passed down decisions against the executive, but it has done little to limit executive power or control electoral fraud and has generally protected the interests of political and economic elites. President Zedillo set out to change its role by replacing all its members in 1995, introducing the power of judicial review, and appointing a member of the opposition party PAN as attorney-general.

The Supreme Court has 11 members, including a chief justice, each appointed for 15-year terms. As in the United States, members are nominated by the president and confirmed by the Senate, but unlike the United States, where only Congress can impeach a justice of the Supreme Court, the Mexican president has the power (with the approval of Congress) to remove a justice. Below the Supreme Court there is a system of circuit courts of appeal and district courts of first instance. The Supreme Court appoints circuit and district judges for renewable four-year terms (their U.S. equivalents are appointed for life by the president, subject to Senate confirmation).

Most English-speaking countries base their legal systems on English common law, but Mexico uses the Roman civil law tradition. The former is unwritten, tends to be adversarial or accusatorial (rather than inquisitorial), and relies heavily on precedent (the principle of *stare decisis*, or standing by previous decisions); the latter is based on written codes and the written opinions of legal scholars, and does not recognize precedent.[20] One of the most important types of cases heard by Mexican federal courts is an *amparo* suit, a concept unique to Mexico for which there is no direct equivalent in the United States. *Amparo*, which literally means favor or protection, can be used in several ways: as a defense of individual rights, as protection against unconstitutional laws, or to force examination of the legality of judicial decisions.[21]

SUBNATIONAL GOVERNMENT

In theory, Mexico has a federal system of administration, with the country divided into 31 states and the Federal District of Mexico City. The states each have a governor elected for a six-year term, a small unicameral Chamber of Deputies whose members are elected for three-year terms, and a number of *municipios*, which may be towns, counties, or consolidated city-county governments. As at the federal level, local government officials cannot serve consecutive terms.

In practice, there are two important differences between the U.S./Canadian and Mexican models of federalism:

- Although Mexican state governments have independent powers, it has been unusual for a state government to contradict or defy a federal government decision or ruling. Even local or state PRI organizations have been all but powerless and obliged to refer back to headquarters in Mexico City on all decisions.[22]

- The federal Senate has the power to remove an elected governor, whose successor may be nominated by the president and confirmed by the Senate. Because each state has its own electoral cycle, and because the *sexenios* of governors do not necessarily coincide with those of presidents, incoming presidents always inherit incumbent governors, over whom they may not have as much control as they would like. Even so, governors are dismissed much less rarely today than they were during the turbulent 1920s and 1930s. On the whole, state governments have a larger measure of autonomy over their routine functions, and the federal government usually intervenes only in cases of extreme corruption or abuse of power.

The other notable point about Mexican local politics is the size and influence of Mexico City.[23] The Federal District itself is home to 9 million people, and the surrounding state of Mexico to a further 12 million. One of the effects of its size has been to create inequalities in the distribution of public investment and in access to public services. The Mexico City area not only contains just over 20 percent of Mexico's population, but it is also the source of more than half of all federal government revenues and receives more than half of all spending on education, health, and public housing. Mexico City is also home to many in the political elite; about 40 percent of all federal government officials are born in Mexico City. No wonder, then, that the job of mayor of Mexico City is considered the second most important in Mexican politics.

ELECTIONS AND PARTIES

The ways in which Mexicans are represented in national politics have changed out of all recognition in recent years. PRI once manipulated the system to ensure continued control, meddled with the results of elections, adjusted the electoral system to give opposition parties enough seats in Congress to keep them cooperative but to deny them power, and was careful to incorporate any groups that might pose a threat to the status quo. In short, key political decisions were made more as a result of competition within PRI than of competition among different parties and interest groups. Elections were used less to determine who would govern than to mobilize support for those who already governed; that is, they were used to legitimize power rather than to distribute power.[24]

Reforms to the electoral system have since allowed opposition parties to win more power. With majorities in both chambers of the legislature, and their victory in the 2000 presidential elections, those parties have now become a more important force in government, and politics has moved outside PRI to a broader public constituency.

THE ELECTORAL SYSTEM

The process of electoral reform first moved into high gear in 1977–1978, when the number of legal political parties grew from four to seven, a mixed single-member and proportional representation electoral system was introduced, and a quarter of the seats in the Chamber of Deputies were effectively reserved for opposition parties (provided that they ran candidates in at least one-third of the electoral districts). Subsequent changes included adding another 180 PR seats in the Chamber of Deputies, doubling the number of Senate seats (from 64 to 128), creating an independent Federal Electoral Institute, introducing tamperproof photo ID cards for voters, and broaching the idea of allowing expatriate Mexicans (there may be as many as ten million) to vote in presidential elections. Most significantly, elections are now subject to such close domestic and foreign scrutiny that it has become difficult for parties to manipulate the outcome.

Several political scientists have theorized that the motive behind all these changes was to build a bipartisan system in which PRI and its main conservative opposition, PAN, became the permanent parties of government, leaving the left-wing Party of the Democratic Revolution (PRD) marginalized.[25] But PAN proved much less willing to cooperate than PRI had hoped, and the PRD has done much better in elections,

TABLE 6.3

Results of Recent Presidential Elections in Mexico

	Candidate	Party*	Number of votes	% share of vote
1994	Ernesto Zedillo Ponce de León	PRI	16,825,607	48.70
	Diego Fernandez de Cavallos	PAN	8,962,141	25.94
	Cuauhtémoc Cárdenas Solórzano	PRD	5,735,217	16.60
	Cecilia Soto Gonzalez	PT	946,656	2.74
	Others		2,079,880	6.02
2000	Vicente Fox Quesada	PAN	15,104,164	43.78
	Francisco Labastida Ochoa	PRI	12,654,930	36.68
	Cuauhtémoc Cárdenas Solórzano	PRD	5,842,589	16.94
	Gilberto Rincón Gallardo	PDS	563,839	1.64
	Others		332,243	0.96

*PRI, Institutional Revolutionary Party; PAN, National Action Party; PDS, Social Democratic Party; PRD, Democratic Revolutionary Party; PT, Workers Party.

creating a fluid situation. The PRI hegemony is gone, Mexican elections are fairer than they have ever been, and voter interest has been piqued.

Mexicans take part in three main sets of elections.

The Presidential Election

The presidential election is held every six years. Each of the major parties fields a single candidate, and there is a straight winner-take-all contest among those candidates. Although PRI once routinely won with an 85 to 95 percent share of the vote, that share has steadily fallen, and in 1994 Ernesto Zedillo became the first PRI candidate to win with less than 50 percent of the vote (see Table 6.3). In the landmark 2000 election, the PRI share of the vote fell to 36.7 percent as Vicente Fox of PAN won the presidency. Turnout at presidential elections has fluctuated from a low of 52 percent (1958) to a high of 77 percent (1994).

The election itself is held in July, but the president does not formally take office until the following December. This gives Mexican presidents one of the longest lame duck periods in the world. In parliamentary systems, new prime ministers typically take office within hours of winning an election; in the United States there is a period of two months between the election and the inaugural. Five months may have suited Mexican presidents during the PRI era, giving incumbents plenty of time to work with successors on ensuring policy continuity and giving PRI officials plenty of time to learn about their new leader. It may also have helped Vicente Fox in 2000 as PAN

FIGURE 6.1

Presidential Electoral Trends in Mexico

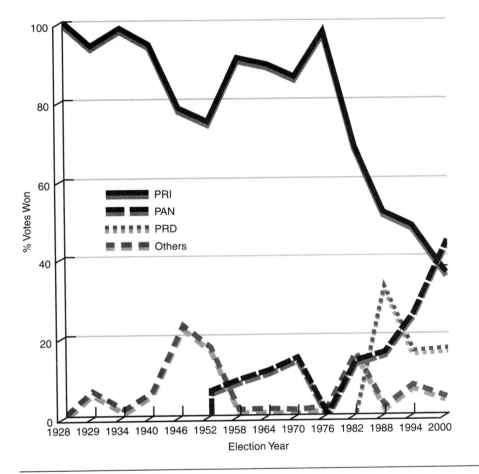

prepared to take office for the first time in its history. But it is doubtful whether such a long period of transition is still useful.

Federal Congressional Elections

Elections to the Senate are held every six years, at the same time as the presidential election, and all Senate seats are contested at the same time. Changes introduced in 1993 reserved three seats in every state for the majority party and gave the fourth seat to the second-placed party.

Elections to the Chamber of Deputies are held every three years. All 500 seats are contested at the same time, but a mixed electoral system is used: 300 seats are decided on the basis of winner-take-all single-member districts, and 200 are decided by

FIGURE 6.2

Legislative Electoral Trends in Mexico

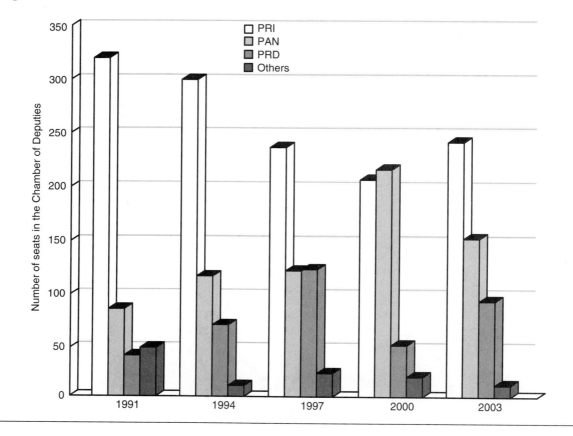

proportional representation (PR). For the PR seats, each party fields a list of candidates, and seats are assigned by a complex formula based on the percentage of the vote won by each party. Voters cast two votes: one for the "uninominal" member for their district and one for a party list of "plurinominal" candidates running at large in the local electoral region, who represent their parties rather than a geographic area. The country is divided into five such regions, and the formula is designed so that no party can win more than two-thirds of the seats altogether. Voter turnout at congressional elections has ranged in recent years as high as 77 percent, but—possibly because of disillusionment with the inter-party bickering of the first three years of the Fox administration—reached an all-time low of 42 percent in 2003.[26]

State and Local Elections

Mexican states operate on their own electoral cycles, which rarely coincide with national cycles. Elections are held for municipal governments (a mayor and council), the single-chamber state assemblies, and state governors (there are no lieutenant governors). As with many such elections, they often provide valuable indications of the possible outcome of national elections. For example, state and local elections in 2003–2005 showed PRI to be making a strong comeback, and to be in contention for the 2006 presidential election.

POLITICAL PARTIES

Mexico has been a multiparty system since 1929, but PRI held a majority in both houses of Congress until 1997, won every presidential election until 2000, and until recently controlled almost every state government. However, five parties won seats in Congress in 1997, and with the PRI stranglehold weakening, the significance of parties has changed. In recent years, three major parties have dominated Mexican politics, with smaller parties playing a supporting role.

Institutional Revolutionary Party (*Partido Revolucionario Institucional*, PRI)

During its heyday, PRI was not a political party in the liberal democratic sense because it was created less to compete for power than to decide how power would be shared; it was not so much a channel for political participation as a means for political control.[27] It kept its grip on power by being a source of patronage, by incorporating the major social and economic sectors in Mexico, by co-opting intellectuals and political rivals on the left, and by mobilizing voters during elections and overseeing the electoral process. In many ways like a Leninist vanguard party, PRI was more a formal part of the state system than an independent arena of political competition. It even identified itself with revolutionary mythology and the symbols of the Mexican state and continues to have the same official colors (red, white, and green) as those in the Mexican national flag.

There were two particular features that made PRI distinctive:

- It had no obvious ideology, but instead shifted with the political breeze and with the changing priorities of its leaders. The **pendulum theory** of Mexican politics described the way that its presidents swung back and forth between conservative and progressive policies.[28] So while Echeverría was progressive, Portillo moved to the right, de la Madrid was a conservative, and Salinas and Zedillo moved back toward the center. Politics in Mexico was not so much about competition among different parties as it was about competition among different factions within PRI—in this sense it was much like the Japanese Liberal Democratic Party. Strands of thought ranged from the conservative traditionalism of the so-called **"dinosaurs"** to the pro-reformism of democrats who wanted more open government.

- Given PRI's dominance, and the power of the executive branch, Mexico was governed by **political centralism.** Paralleling Leninist democratic centralism, this was a phenomenon by which each level of government was weaker and less autonomous than the one above it, and all key policy decisions were made within PRI, as were all choices about who would run for office. Incoming presidents appointed leaders of Congress, PRI, the military, and state-owned industries; they

political centralism
An arrangement by which all key decisions are made within a single, dominant political party.

could veto appointments to lower-level offices; and they could also confirm state governors from PRI, who in turn influenced the appointment of members of courts and state assemblies. Everyone running for office in the name of PRI was chosen by higher levels in the party, and PRI used local political bosses to mobilize peasants and urban workers, encouraging them to vote for PRI.

The signs of PRI's decline can be found as far back as the 1970s, when turnout at elections fell and the party could no longer argue that people had faith in the system. PRI changed the electoral system to encourage greater turnout, but while the plan worked, more people started voting for opposition parties. At the same time, Mexicans were becoming better educated, more affluent, and more worried about Mexico's economic problems, and because PRI had governed for so long, it had no one else to blame. Labor union support for PRI fell, and the number of independent unions grew. The most powerful unions had long been affiliated with PRI and had earned privileges (such as higher wages) in return for their support. But economic problems meant that workers saw their real incomes falling, they became less pliant and more demanding, and an important part of the base of PRI support deteriorated.

In 1989 PRI lost its first state election, and then a political earthquake struck in 1997 when PRI lost its majority in the Chamber of Deputies for the first time in its history. It was still the biggest party, with 239 seats, but the opposition parties among them had 261 seats, which forced PRI to negotiate, bargain, and compromise, something it had never really had to do before. At the 2000 congressional elections its share of Congressional seats fell yet further, it lost its majority in the Senate for the first time, and it lost the jewel in the crown of Mexican politics, the presidency. PRI initially had a crisis of confidence, once again torn between dinosaurs and democrats and failing to stake out a clear place on the political spectrum between PAN on the moderate right and the PRD on the left.[29] But it then found a new role for itself as the party of opposition, and was able to block many of the policy changes planned by Vicente Fox. It also remains the only party that still enjoys nationwide support.

As part of its program to reinvent itself, PRI has tried to appeal to younger voters, who gave most of their votes to PAN in 2000. In the minds of many voters, though, PRI is still associated with corruption. Voters were reminded of this in 2002 when one of the dinosaurs—Roberto Madrazo, a contender for the PRI presidential nomination in 2000—was elected chairman of the party. Madrazo had won the governorship of the state of Tabasco in 1994 in a highly questionable election.[30] In the run-up to the 2003 congressional elections, PRI decided that at least 30 percent of its candidates would be younger than 30 years old and at least half would be women. This tactic seemed to work, because PRI increased its share of congressional seats for the first time in several elections, winning more seats than any other party, if not actually reaching a majority. As this book went to press, Madrazo was seen as the main contender for the PRI nomination for the 2006 presidential race, an indication of how far PRI traditionalists had come to once again dominate the party.

National Action Party (*Partido de Acción Nacional*, PAN)

A moderate right-wing party, PAN was founded in 1939 and until the early 1990s played the role of loyal opposition. Its policies were pro-clerical, pro-American, and pro-business, favoring a limited government role in the economy and the promotion

HOW CORRUPT IS MEXICO?

Corruption is a problem in every country, even in liberal democracies such as the United States, Britain, and Canada, where bribes, kickbacks, misuse of public funds, manipulation of the rules, and nepotism are not unknown. In political systems where power is more concentrated, the opportunities for corruption are greater, so the problem runs deeper. In Mexico, *camarillas*, elitism, and political centralization provide tempting opportunities for political nepotism, while outside government the problem is made worse by the illegal drug trade. The extent of the problem is difficult to measure because it usually involves influence peddling and the trading of favors rather than open bribery or embezzlement, but it persists in government, the bureaucracy, labor unions, and the police, hampering Mexico's efforts to become a successful democracy.

The most infamous recent example of corruption at the highest levels came during the administration of President Carlos Salinas (1988–1994). Once hailed as a world statesman and the leader of a new breed of modernizing Mexican politicians, Salinas came to symbolize continuing doubts about the abilities of the Mexican leopard to change its political spots. The first blemish on his record came in March 1994 when his anointed successor, Luis Donaldo Colosio, was assassinated. Then in September 1994 PRI secretary-general José Francisco Ruiz Massieu was assassinated. In February 1995 the former president's brother Raul was arrested on suspicion of complicity in the

Massieu murder. Then it was found that Raul Salinas had opened Swiss bank accounts into which millions of dollars had been deposited.

Rumors circulated that Carlos Salinas had been involved in a conspiracy either to murder—or to cover up the truth behind the murder of—Colosio, whose independence and public popularity had begun to make PRI hard-liners nervous. It was also clear that a select group of entrepreneurs in Mexico had profited substantially from privatization and had become major sources of funding for PRI. Salinas fled into exile in Ireland, Raul Salinas was found guilty in January 1999 of complicity in the murder of Massieu, and when Carlos Salinas returned briefly to Mexico in June 1999 for a 48-hour visit, he was greeted by so much hostility that he quickly left.

Most of the corruption in Mexico is much more routine and small-scale. The complexity of regulations and laws combines with the inefficiency of bureaucracy to make people conclude that it is cheaper to bribe than to be honest; police and junior officials make matters worse by often demanding *una mordida* (a bite) to take care of business.[31] The Fox administration launched initiatives to address the problem—including sting operations and audits of public bodies—but critics charge that the underlying problems remain. Transparency International ranks Mexico 64th out of 145 countries in terms of how much corruption is perceived to exist among public officials and political leaders.[32]

of private land ownership rather than communal ownership. It was strongest initially among conservative Catholics and northern business interests, and in the urban areas of the wealthier northern and central states, but it was seen as the party of money and drew little support from rural or working-class voters. This began to change in the late 1980s when a new and younger generation of pro-business members joined the party, promoting new policies and irking the old-style party members known as *panistas* who had dominated its leadership until then. It gained the support of urban middle class voters due to disenchantment with PRI and their promises of good government.

In 1989 PAN took control of the government of Baja California Norte, becoming the first opposition party officially to win a state election since the Revolution. It went on to take the state governments of Guanajuato in 1991, Chihuahua in 1992, and Jalisco in 1995. In 1994 PAN candidate Diego Fernandez came in second in the presidential election with nearly 26 percent of the vote, and PAN won the second biggest block of seats in the Chamber of Deputies. Its steady rise to power was capped by its victory in the 2000 presidential election and its gains in Congress, where it became the biggest party. Although PAN remains an essentially conservative party, Vicente Fox has adopted policies more toward the center, putting him at odds with some of his party colleagues. As this book went to press, former interior minister Santiago Creel was being touted as a favorite for the PAN nomination for the 2006 presidential election.

Democratic Revolutionary Party (*Partido de la Revolución Democrática*, PRD)

Founded in 1988, PRD is the major opposition party on the left of Mexican politics. It grew out of mergers involving small left-wing parties, including the Mexican Communist Party (PCM) and the Mexican Worker's Party (PMT), and defectors from PRI. In 1988 the PRD joined with three smaller parties and a group of PRI dissidents to form the National Democratic Front (*Frente Democrática Nacional*, FDN), which provided a platform for the presidential candidacy of Cuauhtémoc Cárdenas and contested that year's congressional elections. Cárdenas had high name recognition, being the son of President Lazaro Cárdenas, the hero of the oil nationalization of the 1930s. Officially, Cárdenas won 31 percent of the vote (the best result ever for an opposition candidate), and he may in fact have won the election, losing only because of fraud. The FDN also won four Senate seats and more than tripled its representation in the Chamber of Deputies.

The 1997 electoral season saw PRD's numbers in the Chamber of Deputies nearly double, from 71 to 124, but Cárdenas came in a disappointing third in the 2000 presidential election, and the party lost more than half its seats in the Chamber of Deputies. It subsequently broke down in factional fighting. One bright spot was the election of Lázaro Cárdenas—grandson of the president and son of the presidential candidate—as state governor of Michoacan in 2001. PRD has also held the office of mayor of Mexico City since 1997: first Cuauhtémoc Cárdenas held the position, and then Andres Lopez Obrador. Obrador stepped down as mayor in July 2005 to run for the PRD nomination for presidency, and was regarded as a favorite for winning the presidency in 2006.

Other Parties

Mexico has long had a cluster of smaller parties, none of which has yet been able to build substantial national support, and some of which have hovered on the brink of extinction. They include the Worker's Party (PT), whose candidate Cecilia Soto Gonzalez in 1994 became the first woman ever to make a showing in a Mexican presidential election, winning nearly 3 percent of the vote. The Popular Socialist Party (PPS), founded in 1948, was for many years the main opposition party on the left, walking a fine line between collaborating with PRI and following instructions from Moscow that communist parties should not form coalitions with other parties. The Mexican Ecological Green Party (PVEM), founded in 1986, surprised almost everyone by winning nine congressional seats in 1997 and finally establishing a national presence. It ran with PAN in an Alliance for Change in 2000 but lost five of its seats. Several smaller parties—notably the Democratic Center Party (CD) and Social Democracy (DS)—were expected to be spoilers in 2000 by drawing votes away from the PRD and PAN, but they ended up having little impact.

POLICIES AND POLICYMAKING

Understanding how public policies are made and implemented is often less a question of knowing the formal rules of government than of appreciating how power is informally manipulated among and within government institutions. In few countries is this more true than Mexico. Policy is supposedly made as a result of the interplay between the federal government, the state governments, and competing political parties, taking into account public opinion. In reality, policy has long been made by a small political elite, through a process that—at least until recently—has been authoritarian, bureaucratic, and corporatist.

Policymaking under PRI could be compared with the workings of an orchestra, with the president as the conductor. Using his formal and informal powers, he worked through his *camarilla* to compel key individuals and institutions to support his program. In large part, his success or failure in determining the tempo of the orchestra depended on his control of the bureaucracy, the party, and the media. At the same time, the president was not a dictator, and political realities demanded that he gauge opinion and consult others within the ruling elite before implementing his program. The tempo of the music depended on the abilities and sensibilities of the lead musicians and the extent to which they followed their conductor.

Much changed after PRI lost the 2000 presidential election. The Fox administration reached out to a broader constituency for policy advice, and because no one party had a majority in Congress, Fox had to take notice of the comments and demands of the political opposition. For the first time, a Mexican president had to amend his policy proposals and objectives to reach a compromise with opposition parties. It is too soon for the old ways to have gone altogether, but the policy process in Mexico has moved several steps closer to the broad-based model of negotiation found in liberal democracies.

ECONOMIC POLICY

Mexican economic policy after the Revolution was driven by two underlying goals:

- Mexico tried to reduce the influence of foreign investors and its dependence on imports of manufactured goods. Along with other Latin American countries, it supported the **Calvo Doctrine** (named for a nineteenth-century Argentinean diplomat), which argues that foreigners involved in economic activities should place themselves on the same footing as the nationals of the country in which they do business, agreeing to abide by its laws, using local courts, and refraining from appealing to their home governments to intervene in disputes.[33] This is a concept that most Americans probably take for granted, but for countries like Mexico—long used to foreigners expecting preferential treatment—it was a novel concept.

■ Mexico worked to achieve sustained economic growth and low inflation. A mixed economy was created, with the government owning and operating key economic sectors (mainly energy production and communications) but also promoting development of the private sector.

These policies worked so well that between 1940 and 1970 it was common to hear talk of a Mexican economic miracle. By the mid-1970s, Mexico had the most successful economy and society of any country where Iberian languages (Spanish and Portuguese) were spoken. It was not very democratic, but it was relatively stable and peaceful, and its economy was growing at a healthy rate. But then came the downturn: poor choices in the wake of the discovery of new oil reserves in the 1960s brought economic problems whose effects are still being felt today. Mexico slipped down the league of Iberian countries, the national debt grew, the purchasing power of the average worker declined, and economic growth in the 1980s was providing less than half the 900,000 new jobs needed every year to keep pace with population growth. Despite an annual growth in GDP of 6 to 7 percent, by the mid-1990s the word *crisis* had begun to appear with depressing frequency in discussions about Mexico's economy.

Over the last decade, the direction of economic policy has shifted significantly.[34] A program of privatization has transformed the economy from one of the most state-dominated and protectionist in Latin America to one of the freest. Mexico is now a vigorous exporter, stability has replaced the economic crises of the 1970s and 1980s, and the government has both created new institutions (such as a competition agency) and given existing institutions (such as the central bank) greater independence. Unfortunately, the benefits of the changes have not yet trickled down to everyone. Poverty is widespread, and there is a significant income gap between the relatively wealthy north of the country and the poorer southern and central regions of Mexico.

The Era of Growth (1940–1970)

Building on the political stability that emerged following the Revolution, Mexico saw sustained economic growth supported by government subsidies to business; protectionism; and the building of basic infrastructure such as roads, irrigation systems, hospitals, and schools. Along with many of its Latin American neighbors, Mexico pursued **import-substitution industrialization**.[35] This strategy involved the use of tariffs, quotas, and other methods to protect domestic industries from the competition posed by imports; the replacement of consumer imports with locally manufactured alternatives; and encouragement by the government to export manufactured goods rather than primary products. This policy brought an average annual economic growth rate of 6 percent, increased the contribution of industry to GDP, and attracted rural people to the cities. The major catalyst in this process was the public sector, which had expanded in the 1930s when the government nationalized the railroads and created Pemex, the state oil company. At the same time, the government provided support for the private sector, giving local entrepreneurs incentives that included subsidies, tariffs on imports, and low tax rates.

Despite the positive changes, Mexico by the late 1960s had painted itself into a corner. By building a large public sector and lowering taxes to promote private investment, the government left itself financially strapped and unable to provide many basic services to the people. Although unemployment was not high, *under* employment was widespread, the income gap between the poor and the wealthy grew, and urban areas attracted a disproportionate share of wealth and investment. To make up some of the shortfall, Mexico began borrowing, and the public debt grew from $810 million in 1960 to more than $6 billion in 1970. By the end of the Echeverría *sexenio* (1970–1976), the debt stood at nearly $20 billion. Inflation grew to 20 to 25 percent, and the peso was overvalued, making Mexican goods expensive abroad.

The Oil Crisis (1978–1985)

Oil was known to the Aztecs and Mayas, but commercial production did not begin in Mexico until the late nineteenth century. With the help of American and British investors, Mexico by the 1920s had become the largest oil producer in the world, accounting for 25 percent of global production. But the role of foreign oil companies was seen as a threat to national independence, so President Lázaro Cárdenas nationalized the oil industry in 1938, creating Pemex and making himself a national hero.

When massive new oil and natural gas reserves were discovered in the Gulf of Mexico in the late 1960s and early 1970s, Mexico was transformed almost overnight into an oil production giant, more than tripling its output and becoming the fourth biggest producer in the world. Unfortunately, Mexico's national debt rose as the government overspent in an effort both to curb unemployment and support the private sector. To make matters worse, domestic political problems combined with the leftward-leaning, anticapitalist postures of the Echeverría regime to lead to a flight of foreign investment. The oil price increases forced by OPEC in the 1970s seemed to offer Mexico a way out of its economic problems, but as Nigeria was also to find to its cost (see Chapter 8), oil is not always the boon it seems. Against the promise of increased profits, the government borrowed heavily from abroad and launched a program of reckless development spending. During the Portillo *sexenio* alone (1976–1982), Mexico borrowed $60 billion.

Western industrialized nations had by then begun to respond to the oil crisis by cutting consumption and investing in alternative energy sources. As a result, oil prices began to fall on the world market, Mexican oil revenues fell, and by 1981 Mexico could not even afford to pay the interest on its debt, which had by then reached $73 billion. Unemployment and inflation grew in tandem, and Mexico's despair was symbolically underlined in 1985 by earthquakes in Mexico City, which not only killed 20,000 people, but also revealed that corruption and kickbacks had led to government buildings being poorly built. This in turn reduced confidence in PRI and added to the support being given to opposition political parties.

Postcrisis Adjustment (1982–)

Hoping to force Mexican companies to become more competitive and to reduce Mexican dependence on oil by promoting non-oil exports, Miguel de la Madrid opened Mexico to greater foreign investment. In the short term, at least, the policy seemed to work. Oil and minerals accounted for 78 percent of the dollar value of

Mexico's exports in 1982; by 2001 they accounted for just 8 percent of exports, and manufactured goods accounted for 90 percent of exports.

maquiladora A factory built in Mexico to manufacture goods for export.

At the heart of this shift was a program launched in 1965 under which factories were built in northern Mexico to make goods for export. Known as **maquiladoras**, these factories allowed foreign corporations to take advantage of cheap Mexican labor and loose environmental standards to make consumer goods for export to the United States (and since 2001 for sale inside Mexico as well). They initially focused on textiles and small electrical appliances, then graduated to more expensive consumer products, including electronic goods, computers, and vehicles parts. Key components were imported duty-free into Mexico, where they were assembled for export. By 2001 the *maquiladoras* employed about 1.2 million people, had helped make Mexico the world's 13th biggest exporter, were providing Mexico with a new source of foreign investment capital, and were exporting nearly $80 billion-worth of goods per year, nearly half of Mexico's total merchandise exports.

Growth in the *maquiladoras* has fallen off in recent years, however, thanks in part to the withdrawal of their duty-free status in 2001, which made imported components more expensive, and thanks in part to the economic downturn in the United States.[36] They have also been controversial because of a combination of poor working conditions, the blatant exploitation of cheap labor, the environmental problems they have caused, and the fact that too few of the profits made by corporations have been reinvested back into local communities in the form of improved housing, roads, and services. And although *maquiladoras* may have helped boost Mexico's industrial sector, they have exacerbated one of the primary worries in Mexican economic policy: the influence of the United States. Consider the following statistics:

- Virtually all of Mexico's external debt—which stood at $140 billion in 2003—is owed to U.S. banks.

- Nearly 90 percent of Mexico's exports go to the United States, and 75 percent of its imports come from the United States.

- U.S. companies account for about 70 percent of all the foreign capital invested in Mexico, and their subsidiaries account for half the manufactured goods exported by Mexico.

One of the effects of Mexican economic dependence on the United States is that the wealthiest states in Mexico are in the north and the poorest in the south. This is partly because workers from northern states are crossing into the United States and bringing their wages back, partly because American tourists visit Mexican border towns in large numbers (700,000 people visit Tijuana from San Diego alone every year), and partly because of the influence of the *maquiladoras*.

Economic reforms over the last decade have had mixed results. A major program of privatization since 1983 has led to the sale or closure of more than 80 percent of the nearly 1,200 businesses once owned by the state, including the two airlines Mexicana and AeroMéxico, the telephone company Telmex, as well as banks and shipyards. The sales have raised $21 billion for the government, but they have also led to the loss of 400,000 jobs, and critics charge that privatization has simply replaced public monopolies with private ones. A prime example is offered by the case of Telmex. Although it was privatized in 1990, it had a monopoly on the long-distance

MEXICO AND FREE TRADE

Inspired in part by the example of the European Union (EU), North Americans for the last decade have been building a free-trade area that—with a population of nearly 425 million and a combined GDP in 2003 of nearly $12.5 trillion—is bigger than the EU. The North American Free Trade Agreement (NAFTA) is not so much a free-trade agreement as a *freer* trade agreement; it is aimed at allowing companies to do business more easily throughout the continent, providing more goods at lower prices, phasing out duties on farm products, making it easier for professionals to live and work in any of the three countries, making companies in the three countries more competitive, and giving each country greater access to each others' markets.

The agreement traces its origins to 1988, when Canada and the United States signed the Canada-U.S. Free Trade Agreement. This was expanded to include Mexico from January 1, 1994, a move that raised many concerns in the United States about loss of jobs, illegal immigration, drug trafficking, and environmental quality. However, NAFTA has raised even more fundamental questions for Mexico:

- It has meant more competition for Mexican companies as Mexico has opened up its markets, and an increased trade deficit because its imports from the United States have grown more quickly than its exports. Membership in NAFTA immediately removed tariffs from nearly half of Mexico's imports from the United States, and by 2009 all U.S.-Mexican

trade is scheduled to be tariff-free. At the same time, there are opportunities for Mexican companies if they can rise to the challenge: They have more access to the U.S. and Canadian markets, more foreign investment is flowing into Mexico, and more jobs are being created in Mexico as U.S. and Canadian companies take advantage of cheap Mexican labor.

- The investment and trade offered by NAFTA may have improved the quality of life for the average Mexican worker, but it has not done so quickly enough to reduce illegal immigration to the United States over the short term.

- NAFTA has meant political and social changes for Mexico because of the links between economic liberalization and democratization. A free-trade partnership with two liberal democracies has brought with it greater pressure for democratic reform. Just as membership in the EU has helped Spain, Portugal, and Greece build stable democracies in the 1980s, and promises to do the same for the EU's newest East European member states, so NAFTA brings Mexico economic benefits that have underpinned its efforts at democratization.

One of the key problems with NAFTA is that it has deepened Mexican dependence on the United States, and so the health of Mexico's economy is driven by the health of the U.S. economy. No surprise, then, that the Fox administration championed the cause of a **free-trade** area covering all of North and South America.

phone market until 1997 and even today dominates the telephone industry. Its controlling shareholder, Carlos Slim, is the richest man in Latin America and has considerable political influence.

Meanwhile, inflation rates have fluctuated from 160 percent in 1987 to just 7 percent in 1994, back up to 17 percent in late 1999, and down again to 5 percent in mid-2005.

free trade The free flow of goods and services between two or more trading partners.

The peso has lost value, falling against the U.S. dollar from 1 peso in 1986 to nearly 11 pesos in 2005. Major investments are needed in infrastructure, Mexicans had less disposable income in 1996 than in 1980, only 55 percent of Mexicans complete their high school education, industrial production fell in the 1990s, and the gap between the rich and the poor has worsened: 37 million Mexicans are still classified as poor or extremely poor (yet Mexico has several U.S. dollar billionaires, most of whom have made their money out of buying newly privatized companies).

The Fox administration continued to free up the market and promote exports, but was too timid for its critics. One of its priorities was to reduce government control over the energy sector, which proved difficult. The 1938 nationalization of the oil industry is still regarded as a landmark event; state ownership of oil and gas, as well as state control over electricity generation and supply, are written into the constitution; and any attempts to privatize the energy industry typically result in a public outcry. However, critics charge that the private sector is better placed to provide the investment so badly needed by the energy industry. The Fox administration made reforms that allowed for more such private investment, but they were only halting steps toward the level of privatization that many think is needed.[37]

FOREIGN POLICY

Mexican foreign policy has traditionally been driven by three major principles: a belief in **universalism**, support for leftist movements in other parts of Latin America, and nonalignment.[38] Universalism can be roughly defined as a willingness to recognize other countries regardless of their ideological leanings. The Estrada Doctrine of 1930 stated that Mexico would give diplomatic recognition to all governments rather than being judgmental about the way they chose to govern themselves. This philosophy long encouraged PRI governments to take a hands-off approach to events around the world.

All three principles pale into insignificance, however, when measured against the single biggest influence on Mexican foreign policy: the United States. No discussion about the relationship between the two is complete without the famous quote by Porfirio Díaz: "Poor Mexico. So far from God and so near to the United States." For many Mexicans, the core goal of foreign policy for decades has been to move out from under the shadow of the United States. As long as the two have been so closely bound in economic terms, however, this has been difficult, and the love-hate relationship has given much of Mexican policy a split personality.

Take, for example, the case of Cuba. While the United States has obsessively (and largely single-handedly) tried to outwit and undermine the Castro regime since it came to power in 1959, Mexico remained a strong supporter of Cuba throughout the cold war. It was the only Latin American country not to break diplomatic ties with Cuba following the Castro revolution, it opposed the U.S. embargo of Cuba, it criticized the 1961 Bay of Pigs invasion, and it helped persuade the Organization of American States (OAS) to lift sanctions against Cuba in 1975. Vicente Fox even made a point of visiting Cuba soon after taking office. At the same time, while refusing to go along with U.S. attempts to isolate Castro, Mexico has helped the CIA track the movements of Cubans in Mexico.

U.S.-Mexican relations have been anything but steady. Although both embarked on independence from roughly similar demographic and territorial bases, the United

States quickly established its superiority. The two countries came into direct conflict over Texas in 1846–1848, resulting in a devastating loss of land for Mexico. Most Americans today know little about the war beyond the myths that have built up around the defense of the Alamo, but Mexicans still carry resentment over "the war of the North American invasion."[39] Mexico's loss gave birth to a strong tradition of nationalism, and concerns about U.S. "imperialism" live on to this day, with criticism coming from both the right and the left of the political spectrum. There is still a strong element of anti-Americanism in Mexico (particularly among elites), and the United States is often used as a scapegoat for many of Mexico's problems. For example, attempting to draw attention away from the failure of his economic policies in 1982, President Echeverría argued that Mexico could not "work and be organized only to have its life blood drained off by the gravitational pull of the colossus to the north."[40]

But the relationship is not as unbalanced as it is often portrayed. For example, there has been a strong historical dependence by the United States on Mexican labor. Mexican workers were first recruited to work on U.S. farms, railroads, and mines in the 1880s, and exports of labor were even institutionalized through the *bracero* program under which—between 1942 and 1964—four million Mexicans were brought to the United States to work in seasonal agriculture. The program ended in 1964 at U.S. insistence, but large numbers of immigrants still cross the border today, most of them illegally. Controlling the flow has always been complicated by the fact that Mexico and the United States share a 2,000-mile (3,220-km) border that is difficult to police.

Controlling what happens on that border has become the key issue that ties the two countries today. Immigration—legal and illegal—has made the border less distinct, and the drug trade has made Mexican stability a critical issue not just for border states but for the entire country. Meanwhile, the cultural balance of the United States is changing thanks to the presence of as many as 21 million Americans of Mexican ancestry (more than 7 percent of the population). The importance to the U.S. of Mexican economic stability was illustrated by U.S.-led bailouts of Mexico in 1982 and again in 1995. Economic problems in Mexico could hurt U.S. corporations and investors, promote civil unrest, and encourage more emigrants to leave for the United States.

The war on terrorism has given Mexico new significance in U.S. policy, and President Fox—rather than trying to keep the Americans at arm's length—has tried to forge a new relationship. He must have been buoyed by the famous utterance by George W. Bush just before the September 2001 terrorist attacks that "The United States has no more important relationship in the world than our relationship with Mexico." With 300 million border crossings between the two countries every year and many places where illegal workers cross into the United States literally within view of border patrols, policing the U.S.-Mexican border is a key element in American national security policy. Vicente Fox lobbied after the attacks for the extension of police, immigration, and customs cooperation among the three members of NAFTA, hoping to reassure the U.S. government that Mexico was not an easy back door into the United States for terrorists. He also pushed for an amnesty for illegal immigrants in the U.S., in return for which he suggested that he would reduce the flow of new immigrants by developing poor regions and by more actively policing

Shanty housing in Tijuana nestles up against a fence marking the Mexican border with the United States. The border has become more porous in recent decades with the movement of an increasing number of Mexicans—legally and illegally—into the United States and the growing economic integration of the two countries.

the border.[41] However, Mexico has so far played no more than a peripheral role in the Bush administration's war on terror.

Beyond its relationship with the United States, Mexico took a more active role in foreign policy under the Fox administration. It helped Colombia in its search for peace by putting pressure on rebels involved in an insurrection, it promoted a multi-national regional development plan for Central America, and was active in its criticism of human rights abuses around the world.

MEXICAN POLITICS IN TRANSITION

Mexico's political development has been driven in recent years by the tensions arising out of two competing sets of forces: the need for economic liberalization against a background of fragile economic growth, and the need for political liberalization against a background of changes in the expectations of Mexican consumers and voters. Mexico seemed to be riding the crest of a wave of modernization and democratic reform in early 1994, but its confidence was shaken by the Chiapas rebellion, the Colosio assassination, and the peso crisis. These all emphasized just how much political and economic change was out of synchronization and brought new attention to the importance of the reforms being made to the electoral process, which resulted in PRI losing the presidency in 2000. But the reforms have come, the clock cannot be turned back, and Mexico is well on its way to absorbing the kind of changes that have moved it further away from its authoritarian one-party past.

The overwhelming presence of the United States has had mixed results for Mexico in the past, but the growth of NAFTA raises the possibility of new economic opportunities for Mexico that will increase the pressures for democratization and economic liberalization. Mexico, which has long had many of the classic features of a newly industrializing country, has the potential to move closer to the realms of liberal democracy if it can balance economic growth, political reform, and the needs of its growing population. It is a substantial regional power, and its membership in NAFTA and the OECD shows just how far it has traveled in its journey away from the old image of the Third World and into the ranks of newly industrializing countries.

KEY TERMS

Calvo Doctrine
camarilla
Chamber of Deputies
Chiapas
corporatism
dedazo
diaspora
dinosaurs
economic nationalism
import-substitution
   industrialization

Institutional
   Revolutionary Party
machismo
maquiladoras
Mexican Revolution
mestizo
North American Free
   Trade Agreement
   (NAFTA)
National Action Party
Pemex

pendulum theory
political centralism
políticos
porfiriato
presidentialism
sexenio
técnicos
universalism

KEY PEOPLE

Cuauhtémoc
   Cárdenas
Lázaro
   Cárdenas

Porfirio Díaz
Vicente Fox
Roberto Madrazo
Andres Lopez Obrador

Carlos Salinas
Ernesto Zedillo

STUDY QUESTIONS

1. Why have the United States and Mexico developed such different sets of political values?

2. What are the implications for the United States and Mexico of the rapid growth of the Mexican diaspora north of the Rio Grande?

3. Is there an element of *machismo* in politics in liberal democracies?

4. Compare and contrast the costs and benefits of a single six-year term for a president with two four-year terms.

5. Should Mexico adopt the U.S. model of holding staggered elections for the Senate?

6. Is democratization in Mexico more a result of decisions made by PRI or a result of pressures arising out of domestic and international economic change?

7. Compare and contrast the handicaps that face the Mexican Congress with those that face legislatures in countries like the United States and Russia in their relations with their respective executives.

8. How does the role of PRI in the Mexican political system compare to the role of the Liberal Democratic Party in Japan?

9. To what extent does corporatism apply to liberal democracies such as the United States or Canada?

10. What would it take for Mexico to become a liberal democracy?

MEXICO ONLINE

Presidency of the Republic: www.presidencia.gob.mx
Senate of the Republic: www.senado.gob.mx
Web sites for the presidency and the federal Senate, both available in English. The Web site for the **Chamber of Deputies** (www.cddhcu.gob.mx) is available in Spanish only.
Mexican Political Parties: www.georgetown.edu/pdba/Parties/Resumen/Mexico/desc.html
Links to the Web sites of Mexico's major political parties, most of which are in Spanish.
Consulate General of Mexico in New York: www.consulmexny.org
Offers links to official news and information on the government, the economy, and Mexican culture.
Latin American Network Information Center: lanic.utexas.edu/la/Mexico
Mexico Channel: www.trace-sc.com
Megasites that both offer links to a wide variety of sites on government, the economy, and the media.
Mexico Daily: www.mexicodaily.com
International news and news from Mexico in English.

FURTHER READING

Camp, Roderic A., *Politics in Mexico: The Democratic Transformation*, 4th Ed. (New York: Oxford University Press, 2002). A general introduction to history and politics in Mexico.

Levy, Daniel C., with Emilio Zebadua, *Mexico: The Struggle for Democratic Development* (Berkeley, CA: University of California Press, 2001). A guide to the political, economic, and social changes taking place in Mexico today.

Oppenheimer, Andres, *Bordering on Chaos: Guerrillas, Stockbrokers, Politicians, and Mexico's Road to Prosperity* (Boston: Little, Brown, 1996). A controversial study of events surrounding Chiapas and the Colosio murder, written by a Pulitzer Prize–winning journalist with the *Miami Herald*.

Preston, Julia, and Samuel Dillon, *Opening Mexico: The Making of a Democracy* (New York: Farrar, Straus and Giroux, 2004). An assessment of recent changes in Mexico, by two journalists from the New York Times.

Rubio, Luis, and Susan Kaufman Purcel (Eds.), *Mexico Under Fox* (Boulder, CO: Lynne Rienner, 2004). An edited collection of studies of political and economic change in Mexico under Vicente Fox.

COMPARATIVE EXERCISE

CONSTITUTIONS

One of the key ideas in Mexican politics is that of the "continuing" revolution. This stems from the argument that the Mexican constitution is a work in progress and that many of its core principles still have not been fully applied. Was this simply an excuse used by PRI to explain away its abuses of power, or is it a genuine explanation of the problems that continue to complicate Mexico's progress toward becoming a liberal democracy? In this Comparative Exercise we will look at constitutions and their record in different societies.

A constitution is a set of rules that typically does at least four things: sets out the general principles by which a country is governed, outlines the structure of government, establishes the procedures used in the political process (such as elections), and outlines the powers of government and the rights of citizens. Most countries have a written or codified constitution, with notable exceptions being Britain and Israel. In other words, the constitution usually takes the form of a structured physical document.

Constitutions do not contain all the rules of government and in fact are usually rife with generalities and ambiguities. They also must be adapted to meet the changing needs of the societies to which they apply, so they are usually supplemented with amendments, laws, and judicial interpretations. Much of what government does also comes down simply to unwritten understandings about acceptable and unacceptable behavior, and political activity is often driven by customs and traditions, few (if any) of which are actually committed to paper. There is nothing in the U.S. Constitution, for example, about political parties or interest groups, yet it is understood that they are a normal and acceptable part of the political process.

There are three key performance indicators for all constitutions: How old are they? How many times have they been amended? and How big is the gap between the principles they espouse and the way government and politics function in reality?

- **Liberal democracies.** Most do well on all three measures. The U.S. Constitution probably does best of all, given that it was the first written constitution in the world (dating back to 1788) and that the U.S. Supreme Court routinely provides dozens of interpretations every year on the meaning of its articles and principles. Not everyone always agrees with these interpretations, but universal agreement is impossible: There will always be debate, for example, on the meaning of freedom of "speech," on whether some of the rights listed in the constitution are relevant any longer (such as the "right" to bear arms, which may or may not be dependent on the existence of militias), and on whether or not some of the procedural rules of government should be changed, such as placing limits on the terms of elected officials.

  Longevity by itself is not a measure of performance; several liberal democracies have undergone relatively recent changes that have led them to rewrite their constitutions. Germany had a new constitution forced on it by the occupying powers after World War II, and France developed an entirely new political system in 1958, adopting its 17th constitution since the 1789 revolution. However, there is nothing to suggest that either the German or the French constitutions are in danger of collapsing, and in fact they may well be the best constitutions that either country has ever had. The same is true of Greece, Portugal, and Spain, all three of which threw off authoritarian regimes in the mid-1970s, adopted new constitutions, and have since enjoyed unprecedented levels of political stability.

- **Communist states.** These did relatively poorly on all three measures. The Soviet Union, for example, had four constitutions in 59 years, they were routinely manipulated by rulers such as Stalin as a means of achieving political and ideological goals, and the gap between their principles and political reality was substantial. China has had four constitutions since 1949, and each has also been changed to reflect the different thinking of new leaders. Both countries included impressive lists of individual rights in their constitutions but also inserted loopholes that made it possible to justify infringements on those rights.

- **Poorer states.** The role and performance of constitutions in poorer or less stable countries varies dramatically. On one hand, the record in NICs has improved: Although many of them have relatively young constitutions, the trends suggest that they are unlikely to collapse or to be rewritten any time soon. In terms of longevity, Mexico is one of the leaders in this group—or actually in any group—with a constitution that is now nearly 90 years old, but it has also been amended so often as to raise questions about the extent to which the original constitution really applies any more. On the other hand, several Latin American states that have experienced persistent political instability have also experienced many short-lived constitutions: The

Dominican Republic has had 25, Haiti has had more than 20, El Salvador has had 16, and Honduras has had 12.

The most important performance indicator of a constitution is the gap between theory and practice. Many constitutions include noble principles and objectives, but they mean little unless they are respected and actually applied. The U.S. Constitution, for example, opens by talking of the need to "establish Justice, ensure domestic Tranquility, … promote the general Welfare, and secure the Blessings of Liberty," but it was written by a group of white men, several of whom owned slaves, and black men were denied the right to vote for nearly 90 years after its ratification, and women for more than 120 years. And despite all the claims made about liberty, freedom, and democracy in the United States, the American model of democracy has important imperfections (see Critical Issues, page 68). However, the principles of the Constitution are promoted and defended (if not always perfectly) by an independent constitutional court that is subject to relatively little political interference. This cannot be said about more authoritarian regimes in other parts of the world, where governments often interfere with the work of courts, intimidate their members, and try to force through amendments that would strengthen their powers relative to their citizens.

INDIA

INDIA: QUICK FACTS

Official name: Republic of India (Bharat Janarajya)

Capital: New Delhi

Area: 1,230,540 square miles (3,174,800 sq. km) (just over one-third the size of the United States)

Languages: Hindi (spoken by 31 percent) and English are the official languages, but there are 16 major languages and 1,400 local dialects

Population: 1,033 million

Population density: 888 per square mile (341 per sq. km.)

Population growth rate: 1.5 percent

POLITICAL INDICATORS

Freedom House rating: Free

Date of state formation: August 15, 1947

System type: Federal republic

Constitution: Published 1950

Administration: Federal; 25 states with a large degree of self-government and 7 union territories

Executive: Prime minister and cabinet

Legislature: Bicameral: Rajya Sabha (250 members, mostly elected for six-year terms by state legislatures) and Lok Sabha (545 members, elected for maximum five-year terms by all eligible voters)

Party structure: Multiparty

Judiciary: Supreme Court (26 members appointed by president after consultation with courts)

Head of state: A. P. J. Abdul Kalam (2002–)

Head of government: Manmohan Singh (2004–)

ECONOMIC INDICATORS

GDP (2004): $692 billion

Per capita GDP: $620

Distribution of GNP: Services 51 percent, industry 27 percent, agriculture 22 percent

Urban population: 28 percent

SOCIAL INDICATORS

HDI ranking: 127

Infant mortality rate: 63 per 1,000

Life expectancy: 63.4 years

Literacy: 68 percent of men aged 15 and older, 44 percent of women

Religions: Hinduism (83 percent), Islam (11 percent), Christianity (2 percent), and Sikhism (2 percent)

INTRODUCTION

India is a land of dramatic contrasts. It has one of the world's oldest cultures, yet it has been an independent nation-state only since 1947. It is the world's largest democracy, yet it has so many social divisions that it seems constantly to hover on the brink of disintegration. It is a nuclear power with its own space program, yet most of its people still live a simple village life. Such apparent contradictions help explain why the West has been fascinated by India for more than 400 years. It was this fascination that led Britain to colonize India and then describe it as the "jewel in the crown" of the British Empire, and this fascination has continued since independence with the charisma and tragedy surrounding the Nehru-Gandhi dynasty, the remarkable size and diversity of India, and its growing importance in the world.

The common Western image of India as crowded and poor is only partly true. It is certainly crowded, with more than one billion people living in an area one-third the size of the United States. And it is certainly poor, with a per capita GDP of just $620. Three-fourths of its people live off agriculture, many of them mired in abject poverty. At the same time, though, India is a multiparty democracy, with a growing middle class and an expanding economy. It not only feeds itself but also is a net food exporter. It is a nuclear power with a bigger consumer market than any European country, and economic liberalization has led to accelerating industrial growth. Like China, India has the potential to become one of the economic superpowers of the twenty-first century, but to do that it must first build political stability.

In social terms, India is home to almost every division known to humanity:

- **Urban-rural.** India is a mainly rural society in which 72 percent of the people live in villages. New agricultural technology has reached many of the rural areas, and so have television and consumer products, but life for many villagers remains tied to the villages in which they live. At the same time, India has some of the biggest and most crowded cities in the world, such as Mumbai (formerly Bombay), Calcutta, Delhi, Chennai (formerly Madras), and Bangalore. Cities cannot keep up with the demand for housing, sanitation, and transport, making life miserable for the poor and frustrating for the middle class.

- **Cultural.** Nowhere else has colonialism forced so many cultures to live together. There are three racial strains (Aryan, Dravidian, and proto-Australoid), 16 major languages, 30 additional languages each with one million speakers or more, and many different scripts. There are two official languages: English and Hindi—the latter is spoken by 31 percent of the population, mainly in the north. Disputes over state and religious boundaries have been common since independence, leading to secessionist movements and insurrections.

- **Religious.** Despite an official separation of religion and the state, religious conflict regularly spills over into politics. More than 80 percent of Indians are Hindu, but India also has a large Muslim community (11 percent of the population) and a vocal Sikh minority (2 percent). Religious disputes were behind the assassinations of Mahatma Gandhi, the champion of Indian independence, in 1948 and of

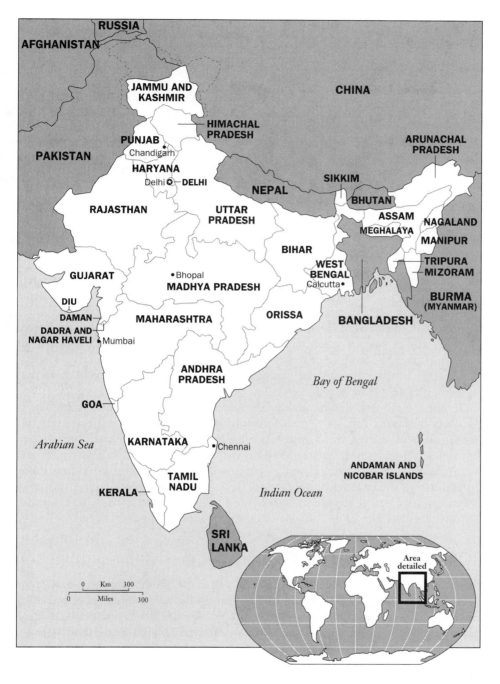

RUSSIA
AFGHANISTAN
PAKISTAN
CHINA

JAMMU AND
KASHMIR

HIMACHAL
PRADESH

PUNJAB
• Chandigarh
HARYANA
Delhi ⊙—DELHI

ARUNACHAL
PRADESH

RAJASTHAN

NEPAL

SIKKIM

BHUTAN

UTTAR
PRADESH

ASSAM
MEGHALAYA

NAGALAND
MANIPUR

BIHAR

WEST
BENGAL
Calcutta •

TRIPURA
MIZORAM

GUJARAT

• Bhopal
MADHYA PRADESH

BANGLADESH

BURMA
(MYANMAR)

DIU
DAMAN
DADRA AND
NAGAR HAVELI • Mumbai

MAHARASHTRA

ORISSA

ANDHRA
PRADESH

Bay of Bengal

GOA

Arabian Sea

KARNATAKA
• Chennai

TAMIL
NADU

ANDAMAN AND
NICOBAR ISLANDS

KERALA

Indian Ocean

SRI
LANKA

| 0 | Km | 300 |
| 0 | Miles | 300 |

Area
detailed

Prime Minister Indira Gandhi in 1984; they have been behind continuing tensions between India and Pakistan over the disputed territory of **Kashmir;** and they have been behind ongoing public violence within India; an estimated 2,000 Muslims died in violence in the western state of Gujarat in February–March 2002 alone. The significance of religion has come to the fore in recent years with growing support for the Hindu nationalist Bharatiya Janata Party.

caste A system of social and economic divisions that pervades the Indian political system.

- **Social class.** The most important of India's social divisions is **caste.** A complex Hindu hierarchy, caste was originally based on family and occupation and went on to become a form of social apartheid, with the behavior of castes restricted and controlled, no intermarriage allowed across castes, and different jobs carried out by particular castes. The more than 3,000 castes and subcastes can be generally aggregated into four broad categories: the Brahmins (who produce most of India's political leaders), the Kshatriyas (warriors), the Vaisyas (traders and merchants), and the Sudras (menial laborers).[1]

At the bottom of the heap are India's 150 million Dalits (formerly called **untouchables**), who were once regarded as almost subhuman and who performed service jobs such as laundry, scavenging, sewage disposal, and removal of the dead. The status of untouchable was formally abolished with the 1950 constitution, but a controversial affirmative action policy has reserved jobs, scholarships, government positions, and even seats in parliament for the so-called "scheduled castes." Recent suggestions that the number of reserved positions be increased led to large-scale rioting by the "forward castes" and remains a bone of contention today, as well as sharpening caste identities.

Despite these divisions and the regular threats they pose to national stability, India is politically vibrant. It has a written constitution that is generally respected, has had 14 free elections and 14 prime ministers since 1947, and has more than half a dozen significant national political parties and many more regional and local parties. Party competition is keen, voter turnout is high, and there is an extensive free press. Unfortunately, the number of political parties has prevented any one from winning a clear majority in recent years, which has led to the creation of unstable coalitions and threatens to undermine India's continuing economic success.

POLITICAL DEVELOPMENT

India has been an independent nation-state only since 1947, but its culture is one of the oldest, most complex, and most sophisticated on Earth, with a history that goes back more than 5,000 years. Unlike many other former colonies, where precolonial political values were largely subsumed to those of the new imperial power, many of the links between the traditional and the modern can still be found in Indian politics today.

The Hindu Heritage

Before the arrival of Europeans, the Indian subcontinent was made up of numerous principalities, kingdoms, and empires. A civilization that paralleled that of Egypt in importance emerged in the Indus River Valley between about 4000 and 2500 B.C. Beginning in about 1500 B.C., waves of nomadic Indo-Aryans began arriving in the northern and central plains from the Caucasus, pushing the native Dravidians further south. The fusion of Aryan and Dravidian culture produced a philosophical system known as the Vedanta; although this is based on a belief in an all-pervasive cosmic system and the unity of all forms of life, the Aryans also imposed a hierarchical structure on Indian society in the form of the caste system.[2] These beliefs formed the foundation of **Hinduism,** now the world's third largest religion after Christianity and Islam.

A second religious and social influence came in the fifth century B.C. with the teachings of Siddhartha Gautama (c. 563–483 B.C.), better known as Buddha. He spent much of his life wandering through northern India teaching his philosophy, which included a rejection of the caste system. By about 250 B.C., what is now India was mainly Buddhist,[3] but Hindu priests countered the influence of Buddhism by arguing that it was subservient to—and part of—Hindu belief. Much of India was unified between 321 and 184 B.C. by the emperor Ashoka and later reunited by the Gupta dynasty (A.D. 300–500).

The most significant alien influence began in about 1000, when Muslims invaded the area. By the early sixteenth century, most of the northern half of India was under the control of the Mughals, a dynasty created by descendants of Genghis Khan. The caste system was strengthened as a defense against Muslim influence, and Hindus refused to cooperate with the invaders on the imposition of taxes and the appropriation of their kingdoms, a policy that was to be paralleled by Mahatma Gandhi's strategy of civil disobedience in the twentieth century.[4] Throughout, India remained a village society, divided into competing kingdoms and principalities but with central authority barely affecting the life of the average villager. Villages were self-sufficient and run by councils of elders, or *panchayat.* Communal self-sufficiency was another idea that Gandhi tried to revive during the drive for independence.

The British Raj (18th Century to 1947)

By the beginning of the nineteenth century, Mughal power in India had all but disintegrated, undermined by internal rebellion. Unlike Japan, which had been united under a strong central authority and so was able to resist European traders, India had a power vacuum into which the Europeans moved relatively easily. Attracted by the prospects of trade, Britain, Portugal, France, and Holland competed for influence in the region, but it was the British who emerged as the dominant power; this was confirmed with the defeat of a Bengali army at Plassey in 1757 by Robert Clive, remembered by history as Clive of India.

From their base in Bengal in the east, the British eventually moved into most of what are now India, Pakistan, Bangladesh, Sri Lanka, and Burma. In some cases they used direct control, and in others they allowed existing leaders to keep power. By setting rulers and religious groups against one another and establishing military dominance, Britain had brought the entire subcontinent under its direct or indirect control by the early 1850s. The creation of the **British Raj** (*raj* is Hindi for reign) was achieved with a remarkably small number of people. At no time in the nineteenth century were there more than 65,000 British troops or 500 administrators in India, and less than 60 percent of India came under direct British control. Until 1857, India was not even directly ruled by the British government but was administered (and in a sense "owned") by the 1,700 shareholders of the East India Company, founded in 1600.

TABLE 7.1

India: A Timeline

Year	Event
1600	Establishment of the British East India Company
1757	Battle of Plassey
1857–1858	Indian Mutiny
1858	Britain assumes direct control over India from the East India Company
1885	Indian National Congress founded
1919	Amritsar massacre
1935	Government of India Act
1942	Launch of the "Quit India" campaign
1947	(August) Independence and partition of India and Pakistan
1948	Mahatma Gandhi assassinated; independence of Burma and Ceylon (the latter renamed Sri Lanka in 1972); dispute with Pakistan over Kashmir
1950	New constitution comes into force; India becomes a republic
1952	First elections in independent India; launch of the first five-year plan
1962	Border conflict with China
1965	War with Pakistan over Kashmir
1971	Pakistan civil war, India-Pakistan war, and creation of Bangladesh
1974	India explodes underground nuclear device
1975–1977	State of emergency; first-ever non-Congress government elected 1977
1984	Indira Gandhi assassinated
1989	Congress loses more than half its seats in general election, and BJP increases its representation from 2 seats to 86; National Front comes to power
1991	Rajiv Gandhi assassinated
1992	(December) Destruction of mosque at Ayodhya leads to widespread rioting, 1,700 deaths and 5,500 injuries
1996	(January) Charges are brought against politicians involved in one of India's biggest ever bribery scandals; (May) voters looking for change inflict major losses on the Congress Party in general election; a BJP-led government soon falls and is replaced by a leftist-regionalist United Front coalition
1998	(March) General election brings BJP-led coalition to power; (May) India carries out five nuclear tests, Pakistan responds with six; U.S. imposes sanctions on both
1999	(April) BJP-led government falls; (May–July) fighting between India and Pakistan over Kashmir; (October) general election returns BJP-led government to power; military coup in Pakistan
2000	(May) Indian population reaches one billion
2001	(January) An estimated 25,000 people die in earthquake in northwestern India; (December) police and gunmen killed in suicide attack on Indian Parliament
2002	(February) More than 800 people killed in Hindu-Muslim violence
2003	Muslim terrorists suspected of exploding two bombs in Mumbai, killing 50
2004	(May) Congress Party returns to power in coalition government; (September) India applies for permanent seat on UN Security Council

Under the British Raj, India was united for the first time and social reforms were made, leading to the abolition of traditions such as *suttee* (the burning of widows on the funeral pyres of their husbands) and *thagi* (institutionalized robbery and murder, from which the English word *thug* is derived). Western education, science, and technology were introduced; English was introduced as the lingua franca; a railroad and communications network was developed; and investments were made in industry and agriculture.

The Raj was shaken by the outbreak of the Indian Mutiny in 1857. British rule relied heavily on a huge army of Indian soldiers (or *sepoys*), many of whom were devoted Hindus or Muslims. Already concerned about the spread of Christian influence, the *sepoys* were even more alarmed in 1857 when they were issued new rifles that used cartridges wrongly rumored to be greased with a mixture of cow fat (which offended Hindus) and pig fat (which offended Muslims). The refusal of some troops to accept the cartridges led to the outbreak of the Indian Mutiny, which lasted 18 months, cost several thousand deaths, and saw appalling savagery on both sides. Although Britain now took over direct administration of India from the East India Company and Queen Victoria was declared empress of India in 1877, the cracks in the edifice of the Raj had begun to show.

The emerging Indian middle class was particularly unwilling to accept foreign domination. In 1885 the Indian National Congress was founded, not so much to campaign for independence as to win greater self-determination and the integration of India into the British Empire on more equal terms. Indians, like Americans before them, did not want to be treated as second-class citizens. The Congress was initially moderate and even had a member elected to the British House of Commons, but as Britain rejected its demands for equality, it became more militant.

A turning point came in April 1919, when Indian troops under British command fired on demonstrators defying a ban on public meetings in the city of Amritsar. According to the official count, nearly 380 were killed and 1,200 wounded. Duly outraged, the Congress—inspired by Mahatma Gandhi—switched from demanding autonomy to campaigning for independence, using nonviolent civil disobedience, or noncooperation. This strategy cut to the heart of the British administrative system, which was based on ruling India mainly through Indians themselves.

India was given a large measure of self-government in 1935 with the Government of India Act. In 1937 elections were held and a new constitution was published, but these changes came too late for the nationalists, who began calling for full independence. Their plans were complicated, however, by divisions between India's Hindus and Muslims. Gandhi and his main associate, Jawaharlal Nehru, hoped that the Congress could represent all Indians and achieve a united, independent India, but Muslims were doubtful about living in a Hindu-dominated state. Their cause was represented by Muhammed Ali Jinnah (1876–1948), leader of the Muslim League. Gandhi had refused to recognize the League's claims to represent Muslims, but Jinnah argued that the Muslims were a nation and refused to cooperate with the "Quit India" movement launched by Gandhi against the British in 1942.

Britain was now faced with two conflicting demands: Jinnah wanted India partitioned into Hindu and Muslim states and then given independence, while Gandhi wanted India to be given independence and to be allowed to settle the religious problem itself. Against a background of mounting violence between Hindus and

MAHATMA GANDHI

One of the greatest political figures of the twentieth century, Mohandas Karamchand Gandhi (1869–1948) was also one of the few leaders of modern independence movements never to have held elective office. Popularly known as the Mahatma (or "great soul"), he was the spiritual leader of India during its struggle for independence.

Born in 1869, Gandhi was trained as a lawyer in Britain. In 1893 he was invited to South Africa to represent South African Indians against discriminatory laws; in that cause, he began experimenting with a brand of nonviolent and passive resistance he described as *satyagraha* (roughly translated as "soul force" or "truth force"). He returned to India in 1915 and by 1920 had emerged as the undisputed leader of the Indian nationalists. Recognizing the administrative and military power of the British, he agitated for Indian independence by using *satyagraha*. Through resistance, noncooperation, hunger strikes, and other symbolic acts for which he was repeatedly imprisoned, he drew attention to the injustices of British rule and focused the attention of a mass movement on achieving independence.

Gandhi also advocated social change among Indians themselves but found himself having to walk a careful line between campaigning for independence and trying to encourage Hindus and Muslims to live together. Before and after independence, violence broke out between Hindus and Muslims, prompting Gandhi to go on hunger strikes until the violence ended. He campaigned for an improvement in the status of untouchables (to the consternation of his caste-ridden Hindu following) and advocated personal simplicity and national self-sufficiency. Clothed in his trademark loincloth and shawl, he would spend at least 30 minutes every day making homespun cloth. The spinning wheel became his symbol and later became part of the national flag of independent India.

India finally won its independence in August 1947, but Gandhi felt this was a hollow victory given partition and the religious and social divisions of India. Five months later, a militant Hindu, disgusted at Gandhi's attempts to maintain peace between Hindus and Muslims, shot the 79-year-old Mahatma to death. India's first prime minister, Jawaharlal Nehru, declared: "The light has gone out of our lives and there is darkness everywhere."

Muslims, Britain concluded that the only option was partition, and so on August 15, 1947, the separate states of India and Pakistan became independent. Partition gave rise to one of the biggest human migrations in history, with Muslims moving to Pakistan and Hindus to India, and the two groups occasionally coming to blows with each other. Altogether, more than 12 million people migrated, and as many as 1 million died in the process.

Nonetheless, 20 million Hindus remained in Pakistan and 40 million Muslims in India, which still has the third biggest Muslim population of any country in the world (surpassed only by Indonesia and Pakistan). Pakistan was faced with the additional problem of forging a new nation out of two separate pieces of territory: West Pakistan, with 34 million people, and East Pakistan, with 46 million people living in an area one-fifth the size of West Pakistan. To complicate the issue, India and Pakistan disagreed over the future of Kashmir, which had a Hindu leader but a predominantly Muslim population.

Independent India (1947–Present)

India entered independence torn by religious turmoil and facing the challenge of forging a nation out of many hundreds of princely states. A new constitution was written, and with its adoption in 1950, the last ties with the British crown were cut and India became a republic. The princes were made to give up their political powers, the old British provinces were abolished, and a federal system was introduced.

India's priorities since independence have been self-reliance, economic development, political stability, and stabilizing relations with its neighbors, especially Pakistan. The Nehru administration (1947–1964) followed a moderately socialist economic line, with a limited land reform program and a series of five-year plans that emphasized the growth of heavy industry. An agricultural program was also launched, which eventually made India self-sufficient in food. But these achievements were offset by India's population growth, its religious and social divisions, and conflicts with its neighbors. India has fought three wars with Pakistan over territorial issues; fought a war with China in 1962; became involved in the Pakistan civil war in 1971; has faced continuing conflict over Kashmir; has seen border disputes with China, which claims part of northern India; has become involved in Sri Lanka's internal problems, which led to Indian peacekeeping troops being stationed in Sri Lanka in 1987; has faced domestic conflict between Hindus, Muslims, and Sikhs; and has had to wrestle with the bigger issue of defining a place for itself in the global system.

India's government was dominated for more than 40 years by the **Congress Party,** which has itself been dominated by a family dynasty: Jawaharlal Nehru was prime minister for nearly 17 years (1946–1964), and his daughter Indira Gandhi (no relation to the Mahatma) was the major character in national politics for the next 20 years (nearly 10 of which she spent as prime minister). She was grooming her son Sanjay to replace her, but when he was killed in a 1980 plane crash, she recruited her son Rajiv to replace her. Following her 1984 assassination, Rajiv took over as prime minister. With his assassination in May 1991, the influence of the family briefly declined, but Congress eventually recruited as its leader Rajiv's Italian-born widow, Sonia; she turned down the opportunity to become prime minister in 2004.

In 1996 the reforming government of Prime Minister Narasimha Rao was found to be riddled with scandal and national elections left the Indian parliament divided among nearly 30 political parties. A five-party coalition government fell in just 12 days and was replaced by a 13-party coalition in which communist and regionalist parties had much influence. It collapsed after 10 months, showing that national government was critically divided at a time when India needed firm leadership, political stability, and economic reform.

The most notable recent developments in Indian politics have been the rise of the Hindu nationalist **Bharatiya Janata Party (BJP)** and the fragmentation of the party system. Where Congress was once dominant and there were a few much smaller parties in opposition, 39 parties were elected to the Indian parliament in 1999, and 24 of them became part of the BJP-led government. Party politics has since settled down into three competing blocs: Congress and its allies, the BJP and its allies, and parties of the left. But all three blocs depend on regional parties intent on putting local interests above those of the general national interest.

Under its leader Atal Behari Vajpayee, the BJP moderated its policy positions, and the talk of militant Hindu nationalism that circulated in the early 1990s all but disappeared. This is not to say that India has not taken an assertive role in foreign policy, however: An invasion of Kashmir in May 1999 by Pakistani and Afghan irregulars led to a two-month conflict, with a death toll estimated to be in the thousands. Although Kashmir continues to be a flashpoint in Indo-Pakistani relations, much more worrisome has been the development of nuclear weapons by both countries. When India carried out five nuclear tests in May 1998, Pakistan responded with six, and both countries were heavily criticized by world leaders. Among the many regional disputes that have come to the fore in the post–cold war world, the persistent disagreement between India and Pakistan ranks among the most potentially dangerous.

India Today

There is no question about India's potential, but there are many questions about how long it will take for that potential to be fulfilled. It has most of the trappings of an emergent democracy, but it also has many problems. These include religious and class conflict, widespread poverty, too many political parties, persistent political corruption, a bureaucracy that is often slow and cumbersome, and a government that is heavily involved in the economy.

The divisions were emphasized in the structure of the government of Atal Behari Vajpayee, a multiparty coalition whose member-parties had so many different platforms and priorities that the work of government was routinely interrupted by internal squabbles. Instead of making progress on badly needed economic reforms, the government found itself torn by small parties driven by vested interests. The opposition Congress Party used the opportunity to make its own attempts to undermine the authority of the BJP-led administration. At the same time, the government was able to make little headway on its most critical foreign policy challenge—the ongoing dispute with Pakistan over the province of Kashmir (see Political Debates, p. 362).

The 2004 elections saw the defeat of the BJP and the return to power of Congress, albeit as part of a 12-party minority coalition. Much was expected of the new government—led by former finance minister Manmohan Singh—but it proved cautious, and critics charged that it failed to produce the economic changes needed to ensure that India caught up with China, which continued to attract much more foreign investment. To be fair, though, a multiparty government will always have difficulty achieving its goals, because of the need to make sure that all partners in the coalition are kept satisfied. The moderate style of the Singh government stood in contrast to the sometimes radical Hindu nationalism of the BJP, but—for many—it was not moving fast enough to bring badly needed change.

POLITICAL CULTURE

Political culture is easiest to define when a political system has settled features and values. Even after nearly 60 years of independence, however, politics in India are unpredictable. Not only do social divisions threaten the viability of the state, but the party system has seen constant change, a modern urban society coexists with a traditional village society, and the role of Hinduism in politics has still not been fully settled. Despite the uncertainties, there are several distinct facets to Indian political culture.

A Dominant State

The most prominent feature of Indian political culture in recent years has been the emergence of a dominant state system, which has come to affect every sphere of Indian life and has promoted a pan-Indian middle-class consciousness at the expense of traditional culture.[5] This has led to a political system based increasingly around popularity contests and American-style elections that have become quasi-presidential. Nowhere has personality more obviously been an issue than in the role played for several decades by the Nehru-Gandhi dynasty; the strength of the dynasty suggested that personality was more important than ideology or administrative ability. But the dominance of the state has not been enough to prevent social, economic, caste, and religious fragmentation.

A Village Society

All societies have their traditional elements, which have varying degrees of influence on politics. Despite the dominance of the modern Indian state and central government, most Indians still live a simple village life that is largely bypassed by national politics, except during elections, when candidates fleetingly become interested in the village vote. Television, satellite dishes, cell phones and the Internet may have reached many villages, but life for average villagers still extends no more than a few miles from their home. The caste system has a strong hold, limiting opportunities for villagers, and traditional local community values still play an important role in Indian politics.

A Society of Violence

Political, social, and religious conflicts regularly lead to physical violence. Perhaps more pervasive and intrusive, though, is the more generalized problem of **structural violence.** Originating in neo-Marxism, this term is used to describe intangible forms of oppression, or the "violence" concealed within a social and political system. Hence the oppression of women is a form of structural violence perpetrated by male-dominated political systems, and extreme poverty is a form of violence perpetrated by one part of society on another. Structural violence in India refers to the invisible effects of poverty, inequality, and caste oppression, which have a psychological impact on the way Indians relate to their political system.

structural violence
The social and economic oppression built into a system of government.

Rising Frustrations

Many people find that the more they have, the more they want, and as their lives improve, they find it harder to compromise. As urban India has modernized and as the middle-class consumer society has grown, so the expectations of Indians (especially urban Indians) have grown and their frustrations risen. Gaps have grown between aspiration and achievement, and the government has been unable to keep up with the demands of new groups entering politics.[6] In particular, the middle classes have become impatient with India's poverty and with what they see as the limits placed on social change by the traditional sector. The gap between expectations and performance goes to the heart of the argument posed by the political scientist Samuel Huntington, who suggests that "the primary problem of politics is the lag in the development of political institutions behind social and economic change."[7] This is certainly true of India.

POLITICAL SYSTEM

India is a federal republic with a parliamentary system of government. It is also a democracy, if democracy is measured by the existence of free political parties, competitive elections, different forms of participation and representation, the stability and continuity of political institutions, and the protection of individual rights and freedoms. But it is far from being a liberal democracy, because there are too many gaps between theory and practice:

- There may be regular elections, but they are often accompanied by violence and fraud; in some cases (such as in the Punjab during the 1980s) elections have been suspended because of violence.

- Indian prime ministers have more potentially dictatorial powers than their liberal democratic counterparts, although their abilities to abuse these powers have become more limited as communications have been modernized and leaders have had to rely on fragile multiparty coalitions as the base of their support.

- India may be federal in theory, but in practice the central government wields so much power over the states that state governments have little real independence. This has been changing, though, with the rise of regional political parties.

- The rights of individuals may be constitutionally protected, but many minorities still rail against the authority of central government and the caste system still exists.

- Despite recent economic growth and liberalization, the vast majority of Indians live a preindustrial lifestyle, many live in crushing poverty, and India is still a poor country.

For now, India is best seen as a newly industrializing country that is working to develop the political and economic form best suited to the needs of its people. It has the potential to become a stable, influential, and wealthy state, but many handicaps must first be removed.

THE CONSTITUTION

The constitution of India created a federal republic based on a parliamentary system of government with guaranteed civil rights and liberties and a separate Supreme Court with the power of judicial review. The constitution is one of the longest in the world, with 395 articles, 8 schedules, and more than 40 amendments. The wording occasionally sounds like parts of the U.S. Declaration of Independence, but the principles come out of the Westminster system of government; nearly 250 articles are taken almost verbatim from the 1935 Government of India Act.

The constitution was drawn up by a Constituent Assembly indirectly elected in 1946 by India's provincial assemblies. The Assembly became the provisional government following independence and oversaw the drafting of the constitution in 1948–1950. Among its priorities were the following: to establish a democratic, sovereign, and independent republic; to ensure the unity of India; to offset the potential for violence and disorder; to set up a secular state; and to establish economic independence and self-sufficiency.[8] Despite the discussions that followed, the dominance of the Assembly by the Congress party meant that a handful of Congress leaders—including Nehru—set the course for the debate and influenced the final form of the constitution, which went into effect on January 26, 1950.

During the debates, some argued that India should be set up as a decentralized state based on village *panchayat*, and some even said that *satyagraha* should be a fundamental right of the people.[9] Others argued that India had long experience with representative parliamentary government and that the unity of India could be ensured only through a strong, centralized authority. At the same time, the need to recognize India's cultural diversity and to keep the princely states happy led to the decision to create a federal system.

The most controversial element of the constitution was the power it gave to the president (on the advice of the prime minister) to suspend or abrogate freedoms during a "grave emergency," that is, when the security of India or its territory were threatened by "external aggression or internal disturbance." Emergencies were declared in 1962 and 1971 during conflicts with China and Pakistan, but emergency powers were given their loosest interpretation by Prime Minister Indira Gandhi in June 1975, when she "advised" the president to declare an emergency in response to an alleged threat to internal security from her political opposition. After she lost the 1977 election, the constitution was quickly changed so that emergency powers could be declared only in the event of external aggression or armed rebellion.

THE PRESIDENT

India's decision to keep the parliamentary system of government after independence was unusual; almost all other former European colonies (except Australia, Canada, and New Zealand) opted for a presidential system with American undertones. Some Indians have called for the creation of a presidential system along French or Russian lines, and Indira Gandhi centralized powers to the point where her administration became quasi-presidential, but the parliamentary system persists and includes a president with about the same (mainly symbolic) powers as the British monarch or Japanese emperor.

The president of India is elected for a renewable five-year term by an electoral college made up of members of both houses of Parliament and of the state legislatures. A vice president is also elected for five-year terms by an electoral college made up of both houses of Parliament, and several have gone on to become president. All presidents to date have been men, and given the long dominance of the Congress Party in Indian politics, most have been the handpicked choices of the party. President K. R. Narayanan, elected in 1997, was notable for being the first Dalit to become president. The current president—A. P. J. Abdul Kalam—is a retired scientist who was architect of India's missile program, for which he earned the nickname "Missile Man." He is India's third Muslim president.

TABLE 7.2

Presidents and Vice Presidents of India

Date	President	Vice president
1950	Rajendra Prasad	—
1952	Rajendra Prasad	Sarvapalli Radhakrishnan
1957	Rajendra Prasad	Sarvapalli Radhakrishnan
1962	Sarvapalli Radhakrishnan	Zakir Hussain
1967	Zakir Hussain*	V. V. Giri
1969	V. V. Giri	G. S. Pathak
1974	Fakhruddin Ali Ahmed*	B. D. Jatti
1977	Neelam Sanjiva Reddy	—
1979		Mohammed Hidayatullah
1982	Giani Zail Singh	—
1984		Ramaswamy Venkataraman
1987	Ramaswamy Venkataraman	Shankar Dayal Sharma
1992	Shankar Dayal Sharma	K. R. Narayanan
1997	K. R. Narayanan	Krishan Kant
2002	A. P. J. Abdul Kalam	Bhairon Singh Sekhawat

*Died in office.

The president technically "appoints" the prime minister and members of the Council of Ministers, although—like the British monarch—all he really does is confirm as prime minister the leader of the largest party or coalition. The president also has several other constitutional powers, but these are exercised on the advice of the Council of Ministers, which is dominated by the prime minister. These powers include the ability to dissolve Parliament, declare a state of emergency, declare an emergency in a state and rule that state by decree, veto parliamentary bills, and promulgate ordinances that have the same power and effect as acts of Parliament. The president is also the commander-in-chief and appoints state governors and Supreme Court justices. The vice president takes over temporarily if the president dies, resigns, or cannot carry out the duties of office, and (like the U.S. vice president) is ex officio chairman of the upper house of the legislature.

Despite having to make almost all their decisions on the advice of the prime minister, presidents have several times had to step in to arbitrate following indecisive elections. For example, after the collapse of the Janata government in 1979, President Sanjiva Reddy asked Charan Singh (leader of a Janata splinter party) to be prime minister. Singh was unable to form a workable government and resigned within three weeks. Reddy then asked Singh to oversee a caretaker government, which held power until the January 1980 elections returned Indira Gandhi to power. Similarly, President Shankar Dayal Sharma had to step in several times during 1996–1997 to identify the politicians in the best position to form a government during the confusion that followed the 1996 national elections. In both cases, the president played an important role as an arbiter and guide during power vacuums.

THE EXECUTIVE: PRIME MINISTER AND THE COUNCIL OF MINISTERS

In theory, Indian prime ministers are the leaders of the majority party or coalition in Parliament. However, the reality has never been quite that simple. For example, Jawarhalal Nehru was never formally selected as party leader by the Congress Party but became leader and prime minister as the political successor to Mahatma Gandhi.[10] More recently, the fluidity of party politics has meant that—in the interests of building a stable coalition—parties may bypass the leadership and look elsewhere. For example, Deve Gowda, who was appointed prime minister in May 1996, was not the leader of any of the parties in the United Front coalition but was chief minister of the southern state of Karnataka. He was recruited by other chief ministers who wanted someone sympathetic to the cause of local government. And current prime minister Manmohan Singh, has never been elected to Parliament—he was an appointed member of the upper house of Parliament, and inherited the job in 2004 when Congress Party leader Sonia Gandhi turned it down.

Prime ministers appoint and oversee the Council of Ministers (although the appointments are technically made by the president on the recommendation of the prime minister). Like the British cabinet, this council consists of the heads and deputy heads of government departments. Ministers either must be members of Parliament (either house) or within six months of their appointment must become members by nomination or by winning a by-election. Unlike the British cabinet, the council is too big (about 45 members) to work effectively as a body and never meets collectively. A tradition has instead evolved of convening a smaller cabinet of the 15 to 20 most important government ministers, which meets weekly, takes collective responsibility, and generally works more like the British cabinet. Indira and Rajiv Gandhi went further by creating "inner cabinets" of close advisors; Indira's was a six-member "kitchen cabinet" which included her son Sanjay, while Rajiv's was known widely as the "Doon clique" after the name of the private school he had attended.

A notable feature of the Indian prime ministership for many years was the dominant role of personality. With some notable exceptions, liberal democratic prime ministers do not usually stamp strong personal influence on their office, but India was ruled for all but four of its first 42 years of independence by the **Nehru-Gandhi dynasty.** This worried many Indians, for several reasons. First, personal leadership is fragile, as emphasized by the traumatic effects of the assassinations of Indira and Rajiv Gandhi, which showed just how far India had come to depend on individuals rather than institutions. Second, leaders who come to power through inheritance need to show little in the way of character or past performance,[11] which means that they may not be battle-hardened by the time they come to power. Finally, dynasties can tend toward authoritarianism, as exemplified by the performance of Indira Gandhi.

The impact of personality on government was consolidated during the first administration of Indira Gandhi, who in 1966 became the world's first female prime minister. Her increasingly authoritarian tactics backfired when she was held personally responsible for food shortages and inflation in 1973–1974, leading her to take her powers to a new extreme by declaring a state of emergency. The role of personality government was further emphasized during the administration of her son Rajiv, who came into politics only because he was recruited by his mother following the death in a 1980 plane crash

TABLE 7.3

Prime Ministers of India

Date	Prime minister	Governing party or coalition
September 1947	Jawaharlal Nehru	Congress
May 1952*	Jawaharlal Nehru	Congress
March 1957*	Jawaharlal Nehru	Congress
January 1962*	Jawaharlal Nehru[†]	Congress
June 1964	Lal Bahadur Shastri[†]	Congress
January 1966	Indira Gandhi	Congress
March 1967*	Indira Gandhi	Congress
March 1971*	Indira Gandhi	Congress (R)
March 1977*	Morarji Desai	Janata Front
July 1979	Charan Singh	Janata (S)
January 1980*	Indira Gandhi[†]	Congress (I)
October 1984	Rajiv Gandhi	Congress (I)
December 1984*	Rajiv Gandhi	Congress (I)
December 1989*	V. P. Singh	Janata Dal–led coalition
November 1990	Chandra Shekar	Janata Dal (S)
June 1991*	P. V. Narasimha Rao	Congress (I)
May 1996*	Atal Behari Vajpayee	BJP-led coalition
May 1996	Deve Gowda	United Front coalition
April 1997	Inder Kumar Gujral	United Front coalition
March 1998*	Atal Behari Vajpayee	BJP-led coalition
October 1999*	Atal Behari Vajpayee	BJP-led coalition*
May 2004	Manmohan Singh	Congress-led coalition

*General elections.
[†]Died in office.

of his elder brother Sanjay, who had been groomed to replace her. Rajiv was transformed in just four years from a commercial airline pilot into a prime minister. After just over five years in office, he lost the 1989 election, but the inability of the opposition to form a workable government contributed to a revival of the Gandhi mystique. Rajiv was on the brink of being returned to office when he was assassinated in May 1991.

Recent events suggest that the power of the office may be on the decline and that parties have become (at least temporarily) the chief centers of power. Narasimha Rao surprised many by holding on to office for a full term (1991–1996), making popular policy decisions, and reducing the influence of personality. However, 27 parties won seats in Parliament after the 1996 elections, the traditional power of Congress was gone (although it remained a key power broker), and confusion reigned as India was ruled by a series of multiparty coalitions. Deals were vigorously pursued behind the

PEOPLE IN POLITICS

MANMOHAN SINGH

© 2005 AFP/Getty Images

Manmohan Singh unexpectedly became India's fourteenth prime minister at the age of 72 in May 2004, when the Congress Party increased its share of seats in parliament and its leader—Sonia Gandhi—turned down the opportunity to become prime minister. Singh is widely regarded as the architect of India's recent economic reforms, and is the first Sikh ever to become prime minister of India.

Born in West Punjab in 1932, he studied economics at Cambridge and Oxford universities in Britain before becoming an academic, teaching both at Oxford and at the prestigious Delhi School of Economics. He then became a bureaucrat, becoming an economic advisor in the Ministry of Commerce in 1971, before working his way up to become governor of the Indian Reserve Bank and to work at the International Monetary Fund. He has never been elected to office, being defeated in his one attempt to be elected to Parliament, and coming to politics instead through appointment to the upper house of Parliament, the Rajya Sabha. He served as India's finance minister from 1991 to 1996 and became a highly trusted confidante of Sonia Gandhi. He was also Leader of the Opposition in the Rajya Sabha from 1998 to 2004.

As prime minister he said that his priorities were to deal with poverty and to continue with India's market-friendly economic reforms, and to build good relations with Pakistan. He presided over a sometimes fractious political coalition, which was supported by communist legislators who were hostile to his economic policies and to his attempts to build good relations with the United States, and had to deal with charges of corruption leveled at several of his cabinet members. Rumors were also rife that he and Sonia Gandhi—still president of the Congress Party—had begun to disagree.

scenes, bringing three prime ministers to office in the space of a year, including one (Atal Behari Vajpayee, leader of the Hindu nationalist Bharatiya Janata Party) who was in office for just 12 days. His two successors held office for 10 months and 11 months, respectively, before Vajpayee came back as prime minister in March 1998, being reconfirmed in office with the elections of October 1999.

The ghosts of the Nehru-Gandhi dynasty still hover in the background, because Congress was led into both the 1999 and the 2004 elections by Sonia Gandhi, the Italian-born, Roman Catholic widow of Rajiv. Congress and its allies lost the 1999 elections, but when they won a plurality of seats in 2004, there was a real prospect that the reluctant and even reclusive Mrs. Gandhi would become prime minister. Even though she had become an Indian citizen and had been elected to Parliament in 1999, her opponents had made political capital out of her origins during the election campaign, although this had largely fallen on deaf ears. After several days of negotiations, however, former finance minister Manmohan Singh was confirmed as prime minister instead. Sonia Gandhi remained leader of Congress, and the Gandhi mystique was continued when her 33-year-old son Rahul was elected by a landslide in 2004 to represent his father's old constituency.

THE LEGISLATURE: PARLIAMENT

As in Britain, the prime minister and the cabinet in India are collectively responsible to Parliament and must keep its confidence to stay in power. When the Congress Party was dominant, Parliament took a subsidiary role in the relationship between executive and legislature, with members of Parliament tying their political careers to the fortunes of the prime minister. On several occasions, though, the support of Members of Parliament (MPs) has been critical to the continued power of the government. This has become clear in recent years as governments have been based on coalitions of multiple parties. Following the May 2004 elections, for example, the Singh government was made up of an astonishing 38 political parties.

Parliament consists of two houses, which have the same powers over legislation but are elected differently.

Rajya Sabha (Council of States)

The Rajya Sabha is the upper house, designed to represent the states. It has 245 members, of which 12 are appointed by the president to represent the professions, the sciences, and the arts and 233 are elected for six-year terms by the state legislatures. The number of members from each state is decided on the basis of population, with the smallest states having one member each and the largest (Uttar Pradesh) having 31. Unlike the lower house, the Rajya Sabha has fixed terms, so it cannot be dissolved by the president. Like the U.S. Senate, its elections are staggered, so one-third of its members stand for reelection every two years. Following the 2004 elections, Congress held 73 of the seats and the BJP held 48.

Lok Sabha (House of the People)

Like many lower houses in bicameral legislatures, the Lok Sabha is the more powerful of the two chambers. It has 545 members, elected from single-member districts by universal suffrage for maximum five-year terms: 525 are elected by voters in the states, 18 are elected by voters in the union territories, and two seats are reserved for Anglo-Indians. The seats are allocated among the states and territories on the basis of population, with each district roughly the same size in terms of population. A notable feature of Indian politics is the relative underrepresentation of citizens at the national level: Whereas the average British MP represents 91,000 people and the average member of the U.S. House represents 650,000 people, the average Indian MP comes from a district of 1.9 million people. For Indians to have the same level as representation as Americans, the Lok Sabha would need to have nearly 1,600 members.

© B. Mather/X01408/CORBIS

The Indian Parliament building in New Delhi. Although it shows the classic style of much British colonial architecture, its role in government is significantly different from that of its British counterpart. The recent dominance of coalition governments has reduced the powers of the prime minister and moved many of the key struggles in Indian politics away from the prime minister's office and into the parliamentary chamber.

The Lok Sabha must meet at least twice per year, with no more than six months between sessions. Like the British House of Commons, it is essentially a debating chamber that provides support and opposition to the government. It has most of the trappings of the Westminster model, such as a neutral speaker elected from among the members of the house, parliamentary committees, and government question time, but—thanks to the forcefulness of many Indian prime ministers and to the high turnover among members after elections—it was for a long time less powerful in real terms than the House of Commons. With the advent of the multiparty coalitions of the 1990s, it took on a much more significant role.

The legislative process in India is similar to those used in the British Parliament and the U.S. Congress. Any bill other than a money bill can be introduced in either house, but most are introduced in the Lok Sabha, where they go through the same process of readings, debates, and consideration by committee as used in the House of Commons. Once passed in the lower house, a bill goes to the Rajya Sabha, where it goes through the same stages. Disagreements between the two chambers are debated, and if they are not resolved, the president can call for a joint meeting of Parliament. Once both houses have passed the bill in the same form, it goes to the president for assent. He can refuse to give it assent and can send it back to Parliament, but if it is passed again, the president must give his assent. Most parliamentary debates take place in English or Hindi.

THE JUDICIARY: SUPREME COURT

India has a Supreme Court responsible for interpreting the constitution and arbitrating in the case of disputes between the states or between the Union (federal) government and the states. The Court originally had eight justices, but the number has been increased to 26. Justices are appointed by the president after consultation with members of the Court and the state courts. Turnover is higher than in the U.S. Supreme Court, because members can hold office only until age 65. Normally, the most senior justice automatically becomes chief justice when the incumbent retires, although Indira Gandhi broke this precedent by promoting her own candidates over senior justices, leading to protests from the legal profession about political interference.

The Court has the power of judicial review, but the Indian constitution is so detailed that the Court has less latitude than its U.S. counterpart. Just as the U.S. Supreme Court spent its early years defining its powers in relation to Congress and the presidency (finally winning the power of judicial review with *Marbury* v. *Madison* in 1803), so the Indian court had a running battle for many years with Parliament, particularly over the issue of the Fundamental Rights contained in Articles 12–35 of the constitution. Several amendments have been passed redefining the relative powers of the Court and Parliament. The 24th Amendment, passed in 1971, gave Parliament the power to amend any part of the constitution, but the Court decision *Keshavananda Bharati* v. *State of Kerala* in 1973 declared that any amendments that attacked the "basic structure" of the constitution would be invalid.

The Supreme Court played a critical role in uncovering and pursuing the scandal that proved to be one of the final straws that broke public support for the Congress Party in 1996. In 1991 police discovered evidence that a business family, the Jains, had been bribing senior members of the government. When four citizens filed a public interest suit with the Supreme Court, its judges took the opportunity to order an investigation. It was finally revealed in January 1996 that 65 politicians and bureaucrats—including perhaps Prime Minister Narasimha Rao himself—had received more than $18 million in bribes.

SUBNATIONAL GOVERNMENT

India is a federal republic, with the Union government at the center and powers over many local issues devolved to the governments of the 25 states and seven union territories. Several of the states are big enough to be countries in their own right: In terms of population, Uttar Pradesh is as big as Russia, Maharashtra is as big as Germany, and Tamil Nadu is as big as Britain.

Every state has its own government, which almost exactly mirrors the structure of the Union government. Each has a figurehead governor appointed by the president of India for five-year terms. To discourage parochialism and encourage objectivity, the governor is usually from another state and is someone who is both politically neutral and acceptable to the state government. Governors appoint the chief ministers, although all they actually do is confirm the leader of the biggest party or coalition in the state assembly. Chief ministers are members of the state assembly, are directly elected by all eligible voters in the state, and rule with the help of a Council of Ministers. Most states have a unicameral Legislative Assembly (Vidhan Sabha), but five of the larger states also have an upper Legislative Council (Vidhan Parishad). The assemblies consist of between 60 and 500 members, depending on the size of the state, and serve five-year terms. (Union territories are ruled by lieutenant governors or administrators appointed by the president of India.)

In the years after independence, the Union government had so many powers that India was described as "quasi-federal."[12] Some observers once denied that India was federal at all,[13] and others spoke instead of a kind of "cooperative federalism." The balance has begun to change in recent years, though, with the rise of regional political parties, some of which have become big enough to be nationally important. Although there were only about 15 to 20 recognized state parties active until the early 1990s, that number has more than doubled in the last decade, leading to the fragmentation of party politics in India.

The southern state of Tamil Nadu has been a notable hotbed of regional politics, with two parties promoting Tamil self-determination: the Dravida Munnetra Kazhagam (DMK) and the Tamil Maanila Congress (TMC). In 1967 the DMK became the first opposition party to win a clear majority in a state assembly. In 1972 a splinter party (the AIADMK) split off from the DMK, claiming that the latter had lost sight of its roots and basic goals. Led by the popular movie star M. G. Ramachandran, the AIADMK went on to win a majority in the Tamil Nadu state assembly. After Ramachandran's death in 1987, the party split into factions, one led by his widow and the other by his former leading actress, Jayaram Jayalalitha. The latter swept to victory in the 1991 state elections and Jayalalitha became chief minister of Tamil Nadu. Her party also won 18 seats in the Lok Sabha, became part of the BJP-led government in 1998, then brought the government down by withdrawing its support in April 1999.[14]

The issue of who has the real power in the relationship between the center and the states in India is debatable. In many respects, the balance lies with the Union government: It has control over defense policy, foreign affairs, and income tax; in a conflict between the Union and the states, Union law always prevails; the Union government has the power to change the boundaries of states, create new states, and even abolish existing states; the president of India, on the "advice" of a state governor, can declare an emergency and transfer powers over the state to the Indian Parliament; an emergency can be declared if a state fails to comply with a law passed by parliament, thereby effectively forcing that state to comply; the Union government has the power of the purse and can decide how to share national revenues out among the states; and finally, a strong prime minister can manipulate and limit state powers, as did Indira Gandhi when she centralized decision making in the Congress Party at the national level and took steps to break the power of state party leaders.

Despite their relative weakness, however, the states cannot be ignored. The Union government relies on state governments to implement policy in several key areas, the performance of national parties at the state level affects the overall strength of those parties, opposition to national parties running in state elections can be turned into opposition at the national level, and recent coalitions at the national level have depended on key regional parties for their support.

ELECTIONS AND PARTIES

It is often claimed that India is the world's biggest democracy, which is true enough if we go by sheer numbers alone; the May 2004 general elections were open to nearly 680 million voters. But while elections are generally free and fair, and India has a free press and a variety of interest groups, political corruption is a problem, with voter intimidation, vote rigging, and occasional breakdowns into violence: nearly 300 people died during the troubled 1991 elections, at least ten people died during elections in 2002 in the northeastern state of Manipur, and there were more deaths in the 2004 elections. For these and other reasons, India ranked 87th out of 145 on the 2004 Transparency International Corruption Perceptions Index.

Nonetheless, national election results generally reflect the preferences of voters, whose political awareness makes them increasingly difficult to manipulate. Political activity and literacy is particularly high among the urban middle classes, and turnout at elections is generally high, even in rural districts. The party system is more fluid than in many liberal democracies, with parties and coalitions coming and going. Party politics was long dominated by the Indian National Congress, which has in recent years had to compete for power with the Hindu nationalist BJP.

THE ELECTORAL SYSTEM

With some notable differences, the Indian electoral system looks much like the British model. Elections to the Lok Sabha and the state assemblies must be held at least once every five years, and all eligible voters take part. Until 1971, elections to the Lok Sabha and the state assemblies were held at the same time. In that year, Indira Gandhi called a general election without calling for state elections. Although her motive was short-term political gain—she was trying to capitalize on her national popularity to neutralize her opponents in the Congress Party and in the states—it has been common since then to hold national and state elections separately.[15]

Everyone older than 18 years of age can vote, and voter turnout increased from nearly 47 percent in 1952 to an average of 60 to 65 percent, before falling off in recent years: it reached a low of 53 percent in the 1991 elections and was up slightly to 56 percent in 2004, helped a little by the use for the first time of electronic voting machines. By every measure, the scale of Indian elections is astonishing: At the 2004 general election, nearly 380 million voters turned out to vote at 800,000 polling stations manned by four million officials. The election was so enormous that it was held in four phases over a period of 12 days—a big improvement since the 1950s, when elections were held over a period of four months.

The General Election

Like Britain and the United States, India uses single-member districts in elections to the lower house (the Lok Sabha), and a plurality on the first ballot is enough to return the winner. The low level of literacy in rural India means that ballots have to be printed

FIGURE 7.1

Election Symbols of Indian Political Parties

Janata Party

Bharatiya
Janata Party

Communist Party
of India

Indian National
Congress (I)

Communist Party
of India (M)

Indian National
Congress (S)

Lok Dal

with the name of the party and an easily recognizable symbol (see Figure 7.1). Election campaigns are short (three weeks), meaning that rural candidates have to undertake a grueling campaign, visiting as many as 600 villages in a single district, often traveling nearly impassable roads. Although most villages now have televisions and there is increased access to the Internet, most candidates still try to reach people through leaflets, speeches, and personal influence. Appeals will often be made on the basis of class, community, caste, faction loyalty, and charisma,[16] but issues are not forgotten. Campaigns have been known to become "waves" or landslides, such as the Indira wave in 1971 and the wave of sympathy that led to the election of Rajiv Gandhi in 1984 in the wake of his mother's assassination. The label wave should not be taken too literally, though, because no one party has ever won a majority of votes.

State Elections

In addition to national elections, Indian voters also take part in regular state assembly elections. These are held at five-year intervals and contested by both national and regional parties. The outcome of state elections often has national implications, particularly given the strength of the bigger regional parties.

POLITICAL PARTIES

The Indian party system has become extraordinarily complex of late. From a time when it was a stable, one-party-dominant system, it has become increasingly unstable, erratic, and fragmented, with new parties coming and going and national parties losing ground to an increasingly messy community of regional parties. The effects of the atomization of the party system were only too clear after the 2004 general election, when 38 parties were represented in Parliament and the government was a coalition of 12 parties (an improvement on the 1999 election, which resulted in a 24-party governing coalition). The number of parties has never been constant, nor does it matter so much as the nature of the coalitions they form. Hence, the best way of trying to understand the Indian party system is not to look at each party in turn, but to follow the different phases in the relationship among the major national parties and the many competing smaller parties.[17]

Congress Dominant (1947–1967)

The first phase of Indian party politics revolved around the Indian National Congress, which was the major force in the independence movement, and—until 1967—routinely won four times as many votes as any other party. Like the Japanese Liberal Democrats, it consisted of several factions bound by a consensus, was flexible enough to absorb policies from other parties, and ran a political machine based on patronage and political favors. Virtually all significant Indian politics took place within Congress, which—thanks to the charisma and ability of Jawaharlal Nehru—had a cohesion and sense of direction that the weak and fragmented opposition lacked.

The centralization of Congress had already begun to break down when Nehru suffered a stroke in January 1964. By the time he died in May, the glue was gone and factional differences had emerged based on personality rather than ideology. The Syndicate, a group of five powerful Congress Party leaders from the states, named Lal Bahadur Shastri prime minister. When Shastri died suddenly in January 1966, a vote was held on the party leadership for the first time, resulting in victory for Indira Gandhi. The end of the unified Congress system was confirmed in the 1967 state and national elections, when Indira Gandhi was returned as prime minister, but Congress lost control of six state governments and had a reduced majority in the Lok Sabha.

Congress Divided (1967–1977)

With Congress now weakened by defections, Gandhi moved to reassert her control of the party, so upsetting the Syndicate that Congress split in two: a group of 226 MPs that supported Gandhi and a rump of 65 that supported the Syndicate. To win a mandate for her wing of Congress, Gandhi called a general election in 1971, which resulted in a landslide for her newly renamed Congress (R) (for Requisitioned, and then for Ruling). Meanwhile, the Syndicate's faction, Congress (O) (for Opposition or Organization), saw its share of seats fall from 65 to 16. Almost immediately, Gandhi found herself caught up in Pakistan's civil war and capitalized on the triumph of the Indian military by calling state elections in March 1972. These resulted in a landslide for Congress (R), which became virtually her personal fiefdom. Whereas Congress had once been a national party that reached through every level of Indian society, Gandhi centralized decision-making power by making senior appointments on the basis of personal loyalty and by regularly reshuffling the cabinet to make sure no one could build a strong opposing base. She even renamed her party Congress (I) (for Indira).

As criticism of her autocratic methods grew, she "advised" the president to declare a national emergency and went on nationwide radio to warn that "a widespread conspiracy" had been growing against her and that the armed forces had been incited to mutiny and the police to rebel. The 1976 general election was postponed, direct rule by New Delhi was imposed on the states, opposition organizations were banned, the bill of rights was effectively abrogated, the press was heavily censored, 110,000 people were arrested and detained without trial, and some of the detainees were tortured and murdered in jail. A new amendment to the constitution was even passed, denying the Supreme Court the power of judicial review. Likening herself to Joan of Arc, Indira Gandhi tried to paint herself as the savior of Indian democracy rather than its enemy.

In March 1977, convinced that Congress (I) could win, Gandhi called a general election. Although taken by surprise, the opposition quickly formed a new coalition, the Janata Front, and campaigned on a manifesto that argued that voters were faced with a choice between "freedom and slavery; between democracy and dictatorship." Janata and its allies won a majority, Gandhi lost her Lok Sabha seat, and her faction of Congress was reduced to 154 seats. She was forced to admit defeat, which to many was vindication that Indian democracy was strong enough to withstand abuses of power.

The Janata Coalition (1977–1980)

The 81-year-old Morarji Desai became prime minister, but despite its mandate, his Janata coalition rapidly fell apart, largely because of a lack of direction, personality clashes, and a series of unpopular policy decisions. Janata leaders also made the mistake of launching personal attacks on Gandhi and even occasionally placing her under house arrest, making her a martyr in the eyes of many. In July 1979 Desai resigned and was replaced by Charan Singh. However, Singh's coalition too was torn by internal dissension, and within a month he had resigned, although he stayed on as head of a caretaker government.

Meanwhile, after briefly considering retirement, Gandhi had rebuilt both her political reputation and her faction of Congress. In November 1978 she won reelection to the Lok Sabha but faced criminal prosecution on charges of misconduct and abuse of authority. After refusing to testify before a parliamentary inquiry into the activities of Maruti, an automobile company founded by her younger son, Sanjay, she was held in contempt and jailed for a week. Before the government could prosecute Gandhi, the Janata government had fallen and new elections were called for in January 1980. Gandhi portrayed herself as the only person capable of forming a strong government, campaigned tirelessly, and was returned to office with a strong majority.

The Gandhis Return (1980–1989)

Gandhi's moment of triumph was short-lived. She had been grooming Sanjay to succeed her, but he was killed in a plane crash in June 1980, forcing her to rethink her plans. She persuaded her elder son, Rajiv, to enter politics, and in a June 1981 by-election he won the Lok Sabha seat left vacant by Sanjay.

In October 1984, in the wake of her attempts to put down an insurrection by Sikh extremists, Indira Gandhi was assassinated by her Sikh bodyguards, leaving Congress (I) without a leader. Rajiv was immediately drafted to replace his mother, automatically becoming prime minister. Two months later, seeking his own mandate, he called a new general election and was returned with a landslide. Rajiv was young and charming, portrayed himself as spokesman for a younger generation, and vowed to end government corruption and prepare India for the twenty-first century. He won the prime ministership partly because of sympathy over the assassination of his mother but also because of the inability of the opposition to offer a credible alternative. His lack of a political past also helped him portray himself as a figure of renewal and change and of stability and continuity.[18]

Despite his 1984 mandate, Rajiv became increasingly arrogant, centralizing power in his office and in the hands of a small group of advisors, and regularly reshuffling his cabinet.[19] An anticorruption program he had promised was run by the new finance minister, V. P. Singh, who pursued his new task with such vigor that many powerful business leaders with close connections to Rajiv Gandhi were investigated. In 1987 Singh was shifted from finance to defense but continued his anticorruption drive with such persistence that he made many enemies and was forced to resign. Then news of the Bofors scandal broke.

In 1986 the Indian government had signed a contract with the Swedish arms manufacturer Bofors for $1.3 billion worth of 155-mm howitzers. In 1987 Swedish radio reported that Bofors had paid Indian middlemen nearly $40 million in "commissions" to make sure that Bofors won the contract. There were even charges that the bribes had reached the highest levels of government, possibly including Rajiv Gandhi himself. (In 2004, an Indian court finally cleared Rajiv of any wrongdoing in the case.) To add to his problems, Rajiv was unable to reduce India's religious tensions, and the conflict and violence between Hindus and Muslims worsened. A united opposition was now able to grow around Rajiv's weaknesses. With his removal from the cabinet in 1987, V. P. Singh created a centrist coalition, called the National Front, consisting of Singh's own Janata Dal, Congress (S), and several local parties. In November 1989, with his five-year term up, Rajiv called a new election.

Congress in Opposition (1989–1991)

India's ninth free election was significant in that—unlike all eight previous elections—the outcome was not a foregone conclusion. For the first time, Indian voters were offered a straight choice between two leaders who were truly being compared as alternatives: Rajiv Gandhi and V. P. Singh. There was no particular crisis, and there were plenty of strong political issues. Singh and his coalition partners ran a co-ordinated campaign, agreeing not to run against each other in most constituencies.

The election resulted in huge losses for Congress and also saw the rise of the Bharatiya Janata Party (BJP), which increased its support from 1 percent to 16 percent, leading some to predict the beginning of a new Hindu nationalist trend in Indian politics. V. P. Singh formed a government with the help of the BJP and communist parties, but his coalition rapidly fell apart. In November 1990 the BJP pulled out of the coalition, and another group of MPs led by the socialist Chandra Shekar broke away. Rajiv Gandhi was invited to form a new government but opted instead to support Shekar. India now witnessed the peculiar sight of a government run by Shekar and his 54 Janata Dal (S) MPs, backed by the 213 Congress MPs and their allies. Shekar was patently a Congress puppet and was unable even to pass a budget.

In March 1991, when Rajiv Gandhi withdrew his support, Chandra Shekar's 117-day government fell, and a new election was called for May—the second in 18 months. On May 21, while campaigning in the southern state of Tamil Nadu and apparently headed for victory, Rajiv Gandhi was killed when a suicide bomber blew herself up only feet away from him. Rajiv's Italian-born wife, Sonia, was asked to take over Congress and to run for prime minister but she refused, and Congress went into the remainder of the election with a new president—the 70-year-old P. V. Narasimha Rao—and several contenders for the post of prime minister. When Congress won, Rao became prime minister.

The Emergence of the BJP (1991–2004)

Following Rajiv's death, India (or Congress at least) seemed obsessed with identifying someone who could take up the Gandhi mantle. No one was found, however, and Narasimha Rao surprised many observers with his abilities as a political tactician and with his popularity, helped in large part by his economic liberalization policies. He quickly ran into problems, however, beginning in December 1992 with the destruction of the mosque at Ayodhya. Rao moved too slowly to control the communal riots that broke out as a result, and the gloss continued to fade as defections weakened his coalition; then news broke in early 1996 of a corruption scandal involving senior politicians and bureaucrats, including Rao himself and seven cabinet ministers.

In the May 1996 elections, Congress was routed, the BJP increased its representation by one-third to become the biggest party in the Lok Sabha for the first time, and parties representing regional interests and the lower castes made notable gains. No one party won more than 30 percent of the seats, however, leaving a leadership vacuum. A BJP-led government collapsed after just 12 days and was replaced by a left-leaning 13-party coalition that lasted just 10 months before collapsing. Its successor fell apart after 11 months, and the March 1998 election resulted in a new government headed again by the BJP and its leader, Atal Behari Vajpayee. Meanwhile, Sonia Gandhi had broken a long silence and taken over the leadership of Congress.

The fragility of India's coalition governments is well illustrated by the events of April 1999. One of the partners in the Vajpayee government was the AIADMK, the regional Tamil party led by former actress Jayaram Jayalalitha. She had apparently entered into

FIGURE 7.2

Legislative Electoral Trends in India

*These parties fought the 1996 and 1998 elections as the United Front.

an agreement with the defense minister, George Fernandes, that if she supported the BJP he would try to weaken charges of corruption made against her during her term as chief minister of Tamil Nadu in 1991–1996. Dissatisfied with the action taken, she demanded that Fernandes be fired, but Vajpayee refused. Jayalalitha responded by withdrawing the support of her 18 MPs, reducing the BJP government to a minority.[20] The government then lost a vote of confidence by a single vote but stayed on as caretaker until a new general election (the third in three years) was held in September–October.

The economic record of the Vajpayee government was poor, but it faced a divided opposition, it had a popular leader, and it profited from a wave of patriotic sentiment with its handling of tensions in Kashmir in May–July. The outcome of the new election was hardly a BJP wave (the party won only three more seats), but Sonia Gandhi's Congress fell to a new low of 112 seats and Vajpayee was able to form a new government, becoming the first prime minister since 1971 to win consecutive elections. The continued rise of the BJP left India at the start of the new millennium with a party system in which the old dominance of Congress had gone, and the membership of the Lok Sabha had become highly fragmented. Following the 1999 election, the BJP held just 33 percent of the seats, Congress held 20 percent, and the remaining 47 percent were divided among a remarkable 37 parties. Of these, 22 operated mainly or exclusively in a single state, 13 had just one seat each in the house, and 11 had between two and five.

The 2004 elections saw the return of Congress in a minority, multiparty coalition. Sonia Gandhi having turned down the opportunity to become prime minister, and sensible minds having turned down the rather bizarre suggestion that her 33-year-old son Rahul—newly elected to Parliament—be recruited in her place, leadership of India fell to Manmohan Singh.

 # POLICIES AND POLICYMAKING

In theory, India is a federal parliamentary republic with a symbolic head of state, an elected prime minister, a council of ministers (all of whom are members of Parliament), a bicameral legislature, a written constitution, a separate supreme court, and elected state governments with separate powers. In practice, political power was so heavily centralized in the prime minister's office until recently that India has often looked more like a unitary than a federal system. Past prime ministers—through the president—have limited or suspended the powers of state governments. The role and power of the center was also intensified by the long dominance of the Nehru-Gandhi dynasty and its Congress Party machine and by the inability of other parties to provide sustained and united opposition. This encouraged Indira Gandhi to accumulate so much power at the center that she took her country to the brink of dictatorship.

As memories of the dynasty fade, the balance of power has begun changing. Recent coalition governments have had to depend for their power on regional political parties, which has shifted the balance of power more toward the states. Furthermore, politics is increasingly driven by competition among class, religious, ethnic, and economic groups. Supporters of centralization say it is the only short-term option if India is to stay united, but critics counter that greater self-determination for the states is the best guarantee for the future of the whole. The challenge is to balance the needs of the parts with the common good of the whole.

ECONOMIC POLICY

India has enormous human resources, some sectors of its economy are growing rapidly, and it has a big consumer market—yet it is still ultimately a poor country. It has a GDP of just over $690 billion, but if the PPP method is used, that figure rises to nearly $3.4 trillion, making India the world's fourth largest economy in absolute terms after the United States, China, and Japan. However, it has a population of one billion, so its per capita GDP is a modest $620. And—using the World Bank definition of a poor person as someone with a daily income of less than a dollar—about two in every five poor people in the world are Indians (a staggering 450 million people).

All is not doom and gloom, however. Given the growth in India's population, the fact that the proportion of poor people has stayed about the same for the last century is a major achievement in itself. Life expectancy for Indians has risen since independence from 32 years to more than 63, the number of children ages 6 to 11 in school has doubled, the number in higher grades has quadrupled, and the literacy rate for men

CLOSE-UP VIEW

PARTIES CONTESTING THE 2004 GENERAL ELECTION

Congress. Congress went into the election lacking unity and ideological coherence. After 42 years under the leadership of the Nehru-Gandhi dynasty, it lost ground during the 1990s to regional and religious parties and saw its membership in the Lok Sabha more than halved. It went into the both the 1999 election and the 2004 election under the leadership of Sonia Gandhi, whose main claim to leadership was her relationship to the party's former leaders. Many within Congress believed that her leadership did not pose a handicap to the party but others did. The 1999 election had seen the Congress share of seats in the Lok Sabha fall to an all-time low; from a peak of 415 seats in 1984, it was down to just 112. In 2004 it won 145 seats, and with its allies in Parliament was able to form the new government.

Bharatiya Janata Party (BJP) (Indian People's Party). A Hindu nationalist party that traces its roots back to 1951 and whose precursor (Jana Sangh) was a partner in the 1977–1980 Janata coalition, the BJP advocated economic nationalism and a re-turn to Hindu values. Its representation in the Lok Sabha grew from two seats in 1984 to 161 in 1996, when its leader Atal Behari Vajpayee formed a short-lived coalition government. He returned to power in 1998, and the BJP won 182 seats in the 1999 election, but it fell back to 138 seats in 2004. It built its power on a wave of Hindu nationalism in the early 1990s but has since moderated its position, leaving the more hard-line policies to one of its coalition partners, Shiv Sena (which won 12 seats in 2004). Other BJP allis include Telugu Desam, a party based in the southern state of Andhra Pradesh and led by N. T. Rama Rao, a for-mer movie star, Dravida Munnetra Kazhagam from Tamil Nadu, the Akali Dal of the Punjab (pro-moting Sikh interests), and the West Bengal–based Trinamool Congress.

Communist parties of India. India has sev-eral communist parties, including the once pro-Beijing Communist Party of India (Marxist) and the once pro-Moscow Communist Party of India (CPI). India had the distinction in 1957 of having the world's first democratically elected commu-nist governments, when the CPI (M) won the state of Kerala. The CPI (M) and CPI between them won 44 seats in the Lok Sabha in 1996 and entered government for the first time as part of the United Front coalition led by Deve Gowda. Their share of seats rose to 53 in 2004, making the Left Front coalition the third-largest in Parliament.

Regional parties. Indian governments have found themselves relying increasingly on regional and state parties, which have not only won signif-icant blocks of seats in the Lok Sabha but also have taken power in several state governments. Notable among them is the Samajwadi Party, which derives most of its support from lower-caste Indians and has its main base of support in Uttar Pradesh, India's biggest state. Eight regional parties won 70 seats in the 1996 Lok Sabha; their share has since risen, sending a strong message to national government about the concerns and aspirations of voters with local interests.

is up from 15 to 68 percent, although women still languish at 44 percent, a sign of their disadvantaged position. The economy has grown 200-fold since independence; the value of exports more than quintupled between 1981 and 2001; and India is now self-sufficient in food, many consumer goods, and basic commodities such as steel and cement. It is 90 percent self-sufficient in energy needs, and its factories build ships, locomotives, trucks, cars, and electronic equipment.

At the same time, India's economy has been strangely staid in comparison with those of neighboring NICs. It often puzzles political scientists and economists that many Indian entrepreneurs living outside their own country can work hard and make themselves rich while many of their compatriots at home remain so poor. Part of the answer lies in the long reliance of India after independence on a series of Soviet-style five-year plans, which set goals for economic development while extending state control over industry. The plans grew in part out of socialist ideas picked up by Congress leaders during visits to pre–World War II Britain, and their aim was to transform India from an agricultural to an industrial economy. The Nehru administration nationalized 17 of India's biggest industries, severely restricted private entrepreneurial activity, set price controls on key commodities such as steel and chemicals, and strictly limited imports. This brought steady economic growth, but it also created a public sector that was overmanned, uncompetitive, and inefficient.

Indira Gandhi initially pursued hands-on economic policies similar to those of her father, but during her second term she opted for limited liberalization. Rajiv Gandhi maintained this policy, cutting income tax and corporation tax, abolishing death duties, relaxing industrial licensing laws and antitrust regulations, and abolishing or lowering quotas and tariffs on many imports. He also set about modernizing the textile industry with the goal of increasing exports and competing with Hong Kong, Taiwan, and South Korea. The Rao government (1991–1996) announced further liberalization, twice devalued the rupee, and cut government spending to qualify for a new loan from the International Monetary Fund. During its administration, India began to transform itself into a market economy.

In many ways, these policies have succeeded. The contribution of industry to GDP has grown from 5 percent in 1950 to nearly 27 percent today, and India has an industrial base that is bigger than that of several European countries. Foreign investment has flowed into the country, inflation in mid-2005 stood at 5 percent (a low rate for a poor country), and GDP and industrial production grew in 2004–2005 at a rate of 6 to 7 percent. India has healthy foreign exchange reserves, its labor market has benefited from outsourcing by European and American companies, its population is young, and there are predictions that India's economy will continue to grow to the point where it will overtake that of Japan by about 2030. In short, India's planners have claimed that the economic fundamentals of India are in good shape.[21]

Another positive trend has been the restructuring of India's business sector. Because most of the world's biggest multinational companies (MNCs) are based in Europe, Japan, and North America, westerners often overlook the possibility of multinationals emerging out of poorer countries. India has several MNCs, however, including Indian Oil, Reliance Industries, Bharat Petroleum, and Hindustan Petroleum, all of which are ranked in the *Fortune* Global 500 list of the world's biggest corporations. Another large corporation is Tata Sons, an 80-company conglomerate on a par with some of the biggest in the West. Founded in 1868, Tata Sons now presides over an industrial empire with annual sales of more than $10 billion, and builds 80 percent of India's commercial road vehicles. It also runs India's biggest steelworks and has interests in everything from iron to chemicals, electricity generation, and computers.

India also stands out from many other poorer countries by virtue of its growing middle class and consumer market. The number of televisions in Indian homes grew from 500,000 in 1976 to nearly 60 million in 2001, the number of home computers and private cars has grown rapidly, Indian vehicle production more than quintupled between 1970 and 1997, and there has been a parallel growth in consumer credit.

Perhaps the greatest challenge faced by India's economic planners lies in bringing its population growth under control—or at least keeping up with the demands of a growing population. With slightly more than one billion people, India is the second most populous country in the world after China and is home to about one in six of all the humans on Earth. Its population is growing at about 1.5 percent annually, and although this is not a high growth rate when compared with many poorer Asian and African states (the average for the latter is 2.6 percent), it still means that India must meet the needs of an additional 20 million people per year (equivalent to a new Australia every year). The United Nations projects that India will overtake China in about 2045, when both countries will have populations of 1.5 billion.

Much of the evidence from population studies suggests that there is an inverse relationship between population growth rates and economic development. For the world's poor, children are a key form of welfare, providing families with labor and security against illness, old age, and unemployment. Thus, in agricultural societies with high infant mortality rates, women tend to have more children in the belief that the more they have, the more will survive to provide for their families. (The absence of contraception contributes to the high fertility rate.) As access to health care improves and infant mortality rates decline, population begins to grow, not because women are having more children, but because more of those children are surviving.

As societies become wealthier and more urbanized, government provides more in the way of social security, women marry and have children later in life, children become more expensive to raise and educate, and parents are able to make choices about the number of children they have. Thus, population growth rates fall to the levels found in liberal democracies: typically in the range of 0.1 to 0.5 percent. Although better education and family planning programs have contributed to bringing population growth under control in many parts of the world, the critical element is an improvement in the quality of life. The downward trend in the population growth rate in India has been one of the effects of its rapid industrialization and of the improvements made in education and health care, but the trend needs to continue if the government is to make progress in its attempts to meet the needs of its people.

Economic changes have brought social and political changes. With the rise of the middle class, the hold of the caste system has been weakened and new groups have entered politics, forcing political parties to appeal to a broader constituency and reducing the influence of the urban elite. At the same time, the benefits of India's economic growth have not been equally spread. The middle class has moved from a "revolution of rising expectations" to a "revolution of rising frustrations." The gap between rich and poor also continues to grow. On one hand, India now feeds itself, and the days when India was a net food importer and famines could leave thousands dead are over. India is now a net food exporter, and bad harvest years are not as serious as they once were. This improvement is thanks in large measure to the "green revolution" of the 1960s, which brought agricultural change to much of Asia, based on improvements in irrigation and seed quality and on the greater use of fertilizers. The result was that output grew while the area of land under crops stayed the same. Growth in the agricultural sector has also brought more investment in villages, which has created new wealth and jobs.

On the other hand, the poorest of India's rural people have been bypassed by economic development, encouraging many of them to seek jobs in cities such as Mumbai

This view of Mumbai (formerly Bombay) is typical of the dramatic contrasts in poverty and wealth that can be found in many newly industrializing countries. In the foreground, families live in shanty dwellings, within view of the affluent high-rise suburb of Bandra in the distance.

(formerly Bombay) and Calcutta. The cities cannot meet the growing need for housing and basic services, further dissatisfying the newly affluent middle class. While urban economic growth has accelerated, real farm incomes have stagnated over the past 30 years. In few places are the effects of rural poverty more marked than in the northeastern state of Bihar, where illiteracy runs at 75 percent, annual per capita income is just over $100, corruption is endemic, hundreds are killed every year in clashes between radical peasant militias and feudal landlords, and most people have never voted.

Even the wealthier parts of India have their problems, though. This was tragically emphasized in January 2001 when the northwestern state of Gujarat was hit by the most destructive earthquake in India's postindependence history. An estimated 25,000 people were killed, and property damage costs ran to nearly $6 billion. Gujarat is one of India's most prosperous states, yet the earthquake revealed that buildings were badly constructed, that inspections and building codes were not enforced, that urban disaster planning was inadequate, and that coordination among emergency agencies was almost nonexistent.

One of India's economic priorities since the early 1990s has been a program of privatization aimed at selling off hundreds of government-owned businesses, which among them make up nearly half of India's capital stock. Analysts suggest that India's relatively low productivity can be blamed in large part on too much government involvement in the economy; the benefits of privatization are already being felt as more competition opens up markets and helps consumers with lower prices and better services.

FOREIGN POLICY

By virtue of its size and location, India is a major regional power, yet there is little question that it operates below its potential in terms of its influence on world affairs. Its population is almost as big as that of China's, and it is much more democratic than China, yet its voice is heard less often in international relations than that of China. Much of the difference can be ascribed to economic policies; while India has been limited by the long-time role of government in the economy, China has been slowly building a large private sector that is exporting all over the world. India is only slowly catching up.

If India's economic voice is not yet heard as loudly as it might be, there is no question about its diplomatic and military influence. It pursued a semiautonomous foreign policy for at least 30 years before independence, and at the time of independence there were calls to have India completely sever its ties with Britain. Nehru, however, took over the foreign policy portfolio, secured India's entry into the Commonwealth, and made India an influential member of the wider Afro-Asian bloc. He used India's influence in the United Nations to promote the cause of decolonization, and Indian troops took part in UN peacekeeping operations in Korea, the Congo, and Cyprus. Nehru argued that India should not align itself with any other power, and in 1955 India became a founding member of the Non-Aligned Movement. For India, nonalignment meant independent action; although refusing to commit itself to any other country or bloc of countries, it reserved the right to take action to protect its security interests whenever necessary.

During the cold war, the United States had a closer relationship with Pakistan than with India, regarding the former as a bulwark against Soviet expansionism and the latter both as an enemy of Pakistan and a friend of the USSR. Certainly the USSR was an important arms and oil supplier and trading partner for India. With the end of the cold war, however, both India and the United States began rethinking their policies in the region. India has intervened militarily in the affairs of all its smaller neighbors, maintains the world's second largest army (with nearly 1.2 million men and women under arms), and has developed its own nuclear weapons. Already saddled with secessionist movements within its borders, India has also had to deal with border disputes with its neighbors. For example, it has been at odds with China since the late 1950s over Kashmir and the Indian state of Arunachal Pradesh. The most serious conflict between the two countries came in 1962, when China invaded northern India and advanced 150 miles before halting. The dispute, which remains unresolved, threatened to become a problem once again in the late 1980s with a buildup of troops on the Chinese side of the border.

Central to India's regional policy has been its relationship with Pakistan. Ever since the 1947 partition of India and Pakistan, relations between the two neighbors have been precarious, a key source of tension being the province of Kashmir (see Political Debates, p. 362). The two countries fought over Kashmir in 1947 and again in 1965 when China—which had its own border disputes with India—took the side of Pakistan, leading to concerns about the broader potential impact of the conflict. The Soviet Union, hoping to check Chinese influence in the region and strengthen ties with both India and Pakistan, stepped in as mediator, and a peace agreement was signed in Tashkent in the central USSR in 1966.

The worst outbreak of fighting between the two countries came in 1971, when India became involved in the Pakistan civil war. The relationship between East and West

Pakistan had been uncertain and unequal from the beginning. Divided by 1,000 miles of Indian territory, the wealthier and mainly Urdu-speaking West dominated the poorer, overcrowded, and mainly Bengali-speaking East. The East provided not only cheap labor but also natural resources such as cotton and jute, earnings from which kept the federal budget balanced. With 55 percent of the total population of the two Pakistans, the East was given only 36 percent of development spending.

In March 1971 the East declared its independence as Bangladesh. The Pakistani army immediately clamped down, heralding nine months of civil war and repression during which untold thousands of East Pakistanis were killed (claims range from tens of thousands to 3.5 million) and 10 million refugees (mainly Hindus) crossed into India. Concerned about the possibility of communal rioting in India, the government of Indira Gandhi began taking a more active interest in the war, and when Pakistan launched a series of air strikes against India on December 3, the Indian response was immediate. On December 6, 1971, India recognized the government of Bangladesh, and just 10 days later its troops entered Dacca and accepted the surrender of Pakistan. India's troops were withdrawn three months later, and Bangladesh was recognized as an independent, sovereign state.

India's role in the war established it as the undisputed power in the subcontinent, a fact that was reemphasized in 1974 when India exploded a nuclear device and became only the sixth country to openly acknowledge a nuclear capability. The explosion was an unmistakable signal to India's neighbors, but it also had global implications, raising concerns in the United States about a nuclear arms race between India and Pakistan. India has been developing missiles—the Agni 1 and the Agni 2—which can carry nuclear and conventional warheads; the latter has a range of 1,375 miles, putting all of Pakistan and much of China in range.

In the 1980s, India accused Pakistan of supplying weapons to Sikh terrorists in the Punjab, and relations between the two countries became so jittery that in 1987, when both countries held military exercises near their joint border, tensions escalated to the point where 340,000 troops were massed on the border in a state of high alert. Problems arose again in May 1999 when Pakistani soldiers infiltrated Indian-held Kashmir. India launched an attack that cost the lives of several hundred soldiers before Pakistani-held positions were recaptured in July.

The most worrisome element of the relationship between the two countries is that they are both now nuclear powers, and the United States in particular fears that a conventional war between them could quickly escalate into a nuclear war. In 1993 the director of the U.S. Central Intelligence Agency was quoted as saying that "the arms race between India and Pakistan poses perhaps the most probable prospect for future use of weapons of mass destruction, including nuclear weapons."[22] The dangers were given graphic illustration in May 1998 when India carried out five nuclear tests and Pakistan responded with six tests of its own. The actions of both governments were universally condemned by other countries.

Indian foreign policy has also included a strong peacekeeping element, as when India sent troops to the Maldives in 1988 to prevent a coup from taking place, and stationed troops in Sri Lanka in 1987–90, supposedly helping underwrite a peace agreement aimed at ending Sri Lanka's civil war. Conflict between the Sinhalese majority and the Tamil minority worsened during the 1970s, leading in 1976 to the creation of a political coalition demanding the creation of an independent Tamil state.

THE MOST DANGEROUS PLACE IN THE WORLD?

In March 2000 U.S. President Bill Clinton described south Asia as "the most dangerous place in the world." He was referring to a potentially lethal combination: two archenemies living next door to each other, both armed with nuclear weapons, and both at odds over a large piece of disputed territory. That territory is Kashmir, claimed by both India and Pakistan, over which the two countries have already twice gone to war (in 1947 and 1965), and which has recently become embroiled in the "war on terrorism."

The dispute dates back to independence and the partition of the two countries in 1947. The Hindu maharajah of Kashmir announced that it would become part of India, a decision Pakistan refused to accept because of the large Muslim population in the province. Fighting then broke out, as a result of which both Pakistan and India moved in troops. A UN cease-fire line was accepted by both sides in 1949, leaving one-third of the state under Pakistani control, but India refused to have an arbitrator appointed to review the problem for fear that this would lead to a plebiscite that would favor Pakistan.

In 1965 tensions increased and the two countries went to war again, Pakistan taking a beating from Indian forces. Since then there has been a deeply troubled peace in Kashmir. The Muslims who make up 60 percent of the population of Indian Kashmir oppose rule by India, militant anti-Indian groups have attracted growing support, and Pakistani leaders have been pressured by right-wing Islamists to support the cause of Kashmir's militants. India has continued to insist on claiming all of Kashmir, and there has been a steady buildup of India's military presence in the region and regular exchanges of fire between Indian and Pakistani troops. A new dimension was added to the problem in 1998 when India and Pakistan formally confirmed that they were nuclear powers (something that had been known informally for many years).

In February 1999 Indian prime minister Vajpayee traveled to Pakistan to meet with Pakistani leader Nawaz Sharif, and the two promised to resolve their differences peacefully. But when Pakistani troops captured territory inside Indian Kashmir, India responded with force. The problem took on a new significance September 11, 2001, because Vajpayee subsequently portrayed himself as the leader of a democracy in a struggle against terrorists. There have been a number of terrorist attacks, including the October 2001 car bomb attack on the legislature of Indian Kashmir. In December 2001, terrorists allegedly trained in Pakistan attacked India's Parliament while it was in session; none of the legislators were hurt, but all six terrorists and five security officers were killed. Three simultaneous bomb explosions in the Indian capital of Delhi in October 2005, that killed 62 people, were suspected of having a connection with Kashmir. International attention has been drawn away from Kashmir by problems in Iraq and North Korea, but the tensions in this very troubled area of the world remain.

The activities of separatist Tamil Tiger guerrillas led to a state of emergency in Sri Lanka in 1983, along with the dispatch of the Indian peacekeeping force (whose numbers grew from 7,000 to 50,000, eliciting charges of Indian imperialism from Tamil separatists). It was a Tamil Tiger who was implicated in the 1991 assassination of Rajiv Gandhi, supposedly over resentment at how the arrival of the Indian peacekeeping force in Sri Lanka had forced the Tigers back on the defensive.

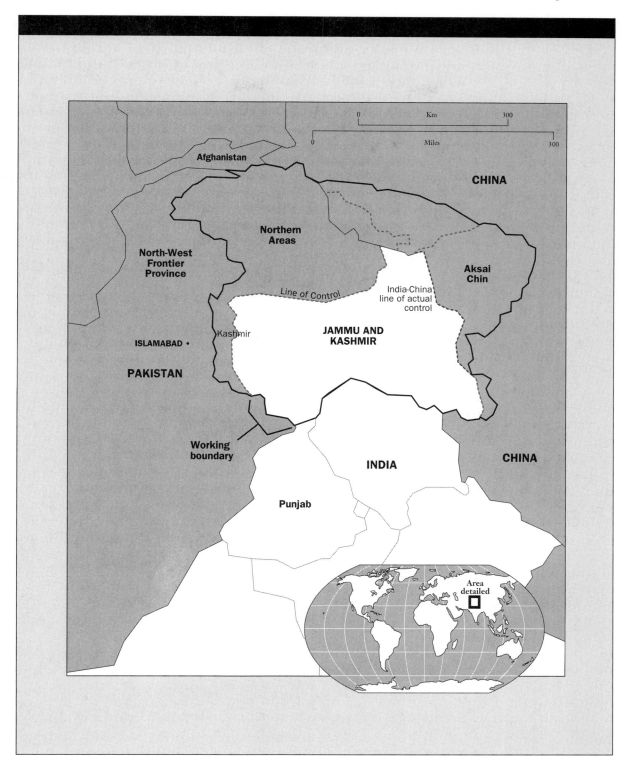

INDIAN POLITICS IN TRANSITION

Questions have been regularly raised since India's independence in 1947 about the country's governability and political stability. Several times it has seemed that India was on the brink of breaking down in religious, social, and economic chaos, yet it has survived. It has come through territorial wars with its neighbors, secessionist struggles by religious minorities, frequent communal violence, a dangerous reliance on a single family for leadership, and attempts by some of its leaders to subvert the democratic process. It still has religious tensions, its population growth is outpacing its ability to meet basic needs for most of its people, and its economy still suffers from the burden of a long history of state intervention. That intervention helped India feed itself and develop an extensive industrial base, but the signs are that it now needs to accelerate the process of economic liberalization and allow its entrepreneurs to create the same opportunities at home as those who have left India have created abroad.

The Rao government began quickening the process of economic liberalization in 1991, and India's economy has since grown ever faster; the architect of many of the economic changes of the 1990s, Manmohan Singh, became prime minister in 2004. If the benefits of economic reform are spread widely enough, then social tensions may be eased and political stability improved, but the fragmentation of party politics reduces the prospects for the latter. India has the potential to become one of the wealthiest and most prosperous countries in the world, but it must first balance its political, economic, and social reforms.

KEY TERMS

Bharatiya Janata Party	Hinduism	Rajya Sabha
British Raj	Kashmir	*satyagraha*
caste	Lok Sabha	structural violence
Congress Party	Nehru-Gandhi dynasty	untouchables

KEY PEOPLE

Indira Gandhi	Sonia Gandhi	Manmohan Singh
Mahatma Gandhi	Muhammed Ali Jinnah	Atal Behari Vajpayee
Rajiv Gandhi	Jawaharlal Nehru	

STUDY QUESTIONS

1. Does structural violence help us understand social problems outside India?

2. Compare and contrast the effects of colonialism on the United States, Mexico, and India.

3. How were Japan and China able to avoid colonization, while India was not?

4. What are the implications for democracy of "emergency" powers in countries such as Russia and India?

5. Which is more appropriate to the needs of a divided society such as India: coalition governments or strong leaders with legislative majorities?

6. Compare and contrast the roles of the prime minister in Britain, Japan, and India.

7. Do dynastic traditions help or hinder the development of emergent states such as India?

8. What reforms (if any) would you make to the Indian electoral system to produce stronger governments?

9. Is there anything wrong with the idea of Sonia Gandhi as prime minister of India?

10. Does India have the potential to become a superpower in the 21st century?

INDIA ONLINE

Prime Minister's Office: http://pmindia.nic.in
Offcial home page of the Prime Minister of India.
The Indian Parliament: http://parliamentofindia.nic.in
Official home page of the Indian legislature, with links to information on the membership, committees, debates, and the budget.
Indian National Congress: www.congress.org.in
Bharatiya Janata Party: http://bjp.org
Official Web sites of India's two major parties.
GOI Directory: http://goidirectory.nic.in
India Image: http://indiaimage.nic.in
Two sites offering an extensive selection of links on government and politics in India.
The Hindu: www.hinduonline.com
The Times of India: http://timesofindia.indiatimes.com
Online versions of two respected daily Indian newspapers.

FURTHER READING

Cohen, Stephen P., *India: Emerging Power* (Washington DC: Brookings Institutions, 2002). A study of the changing economy and society of India, and its emerging global power.

Das, Gurcharan, *India Unbound: The Social and Economic Revolution from Independence to the Global Information Age* (New York: Anchor Books, 2002). An analysis of India's postindependence economic and social changes, written by a former CEO of a major Indian corporation.

Hardgrave, Robert L., and Stanley A. Kochanek, *India: Government and Politics in a Developing Nation*, 6th Ed. (Fort Worth, TX: Harcourt College Publishers, 2000). One of the standard introductions to Indian politics.

Jayal, Niraja Gopal (Ed.), *Democracy in India* (Oxford: Oxford University Press, 2001). An edited collection that includes chapters on the relationship between democracy and different elements of life in India.

Keay, John, *India: A History* (New York: Grove Press, 2000). A lengthy study of more than 5,000 years of Indian history, with an emphasis on the pre-independence eras.

COMPARATIVE EXERCISE

IDEOLOGIES

If a competition were to be held for the most commonly used and most frequently misunderstood terms in political science, *ideology* would make a strong running against terms such as *state*, *democracy*, and *freedom*. It is much abused, has been given multiple meanings, and is often associated with partisans or zealots (if the latter are defined as people of uncompromising or extreme views). "Oh, she's an ideological liberal," we might hear it said of someone with strong left-wing political views.

Although it was coined in 1795 by the French philosopher Antoine Destutt de Tracy to describe the science of ideas, the term has since come to mean a set of ideas or values held by individuals or societies. Put another way, it means a "worldview," or an overall perception that people have about the world around them, made up of a set of attitudes, moral views, and beliefs that provide us with a set of reference points and explanations for the world around us. An ideology helps us organize the complexity of the world in which we live and helps drive our attitudes toward the events we witness and decide how we feel about those events. It is usually applied to politics but is also used in relation to other elements of the social sciences, such as religion and economics.

For purposes of easy reference, most political ideologies are classified on a spectrum running from left to right. This grew out of the practice in the French National Assembly in the late eighteenth century, when—to keep delegates with similar views together and to prevent the outbreak of fistfights—conservative members (pro-monarchists) were seated on the right of the chamber, moderates in the center, and radicals (who wanted an entirely new political system) on the left. We still describe conservatives as right-wing and liberals as left-wing and place all the other "isms" somewhere on that spectrum, from nationalism and fascism on the right

to social democracy, socialism, and communism on the left. If we examine these closely enough, though, we find that the far left and the far right are not that different in terms of their values, so we should really talk in terms of a circle rather than a spectrum.

Ideology plays a very different role in the various political systems examined in this book:

- For most Americans it has little meaning, because ideological identification is low among American voters and American political parties rarely couch their policy positions in terms of ideology. Republicans have conservative leanings and Democrats have liberal leanings, but there are many shades of ideological identification within the two parties, so much so that there is very little difference in Congress between liberal Republicans and conservative Democrats in terms of the views they hold and their positions on bills. When it comes to voters, only about one in three Americans admits to being firmly liberal or conservative or to identifying with either of the two major parties.

- Ideology in almost every other liberal democracy is associated with a variety of economic and social issues (and occasionally regional issues), there is a greater variety of positions represented on the political spectrum than in the United States, and there is more ideological distinction among parties and the voters who support them. Most mainstream parties are either conservative or liberal (as they are conventionally defined). Conservatives take the view (confusingly) that government should pursue classical liberal ideas such as promotion of the free market, a limited role in the economy, and a belief in self-reliance (but a hands-on approach to moral issues). Liberals believe that society's inequalities can best be resolved through government intervention in the form of welfare, subsidized education, and regulation.

At the same time, though, parties with more radical views have won support on the margins, notably communist parties on the left and anti-immigrant nationalist parties on the right. Western Europe has also seen notable gains being made by feminist and green political parties. The latter are commonly associated with environmental issues but actually have a much wider range of interests and often claim that they are "neither left nor right, but in front."

- For emerging countries, ideological divisions are based less on the hands-on/hands-off spectrum seen in liberal democracies, and more on differing attitudes toward reform or national identity. As Russia struggles to reinvent itself, the key division among parties relates to their positions on reform of the economic system—some advocate rapid reforms designed to turn Russia into a free-market liberal democracy, others would prefer a return to centralized state control, and yet others worry about Russia's place in the world as the reforms take place. In Mexico, the key issue is reform of the political and economic system, and left–right differences are less important than differences over the speed of political and economic reform.

- In deeply divided societies such as India, Nigeria, and Egypt, ideology is associated in most people's minds with regional, ethnic, and religious differences. The key driving force in India is the balance between Hindu and Muslim interests, and between the interests of the states versus India as a political entity. In Nigeria, attempts to build an "ideologically driven" party system (that is, a system in which parties are driven by differences over economic and social issues) have failed time and again as parties become ethnically driven, identifying with the interests of the major ethnic groups. In Egypt, the only significant opposition to the governing National Democratic Party comes not from liberal or conservative opposition parties but from a banned Islamist party, the Muslim Brotherhood.

One of the eternal questions in politics is whether people are motivated mainly by their interests, their beliefs, or a combination of the two. It might be logical to assume that rich people in liberal democracies would be conservative (because, among other things, conservative parties are opposed to high taxes) and poor people would be liberal or socialist (because liberal parties are in favor of welfare), but the opposite is often true. It might also be logical to assume that all Indians and Nigerians identify with parties that promote their regional or ethnic interests, but they do not. Ideology may not be a foolproof guide to political attitudes and action, but—used carefully—it can help explain a lot.

Part IV

LESS DEVELOPED COUNTRIES

*True individual freedom cannot exist without economic security and independence.
People who are hungry and out of a job are the stuff of which dictatorships are
made.*

—President Franklin D. Roosevelt

While liberal democracies are stable, democratic, and wealthy, and NICs have made
the kinds of policy changes needed to put them on the path to stability and wealth,
less developed countries (LDCs) have had greater difficulties in finding the formula
for success. They have not yet built stable political structures and processes and their
economic prospects are limited by a heavy reliance on agriculture and minerals
rather than industry or services. Some have made policy changes in recent years that
may lead to long-term stability and prosperity, but most have immature political
institutions, top-heavy or inefficient bureaucracies, often widespread problems with
corruption, economies that depend either on agricultural exports or on a small range
of major products or services, poorly developed social services, and—correspondingly—
little political or economic independence.

Just why this should be so is debatable, and is confused by the fact that even
neighboring countries have followed quite different paths of political and economic
development. Why, for example, is Jamaica (a NIC), which became independent in
1962, more stable than the nearby Dominican Republic (an LDC), which had a 120-year
head start on independence? Why has the West African state of Senegal never had a
military coup, while nearby Nigeria has had at least six since 1966? Why have
Argentina and Brazil become NICs, while neighboring Bolivia, with about as many
years of independence, remains one of the poorest countries in the world? Why is
Tanzania politically stable, when its immediate neighbors Rwanda and Burundi are
not? Are there common structural explanations for the differences? Does the fault
lie with policy choices made by the leaders of these countries, or are they victims of
a global system that has kept them immature and dependent?

CHECKLIST

LESS DEVELOPED COUNTRIES
What Are Their Features?

- A mixed record on representative government, with elections often accompanied by fraud and violence.

- Weak, immature, or poorly defined political institutions and processes.

- Varying degrees of public loyalty to the state. In the most troubled cases, legitimacy undermined by serious external or internal threats.

- A variety of institutionalized forms of political participation and representation, but no guarantees that the voices of citizens will be heard effectively.

- A mixed record on the protection of individual rights under the law.

- A professed belief in human equality, but in reality considerable inequalities.

- A mixed record on political opposition and freedom of speech. At worst, public services and government undermined by incompetence, corruption, or cronyism.

- Inefficient or troubled economies with low per capita GDPs, and based either on one dominant product or a variety of primarily agricultural products.

- Relatively low levels of urbanization, and generally poor infrastructure.

- Low technological development.

- A relatively low quality of life when measured by the provision of education, health care, and other basic services.

- Medium to low ratings on the Freedom House Index and usually low ratings on the Human Development Index.

- Minimal global influence, except in a reactive sense.

Where Are They?

There are 35, and they are mainly in Africa and Latin America:

Belize	Guyana	Peru
Bolivia	Honduras	Samoa
Botswana	Kenya	Senegal
Cameroon	Kiribati	Seychelles
Cape Verde	Marshall Islands	Solomon Islands
Colombia	Micronesia	Suriname
Congo	Namibia	Swaziland
Dominican Republic	Nauru	Tanzania
Ecuador	Nicaragua	Tonga
Fiji	Nigeria	Uganda
Gabon	Palau	Vanuatu
Ghana	Papua New Guinea	
Guatemala	Paraguay	

Western political science has failed to provide general answers to questions like these.[1] Part of the problem is self-imposed: Most political scientists still handicap themselves by approaching the Third World as an amorphous whole, instead of appreciating that it no longer exists. The task is further complicated by the way in which studies of poorer countries are driven more by economic and social factors than by political factors. Look at most of the books published on poorer countries and you will find chapters on economic structures and social change, but there will be little on their political features.

Broadly speaking, LDCs have five major features in common.

Weak Political Institutions

In liberal democracies, political structures have achieved high levels of legitimacy and public acceptance. There are strong and complex institutions, and many channels through which people can take part in politics. By contrast, most LDCs have low levels of **political institutionalization,** a process defined by one political scientist as "the effective establishment of state authority over society through specially created political structures and organs."[2] One of the sources of Nigeria's problems, for example, is that it has yet to develop institutions that have validity among Nigerians or that have the power and authority to compete against the other allegiances (notably ethnicity) that attract public attention. The weakness of civilian institutions in LDCs is reflected in three phenomena that most have experienced at one time or another.

political institutionalization The process through which politics and government become institutionalized and develop regular features.

- **One-party rule.** Many LDCs have seen rule by a single party or a single dominant party, with opposition parties either been banned or controlled. In some cases, the rulers of LDCs have used the Leninist vanguard argument, portraying the party leadership as an educated elite that can lead the masses out of ignorance and division. In other cases, they have argued that the existence of more than one political party is too divisive for young states trying to build national unity. For example, former president Julius Nyerere of Tanzania once argued that African society lacked the class divisions that had encouraged the emergence of multiparty systems in liberal democracies.[3] Similarly, Ugandan president Yoweri Museveni has argued that because most Ugandans are poor, they do not have the social and economic divisions needed to encourage the development of parties with different ideological platforms. Instead, ethnically based parties have developed, thereby creating conflict. To prevent this, he declared Uganda to be a "no-party state."

- **Personal rule.** Where power in liberal democracies is divided and limited, in most LDCs it is centralized and personalized. Where liberal democracies have individuals and groups competing publicly to win the right to govern within the rules of a constitution, LDCs often see power accumulating in the hands of ruling elites, often resulting in leaders holding on to power for many years; thus Omar Bongo of Gabon has been in power since 1967, and Paul Biya of Cameroon has been in power since 1982. For the more ambitious citizens of LDCs, there are fewer opportunities in business, law, or education than in politics, which is partly why it attracts those with a thirst for power. Politics regularly consists of personal or factional struggles to win and keep power, politicians use private agreements and personal ties rather than public rules and institutions,[4] and the ruler often becomes the pivot of state power. He manipulates the law, the police, and the military to keep and express power; he denies power to other groups; and his hold on power breeds corruption retards the development of other political institutions.

- **Military government.** Many LDCs at some point in their recent history have seen themselves either coming under the direct rule of the military, or witnessing a strong military role in civilian political affairs. Why has this been so, and has it been a cause or a consequence of wider political problems? The Kenyan political scientist Ali Mazrui offers several possible explanations for the frequency of military governments in Africa:[5] They may reflect the weaknesses of other political institutions; the military offers social advancement to a country's brightest and most ambitious citizens; a lack of purpose (few LDCs have been to war in recent decades) can lead to boredom and dissatisfaction with incumbent leaders; and military coups are relatively easy to stage because of the concentration of political and economic power in one urban center. The importance of the military in politics was particularly obvious during the 2003 Nigerian elections: the winner (Olusegun Obasanjo) was a former military leader, as was his chief rival (Muhammadu Buhari), while another former military leader (Ibrahim Babangida) was rumored to be pulling strings behind the scenes.

Unstable State Structures

An important prerequisite for democracy is a stable state system, something that many LDCs have found hard to achieve. Whether the spark is internal ethnic, religious, or cultural divisions, or a large gap in income between the poor and the wealthy, many LDCs have struggled to build internal stability. For many African countries, the problem has been the challenge of building viable states within borders created by colonial powers. (The maps in Figure IV.1 show clearly how the borders of modern African states bear no relation at all to the traditional territories of different ethnic groups.) Internal divisions have led to civil wars (such as the Biafran conflict in Nigeria in the late 1960s, a civil war in Uganda in the mid-1980s, and another in the Republic of Congo in 1997–1999), and to border disputes (such as that between Cameroon and Nigeria in the mid-1990s). The scale of these conflicts pales by comparison with those in many marginal countries (see Part VI), but they nevertheless remain a root cause of political turmoil.

Latin American LDCs face relatively few ethnic problems, except where there are large Native American populations, but their sense of national identity has often been weakened by poverty, which—for example—was at the heart of the civil war that raged in Guatemala between 1960 and 1996, involving a combination of the army, right-wing death squads, and antigovernment guerrillas, and leading to the deaths or disappearance of more than 200,000 people. Some political scientists also argue that the stability of several Latin American LDCs has been undermined by Western neoimperialism, whether in the form of cold war military intervention (such as U.S. support for right-wing Nicaraguan counter-revolutionaries (the Contras) in the 1980s), or in the form of demands made by wealthy donor countries and international lending institutions (see following section).

FIGURE IV.1

Comparing Traditional and Modern Boundaries in Africa

Ethnic groups

Political borders

Source: Upper map from Martin Ira Glassner and Harm J. de Blij, *Systematic Political Geography* (New York: John Wiley and Sons, 1989).

A Limited Economic Base

While NICs have attracted foreign investment, opened their markets, and enjoyed broad-based export-led economic growth, the economies of LDCs have grown more slowly, if at all. They are not the poorest countries in the world (that distinction being reserved for marginal countries), but most are industrializing only very slowly, rely heavily on agriculture and/or minerals, have few exports, and have a low per capita GDP (mainly in the range of $300 to $1,500). Some LDCs are building their industrial sectors and developing more diverse economies, but they tend to be the exceptions. Botswana, for example, has invested its earnings from diamond exports in infrastructure, meat production, and the tourist trade. More typical for LDCs, though, are Belize (which relies heavily on sugar exports); Bolivia (zinc, gold, and tin); Congo, Gabon, and Nigeria (oil); Suriname (bauxite); and Kiribati, Palau, and Tonga (fish). The Indian Ocean island state of the Seychelles, meanwhile, is almost entirely dependent upon tourism.

banana republic
A country whose economy is limited to a few agricultural products, whose marketing and profits benefit foreign multinational corporations.

Many LDCs are quintessential **banana republics.** This is a pejorative label, originally coined to describe countries such as Guatemala and Honduras, whose economies relied heavily on the export of bananas, whose economic policies were dominated by U.S. multinationals such as the United Fruit Company, and whose politics were prone to interference by the United States. It could now be applied to almost any country that is dependent on a small selection of agricultural products whose prices are determined by the international market, and the production and marketing of which is often dominated by foreign multinationals. For these and other LDCs, the prospects for economic improvement are dimmed by at least three key problems:

- The prices for most of their exports are determined in foreign markets, and LDCs have little influence over those prices and limited prospects for diversifying their economies to compensate.

- LDC exports are growing only slowly. For example, while the merchandise exports of the Philippines, Mexico, and India grew in the period 1993–2003 by 228 percent, 218 percent, and 159 percent, respectively, Nigeria increased its exports by 104 percent, Senegal by 88 percent, and Botswana and Venezuela by 61 percent. (In more troubled marginal countries, merchandise exports in some cases actually fell; they were down 25 percent in Zimbabwe and down 81 percent in Gambia.)[6]

- Many LDCs have substantial debt problems (relative to the size of their economies), caused by heavy borrowing when commodity prices are high. Ecuador is a case in point; increased income (from oil) encouraged the purchase of more imports and fueled inflation, which became so bad that in 2000 the government replaced the national currency with the U.S. dollar.

To make matters worse, many LDC governments are guilty of mismanagement and waste, and of squandering badly needed foreign aid and investment on low-priority prestige projects—such as new airports, conference centers, highways, and luxury hotels—instead of investing in education, health care, and sanitation. The concentration of power in the hands of governing elites has also increased the opportunities for corruption, and LDCs such as Nigeria, Paraguay, and Honduras have become watchwords for graft and the personal enrichment of politicians, judges, bureaucrats and members of the police.

Inadequate Social Services

LDCs are typically much less urbanized than liberal democracies or NICs, with about 50 to 80 percent of their populations living in rural areas, having little political influence on urban policymakers, and being provided only with basic education and health care. Where there is a significant urban population, it is often blighted by poverty and a lack of investment in housing and other infrastructure, leading to serious social problems. In Honduras, for example, the activities of youth gangs known as *maras*, coupled with widespread police corruption, have made crime the primary issue in public policy. Meanwhile, personal security in Nairobi, the capital of Kenya, has deteriorated to the point that it is widely known as "Nairobbery."

More broadly, most LDCs have poorly developed transport and communications systems, leaving their rural areas isolated and making it difficult for goods to be moved. Among the consequences: few opportunities for farmers and small entrepreneurs to turn a profit, an undereducated workforce, high levels of illiteracy (10 to 40 percent among men), low life expectancy (40 to 60 years), and high rates of infant mortality (30 to 90 deaths per 1,000 live births). On the Human Development Index, most LDCs rank among the lower two thirds of the countries on the list.

To complicate the situation, health care in many LDCs has improved more quickly than economic prospects, which has led to increased population growth. The birth rate may not have changed, but infant mortality rates have declined, leading to an explosion in the number of younger people. The major demographic challenge facing liberal democracies is that their citizens are living longer and the number of elderly people is increasing, placing increased pressure on health care and social security. For LDCs, population numbers are expanding from below, increasing the demand for education and jobs and stretching the ability of the economic system to manage (see Figure IV.2).

For many African LDCs, the absence of adequate education and health care not only has meant too many avoidable deaths from diseases such as malaria (which now kills about a million people in sub-Saharan Africa every year) but has taken on a new significance over the last 20 years with the spread of HIV/AIDS. The lack of preventive health care, coupled with migratory labor systems that oblige many working men to spend many months away from home and social norms that make it difficult to convince many of them to practice safe sex and avoid prostitutes, has led to the rapid spread of HIV/AIDS. Of the more than 39 million people thought to be infected with HIV worldwide in 2005, nearly two-thirds were in sub-Saharan Africa. In the worst affected states in southern Africa (such as Botswana, Swaziland, and Lesotho), more than 20 percent of the population is infected, and deaths from AIDS have begun to lead to falling life expectancy.

Global and Regional Marginalization

Their growing wealth and political stability has given NICs a new level of influence in the world, allowing some of them to act as engines of regional economic growth

FIGURE IV.2

Comparing Population Structure

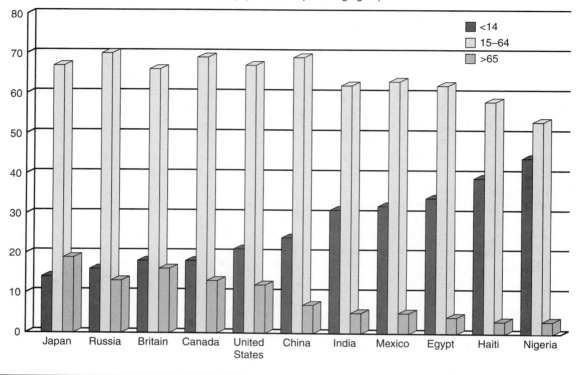

% of population in specific age groups

Source: World Bank, World Development Indicators database, 2005, www.worldbank.org/data. Figures are for 2003.

and drawing more attention from the leaders of the rich industrialized countries. By contrast, most LDCs lack the political or economic power to play an active role in regional affairs or to have much impact on global events. They have less control over their own destinies than do NICs and find themselves in a reactive rather than a proactive relationship with the rest of the world. Most have relatively few sources of national income and the prospects for economic development are further compromised by poor policy choices, centralized decision making, an undereducated workforce, and social problems that undermine attempts to build political stability.

Rich countries and poor countries alike have to borrow to pay the bills, but while rich countries have abundant collateral, poor countries have few sources of income and find it more difficult to service their debts (make the scheduled repayments). A poor country that wants to maintain a positive credit rating with international lending agencies may be required to make policy adjustments demanded by these agencies,

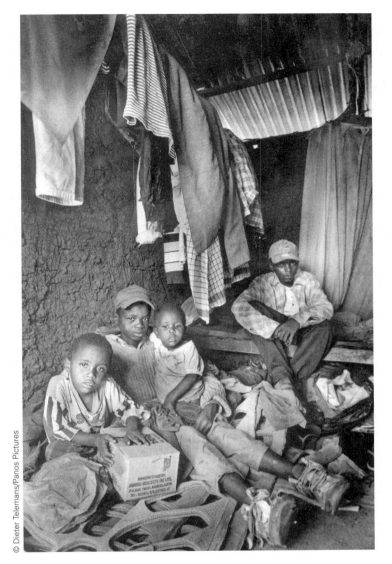

AIDS orphans in their home in one of the slums of Nairobi, Kenya. They survive by scavenging in a dump for anything of value. Their plight is all too common in sub-Saharan African countries struggling with the spread of HIV and AIDS.

or else the agencies may demand that loans be directed at particular economic sectors. This has led to charges that these agencies, most of which are based in (and underwritten by) North America or Europe, are engaging in a form of neoimperialism. Or perhaps they are simply encouraging the kinds of economic changes LDCs need to build self-reliance.

Prominent among the lending agencies are the World Bank and the International Monetary Fund (IMF), both part of the United Nations, both of which were founded in 1945, and both of which are headquartered in Washington, D.C. While the World Bank provides economic development loans, the IMF promotes global monetary stability and economic development. The World Bank has been associated in recent years with so-called **structural adjustment** programs, through which it has required countries seeking loans to balance their budgets, deregulate their financial systems, adopt more liberal trade policies, privatize state-owned industries and services, and remove price controls.

Although these are the kinds of policies associated with liberal democracies, questions have been raised about whether they are the right policies for poorer countries. They helped Asian and Latin American states become NICs, so they may offer the same possibilities for LDCs. However, among the criticisms of the World Bank and the IMF are that (1) they channel government money to poor countries, which may be better served by private investment; (2) they have been prepared to help authoritarian regimes if they are able to guarantee economic stability; and (3) they do not so much encourage self-reliance as incorporation into a Western-dominated global economy. Critics of the lending agencies argue that the best short-term prospects for LDCs may be offered by spillover from neighboring economic powers, such as Mexico, South Africa, and Southeast Asia's tiger economies. This would reduce the dependence of poor countries on Western-brokered lending agencies and move economic development more toward the free market.

EXPLAINING THE PROBLEMS OF DEVELOPMENT

Like almost every NIC, every LDC was colonized at one time or another. However, where NICs have been able to build new levels of postcolonial prosperity, most LDCs have not. Exactly why this has happened is debatable. Social scientists have offered many theories in their attempts to explain the problems of LDCs, variously blaming such potential villains as the international economic system, the greed of Western corporations, the entrapment of LDCs in cold war competition, traditional cultural values, and the incompetence of LDC governments. But there is no universal explanation; instead, we must look to a variety of theories, whether orthodox or radical.

Orthodox Explanations

modernization The process by which traditional societies undergo scientific, technological, social, economic, and political change.

Much of the debate about development in the 1960s centered on **modernization theory.** Looking at the process of decolonization in Africa and Asia, proponents of this theory optimistically argued that emerging countries could follow the same path as liberal democracies; they too had once been "underdeveloped," and look where they were now. Surely the Third World could follow suit—all it needed to do was to adopt modern cultural values and build modern political and economic institutions.[7] This was certainly the view of many colonial administrators as they bade farewell to their former African colonies in the 1950s and 1960s: leave these countries with good infrastructure, they argued, and with an educated elite, a reasonable range of exports, Western political institutions, and helpful injections of foreign aid, they stood a good chance of succeeding. In fact the opposite happened. Modernization turned out to be much more complex than most people thought, and the very process of modernizing often brought instability and violence,[8] making the prospects for these countries worse.

One example of an orthodox approach was the theory spelled out in 1960 by Walter W. Rostow, an economic historian who became an advisor to President Kennedy (and later national security advisor to President Johnson) and whose theories—some charge—helped encourage the United States to become involved in Vietnam. He argued that if poor countries were provided with enough capital, they could be encouraged to "takeoff" and move toward democracy and capitalism rather than communism. He suggested that countries would go through five **stages of growth:** (1) the traditional society, (2) the preconditions for takeoff, (3) takeoff, (4) the drive to maturity, and (5) the age of high mass consumption.[9] Under this analysis, liberal democracies would be at stage 5, most NICs would be between stages 3 and 4, and LDCs would be at stage 2. Rostow's theory was criticized for not explaining how societies moved from one stage to another, for overlooking the extent to which the traditional and the modern coexist in many poorer countries, and for assuming that capitalism and the "age of high mass consumption" are the goals of all economic development.

Radical Explanations

Reacting to the orthodox theories, several scholars in the 1960s and 1970s began arguing that the key to understanding LDCs was to focus on underdevelopment. They talked of a global economic system in which Europeans and North Americans made all the important decisions, and they argued that LDCs were being kept on the periphery, leading to unequal or uneven levels of development. There were several variations on this theme:

- **Imperialism.** Lenin had argued that imperialism was the highest stage of capitalism, that Western capitalists exploited African and Asian workers and peasants, and that by dividing up the rest of the world among themselves, the major powers had created a new proletariat and were promoting global class antagonism.[10] Using Leninist logic, colonialism was—and neocolonialism is—the major obstacle to progress in the LDCs. There is a global commercial and financial system, goes the theory, dominated by a world bourgeoisie at the center (the major industrialized countries) that influences a bourgeoisie on the periphery (the middle class of the LDCs), with a peripheral proletariat (the urban and rural poor of LDCs) at the bottom of the heap.[11] But while no one questions the economic power of liberal democracies and Western multinationals, neither Marxism nor Leninism has been able to explain why some African, Asian, and Latin American countries have become wealthy while others have stayed poor.

- **Vicious circle theory.** This theory argues that poverty perpetuates itself. Because incomes are low, money cannot be saved; without savings there is no capital or investment; without capital, productivity remains low, and the lack of investment leads to low productivity, low incomes, and low exports. In other words, it makes

imperialism The extension of power through superior military or economic force.

CRITICAL ISSUES

THE UNHAPPY TALE OF ZIMBABWE

© Mark Chilvers/Panos Pictures

In previous editions of this book, Zimbabwe has been classified as an LDC. It had all of the characteristic features of an LDC, and until just a few years ago was a country that had strong prospects of being an exception to the rule of the political and economic problems that beset so many of its neighbors. But today Zimbabwe is a country in crisis, one of the pariah nations of the world, governed by an autocratic and venal government that has all but destroyed the economic and social infrastructure of a once promising state. For these reasons, it has been reclassified as a Marginal Country.

Formerly the British colony of Southern Rhodesia (later Rhodesia), it was settled by emigrants from Britain. When Britain began talking of the possibility of giving the country independence under a majority black government, the white minority unilaterally declared independence in 1965. Political tensions rose, leading to a guerilla insurgency fighting for true independence. One of the guerilla groups was led by

Robert Mugabe (pictured left with his wife Grace), who—once a peace settlement had been negotiated and Rhodesia had become independent as Zimbabwe—became first prime minister and then president. Mugabe inherited a country with a vibrant economy, a well-educated population, an efficient government, and a working infrastructure.

After many years of strong and occasionally brutal government, Mugabe in 2000 launched a program of land redistribution, forcibly taking farms back from their white owners in order—he claimed—to give the land to the veterans of the war of independence. In fact much of the land was given to his cronies and supporters, who had no experience of farming. Productive farmland thus fell into misuse, leading to widespread starvation. Mugabe also clamped down on political opposition, and was reelected president in a 2002 election marred by violence and intimidation. The economy suffered as many of Zimbabwe's best educated citizens went into exile, inflation climbed to a high of 600 percent, exports fell, and infrastructure decayed. Meanwhile, Zimbabwe built one of the world's highest rates of AIDS/HIV infection.

This sorry tale suggests that all the theories of underdevelopment do not always hold, and that sometimes poverty is simply the result of bad decisions. In this case, a viable state with strong prospects has been undermined and driven into poverty by the narrow-minded incompetence of an authoritarian government.

the pessimistic argument that poor countries will always stay poor. However, the theory does not explain where and how the circle began (colonialism is usually blamed),[12] says nothing about the role of government and politics, and fails to explain the emergence of NICs or the fact that many LDCs have wealthy elites, emerging middle classes, and successful entrepreneurs.

■ **Dependency theory.** Developed mainly by Latin American social scientists (the *dependencistas*) in the 1960s and 1970s, this theory argues that poor countries will not follow the same path as rich countries (as suggested by modernization theory) because the latter have forever changed the nature of the international system. The rich countries had no major external competition when they first emerged, whereas emerging states in the 1970s faced major competition from the Americans, the Europeans, and the Japanese. Also, the new emerging countries had to borrow money and buy technology from the rich countries, building on a dependency that began during the colonial era. The result was the creation of an unequal world, with a core of rich countries controlling manufacturing and a periphery of poor countries living off the export of raw materials on unfavorable terms. To make matters worse, the rich countries maintained the wealth and power of elites within the poor countries. In short, poverty was not the fault of the poor countries, but of an unequal international system.

dependency
A theory by which a former colony achieves political independence but is still economically dependent on external powers.

The main problem with dependency theory once again was its difficulty in explaining the exceptions to the rule: why were countries such as Argentina, Brazil, Indonesia, Mexico, and Thailand breaking the mold of poverty? Variations on the theme of dependency theory suggested that some of the dependent countries could become wealthier, but they would do so while still remaining dependent on banks and multinationals in the rich countries.[13] As we saw in the case study on Mexico, however, some NICs have become so important as sources of cheap manufactured goods and cheap labor that not only have they undermined key sectors of the rich economies, but their welfare has a direct impact on the overall economic welfare of liberal democracies.

Responding to the problems in all these approaches, and criticizing Western political scientists for their tendency to apply American and European experiences, values, and assumptions,[14] non-Western theorists have responded by arguing the need to look at poorer countries on their own terms. One such line of thought is offered by the Indian theorist Vrajenda Raj Mehta, who argues that Western models take a unidimensional view of humans and society. He supports a multidimensional approach that goes beyond the objective and rational and includes the subjective, intuitive, ethical, and spiritual dimensions of our lives. He argues that "each national community has its own law of development, its own way to fulfill itself," that many of the problems of a country such as India can be linked to its attempts to apply inappropriate Western models, and that India, instead of trying to copy the West, should choose its own goals and "find its own strategy of development and nation-building suited to its own peculiar needs."[15] These are the same kinds of arguments behind the Islamic resurgence since 1979 in the Middle East (see Part V).

LDCs TODAY

Whether because of the international system, because of their own internal weaknesses, because of bad decisions by their leaders, or for some other reason, LDCs today find themselves struggling. And yet there are also signs that at least some of them are slowly developing traditions of political stability, which could help them build and diversify their economies.

For example, several LDCs with a history of military government are now working to build sustainable civilian government. This has happened in countries such as Guatemala and Ghana, but nowhere more dramatically than in Bolivia. During the first 155 years after its independence in 1825, Bolivia had 189 military coups, more than 60 revolutions, 70 presidents, and 11 constitutions—and yet since 1982 it has been under civilian rule. At the same time, new market-oriented economic policies helped bring its inflation rate down from a staggering 11,700 percent in 1985 to about 20 percent in 1997. The switch from military government to civilian government in countries such as Bolivia and Paraguay may now allow them, like Argentina, Brazil, Portugal, and Spain before them, to build democratic institutions.

Similarly, there are signs in some LDCs that power is being decentralized, and that the old habit of leaders holding on to power is beginning to die. In 1985, Julius Nyerere of Tanzania retired after 24 years in office, in 1989 Alfredo Stroessner stepped down after 35 years as leader of Paraguay, in 2000 Jerry Rawlings stepped aside after 19 years first as military leader of Ghana and then as its elected civilian leader, the 19-year leadership of Adbou Diouf in Senegal was ended by elections, and in 2002 Daniel arap Moi of Kenya left office after 24 years in power. Most Latin American LDCs now have multiparty systems (in some cases with so many parties that power is fragmented), and contested elections have been held in more than two dozen African states since 1991.

These could be the first signs that some LDCs may be about to begin resolving the short-term problems that have prevented them from building political stability and economic prosperity. Without internal stability, it is difficult to see them attracting the kind of foreign investment that allowed the United States to develop its resources in the nineteenth century, or Japan and Western Europe to rebuild their economies after World War II, or NICs to achieve the high levels of economic growth they have seen in the past 15 to 20 years. Integration in the global economy on unequal terms is often seen as a possible cause of the continued marginalization of LDCs, yet opening their markets may be the only way of achieving long-term political stability and economic growth.

KEY TERMS

banana republic
dependency theory
imperialism
modernization theory

political
  institutionalization
stages of growth

structural adjustment
vicious circle theory

STUDY QUESTIONS

1. Why are poor countries poor?

2. Is one-party rule an obstacle to political and economic development?

3. Comparing liberal democracies, NICs, and LDCs, what would you say were the minimum prerequisites for the construction of a stable and effective system of government?

4. Which is best for LDCs: changes to economic policies required by the World Bank and the IMF, or private investment from neighboring regional powers?

LDCs ONLINE

International Monetary Fund: www.imf.org
World Bank: www.worldbank.org
Web sites of the IMF and the World Bank; the latter includes useful information on all the countries where the bank is active.
U.S. Agency for International Development: www.info.usaid.gov
Web site of the federal agency responsible for overseeing the U.S. overseas aid program. It includes pages on all the countries where USAID is active.

FURTHER READING

Cammack, Paul, David Pool, and William Tordoff, *Third World Politics: A Comparative Introduction*, 3rd Ed. (Baltimore: Johns Hopkins University Press, 2003). Despite its unfortunate title, a useful introduction to the major political features and institutions of Africa, Latin America, and the Middle East.

Handelman, Howard, *The Challenge of Third World Development*, 3rd Ed. (Upper Saddle River, NJ: Prentice Hall, 2003). An introduction to the theories and realities of underdevelopment.

Harbeson, John W., and Donald Rothchild (Eds.), *Africa in World Politics: The African State System in Flux*, 3rd Ed. (Boulder, CO: Westview, 1999). A series of essays on the history and current problems of Africa, including economic development, democratization, and humanitarian issues.

Kamrava, Mehran, *Politics and Society in the Developing World* (London: Routledge, 2000). A useful study of issues such as democratization, economic development, and social change in poorer states. (Tellingly, it was first published in 1993 as *Politics and Society in the Third World*.)

Wiarda, Howard J. (Ed.), *Non-Western Theories of Development* (Fort Worth, TX: Harcourt Brace, 1999). An edited collection of chapters looking at the impact of Western and non-Western models of development on different regions of the world.

CHAPTER 8

NIGERIA

QUICK FACTS

Official name: Federal Republic of Nigeria

Capital: Abuja

Area: 351,649 square miles (910,770 sq. km) (twice the size of California)

Languages: English (official), Hausa, Yoruba, Igbo, Fulani, and several other languages

Population: 136.5 million

Population density: 361 per square mile (139 per sq. km.)

Population growth rate: 2.4 percent

POLITICAL INDICATORS

Freedom House rating: Partly Free

Date of state formation: October 1, 1960

System type: Presidential republic

Constitution: Published May 1999

Administration: Federal; 36 states and a Federal Capital Territory

Executive: President directly elected for four-year, renewable terms

Legislature: Bicameral National Assembly, consisting of a Senate (109 members) and a House of Representatives (360 members), both elected for four-year renewable terms

Party structure: Multiparty, but in early stages of evolution

Judiciary: Federal Supreme Court

Head of state: Olusegun Obasanjo (1999–)

Head of government: Olusegun Obasanjo (1999–)

ECONOMIC INDICATORS

GDP (2004): $72 billion

Per capita GDP: $390

Distribution of GNP: Services 24 percent, industry 50 percent, agriculture 26 percent

Urban population: 28 percent

SOCIAL INDICATORS

HDI ranking: 151

Infant mortality rate: 98 per 1,000 live births

Life expectancy: 44.9 years

Literacy: 74 percent of men aged 15 and older, 60 percent of women

Religions: About 50 percent Muslim, 30 percent Christian, and 20 percent traditional beliefs (estimated)

INTRODUCTION

Nigeria is an ideal laboratory in which to study African politics, for several reasons. It is a young country struggling to develop a national identity in the face of ethnic and religious divisions. Its political problems have produced both civilian and military governments, which have covered the spectrum from authoritarian to progressive. Its military power and oil wealth give it the potential to become a major regional power. Nigeria holds three particular interests to the United States: many African Americans trace their roots to what is now Nigeria, Nigeria is a major supplier of oil to the United States, and Nigeria is the source of about 40 percent of the heroin that comes into the United States. Finally, a study of Nigeria gives insights into a continent about which most Americans know much too little.

By population, Nigeria is the biggest country in Africa, but no one knows exactly how many Nigerians there are. The last reliable census was held in 1953; a deeply flawed recount in 1991 came up with a figure of 88.5 million; more recent UN estimates put the total closer to 137 million. Growing annually at 2.4 percent, the population is expected to double within 25 years, straining an infrastructure that is already grossly inadequate. Cities face particular problems: just over half of all Nigerians live in the rural areas, but the urban population is growing rapidly as people move to cities such as Lagos, Ibadan, and Enugu in search of jobs. With nearly nine million residents, Lagos is already the biggest city in Africa, and one of the 15 biggest cities in the world.

In economic terms, Nigeria is a poor country, with a GDP of just over $72 billion, or $390 per capita. But if we adjust for purchasing power parity, the GDP rises to nearly $145 billion (or $900 per capita), a reflection of the unrealistically low exchange rate of the Nigerian currency, the naira. If the large Nigerian black market could also be factored in to calculations, the economic picture would look very different. Whatever the size of the economy, however, the biggest problem Nigeria faces is its heavy dominance on oil, which accounts for nearly 99 percent of exports. Not only does this mean that the size and health of the entire economy is driven by the international market price of oil, but so are government revenues. To make matters worse, much of the oil wealth has been squandered and stolen, and there have been bitter political arguments over how to spend the balance. Nigeria also outspent itself during the oil-boom years of the 1970s and now has the biggest external debt in Africa: nearly $35 billion.

In social terms, Nigeria has four critical divisions:

- **Ethnicity.** There are thought to be somewhere between 250 and 400 different ethnic groups living in Nigeria. The biggest are the **Hausa-Fulani** in the north (28 to 30 percent of the population), the **Yoruba** in the southwest (about 20 percent), and the **Igbo** in the southeast (about 17 percent). Every attempt to encourage these groups to think of themselves as Nigerians has so far failed, leading a disgusted Wole Soyinka—the Nigerian novelist and 1986 Nobel laureate for literature—to dismiss the idea of a Nigerian nation as a "farcical illusion."

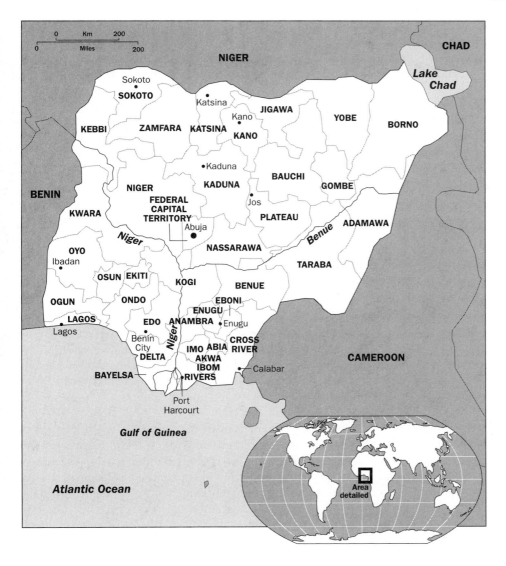

- **Religion.** Nigeria is divided between a mainly Muslim north and a non-Muslim south: Just over half of all Nigerians are Muslim, 30 percent are Christian, and the rest follow traditional religions. In the north there is pressure for the introduction of *sharia*, or Islamic law, and widespread admiration among ordinary people for the Al-Qaeda leader Osama bin Laden. Religious tensions repeatedly turn violent, as they did during 2002 when the Miss World beauty contest was due to be held in Nigeria and a local journalist commented that the participants were so beautiful that the prophet Muhammad might have wanted to marry one. Fighting between Muslims and Christians left about 220 people dead and as many as 1,000 injured.

- **Region.** Nigeria is divided between a north that is dry and poor and a south that is better endowed in resources and basic services: Lagos alone has ten times the elementary school enrollment of the northern region and six times as many hospital beds. Most of the best agricultural land is in the heavily populated south, while most of the northern half of the country is savanna or semi-desert, limiting the potential for agriculture. Regional tensions have been made worse by oil, most of which lies either in the southeast or off the coast of Nigeria, but the profits of which have largely been stolen or squandered by political elites in other parts of the country.

- **Class.** As in many African states, government and business in Nigeria are dominated by a small, educated elite. The wealthiest Nigerians include the new business class, landlords, traders, and self-employed professionals, but social advancement and wealth are also tied to jobs in government and the bureaucracy, which offer high salaries and opportunities for bribery and embezzlement.

In political terms, understanding Nigeria is made more difficult by the lack of settled and predictable political patterns. Since independence in 1960, there have been three civilian governments, five successful and several attempted military coups, a costly civil war, and nearly 30 years of military government. The first civilian government was based on the Westminster system, but Nigerians subsequently opted for the American model, with an elected president and a separate legislature. The first and second attempts at civilian government (1960–1966 and 1979–1983) broke down as leaders lost control and were unable to encourage Nigerians to set aside their ethnic differences. After being delayed several years, a third attempt was launched in May 1999 but faced the same tough challenge of encouraging Nigerians to pull together: estimates suggest that communal violence in the period 1999–2003 alone resulted in the deaths of a staggering 10,000 people (see Political Debates, p. 415).

POLITICAL DEVELOPMENT

Nigeria faces the challenge of trying to build a stable and united state out of a society that is divided along ethnic, religious, and economic lines and in which corruption has become a way of life. The legacy of colonialism could once be blamed for its problems, but Nigerian governments have made matters worse by failing to build a sense of national unity, by failing to tap in to the country's wealth of oil and people, by failing to build successful civilian political institutions, and by allowing incompetence to become a hallmark of the bureaucracy. The cumulative effect has been a story of unfulfilled dreams and missed opportunities, where narrow agendas have undermined the larger goals of building a stable and successful society.

Precolonial Era (900 B.C.–A.D. 1851)

The early history of Nigeria—like that of feudal Europe—is one of a series of states and kingdoms emerging, declining, and combining. From 900 B.C. to A.D. 200, what is now central Nigeria was dominated by the Nok, who discovered how to smelt iron and built a rich and advanced culture. Muslim traders began arriving in about 700, and by the fourteenth century the region was dominated by the kingdoms of Mali, Ghana, and Kanem-Bornu, connected by trade routes that stretched to Europe and the Middle East. By the sixteenth century, what is now northwest Nigeria was part of the Songhai empire, while southern Nigeria saw the rise of the rich and influential Benin culture.

The Portuguese were the first Europeans to explore the area, setting up coastal trading stations in the late fifteenth century, and founding Lagos. With the cooperation of Benin, they shipped slaves to the Americas to work in mines and on sugar plantations, and the **slave trade** became the biggest influence on the development of West Africa. The French, British, and Dutch arrived in the seventeenth century, setting up trading companies and building garrisons to protect their interests. Britain became the biggest slave trader, but when it banned the slave trade in 1807 (it was universally banned in 1833), the Royal Navy was dispatched to enforce the ban. Traders turned their interests to ivory and palm oil, explorers began opening up the interior, and then Christian missionaries arrived.

The Colonial Era (1861–1960)

Britain annexed Lagos in 1861 and then conquered the rest of what was to become Nigeria, driven mainly by concerns about French colonial expansion across the Sahel and North Africa. In 1900 Britain declared separate protectorates over Northern and Southern Nigeria and then combined them in 1914 into the colony and protectorate of Nigeria. It ruled Nigeria as two colonies with different administrative systems: indirect rule in the north through traditional Muslim emirates, which were hierarchical, authoritarian, and bureaucratic,[1] and direct rule in the south through an advisory Legislative Council. The divisions were deepened in 1939 when Britain split Nigeria into three provinces, each based on a different cash crop: peanuts in the North, cocoa in the West, and palm oil in the East. Because the provinces roughly coincided with Nigeria's three major ethnic groups, Nigerians were encouraged to think in regional rather than national terms.

In 1920 the National Congress of British West Africa was founded and began demanding greater political participation for Nigerians. Among the most active of the nationalists was Dr. Nnamdi Azikiwe, who in 1944 helped set up Nigeria's first modern political party, the National Council of Nigeria and the Cameroons. Britain began making arrangements for Nigerian independence after World War II, publishing three experimental constitutions. The third of these—in 1954—created the Nigerian Federation and established a federal parliament with half the seats

TABLE 8.1

Key Dates in Nigerian History

1485	First Portuguese trading post established
1833	Abolition of the slave trade
1861	Lagos annexed by the British
1884–1885	Berlin Conference confirms British claims to the Niger Territories
1914	Creation of the colony and protectorate of Nigeria
1920	Foundation of the National Congress of British West Africa
1944	Creation of the first modern Nigerian political party
1954	Declaration of the Federation of Nigeria
1960	(October 1) Independence
1963	Nigeria becomes a republic with Nnamdi Azikiwe as president
1966	(January) First military coup, Ironsi takes power; (July) second military coup, Gowon takes power
1967–1970	Nigerian civil war
1975	(July) Third military coup, Muhammed takes power
1976	Failed military coup, Obasanjo replaces Muhammed
1979	Fifth constitution
1979–1983	Second Republic; Shagari president
1983	(December) Fourth military coup, Buhari takes power
1985	(August) Fifth military coup, Babangida takes power
1989	Sixth constitution
1991	Abuja becomes Nigeria's new capital
1993	(June) Presidential elections held, but Babangida refuses to release results; (August) Babangida steps down, replaced by transitional civilian government; (November) Abacha takes power
1995	(July) Forty people, including Olusegun Obasanjo, imprisoned on charges of complicity in a coup plot; (October) Abacha regime announces its intention to return Nigeria to civilian rule by October 1998; (November) Ken Saro-Wiwa executed; Nigeria suspended from the Commonwealth
1998	(June) Death of Sani Abacha; (July) death of Moshood Abiola
1999	(February) Olusegun Obasanjo wins presidential elections; (May) civilian rule returns with creation of Fourth Republic; (November) thousands killed in army massacre in Delta region
2000	(August) Visit to Nigeria of President Clinton
2001	(September) More than 500 people killed in religious fighting in Jos; (October) more than 300 people killed in army massacre in Benue
2002	(January) Up to 2,000 people killed following explosion at Lagos army barracks
2003	(April) Olusegun Obasanjo wins election to a second term; (September) Nigeria's first satellite, NigeriaSat 1, launched by Russian rocket.

allocated to the North. Regional elections were held that were contested by several new political parties and movements, almost all of them regionally based. National elections in 1959 produced the first fully elected national government, and on October 1, 1960, Nigeria became independent under the leadership of its first prime minister, a Muslim Hausa-Fulani named Alhaji Sir Abubakar Tafawa Balewa.

Independence and the First Republic (1960–1966)

Nigeria became independent on October 1, 1960, as a federal parliamentary democracy. The British monarch was still head of state, but legislative power was vested in a bicameral parliament, executive power in a prime minister and cabinet, and judicial authority in a Federal Supreme Court. In 1963 Nigeria cut its remaining ties to the British Crown and became a republic with a new nonexecutive post of president, which was filled by Dr. Azikiwe. Unfortunately, the new republic almost immediately became tangled in a web of ethnic and religious divisions. The census proved controversial because the allocation of seats in the federal parliament was based on the number of people in each region. It was also clear that political parties had broken down along regional lines, with each state dominated by a single party. Interparty squabbling broke out, there were strikes by workers complaining about low pay, and charges of political corruption flew. National elections were held in 1964 amid charges of fraud, and regional elections in the west in 1965 were marred by civil unrest and riots. Meanwhile, the military had been quickly Africanized,[2] attracting some of the best and brightest members of Nigerian society, who watched the chaos of civilian politics with growing dismay.

Military Government I (1966–1979)

On January 15, 1966, Nigeria experienced its first military **coup d'etat** staged by a group of Igbo officers headed by Major Johnson Aguiyi Ironsi. Senior national and regional political leaders (including Prime Minister Balewa) were murdered, and the federal system was abolished. Northerners now feared that Igbos planned to establish control over Nigeria, and within days hundreds of northern Igbos had been beaten and killed in outbreaks of civil unrest. Problems reached a head in July when northern army officers staged a second coup, killing Ironsi and replacing him with Lieutenant Colonel Yakubu Gowon, a Christian from Nigeria's central region (sometimes known as the **Middle Belt**). Gowon restored the federal structure and promised a return to civilian rule following agreement of a new constitution. The massacre of Igbos living in the north continued, however, followed by retaliation against northerners living in the south. Tensions boiled over in July 1967, when the Igbo-dominated eastern region declared its independence as the new state of **Biafra,** and civil war broke out, pitting the Nigerian federal government against the secessionist Biafrans led by Lieutenant Colonel Odemegwu Ojukwu.

The war dragged on for 27 months, the Biafrans fighting tenaciously out of fear that northern Muslims were bent on their extermination. Biafra received financial support from sympathizers outside Nigeria, but it was recognized as a sovereign state by only four African governments. Cut off by a naval blockade, it was finally all but starved into submission, with the deaths of between 500,000 and two million

coup d'etat The sudden and forcible overthrow of a government, usually by the military.

Biafrans; the West witnessed the first media images of mass starvation in Africa, a problem that was to become all too common over the next few decades. The war ended in January 1970, Ojukwu went into exile, and Nigeria was reunited.

Gowon was a capable leader who did much to patch up the wounds caused by the civil war, but he was slow to return Nigeria to civilian government and did too little to curb inflation, economic mismanagement, and the squandering of the profit from Nigeria's oil boom of the early 1970s. In July 1975 reform-minded senior officers seized power in a bloodless coup, replacing Gowon with Brigadier Murtala Muhammed, a Hausa-Fulani. He won praise by purging the army, announcing a four-year timetable for the return to civilian rule, and dismissing 10,000 government officials and 150 officers on charges of corruption. But he also upset those who had gained illicitly from the Gowon years, and barely seven months after coming to power, he was assassinated during an attempted coup by followers of Gowon trying to regain power. The coup failed, and Muhammed was succeeded by Lieutenant Colonel Olusegun Obasanjo, notable for the fact that he was Nigeria's first Yoruba head of state. Obasanjo promised to respect the goal of a return to civilian rule by October 1979 and work on the new constitution continued.

The Second Republic (1979–1983)

For its new civilian system of government, Nigeria abandoned the Westminster model, opting instead for the U.S. model, with a directly elected executive, a bicameral National Assembly, and a separate Supreme Court. National elections in 1979 resulted in a clean sweep of the presidency and the legislature by Shehu Shagari and his National Party of Nigeria. Shagari won praise for pardoning Ojukwu and Gowon and allowing them both to return from exile, and—to help promote national unity—he announced plans to move Nigeria's capital from Lagos to Abuja, 300 miles to the north in the exact geographical center of the country. However, Shagari was unable to control corruption, and when the international oil price fell in the early 1980s, his government was undermined by an economy on the verge of collapse. New elections were held in 1983 as planned, but although they were contested by five parties, and Shagari won a second term, the parties again broke down along ethnic and regional lines, and the elections were marred by charges of ballot-rigging and by clashes among supporters of rival parties.

Military Government II (1983–1999)

On December 31, 1983, three months after being returned to office, Shagari was ousted in Nigeria's fourth successful military coup. Although it was welcomed at first, the new leader—Major General Muhammadu Buhari, a Muslim northerner—became increasingly authoritarian and was ousted in August 1985 in yet another coup. He was succeeded by Major General Ibrahim Babangida, a Muslim who was from the Middle Belt, but was widely perceived as a northerner.

Like several of his predecessors, Babangida made the standard promises of a new constitution, an early and orderly return to civilian rule, and economic revival. At first, he won praise both inside and outside Nigeria for his policies, even earning himself the nickname "Maradona," after Argentinean soccer player Diego Maradona, famed for his handling of the ball. Political parties were legalized in 1989, state governments and a new National Assembly were elected in 1990–1992, and the final step in the transition to the new Third Republic was to have been the presidential election of June 1993. This was apparently won by Moshood Abiola of the new Social Democratic Party, but instead of handing over power, Babangida claimed that the election had been rigged and refused to release the results. The outcry that followed persuaded him to step down in August and to hand over power to a transitional civilian government, which was itself ousted within three months by Brigadier Sani Abacha, the defense minister. When Abiola defiantly proclaimed himself president, he was jailed. His wife was later murdered, allegedly by common criminals but more likely for political reasons.

Abacha was openly contemptuous of human rights. He sentenced the respected former military leader Olusegun Obasanjo to life imprisonment in July 1995 on charges of helping plot a coup, and he allowed the execution the following November of Ken Saro-Wiwa and eight activists from the Ogoni tribe of southeastern Nigeria. Saro-Wiwa was a nationally famous novelist and the scriptwriter of a popular Nigerian TV soap, who in the early 1990s had became involved with a movement created to promote the interests of the Ogoni people, who live among the oil fields of the Niger delta. Few of the profits from this oil had been invested back into Ogoniland, which had suffered severe environmental problems. When four pro-government Ogoni chiefs were murdered at a political rally in 1994, Saro-Wiwa was accused of organizing the murders, and was tried by a military tribunal and executed.

Abacha announced plans to return Nigeria to civilian rule and won qualified approval from Western governments for his efforts to control public spending and inflation and to promote privatization. However, Nigeria was suspended from the Commonwealth following the Saro-Wiwa execution, and it became clear that Abacha was manipulating the return to civilian government in order to make sure that he would be elected president. Before he could carry out his plan, however, he died in June 1998 of a heart attack (described by many Nigerians as the "coup from heaven"). When a heart attack also claimed Moshood Abiola the following month, power fell into the hands of General Abdulsalam Abubakar, who moved rapidly to return government to the civilians.

The Fourth Republic (1999–)

Following elections in late 1998 and early 1999, the military stepped down in May 1999, and the Fourth Republic came into being. The new civilian government was headed by Olusegun Obasanjo—who had stepped out of retirement to run for the presidency—and his centrist People's Democratic Party. Like many of his predecessors, Obasanjo made all the usual statements about promoting democracy, putting Nigeria back on the road to economic prosperity, overcoming ethnic and religious tensions, and dealing with corruption. Again like many of his predecessors, he launched a war against corruption by suspending or reviewing government contracts and by replacing several hundred bureaucrats. He also moved to neutralize possible opposition within the military by purging several dozen military officers who had held political office between 1984 and 1999.

On the economic front, Obasanjo moved quickly to renegotiate Nigeria's debt repayment schedule and to repair Nigeria's relations with its major trading partners and sources of lending. It was a calculated risk, because the kinds of reforms that the World Bank and the International Monetary Fund wanted in Nigeria involved the imposition of austerity measures—including a cutback on government spending—that might have undermined the popularity of the Obasanjo government at a time when it desperately needed public support. At the local level, the government was almost immediately faced with outbreaks of community violence as different ethnic groups fought with each other over access to local resources, such as land and jobs. Within months of his inauguration, hundreds of Nigerians had been killed or wounded, mainly in the south. The bloodshed continued throughout his first term in office.

Obasanjo was faced with the same structural problems that had undermined previous attempts to make civilian government work in Nigeria. To address these problems, he had to fundamentally alter the style of Nigerian politics. His first challenge was to build strong political institutions that could sustain democracy and withstand the threats posed by social and economic divisions. He also had to break the power of elites, and as well as dealing with corruption among those in power, he had to take on and defeat the kind of low-level, routine bribery and extortion that has become so much a part of daily life in Nigeria. Finally, questions emerged about the nature of the relationship between national and local governments outlined in the new constitution of the Fourth Republic, with critics calling for a looser association and weaker central government.

The prospects for success were heightened by President Obasanjo's own record in politics. As military leader in 1976–1979, he had proved among the least corrupt of all Nigeria's leaders, and he was the first to actually fulfill his promise of returning power to civilians. Unfortunately, good intentions are a small part of the abilities that a leader of Nigeria must show if he is to help civilian government take root and if he is to help foster a sense of national unity in a country as severely divided as Nigeria. His record during his first term was widely seen as a failure, and many of Nigeria's problems worsened.

Nigeria Today

In April 2003 the second set of elections was held under the constitution of the Fourth Republic. It was surrounded by the usual charges of fraud and by the violence and destruction that have come to be a tragic hallmark of political competition in Nigeria. There were few surprises when Olusegun Obasanjo won a second term in office after having fought a spirited campaign against his main opponent, Muhammadu Buhari, another of Nigeria's former military leaders.

It was remarkable in many ways that Obasanjo should have won, given the problems still faced by Nigeria and the many doubts over his abilities to deal with them. Among the issues at the top of the political agenda: Nigeria's economic problems, the institutionalized corruption that is so much a part of public and political life, the appalling record of religious and ethnic violence that marked his first term in office, problems with crime in the major cities, and the dispute over the place of Islamic *sharia* courts in Northern Nigeria (see later in this chapter). A political leader running for reelection in a liberal democracy on Obasanjo's record would almost certainly lose; it says something about the quality of desperation in Nigerian politics—and perhaps of political manipulation behind the scenes—that the majority of voters apparently believed he was still the best option.

Nigeria promises a great deal, but usually fails to deliver. It could be the economic powerhouse of Africa, but has so far failed to use its oil wealth effectively or to build an economic system that spreads opportunity. Poverty is widespread and persistent, with two-thirds of Nigerians living on less than a dollar per day, and investment in infrastructure has been far from adequate. Nigeria could also be an outstanding experiment in political stability, and while (as this book went to press) it is enjoying its longest-ever spell of uninterrupted civilian government, many doubt the quality of Nigerian democracy, and many also worry about the enormous social problems simmering under the surface. Under the circumstances, it is difficult to be optimistic about the longer-term prospects for Africa's largest country.

POLITICAL CULTURE

In a society as diverse and unstable as Nigeria, it is difficult to distinguish indigenous political values from those created by the mix of African and European political traditions. One Nigerian political scientist argues that the political culture of most countries can be traced back to "some epochal beach-head in its history," such as the American Revolution in the United States or the Bolshevik Revolution in Russia, but that the epochal events in Nigeria were the slave trade and colonialism, which left negative legacies such as corruption, violence, and mistrust.[3] Through all the problems that have been created, however, it is still possible to identify several themes in the country's political culture.

A Belief in Democracy

Despite all the military governments Nigeria has had, they have always been seen by most Nigerians as temporary, and military leaders who were slow in delivering on promises of a return to civilian government (such as Gowon, Babangida, or Abacha) quickly found themselves in trouble. Despite the difficulties experienced by civilian government, Nigerians believe that democratic civilian rule is better than unelected military government, and they support political parties, a free press, interest groups, and social organizations. Although the First and Second Republics both failed, Nigerians do not accept failure as inevitable or enduring.[4]

A Multiethnic State

Ethnic divisions are more important to understanding Nigerian society than social or labor divisions because Nigerians differentiate themselves less by class or occupation than by ethnic group. Whether we call it ethnicity, ethnonationalism, or tribalism, it involves adherence or loyalty to a region or tribe, a sense of exclusivity, and discrimination against people from other regions or tribes (see Close-Up View, p. 396). Ethnicity was not a problem in the precolonial era because different groups had worked out a balance among themselves. It became a problem only when

ETHNICITY AND POLITICS IN NIGERIA

Ethnicity is the feature that most clearly distinguishes one African from another. When outsiders look at Nigeria, they see Nigerians, but when Nigerians look at one another, they are more likely to see Yorubas, Hausas, or Ogonis. The greatest barrier to the creation of a stable state, a workable system of government, and a strong economy in Nigeria is the persistent failure of so many of its people to put the national interest above narrow regional interests.

Ethnicity is a difficult notion to pin down, but it revolves around symbols and experiences that give a group of people a common identity and make them different from neighboring communities. It is usually marked by language, history, customs, experiences, and values. The lines between ethnicity, race, and nation are often fuzzy, but—in general terms—ethnicity and nationality are subdivisions of race. In other words, most Nigerians belong to the same race (Negroid) but are members of different ethnic groups. Similarly, most Europeans belong to the same race (Caucasian) but are members of different national groups: English, German, Italian, Swiss, Slovak, Serb, and so on.

Group identity is a natural inclination for many people and can help give them a sense of who they are, but problems arise when groups become exclusive and think of themselves as superior to other groups (although that superiority often hides feelings of insecurity). Sociologists have long argued that racism in the United States, for example, is a defense mechanism driven by concerns about loss of status or opportunity. This is certainly true of ethnic tensions in Nigeria, where members of one ethnic group—no matter how much they deny it—always have a sneaking suspicion that other groups will gain the upper hand unless their group is well represented in the power structure.

It is difficult to see how Nigeria can rise above its ethnic differences. In precolonial times, ethnic groups had worked out a balance among themselves and largely governed themselves without external interference. The creation of Nigeria forced these groups to live and work together and to build shared systems of government and administration. It also set them on a path of mutual hostility as they competed for power and resources and struggled to preserve their identity. It will take time and considerable moral courage for them to put aside their hostility and to learn to trust each other.

colonial frontiers forced different ethnic groups to live together and to develop a joint system of government. So far, a tradition of Nigerian nationalism has not taken root, and politics routinely breaks down in ethnic rivalry.

The Importance of Community

Closely tied to the issue of ethnic division—and further complicating attempts by Nigeria's leaders to build a sense of national identity—is the priority given by many Nigerians to their local communities. There is no state tradition in Nigeria, and Nigerians find it hard to trust government officials, so they look instead to their communities for stability, and they believe that loyalty to the community is the paramount virtue. One of the more dangerous consequences of this attitude is the persistence of nepotism and corruption, which are distinctive in Nigeria because it is expected that public officials will enrich their constituents and that they are failures if they do not.[5]

The Dominance of the State

Ironically, while the institutions of government and the state are weak in Nigeria, control of state power has come to mean everything. Because it plays such a critical role in creating economic opportunities, winning control of the state has become more important than competing openly over policies. As long ago as 1964, John Mackintosh suggested that "politics count for too much" in Nigeria, the advantages of controlling power being so great that competing groups would use every method available to win and keep power. Little has changed since then. The desperation of these groups is made worse by the absence of enough independent sources of wealth and position to allow democratic institutions to operate the way they should.[6]

 POLITICAL SYSTEM

The study of politics in liberal democracies focuses heavily on institutions: their structure, their sources of power, and the way they relate to each other. By contrast, understanding politics in a less developed country like Nigeria is more a question of understanding the problems experienced in building those institutions and giving them permanence and legitimacy. The return to civilian government under the Fourth Republic in May 1999 meant a switch from rule by military decree to rule by elected bodies with constitutional powers, but the prospects for civilian government in Nigeria still depend heavily on the extent to which institutions can develop roots and overcome the structural problems that have so long plagued Nigerian society. No civilian government has yet lasted more than a few years; it will take a combination of luck, political will, and a massive effort on the part of Nigerians to set aside their differences if the Fourth Republic is to last.

THE CONSTITUTION

Nigeria has had seven constitutions since World War II. The first two (named for the British colonial administrators at the time) were the Richards constitution of 1947 and the Macpherson constitution of 1951. Both were flawed because Nigerians had little say in their creation and because they encouraged regionalism without giving the regions much power. The third—the Lyttleton constitution of 1954—was drawn up with the input and support of Nigerians. It took powers away from the central government, created a federal system of government, and paved the way to self-government in 1956. It was then replaced by the independence constitution of 1960, which was amended in 1963 to declare Nigeria a republic and to replace the British monarch with a Nigerian head of state.

The fifth constitution was published in 1979 as the foundation for the Second Republic, and was based on the American model rather than the Westminster model. It was suspended with the return to military government in 1983, and work was begun by the Babangida administration in 1988 on a replacement, in preparation for the creation of the Third Republic. Early discussions were sidetracked by a controversy about whether Islamic law should be included, with northern Muslims reviving demands that Nigeria be declared an Islamic republic. When it became clear that no agreement would be reached, Babangida ended discussion of the issue and the constitution of the Third Republic was promulgated in May 1989. But before it could be put into force it was suspended by the Abacha regime and was replaced in May 1999 by the constitution of the Fourth Republic, the seventh Nigerian constitution in 39 years.

The new constitution borrows heavily from its predecessors. Unlike the U.S. Constitution, which is full of ambiguities, gaps, and generalities and whose interpretation is left up to the U.S. Supreme Court and its lower courts, the Nigerian constitution is both long and detailed, because its authors went to great pains to cover as many issues as possible. It has 320 articles (the U.S. Constitution has just seven), several schedules, lengthy lists outlining the policy responsibilities of the different branches of government, and—just in case anyone has any doubts—includes a glossary defining the meaning of terms such as *authority, decision, government,* and *law.* Although there are many similarities with the U.S. model, it also contains several features that reflect the peculiar problems and needs of Nigeria:

- National unity is a key theme, emphasized in the opening paragraphs with the argument that Nigeria is an "indivisible and indissoluble" state. The duties of the state include fostering a feeling of belonging and involvement so that "loyalty to the nation shall override sectional loyalties." Remarkably, the state is also responsible for encouraging "inter-marriage among persons from different places of origin, or of different religions, ethnic or linguistic associations or ties." It is hard to imagine this idea being added to the U.S. Constitution.

- Like its predecessors, it includes measures designed to make sure that the national government is not dominated by any one region or ethnic group. For example, the president must win at least 25 percent of the vote in two-thirds of Nigeria's 36 states, and the federal government must include ministers drawn equally from all 36 of those states.

- Seven articles discuss citizenship, and thirteen articles outline the fundamental rights of citizens. These include some unusual ideas. For example, torture, slavery, forced labor, "corrupt practices," and abuse of power are all outlawed; privacy of homes and phone conversations is guaranteed; and—going well beyond the U.S. Constitution—discrimination on the grounds of "place of origin, sex, religion, status, ethnic, or linguistic association or ties" is prohibited.

constitutional engineering A deliberate attempt to change political and social behavior through the rules and goals included in a constitution.

Nigeria's approach to constitutions is a good example of **constitutional engineering.** Where most liberal democratic constitutions have grown out of political and social realities, Nigeria's most recent constitutions have sometimes not only ignored those realities, but have deliberately tried to change political behavior. For example, the committee appointed to write the 1979 constitution was told by the military government to draw up a document that would eliminate "cut-throat political competition," develop consensus politics, promote national interests over regional interests, and eliminate the excessive centralization of power.[7] The constitution of the Fourth Republic is clearly based on attempts to try and get Nigeria past its ethnic and social divisions: a laudable goal, perhaps, but one that also carries many risks.

THE EXECUTIVE: PRESIDENT

Like almost all Britain's former African colonies, Nigeria began independence with a Westminster-style parliamentary system: The legislature and the executive were fused, the government was headed by a prime minister and Council of Ministers, and the British monarch was head of state. Former British colonies with predominantly white populations such as Canada, Australia, and New Zealand took much the same approach, still recognize the British monarch as head of state today, and still use the parliamentary system. By contrast, most predominantly nonwhite former colonies—such as India and Pakistan—rejected the monarchy. In 1963 Nigeria followed suit by

TABLE 8.2

Postindependence Leaders of Nigeria

Date	Head of government	Ethnicity/ region	Religion	Type of government	Reason for leaving office
1960	Sir Alhaji Abubakar Tafawa Balewa	Hausa-Fulani	Muslim	Civilian	Killed in coup
1966	(Jan) Johnson Aguyi-Ironsi	Igbo	Christian	Military	Killed in coup
1966	(July) Yakubu Gowon	Middle Belt	Christian	Military	Coup
1975	Murtala Muhammed	Hausa-Fulani	Muslim	Military	Killed in coup
1976	Olusegun Obasanjo	Yoruba	Christian	Military	Retired
1979	Shehu Shagari	Hausa-Fulani	Muslim	Civilian	—
1983	Shehu Shagari	Hausa-Fulani	Muslim	Civilian	Coup
1984	Muhammadu Buhari	Hausa-Fulani	Muslim	Military	Coup
1985	Ibrahim Babangida	Middle Belt	Muslim	Military	"Retired"
1993	(Aug) Ernest Shonekan	Yoruba	Christian	Interim	"Resigned"
1993	(Nov) Sani Abacha	Northerner	Muslim	Military	Died in office
1998	Abdulsalam Abubakar	Northerner	Muslim	Interim	Retired
1999	Olusegun Obasanjo	Yoruba	Christian	Civilian	—
2003	Olusegun Obasanjo	Yoruba	Christian	Civilian	

becoming a republic and replacing the monarch with a nonexecutive presidency elected by parliament for a five-year term.

Since then, Nigeria has opted to follow the American model for its civilian governments, and instead of having a figurehead president and a prime minister appointed out of the legislature, it has an elected executive presidency sharing powers with a separately elected legislature. Many other African states have done the same thing, and in many cases have seen their presidencies turn into powerful offices with often authoritarian qualities. What are the attractions of the presidential model for a country like Nigeria?

- One explanation is that the Westminster model depends on a nonpolitical head of state, a role that was played until independence by the colonial administration itself, which was anything but nonpolitical.[8] The idea of a neutral figurehead was undermined from the outset, but independence left Nigeria without a strong colonial overlord, so a strong executive presidency was created to fill the void.

- Another argument is that the Westminster model is based on multiparty competition and is too divisive for a society as ethnically diverse as Nigeria, especially since parties often break down on ethnic lines. By contrast, the American model forces the candidates running for election to the presidency to attract support from across the country, and encourages political parties with different ethnic or religious bases to work together.

- A third argument is that the fusion of executive and legislature in the Westminster system increases the chances of a single political party dominating both branches of government. If that party is dominated by a particular ethnic group, then that group will dominate government. With the American model, on the other hand, parties have to build national support in order to control government, and there is also a chance of a president coming from one party and the legislature being dominated by another, thereby dividing power and preventing dominance by one ethnic group.

Under the Fourth Republic, the president is elected by direct universal vote to a four-year term in office, renewable once, and there is a clear division of powers among the executive, legislative, and judicial arms. For example, the president has the power of appointment, but all senior nominations must be approved by the Senate. He cannot declare war without the approval of the National Assembly. He has the power of veto, but this can be overturned by the National Assembly with a two-thirds majority.

The president governs in conjunction with a Government of the Federation, consisting of senior government ministers. The number of ministers—and their portfolios—can be changed by the president without Senate approval, but there must be at least one minister from each of Nigeria's 36 states, and all ministers must be confirmed in office by the Senate. The requirement that every state be represented in the cabinet has stretched the possibilities for the number of meaningful portfolios, so along with important jobs, such as commerce, foreign affairs, defense, and justice, there are less important ones, such as the ministries of aviation, power and steel, solid minerals, and sport.

Nigeria also has a vice president, who would step into the presidency in the event of the death, resignation, or removal of the incumbent. Again with an eye to

OLUSEGUN OBASANJO

The election of Olusegun Obasanjo as the new civilian president of Nigeria in 1999 was generally welcomed inside and outside the country. He had a strong, positive reputation among the elites within Nigerian politics and among key foreign governments, based mainly on his record as military leader of Nigeria in 1976–1979 and on the fact that he had been the first African military leader voluntarily to hand power back to civilians. But his record in office has been less than perfect.

Born in 1937, Obasanjo is a deeply religious Christian Yoruba who first came to national attention as the military officer who accepted the surrender of Biafran forces following the Nigerian civil war of 1967–1970. Six years later, following the assassination of Brigadier Murtala Muhammed, Obasanjo became military leader of Nigeria. Following the creation of the Second Republic, he retired from active politics and set up a pig and poultry farm in his home state in southwestern Nigeria. But he kept up with developments in national politics and was once considered as a possible candidate for the post of secretary-general of the United Nations.

During the Abacha years, Obasanjo became critical of the abuses of power by the military and was imprisoned in 1995 along with several dozen others on charges of plotting a coup. He was released in June 1998 following the death of Abacha. Although he initially refused to reenter politics, he changed his mind and won the People's Democratic Party nomination for the presidency in early 1999, winning the presidential election in May. Distrusted by some for being too close to the military officers who governed Nigeria in the 1980s and 1990s, others saw him as having the credentials of honesty and international statesmanship that were needed to ensure that the Fourth Republic had the best chance of succeeding. Much like Boris Yeltsin, Obasanjo came to power at a critical juncture in the development of his country.

© Brooks Kraft/CORBIS

He moved quickly to rid the country of corrupt government officials and to put the economy back on a stable footing, and he set up a seven-member panel to look into three decades of the abuse of power by military leaders. Once a champion of active government, he now argued instead that he wanted to put the private sector at the heart of Nigeria's revival and launched a halting program of privatization. But he was also widely criticized—at home and abroad—for his failure to control civil conflict, for his use of the army to sometimes brutally put down unrest, and for his unwillingness to criticize the army's excessive use of force. Despite a first term marked by political, economic, and social unrest, Obasanjo was able to fight off challenges to his leadership and—his critics charged—to manipulate the election enough to win a second four-year term in April 2003. By then the gloss had long worn off the optimism surrounding his first election victory, and although many foreign political leaders staked a great deal in the political significance of the Obasanjo government, at home he was deeply unpopular.

ensuring that no single ethnic group dominates government, the constitution requires that vice presidents come from a different part of the country than the president. Obasanjo chose as his vice president Atiku Abubakar, a Muslim northerner who is now seen as a strong contender to win the presidency in 2007. Obasanjo's opponent in the 2003 presidential election—Muhammadu Buhari—was a Muslim northerner whose running mate who was an Igbo from southeast Nigeria.

In both the United States and Nigeria, the formal rules of government say nothing about the role of personality. The true nature of both presidencies is determined by the ability (or inability) of incumbents to manipulate public opinion and the legislative and judicial branches to achieve their goals. Nigerian leaders in particular have had to use the force of their personalities to promote national unity. Military leaders have been helped by their ability to suspend the constitution, rule by decree, and use the military as a means of control, and civilian leaders have been helped by being the only politicians elected from a national constituency. The Second Republic ultimately failed not because it was structurally flawed but because President Shehu Shagari was unable to provide the leadership needed to deal with corruption and ethnic conflict. The survival of the Fourth Republic has so far depended in large part on the ability of Olusegun Obasanjo to lead and to avoid repeating the mistakes of the Shagari administration. Unfortunately, he has often used authoritarian methods to keep control.

THE LEGISLATURE: NATIONAL ASSEMBLY

Nigeria has had more experience with executive politics than with legislative politics. During periods of military government, leadership has been focused in the hands of the soldiers in charge, and during the relatively rare periods of civilian government, legislatures have been trampled in the rush to win control of the only real office that counts: the presidency. During the First Republic, Nigeria followed the Westminster model, with legislative power vested in a bicameral Federal Legislature. The lower House of Representatives had 312 members, elected for five-year terms from single-member districts with roughly equal populations. However, it did little more than rubber-stamp government policy decisions and was further weakened by the fact that it met for fewer than 30 days every year. There was also a 54-member Senate elected by the federal and regional governments and consisting of tribal chiefs and elders.

Under today's Fourth Republic, Nigeria has a bicameral National Assembly based on the model of the U.S. Congress, with powers to check and balance those of the executive.

Senate

Representing the states, the Senate has 109 members: three each from Nigeria's 36 states and one from the Federal Capital Territory of Abuja. Unlike the United States, where U.S. senators represent their entire state, Nigeria has opted for a system in which each state is divided into three senatorial districts, and the candidate who wins the most votes in each district is declared the winner. Senators serve fixed and renewable terms of four years, and they all come up for reelection at the same time.

The Senate is presided over by a president elected from among its members and who is third in line to the presidency of Nigeria after the vice president.

House of Representatives

Representing the people, the lower chamber has 360 members elected on a single-member, winner-take-all basis from districts of roughly equal population size and is presided over by a Speaker elected by the House. As with the Senate, members are elected for fixed four-year and renewable terms, and elections to both chambers are held at the same time. In line with the principle of separation of powers, any members of the National Assembly who are appointed to a position in government or win a seat in state or local government must give up their National Assembly seats.

Both chambers must meet for at least six months each calendar year; have the same powers to initiate, change, and approve legislation; and normally conduct all their business in English. Reflecting concerns about Nigeria's problems with corruption, the constitution requires that before taking up their seats, all National Assembly members must declare their assets and liabilities and must also declare any pecuniary interests they might have in any matters coming up for discussion. The constitution also bars anyone from becoming a member of the Assembly who is a member of a secret society, who is "adjudged to be a lunatic," or who is "declared to be of unsound mind." How these two latter problems are measured or established is not explained.

THE JUDICIARY: SUPREME COURT

Through all the changes in Nigerian politics since 1960, only one institution has remained relatively stable: the judiciary. Military governments usually suspend political parties, abolish civilian political institutions, and sometimes use of military tribunals, but they usually allow the courts to continue functioning, and even use them to underpin the return to civilian rule. During the Second Republic, the judiciary played exactly the same role as the Supreme Court in the United States: acting as guardian and interpreter of the constitution and interceding in disputes between states or between states and the federal government. This is also its role in the Fourth Republic.

The Supreme Court has 15 members overseen by a chief justice, nominated by the president, and either confirmed by the Senate or approved by a judicial commission. Below the Supreme Court is a system of federal and state courts of appeal and high courts, and a separate system of ***sharia* courts** to deal with issues of Islamic law (for more details, see Part V). Since they were created in 2000, *sharia* courts have been controversial. Restricted to 12 northern Nigerian states, they deal only with matters of family law and petty crime, but southern Nigerians worry that their work poses a threat to civil rights across the country. In 2002, worldwide media attention was drawn to the case of Amina Lawal, a woman who was convicted in a *sharia* court of having committed adultery and giving birth to an illegitimate daughter. In line with Islamic law, she was sentenced to be buried up to her waist and stoned to death. She initially accepted the sentence but then appealed her case to a higher court after lawyers took up the case. The court ruled in her favor.

Worshippers leaving the National Mosque in Abuja, Nigeria, after Friday prayers. Among Nigeria's many divisions is religion, which has led to political, economic, and social tensions between the Muslim north and the non-Muslim south.

SUBNATIONAL GOVERNMENT

In their attempts to achieve a balance between state and federal government, the United States and Nigeria have much in common. The question of federal-state relations was at the core of the early political development of the United States, and it took 13 years of confederation before the original states agreed to form a federation. Even then, states' rights were jealously guarded, and there were doubts that the union would last. Tensions between the North and the South led to civil war in 1861, and as recently as the 1950s violence broke out again over the issue of desegregation. Even today, interstate competition continues over the issue of federal government subsidies.

In Nigeria, federal-state tensions have been driven by ethnic hostilities and jealousies, which boiled over with the end of the colonial hegemony in 1960. During its 40 years of independence, Nigeria has seen a civil war, the breakdown of civilian political systems into ethnic and religious rivalry, and an almost routine pattern of civil violence. In their attempts to reduce regionalism, Nigerian governments have changed internal boundaries so often that the map of Nigeria has frequently had to be redrawn (see Figure 8.1).

FIGURE 8.1

Internal Boundary Changes in Nigeria

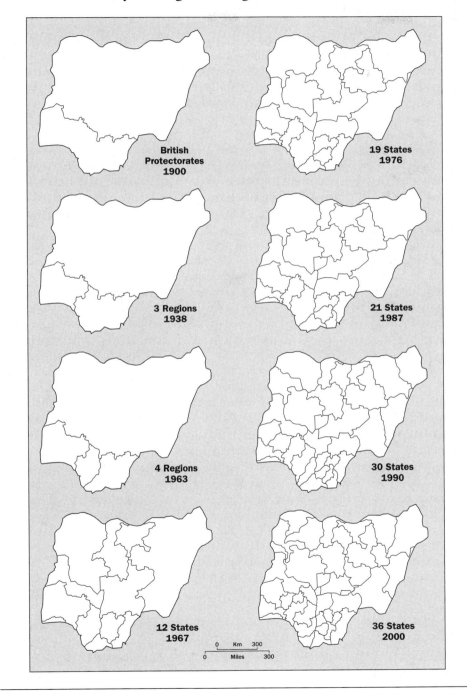

The problems date back to colonial times and to Britain's decision to rule Nigeria first as two separate territories, and then as three regions. Because southerners have always been worried about the power of the predominantly Muslim north (which has produced seven of Nigeria's 11 political leaders), successive governments have divided Nigeria into ever smaller local government units: A fourth region was created in 1963, the four regions were replaced by 12 states in 1967, and the number of states was subsequently increased in increments to its present total of 36. Although the multistate structure has been described as an attempt to break up the power of the major ethnic groups and to make sure that none of the states is dominated by a single ethnic group, the government of the Fourth Republic has still had to work hard to prevent regionalism interfering with attempts to build a unified Nigerian state (and has not done a very good job so far).

Under the Fourth Republic, every state is governed by an elected governor serving renewable four-year terms and a unicameral **House of Assembly.** The House of Assembly has between three and four times as many seats as the state has in the national House of Representatives—it must have at least 24 and no more than 40. Governors have the power of veto, but this can be overruled by a two-thirds majority in the House of Assembly.

Given the repeated failures of national government in Nigeria, the importance of ethnic allegiances, and the identification of many Nigerians with their local community, local politics has much greater significance in Nigeria than is the case in the United States. It not only revolves around the elected members of local and state assemblies but is given another dimension by the role of traditional leaders. As a colonial power, Britain strengthened the position of traditional leaders in many of its colonies by ruling through them; the result in Nigeria is that traditional leaders still have much local influence. Nowhere is this more clear than in the **caliphate of Sokoto.** Created in the nineteenth century, the caliphate replaced the many city-states that had existed for centuries in what is now northern Nigeria and brought together emirates from the different ethnic groups. The caliphate still has its own administrative structure, which coexists with that of federal Nigeria. The leader is the sultan, responsible for the administration of Islamic law, enforcing orthodox Islamic practice, and supervising local taxes.

As happens in many tribal units elsewhere in West Africa, Nigeria's sultans are appointed by a selection council that operates on the basis of consensus to appoint a successor acceptable to the other contenders and to the community. Each has a chief political advisor known as a **sardauna;** among the most influential sardaunas of this century was Ahmadu Bello (1909–1966).[9] Showing how traditional and modern politics often overlap, Bello founded the Northern People's Congress and became prime minister of the Northern region before being murdered during the January 1966 coup. A recent sultan of Sokoto, Sheikh Ibrahim Zakzaky, said that he hoped to promote an "Islamic awakening" in Nigeria and to work toward the creation of an Islamic republic.

Although their power has been reduced in the past century, traditional political units have the advantages over modern, postcolonial units of longevity, legitimacy, and deep roots in local culture.[10] By contrast, elected legislatures and competing political parties are alien and so have had trouble developing a firm foundation. Nigerian federal governments face a dilemma: Should the special place of traditional leaders in the community be exploited to extend the reach of federal government and to support programs of modernization and democratization (which might then weaken the power of traditional leaders), or should traditional leaders be bypassed and their powers reduced, thereby risking the anger of local communities and reducing the credibility and popularity of the federal government?

THE MILITARY

Of the ten countries discussed in this book, the military still plays an important political role in only Nigeria and Haiti. While the political influence of the military in Mexico and Egypt has declined, the Nigerian military has been heavily involved in politics from the outset, and there are few signs of it being marginalized. Weaknesses in the conduct of civilian politics have combined with the zest for power of some of Nigeria's military leaders to ensure that in its first 45 years of independence (1960–2005), Nigeria spent just 16 years under civilian rule. It saw nine changes of leadership, five of which were violent and two of which involved the overthrow of a civilian government by the military. The Shagari government was returned to office in 1983 through a popular vote, but no civilian president has yet been removed from office through a popular vote, nor has there been a transition from one civilian administration to another.

Given the divisions in African civil society, the military is often the only institution with any kind of strength and continuity. In Nigeria, only one coup (in 1976) was an attempt by a deposed regime to win back power; most of the others were responses to political crises, and most were initially welcomed by Nigerians. In every case, the military stepped in—supposedly to restore order—and although Nigeria's military governments routinely suspended the constitution and abolished most civilian political institutions, they allowed the judiciary, the courts, the bureaucracy, the police, and public and private businesses to carry on as usual[11] (although "business as usual" typically meant continued corruption and incompetence).

Just like the military itself, Nigeria's military governments have been centralized and hierarchical and have allowed few significant alternative sources of power. Although most Nigerian military leaders could not be described as autocrats, they have never pretended to be democratic, always arguing that the breakdown of civilian government demanded a strong response. Their definitions of authority have varied:[12]

- The Buhari regime (1983–1985) decided that military-style discipline was the best way of correcting Nigeria's problems, so orderly queues were enforced, the flying of the national flag in public places was mandated, all Nigerians had to stay at home one day per month to help clean up their neighborhoods, and any bureaucrats who arrived late for work were forced to do the frog-jump (jumping up and down in a squatting position with their hands on their ears).

- Concerned about the possibilities of a countercoup, the Babangida regime (1985–1993) in 1990 ordered the execution of 69 army officers, each tried before a military tribunal.

- The Abacha regime (1993–1998), undoubtedly the most despotic and corrupt of all Nigeria's military governments, forced confessions by beating dissidents, hanging them upside down, or starving them; refused public trials for political prisoners; and had convicted criminals shot to death without the right of appeal. Abacha's record was so extreme that, ironically, it did some good: it gave the military such a bad name that the prospects of a return to military government are weaker now than they have ever been.

In order to rule, Nigeria's military governments have created their own subculture of administrative institutions, which have paralleled civilian institutions but have been based on rule by decree. Early military administrations (1966–1979) governed through two bodies:

- A Supreme Military Council (SMC) made up of selected senior officers and which functioned as the principle policymaking forum
- A Federal Executive Council made up of senior federal bureaucrats and which was responsible for implementing the decisions of the SMC

During the Gowon years (1966–1975), Nigeria was ruled by a joint military-bureaucratic government, with civil servants achieving so much influence over the SMC that many were compulsorily retired after the 1975 coup.[13] The Muhammed regime (1975–1976) added three new bodies:

- A National Council of Ministers, which functioned like a cabinet
- A Council of States, consisting of the military governors of the then 12 states and charged with overseeing federal-state relations
- A National Security Organization (NSO), charged with controlling "opponents of the state," but which became a quasi-political organization that intimidated the critics and opponents of the Muhammed and Obasanjo regimes.[14]

During the second military era (1983–1999), all five institutions were initially revived, the only substantial difference being that during the Buhari regime NSO was given greater latitude, and Nigeria came dangerously close to being a police state. (The Buhari regime overstated the degree of Nigeria's problems and rapidly degenerated from being seen as the provider of salvation to being at war with its own people.[15]) When Babangida took power in 1985 he changed the name of the SMC to the Armed Forces Ruling Council (AFRC) and expanded its membership to 28, all of them military officers. He also split the NSO into three agencies responsible for national defense, overseas intelligence gathering, and internal security, and he created bodies responsible for public security and the territorial integrity of Nigeria.

Abacha replaced the AFRC with a 26-member Provisional Ruling Council, which was different from its predecessor only in name. Like all military leaders, Abacha was careful to watch out for opposition and to prevent anyone from building too much power or offering too much opposition to his policies. In April 1996, for example, he dismissed the heads of the army and the air force, allegedly for failure to support some of his more hard-line policies. However, it was clear by then that Abacha was one of the exceptions to the general rule of military leaders who claimed that they had no long-term plans to hold onto power. He used the governing institutions to strengthen his own grip on power and to make sure that when Nigeria returned to civilian rule, it would do so under his control.

ELECTIONS AND PARTIES

Nigerians take politics seriously, sometimes so seriously that their disagreements lead to ethnic and religious conflict. Urban Nigerians tend to be more politically active than those in rural areas, partly because they are closer to the centers of power, partly because of their higher levels of education and standards of living, and partly because the more unscrupulous among them have the most to gain from abusing power. Rural Nigerians have neither the personal mobility nor the access to the channels of participation or communication available to urban Nigerians. Many also value local and community politics over national politics and come under the influence of traditional ethnic and clan leaders.

THE ELECTORAL SYSTEM

The electoral system of the Fourth Republic is fairly simple and straightforward. From local councils to the federal presidency, all elected officials win office through a winner-take-all vote, and all officials serve the same four-year terms, with the president alone being limited to two terms. There are no primaries; the candidates for the presidency from each of the major parties are instead chosen by a vote among senior party members. The successful candidate must win at least half the vote; otherwise a second round is called between the two top-placed candidates in the first round. Although Obasanjo claimed to have won the nomination for his party in 2003 relatively fairly, questions were raised about his opponent, former military dictator Muhammadu Buhari. Twelve candidates contested the nomination for the opposition All Nigeria People's Party, but 11 either withdrew or failed to attend the nominating convention, and Buhari won with 4,328 votes in his favor and just 30 against.

To make sure that the successful candidate wins a broad base of support at the presidential election itself, the candidate must win a majority of all votes cast and at least 25 percent of the vote in at least two-thirds of Nigeria's 36 states. Similarly, state governors must win at least 25 percent of the vote in at least two-thirds of the local government districts within their state. In the event that no candidates meet the terms of this formula, runoff elections are held between the two top finishers, and if neither of them meets these terms, a third runoff is held that requires a simple majority for the winner.

Elections in Nigeria have traditionally been overseen by government commissions, which have come under a variety of different names; the body currently responsible is the Independent Election Commission. Like its predecessors, its job is to oversee the electoral process and make sure that vote rigging and intimidation are minimized, and—on the basis of the census—to redraw electoral districts every ten years as necessary. In this sense, Nigeria has an advantage over the United States, where redistricting is controlled by political parties, which routinely redraw lines so as to give them an advantage in elections.

POLITICAL PARTIES

Nigerian party politics has had a checkered history. The evolution of the party system has three times been interrupted by the intervention of the military, which in each case banned existing parties and insisted on the creation of completely new parties free of allegiances to regions and ethnic groups. Few parties have been able to develop a truly national platform, most have been built on regional differences rather than ideological differences, and none has so far lasted more than a few years.

Before and After Independence (1944–1966)

The roots of the Nigerian party system can be traced to the early twentieth century nationalist movement, which was given an early boost by the foundation of the National Congress of British West Africa, whose first meeting in 1920 was attended by delegates from Nigeria, Gold Coast (now Ghana), Sierra Leone, and Gambia. Party formation moved into a new phase in the 1930s with the return to Nigeria of a growing number of students educated abroad, where they had met one another and been exposed to ideas of democracy and self-determination. The most celebrated was Nnamdi "Zik" Azikiwe (1904–1996), an Igbo who in 1944 co-founded the first party with a national platform, the National Council of Nigeria and the Cameroons (or NCNC, which later changed its name to the National Convention of Nigerian Citizens). The NCNC led the opposition to the 1947 colonial constitution, and Zikism became synonymous for many with Nigerian nationalism, even though the NCNC drew most of its support from eastern Nigeria.

Meanwhile, Obafemi "Awo" Awolowo (1909–1987) founded the Yoruba-based Action Group (AG) in 1948, and northern interests were represented by the Northern People's Congress (NPC), founded in 1949 and led by Alhaji Sir Ahmadu Bello, the religious leader (or Sardauna) of Sokoto in northwest Nigeria. All three claimed to reject tribalism, but they all swept their respective states in the 1951 regional elections, beginning a tradition of close identification between party, region, and ethnic group. They also contested the 1959 federal elections, and when none won a clear majority, the NPC and NCNC agreed to form a coalition. NPC leader Ahmadu Bello would have been expected to become prime minister of Nigeria, but he opted to remain prime minister of the Northern Region, feeling that it was a more important job. In his place, the deputy leader of the NPC, Alhaji Sir Abubakar Tafawa Balewa, became the first prime minister of Nigeria, and AG leader Awolowo became leader of the opposition.

Many other smaller parties were also formed, but it was with this tripartite NCNC-AG-NPC system that Nigeria became independent. Hopes for the perpetuation of a multiparty democracy rapidly disappeared as the Action Group became bogged down by internal divisions and as a crisis developed over the 1962 census and the 1964 federal elections, when northern and southern parties accused each other of rigging the results and the NPC refused even to take part. The chaos that followed led to the January 1966 military coup and the banning of all political parties.

The Second Republic (1979–1983)

During preparations for the return to civilian government in the late 1970s, the Obasanjo regime tried to avoid ethnic politics by laying down detailed rules on party formation. Membership had to be open to all Nigerians, party names and emblems could not reflect regional or ethnic interests, and party headquarters could be situated only in Lagos, the federal capital. A Federal Election Commission (FEDECO) was created to screen all parties, to make sure they met the terms of the new rules, and to oversee the elections. Nineteen associations applied to be recognized as parties, of which only five were allowed to contest the 1979 elections. Despite this, the party system once again boiled down to a tripartite contest strongly reminiscent of the First Republic.

The 1979 presidential election was won by Shehu Shagari of the National Party of Nigeria (NPN), which was seen by many as the successor to the NPC. The NPN also won a plurality in the new National Assembly and the State Assemblies. Meanwhile, Obafemi Awolowo came a close second in the presidential election at the head of the Unity Party of Nigeria (UPN), which looked remarkably like his old Action Group and was ideologically to the left of the NPN. Finally, the spirit of the NCNC was revived in the Nigerian People's Party (NPP), which ran Nnamdi Azikiwe as its presidential candidate. In the lead-up to the 1983 elections, the NPN was accused of manipulating the election, changing the timetable to its own advantage, and refusing to register new parties. The new electoral register drawn up for the election showed a hard-to-believe 34 percent increase in the number of voters, and the elections themselves were marred by charges of abuse and cheating. When Shagari won reelection with a greatly increased share of the vote (up from 34 percent in 1979 to nearly 48 percent in 1983), the credibility of the new administration suffered a fatal blow. Three months later, it was ousted by a military coup.

The Third Republic (1989–1993)

Preparations for the return to civilian rule under the Third Republic closely paralleled those for the Second Republic. In a new attempt to break the regionalism of political parties, the Babangida regime prevented anyone with experience in politics from running for election, hoping (as he put it) to replace "old brigade" politicians with a "new breed" of leaders driven by ideology and unencumbered by the regional ties that had caused so many problems for earlier civilian governments. Announcing his transition plans in 1987, Babangida said he would allow only two parties to contest the new elections. A new National Electoral Commission (NEC) was created, to which 13 political groups applied during 1989 for registration as parties. They were required to show that they had offices and support in every Nigerian state and that membership was open to all, regardless of race or religion. Babangida himself had little respect for parties, which he described as "natural grounds for the idle and illiterate who over the years have failed to qualify for any reputable profession."

The NEC concluded that six of the 13 groups might qualify. But amid suspicions that most were being manipulated behind the scenes by former politicians, Babangida rejected all their applications and told his government to draw up manifestos for two new parties, the Social Democratic Party (SDP) and the National Republican Convention (NRC), "one a little to the left, and the other a little to the right of center," as he described them. Neither was allowed to oppose Babangida's free-market economic policies, and he even provided them with offices, official colors, and election symbols. The two new parties almost immediately developed regional biases; the NRC had a northern tilt, attracting former supporters of Shagari's NPN, while the SDP had a southern tilt, deriving its support from Yoruba and Igbo areas.

The results of local elections in December 1990 seemed to allay fears of a continuation of regionalism. Only 20 percent of voters turned out, but many genuinely made choices between competing candidates, each party won at least one-third of the vote in most states, and each party won local councils outside their region. In October 1991, state gubernatorial primaries were held, but once again old brigade politicians were suspected of pulling the strings. The following month, the NEC canceled the results of primaries in 13 states because of suspicions about manipulation, arrested several old brigade politicians, and arranged new primaries in the affected states.

In December 1991 elections were held for state assemblies and governors. To prevent ballot rigging, secret votes were not allowed; instead, voters at each polling station had to line up behind photographs of their preferred candidates. They were then counted and the results announced immediately. The elections passed off peaceably, with about 20 million Nigerians turning out to vote. The SDP won the governorship and state assemblies in 14 states, including three in the north; the NRC won the governorship and state assemblies in 13 states, including six in the south; and in three states, the NRC won the governorship and the SDP the assembly. The results seemed to bode well for Babangida's attempts to create parties with national appeal, although optimism was tempered by the emergence of factions within both parties.

When presidential primaries were held in August 1992, and contested by 23 candidates, the NEC declared that nearly all of them had cheated and ordered that new primaries be held. With this done, the presidential elections were held in June 1993 and apparently won by Moshood Abiola of the SDP. Although a Muslim, Abiola would have been the first civilian president from the predominantly Christian south, breaking the traditional hold on power of predominantly Muslim soldiers and civilians from the north. Babangida annulled the election amid suspicions that the NRC candidate, Bashir Tofa, had been the army's favored candidate. With the crisis that led to Babangida's resignation in August 1993, the party system was once again suspended.

The Fourth Republic (1999–)

The Abacha regime set up a new national electoral commission, and municipal elections were held in March 1996 on a nonparty or "zero-party" basis. The seeds of new parties, meanwhile, had begun to sprout, much of the opposition to Abacha forming around the National Democratic Coalition (NADECO), formed in May 1994 and led by former state governor Michael Ajasiu. During 1996, 15 new political parties

TABLE 8.3

Results of Recent Presidential Elections in Nigeria

Candidate	Party	% vote
1999		
Olusegun Obasanjo	People's Democratic Party	62.8
Olu Falae	All People's Party/Alliance for Democracy	37.2
2003		
Olusegun Obasanjo	People's Democratic Party	61.9
Muhammadu Buhari	All Nigeria People's Party	32.2
Odemegwu Ojukwu	All People's Grand Alliance	3.3
Other (17 candidates)		2.6

were formed to contest the 1998 elections, but ten were immediately disqualified by the Abacha regime and it became clear that he planned to manipulate the remaining five to his own ends.

Following Abacha's death in 1998, it was decided to wipe the slate clean and start all over again. The new system—overseen by a new Independent National Electoral Commission (INEC)—resulted in the development of three major new parties, with which Nigeria went into the elections for the government of the new Fourth Republic:

- **People's Democratic Party (PDP).** Describing itself as a centrist party, the PDP was led mainly by veteran politicians, including several former military officers brought together by their mutual opposition to the Abacha regime. It did well in local elections in 1998, prompting the two opposition parties to form an electoral pact. The PDP then also did well in elections to the National Assembly in 1999, and its candidate Olusegun Obasanjo rounded off the results by winning the presidency with a solid 62.8 percent share of the vote. Its successes were repeated in 2003.

- **All Nigeria People's Party (ANPP).** The second largest party and therefore the major opposition, the ANPP took moderately conservative positions and was backed by wealthy businesspeople brought together by their support of Sani Abacha and his plans to become the elected president of Nigeria—hence the jibe by its opponents that it should be called the Abacha People's Party. It formed a pact with the Alliance for Democracy, which was mainly of convenience, given that the latter is a moderately liberal party. The ANPP/AD ticket for the 1999 presidential election was won by Olu Falae, a bureaucrat and former finance minister who—ironically—had been jailed by Sani Abacha.

TABLE 8.4

Results of Recent Legislative Elections in Nigeria

Party	1999		2003	
	Senate	House	Senate	House
People's Democratic Party	59	206	76	223
All Nigeria People's Party*	29	74	27	96
Alliance for Democracy	20	68	6	34
United Nigeria People's Party	—	—	—	2
All Progressives Grand Alliance	—	—	—	2
National Democratic Party	—	—	—	1
People's Redemption Party	—	—	—	1
Undeclared/Vacant	1	12	—	1
Total	109	360	109	360

*All People's Party in 1999

- **Alliance for Democracy (AD).** The AD was a regional party with a firm base of support among the Yoruba in southwestern Nigeria, where it won local and state elections in six states. It very quickly became embroiled in controversy, however, when members of the party in the Lagos state legislature broke into two factions supporting different leaders. When they began throwing chairs and tables at each other during a meeting, the police had to be called in to restore order.

In the lead-up to the 2003 elections, there was no certainty that Obasanjo would be nominated once again as the candidate for the PDP. Nigeria had become more democratic under his tenure, but economic problems persisted, thousands of people had died during his term in factional violence and conflict of various kinds (see Political Debates), and Obasanjo had lost much of the support from the Muslim north that had won him the presidency in 1999. Many political leaders also felt that it was time for the election of a president from another part of the country, and Obasanjo was challenged by a former vice president, an easterner named Alex Ekwueme. But Obasanjo safely won the PDP nomination.

According to the Independent Election Commission, about 60 million Nigerians were eligible to vote in 2003 and were given a choice of candidates from 22 registered political parties. Given the low levels of literacy in Nigeria, each party had to be represented on the ballot by a symbol (much like the arrangement in India). The elections were a major test for the credibility of the government because, unlike the military, no Nigerian civilian government had ever organized successful elections.

Although the elections were held during the new civilian political era, and were probably the first ever successfully organized by civilians, all three of the major party

HOW MUCH IS A HUMAN LIFE WORTH?

Imagine if, during the four-year-term of an American president, several thousand people were killed in the United States in a combination of religious and racial conflict, man-made disasters, and army massacres. Imagine some of those massacres taking place after the president himself had sent in troops to restore order, and the president refusing even to issue an apology. Imagine the political and legal ramifications, and the non-stop media analysis. Imagine the chances of that president being reelected.

Consider, then, that an estimated 10,000 people died in Nigeria in violence of one kind or another during the first four-year term of President Olusegun Obasanjo (1999–2003).[17] Examples include the following:

■ In November 1999, after 12 policemen were killed in the Niger Delta region, Obasanjo dispatched tanks and soldiers to restore order, and several thousand people were massacred. Obasanjo refused to apologize, instead promoting the local army commander.

■ In June–July 2001, fighting broke out between two ethnic groups in the south central state of Benue, during which perhaps as many

as 200 people were killed and 50,000 displaced from their homes. In October, after 19 of their colleagues involved in putting down the fighting were killed, Nigerian soldiers went on a three-day rampage through local villages, killing at least 300 people.[18]

■ In September 2001, as many as 500 people were killed and 900 injured in the city of Jos after Muslims and Christians attacked one another with axes, clubs, and machetes. President Obasanjo described the killings as a "disgrace."

■ In January 2002, munitions carelessly stored at a Lagos army barracks exploded. People living near the barracks panicked and many ran toward a nearby canal, where they were trampled or drowned. The official death toll was put at 700, but unofficial estimates went as high as 2,000.

The international press pays remarkably little attention to such incidents. In Nigeria, carnage of this scale is deeply criticized, to be sure, but—remarkably—it was not enough to prevent the reelection of Olusegun Obasanjo in 2003. What does this tell us about the relative value of human life in different societies?

candidates were former Army generals: As well as Obasanjo himself, there was Muhammadu Buhari (military leader in 1984–1985) and the former Biafran rebel leader Odemegwu Ojukwu. Meanwhile, rumors were rife that another former military leader—Ibrahim Babangida—was using his money and influence behind the scenes to influence the outcome of the election. Despite the usual charges of fraud and the usual violence that accompanies Nigerian elections, Obasanjo was elected to a second term in a process regarded by one observer as "hardly credible, but acceptable."[16] This was damning with faint praise, because the elections were marred by irregularities and vote-rigging—it was so bad in 16 states, claimed Muhammadu Buhari, that he was still trying to have the results overturned two years later.

POLICIES AND POLICYMAKING

In contrast to the relatively stable and consistent policymaking structures of liberal democracies, these structures in Nigeria are changeable, and since independence in 1960 have taken three forms:

- Between 1960 and 1966, Nigeria used the Westminster model of a fused executive and legislature, with power divided by a federal system.

- During its periods of military government, Nigeria has been a dictatorship, with decision-making power centered on the military leader and his advisors, the key institutions based around a military-bureaucratic structure, and no substantial competing sources of power.

- Under the Fourth Republic (as it had been during the Second Republic), Nigeria uses the U.S. presidential model, with power shared at the national level among an executive president, a legislature, and an independent judiciary, and further divided between the federal government and state governments.

With all these changes, it is difficult to find any consistent patterns in the policy-making process (other than a high degree of centralization) or to pin down the rules of the process. Superficially, the structure of the Fourth Republic almost exactly follows that of the United States: The powers of the federal government are shared and limited through a system of checks and balances; the presidency is supposed to provide national unity and to place national interests above those of regions or ethnic groups; the National Assembly provides both the states and the people with representation; and the Supreme Court provides a judicial check. At the state level, 36 state governments take care of local administration, represent local interests, and further limit the powers of the federal government.

But just as in a liberal democracy, the bare outline of government overlooks many of its important nuances, and theory and practice do not always coincide. The success of Nigerian government must ultimately be measured in terms of its ability to balance the conflicting demands of the many groups in Nigerian society, to steer a careful course through the minefield of ethnic and religious divisions, and to control corruption and opportunism. Effective government also depends heavily on the legitimacy of the system of government. In contrast to liberal democracies, where the legitimacy of government is rarely seriously questioned, Nigerian governments have had to struggle as much with issues of their own legitimacy as with responding to the everyday needs of simply running the country.

Underlying the challenges of state-building, one of the recurring features of politics in LDCs is the existence of a political elite, which often is cut off from direct contact with the people. Nigeria has been no exception, its problems exacerbated by the relatively small pool of qualified and experienced individuals from which government and the bureaucracy can draw. Nigeria's elite tends to come mainly from three groups: educated or ambitious individuals who win influence through their own efforts (legal or otherwise), people who have won influence through traditional clan or village positions, and senior officers in the military.

The concentration of power in the hands of these elites has limited citizen access to the policy process. Members of the elites set up **patron-client relationships** with networks of political supporters who are obligated to them through the exchange of favors. This is a feature also of politics in the United States, Japan, and Mexico, but leaders in these countries must build a wider base of support. Also, there are many independent channels through which political views can be expressed and opposition exerted that counterbalance the accumulation of power by the elites.

In liberal democratic terms, elitism works against the interests of democracy (even though every liberal democracy has its own elite). However, should liberal democratic criticisms of elitism be applied to Nigeria? Are patron-client relationships an aberration, or do they simply perpetuate traditional clan and tribal hierarchies? Whatever the case, they will continue to exist as long as education and the opportunities for the accumulation of wealth are restricted to a minority, as long as ethnic differences persist, and as long as traditional political leaders continue to have influence. Under these circumstances, policymaking in Nigeria will be based more on limited networks than on any broader notion of the "national interest."

ECONOMIC POLICY

When Nigeria became independent, its economic prospects looked good: It had undergone a careful transition to self-government, it was self-sufficient in food; it had nine major exports (a good range by most African standards); it had a good network of British-built roads, railroads, and harbors; and it had considerable natural and human resources. To add to the optimism, major reserves of good-quality, low-sulfur oil were discovered in the 1950s, setting Nigeria on the road to becoming a major oil producer. (By 2005 it had known reserves that would last about another 20 years at existing rates of consumption and large natural gas deposits that had not yet been fully exploited.)

In the mid-1970s, economic prospects improved even more as the world oil price rose from about $3 per barrel to $15 per barrel. Nigerian oil exports grew rapidly, giving Nigeria a trade surplus. Although most of the exploration and production was done by foreign companies, Nigeria kept a majority shareholding in the oil industry through the state-owned Nigerian National Petroleum Corporation (NNPC) and so was able to restrict the proportion of the profits that left the country. The economy grew by about 8 percent annually, and as a member of the Organization of Petroleum Exporting Countries (OPEC), Nigeria helped engineer the oil price increases of the 1970s that resulted in huge profits for the government.

Nigeria's annual oil income grew from $400 million in 1965 to $9 billion in 1970; in 1980 it reached $26 billion. With money flowing into its coffers, the Gowon government launched the biggest development plan ever adopted by an African country, pledging to spend $100 billion on nothing less than transforming Nigeria from a traditional society into a modern, unified state in five years. The minimum wage was doubled, all civil servants were given a 60 percent pay raise, 50,000 Nigerians were sent to the United States and Europe to learn new skills, and construction plans were announced for seven universities, three airports, 13 television stations, and a new federal capital at Abuja. The United States, the USSR, and Europe showed new interest in closer ties with Nigeria, which was now seen as a major regional economic power.

Then the bottom fell out of Nigeria's ambitions. OPEC unity collapsed, the price of oil fell from a high of nearly $40 per barrel to $12 per barrel,[19] and Nigerian oil revenues fell from $26 billion to $10 billion between 1980 and 1983, just as its foreign debt came due. Nigeria had squandered most of its oil profits, and hopes for economic and social transformation were dashed by political instability, bad planning decisions, waste, hoarding, and profiteering. Instead of investing oil wealth in other economic sectors to prepare itself for the rainy day when the oil price would inevitably fall, the government allowed the agricultural sector to decline. In 1970, oil and cocoa accounted for nearly three-fourths of all exports. Today, oil accounts for nearly 99 percent of exports and 12 percent of GDP. Not only has Nigeria become a single-product economy, its prospects almost entirely driven by changes in the price of oil on the international market, but receipts from oil have been erratic, making it impossible to predict income and to plan development. This dependence on a single valuable product—which afflicts many other poorer countries—is known as "the **resource curse.**"

During the 1980s, Nigeria went from boom to slump. Its currency was overvalued, its foreign exchange reserves plummeted, inflation grew from 20 percent (1980–1984) to 100 percent (1993), and it became a net food importer. GDP fell from $1,100 per capita in 1980 to about $250 in 1989, and even today languishes at just $390. Oil profits also worsened inequalities in the distribution of national wealth, so that the richest 1 percent of Nigerians now control 75 percent of the national wealth. In short, Nigeria was poorer in real terms after the oil boom than it had been in 1970. Instead of becoming rich during the oil years, Nigeria, like Mexico, built a substantial national debt: its external debt in 2005 stood at nearly $35 billion (the biggest in sub-Saharan Africa), and servicing the debt accounted for nearly one-third of Nigeria's export earnings.

As if these problems have not been bad enough, Nigeria under the Obasanjo administration has faced a long list of severe economic and social challenges:

- **Decaying infrastructure.** Roads and railroads are in a bad state of repair, heavy traffic in major cities often leads to severe traffic jams, water and electricity supplies break down daily, the postal service is slow, and there is only one phone per 500 people (compared with more than one per person in the United States). So few telephones work properly that most people find it simpler to make personal visits. A step forward was taken in 2000 with the auction of the first cell phone licenses, since when cell phone use has grown rapidly.

- **Fuel shortages.** Absurd as it may seem in a major oil-producing country where government subsidized fuel is sold at 90 cents (U.S.) a gallon, finding fuel is difficult. The problem is caused partly by the decay in Nigeria's oil refineries, and partly by the smuggling of fuel to neighboring countries, where it is sold at much higher world market prices. The result for Nigerians is that gas stations often run out and customers may have to wait in line for up to 48 hours for new supplies. This not only is a political irritant but wastes time, creating more economic problems as workers miss valuable time at their desks. Meanwhile, demands that the government deregulate the fuel market are opposed by those who have benefited from siphoning off oil profits.

- **A prosperous black market.** Known euphemistically as the "parallel market" or the **informal sector,** the black market can be seen in some ways as a healthy form of free-market economics based on supply and demand, but its existence makes it

A view of downtown Lagos, the rapidly growing former capital of Nigeria. With an official population of nine million (but an unofficial population that is much larger), Lagos is infamous for its poor transport, the bad driving habits of its residents, and its pollution.

difficult for the government to collect taxes or to control economic development. Most Nigerians make their livings wholly or partly from the black market, in part because so few are employed in conventional jobs. The foreign exchange black market alone is estimated to be worth as much as $5 billion annually, or about one-sixth of Nigeria's GDP.[21]

- **A large state sector.** Ever since independence, the government has dominated the business sector; state ownership has meant monopolies and easy pickings for corrupt politicians and bureaucrats, and many of these businesses—such as NITEL, the state telephone company, and NEPA, the electricity company—are infamous for their incompetent management and bad service. The Obasanjo administration promised that it would address this issue, but it privatized just 14 of 107 state-owned companies in its first three years in office. Part of the problem has been a

CRITICAL ISSUES

OIL AND NIGERIA

As the world's sixth-largest producer of oil, producing about two million barrels of crude oil per day and earning about $18 billion annually from oil exports, Nigeria should be a wealthy country. It should be using the oil money to invest in broadening the base of its economy, building new roads and schools, creating the foundations of a welfare system, and—at the very least—bringing wealth and opportunity to the thousands of Nigerians who work for the oil industry and in related segments of the economy. But oil has proved to be the source of many of Nigeria's biggest problems. It contributed to the civil war in 1967, and it continues to cause national tensions by pitting the interests of the six oil-producing southern states against those of non-oil states demanding a cut of the profits. Income from oil exports has proved an irresistible lure to corrupt politicians and military leaders, and oil production has caused major environmental problems in southern Nigeria.

Ironically, economic development problems are among their worst in the oil-producing regions themselves, where little investment has been made in roads, electricity, safe water supplies, or telephones. Particular criticism has been directed at the Dutch-British multinational corporation Royal Dutch/Shell, which produces most of Nigeria's oil. But Shell points the finger of blame at the Nigerian federal government, which collects all of Nigeria's oil revenues. Much goes into paying salaries and overheads, and much of the rest has been siphoned off by corrupt officials. Little has been invested in Nigeria's own oil refineries, which are now in such an advanced state of neglect and disrepair that fuel shortages are common, and Nigeria must import 70 percent of its fuel needs. Meanwhile, the government—remembering that fuel price increases in the past have led to strikes—subsidizes fuel to keep the cost low.

Nigeria has other nonfuel mineral resources, such as tin, bauxite, iron ore, and gold, but it lacks the investment funds needed to develop these resources, and will attract little from abroad until foreign investors can be sure that there is no risk of losing their investments to corruption or to another military government. Unlike many other African countries, Nigeria earns little from tourism. Despite the fact that it has one of the most vibrant cultures on the continent, and a long and fascinating history, little has been done to preserve its heritage (most of its best artifacts were either taken by the British or have since been sold, usually illegally, for the profit of corrupt leaders), and there has been almost no investment in building the infrastructure that tourists demand, including hotels, roads, airports, and communication systems. Tourists are also put off by crime, corruption, and the challenge of even entering the country. Novelist Chinua Achebe once quipped that "Only a masochist with an exuberant taste for self-violence will pick Nigeria for a holiday."[20]

lack of capital within Nigeria to buy these companies, and part has been a lack of confidence in the Nigerian market by potential foreign investors.

- **Widespread poverty.** An estimated two-thirds of Nigerians—nearly 90 million people—live below the poverty line, a problem that feeds into ethnic conflict to produce social unrest. Although liberal democracies also have large numbers of people living in poverty, they have welfare programs that provide a level of support and income that poor Nigerians would define as immense wealth. Americans, for example, are poor if they live in households that earn less than $19,350 (for a family of four), or about $13 per person per day. By contrast, Nigerians are defined as poor if they are earning less than $1 per day.

- **Institutionalized corruption.** Nigeria is one of the most corrupt countries in the world, routinely placed near the bottom of the Corruption Perceptions Index developed by Transparency International.[22] The abuse of power for personal gain in Nigeria poses a threat to political stability on a par only with ethnicity. In the period 1993–1998, for example, it was estimated that Sani Abacha, his family, and his senior advisors and ministers embezzled at least $1 billion, and perhaps as much as $3 billion to $6 billion.[23] President Obasanjo moved quickly within weeks of coming to office to launch an anticorruption crusade: He suspended all contracts, licenses, and appointments made in the five months before he took office; replaced the heads of several public agencies; and gave compulsory retirement to more than 200 government officials, including 99 customs officers. However, it has been normal procedure for every new Nigerian leader to launch an anticorruption drive upon coming to office, without much effect. The only way to remove institutionalized corruption is to ensure that power in the Nigerian political system is shared and checked as widely as possible.

- **An inadequate education system.** Although Nigeria has a free secondary education system, there are too few teachers and classrooms, and the provision of education has been uneven: Southerners have better facilities and more graduates than northerners, and there are too few scientists and professionals being turned out by universities. About 36 percent of Nigerian adults are illiterate, hindering Nigeria's hopes of building a modern, successful society.

- **An inadequate health care system.** Nigeria has 10 doctors and 40 nurses for every 100,000 people (compared with nearly 280 doctors and more than 830 nurses in the United States),[24] infant mortality is 14 times the rate in the United States, life expectancy fell in 1999–2003 from 47 years to 45 years, and only one in five rural people has access to safe drinking water. As with many other African states, AIDS is a critical problem in Nigeria. It arrived later in West Africa than in southern and eastern Africa, but the response has been handicapped by the same social and religious taboos about discussing sex. By 2005, an estimated 3.5 million Nigerians (5 percent of the population) were HIV positive,[25] and there are fears that Nigeria could soon overtake South Africa as the country with the biggest proportion of AIDS cases on the continent. The Obasanjo administration has done little in response.

Nigerian economic policy has been driven in recent years by the demands of the major international lending organizations: such as the World Bank and the International Monetary Fund (IMF). As noted in Part IV, both have typically demanded structural adjustment (fundamental changes to the economy, cuts in public spending, and a reduction of the budget deficit) before providing countries like Nigeria with the "seal of approval" needed to win their support and have its debt repayments rescheduled. In the late 1990s the World Bank was talking of new levels of economic growth in parts of sub-Saharan Africa, with GDP in the previous year having grown by an average of nearly 4 percent and income per person by 1 percent. Unfortunately, Nigeria was not among the higher achievers: its manufacturing output was down, its foreign exchange reserves were low, and it was falling behind on its debt repayment schedule. There were a few hopeful signs, however, notably a fall in inflation from 56 percent to 22 percent, a balanced budget, and an accelerated program of privatization. With its large population and considerable oil wealth, Nigeria has the potential to be the economic rival of South Africa, but only if it can find some means to achieve political stability.

FOREIGN POLICY

The richer a country and the more its economy is geared toward trade, the more active an interest it will take in foreign relations and the more complex its foreign policies will be. Not surprisingly, most liberal democracies have extensive economic and security interests beyond their borders, with the result that most have active and complex sets of foreign policies, covering issues as varied as trade, defense, immigration, and communications. Foreign policy becomes almost as complex as domestic policy, and the leaders of liberal democracies are judged as much by their foreign policies as by their domestic policies.

Poorer countries are more introverted, their attention and resources diverted by pressing domestic issues. For countries like Nigeria, which face no major external security threats, foreign policy is driven mainly by the need to promote economic development and trade. Some political scientists argue that countries such as Nigeria have become so dependent on loans, aid, trade, and foreign investment that the political dependence of the colonial era has been replaced by a postcolonial economic dependence. But Nigeria has advantages; simply by virtue of its size and relative wealth, it is the dominating regional power in sub-Saharan Africa, and since it restored civilian government, it has become one of the two African states (South Africa being the other) that is taken seriously by foreign governments. Nigeria's participation is sought in regional economic and security matters, good relations with Nigeria are now seen as important to any external power looking for influence in the region, and many other African leaders see Nigerian stability as critical for the future development of the entire region.

Notable here has been Nigeria's role in the **Economic Community of West African States (ECOWAS),** which was founded in 1975 and is headquartered in Lagos. With 16 member states and a total population of more than 210 million, ECOWAS set out to achieve first a customs union and then a full common market along the lines of the European Union. To promote cooperation, a development fund was created through which the wealthier ECOWAS members could channel investment funds to the poorer members. With its growing oil revenues in the late 1970s, Nigeria was initially an active member of ECOWAS, exerting regional influence through grants, loans, and technical assistance. During the 1980s, however, as Nigeria began tightening its belt and putting domestic economic priorities above those of regional cooperation, the cracks in ECOWAS began to show. It has suffered from the instability of several of its members (such as Liberia and Burkina Faso), but the major problem has been the unequal size of its members. With 60 percent of the population of ECOWAS, Nigeria is by far the biggest, wealthiest, and most powerful member, a fact that not only makes smaller and poorer members nervous but has also caused resentment among Nigerians who feel that their country has borne too much of the burden of building ECOWAS.

Nigeria is a large and valuable market for the smaller member states, but they have been unwilling to reciprocate by opening their markets to Nigeria and have long suspected Nigeria of working toward regional domination.[26] ECOWAS members often have conflicting economic and trade policies, have made little progress in stabilizing exchange rates among themselves, and regularly fail to pay their membership dues. One of the organization's few tangible achievements has been its role in peacekeeping operations in countries such as Liberia and Sierra Leone. Nigeria has played an active role, and has even contributed to UN operations in Somalia and Bosnia.

Nigerian foreign policy has gone through spells of assertiveness and reticence. During the 1970s it was confident enough to publicly disagree with U.S. involvement in Angola and Belgian involvement in what was then Zaire, was critical of apartheid in South Africa, supported liberation movements in Angola and Zimbabwe, and tried to reduce its dependence on multinational companies, for example when it nationalized British Petroleum interests in 1979. It even campaigned for a permanent seat on the UN Security Council.

But as its economic problems worsened in the early 1980s, Nigeria became more introverted, and by the mid-1990s was too concerned with internal political and economic issues to be an assertive regional power. International leaders have nonetheless courted Nigeria. In 1992 there was the remarkable visit to Nigeria by South African president, F. W. de Klerk. U.S. President Bill Clinton visited in 2000, and British prime minister Tony Blair in 2002. Meanwhile, President Obasanjo has several times visited the United States, meeting with both Bill Clinton and George W. Bush. Such contacts serve to underline Nigeria's potential importance in the region, and its value to non-African states.

Nigeria has taken on a new economic significance for the United States in recent years, as the dependence of energy-addicted Americans on imported oil grows. As part of its strategy to decrease dependence on Persian Gulf oil, the Bush administration in 2002 held talks with the leaders of 11 African oil-producing states, prominent among them being Nigeria. With U.S.-Arab relations worsening, there is a concern that oil supplies from the Gulf could be disrupted, so the United States is looking to increase imports of "secure" oil from African and other oil-producing nations. Some estimates suggest that the United States could be importing as much as 25 percent of its oil from West Africa within the next 15 to 20 years, with Nigeria being the major source.

NIGERIAN POLITICS IN TRANSITION

"The trouble with Nigeria" wrote the novelist Chinua Achebe, "is simply and squarely a failure of leadership. There is nothing basically wrong with the Nigerian character. There is nothing wrong with the Nigerian land or climate or water or air or anything else. The Nigerian problem is the unwillingness or the inability of its leaders to rise to the responsibility, to the challenge of personal example which are the hallmarks of true leadership."[27] He was writing in 1983, just as another of Nigeria's experiments in civilian government was about to collapse. His sentiment still applies today, but—to be fair—Nigeria's problems are so severe that it will take more than strong leadership to solve them.

The Obasanjo administration has addressed several of the core issues relating to corruption, investor confidence in Nigeria has improved under the Fourth Republic, and Nigeria is slowly being taken more seriously in international affairs. But for Nigeria to "work" there will have to be a fundamental transformation in the way

Nigerians relate to one another, and they will have to set aside ethnic and religious differences and try to think of themselves more actively as Nigerians. The worsening level of communal violence suggests that there is still a long road to be traveled. It will also take a fundamental transformation of the economy, with Nigeria moving away from its dependence on oil and broadening the sources of its income, and moving away from the tradition of monopoly and incompetence that characterizes its state-owned businesses, which are in urgent need of privatization.

Nigeria's future remains frustratingly uncertain. It is one of the two biggest and most powerful countries in sub-Saharan Africa, it has a large and energetic population that favors democracy over military government, it has oil wealth that could provide the basis for sound economic development, and it could become an engine for regional economic and political growth. If it can find a way to rise above ethnic and religious division, to channel its oil wealth into building infrastructure and education, and to rid itself of its dependence on military arbitration, it could become Africa's first world power.

KEY TERMS

Biafra
caliphate of Sokoto
constitutional
    engineering
Economic Community of
    West African States
ethnicity
Fourth Republic

Hausa-Fulani
House of Assembly
Igbo
informal sector
Middle Belt
National Assembly
patron-client
    relationships

People's Democratic
    Party
resource curse
sardauna
sharia courts
slave trade
Yoruba

KEY PEOPLE

Sani Abacha
Nnamdi Azikiwe
Ibrahim Babangida

Muhammadu Buhari
Yakubu Gowon
Olusegun Obasanjo

Ken Saro-Wiwa
Shehu Shagari

STUDY QUESTIONS

1. Is Nigeria worth saving?
2. How do Nigeria's experiences in nation-building compare with those of the United States, and is there anything that Nigeria could learn from the U.S. experience?
3. What is the difference between race and ethnicity?
4. Is military government a necessary evil for a country such as Nigeria?
5. If you were Olusegun Obasanjo, what would you be doing to ensure the success of the Fourth Republic?

6. Is strong, authoritarian leadership (like that of Vladimir Putin) the best model for a divided society like Nigeria, or is Nigeria better led by a president who tries to reach out to all groups and accommodate as many of their differences as possible?

7. Should Nigeria accept its ethnic divisions and build a political system that accommodates them rather than subverts them?

8. Should Nigeria respect and build upon traditional local political models, or keep trying to make Western models work?

9. Are political parties the best option for divided societies such as Nigeria, or are there more efficient channels through which citizens can express themselves and be governed?

10. What does Nigeria need to do to wean itself off its economic dependence on oil exports?

NIGERIA ONLINE

The Presidency: www.nopa.net
Web site of the office of the President, with links to sites for other government departments.
Nigeria.com: www.nigeria.com
NigeriaWEB: http://odili.net/nigeria.html
Useful sources of news and information on Nigeria, the first being the Web site of a Lagos-based independent newspaper and the last including a series of links to government Web sites.
allAfrica.com: http://allafrica.com
Panapress: www.panapress.com
Good sources of news on Africa in general, both with regular stories on Nigeria.
Economic Community of West African States: www.ecowas.int
Home page of the regional integration organization.

FURTHER READING

Aborisade, Oladimeji, and Robert Mundt, *Politics in Nigeria*, 2nd Ed. (New York: Longman, 2002). A patchy but useful introduction to Nigerian politics, with chapters on political culture, political structure and processes, and public policy.

Achebe, Chinua, *Things Fall Apart* (New York: Anchor Books, 1994). The classic novel by the acclaimed Nigerian novelist (first published in 1958), which looks into the heart of a family in a small village in Nigeria.

Maier, Karl, *This House Has Fallen: Midnight in Nigeria* (New York: Public Affairs, 2000). A narrative and interpretation of recent events in Nigeria, written by a journalist.

Rotberg, Robert I. (Ed), *Crafting the New Nigeria: Confronting the Challenges* (Boulder, CO: Lynne Rienner, 2004). An edited collection of studies of Nigeria's political, economic and social challenges.

Soyinka, Wole, *The Open Sore of a Continent: A Personal Narrative of the Nigerian Crisis* (New York: Oxford University Press, 1996). A personal and occasionally grumpy set of reflections on Nigeria's political problems, written by the Nobel laureate.

COMPARATIVE EXERCISE

SYSTEMS OF ADMINISTRATION

One of the fundamental problems facing Nigeria is how to achieve a balance between the powers of national and local government. It could decide that its internal divisions are so great that the concept of Nigeria should be abandoned and the country should be split up into smaller states based around different ethnic groups or religions. This is unlikely to happen though, so the only alternative is to try to build national unity, and the nature of its administrative system is the key to winning the battle.

Different administrative systems are distinguished from one another by the relative balance of power between national and local levels of government:

- In **unitary systems,** most significant power rests with the national government, while local units of government have little independence. National government is responsible for almost all key policy areas, taxes are almost all national taxes, national elections are far more significant than local elections in determining the distribution of power, and local government units can be redesigned and abolished by national government. The vast majority of countries have unitary administrative systems, including Britain, France, Japan, China, and Egypt.

- In **federal systems,** local government has more power. There are many competing theories about the nature and the goals of federalism, which comes in many different forms, but its defining characteristic is a system of government in which national and local governments have independent powers, and neither level is subordinated to the other. Federal systems involve the division of powers: national government is typically responsible for broad economic policy issues, foreign policy, and defense, and local government is usually responsible for policing and education.

Both levels of government also have their own taxing and lawmaking powers. There are less than two dozen federations in the world, including the United States, Canada, Australia, Brazil, Germany, Russia, Mexico, India, and Nigeria.

- An even looser arrangement would be found in a **confederation,** an unusual kind of administrative system that was used in the United States in 1781–1789 and in Germany in 1815–1871. Although Switzerland calls itself a federation, the relationship between its cantons is very loose and the Swiss national government has very limited powers, pushing the country close to the definition of a confederation. The European Union also has many of the features of a confederation. The focus of political power in a confederal system rests at the local level, which is responsible for all policy areas except those that local governments agree are better dealt with jointly, such as foreign, defense, and monetary policy.

Unitary systems usually work best in small or homogeneous societies where there are too few political and social divisions to make minorities fearful of the hegemony of the majority. Federalism tends to work best in countries that are big, heterogeneous, or based on the voluntary union of previously independent groups of people. For the United States, federalism was seen as the only arrangement that could unite 13 mutually suspicious colonies that had tried several years of confederalism before they agreed to a closer union. Support for small government in the United States was driven at first by fear of tyranny, but then by desires for self-determination. American federalism has been so successful that there is very little of substance today that differentiates residents of California from those of Arizona, Indiana, or New Hampshire.

In other parts of the world, federalism plays an essential role in providing order and in uniting communities with very different characteristics.

- In Belgium, there is a southern region based on French and a northern region based on Flemish. Each region has its own subgovernment, the capital city of Brussels is bilingual neutral territory in the middle, and visitors wonder what it means to be "Belgian." Belgium has remained intact because the constitution has been amended to give the two language-based regions more power.

- In Canada, French-speaking Quebecois see themselves as so different from their English-speaking compatriots that many want complete independence. Since 1987, the provinces have had new powers over appointments to the Canadian Senate and Supreme Court and veto power over certain constitutional amendments.

- Soviet federalism was little more than a cover for imperialism, and its underlying fragility was illustrated by the speed with which the 15 Soviet republics declared sovereignty following the collapse of the Gorbachev government. Even today, Russia finds itself struggling with demands for self-determination or independence from ethnic minorities living on its borders, developments that could threaten the viability of the entire Russian state.

- In Nigeria, the only attempt to create a unitary state led to the overthrow of the Ironsi government in 1966. The number of states has tripled since 1975 in an increasingly desperate attempt to ensure the unity of Nigeria by breaking up the major ethnic groups and by addressing the fears of minority ethnic groups that one of the larger groups would dominate national government. Ironically, Nigerian national identity is weak, but poorer regions of Nigeria are disinclined to see the country break up because they would then lose access to their current share of the profits from the oil-rich states in the south. Debates continue about the nature of Nigerian federalism and the relationship between national and local government. Among the particular criticisms of the constitution of the Fourth Republic is that it gives the federal government too much power. History may reveal that Nigeria needs a looser confederal relationship in which the balance of power lies with the states, leaving the "national" government responsible for foreign, defense, and monetary policy and for trade issues affecting the country as a whole. A number of Nigeria's ethnic groups are strongly in favor of such a system.

Part V

ISLAMIC COUNTRIES

Islam is the solution.

—Slogan of the Muslim Brotherhood, Egypt

The cold war between communism and the West is over, but a new kind of conflict—between Islam and the West—has emerged to take its place. The old threats of nuclear conflict have been replaced by an ideological and cultural struggle between two protagonists whose failures to understand each other seem to constantly worsen. The fallout is nothing new, because the West and Islam have been at odds with each other for 1,200 years or more. Not even the methods are new: terrorism and conventional state-on-state violence have been elements in the conflict before. What is new is the scale of the conflict and its potential reach in terms of the number of people threatened, the instability promised, and the costs involved.

Islam has long been a factor in global politics, but—at least until the attacks of September 11, 2001—mainstream Western political science had failed to give much serious thought to its broader political significance. The Islamic resurgence that followed the overthrow of the regime of the Shah of Iran in 1979 (see later in this chapter) had been an early indicator of change; thanks in part to September 2001, there is now growing support for the idea that we should try to understand Islamic countries as members of a distinct system type. Although Islamism as a political ideology is more a theory than a reality in most Islamic states, it gives most of them an identity that makes them distinctive from their non-Islamic neighbors.

The West still fails to appreciate that Islam is more than a religion, and to understand the complex interplay between Islamic law, social rules, and politics in countries throughout North Africa and the Middle East. Western liberal democracy supports a separation of church and state, but most Muslims argue that there is no separation of religion (*islam*) and state (*dawla*), and that the followers of Islam are all part of a larger community of the faithful (**umma**) that transcends race, language, and national borders. Unlike any other major monotheistic religion except perhaps Judaism, Islam provides theories of government and the state and a comprehensive

FIGURE V.1

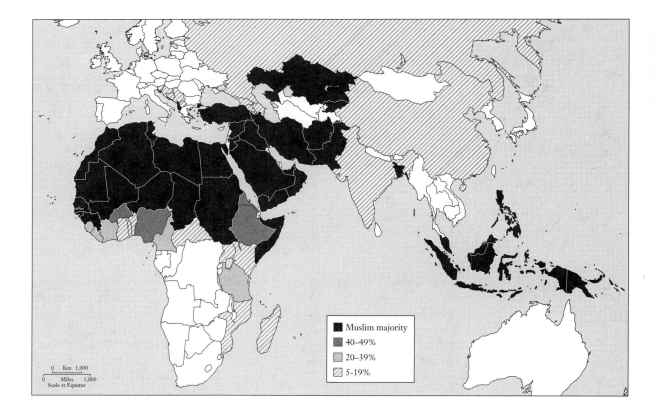

Muslim majority
40–49%
20–39%
5-19%

body of law that can guide the lives of its followers if properly applied. In short, Islam (unlike Christianity) contains a complete program for ordering society.

To be fair, the misunderstandings have also stemmed from the failure of Islamic societies to develop distinctive political institutions. The absence of such institutions is often blamed by Muslims on the problems caused by European colonialism and the imposition of political borders and Western institutions, which caused Islam to lose its way. But Muslims themselves have also disagreed about the role of Islam in politics, which varies from one state to another, not least because of differences in interpretation.[1] One school of Islamic thought sees Islam as an ideology, argues that it needs to become more political, and believes that religion should be tailored toward more radical political ends.[2] Others argue that church and state should be kept separate and that a dominant role for Islam runs the danger of creating a powerful group of religious leaders who would offset the authority of the secular government or could make the people fatalistic and easy to dominate and manipulate.

ISLAMIC COUNTRIES
What Are Their Features?

- A mixed record on representative government, with relatively low levels of political institutionalization

- Weak, immature, poorly defined, and/or unpredictable political processes, with a tendency toward authoritarianism and paternalism

- Relatively low levels of national unity and loyalty to the state

- Most forms of political participation and representation directly or indirectly influenced by Islamic values, with and Islam playing a dominant role—actual or potential—in the forces that drive politics

- Poor records on individual rights under the law

- Poor records on equality, with gender discrimination and little protection for minorities

- Typically ineffective political opposition, the only significant opposition often being proscribed Islamist movements

- Free-market economies, but relatively little variety, and often considerable variations in wealth and poverty

- Typically low levels of urbanization, with considerable urban poverty and mixed infrastructure

- Mixed technological development, but generally improving

- A relatively poor quality of life when measured by the provision of education, health care, and other basic services

- Low ratings on the Freedom House, Economic Freedom, and Human Development indexes

- Varied levels of regional and global influence, mainly in a negative sense

Where Are They?

There are 26, and they are mainly in the Middle East and North Africa:

Afghanistan	Iraq	Pakistan
Algeria	Jordan	Qatar
Bahrain	Kuwait	Saudi Arabia
Bangladesh	Lebanon	Sudan
Brunei	Libya	Syria
Comoros	Maldives	Tunisia
Djibouti	Mauritania	United Arab Emirates
Egypt	Morocco	Yemen
Iran	Oman	

One of the effects of these divisions is the great variety of political structures and situations in Islamic countries: they vary from the absolute monarchies of Saudi Arabia and Brunei to the constitutional monarchies of Jordan and Bahrain, and from Islamic republics such as Pakistan, Iran, the Comoros and Mauritania to states that are legally secular but where Islam is still a central issue in politics, such as Algeria, Egypt, and Syria. At the same time, there is no denying that the Islamic resurgence since the 1970s has been accompanied—as one political scientist puts it—by a re-assertion of Islam in public life: there has been "an increase in Islamically oriented governments, organizations, laws, banks, social welfare services, and educational institutions. Both governments and opposition movements have turned to Islam to enhance their authority and muster popular support."[3] Unfortunately, we tend to hear about political Islam largely in relation to the extremism of groups such as Al-Qaeda, Hamas in Palestine, Islamic Jihad in Egypt, and Hizbollah in Lebanon. This draws attention away from the more important role played by Islam in mainstream politics.

Broadly speaking, Islamic countries have five major features in common.

Patrimonialism and Personalism

Theoretically, Islamic government should be based on mutual consultation (*shura*) involving the community and on rule by the "competent"; that is, rulers with faith, a clear vision of Islam, trustworthiness, initiative, and leadership.[4] In practice, few Muslim leaders could be described as competent, and the concept of *shura* has been distorted to mean that leaders can consult key advisors or experts of their choice.[5] The result in many Islamic states has been a tradition of patrimonialism, where leadership develops around a dominant figure who becomes the source of all important ideas, strategies, and policies, and whose power may be underpinned by a cult of personality. Patrimonial leaders include the sultans, sheiks, and emirs of the Middle East, Muammar Ghaddafi in Libya (in power since 1969), Hafez al-Assad in Syria (in power 1971-2000), or Maumoon Gayoom (president of the Maldives since 1978).

There is a fine line between patrimonialism and authoritarianism; as the nineteenth-century British historian Lord Acton famously noted, "Power tends to corrupt, and absolute power corrupts absolutely." Many Islamic leaders have developed a reputation for accumulating and abusing power and for using Islam as a cloak. Although no Islamic leader since Muhammad has been exclusively a religious leader, many have tried to express their power in religious terms. Anwar Sadat, for example, in a failed attempt to offset criticism that Egypt had become too Westernized and secularized, tried to portray himself as the Believer President and made sure that television news gave prominent coverage to his visits each Friday to the mosque.

personalism
A system of government based around personal links between the rulers and the ruled.

Because power in a patrimonial system depends on access to the leader, he becomes the most important element in the system and tends to govern through an extended network of personal ties that are based on informal links rather than formal contracts or constitutions.[6] Networks are a part of politics everywhere, but they are almost institutionalized in Islamic societies. The royal families of Saudi Arabia and the Gulf emirates are obvious examples, as were the many family and personal links that linked Saddam Hussein's government in Iraq. Family and kinship ties have occasionally turned into extensive bureaucracies and elites based on the military, business, academia, and the mass media.

sharia The body of Islamic law, which functions alongside Western law in most Islamic countries.

Islamic Law

Islam has its own body of law, known as the *sharia,* which tends to make the news in the West only when someone has been sentenced to have a hand cut off for stealing or to be stoned to death for committing adultery. The result is a very narrow and misleading conception of how it works. In fact, Islamic law is deep and sophisticated, with its own system of courts, legal experts, and judges and its own long tradition of jurisprudence.

Muslims believe that God, through Muhammad, outlined universal laws that govern not just human behavior but also explain how nature works. Unlike Western law, where lawbreakers must account only to the legal system, lawbreakers in the Islamic tradition must account to God and all other Muslims. Also unlike Western law, the *sharia* outlines not only what is forbidden for Muslims but also what is discouraged, what is recommended, and what is obligatory. So, for example, Muslims should not drink alcohol, gamble, steal, commit adultery, or commit suicide, but they *should* pray every day, give to charity, be polite to others, dress inoffensively, and—when they die—be buried in anonymous graves.

The use of Islamic law is one of the ideals of an Islamic state, but the *sharia* is not universally applied in any Islamic country. It is widely used in countries such as Iran, Jordan, Libya, Mauritania, Oman, and Saudi Arabia, but the majority of Islamic countries use a mix of Western and Islamic law, turning to the former for serious crime and to the latter for family issues. When Muslims have any doubts about whether something they are considering doing is acceptable, they are encouraged to speak to a Muslim judge, called a *mufti*, who will issue a legal judgment known as a *fatwa*.

A Divided Community

Another of the ideals of an Islamic state is **universalism,** or the unity of the Muslim community. However, Muslims have more that divides them than unites them. First, they are divided by political boundaries developed during the colonial era, which have encouraged Islamic states to put national interests above those of the *umma*, causing deep and sometimes costly divisions. Second, they have doctrinal divisions, with most Muslims being members of one of two major sects: the **Shi'ah** and the **Sunni.** The Shi'ah believe they are the true Muslims in the model of Muhammad and that he was semi-divine, while the Sunni believe that Muhammad was an ordinary human being, and do not believe in religious leaders on earth. With the exception of Iran, Iraq, and Yemen, most Muslim countries are predominantly Sunni.

In addition, Muslims are divided over the role of religion in national life, with some Islamic countries (such as the Comoros, Iran, Mauritania, and Pakistan) claiming to be true **Islamic republics,** based on an Islamic constitution and full application of the *sharia*. Others (such as Albania, Indonesia, and Turkey) are more secular, and believe in a true separation of religion and state. Muslims also disagree over whether they should follow traditional values or adopt Western values. In Saudi Arabia, for example, women are increasingly rejecting their inferior role in society, but in Egypt they have been encouraged to adopt traditional habits, such as the wearing of the *hijab* (veil). Modernization is often equated with Westernization, but standard theories of modernization do not really help explain what is happening in the Islamic world, which is less a process of modernization than of **Islamization.** This can be defined not as wholesale Westernization but as Islamic modernization, or change that borrows from other systems but embodies Islamic principles and values and is not contrary to Islam.[7]

There is a sentimental attraction among many Muslims for the "Islamic cause" and among Arabs for the "Arab cause," but both are difficult to define and neither has had much success. Economic logic suggests that the countries of the Middle East should work more closely together, if only because of their very different sizes,[8] but there has been little progress on regional integration. Two major organizations play an important role in pan-Islamic or pan-Arab affairs: The **Arab League** (founded in 1945) has promoted Arab nationalism, but its members have often disagreed over key international issues such as peace with Israel, while the **Organization of the Islamic Conference,** or **OIC** (founded in 1971), has been unable to overcome the focus by its members on their national interests at the expense of the collective interest of the Islamic *umma*. Its richer members tend to have more influence in the world than the OIC as a collective, its members have often conflicting economic and foreign policy interests, its regular conferences tend to consist of little more than a repetition of the rhetoric of Islamic solidarity, and it has been able to do little to address the problems of poverty and human rights abuses in many of its member states.[9] In many respects, its plight is reflective of the divisions within Islam more generally.

Social and Economic Inequalities

Islamic theory includes ideas about wealth and the economy that reflect elements of both capitalism and socialism. As well as encouraging honesty and criticizing cheating, hoarding, and theft, Islamic economic theory supports material progress and the right to private property (although only in trust from God) and disapproves of monopolies. At the same time, it is hostile to materialism, encourages the equitable distribution of wealth, and emphasizes the importance of placing wider community needs above personal gain.[10] Islam also emphasizes the value of education; criticizes illiteracy and ignorance; and encourages brotherhood, community values, the family, and concern for the poor.

In practice, however, illiteracy and poverty are widespread in the Islamic world, there are often considerable and obvious gaps between the wealthy and the poor, education is handicapped by competition between Western and Islamic ideas, many people lack basic services, and there is little interstate economic cooperation. Militant Islamists have been quick to exploit the dissatisfaction of the poor and to play up the links between the wealthy in the Middle East and Western culture and mass consumption. They have also been keen to promote divisions between men and women. Even though it goes against the teachings of Islam, women are generally treated as inferiors by men, were long denied the right to vote, and do not play a prominent role in politics even today; social inequalities mean that levels of literacy vary between men and women.

THE EVOLUTION OF ISLAM

Most Westerners think of Islam as monolithic and homogeneous, associate it mainly with the Middle East, often associate it with fanaticism, assume that all Muslims are Arabs, and assume that all Arabs are Muslim. They are wrong on every count.

With an estimated 1.2 billion adherents, Islam is the second biggest religion in the world after Christianity and is rapidly on its way to becoming the biggest.

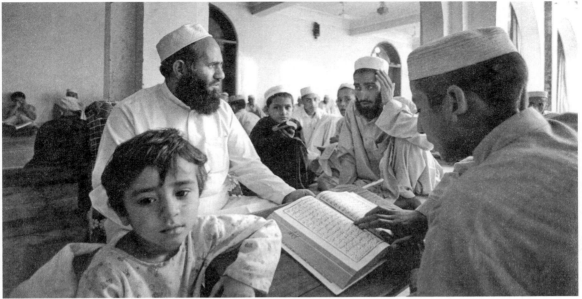

Young boys learning the Quran at an Islamic school in the northern Pakistani town of Peshawar. Islam is the fastest-growing religion in the world, there has been a resurgence of Islamic consciousness since 1979, and the links between politics and religion play an increasingly important role in countries such as Pakistan.

"Islam" means submission to God (or Allah) and is based on taking the **Quran** (the book of revelations supposedly made to the prophet Muhammad by the archangel Gabriel) as the literal word of God. Collected and written down after Muhammad's death, the revelations now constitute the final authority on the religious beliefs and the social system of Islam. Islamic law consists of codes of behavior that evolved over time out of the Quran and the *hadith*, the collected sayings and hearsay statements of Muhammad.

The Founding of Islam (622–632)

Islam was founded by the prophet Muhammad in the seventh century. Although he features prominently in the Islamic faith, he was simply one of a series of prophets supposedly sent from God, among them Abraham, Moses, John the Baptist, and Jesus Christ. For Muslims, Muhammad is the most important of all the prophets because they believe that his revelation was God's last message to humankind. Muhammad was born in about A.D. 570 in Mecca in present-day Saudi Arabia, at a time when the Middle East was in economic and political turmoil, divided by tribal rivalries. Raised an orphan, he made a name for himself as a trader before marrying a wealthy widow at the age of 25. When he was about 40, he claimed to have been visited by the archangel Gabriel, who gave him the first of many messages from God. He began preaching in Mecca, but he met with local hostility and left in 622 with some followers for Medina, 250 miles to the north. This *hijra* (or exodus) is regarded as the beginning of the Muslim era.

In Medina, Muhammad became both the political and religious leader, thereby emphasizing from the outset the fusion of religion and the state in Islam. Using Medina as a base, he raised an army and launched a war against paganism and foreign religions. By the time he died in 632, most of the Arabian Peninsula had come under the influence of his faith, its main attraction being that it was a homegrown religion with mass appeal and more relevance to the lives of local people than imported religions such as Christianity. Distinctively Arab, it united the Arabs for the first (and so far only) time in their history.

The Caliphate (632–1258)

Muhammad's father-in-law succeeded him, becoming the first of many caliphs who would lead Islam for the next 600 years. Within 25 years of Muhammad's death, the Muslims had conquered all of the present-day Middle East. By 750, the Arab empire stretched from Tashkent in central Asia to Marrakech in Morocco. Muslims even conquered Spain and parts of France and southern Italy; the Arab influence can still be seen today in some of the architecture of southern Spain. The turning point came in 732, when the Arabs were defeated by Charles Martel, the Holy Roman emperor, at the battle of Poitiers, just 100 miles from Paris.

At its height, the Arab empire was one of the great cultures of the world. The **Pax Islamica** covered an area greater than that of the Roman Empire at its height. Trade routes grew, towns flourished, political systems evolved, and Arabic became the lingua franca. In the eighth century, the world's best universities, libraries, architects, musicians, scientists, and scholars were Arab. We still feel their influence in our use of Arabic numerals, the decimal system, algebra, geometry, and the concept of zero, which was borrowed by the Arabs from India. Many of the words used in Western science come from Arabic, such as *nadir, zenith, alkali,* and *alcohol.*[11] After peaking in about 950, the Arab empire began declining as a result of internal dissension and division. Although Arab political unity ended, the spread of Islam did not. By 1500, under the leadership of several competing administrations and empires, Islam had spread south into Africa, north into central Asia, and east into what are now India, Bangladesh, and parts of Indonesia.

The Ottoman Empire (c. 1300–1922)

If the Arabs were the first major influence on the evolution of Islam, the Ottomans were the second. Arriving from central Asia, the Ottoman Turks from the late thirteenth century embarked on an expansionist policy, establishing their first capital at Bursa in what is now western Turkey. In 1453 they took the eastern Christian bastion of Constantinople (renaming it Istanbul), and from there moved as far north as what is now Hungary, south into Egypt, and west along the North African coast. The Ottoman Empire eventually covered almost the entire Middle East and remained the major power in the region until well into the nineteenth century. It outlasted the other two Islamic empires, the Safavid, which was based in what is now Iran and collapsed in the eighteenth century, and the Mughal, which covered the

Indian subcontinent and lost power in the early nineteenth century to expanding British influence. In all three, Islam was the major source of law, ideology, and political legitimacy. The Ottoman sultan ruled by divine right and was seen as defender and protector of Islam, and the *sharia* was the official law of the Ottomans.

Modernization and Nationalism (1798–1945)

Ottoman power began declining in the seventeenth century, the beginning of the end coming in 1798 when Napoleon invaded Egypt. Anglo-French influence spread through North Africa, Russian expansionism reached down into central Asia, and Islam itself went through an identity crisis. Surrounded by all these threats, Islamic leaders such as Muhammad Ali in Egypt began arguing that Islam needed to modernize. This was an attempt to respond to, rather than simply react against, Western imperialism. In other words, these leaders believed that they could strengthen their countries by modernizing their military and bureaucracy along European lines, while looking to the Quran and the *sharia* for their guidance.[12] The new policies immediately caused a split between modernists and traditionalists that even today influences politics in Egypt and Iran.

The post–World War I settlement gave Britain a mandate over what is now Iraq, Jordan, and Israel; gave the French a mandate over present-day Syria and Lebanon; and—through the 1917 **Balfour Declaration**—supported the establishment of a Jewish national homeland in Palestine. Central Arabia (Saudi Arabia from 1932) was independent, but most of Persia (Iran from 1935) was under British and Russian control, and the small Gulf states such as Kuwait and Qatar were British protectorates. In short, most of Islam was under European occupation or subject to European and Russian influence. The British and the French began treating their mandates more like colonies, and plans for a Jewish homeland went ahead despite Arab opposition, further deepening resentment against colonialism and promoting a new sense of Arab nationalism and Islamic revival.

During and after World War II, European influence in the Middle East waned, and Islamic states became independent: Lebanon in 1941, Syria in 1945, Jordan in 1946, Pakistan in 1947, and Libya in 1951. The British pullout from Palestine in 1948 was accompanied by the creation of Israel, and the hostility between the Israelis and the Arabs immediately became one of the defining influences in the region (see Political Debates, p. 478). Although British influence in Egypt and Iraq had ended by 1958, and France completely withdrew from North Africa in the period 1958–1962, the United States and the Soviet Union began taking a new interest in the region, or at least in its oil supplies. Some would argue that European colonialism was simply replaced by American neocolonialism, and the U.S. presence came to be seen by many Muslims as just the latest chapter in the history of Western interference in the affairs of Islam.

The Islamic Resurgence (1979–)

In few countries was Western influence more troubling than in Iran. An attempt by Prime Minister Mohammed Mussadeq to nationalize the Iranian petroleum industry in the early 1950s led to his being deposed with U.S. connivance in a 1953 coup

ISLAMISM: RELIGION OR IDEOLOGY?

Particularly since the oil crisis of 1973, there has been a resurgence in parts of the Islamic world of a phenomenon described in the West as fundamentalism or revivalism. Application of the term *fundamentalism* to Islam has at least two problems. First, it comes out of the Protestant Christian ethic and describes a belief that the Bible should be taken literally. But because Islam is already based on taking the Quran literally, it is by definition a fundamentalist religion, so the term is redundant. Second, the term is often used to suggest a restoration of a pure and authentic form of religion, but most Islamic "fundamentalists" are actually looking to revitalize and re-Islamize modern Muslim societies,[13] which is something quite different.

Because of these problems, an increasing number of scholars prefer the term *Islamism*, implying that it should be seen as a rival to "foreign" ideologies such as socialism, fascism, or liberalism.[14] Islamism is usually described either as a movement advocating a revitalization of political Islam or as an attempt to translate the original meaning of the Quran into something like a constitution for a new kind of political movement, with government-sponsored programs that reassert Islam as a primary ideological force.[15] In general, Islamists argue that Western technology, political ideas, and moral standards have corrupted Islam, have taken away the dignity of Muslims, and are used by their followers to keep power by force and deceit. Once Muslims go back to the basics of Islam, argue the Islamists, everything else will fall into place. Exactly how this will happen is irrelevant; what matters is that Muslims have faith. Islam has decayed mainly because it has ceased to be seen as a whole, according to the Islamists. Once Muslims return to the basics of their faith, Islam will be regenerated, and politics will have been "spiritualized."[16] Islamism has had its greatest impact in Iran, where the late Ayatollah Khomeini spearheaded the 1979 revolution against the regime of the shah, who was overtly secular and pro-Western.

and replaced by Shah Mohammed Reza Pahlavi. Iran enjoyed stability and growth under the shah, but he was a tyrannical leader dismissed by his opponents as a puppet of the United States. Pressures for a return to Islam forced the shah into exile in 1979, paving the way for the creation of an Islamic republic under the Ayatollah Ruhollah Khomeini and capping a resurgence of political Islam that had begun in the early 1970s.

Some saw the revolution as symbolic of Muslim disillusionment with Western values and influence and as evidence that revolutionary endeavor had grassroots support in many Islamic states. In December 1979 Islamic militants in Saudi Arabia rebelled, occupying the Great Mosque in Mecca. In October 1981 President Anwar Sadat of Egypt was assassinated by militants critical of the peace treaty he had signed in 1979 with Israel and Sadat's failure to establish an Islamic state in Egypt. In December 1981 militants launched a coup attempt in Bahrain, and in 1985 an attempt was made on the life of the emir of Kuwait. Islamic radicals took several Westerners hostage during the late 1980s and threatened to launch a terrorist offensive against the West. Although the Western media preferred to use the term "Islamic fundamentalism," a new term began to creep into debates about these events: **Islamism** (see Critical Issues, p. 438).

On the political front, Islamism has had a notable impact in several countries:

- In Algeria, sweeping gains by the Islamic Salvation Front in elections in 1990–1991 led to a military coup in January 1992 and the suspension of democratic reforms. Free elections were subsequently postponed, the government suspecting that they would easily be won by Islamists. Civil unrest throughout the 1990s claimed the lives of more than 40,000 people.

- In Afghanistan, Islamist rebels called the Taliban capped several years of mounting conflict with their capture in September 1996 of the capital, Kabul. They said their goal was to establish the world's purest Islamic state, to which end they banned television, music, and cinema; introduced public executions for crimes; and prevented men from shaving or women from working. Their actions were met with widespread criticism from most other governments, including those of the United States, Russia, and Iran; Russia was concerned that their ideas might spread to other Central Asian Islamic communities, and Iran called their policies "medieval." (The Taliban were removed from power by the U.S.-led invasion that followed the September 2001 terrorist attacks.)

- Islamism has been the only significant opposition force in Egypt, where it has been carefully kept under control, but has been active both in the form of a mainstream political party—the Muslim Brotherhood—and of militant Islamist groups that have sometimes used violence to achieve their ends.

- In the Sudan, a civil war broke out in the early 1980s following the imposition on the non-Muslim south of the *sharia* by the government in the Muslim north. Despite the advent of a new military government in 1991 that reversed this decision, the war has continued, so far claiming an estimated 1.2 million lives and raising questions about the continued viability of Sudan as a united state.

Islamism A belief in the basic ideas of Islam, including those relating to government and society.

ISLAMIC COUNTRIES TODAY

Islamic politics today is influenced at one level by concerns about Western involvement in the affairs of the Islamic world. At other levels, it is influenced by the continuing internal debate about the nature of Islam, worries about its social and moral decline, and the gaps that some Muslims see between the will of Allah and the historical development of Islam.[17] In this sense, the Islamic resurgence is really only the latest in a series of revivalist movements that have tried to transform the political, religious, and social life of Islam.

Many Islamic countries were united first by their opposition to Israel (although almost all now recognize its right to exist) and more recently by criticism of Israeli policy toward Palestinians. However, the Islamic world has not been bound more closely by the common thread of Islam. Just as earlier Islamic empires competed with one another, so Islamic countries today are often at odds with one another. The 1980–1988 Iran-Iraq war, one of the most brutal and costly in modern history, was at heart a conflict between Islamic nationalism (Iran) and secular Arab nationalism (Iraq), and it exemplified the ideological disagreements that still exist between

Islamic states. Similarly, several Islamic states fought on the allied side against Iraq during the 1990–1991 Gulf crisis, while others took a pro-Iraqi line. Opinion was divided in 2002–2003 over the issue of how to deal with Iraq and charges that it had developed weapons of mass destruction, with opposition to U.S. policy—ironically—providing many Islamic states with something in common.

The absence of a common purpose—other than the negative philosophy of hostility to (or distrust of) the West—denies the Islamic world many of the threads that pull liberal democracies together. The latter have the common objectives of promoting democracy and capitalism, but critics charge that the Islamic world has lost direction and is failing either to completely rediscover the core values of Islamic philosophy or to adopt the more attractive elements of Western politics and economics. Unless and until it rises above political, doctrinal, religious, or social divisions, Islam will continue to face the identity crisis that has caused it so many problems over the last few centuries.

KEY TERMS

Arab League	Ottoman Empire	Shi'ah
Balfour Declaration	patrimonialism	*shura*
Islamic republic	Pax Islamica	Sunni
Islamism	personalism	*umma*
Islamization	Quran	universalism
Organization of the Islamic Conference	*sharia*	

STUDY QUESTIONS

1. How do the gaps between theory and practice in political Islam compare with those between theory and practice in liberal democracies?

2. Who is to blame for Islam's political problems: Islam, the West, or both?

3. The confrontation between the West and Islam has been likened to that between liberal democracy and communism during the cold war. What are the similarities, and what are the differences?

4. Is Islamism a religion or an ideology?

ISLAM ONLINE

It is difficult to find English-language sites on Islam that do not proselytize and difficult always to know the motives behind these sites. The following provide an interesting variety of options, although they emphasize Arab politics and culture.

ArabNet: www.arab.net
Owned by a Saudi research company, this includes links to sites on a wide variety of Arab-related topics, including news in English.

Arabia.com: www.arabia.com/english
Mainly information on business and culture, with country links (including some to Egypt), political news, links to English-language newspapers in the Middle East, and a link to the Paris-based newsletter *Issues*.
Islamic Gateway: www.ummah.org.uk
A British-based site that contains an interesting set of links to sites relating to Islam.

FURTHER READING

Bill, James A., and Robert Springborg, *Politics in the Middle East*, 5th Ed. (New York: Longman, 2000). The standard introduction to the politics of the region.

Anderson, Roy R., Robert F. Seibert, and Jon G. Wagner, *Politics and Change in the Middle East*, 6th Ed. (Upper Saddle River, NJ: Prentice Hall, 2001). A study of the role of Islam in the Middle East, including its history and its impact on politics and economics.

Esposito, John L., and John O. Voll, *Islam and Democracy* (New York: Oxford University Press, 1996) and Esposito, John L., *Political Islam: Revolution, Radicalism or Reform?* (Boulder, CO: Lynne Rienner, 1997). Two surveys of politics and democracy in Islamic societies; the former includes case studies from six countries, including Egypt.

Husain, Mir Zohair, *Global Islamic Politics*, 2nd Ed. (New York: Longman, 2003). A study of the causes, meaning, and implications of the Islamic revival, with case studies from throughout the Islamic world.

EGYPT

EGYPT: QUICK FACTS

Official name: Arab Republic of Egypt (Jamhuriyat Misr al-Arabiya)

Capital: Cairo (el-Qahira)

Area: 382,865 square miles (991,620 sq. km) (three times the size of New Mexico)

Languages: Arabic (official), English and French widely understood by educated classes

Population: 67.6 million

Population density: 167 per square mile (64 per sq. km)

Population growth rate: 1.8 percent

POLITICAL INDICATORS

Freedom House rating: Not free

Date of state formation: February 28, 1922 (nominal independence from British protection established 1922; legal independence 1936, effective independence 1952)

System type: Presidential, limited democracy

Constitution: Published 1971

Administration: Unitary

Executive: President, serving six-year renewable terms

Legislature: Bicameral: People's Assembly of 454 members, elected for five-year terms, and a Consultative Assembly of 264 members

Party structure: Multiparty; 14 parties now recognized, but party activity controlled and system dominated by National Democratic Party

Judiciary: Supreme Constitutional Court

Head of state: Hosni Mubarak (1981–)

Head of government: Ahmed Nazif Ebeid (2004–)

ECONOMIC INDICATORS

GDP (2004): $75 billion

Per capita GDP: $1,310

Distribution of GNP: Services 50 percent, industry 34 percent, agriculture 16 percent

Urban population: 45 percent

SOCIAL INDICATORS

HDI ranking: 120

Infant mortality rate: 33 per 1,000 live births

Life expectancy: 69.1 years

Literacy: 55 percent of people aged 15 and older

Religions: Islam is the state religion; 94 percent of the population is Muslim, the rest is Christian and other religions

INTRODUCTION

Egypt is not as much in Western news headlines as Iraq or Iran, but behind the scenes it has been the dominant political and economic actor in the Middle East for most of the past century. This has been due partly to its size (there are about 68 million Egyptians), but mainly to its strong national identity and the fact that Egypt has been a distinct polity for nearly 5,000 years. The Egyptian nationalism that brought Gamal Abdel Nasser to power in a 1952 military coup had a long history, and Nasser went on to inspire at least two generations of Arab leaders. Between 1948 and 1979, Egyptian-Israeli hostility was at the heart of international relations in the region, and although Egypt and Israel are now at peace, Egypt remains a power broker between warring factions in the Middle East and a key point of contact for the West. Egypt also exerts a strong cultural influence: Its television programs, films, and music are watched or heard throughout the Arab world.

Egypt occupies a strategically important position at the junction of Asia and Africa and at the crossroads of the Middle East, the Arab world, and Islam. The heart of Egyptian culture and society has always been the fertile Nile River valley and delta, a ribbon of green and brown that bisects the country and supports 99 percent of the population. The major cities of Egypt—Cairo, Alexandria, Giza, Mansoura, and Zagazig—are all within 160 miles of one another at the mouth of the Nile. With more than 10 million people, Cairo is one of the biggest and most crowded cities in the world, and the Egyptian population, which is growing at 1.8 percent annually, is expected to double in the next 25 years.

In economic terms, Egypt is not a rich country. It has the second biggest economy in the Arab world after Saudi Arabia, but its per capita GDP of $1,310 makes it one of the poorest countries in the Middle East. The contribution of agriculture to national wealth has fallen since the mid-1960s as the contribution of industry and manufacturing has grown, but Egypt's major handicap is its lack of natural resources. About 95 percent of Egypt is too barren and dry to be habitable or cultivable, and although Egypt is an oil producer, its oil reserves are small. The only other major sources of revenue are foreign aid, tourism, revenues from the Suez Canal, and remittances from Egyptian workers living abroad. To complicate matters, Egypt has a national debt of $31 billion, and no government has succeeded in giving Egypt a strong economic base or in closing the wealth gap between the masses and the urban elite. There have been some signs of a modest economic upturn in recent years, but many problems remain.

In social terms, Egypt has none of the disruptive ethnic divisions of countries such as India or Nigeria. Most Egyptians are Muslim, Arab, and speak Arabic. The only significant minority are the Copts, direct descendants of the early Christian Egyptians, who make up 6 percent of the population. But while Islam may give most Egyptians a strong common bond, it is also at the heart of the country's political divisions. There is an ongoing tension between secularism and Islamism, and militants have done their best to undermine government. They assassinated President Anwar Sadat in 1981, have made several attempts on the life of President Hosni Mubarak, and during the 1990s launched attacks on tourists in an attempt to hit at one of

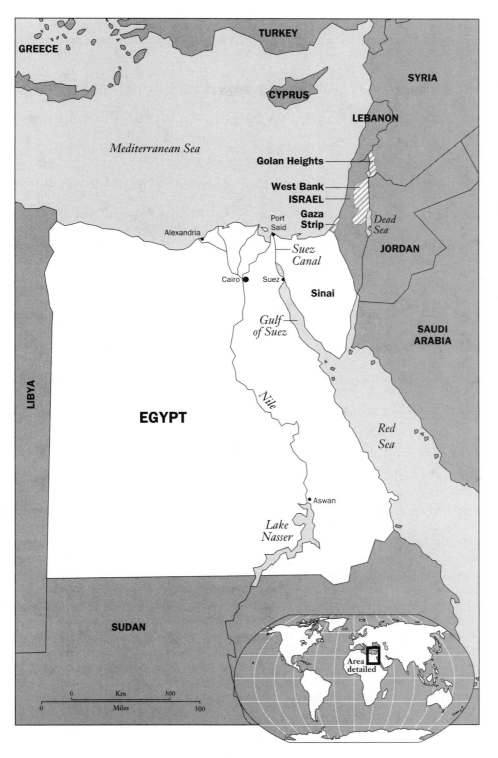

GREECE

TURKEY

CYPRUS

SYRIA

LEBANON

Mediterranean Sea

Golan Heights

West Bank

ISRAEL

Gaza
Strip

*Dead
Sea*

JORDAN

Port
Said

Alexandria

*Suez
Canal*

Cairo   Suez

Sinai

*Gulf
of Suez*

SAUDI
ARABIA

Nile

EGYPT

*Red
Sea*

LIBYA

Aswan

*Lake
Nasser*

SUDAN

Area
detailed

| 0 | Km | 300 |
| 0 | Miles | 300 |

Egypt's major sources of foreign income. Although the last few years have been relatively peaceful, Islamism remains at the heart of a debate over the goals of economic development and modernization and has had much influence on social values.

In political terms, Egypt has evolved since 1952 into a multiparty civilian system of government, but one in which power is centralized in the office of the president, supported by political, business, and military elites, and underpinned by a large and cumbersome bureaucracy, and by the monopoly held by the ruling **National Democratic Party.** Egypt today is more democratic than before, but the process of democratization has been limited and halting and the control of opposition groups has left most Egyptian voters cut off from the political process. Political centralization has been heightened by Egypt's geography, which has concentrated most of its people along the Nile, and has been promoted by a tradition of personalism and rule by an elite rather than rule by law. There are signs, though, of change. Criticism of government methods is growing, more information is available about human rights abuses, pressures are growing from opposition media, and the Egyptian people are not quite so tolerant of authoritiarianism as they once were.

POLITICAL DEVELOPMENT

Despite its long and rich history, Egypt has spent most of the last 2,500 years under foreign domination. Only in 1952 did it finally establish political independence, but even then it found itself caught in rivalries involving first the British and the French, then the USSR and the United States, and then the West and Islam. For all these reasons, the emergence of the nation-state in Egypt has been a recent phenomenon, and state-building is still a work in progress.

The Era of the Pharaohs (3100–525 B.C.)

What we loosely define as civilization began in the fertile valley of the Nile River about 7,000 years ago. Nomadic peoples were attracted to the region by the rich silt deposited along the banks of the Nile. As more people arrived, an organized political and social system emerged. In about 3100 B.C., the first of many dynasties of pharaohs was established at Memphis, near present-day Cairo. This led to the unification of the country from the Nile Delta to Upper Egypt and the creation of one of the most sophisticated and successful cultures in history. The era of the independent pharaohs ended in 525 B.C. with Egypt's defeat by the Persians. Except for a short break between 380 and 343 B.C., Egypt was to be dominated for the next 2,400 years by one foreign power after another: First came the Persians, then the Greeks under Alexander the Great, then the Romans and the Byzantines, and then in 642 the Arabs, who brought with them Islam.

From the Arabs to the Ottomans (642–1875)

Arab rule lasted for about 600 years, established Arab hegemony over Egypt, and led to the conversion of Egyptians from Christianity to Islam. In the tenth century a group of Shi'ah Muslims based in what is now Tunisia attacked Egypt and set up a new capital at el-Qahira (Cairo). In the face of growing external threats to Egypt, one of the last of the Arab rulers created a new regiment of Turkic slaves known as Mamluks (the owned). In 1250 the Mamluks became the new rulers of Egypt, which became the new center of Islamic culture and political power. This lasted until 1517 when the lower Nile valley became part of the growing Ottoman Empire. The Ottomans ruled indirectly through a corrupt and despotic group of Mamluks who took Egypt to the edge of ruin.

In 1798 Napoleon arrived in Egypt, presenting himself as a liberator but actually aiming to establish a foothold in the Middle East as a means of threatening British power in India. Despite cloaking his administration in Islamic principles, Napoleon was not widely welcomed and had to suppress two uprisings before finally being driven from Egypt in 1802 by the British and the Ottomans. Egypt now came under the rule of Muhammad Ali (1769–1849), an Albanian who had risen through the ranks of the Egyptian army. He became governor in 1805, launching a dynasty that would rule Egypt until 1952. He tried to modernize Egypt by building a Western-trained army; introducing cotton in 1820; reforming local agriculture; building canals and dams to provide transport and a steady supply of water; and building iron foundries, munitions plants, a shipyard, and textile plants. His administration also marked the beginning of the Egyptian state, and Egypt was unified for the first time in 300 years under a central authority based in Cairo.

The modernization was not to last: There were too few qualified Egyptians to maintain the new economic system, and Europeans (the British in particular) undermined the monopolies created by Muhammad Ali. He died in 1849, leaving behind a durable administrative system that gave Egypt a new prominence in the Middle East and reduced its allegiance to the Ottoman Empire. That prominence grew in 1854 when the French engineer Ferdinand de Lesseps was given a concession to build the **Suez Canal.** Opened to shipping in 1869, it was owned by Egypt and managed by French operators, but most of the shipping going through the canal was British.

The Era of the Europeans (1875–1952)

In the early 1870s, Egypt faced bankruptcy as cotton prices fell after the U.S. Civil War and a series of extravagant economic development schemes failed. Unable to pay its foreign debts, Egypt agreed in 1875 to sell its shares in the Suez Canal to Britain. To protect its new interests, Britain landed troops in 1882, and Egypt became an informal British protectorate, despite still being a province of the Ottoman Empire. Britain continued to modernize Egypt but spent little on education or industry and gave Egyptians little say in government. A nationalist undercurrent developed, but its adherents disagreed on the role of Islam: Egypt was never declared an Islamic state, and its politics, government, and law leaned toward the secular and the Western.

In 1914 Britain went to war with the Ottoman Empire, which sided with Germany in World War I, and formally declared Egypt a protectorate. With British control over Egypt expanding, nationalists led by Saad Zaghlul (1857–1927), a high ranking civil servant, formed *Wafd al-Misri* (the Egyptian Delegation) and began agitating for independence. When Zaghlul was deported in 1919, a mass insurrection grew,

TABLE 9.1

Egypt: A Timeline

642	Arab conquest of Egypt
1798	Invasion by Napoleon
1805–1848	Muhammed Ali
1854–1869	Construction of the Suez Canal
1875	Egyptian shares in the Suez Canal sold to Britain
1914	British protectorate declared
1922	Independence granted under a League of Nations mandate
1936	Anglo-Egyptian Treaty
1937	Farouk succeeds to the throne
1948	Creation of Israel; first Arab-Israeli war
1952	Military coup (July 23); King Farouk abdicates
1953	(June 18) Egypt becomes a republic
1954	Nasser becomes president
1956	(July) Suez Canal nationalized by Nasser; (October) invasion by Israeli, British, and French forces; Israel occupies Gaza strip
1958–1961	United Arab Republic (Egypt and Syria)
1967	(June) Six-Day War with Israel; Suez Canal closed; Israel occupies Sinai Peninsula
1970	Death of Nasser; succeeded by Anwar Sadat
1971	Corrective Revolution; new constitution; completion of Aswan High Dam
1973	Yom Kippur War with Israel
1979	(March) Peace treaty with Israel signed; Sinai returned to Egypt; Egypt suspended from the Arab League
1981	Assassination of Anwar Sadat; succeeded by Hosni Mubarak
1989	Egypt readmitted to the Arab League
1990	Egypt forges Arab coalition to free Kuwait following Iraqi invasion and takes part in the subsequent allied offensive
1991	Egypt signs agreements with the IMF and the World Bank in response to continuing debt problems
1993	Islamic militants make attempts on the lives of Egypt's information and interior ministers, and—in November—on Prime Minister Atef Sidqi
1995	Assassination attempt on Hosni Mubarak
1997	Construction begins on $1 billion Peace Canal to irrigate Sinai; (November) 58 tourists killed by Islamic militants in attack at Luxor
1999	(September) Assassination attempt on Hosni Mubarak, who is reelected for fourth term
2002	(July) Egypt celebrates 50th anniversary of Free Officers coup
2004	(October) Bomb attacks target Israeli tourists on Sinai peninsula, killing 34 people; (November) Funeral of Palestinian leader Yasser Arafat in Cairo
2005	(February) Mubarak announces a change in the constitution to allow for multicandidate presidential elections; (July) Nearly 90 people killed in bomb attacks on Egyptian resort of Sharm al-Sheikh; (September) Mubarak elected to a fifth term in office

leading to an agreement by Britain to end the protectorate in 1922. Egypt now became a monarchy under King Fuad I, but British troops remained in the Suez Canal zone and Britain still controlled foreign and defense policy. A new constitution was drawn up, giving the king extensive powers but giving the new Egyptian parliament the power of veto. The Wafd Party won a majority in the 1924 elections, and Zaghlul became prime minister.

In 1936 King Fuad died and was succeeded in 1937 by his son Farouk. An Anglo-Egyptian Treaty was signed and brought an end to the British military occupation, except along the Suez Canal. With the outbreak of World War II, however, British troops returned when Egypt was used as a base for the war against the Germans in North Africa. One of the most decisive battles of the war was fought in October 1942 at El Alamein, 70 miles west of Cairo, when the German Afrika Korps was turned back by British and Empire troops. Egypt benefited from Allied spending on industry and labor, but the new wealth was unevenly spread and land ownership was concentrated in the hands of Farouk and his supporters. Farouk made matters worse by developing a reputation as a playboy with a taste for food, yachts, and fast women.

Anti-British sentiment was strongest among the new corps of professional officers coming out of the Egyptian Military Academy, founded in 1936. For them, one of the last straws was the 1948 creation of the state of Israel. This sparked the outbreak of the first Arab-Israeli war, aimed at preventing the creation of the Jewish state. When Israel survived, nationalists blamed Egypt's poor showing on the weakness of the Farouk government and the incompetence of his commanders. Among the secret societies plotting against the monarchy was the **Free Officers,** a group of about 300 junior military officers. On July 23, 1952, they overthrew Farouk, meeting little resistance.

Nasser and the Arab Republic (1952–1970)

The military emerged from the 1952 coup in a strong position, but the Free Officers had few plans about how to proceed. Farouk was sent into exile (he died in Italy in 1965), and the monarchy was abolished in 1953. All political parties were banned, and a nine-member Revolutionary Command Council (RCC) took power. General Mohammed Naguib became the first president of the republic in June 1953, but it soon became obvious that the real power behind the throne was Colonel Gamal Abdel Nasser. In November 1954, Naguib was arrested and Nasser became president.

Nasser saw a continued division between Islam and the state, but he increasingly used Islam as a means of legitimizing his brand of Arab socialism and of underpinning Egypt's claims to be leader of the Arab world.[1] Those claims were given new credibility with the **Suez crisis** of 1956, one of the major turning points in the history of international relations since 1945. The crisis grew out of Nasser's plan to build the $1.4 billion **Aswan Dam** on the upper Nile. Britain and the United States agreed to provide part of the financing, but when Nasser bought arms from Czechoslovakia in 1955, and announced his intention to recognize communist China, the United States withdrew its financial support. Looking for another source of funding, Nasser nationalized the Suez Canal in July 1956, guaranteeing freedom of shipping and compensation for the mainly British and French stockholders. The British government considered Nasser to be a fascist dictator and made clear its plans to use

GAMAL ABDEL NASSER

Not only is he widely regarded as the founder of modern Egypt, but Gamal Abdel Nasser (1918–1970) is still revered by many in the Middle East as one of the great heroes of the Arab cause. He led a coup that (he argued) gave Egypt its first truly Egyptian government since the fifth century B.C., and he was also responsible for a program aimed at modernizing Egypt and ending its subservient position in the global system. By so doing, he symbolized Arab resistance to the West.

Born in Alexandria in 1918, Nasser graduated from the Egyptian Military Academy, becoming an army officer in 1938. Almost immediately, he began plotting to overthrow the government and remove the British. He fought in the 1948 Arab-Israeli war, and in the same year helped form the Free Officers Movement, which elected as its leader General Mohammed Naguib and launched the coup of July 1952. In 1954 Nasser replaced Naguib first as prime minister and then as president. In June 1956 he was "elected" president and in 1958 became leader of the short-lived United Arab Republic.

Nasser not only built enormous popularity among Egyptians but was also popular in the wider Arab world for his stand against the West with the 1952 coup, for the 1956 nationalization of the Suez Canal, and for his hostility toward Israel. He played a leading role in the creation of the Non-Aligned Movement in 1955, coming to be regarded as one of its leaders alongside Yugoslavia's Marshal Tito, India's Jawaharlal Nehru, and China's Zhou Enlai. Despite his "nonalignment," however, he accepted military aid from Czechoslovakia in 1955, a move that the United States saw as an unwelcome extension of Soviet influence in the region.

Nasser died of a heart attack on September 28, 1970, at the early age of 52, and was succeeded by Anwar Sadat. Despite his authoritarianism, his occasional arrogance toward his Arab neighbors, and his unwillingness to tolerate dissent or opposition, Nasser's stature in the Arab world remains virtually unassailable. Just as many Americans and Europeans who were alive in 1963 remember where they were when they first heard of the assassination of John F. Kennedy, many Arabs who were alive in 1970 remember where they were when they first heard the news of Nasser's death.

force to regain the canal, even in the face of U.S. opposition. As a result of secret meetings with Britain and France, Israel attacked Egypt in October and Britain and France responded in November by invading the canal zone, supposedly to protect their interests. The Soviet Union, which had approved the nationalization of the canal, strongly criticized the invasion, and the United States demanded a withdrawal of all three armies. They were finally pulled out in March 1957 and replaced by a UN peacekeeping force.

The Suez crisis had several consequences: It sparked Britain's biggest postwar financial crisis, and led to the resignation of prime minister Anthony Eden; it hammered the last nails into the coffin of the ailing French Fourth Republic, which collapsed in 1958; it ended Anglo-French control over the canal and symbolized the end of Britain and France as major world powers; it confirmed the status of the

United States as a military and political superpower, showing clearly to any remaining doubters that it was the senior partner in the Atlantic alliance; and it bolstered Nasser's reputation in the Arab world, where his actions were seen as a slap in the face to the West. It also led to an increase in Soviet influence in the Middle East when the Soviets gave Nasser the aid he needed to build the Aswan Dam, which finally went into operation in 1971.

Nasser's reputation was further strengthened by an invitation from Syria in 1958 to become leader of a new Syrian-Egyptian federation, the **United Arab Republic (UAR).** Syrian political parties were abolished, Cairo became the capital of the UAR, and Nasser became president of the new state. The marriage was not to last long, however, because it was patently unequal and the physical distance between the two countries made it impractical. The union collapsed after anti-unionists took control in Syria in 1961.

In 1962 Nasser created the **Arab Socialist Union (ASU),** which had all the outward appearances of a political party but actually was little more than an institution he could use to extend his control. Through the Union, he promoted a philosophy of "scientific Arab socialism," which he argued was compatible with Islamic principles and would allow the Arab world to build a political and economic position independent of either superpower. (Despite his claims that Egypt was nonaligned, Nasser bought weapons from the USSR and invited thousands of Soviet military advisors into Egypt, causing many sleepless nights in the U.S. State Department.)

If the 1950s had seen Nasser's rise as a leader of the Arab cause, the 1960s saw his credibility diluted, notably when Egypt was defeated in the 1967 Arab-Israeli war, otherwise known as the **Six-Day War.** Responding to border incidents, acts of sabotage, verbal threats, and the signing of a mutual defense treaty between Egypt and Jordan, Israel launched a preemptive strike on June 5 against Egypt, Jordan, Syria, and Iraq. Within hours, the air forces of all four Arab states had been virtually destroyed, and by June 10 the Israelis had overrun the **Sinai Peninsula** and forced a ceasefire. The defeat left Egypt battered and demoralized, and—for some—seemed to confirm Islam's impotence. Nasser took responsibility for the defeat and resigned, but such was his popularity that he was persuaded to return to office. In March 1969 Nasser launched a War of Attrition against the Israelis in the Sinai, which brought costly counterattacks by Israeli artillery and jets. Nasser accepted Soviet military aid but said he would also accept a U.S.-sponsored ceasefire. With his death in September 1970, plans for the ceasefire were suspended.

Peace with Israel (1979–)

Egypt since 1970 has been led by two men: Anwar Sadat (1970–1981) and Hosni Mubarak (1981–). A veteran of the Free Officers Movement who was obsessed with moving out from under the shadow of Nasser, Sadat continued Egypt's economic development. He also made it his priority to take back the Sinai Peninsula and reduce Egyptian dependence on the USSR. In October 1973 came the **Yom Kippur War.** During Yom Kippur (the Jewish Day of Atonement), Sadat launched a surprise attack against Israel. Crying "Allahu Akbar!" ("God is Great!"), Egyptian troops crossed the canal and took some Israeli fortifications. Israel immediately counterattacked and recrossed the canal within hours, but Egypt's moment in the sun was enough to earn Sadat the title "Hero of the Crossing." A ceasefire was arranged, but the exchange gave Sadat the opportunity to look for a diplomatic resolution of the Arab-Israeli impasse.

The failure of U.S.-mediated negotiations in 1974–1976 prompted Sadat to make the bold and ultimately fatal gesture of flying to Jerusalem, becoming the first (and still only) Egyptian leader ever to visit Israel. Negotiations led to the **Camp David Accords** of 1978, agreed to under the sponsorship of President Jimmy Carter. When Egypt and Israel signed a peace treaty in 1979, the Sinai was finally returned to Egypt. Despite this, Sadat was accused by other Arab leaders of selling out to the United States and Israel, and he never won the same level of trust and admiration in the Arab world as Nasser.

The Egyptian economy improved little during Sadat's tenure, despite his policy of liberalizing the economy (known as *Infitah*, or "the opening") and allowing new foreign investment in Egypt. On the political front, he tried to offset criticisms of the peace treaty with Israel by allowing three factions to emerge within and eventually supersede the ASU. He also allowed Islamic opposition groups to operate, but when they openly criticized the peace treaty, he cracked down. Their response was deadly. On October 6, 1981, while reviewing a military parade on the outskirts of Cairo, Sadat was shot to death by members of a group of Islamic radicals. Showing how he had become more popular outside Egypt than within, three U.S. presidents attended his funeral, but he was barely mourned in the Arab world.

Sadat was smoothly succeeded by Hosni Mubarak, his vice president. As well as continuing to promote economic growth, Mubarak has had to walk a fine line between restoring Egypt's reputation among its Arab neighbors and maintaining good relations with Israel. Careful diplomacy led to Egypt's readmission to the Arab League in May 1989, ten years after it was expelled in retaliation for signing the peace treaty with Israel. In August 1990 Egypt played a pivotal role in organizing an Arab response to the Iraqi invasion of Kuwait and sent 32,000 troops to the region, a contingent second in size only to that of the United States.

Egypt Today

Mubarak has had to balance the demands of Islamists with his plans to promote a secular Egyptian state. He has continued to democratize Egypt in a carefully controlled process, and most opposition parties consider him preferable to a more authoritarian or radical Islamic alternative.[2] Egypt has been under a state of emergency since the assassination of Sadat, and Mubarak used his emergency powers to clamp down on Islamic militancy during the 1990s; in spite of this, more than 1,200 people were killed in acts of violence between 1992 and 1999, the worst being an attack on tourists at Luxor in the Nile valley in November 1997, which left 52 people dead. Militants also tried to assassinate Mubarak during a visit to Ethiopia in June 1995, but following the declaration of a ceasefire in March 1999, the government became more lenient toward the militants, despite another attempt on Mubarak's life in September 1999.

Meanwhile, the economic news has been mixed, with falling inflation, growing unemployment, not enough foreign investment, and a halting program of privatization. Mubarak has clamped down on political corruption and has allowed opposition parties to expand their activities. He also arranged for the first multicandidate presidential elections in 2005, although it is questionable how much chance his opponents really stood of winning, and Mubarak—according to official results—was easily reelected for a fifth term in office. He has no obvious successors (unless one believes gossip that he is grooming his son Gamal to take over) and has so far opted not to appoint a vice president to help ensure the continuity of government and of his policies.

POLITICAL CULTURE

When the Free Officers took power in 1952, there was little in the way of an established political structure that they could build on, reform, or even abolish. There had been little popular participation; there were few organized economic, social, or political groups; and there was no tradition of political accountability. However, there had been a tradition of centralization and a strong, bureaucratized state.

A Dominant State

For most of its history, Egypt has been governed by strong leaders using authoritarian methods. It has been argued that Egyptians during the Sadat years came to expect "harsh government as almost a natural phenomenon about which little could be done except to adapt or to evade its exactions."[3] Having become used to a strong state system with little public accountability, Egyptians see themselves as separated from the state. There is little sense of belonging or of mutual responsibility between the governors and the governed, creating a political gulf that limits the growth of political consciousness and participation. An example of the lengths to which the Mubarak administration is prepared to go to stifle opposition came in June 2002, when Dr. Saadeddin Ibrahim—an American-educated sociology professor—was jailed for seven years, charged with tarnishing Egypt's image abroad. One of Egypt's best-known champions of clean government, Ibrahim ran an independent research institute and was deeply critical of the way recent elections had been managed. He was held under the state of emergency that has been in force in Egypt since 1981.

A Patrimonial Society

Patrimonialism and personalism have always been important features of Islamic society, building on the patriarchal system at the core of all traditional societies. While the patriarch operates at the family level with no machinery in place to enforce his will, the patrimonial leader sets up an identifiable administrative structure and rules through an extensive bureaucratic network.[4] Patrimonialism has been a theme in Egyptian political leadership since the pre-coup days, monarchs and presidents alike portraying themselves as father figures and using networks of supporters to keep a grip on power and limit the growth of autonomous political institutions. Before 1952, the king was at the hub of the system. With Nasser, army officers became the new elite, and they were subsequently joined by the bureaucracy, business leaders, and party leaders. Sadat and Mubarak have both exploited the patrimonial tradition and the attendant shortcuts it provides to authoritarian government.

Localism and the Peasant Society

More than half of all Egyptians are peasants (or *fellahin*) and live in 7,000 villages scattered along the Nile. Much like Indian villagers, their lives are tied to the land, reach no more than a few miles from the village, and are inherently conservative. Recent studies have shown a growing awareness among peasants about events in Cairo and beyond, but those studies have also shown little inclination among peasants to respond or take part. Even Nasser realized that the traditional mistrust of the *fellahin* toward government would make it dangerous to give the impression that the government wanted to make them into state functionaries by nationalizing or collectivizing farms. Nasser's interest in improving the quality of life for the peasants, combined with the changes he made with land reform and the expansion of social services, made him a hero among the *fellahin*.[5]

As economic development and urbanization change the social structure of Egypt, the *fellahin* population is declining in relative terms, and the new urban middle and working classes are growing. As this happens, traditional culture is being undermined, forcing the government to respond by allowing more public access to the political process. Centralization and patrimonialism are becoming less acceptable, and although they are still weak, autonomous political institutions such as the legislature, political parties, and the media are winning more power.

Religious-Secular Tension

Islam is the state religion of Egypt, and all three of its modern presidents have claimed to be true believers and have felt obliged at least to go through the motions of identifying themselves with Islam. In fact, there has been a tendency toward secularism in government and public policy, even though Islamists have worked hard to encourage Egyptians to adopt traditional Islamic values. There were signs during the late 1980s that these values were slowly spreading—notably as more women wore veils or completely covered their bodies—but they now seem to be on the wane. The shift has been a result of the ongoing debate within Islam about the nature of modernity. Physical signs of that modernity are everywhere, with fast food, cell phones, satellite dishes, early signs of a Muslim feminist movement, and more Egyptians hooked up to the Internet. This does not mean that Muslims are rejecting their religion, but rather that they are increasingly adapting it to modern pressures.

 POLITICAL SYSTEM

Egypt is an emerging democracy in the sense that political power has been devolved since 1952 from a military elite to a broader, popular constituency. This is still a limited constituency, however, and the average Egyptian has little influence over politics or government. Opposition groups are controlled, political institutions are still evolving, and the pace of democratization has been carefully regulated. Anwar Sadat spoke of his support for the rule of law and his desire to create a "state of institutions,"

but he was not prepared to give these institutions autonomy. Hosni Mubarak has allowed the creation of new political parties, but government control of the electoral system has prevented them from winning more than a handful of seats. The constitution describes Egypt as a "democratic socialist state" and condemns exploitation and income differences, yet levels of personal income vary widely.

It has been argued that a common feature of politics in poorer states is the dominance of policy-implementing institutions (such as the military and bureaucracy) over policymaking institutions (such as legislatures and parties).[6] This is certainly true of Egypt, where politics revolves around personalities rather than institutions and where power is expressed through an unwieldy bureaucracy, creating a phenomenon once described as "bureaucratic feudalism."[7] The 1952 coup was not a popular revolution but instead was carried out by a small group of army officers working in what they thought was the public interest. Once in power, the Free Officers were driven less by ideology than by a belief in change, a concern to avoid the worst mistakes of capitalism and communism, and a desire to end Egypt's subordination to the West.

Arguing that discipline rather than democracy was the key to changing Egypt,[8] and worried about opposition from every quarter, the officers created a political system that remains authoritarian, centralized, bureaucratic, and elitist and that revolves around personality politics, nepotism, and patronage. The president sits at the center and rules through personal networks rather than through well-defined institutions. The president's power is underpinned by a network of elites, whose influence radiates in concentric circles. Closest to the president is the **core elite.** Under Nasser this elite consisted mainly of the military and a few influential civilians; under Mubarak it has included ministers, military commanders, senior civil servants, managers of public sector businesses, newspaper editors, religious and academic leaders, heads of syndicates and chambers of commerce, members of parliament, and party leaders.

The support of the elite has been encouraged under Mubarak with rewards and inducements such as job offers in government, the bureaucracy, joint-venture business enterprises in which the government has a stake, public organizations, or the governing National Democratic Party.[9] Dissent and opposition are contained, notably through the state security apparatus and other government ministries. Given the extent to which political participation is controlled, Islamists have become the only significant source of opposition to the government.

THE CONSTITUTION

Egypt's first constitution—published in 1923—created a limited democracy that might have laid the foundations of a lasting parliamentary democracy had it not been changed to give the monarch the right to appoint the prime minister, dismiss the cabinet, and dissolve parliament. It was suspended in 1952 and replaced in 1956 by a new document that made Egypt a republic, gave considerable power to the president, and included a commitment to economic planning and social welfare. During his 16-year tenure, Nasser drew up five more constitutions, the 1964 version of which described Egypt as a "democratic socialist" state and declared Islam to be the state religion.

The eighth (and most recent) constitution was drawn up in 1971, and—like constitutions in most authoritarian states—it includes ideas that are still not put into practice. For example, it declares that the *sharia* is the "principal" source for law and the legal system, yet Egypt remains a secular state. Opposition parties have called for a new constitution that would guarantee human rights, give the legislature more powers, and limit the president to two four-year terms, but few changes of a democratic nature have been made beyond the holding of multicandidate presidential elections for the first time in 2005.

THE EXECUTIVE: PRESIDENT

The Egyptian political system is often compared with that of France or Russia, which have a **dual executive:** a powerful president, separately elected from the legislature, and a prime minister, who is appointed and dismissed by the president. French presidents tend to act as guides and arbiters, while prime ministers roll up their sleeves and jump into the fray of day-to-day politics. The Egyptian model has more of the features of the Russian dual executive, because the balance of power lies much more with the president. Predictably, the Egyptian system is often described as having a pyramidal structure with the president sitting at the peak in the role of a modern-day pharaoh. He so dominates the system that all other institutions are peripheral, although the legislature and political parties are becoming more important.

The Egyptian president has an array of powers greater than those of any other leader covered in this book:

- He can hire and fire a large number of people, including his vice president, prime minister, the cabinet, the governor of the Central Bank, senior military leaders, managers of public businesses, newspaper editors, party leaders, judges, university presidents, and provincial governors. He can even make himself prime minister, as Mubarak did in 1981–1982.

- He suggests all major legislation, has the power of veto, determines all major policies, and effectively handpicks members of parliament. Through favors, appointments, and rewards, the president can make sure that his legislation is accepted. If he finds the People's Assembly uncooperative, he can dissolve it and call new elections, provided only that he wins the approval of a majority in a referendum.

- He can issue decrees and decisions that have the power of law, he can call and chair meetings of the Council of Ministers, and he can call public referenda to change the constitution, as did Sadat in 1980 when he gave himself an unlimited number of 6-year terms in office.

- He can use emergency powers if "national unity or safety" is threatened (notions which are open to wide interpretation) or if the "Constitutional role of state institutions" is obstructed or threatened. A **state of emergency** was declared in 1981 following the assassination of President Sadat and has since been renewed every three years.

- He is commander-in-chief, can declare war with legislative approval (which is guaranteed), has complete control over foreign and defense policy, and can conclude treaties with other countries, not all of which need legislative approval.

state of emergency
A situation in which normal government is suspended or bypassed in order to deal with an emergency.

Given all these powers, understanding the presidency is less a question of appreciating the formal rules of the office than of understanding how incumbents have defined the office. Each Egyptian president has stamped a unique character on the job, although the nature of personal authoritarian rule has remained unchanged throughout each of their administrations.[10]

The Nasser Presidency (1956–1970)

The Nasser administration was a benevolent dictatorship. He and the other Free Officers had no clear plan for Egypt, but they were convinced that the old regime would mean continued social divisions and poverty for the majority of Egyptians. They believed that a new system based on equality and justice would somehow evolve out of the ashes of the old regime. When this did not happen, and when it seemed clear that the old elite was being replaced by a new one, Nasser argued the need for a transitional phase in which changes could be generated by his leadership; he called this "guided democracy."[11]

Intolerant of criticism, Nasser—popularly known as *El-Rais*, or the Boss—surrounded himself with a core elite recruited mainly from the military. To some extent this elite worked as a communal leadership; policy was made within the elite and imposed through the military and the bureaucracy. The army was the basis of his support, but Nasser also controlled the internal security apparatus and the one proto party (the Arab Socialist Union, or ASU), and he regularly reshuffled ministers and other senior officials to prevent anyone from building an independent base of support. His power was underpinned by a **cult of personality,** reflected in the many titles by which he was known, including "Father Gamal," "Destroyer of Imperialism," and "Hero of Heroes."

Because he depended so much on his charisma and on the personal link between him and his followers, power was not institutionalized. The stability that Nasser himself provided stood in sharp contrast to the instability of other institutions; his parliaments lasted two years on average and his cabinets 13 months, and he promulgated six constitutions in 16 years.[12] Despite his criticism of the Farouk regime and its elitism, his own administration came to look much like the old elite. He became less interested in the wider needs of Egyptians and more concerned with personal power. Egypt's humiliation in the 1967 Arab-Israeli war seemed to confirm just how ineffectual and corrupt the system had become. Despite the defeat and mass demonstrations in 1968 that seemed to suggest that the people wanted a greater say in politics and government, Nasser himself survived, his popularity barely dented. Part of the problem was that most Egyptians did not know just how badly their country had been beaten in the war; had they known, they might have been less charitable toward the Boss.

The Sadat Presidency (1970–1981)

The importance of personality in the Egyptian political system was reflected in the power struggle that followed Nasser's death. He had made few plans for a succession, and there was no formal process in place by which a new president could be elected. The office of vice president had been abolished in 1968, but it was revived in 1969

cult of personality
A program through which leaders perpetuate their power by ensuring that they are always present in the consciousness of their subjects.

TABLE 9.2

Modern Leaders of Egypt

Head of state	Prime minister
1936 Farouk	(12 in the period 1944–1952)
1952 Ahmad Fouad II	1952 Mohammed Naguib
1953 Mohammed Naguib	
1954 Gamal Abdel Nasser	1954 Gamal Abdel Nasser (February–March)
	Mohammed Naguib (March–April)
	Gamal Abdel Nasser (April–)
	1962 Ali Sabri
	1965 Zakariya Mohieddin
	1966 Muhammad Sedki Sulayman
	1967 Gamal Abdel Nasser
1970 Anwar Sadat	1970 Mahmoud Fawzi Desoqi Gohari
	1972 Aziz Sedki
	1973 Anwar Sadat
	1974 Abdel-Aziz Hejazi
	1975 Mahmoud Muhammad Salem
	1978 Mustafa Khalil
	1980 Anwar Sadat
1981 Sufi Abu Talib (acting)	1981 Hosni Mubarak
1981 Hosni Mubarak	1982 Ahmad Fuad Mohieddin
	1984 Kamal Hassan Ali
	1985 Ali Mahmoud Lufti
	1986 Atef Sidqi
1987 Hosni Mubarak	
1993 Hosni Mubarak	
	1996 Kamal al-Ganzouri
1999 Hosni Mubarak	1999 Atif Ebeid
	2004 Ahmed Nazif
2005 Hosni Mubarak	

and given to Sadat, who became such a trusted lieutenant of Nasser's that he earned the nickname "Colonel Yes-Yes." Sadat succeeded Nasser, and although he inherited the strength of the presidency, little was known about him, few Egyptians even knew what he looked like, and few expected him to last long. They were to be proved quite wrong.

Born the same year as Nasser, Sadat had been a member of the Free Officers and from 1961 to 1969 was speaker of the Egyptian legislature. Regarded by many Nasserites as a usurper, the way Sadat confirmed his position and made the presidency his own says much about how Egyptian politics works. Although he was quickly confirmed as president by both the ASU and the National Assembly, his position was far from secure, and he faced opposition from his vice president, Ali Sabri, and from the Central Committee of the ASU. The army and the legislature were on his side, though, and Sadat was able to bide his time and build support. His position was finally confirmed in a series of rapid-fire events in May 1971, described by Sadat as the **Corrective Revolution:** He fired Sabri; purged senior members of the military, the police, the ASU, and the intelligence service; reorganized the cabinet; appointed key governors; arranged street demonstrations in his support; disbanded the ASU Central Committee; and set up a committee to oversee elections to the ASU.[13] By the end of May, Sadat was firmly in charge. Within months, a new constitution had been published on his instructions, and the anniversary of the Corrective Revolution later became a national holiday.

Sadat may have been more liberal than Nasser, but his methods regularly bordered on autocratic. His tenure has been described as a "presidential monarchy": He wanted political institutions to function, but if they deviated from his definition of the public interest, he saw it as his job to set them right. Whereas Nasser addressed the Egyptian people as "brothers," Sadat was more paternalistic. He saw himself as *rabb alaila al-misriya* (head of the Egyptian family), described the people as "my children," and talked about "my constitution," "my parties," and "my opposition."

Although Sadat had removed his opponents, he also believed it was important to build a popular base of support and to give his government legitimacy. Claiming to abhor the personalism and mistrust that had surrounded Nasser, he began devolving power to the legislature, the press, and a multiparty system, while at the same time making sure that the presidency monitored and controlled all these other centers of power. In May 1980 he took the job of prime minister for himself, arranged a referendum to end the constitutional limit of two terms for a president, and effectively became president for life. He also created a new upper house designed to strengthen his control of the legislature.

The Mubarak Presidency (1981–)

Mubarak became president by virtue of being vice president when Sadat died. Just 24 years old at the time of the Free Officers coup, he represented a new generation of political leaders, and has gone on to be more low-key, cautious, pragmatic, and conciliatory than his predecessors. He claims to be a religious moderate, has avoided the cult of personality, and argues that he is an exception to traditional Islamic paternalism. But this has not stopped him from holding on to power for a quarter of a century. (See People in Politics, p. 460.)

HOSNI MUBARAK

© AP/Wide World Photos

Hosni Mubarak has been president of Egypt since 1981, making him one of the longest serving heads of state in the world. Despite his longevity, and despite the importance of Egypt to U.S. interests in the Middle East, Americans know much less about him than they did about his predecessor, Anwar Sadat. While Sadat became a world statesman, both praised and pilloried for his overtures to Israel, Mubarak has kept his head below the barricades and is not known for bold initiatives.

Born in 1928 in the Nile delta village of Kafr-El Meselha, Mohamed Hosni Mubarak was one of five children of an inspector in the ministry of justice. He graduated from the national military academy in 1947 with degrees in military and aviation sciences, trained as an air force fighter pilot and instructor (spending time in the Soviet Union), was appointed director of the air force academy in 1968, was made air force chief of staff in 1969 by Nasser, and was promoted to commander of the air force by Sadat in 1972. He led the air force during the 1973 Yom Kippur War and—to the surprise of many—was made vice president in 1975, probably because he was competent and dependable without being a political threat to Sadat; Nasser had made Sadat his vice president for similar reasons.

Mubarak was sitting beside Sadat when he was assassinated in October 1981 but was only slightly wounded. Within a week he had been nominated as president, and his "election" was confirmed in a national referendum. Mubarak subsequently made the office his own but used less authoritarian methods than his predecessor. His priorities have included greater freedom for opposition parties; taking on—and ultimately defeating—Islamic militancy during the 1990s; keeping on good terms with Israel, the United States, and the Arab world; and maintaining a steady program of privatization aimed at strengthening the private sector in Egypt. He has survived at least six assassination attempts and was "reelected" to his fourth term in office in 1999. Given his advancing age, speculation mounted during 2003 that he was grooming his son Gamal—a former banker—to succeed him, appointing him as political secretary of the NDP, the third most senior position in the party. In September 2005, aged 76, he won a fifth term in office.

Then Prime Minister Atef Ebeid (right) addresses the People's Assembly in Cairo. Unlike dual executives in countries such as France, the Egyptian version is heavily weighted toward the president, and the People's Assembly has been little more than a rubber stamp and a safety valve to keep opposition parties under control.

In policy terms, Mubarak's options have been limited by Egypt's severe economic and social problems, by the need to contain the Islamic opposition, and by Egypt's position at the hub of the Arab world. Mubarak has maintained a state of emergency during his entire term, although he has won the confidence of opposition parties by including them in policy debates.[14] He has allowed an opposition press to operate and has increased the number of parties from 4 to 14. At first he showed little inclination for holding on to power indefinitely, but he stood for—and won—a third six-year term in October 1993. He said it would be his last, but then allowed himself to be "elected" unopposed to a fourth term in September 1999, and engineered a more "democratic" election to win a fifth term in September 2005.

THE LEGISLATURE: PEOPLE'S ASSEMBLY

The legislative arm of the Egyptian government consists of a prime minister, a Council of Ministers (or cabinet), and a quasi-bicameral legislature. The prime minister and other ministers are all appointed and removed by the president, do not need to be members of the legislature, and are often chosen more for their loyalty than for their abilities. To prevent anyone from developing enough power to oppose the president, cabinet posts are regularly reshuffled.

Prime ministers tend to be functionaries of the president, overseeing the government's legislative program, focusing on domestic issues, coming and going very quickly, and being almost unknown outside Egypt. They also have a thankless task, having to deal with all of Egypt's problems without upsetting the army or the president, and meanwhile having to take all the blame when those problems are not resolved.[15] The most notable holder of the office was Atef Sidqi, who also was the longest holder of the office: 1986–1996. Much like Viktor Chernomyrdin in Russia, Sidqi was loyal, dull, and dependable; posed no threat to Mubarak's position; and overall was a safe choice for the post. He pushed Egypt steadily toward a market economy before being replaced in 1996 by Kamal al-Ganzouri. In an attempt to inject some new blood into the cabinet at the beginning of his fourth term in 1999, Mubarak replaced al-Ganzouri with Atif Ebeid. American-educated (with a Ph.D. from the University of Illinois), Ebeid was centrally involved in Mubarak's privatization program, and his promotion was seen as an indication of the importance of that program to Mubarak's new term in office. He was replaced in July 2004 by Ahmed Nazif, a computer expert and former communications minister. His appointment was seen as part of a trend to appoint technocrats to leading positions in government, and as part of an indication that change was in the air; Mubarak also replaced half of his cabinet and half of the regional governors at the same time.

Egypt has had a legislature since 1923, when a bicameral parliament was created, with a Senate and a Chamber of Deputies. It could override the king with a two-thirds majority, but the king appointed the ministers and 40 percent of the senators and could dissolve parliament and rule by decree, so it was little more than a legislative façade. Under the 1956 constitution, a unicameral National Assembly was created, with 350 members. It was replaced in 1958 with the National Assembly for the United Arab Republic (with 400 members from Egypt and 200 from Syria), which did little more than rubber-stamp Nasser's policies.

Changes made by Sadat created the current arrangement.

Consultative Assembly (*Majlis al-Shura*)

Established by Sadat in 1980, the Consultative Assembly is not a full-fledged upper chamber, but it has many of the features of a legislative body. Although its powers are limited and it was once dismissed as "a retirement haven for burned-out top-level bureaucrats, ministers, and politicians,"[16] it must be consulted on constitutional amendments, treaties, draft laws referred by the president, and any policy issues referred by the president. It has 264 members, of whom 176 are elected to renewable six-year terms and the rest are appointed by the president. Half come up for reelection or reappointment every three years, and half of the elected members must be workers or farmers. In recent elections, the ruling National Democratic Party has won a monopoly in the chamber.

People's Assembly (*Majlis al-Shaab*)

Replacing the National Assembly in 1971, the People's Assembly has 444 elected members (deputies) and 10 members appointed by the president. Between 1983 and 1990, 400 deputies were elected using proportional representation; the remaining 44 seats were reserved for independents. This was declared unconstitutional by the Constitutional Court, so the electoral system was changed for the 1995 elections to one based on 222 districts, with the top two vote winners in each district being elected. As with the Consultative Assembly, half the members must be workers or farmers. The Assembly is elected for five-year terms, but it can be dissolved by the president before the five years are up if he wins public support in a referendum, which he always does. New elections must then be held within 60 days.

The People's Assembly has several constitutional powers that seem to limit those of the president: It can reject laws proposed by the government or decreed by the president, can propose laws of its own, and has close control over the national budget. It also has the power of oversight: It can monitor the performance of the government, ask ministers to appear before it to be questioned, relay problems or grievances from citizens, and hold investigations and hearings into government activities. Finally, it can debate government policy, although this means little in real terms. Parliamentary debates in Egypt were once described as follows: "The normal pattern . . . has been to tear a given policy to pieces in committee . . . , to give ample newspaper . . . coverage to the findings, and then to have the Assembly as a whole approve the policy with marginal modifications."[17]

The lack of independence of the Assembly is reflected clearly in election results; at no time has the governing National Democratic Party ever won less than 70 percent of the seats. Because the president controls the party, sets the legislative program for the Assembly, and can bypass the Assembly any time he likes, it is no more than a legislative façade designed to support the authority of the presidency.

THE JUDICIARY: SUPREME CONSTITUTIONAL COURT

Despite the weaknesses of the constitution, Egypt has a Supreme Constitutional Court that is responsible for interpreting the constitution and occasionally influences government policy. The work of the Court is undermined by at least two major problems: First, Egyptian law is confusing, because it consists of a mixture of Islamic, French, British, and Soviet-inspired influences and can easily be counteracted by presidential decrees and states of emergency. Second, judges are overworked and underpaid.

The Court has played an important role in revealing the weaknesses in the Egyptian definition of democracy. It has been particularly active on the issue of elections, beginning when it voided the 1984 and 1987 elections to the People's Assembly on the grounds that electoral law discriminated against independent candidates. This led to changes in the electoral law and the holding of new elections in December 1990, nearly 18 months early. But the Court declared that the governing National Democratic Party had interfered in the outcome of the 1990 and 1995 elections as well, casting doubts on the legitimacy of the entire legislative process. These decisions emphasize the role of the Court as the only significant opposition to the powers of the government. Critics of those powers argue that there is so much confusion in the existing system that nothing less than a new constitution will solve Egypt's legal problems.

THE MILITARY

Since the 1952 Free Officers coup, the military has played an important role in Egyptian government and society, not least because all three of its presidents have been former military officers (the army for Nasser and Sadat, the air force for Mubarak). Nasser claimed that he saw the military as a vanguard in the vein of Lenin's Bolsheviks: a group that would take power on behalf of the people and then hand over that power when the people wanted it.[18] In fact, power in Egypt from 1952 until 1967 lay in a mutually supportive relationship between the government and the military, which was without doubt the strongest institution in the political system.

Sadat continued to promote the power of the military over that of civilian institutions, using the success of the armed forces in the 1973 crossing of the Suez Canal to restore the prestige of the military (but keeping the full truth of their performance from the Egyptian people). He also gave officers promotions, secondments to the government, and salary increases. Part of the reason Hosni Mubarak was chosen as vice president was so Sadat could be sure that the air force was controlled by the government.[19]

A major challenge for Mubarak when he came to office was to give the military a sense of purpose in the aftermath of the 1979 peace treaty. The military had been almost halved in size during the late 1970s (from 900,000 personnel to 500,000), and its mission was changed from preparing for war with Israel to becoming a rapid strike force with the ability to intervene in other regional trouble spots. Mubarak ended the reductions and appointed as chief of staff—and eventually minister of defense and deputy prime minister—a former classmate named Abd al-Halim Abu Ghazala. In recent years, the military has expanded its interests into the civil sphere, even going so far as to build highways, clean polluted beaches, and run new farms. The military is still a key institution in the political system, compelling the government to maintain a balance between the civilian and military sectors of society.

SUBNATIONAL GOVERNMENT

Given that Egypt is a unitary state, that almost all Egyptians live in the vicinity of a single river, and that its rulers have long favored centralized control, local government is a relatively minor element in the political system. This is not to say that the local community—particularly the peasant community—has no importance; it just has little independence. In the rural areas, the village is the basic social unit, and villagers have traditionally owed their allegiance to the village headman, or *umdeh*. Clientelism is still so strong in these communities that an *umdeh* might be able to deliver the entire vote of his village to the governing party, in return for policies that support his position and his privileges.

The highest level of local government in Egypt is the governorate (or *muhafazah*), of which there are 26, each with its own governor appointed by the president.

Below these are 133 districts and hundreds of villages, each with an appointed executive officer and executive council. The higher-level executives are hired and fired at the discretion of the president of Egypt.

ELECTIONS AND PARTIES

The average Egyptian has little influence on politics. There are several legal political parties, but none have enough power to overrule the government-sanctioned National Democratic Party. There are elections, but turnout is low and the results prove little beyond the regime's control of the electoral system.[20] Egypt has a poor record on human rights, and Egyptian leaders have little public accountability, mainly ignoring the principle of *shura* (consultation). At the same time, some recent trends point toward democratization, and public opinion is taken more seriously than before. The Mubarak era in particular has seen the rise of opposition political parties and an opposition press, and more leniency has recently been shown toward the Islamist opposition.

THE ELECTORAL SYSTEM

Egyptian elections are neither free nor fair. Official turnout figures are inflated, the results lead to few changes in policy or the makeup of government, and the choices facing Egyptian voters have been controlled by the government. The 1956 constitution created the National Assembly, but all candidates had to be screened by the only legal party, the National Union, and official electoral turnout figures were high only because voting was compulsory or the figures were exaggerated. No competing parties ran in the election, and the Assembly was little more than a rubber stamp for the policies of the Nasser government.

The choice for Egyptian voters broadened during the Sadat administration, when three officially sanctioned parties were created. But they were so patently manipulated by the government that the 1976 elections could hardly be described as competitive. Hosni Mubarak has allowed more parties to be licensed during his administration, and although the governing party wins a near monopoly of seats in the legislature, elections are at least contested by groups that look like political parties. However, the election process is controlled by state agencies, and banks and agricultural loan agencies are used in rural areas to give incentives to voters to turn out. State control goes so far as regulating the flow of information, intimidating voters and candidates, and "correcting" results. Candidates are selected less on the basis of what they know than whom they know, with members of the elite often stepping in to make sure that friends or relatives are nominated.

The Presidential Election

Elections for the presidency are held once every six years, but they are not elections in the democratic sense of the word. Until 2005, there was no direct election;

instead, the People's Assembly nominated a single candidate for the presidency, who was then confirmed in a national referendum. At least one-third of the members of the People's Assembly had to make the nomination, which had to be confirmed by at least two-thirds of the members. The public referendum that followed—in which voters were given a simple yes/no option—was not so much an election as confirmation of the choice of the Assembly, and since the Assembly has long been dominated by the National Democratic Party, the party's nominee has always won. In the 1999 "election," President Mubarak allegedly had the support of 98 percent of the members of the legislature and was allegedly confirmed by nearly 94 percent of the nearly 80 percent of registered voters who took part in the referendum.

This all changed in 2005, when the constitution was changed to allow multiple candidates to stand for election for the first time in Egypt's history. While some hailed this as a positive step forward, skeptics charged that the election would provide no more than the appearance of democracy, and their worst fears were confirmed when it was revealed that the NDP would have the right to vet all the candidates, and in essence to manipulate the election to make sure that their candidate won. In the event, ten candidates were approved for the 2005 election, another 20 were not approved, and—as anticipated—Hosni Mubarak won a fifth term in office. Against a background of low voter turnout (less than one in four Egyptian voters took part), he claimed to have won nearly 87 percent of the vote, drawing immediate charges from defeated opponents of fraud, and demands for a rerun.

Legislative Elections and Referendums

Every four years, all but ten of the 444 members of the People's Assembly run for reelection. The country is divided into 222 districts, and candidates from all legal political parties run off against each other, the top two candidates from each district winning. According to the Constitution, at least half the deputies must be "workers and farmers" and the balance are "professionals." Official figures suggest that turnout at the elections is 80 percent or more, but the figures are inflated by the government. In 1990, with most of the opposition parties boycotting the election in protest at government controls over the process, only 15 percent of eligible voters turned out and only one opposition party won enough votes to be represented in the People's Assembly. At the 1995 elections, turnout was back up to 48 percent but only 13 opposition deputies were elected, and in more than half the districts, opposition candidates challenged the results in court. Turnout in 2000 was back down to about a quarter.

Following a speech in 1999 by President Mubarak in which he indicated that he wanted more democracy and opposition participation in politics, rumors began to circulate that he might change the electoral system to allow more opposition deputies to be elected in the 2000 People's Assembly elections. It was thought that this might be a reward for the support given him by several parties in the 1999 presidential referendum, but cynics suggested that the proposal was aimed simply at improving Egypt's international image and that the number of opposition deputies would still be restricted. In fact, the NDP did remarkably badly, and although its share of seats went up by 11 percent, this was only because the party was able to encourage 218 "independent" candidates to declare themselves as NDP members.

FIGURE 9.1

Legislative Electoral Trends in Egypt

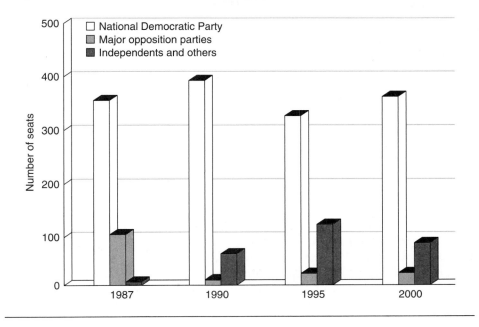

Meanwhile, the number of opposition deputies grew by just one, to a paltry total of 14. The 2005 elections took place in three stages during November and December, and were contested by 13 political parties.

In addition to elections, Egyptians also take part in referenda or plebiscites, whose results are also engineered. The president has the power to call a public referendum on issues of national importance, such as changes to the constitution, and his own position in office has also been confirmed in recent years by a referendum. If the figures are to be believed, turnout at referenda is always 85 percent or more, and presidents always win at least 90 to 95 percent of votes. No surprise, then, that the referendum has been described as "a government tool of extreme cynicism."[21] A recent example of a referendum was the May 2005 vote on the proposal to allow constitutional changes clearing the way for multicandidate presidential elections. The government claimed a turnout of 53 percent of registered voters, of whom about 83 percent agreed with the proposal. There were unofficial reports, however, of very low turnout in Cairo, possibly contributed to by a call from critics of the government to boycott the referendum.

POLITICAL PARTIES

Egypt has a long history of party politics, but parties have always been carefully manipulated by the governing regime to suit its goals. A multiparty system was in place between 1923 and 1953, but real power was centralized in the monarchy, and the

Wafd Party (formed in 1918 to campaign for independence) was the only organization with the support, resources, and local branches to be able to function like a party. The legislature also contained independent members, a Communist Party founded in 1922, and a Wafdist breakaway party (the Saadists). The only other significant political groups were the **Muslim Brotherhood** and the right-wing Young Egypt (*Misr al-Fatat*, founded in 1933), neither of which operated as formal political parties.

Following the 1952 coup, political parties were abolished and replaced by mass membership movements. Designed to rally support for Nasser's government, these movements encouraged people to back his policies rather than debate them; meanwhile, all other political activity was banned. The first of the movements was the Liberation Rally, which was created in 1953 and then replaced in 1957 with the National Union. Much like a Soviet-style vanguard party, the National Union was used by Nasser as a means of generating public approval, stifling opposition, excluding other groups from politics, and building a "national consciousness."[22]

In 1962, following the collapse of the United Arab Republic, Nasser proclaimed that Egypt would be a revolutionary model for the rest of the Arab world and created the Arab Socialist Union (ASU). Modeled on the Communist Party of the Soviet Union (CPSU), its higher levels were locked into the government structure in much the same way as the CPSU related to the Soviet government, and it had a National Congress (equivalent to the People's Congress of the CPSU), a Central Committee, and a 10-member Supreme Executive Committee that looked much like a politburo. At the apex of both party and government was Nasser himself, who so dominated the "party" that it never really took root in Egyptian society. There were signs in later years that Nasser was prepared to tolerate more criticism and dissent so long as it took place within the one-party system. Dying before he was able to develop his ideas, he left Sadat to deal with an immature political system.

Once Sadat had consolidated his power, he allowed opposing political views to be more freely expressed, seeing this as a way of making his administration different from Nasser's, satisfying public demand for greater participation, winning support from the liberal elements of the Egyptian bourgeoisie that formed the basis of much of his power, pleasing the United States, and encouraging his economic liberalization program.[23]

Although he was opposed to a multiparty system, Sadat announced in July 1975 that he would allow more debate and a greater diversity of viewpoints within the ASU and he encouraged the establishment within the party of what he called "pulpits" or "platforms." By the end of 1975, more than 40 platforms had been declared, but Sadat approved only three, and these now became "organizations," supposedly representing the right, center, and left of the ASU. The centrist Arab Socialist Organization (ASO) took over the structure and policies of the ASU, while the right was represented by the Socialist Liberal Organization and the left by the National Progressive Union Organization. All three organizations were allowed to compete in the 1976 elections, which resulted in a landslide for the ASO.

The three organizations were now allowed by Sadat to become full-fledged parties; the word *Organization* in their titles was replaced with Party. However, he made sure that the center dominated; the right-wing and left-wing parties (and independent deputies) were allowed to act only as safety valves for government opponents.

When Sadat announced in July 1978 that he was organizing his own party, the National Democratic Party, it immediately absorbed the Arab Socialist party, which it mirrored in everything but name.

Hosni Mubarak continued to encourage the development of this multiparty system, allowing ten more parties to be licensed. Although Egypt now looks like a true multiparty system, no opposition party has been able to develop a firm social base, so they all remain to some extent artificial. Mubarak has continued to defend the constitutional ban on parties based on religion, class, or region, and he has banned parties opposed to the peace treaty with Israel. His government has also undermined the strength and credibility of opposition parties by exploiting their internal divisions.[24] The opposition is further handicapped by restrictions placed on its activities, by its lack of access to state-run radio and television, and by its lack of new ideas.

There are now several legal parties in Egypt, including the following:.

The National Democratic Party (NDP)

Successor to Nasser's Arab Socialist Union and Sadat's Arab Socialist Party, the National Democratic Party has been more streamlined in ideological terms than the catch-all ASU, but its position is difficult to pin down. It calls itself pro-Arab, pro-Palestinian, and nonaligned, and yet it is also pro-Western. The NDP supports some of the socialist elements of the Nasser revolution, yet it has also stood for Mubarak's policy of strengthening the private sector. It claims to be concerned less with ASU-type propaganda and indoctrination and more with recruiting leaders and mobilizing the people, yet it is still dominated by the core elite, contributes little to government policy, and has little sense of purpose or ideological identity. Despite these contradictions, the NDP has dominated the People's Assembly, winning 80 percent of the seats in the 2000 election.(To be accurate, though, many of its Assembly members are independents who have allied themselves with the NDP.)

Socialist Labor Party

Although not very different ideologically from the NDP, this oddly named party is in fact conservative and was once something like an authentic opposition. It criticized the warming of Egyptian relations with Israel and became so critical of Sadat's style of leadership that its leaders were arrested in a 1981 purge. It became part of the coalition opposition in 1987, but it boycotted the 1990 elections and lost its 16 seats in the People's Assembly, winning none of them back in 1995 or 2000.

Socialist Liberal Party

Despite their name, the Socialist Liberals were the successors to the right-wing platform of the ASU. Once again, they were ideologically little different from the NDP, and Sadat even arranged for some of his supporters to join the party to limit its powers of opposition. It has since become more centrist, emphasizing the importance of free enterprise and arguing in favor of privatization and political liberalization. It joined the opposition coalition in 1987, boycotted the 1990 elections and lost its six seats, and won only one of its seats back in 1995 and 2000.

New Wafd Party

The New Wafd is a liberal party that was founded in 1978, quickly banned, then revived in 1983. It favors political and economic liberalization and is strongly nationalist and secularist, although it confused its followers by joining in a brief alliance with the Muslim Brotherhood in 1984. The New Wafd won nearly 11 percent of the vote and 35 seats in 1987, and it was one of the few parties not to denounce the Iraqi invasion of Kuwait in 1990. It boycotted the 1990 elections, but 14 of its members ignored the boycott and won seats as independents. It won seven seats in the 1995 elections and retained them in 2000.

The Muslim Brotherhood

Although the constitution makes it illegal to form parties based on religion, this has not stopped the Muslim Brotherhood—the nearest thing in Egypt to a bona fide Islamist political party—from being a major force on the margins of Egyptian politics. The Brotherhood bypassed the law by first making an electoral pact with the New Wafd Party and then running in the 1987 elections in an alliance with the Socialist Labor and Socialist Liberal parties. The alliance campaigned under the slogan "Islam is the Solution" and called for the abrogation of the 1979 treaty with Israel and full application of the *sharia*. It won 17 percent of the vote and 60 seats and—as the Socialist Labor Coalition—briefly constituted the opposition to the NDP.

The Brotherhood was founded in 1928 by a schoolteacher named Hasan al-Banna (1906–1949). Members argued that because Islamic principles were not being followed in the government of Muslim countries, Islam had been vulnerable to outside influences from the days of the Crusades right up to the twentieth century. They argued that there was too much Western orientation in the thinking of Islamic leaders, that neither capitalism nor communism provided the answer, and that only a return to Islamic principles promised any future for the Muslim world. They called for an Islamic revolution, the use of the Quran as a constitution, and the creation of a new political order based on the *sharia*, although they did not spell out the details of how the new Islamic government would work.

Accused of complicity in the 1948 assassination of the Egyptian prime minister, the Brotherhood was banned, and al-Banna was murdered by Egyptian secret police in 1949. The Brotherhood was further marginalized in 1952 by the success of the Free Officers coup and the popularity of Nasser's brand of Arab socialism. When a member of the Brotherhood fired six gunshots at Nasser while he was addressing a crowd in Alexandria in October 1954, Nasser arrested several thousand of its members. The Brotherhood was further weakened by internal divisions and a lack of leadership, and it was finally driven underground in 1965 following charges that it was implicated in an attempted coup.

Sadat apparently encouraged the revival of an Islamic opposition, but only as a means of providing an ally against his left-wing opponents. The Brotherhood initially supported Sadat, was allowed to openly hold prayer meetings in Cairo, and was allowed to revive its journal *Al-Dawa* in 1976. Following Camp David, however, the Brotherhood began to criticize Sadat's overtures to the West, his rapprochement with Israel, and the isolation from the Arab world that followed. It warned of the

CLOSE-UP VIEW

ISLAMIC RADICALS IN EGYPT

The Muslim Brotherhood and pro-government clergy are the mainstream representatives of Islamist ideas in Egypt, but the opposition also includes two more militant strands: underground groups known as *jamaat* and local associations known as *jamiyat*.[26] The *jamaat* have won the most publicity in recent years and between 1992 and 1999 were at the heart of a campaign of violence aimed at overthrowing the Mubarak administration; as many as 1,300 people died and 30,000 were imprisoned. Their members argue that the Brotherhood has sold out to the secular system, that state and society have become un-Islamic, and that Muslims must rise in a *jihad* (holy war) that would lead to a new Islamic state.

Radicals were behind the assassination in 1981 of Anwar Sadat, an event that was supposed to have preceded the foundation of an Islamic caliphate; preparations included the infiltration of the armed forces by members of radical groups. Hundreds were arrested following the assassination, and the five chief alleged conspirators were executed in April 1982. In 1986 radicals were implicated in a plot to overthrow the Mubarak government; among the 30 conspirators arrested were several army officers, a fact that raised concerns about the extent to which radicals had infiltrated the military. The radicals went on to claim responsibility for attempts on the lives of Prime Minister Atef Sidqi in 1993 and of President Mubarak in June 1995.

The mid-1990s saw them attacking tourists in an attempt to undermine one of Egypt's major sources of income. During 1992–1993, attacks on tourists left 290 people dead and 670 wounded, contributing to a falloff in tourist arrivals from 3.2 million in 1992 to 2.6 million in 1993.[27] One of the most active of the organizations targeting tourists was *Jamaat Islamiya* (Islamic Group), founded in the late 1970s as the student wing of the Muslim Brotherhood. They were behind an attack in November 1997 at Luxor, during which 58 tourists and four Egyptians were machine-gunned and stabbed to death. The attack was widely condemned by Islamist groups outside Egypt, lost *Jamaat Islamiya* much of its following, and led to a split within its ranks about the policy of tourist attacks. One of its more notorious leaders was the Egyptian physician Ayman al-Zawahiri, who in the 1980s developed links with Al-Qaeda leader Osama bin Laden. Al-Zawahiri has since gone on to be described as bin Laden's second-in-command, although—given the nonhierarchical structure of Al-Qaeda, this is not entirely accurate; he is better described as the operational and ideological leader of the organization. In 1999 he was sentenced to death in absentia by Egypt for his alleged role in the Luxor killings, in 2001 Interpol issued an arrest warrant for him in connection with the terrorist attacks of September 2001, and the U.S. Department of State has placed a reward of $25 million on his head.

dangers of more Western involvement in Egyptian affairs in the wake of economic liberalization, and it continued to argue that only the introduction of Islamic principles based on the sharia could end corruption and contamination from the West. Brotherhood members became particularly active on university campuses, encouraging women to wear more modest dress, recruiting new members, encouraging the segregation of sexes in lectures, and exploiting the frustration among recent graduates unable to find jobs or afford adequate housing. By 1986 the Brotherhood was claiming a membership of one million, although other estimates were in the region of 250,000 to 400,000.[25]

Today the Muslim Brotherhood is a political party in all but name. It has a strong institutional base, rejects violence, and even refuses to take part in demonstrations. Despite this, it remains frustrated by the unwillingness of the government to give it formal recognition as a political party. How long it takes for this frustration to be transformed into militancy remains to be seen. Mubarak initially tolerated limited political activities by the Brotherhood, but he began to crack down on it in the mid-1990s as part of his government's program to contain militant Islam, and hundreds of its members were imprisoned or tried.[28]

POLICIES AND POLICYMAKING

The policymaking process in Egypt is relatively simple. Policy is made almost entirely by the president and the core elite, influenced by groups with access to that elite, and implemented by a large and mainly inefficient bureaucracy. Institutions outside the center—such as the legislature, opposition political parties, and the opposition media—tend to be controlled by the core elite, have little independent freedom of action, and have only a marginal effect on policymaking. Despite the emphasis on the Islamic theory concerning consultation, the input of "the people" is strictly limited, and citizens have tended to follow rather than lead in the design of public policy. Nevertheless, policies do change from one administration to another.

- Under Nasser, the public sector had priority, the government was heavily involved in economic planning and management, and Egypt followed a supposedly nonaligned foreign policy. Nasser tried to impose his brand of Arab socialism on Egypt and to marginalize the Islamic opposition.

- Under Sadat, state control over the economy was reduced, foreign investment was encouraged, and—toward the end—Egypt followed a more conciliatory policy toward Israel and a more pro-Western foreign policy.

- Under Mubarak, Egypt has seen slow democratization and economic liberalization, and the centrality of the president and the elite in the political structure has been reduced. The trend in policymaking continues to be toward greater input by other institutions, and Egypt plays an important role in bringing together different parties in Middle Eastern political disputes.

All three presidents had at least one common problem: a bureaucracy that is big, overworked, and riddled with corruption, inertia, and inefficiency. The bureaucratization of modern Egypt began with Nasser's policies of nationalization and centralization. In 1952 there were only 250,000 bureaucrats in Egypt. Thanks to a guarantee made by Nasser of a job in government for every university graduate, the numbers rose so rapidly that by 1985 public employees made up one-third of the labor force. Sadat missed several opportunities to reform the system, being too preoccupied with foreign policy to provide the leadership needed for economic reform and too naively optimistic that simply returning Egypt to market policies would bring prosperity. Without the necessary drive and cohesion that strong leadership would have brought, decision making was fragmented among many agencies and committees.[29] The guaranteed-job policy has been quietly ignored of late, but there are still about six million public employees in Egypt, making up about 25 percent of the labor force. (In the United States, bureaucrats at all levels make up about 15 percent of the labor force.) Most bureaucracies are inherently conservative, but the Egyptian bureaucracy has been particularly cumbersome and resistant to change.

In short, the good of Egypt as a whole has been sacrificed to interagency rivalries and empire building, and these problems have been compounded by the effects of bribery, corruption, and the demands of special interests. The cumbersome bureaucracy is both a cause and an effect of the tendency for policymaking and implementation to bypass established channels, and is a large part of the reason why Egypt was ranked 74 out of 145 on Transparency International's Corruption Perceptions Index for 2004. The process of government tends to bypass the bureaucracy, relying instead on decrees and personal contacts.

ECONOMIC POLICY

In economic terms, Egypt is both poor and vulnerable. Many Egyptians live in crushing poverty, especially those who have moved to Cairo in search of work. According to unofficial estimates, about 18 to 20 percent of the labor force is unemployed (the government claims the rate is only 9 percent), another 30 to 35 percent is underemployed, and many of those with work are paid minimal wages: 75 to 80 percent of Egyptians have family incomes of less than $50 per month, forcing many to take second jobs, often as laborers or taxi drivers. The contribution of agriculture to GNP has fallen, but it still accounts for 16 percent, while industry accounts for 34 percent, and half comes from services. As with many poorer countries (and even some richer ones), there are big gaps in income between the rich and the poor, promoting resentment among the poor, which has been exploited by the Islamist opposition.

Throughout its modern history, Egypt has depended almost entirely on a single export at a time. Cotton was king until the worldwide collapse of the cotton market in 1951–1952. Since then oil has taken over and now accounts for about 25 percent of exports, with cotton, textiles, and agricultural goods making up much of the rest. Like Nigeria, the dominance of oil makes Egypt vulnerable because its economy is affected by changes in the price of oil on the international market. To make matters worse, Egypt is a relatively small oil exporter compared with some of its Arab neighbors, oil production has been developed only relatively recently, and the level of production will fall as Egypt's limited reserves are used up.

Apart from oil, Egypt has little in the way of natural resources. Less than 5 percent of its land is cultivable, the rest being desert and semi-desert. It has a few small mineral resources and some natural gas, and it meets about 15 percent of its energy needs with hydroelectricity from the Aswan Dam. Beyond oil, Egypt has only four significant sources of income: revenues from tourism (about $4.3 billion in 2000–2001), $2.4 billion in annual foreign aid (about 80 percent of it from the

© Mark Henley/Panos Pictures

A group of Japanese tourists visiting the Sphinx and the pyramids at Giza, near Cairo. Tourism is one the major sources of income for Egypt, a point that Islamic extremists exploited in the 1990s when they launched a series of attacks on tourists—a policy that backfired when the death toll became too great.

United States), revenues from the Suez Canal (about $2 billion annually), and remittances from the more than four million Egyptians who work in nearby oil-exporting countries (such as Libya and the Gulf states, where they can often earn ten times as much as they would at home).[30] These are all modest sources of income, so Egypt needs to diversify its economic base and look for new sources of domestic income. The problem is made all the more urgent by the population growth rate of 1.8 percent (down from 2.2 percent in 2001), which adds one million more people to the total every ten months. There is also a steady movement of people from rural areas to the cities, exerting growing pressure on urban infrastructure.

The dominance of the Egyptian political system by the president means that the evolution of the country's public policies has been driven by the personal tastes and objectives of Nasser, Sadat, and Mubarak. In many ways, Egyptian economic policy today is still influenced by Nasser's early priorities of heavy centralization and ridding Egypt of foreign domination and dependence upon the West. That influence can be summarized as follows.

- **Economic centralization and bureaucratization.** Nasser created a large public sector and introduced Soviet-style economic plans, which led to an increase in the size and power of the bureaucracy, a problem that spilled over into the inefficiency of state-run industries, which made overpriced goods of inferior quality. Unable to export these anywhere outside the Soviet bloc, Egypt was unable to earn much hard currency.

- **Nationalization of the Suez Canal.** Following nationalization in 1956, the canal almost immediately became a major source of revenue for Egypt, a source that was temporarily cut off when the canal was closed following the 1967 Arab-Israeli war. Revenues increased sharply following the reopening of the canal in 1975, but they are unlikely to grow much beyond today's levels. If the government were to try to increase its profits by raising tariffs, it would discourage shippers from using the canal.

- **The building of the Aswan Dam.** The help given by the USSR in building the dam reinforced the tendencies toward centralized economic planning. The dam quickly paid for itself, created an inland fishery, and became a valuable source of electricity and water for irrigation, but the demands of energy generation and irrigation often conflict; depending on the season, the flow of water needed for irrigation is either too low or too high for electricity generation. The dam has also cut the flow of silt to land downstream, increasing Egypt's need for artificial fertilizers, causing a dangerous accumulation of salt in neighboring soils, and leading to a deterioration of the Nile delta and its fishing industry.

To complicate Egypt's economic development plans, conflicts with Israel were expensive, not only in the direct costs of maintaining a large military and going to war but also in the revenues lost while the Suez Canal was closed to shipping, oil fields in the Sinai were under Israeli occupation, and tourists stayed away. The 1979 peace treaty with Israel at least reduced the costs of defense and gave Egypt a "peace dividend."

Whereas Nasser believed in centralized government control over the economy, Sadat took a more liberal approach. Soon after becoming president, he expelled Soviet military advisors, and with them went significant Soviet influence over Egyptian economic policy. Having won a psychological victory in foreign policy with the crossing of the Suez Canal, Sadat turned his attention to the domestic front, where he had plans for an economic "crossing." The result was the ***Infitah*** (*al-infitah al-iqtisadi*, or economic opening), an attempt to open the Egyptian market and combine its basic strengths with the benefits of foreign investment and technology. Sadat allowed a dramatic increase in foreign investment in Egypt, relaxed currency and import restrictions, and encouraged growth in the private sector. His hope was that Western technology could be combined with Arab capital and Egypt's natural resources and abundant labor to promote economic development.

In many ways, the *Infitah* had exactly the opposite effect. First, foreign investment did not reach the levels hoped for by Sadat. Second, while that investment should have promoted industrial development, industrial activity as a percentage of total economic activity actually declined. Capital was instead invested in the financial sector, tourism, and construction, all of which benefited tourists and the middle class. Third, the most profitable imports were luxury and consumer goods, which could be afforded by only a few and raised questions about how long Egypt could support a consumer market without increasing its domestic levels of consumption.[31] The output of goods and services in Egypt could not meet the growing demand, so Egypt had to borrow to pay for imports, leading to the rapid growth of its national debt.

As Egyptian workers began to realize that there would be few benefits in the *Infitah* for them, labor unrest grew, and the Sadat administration had to act to forestall Egypt's growing debt problems. In 1976 the United States and the International Monetary Fund (IMF) convinced Sadat to end the subsidies on basic commodities such as flour, rice, sugar, beans, and bread, which made them cheap to Egyptians but drained the national treasury. Sadat lifted the subsidies in January 1977, the price of bread doubled, and for two days in mid-January, Egypt was torn by riots that brought the country to a halt. Officially, 80 people were killed during the riots and 800 injured, although the true figures were probably much higher. Sadat immediately reintroduced the subsidies, but his political reputation had been irreparably damaged.

Hosni Mubarak has continued to liberalize the economy, directing more investment toward industry and agriculture and trying to broaden Egypt's economic base. He has been driven in part by economic reforms forced on Egypt by the terms of debt-relief programs agreed with the IMF and the World Bank. The IMF has encouraged Egypt to move to a market-oriented economy and to sell off some of its inefficient state-owned industries. By mid-1999, about 40 percent had been privatized, and the government was making plans to sell off seven regional electricity companies and the telecommunications company Telecom-Egypt. The public sector now accounts for 70 percent of GDP.

Much of Egypt's industry is linked to agriculture, through food processing and textile manufacture, for example. More investment is now being geared toward energy generation and the development of heavier industries, such as vehicle manufacture. Agricultural growth is limited by the shortage of arable land, a problem that is worsening in the face of urban sprawl. The only options available are investments in mechanized farming techniques and new technology or land-reclamation schemes, either of which will be expensive. The biggest and most controversial example of land reclamation was launched in 1997; nearly 20 years after it was first proposed by Anwar Sadat, construction began on the 190-mile Peace Canal, aimed at using wastewater to irrigate 500,000 acres of desert in the Sinai at an estimated cost of nearly $1 billion. An even more ambitious project in southern Egypt—the New Delta scheme—proposes taking water from the Aswan Dam and transporting it along a canal linked by a series of oases into the center of Egypt, creating a "parallel Nile."

Prospects for the Egyptian economy began to improve in the 1990s. Inflation was down from a high of 20 percent to just 2 percent in 1999, the economy grew at a healthy 5 to 6 percent annually during the second half of the decade, foreign investment was pouring in to the country, and the quality of public services and infrastructure was improving. The campaign against militant Islamism meant that more effort was being expended on the tourist industry, more money was being spent in the poor urban areas that were long hotbeds of discontent, and there was an expansion of electricity and water supply to villages.

Then came the events of September 11, 2001. The global economic downturn that followed had a particularly damaging effect on Egypt, as reliant as it is on foreign sources of income. Oil revenues fell, and so did tourist arrivals as jittery foreigners cancelled their vacations. The impact of 50 years of central planning continues to be felt, limiting the attractions of government-owned industries to private investors. Unemployment is growing, inflation was up to nearly 6 percent in 2005 and industrial production was growing at only 3 percent, capital is leaving the country, exchange rates are falling, property values were halved in 1999–2002, and although government figures show a growth in GDP, independent economists have cast strong doubt on those figures.[32] A combination of long-term structural problems and short-term international problems raise many questions about Egypt's economic future.

FOREIGN POLICY

Egypt is the closest ally of the United States in the Arab world and has always been an influential force in the Middle East, not least because of its size and location. This was made clear once again in 2002–2003 as the United States increased the pressure on the Iraqi regime of Saddam Hussein and Hosni Mubarak found himself once again playing an important role in the debate over whether and when the United States should attack Iraq or whether a peaceful resolution to the problem could be brokered.

Egyptians see themselves as the natural leaders of the Arab world, but that role has been expressed in different ways. During the Nasser era, Egypt was officially nonaligned, hostile to Israel, and lukewarm toward the United States. Since then, it has reached an accommodation with Israel and become closer to the United States—helped, of course, by the large amounts of aid given to Egypt by the United States. The Middle East has been one of the most volatile regions in the world for more than two generations now, and so to understand Egyptian foreign policy today we have to review events going back several decades.

Foreign Policy Under Nasser

Nasser's priorities in foreign policy were twofold. First, he worked to end Anglo-French control over the Suez Canal and to establish an independent position for Egypt in the global system. To this end, he attended the founding meeting of the Non-Aligned Movement in Bandung, Indonesia, in 1955; sought Soviet military and economic assistance; and ultimately sparked the 1956 Suez crisis. By 1970, there were an estimated 15,000 to 20,000 Soviet military advisors in Egypt, leading some to argue that Egypt had simply replaced dependence on the West with dependence on the Soviet bloc.

Second, Nasser worked to establish Egypt as the leader of the Arab world, building on the praise he won at Suez in 1956. He set up the abortive union with Syria in 1958, sent Egyptian troops to Yemen to back up a republican military regime that took power in 1962, and pursued an aggressively anti-Israeli policy. Egypt's defeat in the 1967 Six-Day War led Nasser to tone down his revolutionary rhetoric in foreign policy. Not only did the war leave the Sinai Peninsula and half of Egypt's oil resources under Israeli occupation, but revenues from the Suez Canal came to a halt and nearly 25 percent of national income was being spent on the military.[33]

CAN THE ARABS AND ISRAELIS LIVE TOGETHER?

The dominating foreign policy concern of Egypt for the last two generations—and one of the most troubling issues in Middle Eastern politics generally—has been the relationship between Israel and its Arab neighbors. The creation of the Jewish state of Israel in 1948 had an effect much like throwing a large rock into a pond: There was a large splash, waves were sent out in all directions, and the ripples continue to move back and forth even today.

Calls for an independent Jewish homeland in **Palestine** date back to the nineteenth century, and Jews began to immigrate to the region in 1870. In 1920 Palestine was placed under the administration of the British, who quickly found themselves caught between Jews wanting to settle there and indigenous Arabs opposed to the idea. A plan to partition the region was accepted by the Jews and the new United Nations but not by the Arabs, and when the British mandate ended in May 1948, Jewish leaders immediately proclaimed an independent state of Israel in Palestine.

While Israel was widely recognized in the non-Arab world, there were four wars between Arabs and Israelis (in 1948, 1956, 1967, and 1973). Meanwhile, Jews immigrated in growing numbers to the new state, and many of its Arab residents fled into exile. President Nasser led the opposition to Israel, and the 1967 Six-Day War was designed to deal the fatal blow. Rather than destroying Israel, however, the war left Egypt's military in disarray and left Israel in occupation of Egypt's Sinai Peninsula (it had taken over the Gaza strip during the 1956 Suez crisis) as well as Jerusalem, the Golan Heights in southern Syria, and the West Bank area of Jordan.

Israel had withdrawn completely from the Sinai by 1982, but the Israeli-Palestinian conflict continued to destabilize the region, as did the decision by Israel to move settlers into the territories it had illegally occupied since the Six-Day War. Meanwhile, the Palestinians continued to lobby for their own homeland in the West Bank and Gaza, the pressure increasing in 1987–1991 with the *intifada*, an uprising among Palestinians. In September 1993, an agreement was reached in Oslo, Norway, under which the Palestinians recognized the right of Israel to exist, and Israel recognized partial Palestinian self-rule. Following the failure of an attempt by the Clinton administration to broker a treaty that would have created a Palestinian state, violence between the two sides escalated. Palestinian suicide-bombers launched attacks on Israel, which responded with aggressive military action. The unwillingness of successive U.S. administrations to criticize Israeli policy on the occupied territories has fed into the anti-Americanism of Islamic radicals (and even of Arab moderates). The death of Palestinian leader Yasser Arafat in November 2004 raised the prospects of peace once again (if only because the Bush administration had refused to talk to him), as did the promised pull-out of Israeli settlers from the Gaza Strip in 2005. But hopes for peace have been raised in the Middle East many times, only to be dashed.

Foreign Policy Since Nasser

Sadat's foreign policies stood in stark contrast to those of Nasser, in several respects. Within a year of coming to power, Sadat had expelled all Soviet advisors and other personnel and had begun working toward a closer alliance with other richer Arab states. In 1973 he launched the attack on the Israeli occupation of the Sinai, which resulted in the much-vaunted crossing of the Suez. Sadat subsequently felt that Egypt had regained enough of its self-esteem for his government to embark on a policy of accommodation with Israel. His historic visit to Jerusalem in November 1977—the first by an Egyptian leader—heralded the Camp David meetings between Israel and Egypt in September 1978 and the signing of the Egypt-Israel Peace Treaty in March 1979. Sadat's supporters say his actions were an example of statesmanship; others argue that Egypt's economic problems left him with no choice but to make a deal with Israel and the West. The bread riots of 1977 emphasized the importance of redirecting military spending into investment in economic growth at home.

Hosni Mubarak has followed a more overtly pro-U.S. policy than Sadat, irritating the Islamist opposition. Mubarak has had to maintain a fine balance between peace with Israel and ensuring that he is not seen by the Arab world as having sold out to the West. Significantly, he has never visited Israel, but he has always made sure that he is seen to be open to overtures from progressive Israeli governments. During the Reagan and first Bush administrations, the United States shifted its foreign policy interests in the Middle East from Egyptian-Israeli relations to the Gulf region but continued to underwrite the Camp David Accords with aid to both Israel and Egypt: Given on a 3:2 ratio, Israel receives nearly $3 billion and Egypt nearly $2 billion. (It is slowly being phased out, but still accounts for one-third of U.S. foreign aid.) Much of the aid to Egypt is used to subsidize prices on basic food needs, helping stave off a repetition of the 1977 bread riots. Egypt today has a more influential role in Arab politics than it has had since the 1970s; its new confidence came through in the active support it gave to the allied coalition in the 1990–1991 Gulf War (in return for which $15 billion in foreign debt was written off).

The relationship between Egypt and the United States was put to its sternest test in 2002–2003, as the Bush administration increased the pressure on Iraq against the background of charges that it had developed weapons of mass destruction. Unlike the 1990–1991 Gulf crisis, when there was strong support both within the Arab world and outside for an attack on the Iraqi regime following its invasion of Kuwait, there was much less support for the attack that came in March–April 2003. American policy was widely criticized within Egypt, where many asked why the United States did not first use its influence to compel Israel to withdraw from its illegal occupation of the West Bank. President Mubarak downgraded relations between Egypt and Israel, accused the latter of "state terrorism" and of "perpetuating horrific human rights abuses" in Palestinian territories, and lobbied the United States and other Western governments to adopt a peace plan by which a Palestinian state would be created and Israel would withdraw from the occupied territories. The two crises once again placed Egypt in a difficult position, torn between pleasing its American allies and its Arab neighbors.

EGYPTIAN POLITICS IN TRANSITION

Egypt is a poor and overpopulated country that walks a fine line between Islamism and secularism, between tradition and modernity, between the Arabs and the West, and between democracy and authoritarianism. It has maintained a balance of sorts and earned a reputation for itself as the most influential state in the Arab world, but at the cost of sluggish democratic and economic progress. It is a nation of Muslims, but although Islamists influence social and moral issues in Egypt, it is still far from being an Islamic state of the kind they want. Islamism continues to feed off the poverty of Egypt and off concerns about the influential role that the West (and the United States in particular) plays in Middle Eastern affairs.

Egypt has been the key power broker in Middle Eastern and Arab relations over the last two generations, but it has not yet reaped the kind of economic rewards that often come to powerful regional actors. There has been a gradual process of democratization over the last 20 years, and attempts have been made to deal with Egypt's pressing economic problems, but these have had mixed results. The future is likely to see Mubarak continuing the process of democratization, but he will need to move more quickly and effectively if he is to provide the kind of sustained political stability, bureaucratic efficiency, and economic growth needed to address the plight of the Egyptian people. Meanwhile, all attempts at political and economic change in the region continue to be impacted by the tensions between Islam and the West.

KEY TERMS

Arab Socialist Union
Aswan dam
Camp David Accords
core elite
Corrective Revolution
dual executive
fellahin

Free Officers
Infitah
jamaat
Muslim Brotherhood
National Democratic
  Party
Palestine

People's Assembly
Sinai Peninsula
Six-Day War
Suez Canal
Suez crisis
United Arab Republic
Yom Kippur War

KEY PEOPLE

Hasan al-Banna
King Farouk
Hosni Mubarak

Gamal Abdel Nasser
Ahmed Nazif
Anwar Sadat

Atef Sidqi
Saad Zaghlul
Ayman al-Zawahiri

STUDY QUESTIONS

1. Of the many historical influences on Egypt, which are the most politically prominent today?

2. Egypt had a relatively limited experience of colonialism. Compare and contrast the effects of that experience with the effects of the much longer and deeper history of colonialism in India and Nigeria.

3. Does Egypt need a strong, centralized government?

4. Compare and contrast the role of personality in the presidencies of the United States and Egypt. Why—and in what ways—does the personality of the incumbent influence the character of the office?

5. Compare and contrast the dual executive in Russia and Egypt. How are the roles of the legislatures different?

6. Why is the military so much more politically significant in Nigeria than in Egypt?
7. What does Hosni Mubarak have to fear from honest and fair elections?
8. Compare and contrast the relative roles in their respective countries of strong political parties such as the LDP in Japan, PRI in Mexico, and the NDP in Egypt.
9. Why has the party system in Egypt been more enduring than it has in Nigeria?
10. What are the most realistic options for Egypt to pull out of its economic malaise?

EGYPT ONLINE

The Egyptian Presidency: www.presidency.gov.eg
An official government site with information on the presidency and on Egypt.
People's Assembly: www.assembly.gov.eg
The home page for the People's Assembly, which includes information on Assembly members and the text of the Egyptian constitution.
National Democratic Party: www.ndp.org.eg/index_en.htm
Official Web site for Egypt's governing party.
Egyptian State Information Service: www.sis.gov.eg
An official government site that provides links to information on Egyptian politics, current events, and economic matters.
Egypt WWW Index: http://ce.eng.usf.edu/pharos
Megasite maintained by the University of South Florida, with links to sites on politics, business, history, and news about Egypt.
Middle East Times: http://metimes.com
A source of English-language news on Egypt and the Middle East.

FURTHER READING

Fahmy, Ninette S., *The Politics of Egypt: State-Society Relationship* (New York: RoutledgeCurzon, 2002). A study of the interactions between the Egyptian state and society, including chapters on the political system, political parties, and the legal system.

Goldschmidt, Arthur, *Modern Egypt: The Formation of a Nation-State*, 2nd Ed. (Boulder, CO: Westview Press, 2003). A history of Egypt, with an emphasis on the modern era (post-1850s).

Kassem, Maye, *Egyptian Politics: The Dynamics of Authoritarian Rule* (Boulder:CO: Lynne Rienner, 2005). A study of authoritarian rule in Egypt.

Long, David E., and Bernard Reich (Eds.), *The Government and Politics of the Middle East and North Africa*, 4th Ed. (Boulder, CO: Westview, 2002). An introduction to the politics of the Middle East, placing Egypt in the context of regional political, economic, and social change.

Rubin, Barry, *Islamic Fundamentalism in Egyptian Politics* (New York: Palgrave Macmillan, 2002). A study of Islamic fundamentalism in Egypt, looking at the different groups and their policies and philosophies.

COMPARATIVE EXERCISE

TERMS OF OFFICE

Hosni Mubarak's "reelection" to office for a fifth six-year term as president in 2005 made him one of the longest-serving heads of state in the world, and raised once again the issue of the appropriate limits that should be placed on the terms of office of elected officials. Questions continue to be asked—in Egypt and elsewhere—about how many terms government officials should be allowed to serve, how long each term should be, and whether the terms should be of fixed or of flexible duration. When Bill Clinton left office in 2001 after his two terms, liberals bemoaned the fact that he was not allowed to stay for a third term, while conservatrives were only too happy to see him replaced by George W. Bush.

Different governments have developed different combinations of limits on different offices, with varying results.

- **Limited vs. unlimited terms.** The United States—and other systems that have adopted the American model—has opted for a combination of limited and unlimited terms in its executive and legislature: The president can serve a maximum of two four-year terms, while members of Congress can serve an unlimited number of two- or six-year terms. The U.S. Constitution said nothing about limits on the terms of the presidency, but George Washington set a precedent by stepping down after two terms. All his successors honored that precedent until Franklin Delano Roosevelt, who was reelected twice to the office, serving a total of 13 years as president. The 22nd Amendment to the constitution, ratified in 1951, limited subsequent presidents to two terms in office.

  The main advantage of term limits is that they encourage regular turnover in office. Not only does this avoid the dangers of authoritarian tendencies, complacency, or the development of a ruling elite, but it also ensures that new ideas and policies are brought into government. Term limits also cancel out the sometimes unfair advantages of incumbency, which include name recognition and the ability to attract greater media attention and more campaign funding.

  The arguments against term limits include the following: they prevent good leaders and legislators from staying in office; they are undemocratic in the sense that they restrict the ability of voters to elect whomever they like to office; they do not allow for the development of career politicians who can develop the experience, contacts, and reputation needed to do the best possible job for their constituents; and they weaken the powers of elected officials relative to lobbyists and bureaucrats, who can build many years of experience in government and thus can be at an advantage over elected officials.

  With their restriction on executives to a single six-year term in office and their ban on consecutive terms in legislative office, the Mexicans have developed something of a compromise. However, it has the effect of cleaning out government completely every six years, and the confusing effect of encouraging politicians to move back and forth among different offices.

- **Short vs. long terms.** Terms in office vary substantially, from as little as two years to as much as a lifetime appointment that can result in a leader staying in office for several decades. The U.S. House of Representatives is at the low end of the scale, its two-year terms being among the shortest in the world. Just down the street in Washington, D.C., however, justices of the U.S. Supreme Court enjoy appointments for life, and can be removed only for committing "high crimes and misdemeanors" (which are not defined in the constitution). Elsewhere, the most common terms of office are in the range of four to six years, the length increasing for constitutional courts, whose members are commonly appointed for anything between 12 years and life.

The main advantage of short terms is that they ensure that voters often have the opportunity to comment through the ballot box on the performance of their elected officials. They also keep representatives accountable and discourage them from taking voters for granted. The disadvantages, however, are many: Frequent elections court the danger of promoting voter apathy; unless elections are paid for out of the public purse, they force parties and candidates to spend less time on government business and more time raising campaign funds; they interfere with the development of long-term views on public policy; and they heighten the danger of high turnover in public office.

Lifetime appointments to constitutional courts reduce the political pressures on the work of the judiciary and make it more likely that courts will develop more consistent positions on judicial issues. At the same time, however, they reduce the introduction into the courts of new ideas, raising the danger that courts might fall out of step with the prevailing views of government and society.

- **Fixed vs. flexible terms.** While the United States and other countries using the U.S. model have opted for fixed terms for elected officials—two years for representatives, four years for presidents, and six years for senators—most parliamentary systems have adopted a system of maximum terms, where elections can be held any time within an agreed limit, which is typically four or five years.

The main advantage of fixed terms is that they allow both voters and elected officials to plan around a predictable timetable, and to know how much time is left for a legislative program before the next election. The use of staggered terms also allows voters to change the makeup and direction of government in increments and reduces the likelihood of temporary emotions producing a massive switch in the makeup and direction of government.

Flexible terms inject a note of uncertainty into the electoral process, which affects elected officials, parties, and voters alike. Everyone knows the final permissible date for an election, but no one except the leader and his or her advisors knows when it is most likely to come. Cynics who argue that elected officials think only about elections would probably conclude that flexible terms force those officials to be thinking about being responsive to the needs of constituents constantly, rather than only in the weeks or months leading up to the election. Finally, flexible terms allow leaders to manipulate the electoral system by calling elections only at times when there is the greatest likelihood of their party winning.

Although there is universal agreement that representative democracy demands that limits be placed on the terms in office of elected officials, there is no agreement concerning the number and length of those terms.

Part VI

MARGINAL COUNTRIES

America is now threatened less by conquering states than we are by failing ones.

—U.S. National Security Strategy, 2002

Marginal countries are the most troubled in the world: the most politically unstable, the poorest, the least successful at meeting the basic needs of their people, and the furthest from achieving workable state systems. We hear and see relatively little about them in the news, at least until there is another natural or man-made disaster of some kind that briefly draws our attention to the plight of their people. And yet the problems of these countries can create an instability in the international system that poses a direct threat to wealthy countries, whether by being staging posts in the drug trade, becoming hotbeds of terrorist activity, challenging rich countries to deal with the problem of genocide or mass starvation, becoming the source of refugee crises, or threatening their more stable and successful neighbors. In short, we ignore these countries at our peril.

Many marginal countries are home to the most dramatic tales of hardship, and often witness human tragedy on an immense scale. Consider the following examples:

- **Democratic Republic of Congo** covers a vast swathe of central Africa that was once known as Zaire and has enormous mineral wealth. It was long run by the corrupt and authoritarian regime of President Mobutu Sese Seko, a firm U.S. ally because of his anti-Soviet policies. After stealing and amassing a personal fortune estimated at $4 billion, Mobutu fled into exile in 1996 after a rebellion (he died in 1997), and Zaire—by then renamed Democratic Republic of Congo—broke down in civil war. In the period 1997–2003 an estimated *three million* Congolese died from a combination of fighting, disease, and malnutrition (mainly the latter). This is an astonishing figure, and the highest casualty figure for any war since World War II, yet it attracted almost no media or political attention in the West.

- **Cote d'Ivoire** is a former French colony in West Africa that for more than 30 years was seen as a model of stability, but has recently been plagued by widespread political violence that seems to have no solution. The military took power by force

CHECKLIST

MARGINAL COUNTRIES   *essay!*
What Are Their Features?

- Partially developed or absent democracy, with sometimes persistent military government, and even breakdown into anarchy
- Poorly defined, inconsistent, and unpredictable political institutions and processes
- Mixed levels of public loyalty to the state, with often deep social divisions and sometimes civil war and genocide, deliberate isolation from the international community, and occasionally disputed legal status
- Few independent or competing sources of political power
- Poor records on human rights
- Little respect or support for human equality
- No significant, effective political opposition

- A limited economic base, with a low per capita GDP, extensive black markets, a primarily agricultural workforce with few natural resources or exports (or exports that benefit only the corrupt elite), and a heavy dependence on foreign aid
- Relatively low levels of urbanization, and poor infrastructure
- A lack of basic infrastructure and low levels of technological development
- A low quality of life, with sometimes serious public health problems
- The lowest ratings on the Freedom House and Human Development indexes
- No regional or global influence, except in a negative sense

Where Are They?

There are 36, and they are mainly in Africa and Asia:

Angola	Eritrea	Nepal
Benin	Ethiopia	Niger
Bhutan	Gambia	Rwanda
Burkina Faso	Guinea	Sao Tomé and Principe
Burma	Guinea-Bissau	Sierra Leone
Burundi	Haiti	Somalia
Central African Republic	Lesotho	Tanzania
Chad	Liberia	Togo
Congo, Democratic Republic of	Madagascar	Tuvalu
Côte d'Ivoire	Malawi	Western Sahara
East Timor	Mali	Zambia
Equatorial Guinea	Mozambique	Zimbabwe

in 1999, displacing a leader who had made a point of sowing discord between southern Christians and Muslim northerners. A civil war broke out in 2002 that took thousands of lives and left the country divided into two halves, the northern half controlled by rebels. A buffer zone between the two is today patrolled by foreign peacekeepers, and all attempts to reach a political solution have so far failed.

- **Equatorial Guinea** is a small oil-rich enclave on the west coat of Africa that has been ruled since independence in 1968 by just two men: Francisco Nguema and his nephew Obiang. The older Nguema declared himself president for life in 1972 and launched a reign of terror that ended in 1979 when he was overthrown by his nephew, who had him tried and executed. Few citizens benefit from their country's oil wealth, and the current president Obiang Nguema has declared figures on oil revenues to be a state secret. Life expectancy is about 50.

- **Bhutan** is a small central Asian kingdom that remained cut off from the outside world until the 1970s. Governed by a Western-educated king with four wives (all of whom are sisters), its major export is electricity. Attempts to preserve Buddhist culture led to riots in the 1990s among the Nepali minority, more than 100,000 of who fled to refugee camps in neighboring Nepal.

- **Western Sahara** is a territory in northwest Africa consisting mainly of desert, whose status under international law has been in dispute since it gained independence from Spain in 1976. It has been claimed by both Morocco and Mauritania, but the Polisario Front has been campaigning to have it set up as an independent state for the Sahara Arab people. Various attempts by the United Nations to resolve the standoff have failed.

These examples provide a taste of the kinds of problems faced by marginal countries. The problems are often different in both their causes and effects, but what all these countries have in common is that they exist on the margins of political viability; have mainly failed to develop workable systems of government or to establish workable economies; lack access to the capital, technology, health care, and education that have been the building blocks of more successful societies; and have not been successfully integrated into the global system of which we are all now a part.

Broadly speaking, marginal countries have five major features in common.

Political Instability

Where LDCs have weak political institutions, in marginal countries those institutions are ineffective at best, hover on the brink of collapse, and in rare cases have disappeared altogether, afflicted by a breakdown in law and order that has led—in the most extreme cases—to domestic **anarchy.** The divisions that color marginal countries are often so intense, and their citizens so powerless, that society breaks down in civil conflict and war, with armed factions fighting for control and the innocent majority caught in the crossfire. In those countries that have at least a core governing structure in place, elections are often manipulated and dissolve into open violence, the competition for power is undermined by corruption and bribery, and it is relatively easy for the group in control to accumulate more power and to build a dictatorship. Human rights violations are the norm rather than the exception.

The most troubled countries in the world are described as **failed states.** The idea of failure in this context can be defined in many ways, and there are no precise qualities that a country must have either to be failing or to have failed. Generally, though, these are countries where civil violence and poverty are so extreme that government

anarchy A political theory based on the argument that society does not need government.

failed states Countries where conditions are so dire that government barely functions, and the basic needs of people are no longer met.

can no longer function, and the basic needs of people—such as security, education, and health care—are no longer met. There is usually no working system of law and order, there are disputes about who is in charge, there are no working institutions of government, and there are no institutions capable of representing the country to the outside world.[1] Failed states are in such dire straits that the UN and foreign governments often step in to restore order or provide basic services. Estimates of the number of failing or failed states in the world vary,[2] but most lists include such countries as Burundi, Chad, Democratic Republic of Congo, Guinea, Haiti, Liberia, and several Islamic states (such as Afghanistan, Bangladesh, Iraq, Sudan, Syria, and Yemen).

An Unstable State System

In the world's most troubled states, there is either too much government—with all power focused in the hands of a small ruling elite—or too little government, with no predictable system of government, a legal system that is either weak or ignored altogether, and a sense of national identity that may be shaky or completely absent. In either case, the political opposition may be weak or nonexistent, encouraging people to ally themselves with warlords, private armies, rebel groups, or ethnic nationalists.

We have already looked at the problems faced by Cote d'Ivoire, Democratic Republic of the Congo, and Western Sahara. Consider also the plight of Eritrea in northeast Africa, and the difficulties it faces in building stability. A former Italian colony, it was annexed by Ethiopia in 1962, setting off a 32-year civil war. It won its independence in 1993, but its relationship with Ethiopia remains strained; when a border dispute broke out in 1998, tens of thousands of soldiers on both sides died. Decades of war left Eritrea with very little infrastructure, and President Isaias Afewerki—who was elected by the country's national assembly in 1993—has since refused to hold new presidential elections, has only allowed one political party to function, tolerates no public criticism, and allows no private newspapers or radio or TV stations.

Economic Stagnation or Decline

Marginal countries are the poorest in the world, with a wide range of economic problems, or with economic foundations that are so small or restricted that they offer their people little opportunity to better their lives. For the governments of liberal democracies, one of the key challenges is to make sure that as many people as possible have access to the opportunities provided by the free market, and to deal with problems such as unemployment and closing the gap between the wealthy and the poor. But for marginal countries, those economic opportunities are missing. Since resources are typically concentrated in the hands of the state, the struggle for power becomes more intense, creating a winner-take-all system where losers cannot be successfully reabsorbed into society. When Guinea-Bissau, a former Portuguese colony on the west coast of Africa, lives almost entirely off the production of cashew nuts, or when Gambia, a nearby former British colony, lives almost entirely off the production of peanuts, the chances of creating wealth and opportunity are greatly reduced.

Because the risk is often too high, or because there are not enough skilled or semi-skilled workers, foreign corporations and governments will not invest in marginal countries, with the significant exception of lucrative natural resource extraction and all the problems this creates. This means that the economies of these countries remain heavily based on agriculture. And without some form of centralized control, the black market dominates and most people produce only enough to take care of their own immediate needs. Without working economies, the situation in marginal countries can deteriorate to the point where agricultural systems break down, leading to mass starvation and to refugee crises as thousands leave their homelands and move to other parts of the country or to neighboring countries seeking sustenance.

The economic problems faced by marginal countries may be made worse by environmental degradation, civil war, ethnic conflict, genocide, corruption, bad governance, or natural handicaps (including tropical diseases) that poor countries find hard to fight. For example, international news headlines were briefly dominated in mid-2005 by a drought in Niger, an arid country that sits on the edge of the Sahara Desert. Under almost constant military rule since its independence from France in 1960, the economic prospects for Niger are undermined by its heavy dependence on exports of uranium, and its agricultural prospects are undermined by repeated droughts and the encroaching desert. In 2005, yet another drought and a locust infestation left about 2.5 million people facing food shortages and starvation. Their problems were made worse by mismanagement in the distribution of emergency food aid, which—according to the local offices of international organizations—was not reaching the right people at the right time.

A Low Quality of Life

The combination of political instability, civil conflict, and economic stagnation has gone hand-in-hand to leave marginal countries with some of the worst social conditions in the world. They typically have the lowest literacy and the lowest primary school completion rates, the highest rates of infant mortality, the lowest life expectancy, the lowest levels of access to clean water and sanitation (see Figure VI.1), and minimal access to the kind of modern transportation systems, infrastructure, and new technology that liberal democracies take for granted. Where liberal democracies have welfare systems that act as safety nets for their poorest or more disadvantaged citizens, there is not much welfare for the world's poorest people beyond their immediate families, and even that may be no guarantee if they are held hostage to war or drought.

Global Marginalization

This idea should not be taken too literally, because although failing countries are at the margins of viability and sustainability, it is also becoming clear that they are having an increasing impact on the international system by becoming critical sources of instability. "Weak or failed states," argues Francis Fukuyama, "are the source of many of the world's most serious problems."[3] The problems of marginal states can spill over onto their neighbors through the drug trade, the spread of disease, refugee problems,

FIGURE VI.1

Comparing Life in Rich and Poor Countries

Source: World Bank, World Development Indicators database, 2005, www.worldbank.com. Figures are for 2002–2003.

and civil war. People living in abject poverty, their lives disrupted and threatened by chaos and violence all around, can become so desperate that they can fall under the influence of demagogues and hate mongers, who may blame wealthy countries for their plight, and thereby feed into international terrorism.[4] As focused as they have been for so long on big power competition, North Americans and Europeans have not fully addressed the problems of marginal countries, nor have they developed the tools needed to deal with the problems of poverty. Most notably, they have failed to address a debt crisis afflicting the world's poorest countries, which has been on the agenda for more than twenty years. They have also failed to liberalize trade in agriculture and textiles, which would offer opportunities for economic growth.

ADDRESSING THE PROBLEMS OF MARGINAL COUNTRIES

We saw in Part III how newly industrializing countries—most of them former colonies—have been able to move beyond the heritage of colonialism and build democratic stability and vibrant export-led economies, attract foreign investment, create new jobs and wealth, and invest in human capital by building infrastructure, schools, and hospitals that provide the foundations for social development. Then we saw in Part IV how less developed countries have the potential to follow the same path, but are handicapped by a variety of problems, some self-imposed, some growing out of their history, and some imposed by the international system—but at least they have political, legal, and economic systems that function.

In the case of marginal countries, the handicaps are both more obvious and more serious, but this does not mean that there is much agreement on either the causes of their difficulties or on the best way of addressing them. One school of thought focuses on internal problems, emphasizing the challenge of building workable systems of government out of deeply divided societies. Whether the divisions are economic, cultural, ethnic, gender-based, or religious—runs the thinking—they interfere with attempts to build a sense of national identity and to work toward common goals. Some of the divisions are blamed on colonialism, in the sense that colonial borders were drawn without regard to different ethnic or religious groups. Some of the divisions are blamed on bad government, where a corrupt governing elite exploits power to enrich itself.

Another school of thought focuses on geography and environmental factors. One reason rich countries have been successful is that they have had the kind of natural resources, temperate climate, river systems, and absence of disease that first allowed organized and profitable agriculture to develop and then provided the foundations for the industrial revolution. But these kinds of limitations might be overcome in marginal countries if enough was invested in transportation, health care, and the management of natural resources, such that access to them was opened as widely as possible, and scarce financial resources were wisely used.

Yet another school of thought argues that the international community makes life worse for poor countries. This may be because of the history of exploitation of the poor by the rich, whether through colonialism, slavery, or unfair trading practices—although there is the argument that exploitation does not cause poverty so much as

CRITICAL ISSUES

GIVE WAR A CHANCE

© Carlos Mhula/Panos Pictures

A problem common to many poor countries is civil war. With all the disruption, loss of life, destruction of property and infrastructure, and misuse of limited resources that it generates, civil war can obviously slow development, particularly in cases where the conflict drags on for many years. There is no question that war is a great evil, particularly when society's most innocent members are caught in the crossfire; few images are more tragic than those of young children killed or injured in war, and in some cases even conscripted to take part in the fighting (the photo shows a child soldier conscripted by a rebel group in Mozambique). The problem of **child soldiers** taking part in wars as far afield as Sierra Leone, Liberia, Congo, Sudan, and Sri Lanka has attracted new attention in recent years; they may join voluntarily or involuntarily, they may be indoctrinated to kill, they may be used as child terrorists, or they may be used as sexual slaves for the leaders of armies. An estimated six million child soldiers have been killed in conflict since the mid-1990s.[5]

But it has been suggested by some that despite the horrors of war, it may have at least one virtue: it can resolve conflict and perhaps bring about a lasting peace. Allowing enemies to fight it out and reach their own kind of accommodation, argues Edward Luttwak, may be better than allowing external powers or the UN to interfere, keeping resentful groups of combatants in refugee camps and sometimes supplying both sides in armed conflicts. In other words, says Luttwak, perhaps the international community should (turning on its head the title of the famous song by John Lennon) "give war a chance."[6] Most liberal democracies—especially those in Europe—reached the state of stability and equilibrium they have today only after centuries of fighting, so perhaps postcolonial countries should be allowed the same opportunity. Of course, at least one flaw in this argument is that most European countries were not being supplied by external powers, nor was there always the prospect of their wars spilling over to and threatening the security of those powers, and nor did those external powers have to worry about the impact of television coverage on public opinion at home.

poverty invites exploitation, since poor countries are vulnerable to abuse.[7] It may also be because rich countries become involved in the internal affairs of divided countries, whether for well-meaning humanitarian reasons or for not-so-well-meaning political reasons. Haiti provides an example of this; the United States has intervened in its internal affairs many times, supposedly to help restore order and build democracy, but critics of U.S. policy argue that the interventions have done more harm than good.

Others suggest that the problem lies not with intervention by rich countries, but with the quality or the focus of that intervention. For example, Francis Fukuyama has argued that the West has been right to intervene militarily or economically in failed or weak states, but that it has failed to create the kind of self-sustaining state institutions that can survive the withdrawal of that outside intervention. He claims that poverty is not the proximate cause of terrorism, but rather that the West offers an attractive package of material prosperity and political and cultural freedom that many people in the world want but find difficult to achieve. But while the West has been busy reducing the role of the state, what is really needed to help poor countries is a growth of state power and the transfer of functioning public institutions.[8]

This is all very well, respond the critics, but who is to say that Western ideas about how state institutions should be structured and function are always appropriate to the needs of poorer countries? European and American institutions evolved out of the particular needs and circumstances of Europe and North America—they may not be appropriate for other societies. In economic terms, for example, one critic of Western policy argues that Western governments should "just get out of the way." Rather than trying to help developing countries by pursuing the kinds of policies used at home, they should instead focus on the particular features of poor countries, such as corruption and cronyism, support much simpler market-oriented policies to encourage home-made development, and focus on the private sector as an engine of growth.[9]

The Bush administration has routinely played up the strong prospects of building democracy in Iraq, and the likelihood of a post-Saddam, post-war Iraq becoming a beacon for democracy in the Middle East. The idea that democracy can be transferred to non-Western societies features in much of the thinking of American policymakers and analysts.[10] So, for example, as the Soviet Union began to crumble, President Reagan claimed that freedom had a momentum that could not be halted. Speaking in 2003, President George W. Bush claimed that number of democracies in the world had grown from about 40 in the late 1970s to about 120, with more on the way.[11] It was difficult to square these ideas, however, with indications that Iraq was steadily deteriorating into civil war, and with the persistence of instability in countries such as Haiti, Democratic Republic of the Congo, Sudan, Niger, Chad, Ethiopia, and Zimbabwe.

Turning to economic issues, one of the problems facing failing or failed states is the absence of a structured economic system. Instead of being used as a foundation for economic development, the most valuable resources—such as diamonds or oil—are typically plundered by those who control the country, or are fought over in civil war, and the benefits of those resources rarely if ever reach the poor majority. One explanation of the problems faced by some marginal countries is the so-called **"resource curse."**[12] This theory argues that where poor countries are relatively well endowed in natural resources, those resources may actually pose more of a handicap to development than an opportunity.

The "curse" stems from a combination of factors. First, because these resources are easy to exploit and can bring quick returns, a country will focus its development efforts almost entirely in that sector, investing little in other sectors, and becoming heavily dependent on a product whose value may be held hostage to fluctuations in its price on the international market, over which the producing country has little influence. Second, the profits that come from these products can encourage corruption, ensuring that they find their way into the bank accounts of the rich and powerful rather than being reinvested back into the community. The resources can also encourage internal conflict, when poorer regions of the country find that they are not benefiting equally from the profits of resources found in other parts of the country.

One controversial issue relating to poverty is the question of the **overseas development assistance (ODA)** provided by rich countries: Is there enough, is it invested in the right kinds of activities, and does it breed independence rather than dependence? The answer for most critics of aid is "No" on all three counts. In 1970, the UN General Assembly set a target of 0.7 percent of GNP for donor countries for foreign aid, but only four countries have so far met that target: Denmark (0.84 percent), Luxembourg (0.81 percent), the Netherlands (0.80 percent), and Sweden (0.79 percent). Meanwhile, the world's biggest providers of aid in absolute terms have fallen far short: in order, they are the United States (0.15 percent), Japan (0.20 percent), France (0.41), Germany (0.28 percent), and Britain (0.34 percent) (see Table VI.1). Defenders of U.S. aid argue that the United States provides more aid than anyone else (actually, it provides less than half as much as the European Union), and that private philanthropy makes up for the shortfall in meeting the UN target (actually, adding in private spending only pushes the total up to 0.21 percent of GNP).[13]

The jury is still out on the question of whether aid is being used effectively. Many critics of foreign aid argue that it is based too much on taking a Band-Aid approach rather than on helping poor countries help themselves. Much ODA is also given with strings attached, with the choices about which countries and communities receive the most sometimes being driven by political and ideological agendas. For example, the Bush administration, while allocating $15 billion to the global fight against AIDS, stipulated that the spending should be channeled to programs that promoted abstinence rather than condom use, and could not be used for abortions or to treat prostitutes. It also refused to allow aid funds to be used by groups that carry out or provide advice on abortions.

MARGINAL COUNTRIES TODAY

The prospects for the world's poorest and most unstable countries are not good. Many seem to be caught in an endless downward spiral of crises, and when even potentially successful countries—such as Cote d'Ivoire and Zimbabwe—start down that spiral, it becomes obvious just how fragile the political and economic structures of many countries can be.

What of the future? In 2000, at the UN Millennium Summit, a series of eight Millennium Development Goals were set, aimed at reducing extreme poverty.

TABLE VI.I

Overseas Development Aid

	$ million	% of GNP
EU-15 total	37,139	0.35
US	16,254	0.15
Japan	8,880	0.20
France	7,253	0.41
Germany	6,784	0.28
UK	6,282	0.34
Netherlands	3,981	0.80
Italy	2,433	0.17
Sweden	2,400	0.79
Spain	1,961	0.23
Belgium	1,853	0.60
Denmark	1,748	0.84
Finland	558	0.35
Austria	505	0.20
Ireland	504	0.39
Greece	362	0.21
Portugal	320	0.22
Luxembourg	194	0.81
Total	69,029	

Official government aid only, ranked by dollar amount. Figures are for 2002.

EU-15 = the 15 member states of the European Union.

Source: Organization for Economic Cooperation and Development.

These included the achievement of universal primary education; the promotion of gender equality and the empowerment of women; a reduction in child mortality; an improvement in maternal health; the fighting of HIV/AIDS, malaria, and other diseases; and environmentally sustainable development. To even begin to achieve these goals, it has been estimated that present levels of ODA must be doubled to about $160 billion per year, or 0.5 percent of the GDP of rich countries.[14] These are all noble goals, but they will take a change in the priorities of wealthy countries, and will demand a better understanding of how to achieve the kind of political stability that marginal countries must have to make development more effective. This will not be easy.

KEY TERMS

child soldiers   overseas development aid
failed states   resource curse

STUDY QUESTIONS

1. How seriously should great powers take the threat posed by instability in marginal countries?

2. Should we "give war a chance," and allow marginal countries to fight over their differences until they have reached a state of equilibrium?

3. Does globalization pose a threat or offer an opportunity to marginal countries?

4. What are the best approaches to dealing with the problems of marginal countries?

MARGINAL COUNTRIES ONLINE

World Bank: www.worldbank.com
The best source of data and information on marginal countries.

FURTHER READING

Herbst, Jeffrey, *States and Power in Africa: Comparative Lessons in Authority and Control* (Princeton: Princeton University Press, 2000). A theoretical and historical examination of the difficulties African leaders have faced in establishing viable states. Includes some controversial recommendations for addressing state failure in Africa today.

Holsti, Kalevi J., *The State, War, and the State of War* (Cambridge: Cambridge University Press, 1996). A detailed examination of the relationship between state strength or weakness and the prevalence of war in the contemporary era.

Lomborg, Bjørn, (Ed.), *Global Crises, Global Solutions* (Cambridge: Cambridge University Press, 2003). A weighty tome with chapters on some of the key problems facing the world, most of which—including conflict, access to education, corruption, malnutrition, and migration—affect marginal countries more than others.

Migdal, Joel S., *Strong Societies and Weak States: State-Society Relations and State Capabilities in the Third World* (Princeton: Princeton University Press, 1998). Emphasizes the difficulties states have in penetrating and establishing authority over societies in poor countries.

Sachs, Jeffrey, *The End of Poverty: Economic Possibilities for Our Time* (New York: Penguin, 2005). A best-selling economist explains why the poorest countries have been unable to improve their lot, and offers a nine-part set of solutions based on dealing with a combination of political, economic, social, and environmental problems.

HAITI

QUICK FACTS

Official name: Republic of Haiti

Capital: Port-au-Prince

Area: 10,714 square miles (27,750 sq. km.)

Languages: Creole and French

Population: 8.4 million

Population density: 784 per square mile (301 per sq. km)

Population growth rate: 1.8 percent

POLITICAL INDICATORS

Freedom House rating: Not Free

Date of state formation: 1804

System type: Unitary presidential republic

Constitution: Published 1987

Administration: Unitary

Executive: President, serving five-year renewable terms

Legislature: Bicameral: Senate of 27 members, elected for six-year terms, and Chamber of Deputies of 83 members, elected for four-year terms

Party structure: Fluid multiparty system

Judiciary: Supreme Court

Head of state: Boniface Alexandre (interim) (2004–)

Head of government: Gerard Latortue (interim) (2004–)

ECONOMIC INDICATORS

GDP (2004): $3.5 billion

Per capita GDP: $390

Distribution of GDP: Services 55 percent, industry 17 percent, agriculture 28 percent

Urban population: 36 percent

SOCIAL INDICATORS

HDI ranking: 153

Infant mortality rate: 76 per 1,000 live births

Life expectancy: 52 years

Literacy: 54 percent of people aged 15 and older

Religions: Christianity (Roman Catholicism) and voodoo

INTRODUCTION

dictatorship
A political system in
which all power is
held by one person
or group of people.

Few countries in the world more graphically illustrate the idea of "crisis" than Haiti. Decades of **dictatorship**, political instability, poverty, economic mismanagement, environmental degradation, and public violence have left it one of the poorest and most troubled countries on the face of the earth. Some have even dubbed it a failed state. Ironically, it has been independent longer than any other country in the Americas except the United States, and yet it remains one of the most chaotic, corrupt, and unstable countries in the western hemisphere. In virtually every international comparative ranking system, whether political, economic, or social, Haiti appears close to the bottom, or in last place. So desperate is its situation that Mother Theresa, with decades of experience in the slums of Calcutta, was moved to describe the Port-au-Prince slum of Cité Soleil (City of the Sun) as the "fifth world."

In economic terms, Haiti faces a host of problems, from widespread poverty to high unemployment, poor infrastructure, and a heavy dependence on agriculture. With a GDP of $3.5 billion in 2004, it ranked 133rd in the world in terms of national wealth. Its per capita GDP of just $390 made it one of the poorest countries in the world, and the poorest by far in the western hemisphere. And rather than growing, its economy has actually shrunk in recent years. Thanks in large part to more than $1 billion in foreign aid, there have been some positive recent short-term trends, with greater access to electricity and clean water, the creation of jobs and the recruitment of police officers, and an anticorruption program, but Haiti faces too many ingrained structural problems to see much hope of permanent, long-term changes in its near future. Huge investment is needed in education, health care, and the development of infrastructure, but this will pay few dividends as long as Haiti's political system remains on rocky ground, and as long as its system of law and order is unable to provide the stability that ordinary Haitians need.

In social terms, life in Haiti is dismal. It has the lowest life expectancy, highest poverty rate, highest incidence of HIV/AIDS, and highest infant mortality rate in the western hemisphere, it has a literacy rate of less than 50 percent, and—according to the UN—about half its people lack enough food to live a healthy and active life. Its problems are reflected in its ranking of 153rd out of 177 in the 2004 Human Development Index. Although it practices religious toleration, it has racial problems; the small and mainly urban French-speaking mulatto community controls the economy to the detriment of the 95 percent of Haitians who are of African descent. There are also deep divisions between urban and rural Haitians, the latter having relatively little direct contact with government. The economic divisions are reflected in language, which has become a social barrier: Creole is spoken by most people, and French is spoken by the educated elite, but very few Haitians are fluent in both.[1] Meanwhile, an increasing number of educated Haitians also speak English.[2]

In political terms, Haiti is the antithesis of a democracy. Formally, it is a unitary presidential republic with three branches of government and a separation of powers. But in reality it has never been able to achieve any kind of long-term political stability, its politics routinely being disrupted by the army, and civilian leaders routinely engaging in electoral fraud, denying citizens the rights of free speech and

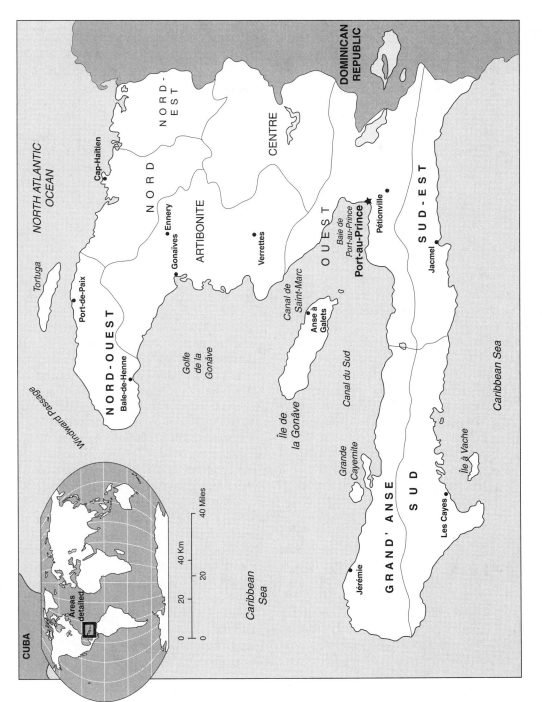

NORTH ATLANTIC OCEAN

CUBA

Windward Passage

Tortuga

NORD-OUEST

Port-de-Paix

Baie-de-Henne

Cap-Haïtien

NORD

NORD-EST

Ennery

Gonaïves

ARTIBONITE

Verrettes

CENTRE

DOMINICAN REPUBLIC

Golfe de la Gonâve

Canal de Saint-Marc

Anse à Galets

Île de la Gonâve

Canal du Sud

OUEST

Baie de Port-au-Prince

Port-au-Prince

Pétionville

SUD-EST

Jacmel

Grande Cayemite

GRAND'ANSE

SUD

Jérémie

Les Cayes

Île à Vache

Caribbean Sea

Caribbean Sea

Areas detailed

40 Miles

40 Km

20

20

0

0

free assembly. So dire is Haiti's political situation that—according to the World Bank Governance indicators described in the Introduction—Haiti is in the first percentile on the rule of law, and in the 14th percentile in political stability. Along with China, it was one of only two of the case studies in this book to appear in the 2005 Freedom House report *The Worst of the Worst: The World's Most Repressive Societies*.[3]

Under the circumstances, it is hard to know what to expect out of Haiti, except more bloodshed and instability. There was a brief spell of optimism in 1990 when democratic elections were held, but President Jean-Bertrande Aristide was removed within months by a military coup. Democracy was restored in the mid-1990s, but the elections of 2000 were held under a cloud of suspicions of vote-rigging and threats of violence, and in 2004 Haiti tottered on the brink of civil war. As this book went to press, new elections were scheduled but many questions remained about the prospects for the development of long-term political stability.

POLITICAL DEVELOPMENT

Like so many countries of the developing world, Haiti today is in large part a product of the colonial era. The native peoples of the island of Hispaniola were the Arawak, who populated the Bahamas and the Greater Antilles of the Caribbean. They were the first natives to be seen by Christopher Columbus when he arrived in the Americas in 1492, and in 1493 established the first Spanish colony in the New World. The Arawaks had their own organized government and religion, had developed productive systems of agriculture, and traded with the peoples of other islands in the Caribbean and of the mainland of what is now South America. But all this was quickly swept aside with the arrival of the Spanish, who pursued a policy of genocide and introduced diseases such as smallpox, measles, and typhus to which the Arawaks had no resistance. The result was that hundreds of thousands died (estimates vary on the exact figure) and by the middle of the sixteenth century barely 150 Arawaks remained.

Spain used Hispaniola as a base for their conquest of the Americas, introducing the policy of *repartimiento*, under which colonists would be given large parcels of land and the right to force Indians into a labor force. Spain insisted that the remaining population of natives and settlers move to the eastern half of the island of what they were calling Santo Domingo, so that it could be more closely controlled by officials in the capital city of Santo Domingo de Guzmán. Into the vacuum that remained, African slaves were imported to work on sugar plantations, and French pirates used the western part of the island as a base from which to attack passing English and Spanish ships. In 1697, Spain ceded the area to France, dividing the island into the French colony of Saint-Domingue and the Spanish colony of Santo Domingo. The French encouraged an agricultural economy based on sugar and coffee that transformed the region into one of the richest colonies in the French empire, and more slaves were imported to work the plantations.

Independence from France (1804–1915)

Violent conflict between French colonists and bands of runaway slaves were common throughout the eighteenth century, and one outbreak in the 1750s left several thousand people dead. The outbreak of revolution in France in 1789 encouraged a debate within the small white population of Saint-Domingue about its implications, with freed slaves and the mixed-race descendants of planters and their slave mistresses (known as *gens de couleur*, or people of color) demanding the same rights as the white French colonists. In August 1791, a revolt among slaves led to the Haitian Revolution, led by François-Dominique Toussaint Louverture (a former domestic servant), Jean-Jacques Dessalines (who was born a slave but later served in the French army), and others who were to become heroes of the Haitian struggle for independence. By 1800 the slaves had taken control, and when Napoleon sent a French army to the island to put down the revolt in 1803, it was defeated by Dessalines. On January 1, 1804, the colony declared itself independent from France and—reviving its original native name of *Ayiti* (meaning "mountainous")—renamed itself Haiti. It was now established as the second independent nation in the western hemisphere (after the United States), and the first free black republic in the world.

Dessalines became governor general of Haiti, but in 1805 declared himself Emperor Jacques I. His term in office was marked by racial tensions, with the mainly black peasants living off the land and lighter skinned Haitians dominating business and politics. Dessalines declared Haiti to be an all-black nation, and he made it illegal for whites to own land or property; most whites left Haiti, and many of those who remained were murdered on his orders. His authoritarian regime centralized power in the hands of the state and networks of Dessalines supporters, creating resentment that led to his assassination in October 1806.

Haiti was now divided between a black-controlled north and a south controlled by mulattoes (people of mixed African-European heritage), and although Jean Pierre Boyer reunited the country in 1820, he excluded blacks from government. He quickly invaded the newly independent neighboring state of Santo Domingo, uniting the entire island of Hispaniola and ruling as president from 1822 until 1843. Haiti was not generally recognized by the international community, and lived under constant fear of invasion by France. In 1825, with French warships sitting in the harbor of the Haitian capital of Port-au-Prince and the United States supporting French demands, Boyer signed an agreement to pay reparations to French slaveholders for their losses during the revolution. With Haiti in debt to France for the next 40 years, its attempts to build economic viability were undermined. Boyer was removed from office in an uprising in 1843, moving into exile in France. Santo Domingo declared independence from Haiti in 1844, and is now the Dominican Republic.

Following another peasant revolt and confusion in the leadership of Haiti, with a string of four presidents who served barely a year each in office, General Faustin Soulouque—a veteran of the 1791 slave revolt—was elected president in 1847, and in 1852 declared himself Emperor Faustin I. His authoritarian rule succeeded in once again uniting the country, but he was overthrown in 1858 by General Fabre Geffrard, who was elected to the presidency the following year. Catholicism was reintroduced to Haiti during his administration, and he voluntarily stepped down in 1867 after drawing up a new constitution, Haiti's third. The country now entered a period of relative peace and calm, paying off its debt to France in 1879, and injecting some stability into the economic system. But Haiti was still unable to develop any kind of consistent leadership, and between 1867 and 1915 there were no less than 21 presidents (compared to just 12 in the United States).

TABLE 10.1

Haiti: A Timeline

1492	(December) Christopher Columbus makes landfall on the northern shore of Hispaniola
1697	Spain cedes the western third of Hispaniola to France
1789	French Revolution
1790	Civil war breaks out in Sainte-Domingue
1791	(August) Outbreak of the Haitian Revolution
1804	(January 1) Independence from France
1822–1844	Haiti united with neighboring Santo Domingo
1915	(July) Beginning of U.S. occupation of Haiti
1932	U.S. withdrawal from Haiti
1957	Papa Doc Duvalier elected president
1964	Duvalier declares himself president for life
1971	(April) Duvalier dies and is succeeded by his son Jean-Claude
1983	(March) Visit to Haiti of Pope John Paul II; new constitution published
1986	(February) Baby Doc removed from power in a coup
1987	New constitution published
1988	Leslie Manigat is elected president, but is removed in a coup after four months
1990	Jean-Bertrand Aristide elected president, but removed in a coup in September; massive exodus of boat people follows
1994	(October) Under international pressure, military steps down and Aristide returns to Haiti to finish out his term
1995	(December) Rene Préval elected president; takes office February 1996
2000	(November) Aristide elected to second term in deeply flawed election
2001	(July) Allegations of attempted coup; (December) 12 people die in another apparent coup attempt
2003	(April) Voodoo formally recognized as a religion
2004	(January) 200th anniversary of Haitian independence; celebrations develop into an uprising against Aristide, who flees into exile in February; (March) Boniface Alexandre inaugurated as interim president

Occupation by the United States (1915–1934)

In 1915, the president of Haiti—Jean Vilbrun Guillaume Sam—was overthrown after barely four months in office by a revolt led by a critic of Haiti's ties with the United States, and sparked by Sam's order to execute 167 political prisoners, including a former president. He took refuge in the French Embassy, but this was attacked and taken over by a mob that literally ripped Sam to pieces, parading the pieces through the streets of Port-au-Prince. Against a background of engineered hysteria in the United States about the possibility of an invasion of Haiti by Germany, and concerned that an anti-American leader might succeed Sam and threaten American property and investments in Haiti, President Woodrow Wilson ordered American troops to be landed in Haiti, setting off a 19-year occupation during which the island came under the administration of the U.S. Marine Corps and enjoyed one of its longest periods of stability. Although Haiti remained nominally independent during the occupation and was never formally colonized by the United States, all key decisions were overseen by representatives of the U.S. government. The education system was reformulated, infrastructure was redeveloped, and a new form of order was imposed on Haiti. However, the ruling elite was clearly American and white, racist attitudes tended to color the approach of many of the American administrators, and the occupation force made use of what was—to all intents and purposes—slave labor to help rebuild infrastructure. To make matters worse, a local military force was built that murdered many of those opposed to the occupation and established the foundations for the authoritarian military governments that would follow.

Local opposition to the occupation began almost from the first day, rebels taking action to resist the decisions of the U.S.-supported government. Several presidential candidates refused to accept the office on a matter of principle, and those who accepted were seen as little more than figureheads. A new constitution was even drawn up for Haiti by the United States, the primary author being Franklin D. Roosevelt, then Secretary of the Navy. The legislature refused to accept the constitution, however, which was only promulgated after being put to a national referendum. A rebellion in 1918 was put down at the cost of more than 2,000 Haitian lives. One of the most popular critics of the occupation—Charlemagne Péralte—was even assassinated by a U.S. Marine disguised as one of his followers.

In the wake of the findings of two government commissions, the United States began a withdrawal from Haiti in 1932, the general conclusion being that while there had been stability during the occupation, the underlying causes of poverty and instability remained. However, the United States was to retain control over fiscal policy until 1947. During the 1940s and 1950s Haiti was shaken by a series of coups and changes of leadership (it had nine leaders between 1941 and 1957) that were brought to an end by the election to the presidency in 1958 of Dr. François "Papa Doc" Duvalier, a rural medical doctor. Haiti now embarked on an era in which it became more like a monarchy than a republic.

The Duvaliers Take Charge (1957–1986)

The Kennedy administration was critical of the rule of Duvalier, but the Johnson and Nixon administrations—as so many U.S. administrations were to do—began to

PAPA DOC DUVALIER

The most notorious character in modern Haitian history was undoubtedly Francois Duvalier, known more generally as "Papa Doc." He ruled Haiti between 1957 and 1971, becoming a byword for despotic rule and bequeathing the country a political system in which authoritarian rule was all too easy to achieve and the prospects for the development of a civil society in Haiti were starved to death. He is thought to have survived at least six assassination attempts while in office.

Born in 1901 in Port-au-Prince, and educated as a medical doctor at the University of Haiti, Duvalier worked between 1934 and 1946 in mainly rural hospital and clinics, specializing in yaws, a tropical disease. From 1946 to 1950 he was director of the national public health service and Secretary of Labor. After opposing the election in 1950 of President Paul Magloire, he went into internal exile, practicing medicine until an amnesty was declared in 1956. In 1957 he was elected president of Haiti, starting out on an encouraging note when he brought some stability to the country. But after surviving an attempted coup in 1958 he had the legislature declare a state of siege, and two months later began to rule by decree. He also cleared out opposition within the army and created his own paramilitary group for-

mally known as the Volunteers for National Security, but more widely known as the ***tonton macoutes*** (slang for "bogeymen"). Drawing no formal salary, the *macoutes* lived off extortion, became more powerful than the army, and were used by Duvalier to murder and intimidate his opponents; estimates of the number of Haitians killed during his regime range as high as 30,000.

Duvalier exploited **voodoo**—a religion that combines Roman Catholic ritual and the animism of West African traditional beliefs—to support his methods and build a cult of personality that allowed him to claim to be the embodiment of the spirit of Haiti. In 1961 he dissolved the existing Haitian legislature, created a new one, and arranged elections in which all the candidates were his followers. With the support of the army, he also staged an election in which he was the sole candidate and claimed to have won every one of the more than 1.3 million votes cast. In 1964 he engineered a change to the constitution that made him president for life, and gave him the power to nominate his son Jean-Claude as his successor, which he did. He died in April 1971. In 1986, after his son Baby Doc had fled from Haiti in the wake of his ouster, Papa Doc's body was exhumed and posthumously "executed" by being beaten.

accept him, in large part because of his opposition to communism and because of Haiti's strategic location so close to Cuba. This unfortunate habit of cohabiting with anti-communist dictators was to be the motivation behind U.S. support—for example—of the Trujillo regime in the neighboring Dominican Republic, the Mobutu regime in Zaire, and the Shah of Iran. Single-minded opposition to communist leaders has also been one factor behind the unwavering U.S. attempts to undermine the Castro regime since it came to power in 1959.

If anything positive can be said about Duvalier, it is that—like so many authoritarian leaders—he brought stability to Haiti. In the 14 years before he came to power, Haiti had eight leaders, five of whom each served no more than a few months in office, and two of whom were removed by the army. Duvalier ruled Haiti for 14 years, giving Haiti its longest spell of uninterrupted government in decades. But he kept control with an iron grip, using terror tactics to maintain his hold on power and retarding the development of civil society and democratic political institutions in Haiti (see People in History). His reign of terror also led to a massive brain drain as the educated elite left Haiti for the United States and Europe, undermining the country's economic prospects.

Duvalier died in 1971 and was succeeded by his 19-year-old son Jean-Claude, otherwise known as "Baby Doc." He had never shown any interest in politics or aptitude for government, and although he often promised to return Haiti to democracy, little real change took place during his term in office. Day-to-day government was left largely in the hands of his mother, Simone, while he enjoyed the trappings of office without responsibility, living life as a playboy and building the Duvalier family bank accounts. In 1980 he reputedly spent $3 million on a wedding to the daughter of one his late father's political enemies. In 1983, attention was draw to the plight of Haiti by the visit of Pope John Paul II, who publicly criticized the poverty of the country.

In 1985 Baby Doc announced that political parties would be legalized and that he would appoint a prime minister, but the changes came too late, a popular uprising grew, and Duvalier was removed in a coup in 1986, fleeing into exile in France. The new U.S.-sponsored administration of Lt.-General Henri Namphy promised the establishment of a democratic system of government, and a new constitution was adopted in 1987. Legislative elections at the end of 1987 were marred by widespread fraud, were stopped after just a few hours of voting, and were run again in January 1988. Leslie Manigat was appointed president by the interim governing civil-military council, and confirmed just three days later in elections in which less than 5 percent of Haitians took part. Manigat was removed from power in a military coup just eight months later, and replaced by General Prosper Avril. An attempted coup against him in April 1989 failed.

New hope was raised for the prospects of democracy in Haiti in 1990 when Jean-Bertrand Aristide was elected president in what was widely acclaimed as Haiti's first democratic presidential election. But within just eight months—after promising increases to the minimum wage, improvements in literacy, and an improvement in Haiti's human rights record—he too had been deposed by the military and sent into exile. The new regime used paramilitary thugs to impose rule by terror and engaged in blatant narcotics trafficking, drawing an oil and trade embargo from the United States and the United Nations. Facing the threat of an imminent U.S. invasion, the officers stepped down in September 1994, U.S. troops once again occupied Haiti, and Aristide was returned to office. New parliamentary elections were held in June 1995, but many questions were raised about their legitimacy. With UN troops still in place, a presidential election was held in December 1995 and won by Aristide's former prime-minister, René Préval (the constitution prevented Aristide himself from running for a second consecutive term). After serving one term, Préval was succeeded by Aristide in elections held in 2000 that were boycotted by all major opposition parties and were held against a background of widespread civil unrest. When Aristide claimed to have won 92 percent of the vote, and when his party won 80 percent of the seats in the lower House of Deputies and all but one seat in the Senate, the credibility of his government was pushed to the breaking point.

Aristide took office in February 2001, but without the welcome that had greeted him in 1990. His legitimacy was never acknowledged by opposition parties, and in a throwback to the bad old days of Duvalier, armed gangs called *chiméres* were used to bolster his position. Public disquiet fed into an armed insurrection led by a rebel group that went through several changes of name, including the Front de Resistance. Aristide held on as long as he could in the presidential palace in Port-au-Prince, but in the face of mounting civil unrest, and amid widely held suspicions of involvement by the United States and the Dominican Republic, he stepped down in February 2004 and went into exile. The United States—along with France—once again intervened militarily in Haiti's affairs, landing 20,000 troops to try to keep the peace and prevent another military coup. After 90 days, the U.S. troops were replaced by a 7,400-member multinational UN stabilization force.

Haiti Today

In line with the terms of the constitution, Aristide was replaced by Boniface Alexandre, Chief Justice of Haiti's Supreme Court. Meanwhile, Gerard Latortue (a former foreign minister of Haiti) was appointed prime minister, and he in turn appointed a new cabinet that consisted mainly of leaders from the political opposition. Alexandre was intended to be no more than an interim leader who would govern Haiti while preparations were made for new elections and a return to an elected civilian government. The elections were postponed twice, and as this book went to press legislative and presidential elections were scheduled for the end of December 2005, with the expectation that a new government would be sworn in to office in early February 2006. The prospects for an orderly transition were not strong. The Haitian police force, already small and badly trained, had all but collapsed, and a combination of easily available weapons, political division, and widespread poverty made sure that political violence persisted despite the presence of the UN peacekeepers. Foreign observers felt that Haiti's gun culture was still too dominant, and that adequate preparations had not been made to ensure accurate and complete voter registration.

POLITICAL CULTURE

Like so many failed or failing states, the key to understanding Haiti is to understand its deep social, economic and political divisions. Liberal democracies too are often divided, but on the whole they have been able to rise above and live with those divisions, which never seriously threaten the fabric of the state or undermine the system of government. But in Haiti, such divisions define and drive the relationships between people and government, and have been at the heart of the channels through which power is determined and manipulated. The main features of political culture in Haiti are a weak state, strong centralized political control, and unfortunate traditions of political violence and corruption.

A Weak State

Despite more than 200 years of independence, Haiti has so far been unable to build a strong state system. Too many people still feel cut off from the state, and are discouraged from participating in the political process. This denies Haiti the kind of political stability that it so urgently needs, making it difficult for even the most well-meaning of its leaders to encourage the development of a democratic ethic. There is no tradition of strong political institutions or processes, nor of an efficient bureaucracy, judiciary, or police force. Without the basic building blocks of a working state system, it is difficult to see how Haiti can develop a political system that citizens can use to achieve their objectives, and that will respond to the needs of the majority of Haitians.

A Semi-Monarchical Tradition

Haiti has always claimed to be a republic, and the rebellion that led to its independence in 1804 was encouraged by the republican principles of the American Revolution and the French Revolution. But despite the claims, it has often looked like a monarchy. The tradition of rule-for-life and hereditary succession dates back to Henri Christophe in 1807–1820 and Faustin Soulouque in 1847–1859, but it can be found up to the recent past. As well as the many rulers of Haiti who have declared themselves presidents-for-life (at least five in the nineteenth century), Papa Doc Duvalier went a step further by trying to create a hereditary system, which might have lasted longer were it not for the lack of interest that his successor Baby Doc showed in politics. Against a background of the weakness of other institutions, the presidency has always been the strongest—or at least the most visible—of Haiti's political institutions, and the principle of a separation of powers has rarely been allowed to function in practice. The focus of Haitian politics lies firmly in the presidential palace rather than in the hallways and chambers of the National Assembly.

Political Violence

Haitians have had little real experience of democratic politics, but instead have had to live with a long and unhappy history of political violence. Whether this has come in the form of the tactics used by authoritarian leaders to hold on to power or in the form of the rebellions that have repeatedly been the source of political change, Haitians have come to expect that the bullet will always play a stronger role in politics than the ballot. Popular insurrections have often been at the heart of changes in political regime, most recently in the removal of Jean-Bertrand Aristide from power in 2004. Political violence persisted during the administration of the interim regime that followed Aristide, reaching a level during 2005 that raised questions about the viability of holding new elections.

Institutionalized Corruption

To a greater extent even than is true of Mexico and Nigeria, corruption has been institutionalized in Haiti, promoted by the ease with which those in power can use their position for personal and political gain. The problem is so great that, in its 2004 report, Transparency International ranked Haiti last in a list of 145 countries in its Corruption Perceptions Index. Spectacularly illustrating the dictum that absolute power corrupts absolutely, Haitian leaders have typically been willing to place their own enrichment before the welfare of the Haitian people or of the survival of the state. There were hopes that Jean-Bertrand Aristide might mark the beginning of a new way of doing political business in Haiti, but even he fell foul of the atmosphere of corruption, being unwilling to deal with corruption in the police force, criticize the activities of pro-government gangs, or support freedom of the press.

POLITICAL SYSTEM

Haiti became independent not long after the United States, was one of the first countries to abolish slavery, and might have become a model for democratic change in nonwhite societies. But its political system was never able to build any stability or consistency, it never developed substantial political institutions or predictable political processes, it never bred an efficient bureaucracy or police system, and throughout the nineteenth century it veered more toward authoritarianism than democracy. At the centennial celebrations in1904, President Rosalvo Bobo lamented his country's history of violence and instability, declaring that he was "tired … of our stupidities" and of "a century of slavery of Negro by Negro," urging Haitians to work hard to make sure that by the time of the bicentennial in 2004, there would be something to celebrate.[4] But there was little to celebrate in 2004, and in fact the bicentennial celebrations sparked yet another popular uprising against the government, and the final fall of the Aristide administration.

If Haiti has a political system as such, rather than a series of variations on a central theme of ongoing instability, then that system is both underdeveloped and marked more by unpredictability than by predictability. Its institutions exist more firmly on paper than in reality, and the daily life of most Haitians is affected more by the tribulations and uncertainties brought by poverty and violence than by any meaningful application of the letter of the constitution. On paper, Haiti is a presidential unitary republic with a dual executive, a bicameral national legislature, and an independent judiciary. In reality, it is whatever the incumbent leadership is able to impose or get away with.

THE CONSTITUTION

Not surprisingly for an unstable state such as Haiti, it has had a troubled constitutional history, with multiple constitutions adopted over the years, and none ever achieving any permanency. The first constitution was drawn up in 1805 under the administration of Jean-Jacques Dessalines. Another was drawn up in 1843 following the removal of Jean Pierre Boyer from office. Two more came in 1867 and 1874, and in 1918 a new one was drawn up by occupying U.S. government representatives. Papa Doc Duvalier drew up his own constitution in 1957 which he quickly ignored, replacing the bicameral legislature with a unicameral body, and then declaring himself president for life. His son also drew up his own constitution in 1983.

The current constitution was adopted in 1987, soon after Baby Doc's fall from power, in preparation for new elections. Approved in a public referendum, the new document drew heavily on the basic principles found in the U.S. and French constitutions.

It was progressive and democratic, declaring the intent to establish democracy in Haiti, guaranteeing basic human rights, and setting up an institutional system with a separation of powers. Reflecting the fragility of Haitian constitutions, the new constitution was suspended by a decree from President Henri Namphy within months of his taking office in a coup in 1988. It was only partly reinstated the following year by the administration of General Prosper Avril, and although it is still in place today, it has yet to develop roots or to have a substantial impact on the way political business is conducted in Haiti. The problem, argues Stotzky, is that "the Haitian people … have not internalized the significance and legitimacy of a constitutional system based on the rule of law." Instead, they have internalized "a belief in the overpowering importance of status and connections, thus crippling the transition to a constitutional democracy."[5]

THE EXECUTIVE: PRESIDENT AND PRIME MINISTER

Under the terms of the 1987 constitution Haiti has a dual executive, with a president elected for five-year terms and a prime minister appointed by the president with the support of the legislature, the National Assembly. To guard against executives holding on to power indefinitely, and even declaring themselves presidents-for-life (as have so many of their predecessors), the president is not allowed to hold successive terms in office. Thus Aristide had to step down in 1996, but ran again for election in 2000. Superficially, the president has many of the same powers as those of the president of the United States, but Haiti's political instability has meant that the terms of the 1987 constitution have barely had the opportunity to be put into effect, and of the ten people who held office between 1987 and 2005, six were there in a provisional capacity, running Haiti while plans were made to return to a constitutional presidency.

As with all authoritarian political systems, the formal powers of the president are less important to an understanding of Haitian politics than the personality of the officeholder. The job depends heavily on the personal networks the president has built, how he (all presidents have been men except Ertha Pascal-Trouillot, drafted from the Supreme Court as interim leader in 1990) uses those networks, and the kind of relations he builds with social groups such as rural peasants, the urban poor, students, and civic groups, as well—of course—as the army. Aristide was successful as long as he had their support, but once he lost it he was quick to lose control, and then power.

The president governs in cooperation with a prime minister, appointed from the National Assembly. The last prime minister formally appointed under the constitution was Yvon Neptune, who took office in March 2002 after being appointed by Jean-Bertrand Aristide. Shortly after the March 2004 overthrow of the government and Aristide's resignation, Neptune was assailed by a mob that tried to arrest him on charges of corruption. A few days later gunmen tried to break into his residence and were killed by U.S. Marines standing guard. The interim government of Boniface Alexandre replaced Neptune as interim prime minister with Gérard Latortue, and Neptune was banned from leaving the country in order that corruption charges

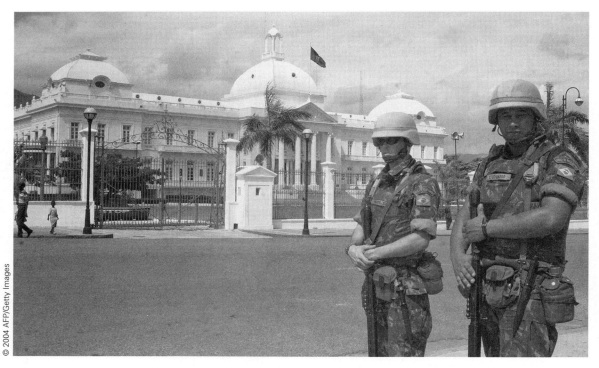

© 2004 AFP/Getty Images

UN peacekeepers stand guard outside the Presidential Palace in Port-au-Prince. With political power in Haiti focused so centrally in the executive, the palace is at the heart of Haitian politics, being both the seat of civilian governments and the target of popular opposition to civilian and military leaders.

against him could be investigated. Neptune turned himself in to the police and was held without charge, eliciting criticism from the UN mission in Haiti.

THE LEGISLATURE: NATIONAL ASSEMBLY

The legislative arena is only marginal to an understanding of power in Haiti, in part because so much control typically rests with the president, and in part because Haiti lacks the kind of permanent and significant political parties that would give its legislature the focus and direction needed to make it an important political actor. The Haitian legislature—the National Assembly—consists of two chambers.

Senate (*Sénat*)

Under normal circumstances, the Haitian Senate would have 27 members, who—on the U.S. model—would be elected for six-year renewable terms, with one-third coming up for reelection every two years. Part of the reason the 2000 elections were disputed was that Jean-Bertrand Aristide's Lavalas Family Party allegedly won 26 of those seats, a highly unlikely result under any circumstances. The Senate was

TABLE 10.2		

Modern Leaders of Haiti

Term	Name	Party or base of power
1941–1946	Élie Lescot	
1946	Colonel Franck Lavaud	Interim (military)
1946–1950	Dumarsais Estimé	
1950	General Franck Lavaud	Interim (military)
1950–1956	Colonel Paul Magloire	Military
1956–1957	Nemours Pierre-Louis	Provisional
1957	Franck Sylvain	Provisional
1957	Daniel Fignolé	Provisional
1957	General Antoine Kébreau	Provisional (military)
1957–1971	François Duvalier	National Unity Party
1971–1986	Jean-Claude Duvalier	National Progressive Party
1986–1988	Lt. General Henri Namphy	Provisional (military)
1988	Leslie Manigat	
1988	Lt. General Henri Namphy	Provisional (military)
1988–1990	Lt. General Prosper Avril	Provisional (military)
1990	Ertha Pascal-Trouillot	Provisional (judicial)
1991	Jean-Bertrand Aristide	Lavalas coalition
1991	Raoul Cédras	Military
1991–1992	Joseph Nérette	Provisional
1992–1993	Marc Bazin	Acting
1993–1996	Jean-Bertrand Arisitide	
1996–2001	René Préval	
2001–2004	Jean-Bertrand Aristide	Family Lavalas Party
2004–	Boniface Alexandre	Provisional (judicial)

suspended following the 2004 overthrow of the government, and new elections were scheduled for late 2005.

Chamber of Deputies (*Chambre des Députés*)

Again, under normal circumstances the Chamber of Deputies would have 83 members serving renewable four-year terms. Candidates from the Lavalas Family Party won 73 of those seats at the 2000 elections. New elections should have been held in

JEAN-BERTRAND ARISTIDE

© Reuters/CORBIS

Although he is currently in exile, making him the only subject of a "People in Politics" profile in this book who was not actually in power as the book went to press, Aristide's role in recent Haitian politics has been sufficiently important to make him worth closer study. Once enormously popular in Haiti, particularly among the poor, he now lives in exile after having been driven from power by an alliance of opposition parties and civic groups, his reputation as a democrat severely tarnished.

Born in Port-Salut, Haiti, in July 1953, Aristide studied to become a Catholic priest, and was ordained in 1983. Appointed to a parish in one of the slums of Port-au-Prince, he was affectionately known as "Titide" ("Tiny Aristide") and was criticized by the Duvalier regime for his membership in the radical wing of the Catholic Church. His opposition to the military governments that followed the Duvaliers earned him a reputation as a Caribbean version of Nelson Mandela, and he was recruited by a coalition of left-to-center political groups to run as their presidential candidate in the elections of 1990. During the campaign he described his followers as *Lavalas*, meaning "the flood" or "the torrent" in Creole. He won the election with more than two-thirds of the vote.

Aristide took office as Haiti's first democratically elected president in February 1991, but in

September was removed in a military coup and fled into exile in Venezuela. The collapse of his government helped spark a massive exodus of boat people looking to escape Haiti's poverty by moving to the United States and other neighboring countries. Aristide worked to build support for his presidency from abroad, and with international support building, the military regime of Marc Bazin stepped down, U.S. troops were sent in to keep the peace, and Aristide was returned to office in October 1994. His term ended in February 1996, and because the constitution does not allow consecutive terms, he left office (but only after a debate about whether he should be allowed to serve out the time that he had been in exile). He had left the priesthood in 1995 and was married in 1996.

The 1995 elections saw the victory of one of his allies, René Préval (who had been Aristide's prime minister in 1991), and February 1996 saw the first peaceful transition of power in the nearly 200-year history of Haiti. While in temporary retirement, Aristide created a new political party—the Family Lavalas—with which he ran in the November 2000 elections. These elections were marred by allegations of widespread fraud, and were boycotted by most opposition parties. Disillusionment with the new Aristide government led to as many as two attempted coups in 2001. The 2003 elections were postponed and Aristide began ruling by decree, leading to demands from opposition parties for his resignation. In December 2003 outrage was sparked when pro-Aristide gangs, with police support, broke into the Haitian national university and attacked students and administrators. Aristide condemned the incident, but also criticized the students. A general strike in mid-December closed all businesses in Haiti.

Political violence escalated in early 2004, and the beginning of the end came when a rebel group took control of two of Haiti's biggest cities, Gonaïves and Cap-Haïtien. With international criticism against his government mounting, Aristide left Haiti in February, flying into exile first in the Central African Republic, then in Jamaica, and then in South Africa.

2004 but were postponed. Like the Senate, the Chamber was suspended in 2004, and new elections were scheduled for late 2005.

THE JUDICIARY

Haiti has a Supreme Court (*Court de Cassation*) as well as a system of courts of appeal and other smaller courts. The Supreme Court consists of a president, a vice president, and ten judges appointed for ten-year terms. The president nominates judges on the basis of lists submitted by the Senate, municipal assemblies, and various other bodies; Supreme Court judges must be at least 30 years of age, and must have practiced law for ten years and held the position of judge or public attorney for at least seven years. But where courts in other troubled states have often been the only institutions that have continued to function when the executive and the legislature have been in trouble or have been suspended, the Haitian court system has been weak, corrupt, and inefficient. It has never had more than a marginal relationship with ordinary Haitians, it has been handicapped by outdated legal codes and poor facilities, and its authority has been undermined by a police force that is badly trained, riddled with corruption, often resorts to violence to achieve its goals, and has been unable (or unwilling) to deal with a generalized breakdown in law and order.

SUBNATIONAL GOVERNMENT

Haiti is a small country (about the size of Massachusetts) and is largely homogenous, with most of its people coming from the same ethnic background and speaking the same language, so—not surprisingly—it is a unitary state. It is divided (along the lines of the French model) into nine *departments* (or provinces), but these have only marginal significance in Haitian government; for many years, the army played a more important role in local politics than regional government institutions. The focus of power in Haiti is in the major cities such as Port-au-Prince, Gonaïves, and Cap-Haïtien, where the educated middle-class lives, which are the major recruiting grounds for political leaders, which are the major sources of government revenue, and which attract the bulk of government spending; recent estimates suggest that Port-au-Prince, with about one-fifth of Haiti's population, is the target of about two-thirds of government spending. The urban-rural divide is one of the distinctive features of life in Haiti, and the relative lack of political influence of the rural majority is both a cause and effect of the centralization of power in the presidential palace in Port-au-Prince.

THE MILITARY

The military has long played a core role in Haitian politics. So central was it to political change in the nineteenth and early twentieth century that one of the most common channels for bringing about a change in government was the so-called insurrection-*coup d'etat*. Unlike a conventional modern *coup*, which usually involves the

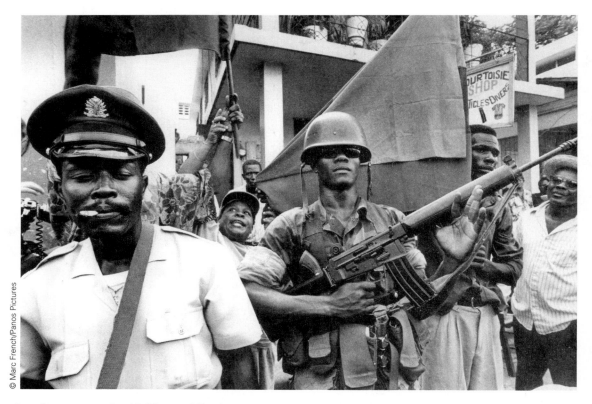

© Marc French/Panos Pictures

A policeman and a Haitian soldier keep a wary eye on a public rally in Port-au-Prince. The weaknesses of civilian government in Haiti have created an unfortunate and destabilizing tradition of power passing to noncivilian authorities, which have had a tradition of using force to maintain control and keep a grip on power.

forceful removal of a leader by the military, the insurrection-*coup d'etat* began with an uprising that called for broader public participation, which in turn sparked a *coup* led by a combination of the military and civilian groups.[6] Most of Haiti's leaders during this time were military men (most of them generals), as were most of the country's regional political leaders. Haiti's first civilian political leader was Michel Oreste, who became president in May 1913 but served less than eight months before being overthrown by the military.

The U.S. occupation transformed the army, turning it into a professional organization with a centralized bureaucracy, but this created future problems because the army developed a stronger and tighter identity than did civilian institutions. It was involved in several coups and changes of government in the 1940s and 1950s, finally being reigned in by the Duvalier regime. Concerns about the ongoing power of the army led to its formal disbanding in 1994, in the hope of limiting its impact on civilian politics. A little hope at least can be gleaned from the fact that no recent Haitian leader has been from the military.

ELECTIONS AND PARTIES

The focus of political activity in Haiti lies not with its people—except in a negative sense whenever popular movements arise to remove those in office—but within the small power elite that has governed the country for most of its history. For this reason, an understanding of the channels through which Haitians become involved in politics is only marginal to an understanding of how power is manipulated and structured. There are elections, but they are rarely honest or efficient. And while Haiti has a long history of political party activity, it has never seen the development of long-lived parties with significant roots in society. Party activity is at its greatest during presidential election seasons, when new parties emerge around the campaigns of the leading candidates; these parties have represented a wide range of issues, from Haitian nationalism to the interests of rural peasants, Haitian youth, communism, workers rights, and opposition to the incumbent government. But parties have rarely survived much longer than the terms in office of the leaders with whom they are associated (or whom they oppose), and so parties play only a peripheral role in Haitian politics.

POLICIES AND POLICYMAKING

Just as the policymaking process in Haiti lacks any consistency or sense of permanence, so policies have been unable to give Haiti the kind of direction or upward trajectory of development that it so desperately needs. Since ideas almost entirely emanate from the executive, and since the vast majority of Haitians are kept out of the political process, the direction that Haiti takes is a reflection of the views of a minority, many of whom have limited objectives that are driven less by the goal of building Haiti into a successful society than by promoting narrow personal agendas.

ECONOMIC POLICY

Haiti's economic situation is dire, its problems generated by a combination of mismanagement, corruption, limited natural resources, minimal investment, and natural handicaps. Already the poorest country in the Americas, and one of the poorest countries in the world, its economy has been shrinking in recent years. According to World Bank figures, it grew smaller by an average of 0.2 per cent annually during the 1980s and an average of 0.4 percent annually during the 1990s. Two-thirds of Haitians live in poverty, two-thirds depend on agriculture to make a living—mainly in the form of small-scale subsistence farming—and two-third have no formal jobs; these three groups almost entirely overlap, although there is also massive poverty in parts of Haiti's biggest cities.

Haiti is essentially an agricultural economy heavily reliant on exports of coffee, cocoa, mangoes, and other products whose prices have fallen on the international market because of overproduction. Attempts to build exports of clothing have been undermined by attempts to build a Central American free-trade bloc to which Haiti would be able to contribute very little. Only about 28 percent of its land is arable, limiting its prospects of developing its agricultural base. It might be able to improve its prospects if it was to invest more of its resources—and loans or aid from the international community—in infrastructure, but it has not. Barely 25 percent of its roads are paved, there is no passenger train service, only 4 of its 13 airports have paved runways, there is only limited telephone service in the rural areas, and only a small fraction of Haitians—perhaps 1 percent—have access to the Internet.

Its economic prospects are undermined by its mountainous terrain and its lack of navigable rivers, and by its location in the middle of the hurricane belt; not only must it wrestle with flooding, earthquakes, and occasional droughts, but it has made matters worse by environmental mismanagement. Much of its forest cover has been removed as land was cleared for agriculture and firewood—so much has gone that the frontier between Haiti and the Dominican Republic is immediately visible to anyone flying over the two countries; to the east there is still considerable forest cover, but to the west much of it is gone. The lack of trees to absorb rainwater worsens soil erosion and flooding.

The challenge of meeting the economic needs of Haitians has been made worse by its fast-growing population. With a growth rate of 1.8 percent, the population of Haiti between 1985 and 2005 grew from five million to eight million, putting additional pressure on an economic system that is already incapable of meeting basic demand. Like most poor countries, Haiti is heavily dependent on foreign aid, most of it coming from the United States, the European Union, and the World Bank. But endemic corruption has meant that much of that aid has been siphoned off by government officials intent on lining their own pockets. Not only have the poor not received much of that aid, but donors are wary about providing any more. Poverty and the absence of opportunity has fueled an exodus of Haitians to the United States and Canada, with the U.S. Coast Guard reporting that it has picked up more Haitian boat people in recent years than refugees from any other Caribbean nation.

Haiti's economic problems are reflected in the quality of life suffered by most Haitians: barely half the population is literate, more than half has no access to clean water or sanitation, about half of all Haitians are undernourished, life expectancy lingers at just 49 years, most Haitians have no access to basic healthcare—which means that diseases such as tuberculosis are spreading—and Haiti has the highest incidence of HIV/AIDS in the Americas: nearly one in 20 Haitians is infected (see Critical Issues).

Tourism has become a major money-earner for neighboring Dominican Republic, and could be a potential savior of the Haitian economy, but Haiti has neither the infrastructure nor the necessary record on public safety to sustain a tourist trade. Problems with public safety have also scared off foreign industries that might be a source of investment in Haiti, creating jobs and investing in badly needed infrastructure.

Is there much—or even any—any good economic news for Haiti? Not really. It would take a substantial and systemic change of approach, supported by aid from rich countries, to bring about a change in its economic prospects. It would take a combination of a substantial investment in infrastructure, enduring political stability, and the development of an efficient and effective bureaucracy, judiciary, and police

CRITICAL ISSUES

HAITI AND AIDS

As if Haiti's political and economic challenges were not enough, the country is also afflicted with a widespread HIV/AIDS problem; it is the leading cause of death among Haitians, killing about 30,000 people per year and leaving tens of thousands of children orphaned. And yet there is a sliver of hope to be salvaged from the problem, because Haiti has a relatively successful record in dealing with the problem.

Haiti was one of the first countries to be severely affected by AIDS because of its popularity as a destination for sex tourism in the 1970s; the earliest reported case of HIV infection in Haiti came in 1978. So widespread had the affliction become that when it first captured international news headlines in the 1980s, it was infamously associated with the Four Hs: hemophiliacs, homosexuals, heroin addicts, and Haiti. The Haitian Red Cross did not begin screening the blood supply for infection until 1986, and by 1993 about 6 percent of the adult population was thought to be infected, the highest rate outside Africa. Haitians had also been implicated in the spread of the

disease to the United States and to other liberal democracies (although medical professionals in Haiti argue that it was actually tourists coming to Haiti who brought it with them). Extreme poverty and the lack of access to health clinics made the problem worse, and it has been compounded by a widespread belief in the rural areas that voodoo or magic is involved in the spread of the disease—this makes it difficult to convince people that it is spread by human contact, and to encourage them to seek aid from medical professionals rather than from voodoo priests.[7]

But recent research suggests that the number of HIV/AIDS cases may have been cut to 3 percent since the mid-1990s thanks to public education, the wider use of condoms, strong political support, and greater access to anti-retroviral drugs.[8] The successful delivery of AIDS treatment to so many of Haiti's poorest citizens, in locations where there is often no reliable electricity supply nor access to adequate testing conditions, is also seen as a sign of hope of what could be achieved in other poor countries.

force to turn Haiti around, and on the record of the last 200 years, none of this seems likely to happen any time soon.

FOREIGN POLICY

Like all poor countries, Haiti is an introspective society with very little in the way of foreign policy interests beyond the actual or potential role played by foreign powers—mainly the United States—in its internal politics, or by the United Nations in helping both keep the peace and rebuild the Haitian economy. There has been a long history of actual or threatened U.S. interventions in Haitian politics, the most substantial being the 18-year semi-occupation between 1915 and 1932. Most recently, the United States spearheaded the creation of a 31-country Multinational Force (MNF) which landed in Haiti in 1994 to restore order following the military coup. The United States was again the lead participant in the 2004 intervention designed to restore order following the removal from power of Jean-Bertrand Aristide.

HAITIAN POLITICS IN TRANSITION

It is difficult to find much in the Haitian experience that offers hope for its people. It has all the core features of a marginal country: ongoing political instability, an unstable state system, economic stagnation, a low quality of life, and existence on the margins of viability. It may entirely have failed as an exercise in state-building, and it is far from succeeding in developing the core requirements of a political system that works. While explanations of the difficulties faced by marginal countries in other parts of the world often point to the disjunctions caused by colonialism, Haiti has been independent for more than 200 years. Of course, those who support external explanations for the problems of marginal countries can point to more recent noncolonial interventions in Haiti, such as the U.S. occupation and more recent military interventions and economic influences, but this line of reasoning will only go so far. Haiti has largely failed itself. Haitians have not been able to organize or build a functioning civil society, making it relatively easy for a power elite to emerge and sustain itself over a long period of time. As much as anything, the ability of Haiti to address and deal with its problems must come from within, but the kind of changes needed to achieve the transition to success are not likely to happen any time soon.

KEY TERMS

tonton macoutes   voodoo

KEY PEOPLE

Jean-Bertrand Aristide   François "Papa   Jean-Claude "Baby Doc"
                                Doc" Duvalier   Duvalier

STUDY QUESTIONS

1. What are the chief causes of Haiti's political and economic problems?
2. Is Haiti its own worst enemy?
3. Are the "stupidities" that Rosalvo Bobo lamented in 1904 still present in Haiti, and—if so—what are they?
4. Where does the focus of power lie in Haiti?
5. Should the international community step back and allow Haiti to resolve its own problems, no matter what the cost?

HAITI ONLINE

Another sign of the poverty of a country like Haiti is its poor connections to the Internet. Limited news and information about Haiti (much of it in French) can be found on the Web site of the Haitian embassy in Washington DC (www.haiti.org). Otherwise, almost all Web-based information about Haiti can be found only on the sites of foreign governments (such as the CIA World Factbook), interest groups (such as the National Coalition for Human Rights at www.nchr.org, or the Haiti Action Committee at www.haitiaction.net), or media sources.

FURTHER READING

Farmer, Paul, *The Uses of Haiti*, 3rd Ed. (New York: Common Courage Press, 2005). A controversial indictment of U.S. policy in Haiti, written by a medical doctor with many years of experience working with the rural poor in Haiti.

Fatton, Roger, *Haiti's Predatory Republic: The Unending Transition to Democracy* (Boulder, CO: Lynne Rienner, 2002). A study of Haitian politics between 1986 and 2001, which argues that the absence of strong political institutions has led to a power vacuum, placing the achievement of democracy frustratingly beyond reach.

Greene, Graham, *The Comedians* (London and New York: Penguin, 1966). A classic modern novel that gives some insight into the quality of life in Haiti under Papa Doc Duvalier and the *tonton macoutes*.

Stotzky, Irwin P., *Silencing the Guns in Haiti: The Promise of Deliberative Democracy* (Chicago: University of Chicago Press, 1997). An analysis of the problems facing Haiti in the wake of the restoration to power of Jean-Bertrand Aristide. Although dated, it has useful chapters on the history and politics of Haiti.

COMPARATIVE EXERCISE

JUDICIARIES

One of the defining features of a successful and stable political system is a belief in the rule of law: the idea that the distribution of power is determined and limited by a system of laws to which all citizens are equally subject. An effective legal system has at least three requirements: lawmaking institutions that can develop laws that respond to the needs of the majority while protecting the minority (and allow both groups adequate input into the lawmaking process); the effective implementation of those laws by an efficient bureaucracy and police force; and the existence of judiciaries that can be arbiters over the lawmaking process, ensuring that the actions of government, individuals, corporations, and other bodies meet the letter of the law.

The main job of a judiciary (also known as a judicature) is to adjudicate legal disputes and interpret the meaning of laws. Members of a judiciary are not expected to make law—that responsibility lies with legislatures—but only to issue judgments on laws in relation to the constitution. They are also expected to follow rather than lead, in the sense that they are not expected to significantly change the meaning of the law. And finally, they are expected to be independent, and to be protected from any kind of external pressures or influences. But the ideal of being objective and independent is difficult to achieve—judges come to the job with their own sets of values and their own ideologies, and these values color how judges see the world and how they interpret the law. This in turn will make them dependent, in the sense that they are more likely to be sympathetic to views and problems that coincide with their own values.

Every country has a judiciary, although their effectiveness can vary. Two extremes are posed by the United States and Haiti. In the former, politics is very much law-based (some would say that the role of law in the political process has gone too far, because Americans are too ready to look to the legal

system to resolve disputes, rather than trying to resolve them outside the courts.). The United States has a judicial structure that has become a critical part of government, and—most of the time—is both efficient and respected. Courts play a critical role in interpreting the constitutionality of the actions of governments and individuals, whether at the federal level or the state level. By contrast, Haiti's judiciary is inefficient and ineffective. Unlike Zimbabwe, where the courts have been able to protect their independence in the face of the abuses of power by the Mugabe regime, Haitian courts have been weak and inefficient, and have added to the problems of the country rather than helping address them.

The terms of office of judges can have a significant impact on how the courts function, and on their relationship to the political system.

- **Unlimited terms.** Judges in the U.S., Belgian, Danish, Dutch, Israeli, Portuguese, and Russian constitutional courts have lifetime appointments, and can only be removed for serious dereliction of duty. Life terms help give them independence—they do not face the problem of being threatened with nonrenewal for not agreeing with the incumbent administration—provide continuity and stability, and ensure that the accumulated abilities and knowledge of judges can be brought to bear on the judicial system. But life terms also run the danger of creating courts that are increasingly out of touch with political opinion, and of providing few opportunities to inject new thinking and values into the work of courts.

- **Limited terms.** Judges in the European Court of Justice serve ten-year renewable terms, while Indian judges must retire at 65, and Brazilian judges at 70. This creates advantages and disadvantages that are opposite to those of lifetime appointments. Term limits open the door to greater political manipulation, raise the danger of too many changes in the direction of judicial thinking, and can result in experienced judges being replaced too quickly by new judges. But they also ensure that fresh thinking is regularly injected into the work of courts, helping them better keep up with the needs of society.

The work of courts can also be impacted by the different ways in which judges become members (whether it is by election or by appointment), and which institutions are involved in the process. For example, U.S., Argentinean, Mexican, and Russian judges are nominated by the president and confirmed by the upper chamber of the legislature. France and Poland turn this around, giving the president the power of confirmation, choosing from a list nominated by a judicial council. Italy has 15 judges, of whom five are appointed by the president, five by the legislature, and five by lower courts. Japanese judges are appointed by the legislature, with the chief justice appointed by the emperor. In most constitutional monarchies, judges are appointed by the king or the queen, which gives those judges less political significance than the appointments made by the president of the United States. Meanwhile, German judges are elected by the German legislature, with half being decided by the upper house and half by the lower house.

A critical question about judiciaries is whether or not they can be independent and make judgments that are not affected by political considerations. In talking about the prospects of appointments to the U.S. Supreme Court in 2005, George W. Bush often talked about the importance of having judges who would respect the rule of law and not "legislate from the bench." But how can we be sure that judges are not injecting personal values and considerations into their decisions? If the debate that takes place over Supreme Court justices is any indication, then most Americans do not believe that objectivity is possible.

CONCLUSIONS

There is nothing predictable about life except change, but perhaps no generation has seen such all-encompassing changes in its time as ours has. Advances in science, technology, and communications have dramatically redefined our relationships with others; we can watch unfolding events from all over the world live on 24-hour TV news stations; we can travel to another continent—and even to the other side of the earth—in a matter of hours; political events in one part of the world can have immediate implications in another; financial markets are affected around the clock by developments all over the world; and the Internet has turned the way we do business on its head and given us instant access to a huge new storehouse of information that once took days or even weeks to collect, assuming we could find it at all.

In political, economic, and social terms, many of the changes have been positive. Consider the following:

- The collapse of Soviet-style communism and the spread of democratic, freemarket ideas in Russia and its former Eastern European satellites
- The economic and political integration of Europe, which has now enjoyed its longest spell of peace since medieval times, and has emerged as a new economic and political superpower
- The expansion of free-market principles in China and India, potentially the consumer giants and superpowers of the future
- The emergence of newly industrializing countries with new political stability and economic confidence
- The expansion of democracy in Latin America
- The end of nearly five decades of apartheid in South Africa, 16 years of military rule in Nigeria, and a generation of political violence in Northern Ireland

Unfortunately, there are just as many—if not more—examples of new and ongoing problems:

- Conflicts in many parts of the world—including Israel/Palestine, Kashmir, and many parts of Africa—that almost seem to defy resolution
- An almost perpetual cycle of poverty and instability that grips much of sub-Saharan Africa, to which has been added the worsening specter of HIV and AIDS
- Religious and ethnic strife in India, Nigeria, the Balkans, and many other parts of the world
- Global and regional environmental problems caused by a combination of the thoughtless overconsumption of wealthy states and the desperate struggle for existence of poor states
- A resurgence of nationalism in parts of Eastern Europe, Asia, and Africa
- The persistence of authoritarian governments in Africa and Latin America

Most troubling of all at the beginning of the new century is the resurrection of the age-old misunderstandings between Islam and the West. The attacks of September 11, 2001, were just the most deadly and violent of a string of terrorist attacks in the United States, Western Europe, East Africa, Southeast Asia, and the Middle East that have represented a revival of an old struggle, using old methods but at a greatly heightened level. The uneasy peace that prevailed during the cold war was always ultimately protected by the certainty of mutually assured destruction: If one side launched its weapons on the other, the other would respond in kind—and both sides could be sure that the costs of war would greatly outweigh the benefits. Today we live in a world where states are terrorized by people and groups that are happy to die for their cause, are difficult to identify and pin down, and whose operations cannot easily be related to national boundaries.

The importance of understanding all these political and economic changes remains. When events on another continent can have a direct and almost immediate impact on our own lives, we need to understand those events. Unfortunately, too many of us live in splendid isolation and allow our interests to reach little further than our homes, our families, and our neighborhoods. Many Americans watch changes unfolding in Iraq, Russia, the Koreas, the Balkans, South Africa, Israel, Kashmir, and Mexico without the ability to put them in perspective, or even to understand their causes or significance. Sometimes they cannot even find the countries involved on a map.

The United States is a large, rich, powerful, generous, dynamic, and well-endowed country that has become used to leading rather than following. However, one of the problems with power is that it can breed arrogance and complacency. History has shown, time after time, that great powers have assumed they are the keepers of their own destinies, only to find that the world has changed around them more quickly than they realized. The challenges to the global role of the United States reveal themselves in many ways. They can be seen in the way that traditional American export markets are being undercut by cheaper and often better-manufactured goods from East Asia. They can be seen in the way that jobs are being lost to economic competition and cheaper labor. They can be seen in the way that the best military technology in the world is not always enough to deal with an enemy that may be less well-equipped but that may be fighting for its independence or its survival.

Closer to home, challenges to the power of the United States are posed by the persistence of poverty, violence, and discrimination; by falling SAT scores; by reduced opportunities; by a growing gap between the rich and the poor; by dulled ambition; and by political divisions. The United States may have the best medical technology in the world, but many people lack health insurance and are denied the benefits of that technology. The United States may have some of the most innovative entrepreneurs in the world, but many Americans are still denied access to the opportunities they create. The United States may have some of the best colleges and universities in the world, but thousands of Americans can do little more than read a road sign. Meanwhile, ethnic minorities suffer low life expectancy, poor education, high murder rates, and high rates of illiteracy.

These two sets of developments—abroad and at home—are intimately linked. For nearly two generations, the place of the United States in the world was determined by cold war thinking. Americans were raised to think of global relations as a struggle between the forces of capitalism and socialism, or good and evil, and to think of the United States as the leader in the Western response to the Soviet challenge. But the world is no longer quite so neatly predictable (assuming it ever was), and the military tensions of the cold war have been replaced by an increasingly complex web of political, economic, and social tensions, spearheaded by the threat of terrorism.

You have just finished reading a book designed to introduce you to the variety of political systems in the world, and—by comparing their political structures, values, and processes—to illustrate the differences and similarities among political systems with a view to shedding light on the changes the world is undergoing. There are 188 independent countries in the world, and although we have looked at just ten of them, the examples used in this book were picked because they underline several themes that comparativists have been able to identify through their study of different societies:

- **All societies are interrelated.** The only way that each of us as individuals can effectively relate to our social environment is to understand how we fit in and what drives others. The same is true of countries. Domestic policy of every kind in every country is influenced by outside political, economic, and social forces, and we cannot develop effective policies without understanding those forces. We saw the impact of colonialism on Africa, Asia, and Latin America, and—more recently— we have seen how even the world's richest countries have come to be affected by developments from some unexpected quarters.

- **Political, economic, and social issues are intimately interlinked.** Systems of government are the product of the societies in which they function, and no study of those systems would be complete without an understanding of the links between government, markets, and people. We saw how political culture has brought significant differences to the expectations of government in liberal democracies such as the United States, Britain, and Japan, and how it resulted in different interpretations of Marxism-Leninism in the USSR and China.

- **The success of a system of government depends on the extent to which it meets the needs of its citizens.** We saw how political systems that fail to take root and respond to the changing needs of their people (such as the USSR and former colonies such as Nigeria) will ultimately collapse under the weight of their internal contradictions. We saw that the United States, Britain and Japan enjoy high levels of legitimacy, while Russia, China, Mexico, and India struggle to find a workable formula, Nigeria and Egypt still have large gaps between the goals of government and the needs of the people, and Haiti has not yet found a formula at all.

- **No political system is perfect, and none is necessarily better than any other.** Each meets different needs in different ways and with different levels of efficiency. Americans often talk about the United States as the world's brightest beacon of liberty and democracy; Britons assume that their political system has endured because it was built on more solid foundations than those of their European neighbors; Westerners look on the chaos of politics in countries like Nigeria, Egypt, and Haiti with horror and wonder why liberal democracy does not take root in those societies. But the way things are done in liberal democracies is not necessarily the way they are done or even should be done in other political systems. The competitive multiparty democracy used by liberal democracies, for example, may not be the best option for societies that put a premium on consensus.

- **Nothing is predictable about politics except its unpredictability.** Political scientists have tried for decades to understand human society and to draw up predictive rules about politics, but they have been tripped up by the idiosyncrasies of human relationships. The environment in which politics takes place constantly changes, making it difficult to predict the outcome of political change. Imagine, for example, political science professors in 1970 making forecasts about the world in 2005. Not many would have foreseen the reunification of Germany, the emergence of the European Union, the rise of international terrorism, or economic liberalization in China and India.

- **Social divisions are a fact of life in virtually every political system.** Whether they are based on class, ethnicity, religion, gender, region, or wealth, these divisions play a major role in determining how well a political system meets the needs of its citizens. We saw how politics in countries such as India and Nigeria is driven in large part by the need to address social conflict, but even relatively stable democracies such as the United States and Britain are faced with resolving internal ethnic, religious, and economic divisions.

Opinion is divided on what the future holds. Optimists believe that we are headed toward global democracy and that one government after another is improving its ability to respond to the needs of its citizens. They argue that peace has broken out in many nations that have a tradition of instability and war (like those of Europe) and that economic prosperity and political stability are coming to other nations that were once destabilized by colonialism (like those in Southeast Asia).

Pessimists point to the regional and local wars that continue to disrupt life in many parts of the world; at the continued conflicts caused by nationalism; at questions about the transition to democracy in Russia, Eastern Europe, and other parts of the world; at the social problems that trouble societies on every continent; at the widespread poverty in sub-Saharan Africa and Latin America; at global population growth and environmental problems; and at the repeated inability of political leaders to meet the needs of all their citizens. But wherever we are headed, comparative politics can give us insight into the paths we are taking and perhaps help us make decisions that will make the world a better, safer, and more fulfilling place in which to live.

GLOSSARY

Many of the terms used in political science have different meanings, either because they have been applied differently over time or because they have been regularly misused. This glossary contains brief definitions of key terms and concepts used in the text, defined according to the way they are generally applied today.

absolute government A system in which there is no limit to what government may do.

anarchy Literally, an absence of government. Although the term implies chaos, anarchism is actually a political theory based on the arguments that society does not need government and that no government is legitimate unless it is based entirely upon the consent of the governed.

autocracy Self-rule, or rule by one person who usually exercises power without reference to anyone else. Compare with *monarchy*.

bourgeoisie Literally "town-dwellers" (from the French). A term appropriated by Karl Marx to describe the class of property owners created by the capitalist system. Coincides roughly with today's middle or upper-middle classes. Compare with *proletariat*.

bureaucracy A collective term for people employed directly by a government to implement policy and to carry out the daily administration of a society.

cabinet The group of heads of government departments and senior administrators who act collectively as the government in parliamentary systems of government (such as Britain or Japan) or as administrators and advisors to the executive in presidential systems (such as Mexico or the United States). Also sometimes known as a council of ministers.

capitalism An economic system dominated by private ownership of services, industry, and agriculture, where production and distribution are driven by the profit motive, prices are set by supply and demand, and employees sell their labor for wages.

civil liberties The rights that protect individuals from the arbitrary actions of government. They include freedom of speech, movement, association, and religion.

civil rights The rights that protect individuals from exploitation or harm by other individuals. They include the right not to be discriminated against on the basis of being a member of a group (for example, gender, race, age, religion, or sexual orientation).

cold war The war of words, ideas, ideologies, and threats that took place between the Western bloc (the United States, Canada, and Western Europe) and the Soviet-Chinese bloc between 1945 and 1990. The war involved few direct military conflicts between the two sides, but many conflicts between their client states.

collective responsibility An understanding that all decisions made by a group are made collectively and that all members must stand or fall by those decisions. It applies, for example, to the cabinet in Westminster-style government.

colonialism   The theory and practice by which citizens of one territory or political unit have a physical presence in another territory, and—while sustaining themselves in the new territory—show allegiance to and retain the language and customs of the mother territory.

communism   A social, economic, and political system in which power and property are held in common, all decisions are made communally, and all members of the system are equal in the eyes of the law.

comparative politics   One of the major branches of the academic study of politics. It involves the systematic study of the differences and similarities between and among political systems, with the goal of understanding those systems and of making generalizations and drawing up rules about politics.

consensus   A decision-making system in which all opinions converge to reach a common conclusion with which everyone can agree.

conservatism   A political ideology that sprang from a desire to maintain or conserve the status quo, but has gone on to include a belief in "traditional" customs and values, a limited economic role for government, self-reliance, and the exercise of power through a strong legal system.

constitution   A set of rules (usually written in a single document) outlining the structure, operating rules, and powers of a government; defining the responsibilities of government; and stating the relative rights of the governors and the governed.

corporatism   A political system based on corporate bodies or associations playing an intermediary role between their members and the state. This was a key feature of Mussolini's Italy and Franco's Spain, and elements remain today in countries such as Mexico.

coup d'etat   Literally "blow against the state" (from the French). A term describing the sudden and forcible overthrow of a government, usually by the military or other armed opponents.

cult of personality   A program through which a leader perpetuates his power by ensuring that he is omnipresent in the consciousness of his subjects and by ensuring that he is strongly associated in their minds with positive images of the state.

culture   A sociological or anthropological term referring collectively to the customs, habits, beliefs, norms, and values of a group of people.

democracy   Literally "government by the people as a whole" (from the Greek). An immensely complicated concept generally understood to mean a political system in which government is based on a mandate from the people and in which power is constitutionally limited, and is given to—or taken from—leaders by those they lead. What democracy means in practice is debatable.

democratic centralism   A Leninist concept describing a society governed by a single, strictly hierarchical party operating on democratic principles, with free political discussion and free elections, but only within the party. Each level of the party is elected by the level below and is accountable to that lower level.

dependency   A theory describing a relationship in which a former colony has achieved political independence but is still economically dependent on the Western capitalist powers.

dictatorship   A system of government in which all political power is held by one person or group of people who is/are accountable to no other person or group and who is/are able to use that power to direct and govern society and compel obedience.

divine right   The belief in medieval Europe that monarchs or sovereigns ruled by the consent of God and might even be gods. The sovereign, answerable only to God, rules without a contract or the common consent of the people.

dual executive   A political system in which executive power is shared between an elected president and a prime minister appointed out of the legislature. Used in Russia, France, Poland, Egypt, and Haiti, among others.

ethnocentrism   A view of the world based on a belief in the cultural or ethnic superiority of the observer and of the culture or race to which he or she belongs.

executive   The element of government responsible for implementing policy and executing laws passed by the legislature (for example, the presidency of the United States).

failed states   Countries where civil violence and poverty are so extreme that government can no longer function, and the basic needs of people are no longer met.

fascism   A political ideology characterized by a belief in strong, centralized leadership, a cult of personality, nationalism, collective organization, social discipline, and hostility to democracy (all features of Nazi Germany or Italy under Mussolini). "Fascist" is now widely used as a derogatory term to describe anyone supposedly hostile to liberal or democratic ideas.

federalism   An administrative system in which local units of government have powers independent of those of the national government and in which authority is divided between the two.

feudalism   A hierarchical political, social, and economic system (usually associated with medieval Europe or Asia) in which most people own little or nothing and are subservient to an aristocracy that owns most of the land (and has most of the political power) and grants access to land in return for service (usually military).

free trade   An arrangement in which there is a free flow of goods and services between two or more trading partners, and trade is not subject to tariffs, quotas, or any other limits.

glasnost   Literally "openness" (from the Russian). A term used to describe Soviet President Mikhail Gorbachev's policy of encouraging more open debate about the problems facing the USSR and of showing a greater willingness to acknowledge the problems of the Soviet government and economy.

globalization   The process by which changes in international trade, cultural exchange, transport, communication, and political links have created a global society that is no longer limited or constrained by national frontiers.

government   The exercise of influence over a group of people, either through law or coercion. Also used (as a noun) to describe the body that exercises that control.

gross domestic product   The basic measure of economic output of a country, expressed as the sum value of the final goods and services produced within the borders of a country.

gross national product   The sum value of the final goods and services produced by a country, both domestically and through investments abroad.

head of government   The individual who directs the government of a country and in whom executive power is normally vested. In liberal democracies, this would be a partisan politician elected to that position for a fixed term.

head of state   The individual who symbolically represents the state and all the citizens of that state, irrespective of their backgrounds and beliefs. This is usually a nonexecutive, figurehead position. In the United States, Mexico, and Egypt, the president is both head of state and head of government; in Britain, the prime minister is head of government and the monarch is head of state.

human rights   Rights that are determined by mutual agreement to belong to all humans, whether or not the rights are protected by law. Examples include freedom from hunger, want, persecution, and discrimination.

ideology   A systematic, consistent, and (ideally) coherent set of political beliefs, ideas, and values. For examples, see *conservatism, fascism,* and *liberalism.*

imperialism   The extension of power (political, economic, social, or even cultural) through superior force.

industry   Any economic activity that involves the transformation of raw materials, such as minerals and wood, into tangible and usable products.

interest group   A group of people who use their collective power to influence public policy, opinion, or behavior toward a particular end.

Islam   The political, social, and economic values and goals associated with adherents to Islamic religious beliefs. Also describes the worldwide community of Muslims.

Islamism   The term preferred by some Muslims to describe their belief in a return to the basic ideas of Islam, including those relating to government and society.

judiciary   The collective body of judges within a legal system. Their powers vary from one system to another, but they are commonly involved in interpreting and applying constitutional law.

legislature   The part of government concerned with making law, that is, introducing, discussing, and voting on new laws. Usually an assembly of elected officials (such as Congress in the United States, the Diet in Japan, and the Federal Assembly in Russia).

Leninism   An ideology associated with Lenin's revolutionary principles, which included the establishment of a vanguard party, the promotion of democratic centralism, and worldwide revolutionary activity aimed at the overthrow of capitalist imperialism.

less developed country   A country at an early stage of political and economic development, whose recent history may have been disrupted by colonialism and that has yet to develop consistent political institutions or to build economic or social stability.

liberal democracy   A political system built around a belief in representative and limited government, regular and competitive elections, the rule of law, multiple channels for political participation, limited state control over the economy, and the protection of civil rights and liberties.

liberalism   A political philosophy based on a belief in limited government, the freedom of the individual, toleration in matters of morality and religion, and the redistribution of resources to the equal benefit of all in a society.

limited government   A form of government in which sovereign power is limited by law. The opposite of *absolute government.*

Maoism   Mao's interpretation of communism, adapted to fit rural societies such as China in the 1950s. Includes a rejection of elitism, hierarchy, and technical expertise and a stress on communalism, small-scale organization, and social experimentation.

marginal country   A country existing on the margins of viability, with a weak system of government (bordering on none), a poor record on human rights, an underdeveloped economy, poor infrastructure, low levels of human development, internal conflicts, and occasionally a complete breakdown in civil order. See also *failed states.*

martial law   The imposition of military rule over a civilian population. Sometimes imposed during a state of emergency or during military occupation of a foreign territory.

Marxism   The philosophy of Karl Marx, who argued that the structure and inequalities of industrialized societies could be explained by understanding the tensions arising out of class struggle, which would ultimately lead to the overthrow of capitalist society.

Marxism-Leninism   A combination of the economic theories of Marx and the revolutionary methods described by Lenin, the latter being used to bring about the end of the political and social inequalities resulting from *capitalism.*

modernization   The process by which traditional societies are transformed by scientific, technological, social, economic, and political change. Usually implies a transition toward the model provided by Western liberal democracies.

monarchy   Literally "rule by one," but generally applied to an institution characterized by nobility, aristocracy, and heredity. Most monarchs are heads of state (and occasionally even of government), inherit their position from a parent, and hold power for life or until they voluntarily renounce that power. Their power is usually constitutionally limited.

nation   A cultural concept describing a group of people sharing a common cultural heritage, language, customs, and traditions, and usually inhabiting a fixed territory.

nation-state   A state organized for the government of a nation. In practice, most nation-states consist of a single state system bringing together two or more nations.

nationalism   The promotion of ideas associated with the nation, or putting national values and interests above those of the wider community. May spill over into aggressive behavior toward anything considered a threat to the identity of a national community.

newly industrializing country   A country that has undergone recent, relatively rapid, and sustained economic growth, largely as a consequence of the development of manufacturing and exports. This economic growth is underpinned by—and promotes—political stability.

nonalignment A philosophy supported by the leaders of a number of newly independent African and Asian countries in the 1950s, including the promotion of mutual solidarity, a refusal to take sides in the cold war, and a reduction of dependence on the superpowers.

oligarchy Literally "rule by a few" (from the Greek). A political system in which all real power is held by a group. Could be used to describe the relationship between administrators and students in a university.

orientalism The tendency of Westerners to use misleading stereotypes and generalizations in describing the East (or the Orient).

parliament The legislative body in the Westminster system of government (from the French word *parler*, to talk). Normally consisting of elected members, its main function is to debate and vote on proposals for new laws.

parliamentary system A political system, based on the Westminster model, in which supreme legal authority is vested in parliament, of which all elected government officials are members. Distinct from the separation of powers used in the U.S. system of government.

patrimonialism A political system based on a leader as a father figure who has limited accountability to his people but who claims to understand their interests and needs. Found in many Middle Eastern societies and African tribal societies.

perestroika Literally "restructuring" (from the Russian). The policy instituted by Mikhail Gorbachev of restructuring the Soviet Union's political and economic system to reduce the control of central government and promote efficiency.

personalism A system of government in which power revolves around personal links between the rulers and the ruled. Occasionally also known as cronyism.

pluralism A belief in the distribution of power among several institutions and in allowing government to be influenced by competition among competing groups, systems of values, and sets of demands.

plurality Term used to describe the outcome of an election in which the candidate with the most votes wins, without having a majority.

police state A state in which power is distributed and stability maintained by force, usually through the police. Commonly involves the use of secrecy and the granting to the police of almost unlimited powers over the lives of citizens.

political culture The political norms and values of a society. Political culture helps explain what citizens and leaders regard as acceptable or unacceptable behavior.

political party A group of like-minded individuals formed to put forward a set of ideas and objectives concerning government and to compete for power in open elections.

political science The systematic study of politics, with the goal of drawing up rules about government, political culture, representation, participation, and public policy.

politics The process by which individuals compete for power and resources and by which competing interests are reconciled. Sometimes described as the process that determines who gets what, when, and how.

polity A politically organized society, or the structure and form of government in that society.

polycentrism   The division of a political organization into competing centers of power. Usually applied to the many competing interpretations of communism and to indicate the emergence of competing communist parties in different countries.

postindustrial society   A society that has undergone agricultural and industrial revolutions and where most economic activity is based on the provision of services (such as retailing, financial services, transport, and information).

power   The ability to have another person or group act in accordance with your wishes. Power comes in many forms, including political, social, economic, military, personal, psychological, ideological, legal, moral, and inspirational.

privatization   The process by which government-owned businesses, industries, and services are sold to private owners and/or shareholders.

proletariat   A term associated with Marxism, describing the class of workers in a capitalist industrial society who have little or nothing to sell other than their labor and so have little or no political or economic power.

proportional representation   An electoral system in which political parties win seats in a legislature in direct proportion to their share of the popular vote. Used in a number of European countries, such as Italy and Sweden. Contrast with the *winner-take-all* or *plurality* system.

public policy   The deliberate actions and inactions of governments and elected officials: whatever they do (or do not do) to govern or change society. The concept usually assumes a set of logically planned objectives, but it is often driven by inspiration and opportunism and characterized by incremental change and muddling through.

purchasing power parity   A different method of calculating the GDP or GNP of a country, by which the total is expressed not in absolute terms but according to the purchasing power of the national currency.

republic   Literally "the public thing" (from the Latin). A political system in which all members of the government are elected (as opposed to a monarchy, where at least one is not).

revolution   Political, economic, or social change that represents a marked break with what came before. It may happen suddenly and be accompanied by violence (as with the American, French, and Russian revolutions), or may take longer and be achieved through changes in law or policy (as with the Thatcher and Gorbachev revolutions).

rule of law   A system of government in which the distribution of power is determined and limited—and conflicts resolved—according to a mutually agreed-upon body of laws, to which every citizen is equally subject.

services   Any economic activity that does not result in the production of a physical commodity, but rather in the provision of an intangible service (such as retailing, banking, transport, and communication).

single-member districts   Legislative districts represented by a single person in a local or national legislature (as opposed to multimember districts, which are represented by more than one person).

social democracy   A political and economic ideology seeking social change and the redistribution of wealth and political power through democratic rather than radical means. A less radical form of *socialism.*

socialism   A political and economic ideology based on a redistribution of wealth, political power, and social services; the promotion of social and economic equality; and the elimination of social control (notably through ownership of property).

sovereignty   An attribute possessed by a person or institution, giving them power over a particular constituency. In the United States, sovereignty is shared by the three major arms of government. In parliamentary systems, sovereignty rests largely with the legislature. All nation-states have sovereignty over the lands within their borders (provided they are recognized in international law).

Stalinism   The political, economic, and social values, methods, and policies associated with the administration of Joseph Stalin in the USSR. These included centralized economic planning, the systematic elimination of all opposition, a cult of personality, a police state, and mass terror and propaganda. Used to describe North Korea today.

state   One of the most hotly debated concepts in political science. Generally connotes a community of individuals living within recognized frontiers, adhering to a common body of law, and coming under the jurisdiction of a common government. Also used to describe collectively the officials, laws, and powers of that community.

state of emergency   A situation in which normal legislative and judicial powers—and perhaps even the rights of citizens—are suspended or bypassed in order to deal with an emergency situation, such as a threat to government or the state.

state-building   The process by which a community of individuals builds a state system and an identity, to which they feel common allegiance.

state socialism   A system in which the state owns the means of production and in which government and party institutions encourage the people toward the ultimate goal of creating a classless communist society.

structural violence   As distinct from physical violence, this term connotes social and economic oppression built into a system of government. Anyone suffering political, economic, or social discrimination or hardship as a consequence of prevailing conditions becomes the victim of structural violence.

terrorism   The use of physical or psychological violence for political ends. It is usually aimed against civilian targets with the goal of arousing fear and achieving political change.

Third World   The group of countries that, during the cold war, supposedly took the side of neither the Western alliance nor the Soviet bloc. More generally used to describe the countries of Latin America, Africa, and Asia, most of which were at one time or another European colonies.

totalitarianism   A political system in which all institutions and activities are subject to total state control and in which no individual rights or privileges are formally recognized (for example, the USSR under Stalin or Germany under Hitler).

unitary state   A state in which all significant executive power is vested in the national government, with little or no independent power vested in local units of government.

vanguard party   The Leninist concept of a revolutionary party created to bring change or revolution on behalf of the masses.

welfare state   A state that provides through law for people in need, such as the poor, the elderly, the handicapped, or anyone otherwise economically or physically disadvantaged.

Westminster model   The system of government associated with the British parliamentary model, the key features of which are: a fused executive and legislature, two legislative chambers representing different constituencies, a cabinet exercising key executive powers, an elected head of government, and a separate head of state.

winner-take-all   An electoral system in which the candidate winning the most votes (a plurality) wins office.

ABBREVIATIONS AND ACRONYMS

AFRC	Armed Forces Ruling Council (Nigeria)
ASU	Arab Socialist Union (Egypt)
CCP	Chinese Communist Party
CNN	Cable News Network
CPC	communist and postcommunist countries
CPSU	Communist Party of the Soviet Union
ECOWAS	Economic Community of West African States
EU	European Union
G-8	Group of 8
G-77	Group of 77
GATT	General Agreement on Tariffs and Trade
GDP	gross domestic product
GNP	gross national product
IMF	International Monetary Fund
LDC	less developed country
LDP	Liberal Democratic Party (Japan)
MNC	multinational corporation
MP	Member of Parliament (Britain)
NAFTA	North American Free Trade Agreement
NATO	North Atlantic Treaty Organization
NDP	National Democratic Party (Egypt)
NIC	newly industrializing country
NIEO	New International Economic Order
NPC	National People's Congress (China)
NRC	National Republican Convention (Nigeria)
ODA	official development assistance
OECD	Organization for Economic Cooperation and Development
OIC	Organization of the Islamic Conference
OPEC	Organization of Petroleum Exporting Countries
PAN	National Action Party (Mexico)
PLA	People's Liberation Army (China)
PPP	purchasing power parity
PR	proportional representation
PRC	People's Republic of China
PRD	Party of the Democratic Revolution (Mexico)
PRI	Institutional Revolutionary Party (Mexico)
SCAP	Supreme Commander for the Allied Powers (Japan)
SDP	Social Democratic Party
SDPJ	Social Democratic Party of Japan
SMC	Supreme Military Council (Nigeria)
UAR	United Arab Republic
UK	United Kingdom
UN	United Nations
UNAM	National Autonomous University (Mexico)
UNCTAD	United Nations Conference on Trade and Development
USSR	Union of Soviet Socialist Republics
WTO	World Trade Organization

ENDNOTES

Introduction

1. Dogan, Mattei, and Dominique Pelassy, *How to Compare Nations: Strategies in Comparative Politics* (Chatham, NJ: Chatham House Publishers, 1984), p. 5

2. Yin, Robert K., *Case Study Research: Design and Methods* (Beverly Hills, CA: Sage, 1989), p. 21.

3. See, for example, Gabriel Almond et al., *Comparative Politics Today*, 8th Ed. (New York: Longman, 2003).

4. Weber, Max, *The Theory of Social and Economic Organizations* (Glencoe, IL: Free Press, 1947).

5. Moore, Barrington, *Social Origins of Dictatorship and Democracy* (London: Methuen, 1967).

6. Safire, William, *Safire's Political Dictionary: The New Language of Politics* (New York: Random House, 1978).

7. Wolf-Phillips, Leslie, "Why Third World?" in *Third World Quarterly* 1:1, February 1979, pp. 105–114.

PART I: Liberal Democracies

1. Bloom, Alan, *The Republic of Plato*, 2nd Ed. (New York: Basic Books, 1991).

2. Dahl, Robert, *Polyarchy: Participation and Opposition* (New Haven, CT: Yale University Press, 1971).

3. Moore, Barrington Jr., *Social Origins of Dictatorship and Democracy: Lord and Peasant in the Making of the Modern World* (Boston: Beacon, 1967), p. 417.

4. Hobbes, Thomas, *Leviathan* (Oxford: Oxford University Press, 1998).

5. Landes, David, *The Unbound Prometheus: Technological Change and Industrial Development in Western Europe from 1750 to the Present* (Cambridge, UK: Cambridge University Press, 1969), pp. 42–54.

6. Smith, Adam, *The Wealth of Nations*, Ed. Edwin Cannan (New York: Modern Library, 1994).

7. Landes, David, *The Unbound Prometheus: Technological Change and Industrial Development in Western Europe from 1750 to the Present* (Cambridge, UK: Cambridge University Press, 1969), p. 10.

8. Mill, John Stuart, *On Liberty* (New York: W.W. Norton, 1975).

9. Tucker, Robert (Ed.), *The Marx-Engels Reader* (New York: W.W. Norton, 1978), p. 287.

10. Landes, David, *The Unbound Prometheus: Technological Change and Industrial Development in Western Europe from 1750 to the Present* (Cambridge, UK: Cambridge University Press, 1969), pp. 35–36.

Chapter 1: United States

1. U.S. Census Bureau Web site, 2005, www.census.gov.

2. U.S. Bureau of the Census, *Projections of the Population of the U.S. by Age, Sex and Race: 1995 to 2050* (Washington, DC: U.S. Bureau of the Census, 1996).

3. For discussion, see Seymour Martin Lipset, *American Exceptionalism: A Double-Edged Sword* (New York: W.W. Norton, 1996).

4. Madsen, Deborah L., *American Exceptionalism* (Jackson: University Press of Mississippi, 1998), p. 1.

5. Hoogenbloom, Ari, "American Exceptionalism: Republicanism as Ideology," in Elizabeth Glaser and Herman Wellenreuther, *Bridging the Atlantic: The Question of American Exceptionalism in Perspective* (Washington DC: Cambridge University Press, 2002), p. 45.

6. Koh, Harold Hongju, "Foreword: On American Exceptionalism," in *Stanford Law Review*, 55:5, May 2003, pp. 1479–1527.

7. World Values Surveys, various years.

8. See, for example, the discussion in John Micklethwait and Adrian Wooldridge, *The Right Nation: Conservative Power in America* (New York: Penguin Press, 2004), and Thomas Frank, *What's the Matter with Kansas? How Conservatives Won the Heart of America* (New York, NY: Metropolitan Books, 2004).

9. For a discussion of this, see Stephen Graubard, *Command of Office: How War, Secrecy and Deception Transformed the Presidency from Theodore Roosevelt to George W. Bush* (New York: Basic Books, 2005).

10. Burns, James MacGregor, J. W. Peltason, Thomas E. Cronin, David B. Magleby, David M. O'Brien, and Paul C. Light, *Government by the People*, 20th Ed. (Upper Saddle River, NJ: Prentice Hall, 2003), p. 365.

11. Greenstein, Fred I., *The Presidential Difference: Leadership Styles From FDR to Clinton*, 2nd Ed. (Ithaca: Princeton University Press, 2004).

12. Greenstein, Fred I., *The Presidential Difference: Leadership Styles From FDR to Clinton*, 2nd Ed. (Ithaca: Princeton University Press, 2004), p. 369.

13. Hibbing, John, and Elizabeth Theis-Morse, *Congress as Public Enemy* (Cambridge, UK: Cambridge University Press, 1995).

14. Federal Election Commission Web site, 2005, www.fec.gov.

15. University of Michigan Survey Research Center figures.

16. Welch, Susan, John Gruhl, John Comer, and Susan M. Rigdon, *Understanding American Government*, 9th Ed. (Belmont, CA: Wadsworth, 2003), p. 145.

17. Federal Election Commission Web site, 2003, www.fec.gov.

18. For a controversial assessment of this argument, see Michael Parenti, *Democracy for the Few*, 7th Ed. (Belmont, CA: Wadsworth, 2001).

19. Federal Election Commission Web site, 2003, www.fec.gov.

20. See Michael Ignatieff (Ed.), *American Exceptionalism and Human Rights* (Ithaca: Princeton University Press, 2005).

21. For a discussion of the structure of policymaking in the United States, see B. Guy Peters, *American Public Policy: Promise and Performance*, 6th Ed. (Washington DC: CQ Press, 2003).

Chapter 2: Britain

1. Jacobs, E., and Robert Worcester, *We British* (London: Weidenfeld and Nicolson, 1990), pp. 138–139.

2. Jones, Bill, and Dennis Kavanagh, *British Politics Today*, 6th Ed. (Washington, DC: CQ Press, 1998), pp. 179–185.

3. Norton, Philip, *The British Polity*, 4th Ed. (New York: Longman, 2001), p. 44.

4. See Budge, Ian, Ivor Crewe, David McKay, and Ken Newton, *The New British Politics*, 3rd Ed. (Harlow: Pearson Educational Limited, 2004), Chapter 11.

5. Hart, Vivien, *Distrust and Democracy* (Cambridge, UK: Cambridge University Press, 1978), pp. 202–203.

6. Dahl, Robert (Ed.), *Political Oppositions in Western Democracies* (New Haven, CT: Yale University Press, 1966), p. 353.

7. Almond, Gabriel A., and Sidney Verba (Eds.), *The Civic Culture Revisited* (Newbury Park, CA: Sage Publications, 1989).

8. Wallace, M., and J. Jenkins, "The New Class, Postindustrialism and Neocorporatism: Three Images of Social Protest in the Western Democracies," in J. Jenkins and B. Klandermans (Eds.), *The Politics of Social Protest* (London: University College London Press, 1995).

9. Office for National Statistics, *UK 2002: The Official Yearbook of Great Britain and Northern Ireland* (London: The Stationery Office, 2001), p. 238.

10. Kavanagh, Dennis, *British Politics: Continuities and Change*, 4th Ed. (Oxford: Oxford University Press, 2000), pp. 47–49.

11. Norton, Philip, *The British Polity*, 4th Ed. (New York: Longman, 2001), p. 57.

12. Bagehot, Walter, *The English Constitution* (Ithaca, NY: Cornell University Press, 1963).

13. Norton, Philip, *The British Polity*, 4th Ed. (New York: Longman, 2001), p. 308.

14. Norton, Philip, *The British Polity*, 4th Ed. (New York: Longman, 2001), p. 308.

15. For details on the roles of the prime minister, see Bill Coxall, Lynton Robins, and Robert Leach, *Contemporary British Politics*, 4th Ed. (Basingstoke: Palgrave Macmillan, 2003), pp. 189–193.

16. Kavanagh, Dennis, *British Politics: Continuities and Change*, 4th Ed. (Oxford: Oxford University Press, 2000), p. 50.

17. For more details, see Peter Hennessy, *The Prime Minister: The Office and its Holders Since 1945* (New York: Palgrave, 2001), p. 178.

18. Hennessy, Peter, *The Prime Minister: The Office and its Holders Since 1945* (New York: Palgrave, 2001).

19. Coxall, Bill, Lynton Robins, and Robert Leach, *Contemporary British Politics*, 4th Ed. (Basingstoke: Palgrave Macmillan, 2003), pp. 228–243.

20. Fielding, Steven, "A New Politics?" in Patrick Dunleavy, Andrew Gamble, Ian Holliday, and Gillian Peele (Eds.), *Developments in British Politics 6* (New York: Palgrave, 2000), p. 27.

21. Thomas, Rob, "UK Economic Policy: The Conservative Legacy and New Labour's Third Way," in Stephen P Savage and Rob Atkinson (Eds.), *Public Policy Under Blair* (Basingstoke: Palgrave Macmillan, 2001).

22. For more discussion, see Sanders, David, "Voting and the Electorate," in Patrick Dunleavy, Andrew Gamble, Ian Holliday and Gillian Peele (Eds.), *Developments in British Politics 5* (Basingstoke, UK: Macmillan, 1997).

23. Sanders, David, "Voting and the Electorate," in Patrick Dunleavy, Andrew Gamble, Ian Holliday and Gillian Peele (Eds.), *Developments in British Politics 5* (Basingstoke, UK: Macmillan, 1997).

24. Young, Hugo, *One of Us* (London: Pan Books, 1990), p. 371.

25. Figures from Riddell, Peter, *The Thatcher Decade* (Oxford: Basil Blackwell, 1989), pp. 53, 72, 75, 118.

26. Riddell, Peter, *The Thatcher Decade* (Oxford: Basil Blackwell, 1989), pp. 93–94.

27. Kaltesky, Anatole, "Sour noises, but what a sweet taste," in *The World in 2003* (London: The Economist, 2002).

28. For more details, see John McCormick, *Understanding the European Union*, 3rd Ed. (Basingstoke: Palgrave Macmillan, 2003).

29. For a discussion of this problem, see Andrew Gamble, *Between Europe and America: The Future of British Politics* (Basingstoke: Palgrave Macmillan, 2004).

Chapter 3: Japan

1. Miyamoto, Masao, *The Straitjacket Society: An Insider's Irreverent View of Bureaucratic Japan* (New York: Kodansha International, 1994).

2. McClain, James L., *Japan: A Modern History* (New York, NY: W.W. Norton, 2002), p. 135.

3. Umegaki, Michio, *After the Restoration: The Beginning of Japan's Modern State* (New York: New York University Press, 1988), p. 54.

4. Gordon, Andrew, *A Modern History of Japan: From Tokugawa Times to the Present* (New York: Oxford University Press, 2003), pp. 229–234.

5. Hrebenar, Ronald J., *Japan's New Party System*, 3rd Ed. (Boulder, CO: Westview, 2000).

6. Gordon, Andrew, *A Modern History of Japan: From Tokugawa Times to the Present* (New York: Oxford University Press, 2003), p. 320.

7. *The Economist*, "What Ails Japan? A Survey of Japan," April 20, 2002.

8. Stockwin, J. A. A., *Governing Japan: Divided Politics in a Major Economy*, 3rd Ed. (Oxford: Blackwell, 1999), p. 28.

9. Mouer, Ross, and Yoshio Sugimoto, *Images of Japanese Society: A Study in the Social Construction of Reality* (London: Kegan Paul International, 1990).

10. Berry, Mary Elizabeth, *Hideyoshi* (Cambridge, MA: Harvard University Press, 1989), p. 111.

11. Neary, Ian, *The State and Politics in Japan* (Cambridge: Polity Press, 2002), pp. 202–207.

12. See James L. McClain, *Japan: A Modern History* (New York, NY: W.W. Norton, 2002), pp. 203–205.

13. Hayao, Kenji, *The Japanese Prime Minister and Public Policy* (Pittsburgh: University of Pittsburgh Press, 1993).

14. Stockwin, J. A. A., "Parties, Politicians and the Political System," in J. A. A. Stockwin et al., *Dynamic and Immobilist Politics in Japan* (Honolulu: University of Hawaii Press, 1988), p. 53.

15. Stockwin, J. A. A., "Parties, Politicians and the Political System," in J. A. A. Stockwin et al., *Dynamic and Immobilist Politics in Japan* (Honolulu: University of Hawaii Press, 1988), p. 54.

16. See J. A. A. Stockwin, *Governing Japan: Divided Politics in a Major Economy*, 3rd Ed. (Oxford: Blackwell, 1999), pp. 166–170

17. Hayes, Louis D., *Introduction to Japanese Politics* (New York, NY: Paragon House, 1992), p. 112.

18. Krauss, Ellis S., *Japan's Democracy: How Much Change?* (New York: Foreign Policy Association Headline Series No. 305, 1995), p. 37.

19. Neary, Ian, *The State and Politics in Japan* (London: Blackwell, 2002), p. 67.

20. Krauss, Ellis S., *Japan's Democracy: How Much Change?* (New York: Foreign Policy Association Headline Series No. 305, 1995), pp. 39–40.

21. van Wolferen, Karel, *The Enigma of Japanese Power: People and Politics in a Stateless Nation* (London: Macmillan, 1989).

22. Johnson, Chalmers, *MITI and the Japanese Miracle: The Growth of Industrial Policy 1925–75* (Stanford: Stanford University Press, 1985), p. 154.

23. Hayao, Kenji, *The Japanese Prime Minister and Public Policy* (Pittsburgh: University of Pittsburgh Press, 1993), pp. 7–8.

24. *The Economist*, "What Ails Japan? A Survey of Japan," April 20, 2002.

25. *The Economist*, July 6, 2002, p. 49.

26. Nathan, John, *Japan Unbound: A Volatile Nation's Quest for Pride and Purpose* (New York: Houghton Mifflin, 2004).

27. *The Economist*, "What Ails Japan? A Survey of Japan," April 20, 2002.

28. *The Economist*, May 19, 2001.

PART II: Communist and Postcommunist Countries

1. Barry, Donald B., and Carol Barner-Barry, *Contemporary Soviet Politics: An Introduction* (Englewood Cliffs, NJ: Prentice Hall, 1982), p. 362.

2. Lieberthal, Kenneth, *Governing China: From Revolution Through Reform* (New York: W.W. Norton, 1995), pp. 293, 329.

3. Lane, David, *The Socialist Industrial State: Towards a Political Sociology of State Socialism* (London: George Allen & Unwin, 1976), p. 73.

4. Lenin, Vladimir Ilyich, *What Is To Be Done?* (New York: Penguin, 1988).

5. Lenin, Vladimir Ilyich, *Imperialism: The Highest Stage of Capitalism* (New York: International Publishers, 1939).

6. Schram, Stuart, *The Thought of Mao Tse-Tung* (Cambridge, UK: Cambridge University Press, 1989).

Chapter 4: Russia

1. Pipes, Richard, *The Russian Revolution 1899–1919* (London: Harrill, 1989).

2. Arendt, Hannah, *The Origins of Totalitarianism* (New York: Harcourt, Brace, 1968).

3. Hammer, Darrell P., *The USSR: The Politics of Oligarchy* (Boulder, CO: Westview Press, 1990), p. 36.

4. Lucas, Edward, "Putin's Choice: A Survey of Russia," in *The Economist*, July 21, 2001.

5. Sakwa, Richard, *Russian Politics and Society*, 3rd Ed. (London: Routledge, 2002), p. 425.

6. White, Stephen, *Political Culture and Soviet Politics* (New York: St. Martin's Press, 1979), p. 64.

7. Rhodes, Mark, "Political Attitudes in Russia," in *RFE/RL Research Report*, January 15, 1993, pp. 42–44.

8. Barry, Donald D., and Carol Barner-Barry, *Contemporary Soviet Politics: An Introduction* (Englewood Cliffs, NJ: Prentice Hall, 1982), p. 13; White, Stephen, *Political Culture and Soviet Politics* (New York: St. Martin's Press, 1979), pp. 110–111.

9. Biryukov, Nikolai, and V. M. Sergeev, *Russia's Road to Democracy: Parliament, Communism and Traditional Culture* (Aldershot, England: Edward Elgar, 1993).

10. Cohen, Stephen R., *Rethinking the Soviet Experience: Politics and History Since 1917* (New York: Oxford University Press, 1986), Chapter 5.

11. For details, see Richard Sakwa, *Russian Politics and Society*, 3rd Ed. (London and New York: Routledge, 2002), pp. 55–60.

12. Hughes, James, "From Federalization to Recentralization," in Stephen White, Alex Pravda, and Zvi Gitelman (Eds.), *Developments in Russian Politics 5* (Durham, NC: Duke University Press, 2001).

13. Sakwa, Richard, *Russian Politics and Society*, 3rd Ed. (London and New York: Routledge, 2002), p. 112.

14. See Thomas M. Nichols, *The Russian Presidency: Society and Politics in the Second Russian Republic* (New York: Palgrave, 2000), Chapter 7.

15. For an assessment of the role of the Federal Assembly in the policy process, see Tiffany A. Troxel, *Parliamentary Power in Russia, 1994–2001: Resident vs. Parliament* (Basingstoke: Palgrave Macmillan, 2003).

16. Remington, Thomas F., "Putin, the Duma, and Political Parties," in Dale R. Herspring (Ed.), *Putin's Russia: Past Imperfect, Future Uncertain*, 2nd Ed. (Lanham, MD: Rowman and Littlefield, 2005).

17. Government figures quoted by Thomas F. Remington, "Parliamentary Politics in Russia," in Stephen White, Alex Pravda, and Zvi Gitelman (Eds.), *Developments in Russian Politics 5* (Durham, NC: Duke University Press, 2001).

18. McFaul, Michael, *Post-Communist Politics: Democratic Prospects in Russia and Eastern Europe* (Washington, DC: Center for Strategic and International Studies, 1993), p. 55.

19. This categorization follows that used by *The Economist*, December 13, 2003, p. 25.

20. Herspring, Dale R. (Ed.), *Putin's Russia: Past Imperfect, Future Uncertain*, 2nd Ed. (Lanham, MD: Rowman and Littlefield, 2005), p. 3.

21. Willerton, John P., "The Presidency," in Stephen White, Alex Pravda, and Zvi Gitelman (Eds.), *Developments in Russian Politics 5* (Durham, NC: Duke University Press, 2001).

22. "Vlad the Impaler," in *The Economist*, November 1, 2003, pp. 13–14.

23. Jensen, Donald, "How Russia is Ruled," RFE/RL Web site, 1999, www.rferl.org/nca/special/rywhorules.

24. *The Economist*, "Putin's Choice: A Survey of Russia," July 21, 2001, p. 12.

25. Harvard economist Jeffrey Sachs, quoted in *The Economist*, March 23, 2002, p. 67.

26. Transparency International Web site, 2005, www.transparency.org.

27. Shaw, Denis J. B., *Russia in the Modern World: A New Geography* (Oxford: Blackwell Publishers, 1999), p. 58.

28. Millar, James R., "Putin and the Economy," in Dale R. Herspring (Ed.), *Putin's Russia: Past Imperfect, Future Uncertain*, 2nd Ed. (Lanham, MD: Rowman and Littlefield, 2005),

29. Truscott, Peter, *Russia First: Breaking with the West* (Ilford, UK: Frank Cass, 1997).

30. *The Economist*, December 1, 2001, pp. 46–47.

31. See Dale R. Herspring, "Putin and Military Reform," in Dale R. Herspring (Ed.), *Putin's Russia: Past Imperfect, Future Uncertain*, 2nd Ed. (Lanham, MD: Rowman and Littlefield, 2005).

Chapter 5: China

1. See, for example, William H. Overholt, *The Rise of China: How Economic Reform is Creating a New Superpower* (New York: W.W. Norton, 1994); David Shambaugh (Ed.), *Greater China: The Next Superpower?* (Oxford: Oxford University Press, 1995); Geoffrey Murray, *China: The Next Superpower: Dilemmas in Change and Continuity* (New York: St. Martin's Press, 1998); Lawrence J. Bramh, *China's Century: The Awakening of the Next Economic Powerhouse* (New York: John Wiley & Sons, 2001); and Ted Fishman, *China, Inc.: How the Rise of the Next Superpower Challenges America and the World* (New York: Scribner, 2005).

2. Derbyshire, Ian, *Politics in China: From Mao to the Post-Deng Era* (Edinburgh, Scotland: W & R Chambers Ltd., 1991), p. 1.

3. Schram, Stuart, *The Thought of Mao Tse-Tung* (Cambridge, UK: Cambridge University Press, 1989), p. 195.

4. Mao Zedong, *Quotations from Chairman Mao Tse-Tung* (Beijing: Foreign Languages Press, 1972).

5. Lin, Nan, *The Struggle for Tiananmen: Anatomy of the 1989 Mass Movement* (Westport, CT: Praeger, 1992), pp. 1–17.

6. Harding, Harry, "Political Development in Post-Mao China," in A. Doak Barnett and Ralph N. Clough, *Modernizing China: Post-Mao Reform and Development* (Boulder, CO: Westview Press, 1986), p. 33.

7. *The Economist*, November 23, 2002, p. 40.

8. Pye, Lucian, *China: An Introduction* (New York: Longman, 1991), p. 72.

9. Lieberthal, Kenneth G., and Michel Oksenberg, *Policy Making in China: Leaders, Structures and Processes* (Princeton, NJ: Princeton University Press, 1988), pp. 162–163.

10. Shirk, Susan L., "The Chinese Political System and the Political Strategy of Economic Reform," in Kenneth G. Lieberthal and David M. Lampton, *Bureaucracy, Politics and Decision-Making in Post-Mao China* (Berkeley, CA: University of California Press, 1992).

11. Shirk, Susan L., "The Chinese Political System and the Political Strategy of Economic Reform," in Kenneth G. Lieberthal and David M. Lampton, *Bureaucracy, Politics and Decision-Making in Post-Mao China* (Berkeley, CA: University of California Press, 1992).

12. Townsend, James R., and Brantly Womack, *Politics in China*, 3rd Ed. (Chicago: Scott Foresman, 1998), p. 352.

13. Shirk, Susan L., "The Chinese Political System and the Political Strategy of Economic Reform," in Kenneth G. Lieberthal and David M. Lampton, *Bureaucracy, Politics and Decision-Making in Post-Mao China* (Berkeley, CA: University of California Press, 1992), p. 61.

14. Long, Simon, "Leadership Politics Since 1989," in Robert Benewick and Paul Wingrove (Eds.), *China in the 1990s* (Basingstoke, UK: Macmillan, 1999).

15. Saich, Tony, *Governance and Politics of China* (New York: Palgrave, 2004), p.110.

16. Hamrin, Carol Lee, "The Party Leadership System," in Kenneth G. Lieberthal and Michel Oksenberg, *Policy Making in China: Leaders, Structures and Processes* (Princeton, NJ: Princeton University Press, 1988).

17. Wang, James C. E., *Contemporary Chinese Politics: An Introduction*, 7th Ed. (Upper Saddle River, NJ: Prentice Hall, 2001), p. 82.

18. Chang, Parris, "The Last Stand of Deng's Revolution," in *Problems of Communism* 30 (January–February 1981), pp. 3–19.

19. "China's Leader Shows His Stripes," on BBC News Online, news.bbc.co.uk, January 11, 2005.

20. Chang, Parris, "The Last Stand of Deng's Revolution," in *Problems of Communism* 30 (January–February 1981), pp. 3–19.

21. Wang, James C. E., *Contemporary Chinese Politics: An Introduction*, 7th Ed. (Upper Saddle River, NJ: Prentice Hall, 2001), p. 102.

22. Wang, James C. E., *Contemporary Chinese Politics: An Introduction*, 7th Ed. (Upper Saddle River, NJ: Prentice Hall, 2001), p. 117.

23. Moody, Peter, *Tradition and Modernization in China and Japan* (Belmont, CA: Wadsworth, 1995), p. 214.

24. Saich, Tony, *Governance and Politics of China* (New York: Palgrave, 2004), p. 114.

25. Jencks, Harlan W., "The Chinese People's Liberation Army: 1949–89," in David Goodman and Gerald Segal (Eds.), *China at Forty: Mid-Life Crisis?* (Oxford: Clarendon Press, 1989), pp. 93–94.

26. For example, they are barely mentioned by either Tony Saich, *Governance and Politics of China* (New York: Palgrave, 2004), or James C. E. Wang, *Contemporary Chinese Politics: An Introduction*, 7th Ed. (Upper Saddle River, NJ: Prentice Hall, 2001).

27. Saich, Tony, *Governance and Politics of China* (New York: Palgrave, 2004), p.76.

28. Wang, James C. E., *Contemporary Chinese Politics: An Introduction*, 7th Ed. (Upper Saddle River, NJ: Prentice Hall, 2001), p. 98.

29. *The Economist*, June 1, 2002, p. 40.

30. See Saich, Tony, *Governance and Politics of China* (New York: Palgrave, 2004), pp. 81–85.

31. Houn, Franklin, *A Short History of Chinese Communism* (Englewood Cliffs, NJ: Prentice Hall, 1967), p. 89.

32. Lieberthal, Kenneth G., and Michel Oksenberg, *Policy Making in China: Leaders, Structures and Processes* (Princeton, NJ: Princeton University Press, 1988).

33. Lampton, David M., "The Implementation Problem in Post-Mao China," in David Lampton (Ed.), *Policy Implementation in Post-Mao China* (Berkeley, CA: University of California Press, 1987), pp. 7–8.

34. Lampton, David M., "The Implementation Problem in Post-Mao China," in David Lampton (Ed.), *Policy Implementation in Post-Mao China* (Berkeley, CA: University of California Press, 1987), pp. 49–51; Samuel S. Kim (Ed.), *China and the World: New Directions in Chinese Foreign Relations* (Boulder, CO: Westview Press, 1989).

35. *The Economist*, "A Survey of China," June 15, 2002, p. 3.

36. Warshaw, Steven, *China Emerges* (Berkeley, CA: Diablo Press, 1991), p. 93.

37. Levine, Steven I., "Sino-American Relations: Renormalization and Beyond," in Samuel S. Kim (Ed.), *China and the World: New Directions in Chinese Foreign Relations* (Boulder, CO: Westview Press, 1989).

38. Cumings, Bruce, "The Political Economy of China's Turn Outward," in Samuel S. Kim (Ed.), *China and the World: New Directions in Chinese Foreign Relations* (Boulder, CO: Westview Press, 1989).

39. Wang, James C. E., *Contemporary Chinese Politics: An Introduction*, 7th Ed. (Upper Saddle River, NJ: Prentice Hall, 2001), pp. 319–320.

40. Wang, James C. E., *Contemporary Chinese Politics: An Introduction*, 7th Ed. (Upper Saddle River, NJ: Prentice Hall, 2001), pp. 363–364.

PART III: Newly Industrializing Countries

1. See, for example, Timothy M. Shaw and Jerker Carlsson, "Newly Industrialized Countries and South-South: Concepts, Correlates, Controversies and Cases," in Carlsson and Shaw (Eds.), *Newly Industrialized Countries and the Political Economy of South-South Relations* (New York: St. Martin's Press, 1988), p. 7; Mortimer, Robert A., *The Third World Coalition in International Politics* (Boulder, CO: Westview Press, 1984).

2. For more information on outsourcing, see Daniel W. Drezner, "The Outsourcing Bogeyman," in *Foreign Affairs* May/June 2004.

3. Garten, Jeffrey, *The Big Ten: The Big Emerging Markets and How They Will Change Our Lives* (New York: Basic Books, 1997), pp. 70–71.

4. Sauvant, Karl P., *The Group of 77: Evolution, Structure, Organization* (New York: Oceana Publications, 1981).

Chapter 6: Mexico

1. Needler, Martin C., *Mexican Politics: The Containment of Conflict* (New York: Praeger, 1990), p. 13.

2. Paz, Octavio, "Reflections: Mexico and the United States," in *New Yorker*, September 17, 1979.

3. Camp, Roderic Ai, *Politics in Mexico: The Democratic Transformation*, 4th Ed. (New York: Oxford University Press, 2002), pp. 21–24.

4. Purcell, Susan Kaufman, "Mexico," in Howard J. Wiarda and Harvey F. Kline (Eds.), *Latin American Politics and Development* (Boulder, CO: Westview Press, 1990), p. 397.

5. Grayson, George W., *Mexico: From Corporatism to Pluralism?* (Fort Worth, TX: Harcourt Brace, 1998), pp. 17–18.

6. See Julia Preston and Samuel Dillon, *Opening Mexico: The Making of a Democracy* (New York: Farrar, Straus and Giroux, 2004), Chapter 15.

7. Baer, M. Delal, "Mexico at an Impasse," in *Foreign Affairs* 83:1, January/February 2004, pp. 101–113.

8. Wiarda, Howard J., and Harvey F. Kline (Eds.), *Latin American Politics and Development* (Boulder, CO: Westview Press, 1990), p. 15.

9. Wiarda, Howard J., "Constitutionalism and Political Culture in Mexico: How Deep the Foundations?" in Daniel P. Franklin and Michael J. Bann, *Political Culture and Constitutionalism: A Comparative Approach* (Armonk, NY: M. E. Sharpe, 1995).

10. For more discussion on this, see George W. Grayson, *Mexico: From Corporatism to Pluralism?* (Fort Worth, TX: Harcourt Brace, 1998).

11. Camp, Roderic Ai, *Politics in Mexico: The Democratic Transformation*, 4th Ed. (New York: Oxford University Press, 2002), pp. 116–120.

12. Camp, Roderic Ai, *Politics in Mexico: The Democratic Transformation*, 4th Ed. (New York: Oxford University Press, 2002), pp. 135–138.

13. Camp, Roderic Ai, *Politics in Mexico: The Democratic Transformation*, 4th Ed. (New York: Oxford University Press, 2002), p. 11.

14. Needler, Martin C., *Mexican Politics: The Containment of Conflict* (New York: Praeger, 1990), p. 92.

15. Needler, Martin C., "The Government of Mexico," in Michael Curtis (Ed.), *Introduction to Comparative Government*, 4th Ed. (New York: Longman, 1997), pp. 530–531.

16. For an assessment of the Fox presidency, see Luis Rubio and Susan Kaufman Purcel (eds), *Mexico Under Fox* (Boulder, CO: Lynne Rienner, 2004).

17. See Julia Preston and Samuel Dillon, *Opening Mexico: The Making of a Democracy* (New York: Farrar, Straus and Giroux, 2004), Chapter 6.

18. Camp, Roderic A., "Mexico's Legislature: Missing the Democratic Lockstep," in David Close (Ed.), *Legislatures and the New Democracies in Latin America* (Boulder, CO: Lynne Rienner, 1995).

19. *The Economist*, January 5, 2002, p. 32.

20. Avalos, Francisco A., *The Mexican Legal System*, 2nd Ed. (New York: Fred B. Rothman Co., 2000) p. 16.

21. Avalos, Francisco A., *The Mexican Legal System*, 2nd Ed. (New York: Fred B. Rothman Co., 2000), p. 12.

22. Ugalde, Antonio, *Power and Conflict in a Mexican Community: A Study of Political Integration* (Albuquerque: University of New Mexico Press, 1970), p. 95.

23. For an assessment of its role and significance, see Alan Riding, *Distant Neighbors: A Portrait of the Mexicans*, 3rd Ed. (New York: Vintage Books, 2000), Chapter 13.

24. Camp, Roderic Ai, *Politics in Mexico: The Democratic Transformation*, 4th Ed. (New York: Oxford University Press, 2002).

25. Alcocer, V. Jorge, "Recent Electoral Reforms in Mexico: Prospects for a Real Multiparty Democracy," in Riordan Roett (Ed.), *The Challenge of Institutional Reform in Mexico* (Boulder, CO: Lynne Rienner, 1995).

26. Baer, M. Delal, "Mexico at an Impasse," in *Foreign Affairs* 83:1, January/February 2004, pp. 101–113.

27. Teichman, Judith A., *Policymaking in Mexico: From Boom to Crisis* (Boston: Allen and Unwin, 1988), p. 13.

28. Grayson, George W., *Mexico: From Corporatism to Pluralism?* (Fort Worth, TX: Harcourt Brace, 1998), p. 53.

29. *The Economist*, August 11, 2001, p. 30.

30. *The Economist*, January 11, 2003, p. 27.

31. *The Economist*, May 12, 2001, p. 42.

32. Transparency International, Corruption Perceptions Index 2004, www.transparency.org/surveys/index.html.

33. Needler, Martin C., *Mexican Politics: The Containment of Conflict* (New York: Praeger, 1990), p. 118.

34. *The Economist*, "After the Revolution: A Survey of Mexico," October 28, 2000.

35. Grayson, George W., *Mexico: From Corporatism to Pluralism?* (Fort Worth, TX: Harcourt Brace, 1998), pp. 26–38.

36. Smith, Geri, "The Decline of the Maquiladora," in *Business Week Online*, April 29, 2002, www.businessweek.com.

37. *The Economist*, July 13, 2002, p. 31.

38. Levy, Daniel, and Gabriel Szekely, *Mexico: Paradoxes of Stability and Change* (Boulder, CO: Westview Press, 1987), p. 189.

39. Smith, Peter H., *Mexico: The Quest for a U.S. Policy* (New York: Foreign Policy Association, 1980), pp. 6–7.

40. Quoted by George W. Grayson, *Mexico: From Corporatism to Pluralism?* (Fort Worth, TX: Harcourt Brace, 1998), p. 242.

41. *The Economist*, July 21, 2001, p. 31.

Chapter 7: India

1. Government of India, *Report of the Backward Classes Commission* (Delhi: Government of India, 1981).

2. Lall, Arthur, *The Emergence of Modern India* (New York: Columbia University Press, 1981), p. 2.

3. Lall, Arthur, *The Emergence of Modern India* (New York: Columbia University Press, 1981), p. 3.

4. Lall, Arthur, *The Emergence of Modern India* (New York: Columbia University Press, 1981), p. 6.

5. Nandy, Ashis, "The Political Culture of the Indian State," in *Daedalus* 118:4 (Fall 1989), p. 1–26.

6. Hardgrave, Robert L., and Stanley A. Kochanek, *India: Government and Politics in a Developing Nation*, 6th Ed. (Fort Worth, TX: Harcourt Brace, 2000), pp. 11–13.

7. Huntington, Samuel P., *Political Order in Changing Societies* (New Haven, CT: Yale University Press, 1968), p. 5.

8. Brass, Paul R., *A New Cambridge History of India*, Vol. I, V:I (Cambridge, UK: Cambridge University Press, 1990), pp. 10–13.

9. Brass, Paul R., *A New Cambridge History of India*, Vol. I, V:I (Cambridge, UK: Cambridge University Press, 1990), p. 9.

10. Brass, Paul R., *A New Cambridge History of India*, Vol. I, V:I (Cambridge, UK: Cambridge University Press, 1990), p. 36.

11. Hart, Henry C., "Political Leadership in India," in Atul Kohli (Ed.), *India's Democracy: An Analysis of Changing State-Society Relations* (Princeton, NJ: Princeton University Press, 1988), p. 55.

12. Wheare, Kenneth, *Federal Government* (New York: Oxford University Press, 1951), p. 28.

13. Chanda, Asok, *Federalism in India* (London: George Allen & Unwin, 1965), p. 124.

14. For more details, see Hardgrave, Robert L., and Stanley A. Kochanek, *India: Government and Politics in a Developing Nation*, 6th Ed. (Fort Worth, TX: Harcourt Brace, 2000), pp. 318–319.

15. Brass, Paul R., *A New Cambridge History of India*, Vol. I, V:I (Cambridge, UK: Cambridge University Press, 1990), p. 83.

16. Brass, Paul R., *A New Cambridge History of India*, Vol. I, V:I (Cambridge, UK: Cambridge University Press, 1990), p. 86.

17. For more details, see Robert L. Hardgrave and Stanley A. Kochanek, *India: Government and Politics in a Developing Nation*, 6th Ed. (Fort Worth, TX: Harcourt Brace, 2000), Chapter 6.

18. Shah, Ghanshyam, "Grass-Roots Mobilization in Indian Politics," in Atul Kohli (Ed.), *India's Democracy: An Analysis of Changing State-Society Relations* (Princeton, NJ: Princeton University Press, 1988).

19. Hardgrave, Robert L., and Stanley A. Kochanek, *India: Government and Politics in a Developing Nation*, 6th Ed. (Fort Worth, TX: Harcourt Brace, 2000), p.275.

20. *The Economist*, April 17, 1999, p. 44.

21. See "India's Shining Hopes: A Survey of India," in *The Economist*, February 21, 2004.

22. *The Economist*, May 22, 1999.

PART IV: Less Developed Countries

1. Kamrava, Mehran, *Politics and Society in the Developing World* (London: Routledge, 2000), p. 209.

2. Kamrava, Mehran, *Politics and Society in the Developing World* (London: Routledge, 2000), p. 2.

3. Nyerere, Julius, *Freedom and Unity* (Dar-es-Salaam and London: Oxford University Press, 1966), p. 198.

4. Jackson, Robert H., and Carl G. Rosberg, *Personal Rule in Black Africa* (Berkeley, CA: University of California Press, 1982), p. 1.

5. Mazrui, Ali A., *The Africans: A Triple Heritage* (London: BBC Publications, 1986), pp. 182–183.

6. Figures from World Trade Organization Web site, 2003, www.wto.org.

7. Handelman, Howard, *The Challenge of Third World Development*, 3rd Ed. (Upper Saddle River, NJ: Prentice Hall, 2003), p. 14.

8. Moore, Barrington, *The Social Origins of Dictatorship and Democracy* (Boston: Beacon Press, 1966), p. 418

9. Rostow, Walter W., *The Stages of Economic Growth: A Non-Communist Manifesto* (New York: Cambridge University Press, 1960).

10. Lenin, Vladimir Ilyich, *Imperialism: The Highest Stage of Capitalism* (London: Lawrence and Wishart, 1948).

11. Amin, Samir, *Accumulation on a World Scale: A Critique of the Theory of Underdevelopment* (New York: Monthly Review Press, 1974); and *Unequal Development: An Essay on the Social Transformations of Peripheral Capitalism* (New York: Monthly Review Press, 1976).

12. Reitsma, H. A., and J. Al. G. Kleinpenning, *The Third World in Perspective* (Assen, Netherlands: Rowan and Allanheld, 1985), p. 215ff.

13. See, for example, Fernando Henrique Cardoso and Enzo Falletto, *Dependency and Development in Latin America* (Berkeley, CA: University of California Press, 1979).

14. Chilcote, Ronald, *Theories of Comparative Politics: The Search for a Paradigm* (Boulder, CO: Westview Press, 1981), p. 287.

15. Mehta, Vrajenda Raj, *Beyond Marxism: Towards an Alternative Perspective* (New Delhi: Manchar Publications, 1978), p. 92.

Chapter 8: Nigeria

1. Whitaker, C. S., "Second Beginnings: The New Political Framework in Nigeria," in Richard L. Sklar and C. S. Whitaker, *African Politics and Problems in Development* (Boulder, CO: Lynne Reinner Publishers, 1991), p. 230.

2. Aborisade, Oladimeji, and Robert J. Mundt, *Politics in Nigeria*, 2nd Ed. (New York: Longman, 2002), pp. 13–15.

3. Ekeh, Peter, "Nigeria's Emergent Political Culture," in Peter Ekeh et al. (Eds.), *Nigeria Since Independence: The First Twenty-Five Years* (lbadan, Nigeria: Heinemann Educational Books, 1989), pp. 2–6.

4. Diamond, Larry, "Nigeria: Pluralism, Statism, and the Struggle for Democracy," in Larry Diamond et al. (Eds.), *Democracy in Developing Countries Vol. 2: Africa* (Boulder, CO: Lynne Reinner Publishers, 1988), p. 60.

5. Ekeh, Peter, "Nigeria's Emergent Political Culture," in Peter Ekeh et al. (Eds.), *Nigeria Since Independence: The First Twenty-Five Years* (lbadan, Nigeria: Heinemann Educational Books, 1989), p. 4.

6. Mackintosh, John, "Nigeria Since Independence," in *World Today* 20:8 (1964), p. 337.

7. Graf, William D., *The Nigerian State: Political Economy, State Class and Political System in the Post-Colonial Era* (London: James Currey, 1988), pp. 65–66.

8. Oyinbo, John, *Nigeria: Crisis and Beyond* (London: Knight, 1971), p. 9.

9. Paden, John N., *Ahmadu Bello: Sardauna of Sokoto* (Zaria, Nigeria: Hudahuda Publishing, 1986).

10. Graf, William D., *The Nigerian State: Political Economy, State Class and Political System in the Post-Colonial Era* (London: James Currey, 1988), p. 186.

11. Graf, William D., *The Nigerian State: Political Economy, State Class and Political System in the Post-Colonial Era* (London: James Currey, 1988), p. 41.

12. *The Economist*, "Nigeria Survey," January 15, 2000, p. 4.

13. Elaigwu, J. Isawa, "The Political Trio on Nigeria's Military Government: The Dynamics of Inter-Elite Relations in a Military Regime, 1967–75," in *The Nigerian Journal of Public Affairs*, VI:2 (1976).

14. Dudley, Billy, *An Introduction to Nigerian Government and Politics* (Bloomington, IN: Indiana University Press, 1982), p. 103.

15. Joseph, Richard A., "Principles and Practices of Nigerian Military Government," in John W. Harbeson (Ed.), *The Military in African Politics* (New York: Praeger, 1987), pp. 83–84.

16. Kew, Darren, "The 2003 Election: Hardly Credible, But Acceptable," in Robert I. Rotberg (Ed.), *Crafting the New Nigeria: Confronting the Challenges* (Boulder, CO: Lynne Rienner, 2004).

17. For a discussion of the roots of the problem, see William Reno, "The Roots of Sectarian Violence, and its Cure," in Robert I. Rotberg (Ed.), *Crafting the New Nigeria: Confronting the Challenges* (Boulder, CO: Lynne Rienner, 2004).

18. The Economist, July 7, 2001, p. 45 and November 3, 2001, p. 54.

19. For a chronology of world oil prices, see the U.S. Department of Energy Web site at www.eia.doe.gov/emeu/cabs/chron.html.

20. Achebe, Chinua, *The Trouble with Nigeria* (Oxford: Heinemann, 1983).

21. *The Economist*, August 3, 2002, pp. 59–60.

22. For the latest rankings, based on the extent to which corruption is perceived to exist among politicians and public officials, visit Transparency International's Web site at www.transparency.org.

23. Economist Intelligence Unit Country Report, *Nigeria*, 3rd quarter 1999, p. 19.

24. Nigerian data from World Bank, 2003, www.worldbank.com; U.S. data from Bureau of Health Professions, quoted by Centers for Disease Control, 2003, www.cdc.gov.

25. BBC News Online, May 12, 2005, http://news.bbc.co.uk.

26. Aluko, Olajide, *Essays on Nigerian Foreign Policy* (London: George Allen &Unwin, 1981), p. 17.

27. Achebe, Chinua, *The Trouble with Nigeria* (Oxford: Heinemann, 1983).

PART V: Islamic Countries

1. Bannerman, Patrick, *Islam in Perspective: A Guide to Islamic Society, Politics and Law* (London: Routledge, 1988), pp. 60–82.

2. Piscatori, James P., *Islam in the Political Process* (Cambridge, UK: Cambridge University Press, 1983), p. 4.

3. Esposito, John L., *The Islamic Threat: Myth or Reality?* (New York: Oxford University Press, 1992), p. 12.

4. The information here on the theoretical features of Islamic politics and economics is drawn from Ismail Raji al Faruqi, "The Islamic Critique of the Status Quo of Muslim Society," in Barbara Freyer Stowasser (Ed.) *The Islamic Impulse* (London: Croom Helm, 1987).

5. Rahman, Fazlur, "The Law of Rebellion in Islam," Paine Lecture in Religion, published by the University of Missouri-Columbia, 1983, p. 8.

6. Bill, James A., and Robert Springborg, *Politics in the Middle East* (New York: Longman, 2000), p. 152ff.

7. Esposito, John L., *Islam and Politics* (Syracuse, NY: Syracuse University Press, 1991), p. 296.

8. Bill, James A., and Robert Springborg, *Politics in the Middle East* (New York: Longman, 2000), p. 415.

9. Husain, Mir Zohair, *Global Islamic Politics*, 2nd Ed. (New York: Longman, 2003), pp. 212–215.

10. Bannerman, Patrick, *Islam in Perspective: A Guide to Islamic Society, Politics and Law* (London: Routledge, 1988), pp. 97–98.

11. Peretz, Don, *The Middle East Today* (Hinsdale, IL: The Dryden Press, 1971), pp. 40–41.

12. Esposito, John L., *The Islamic Threat: Myth or Reality?* (New York: Oxford University Press, 1992), p. 42.

13. Beinin, Joel, and Joe Stork, *Political Islam* (Berkeley, CA: University of California Press, 1997), p. 3.

14. Khalid, Detlev, "The Phenomenon of Re-Islamization," in *Aussenpolitik* XXIX (Winter 1978), pp. 433–453.

15. Husain, Mir Zohair, *Global Islamic Politics*, 2nd Ed. (New York: Longman, 2003), p. 53.

16. Piscatori, James P., *Islam in the Political Process* (Cambridge, UK: Cambridge University Press, 1983), pp. 3–4.

17. Esposito, John L., *The Islamic Threat: Myth or Reality?* (New York: Oxford University Press, 1992), p. 32ff.

Chapter 9: Egypt

1. Esposito, John L., *Islam and Politics*, 4th Ed. (Syracuse, NY: Syracuse University Press, 1998), p. 131.

2. Beattie, Kirk, J., "Prospects for Democratization in Egypt," in *American-Arab Affairs* 36, Spring 1991, pp. 31–47.

3. Hinnebusch, Raymond A., *Egyptian Politics Under Sadat* (Cambridge, UK: Cambridge University Press, 1985), p. 223.

4. Weber, Max, *The Theory of Social and Economic Organization* (New York: The Free Press, 1947).

5. Hopwood, Derek, *Egypt: Politics and Society 1945–1990*, 3rd Ed. (London: Routledge, 1992), p. 172; Ibrahim, Saadeddin, "Religion and Politics Under Nasser and Sadat, 1952–81," in Barbara Freyer Stowasser (Ed.), *The Islamic Impulse* (London: Croom Helm, 1987), pp. 123–124.

6. Bill, James A., and Robert Springborg, *Politics in the Middle East*, 5th Ed. (New York: Longman, 2000), p. 230.

7. Baker, Raymond William, *Egypt's Uncertain Revolution Under Nasser and Sadat* (Cambridge, MA: Harvard University Press, 1978), p. 70ff.

8. Hinnebusch, Raymond A., *Egyptian Politics Under Sadat* (Cambridge, UK: Cambridge University Press, 1985), pp. 12–13.

9. Springborg, Robert, *Mubarak's Egypt: Fragmentation of the Political Order* (Boulder, CO: Westview Press, 1989), pp. 30–33.

10. Kassem, Maye, *Egyptian Politics: The Dynamics of Authoritarian Rule* (Boulder, CO: Lynne Rienner, 2005).

11. Andersen, Roy, Robert Seibert, and Jon Wagner, *Politics and Change in the Middle East: Sources of Conflict and Accommodation*, 7th Ed. (Upper Saddle River, NJ: Prentice Hall, 2003), pp. 88–89.

12. Vatikiotis, P. J., *The History of Modern Egypt: From Muhammad Ali to Mubarak*, 3rd Ed. (Baltimore: Johns Hopkins University Press, 1986), p. 422.

13. Cooper, Mark N., *The Transformation of Egypt* (Baltimore: Johns Hopkins University Press, 1982), p. 70.

14. McDermott, Anthony, *Egypt from Nasser to Mubarak: A Flawed Revolution* (London: Croom Helm, 1988), p. 73ff.

15. *The Economist*, "New Surgeon, Same Old Scalpels," July 17, 2004.

16. Springborg, Robert, *Mubarak's Egypt: Fragmentation of the Political Order* (Boulder, CO: Westview Press, 1989), p. 139.

17. Waterbury, John, *The Egypt of Nasser and Sadat: The Political Economy of Two Regimes* (Princeton, NJ: Princeton University Press, 1983), p. 16.

18. Nasser, Gamal Abdel, *The Philosophy of the Revolution* (Cairo: The National Publication House, 1954), pp. 33–34; Springborg, op. cit., p. 96.

19. Marsot, Afaf Lutfi Al-Sayyid, *A Short History of Egypt* (Cambridge, UK: Cambridge University Press, 1985), p. 143.

20. Beattie, Kirk, J., "Prospects for Democratization in Egypt," in *American-Arab Affairs* 36, Spring 1991, pp. 31–47.

21. McDermott, Anthony, *Egypt from Nasser to Mubarak: A Flawed Revolution* (London: Croom Helm, 1988), p. 102.

22. Hopwood, Derek, *Egypt: Politics and Society 1945–1990*, 3rd Ed. (London: Routledge, 1992), p. 89.

23. Hinnebusch, Raymond A., *Egyptian Politics Under Sadat* (Cambridge, UK: Cambridge University Press, 1985), pp. 158–159.

24. Springborg, Robert, *Mubarak's Egypt: Fragmentation of the Political Order* (Boulder, CO: Westview Press, 1989), pp. 198–202.

25. Beattie, Kirk, J., "Prospects for Democratization in Egypt," in *American-Arab Affairs* 36, Spring 1991, pp. 31–47.

26. Rubin, Barry, *Islamic Fundamentalism in Egyptian Politics* (New York: Palgrave Macmillan, 2002).

27. *New York Times*, February 3, 1994; tourist arrival figures from Egyptian Tourism Authority, quoted in Economist Intelligence Unit, *Egypt Country Profile 1995–96* (London: Economist Intelligence Unit Ltd., 1995).

28. For a study of Mubarak's attitude toward the Brotherhood, see Hesham Al-Awadi, *In Pursuit of Legitimacy: The Muslim Brothers and Mubarak, 1982–2000* (New York: Tauris Academic Studies, 2005).

29. Hinnebusch, Raymond A., *Egyptian Politics Under Sadat* (Cambridge, UK: Cambridge University Press, 1985), p. 259.

30. Economist Intelligence Unit Country Report, *Egypt*, 3rd Quarter 1999, pp. 13–14.

31. Marsot, Afaf Lutfi Al-Sayyid, *A Short History of Egypt* (Cambridge, UK: Cambridge University Press, 1985), p. 142.

32. *The Economist*, January 5, 2002, p. 36.

33. Vatikiotis, P. J., *The History of Modern Egypt: From Muhammad Ali to Mubarak*, 3rd Ed. (Baltimore: Johns Hopkins University Press, 1986), p. 409.

PART VI: Marginal Countries

1. Daniel Thürer, "The 'Failed State' and International Law," December 31, 1999, Global Policy Forum, www.globalpolicy.org.

2. *Foreign Policy* journal notes that the CIA puts the number at 20, the World Bank puts the number at about 30, and Britain's Department for International Development talks of 46 "fragile" states of concern. See *Foreign Policy*, www.foreignpolicy.com.

3. Fukuyama, Francis, *State-Building: Governance and World Order in the 21st Century* (Ithaca: Cornell University Press, 2004).

4. See Stuart Eizenstat, John Edward Porter, and Jeremy Weinstein, "Rebuilding Weak States" in *Foreign Affairs* 84:1, January/February 2005, pp. 134–145, and

Stephen D. Krasner and Carlos Pascual, "Addressing State Failure," in *Foreign Affairs* 84:4, July/August 2005, pp. 153–170.

5. Singer, P.W., *Children at War* (New York: Pantheon, 2005).

6. Luttwak, Edward N., "Give War a Chance" in *Foreign Affairs* 78:4, July/August 1999, pp. 28–42. See also V.L. Elliott et al, *Breaking the Conflict Trap: Civil War and Development Policy* (Washington DC: Worl Bank, 2003), Chapter 2.

7. Sachs, Jeffrey, "Can Extreme Poverty be Eliminated?" in *Scientific American*, September 2005, pp. 56–65.

8. Fukuyama, Francis, *State-Building: Governance and World Order in the 21st Century* (Ithaca: Cornell University Press, 2004).

9. Anderson, Robert E., *Just Get Out of the Way: How Government Can Help Business in Poor Countries* (Washington DC: Cato Institute, 2004).

10. See, for example, James Dobbins et al., *America's Role in Nation-Building: From Germany to Iraq* (Santa Monica, CA: RAND, 2003), p. 204.

11. Speech by President George W. Bush to the U.S. Chamber of Commerce, November 2003.

12. Auty, Richard M., *Sustaining Development in Mineral Economies: The Resource Curse Thesis* (London: Routledge, 1993). See also Paul Collier and Ian Bannon (Eds.), *Natural Resources and Violent Conflict: Options and Actions* (Washington DC: World Bank, 2003).

13. Sachs, Jeffrey, "Can Extreme Poverty be Eliminated?" in *Scientific American*, September 2005, pp. 56–65.

14. Sachs, Jeffrey, "Can Extreme Poverty be Eliminated?" in *Scientific American*, September 2005, pp. 56–65.

Chapter 10: Haiti

1. Stotzky, Irwin P., *Silencing the Guns in Haiti: The Promise of Deliberative Democracy* (Chicago: University of Chicago Press, 1997), p. 21.

2. Freedom House, *The Worst of the Worst: The World's Most Repressive Societies* (New York: Freedom House, 2005).

3. Freedom House, *The Worst of the Worst: The World's Most Repressive Societies* (New York: Freedom House, 2005), pp. 39–40.

4. Quoted in *The Economist*, December 20, 2003, p. 47.

5. Stotzky, Irwin P., *Silencing the Guns in Haiti: The Promise of Deliberative Democracy* (Chicago: University of Chicago Press, 1997), p. 85.

6. Laguerre, Michael S., *The Military and Society in Haiti* (Basingstoke: Macmillan, 1993), p. 23.

7. Caistor, Nick, "Haiti's AIDS and Voodoo Challenge," in BBC News Online, November 20, 2003, http://news.bbc.co.uk.

8. *The Economist*, "H for Hope," June 19, 2004, p. 39.

NAME INDEX

Abacha, Sani, 393, 395, 398, 407–408,
    408–409, 412–413, 413, 421
Abiola, Moshood, 393, 412
Abubakar, Abdulsalam, 393
Abubakar, Atiku, 402
Achebe, Chinua, 420, 423
Acton, Lord, 432
Afewerki, Isaias, 488
Ajasiu, Michael, 412
Akihito, Emperor, 139, 140
Alexander III, Tsar, 176
Alexander the Great, 446
Alexandre, Boniface, 508, 511
Andrew, Prince, 94
Andropov, Yuri, 190
Aoshima, Yukio, 148
Arafat, Yasser, 478
Aristide, Jean-Bertrand, 502, 507,
    507–508, 509, 510, 511, 512, 519
  biography, 514
Aristotle, 2, 4
Arthur, Chester, 51
al-Assad, Hafez, 432
Avril, Prosper, 507, 511
Awolowo, Obafemi, 410, 411
Azikiwe, Dr. Nnamdi, 389, 391, 410,
    411

Babangida, Ibrahim, 372, 392, 395, 398,
    407, 408, 411, 412, 415
Bagehot, Walter, 93, 94
Balewa, Alhaji Sir Abubakar Tafawa,
    391, 410
al-Banna, Hassan, 470
Bazin, Marc, 514
Bello, Alhaji Sir Ahmadu, 406, 410
Berezovsky, Boris, 212
Blair, Tony, 84, 88, 89–90, 91, 95, 98,
    99, 102, 103, 107, 108, 110–111,
    113, 114, 115, 117, 120, 423
  biography, 97

Bobo, Rosalvo, 510
Boldyrev, Yuri, 210
Bongo, Omar, 371
  Booth, Cherie, 97
Boyer, Jean Pierre, 503, 510
Brezhnev, Leonid, 179, 189, 190, 208,
    217
Brown, Gordon, 97
Brundtland, Gro Harlem, 136
Buddha, 331
Buhari, Muhammadu, 372, 392, 394,
    402, 407, 408, 409, 415
Buja, Paul, 371
Bukharin, Nikolai, 190
van Buren, Martin, 51
Bush, George H. W., 6, 54, 67, 71, 74,
    479
Bush, George W., 24, 45, 46, 51, 52,
    55, 62, 67, 68, 69, 72, 74, 218, 319,
    423, 482, 493, 523
  biography, 53
Bush, Jeb, 53

Calles, Plutarco Elías, 290
Cameron, David, 109
Campbell, Kim, 136
Cárdenas, Cuauhtémoc, 299, 312
Cárdenas, President Lázaro, 290, 312,
    315
Cárdenas, Governor Lázaro, 312
Carranza, Venustiano, 288
Carter, Jimmy, 52, 67, 452
Castro, Fidel, 178, 318
Charles, Prince, 94, 95
Chen Yun, 241
Chernenko, Konstantin, 190
Chernomyrdin, Viktor, 198, 210, 462
Chiang Kai-shek, 230, 233, 260
Christophe, Henri, 509
Chubais, Anatoly, 199
Churchill, Winston, 23, 117, 219

SUBJECT INDEX